THAT LINE OF
DARKNESS

V O L U M E   T W O

The Gothic from Lenin to bin Laden

The Night
1918-1919
Max Beckmann
Germany

ROBERT A. DOUGLAS

THAT LINE OF DARKNESS

VOLUME TWO

The Gothic from Lenin to bin Laden

encompass
EDITIONS

Published by Encompass Editions, Kingston, Ontario, Canada. No part of this book may be reproduced, copied or used in any form or manner whatsoever without written permission, except for the purposes of brief quotations in reviews and critical articles.

For reader comments, orders, press and media inquiries:
www.encompasseditions.com

FIRST EDITION 2013

ISBN: 978-1-927664-00-1

Cataloguing in Publication Program (CIP)
information available from Library and Archives Canada at
www.collectionscanada.gc.ca

FRONT COVER
A detail from Max Beckmann's
The Night (1918-19)

BACK COVER
A detail from Max Beckmann's
The Night (1918-19)

COVER DESIGN
by Robert Buckland

TEXT DESIGN
by Jean Shepherd

encompass
EDITIONS

If only there were evil people somewhere committing insidiously evil acts, and it were necessary only to separate them from the rest of us and destroy them. But the line dividing good and evil cuts through the heart of every human being. And who is willing to destroy a piece of his own heart?

—*The Gulag Archipelago*
Alexander Solzhenitsyn

There must be a moment at the beginning, where we all could have said no.
But somehow we missed it.

—*Rosencrantz and Guildenstern*
Are Dead
Tom Stoppard

When you cross over that line of darkness, it's hard to come back. You lose your soul.

—Former CIA officer

Acknowledgments

In Volume One, I named several individuals who supported my efforts by critiquing chapters in what was originally conceived as a single volume. I was remiss in not naming Ted Tennant, Tiska Wiedermann and Jenifer Sutherland for their contributions. In the preparation of Volume Two, I wish to acknowledge Linda Jones, Susan Chisholm and Jane Deeks for their reading and helpful comments on different chapters. I also would want to thank my friend Kevin Courrier for his continuing support and particularly his invaluable assistance in the editing of visual material that I used in teaching a six-week course on the two volumes of *That Line of Darkness* for the Life Institute at Ryerson University in Toronto. I want to thank Robert Buckland and Jean Shepherd at Encompass Editions for their guidance and patience in transforming a manuscript into a book worthy of publication. I am particularly indebted to author James FitzGerald and Dr. Leonard Friesen for reading both volumes in manuscript and kindly writing glowing blurbs. Finally, I want to acknowledge the tremendous support of my wife Gayle for her careful reading, her suggestions for improvements and her moral support and love that sustained me throughout this long process.

To Gayle as always

Table of Contents

Preface

The first volume of *That Line of Darkness* explores the anxieties of late Victorian and pre-war England through the lens of the Gothic genre that frequently involved the transgression of boundaries into a dark underbelly of Victorian life. Its conventions set the stage for illuminating the Great War. Rather than literary texts, the war itself becomes the text and Gothic filters the template for interpreting it. If that book illustrated the possibility that the transgression or the challenging of boundaries could remedy or at least highlight an injustice—for example, the case studies of Josephine Butler and Oscar Wilde—the second volume sets out a darker scenario as it looks through a Gothic prism at the Soviet Union during the time of Lenin and Stalin, Nazi Germany throughout the 1930s, and America during the early Cold War and the post 9/11 present. But it is not a general overview of these epochs. There is little or no discussion of international relations, diplomacy or, apart from the Soviet Union, economics. When addressing the two police states, culture is only examined for how it served the dominant ideology; there is, for example, no discussion of the radical avant-garde in the 1920s in the U.S.S.R. The focus for this book is to explore what happens to individuals and groups, who for reasons of ideology, opportunism, national security or the perks of power, cross the line and shed their humanity.

Gothic elements are incorporated into *That Line*. For example, a common Gothic motif—how a primitive, even primeval, past threatens a modernist technological, scientific present—can be grafted onto the ideology of the Soviet Union under Lenin and Stalin. Consider how Maxim Gorky's attitude toward the peasantry

1

mirrors that of a protagonist toward a villain in a Gothic novel: he referred to them as another species, benighted in being "not yet human [and therefore]...our enemy."[1] In his narrative, the peasant embodies the atavistic past that endangers not only the transient present but the radiant future, one that is "scientifically" predetermined by Marxist ideology. Another Gothic feature, the threat to bloodlines, was calcified into an ideological obsession that overrode all other policy considerations in Nazi Germany. Although interest groups and policy makers elsewhere advocated, and in some cases implemented, policies to protect the "healthy" gene pool, Germany vastly surpassed all other countries in its aggressive efforts to "cleanse the racial self" of supposedly polluting elements. Psychic vampirism, when one mind is replenished by the energy that is leeched or siphoned from another, applies not only to these states, but to a comparatively open society in America where it took the form of funding mind-control experiments during the Cold War. After 9/11 this dynamic was more diffuse as it emerged in political manipulation during the lead-up to the war in Iraq.[2]

An epitet frequently used to describe the Soviet Union and Nazi Germany, the subjects of Part One and Part Two, is "totalitarian." Recent research has shown that the two regimes were not top-down monoliths where omnipotent states exercised absolute power over passive victimized citizens. A degree of private enterprise was allowed in Nazi Germany and even in the Soviet Union during the 1920s. There were even constituencies that supported the repression of other groups. Many citizens, owing to a variety of motives, actively embraced or passively assented to the values of their respective states. Despite the absolute power of Stalin, the decision-making was often left to his senior lieutenants even though they made every effort to comply with his general wishes and to consult with him when they were uncertain of how to act. Similarly, Hitler often left day-to-day decisions to those beneath him. This vacuum at the top meant that more power was assumed by local authorities. The "working toward the Führer" principle embraced by hundreds of thousands of Germans who acted upon what they understood to be goals of the Nazi leader, more than compensated for the lack of coordinated central specifics.[3] Historian Lynne Viola characterizes the Soviet Union under Stalin as "an extraction state" in which the peasantry was required to pay a "tribute" in the form of grain to finance industrialization. Peasant labour, including forced labour in the camps, was deployed to appropriate natural resources and to provide soldiers in its wars. She describes the Soviet Union as an empire in which the countryside was an "internal colony" wherein the peasantry was comparable to the indigenous peoples in overseas colonies that served the economic interests of European powers of an earlier era. This may be a distinctive feature of imperialism, but Viola charts how Stalin's perception of these peasants as a threat to collectivization led to their being uprooted and transplanted regardless of the human cost involved, even if it entailed (which it did) a huge financial price to the nation. Viola describes that policy as "an unmitigated disaster." Yet she contends that Moscow had little control over what transpired in the day-to-day operations of the hinterland. The exploitation and brutality with which the resettled peasantry was treated was dependent on a "weakly developed rural government often run by poorly educated individuals reared in civil war and class warfare." They would have regarded the most entrepreneurial peasants (kulaks) as the unredeemable *other*. Given these conditions—when ideology allows zealotry, inhumanity and incompetence to overrule even a smattering of pragmatism—totalitarianism seems a more apt designation than imperialism to describe the Soviet Union.

Nonetheless, despite the difficulties of local conditions—transportation, communication and distance—leadership at the top (including in democratic societies) initiates policy and sets the tone of its ideological message through public pronouncements for how local authorities should enforce its power. Even if the U.S.S.R. and Germany did not possess the resources to exercise complete control, their totalitarian aspirations were evident in their ruthless persecution of scapegoated groups for being who they were, and their demands that individual initiatives and freedoms be subsumed under the exigencies of the collective. Both regimes foisted an exclusive totalitarian ideology onto the fabric of daily life: few areas, public or private, including the arts, were immune from Party control and surveillance. If the function of the arts, as British poet W. H. Auden believed, was to make us more human and more difficult to deceive, that might explain why "all totalitarian theories of the state...have deeply distrusted the arts. They notice and say too much, and the neighbours start talking."[4] Given the attention to and the need of the potentates in the Soviet Union and Nazi Germany to ensure that the arts conformed to prescribed values,

Auden's musings only strengthen the case that totalitarianism remains an effective characterization of these states and of the radical evil that permeated them.

Part Three, which addresses America and international terrorism, explores the fundamentalist absolutism of the Bush presidency and militant Islamism. American actions at home and abroad reveal not only a mirror image of the monster America wished to destroy, but convey a disturbing continuity with those states that have been consigned to history's graveyards. All three of them, albeit with radically different degrees of intensity, heightened the politics of fear to further their national or imperial agendas. I am not suggesting a moral equivalence or comparison between the callous disregard for civilian life shown by Islamist terrorists or the magnitude of the murderous actions perpetrated in Nazi Germany and the Soviet Union, and the cavalier dismissal of the rule of law that operated during the Bush years. In America, countervailing institutions, personal freedoms and respect for human dignity existed in ways that were inconceivable in Germany, the U.S.S.R. and in the liberty-lashing culture of al-Qaeda. Nonetheless, American contempt for the "towel people" at both the official and main-street level made it possible to sanction constitutional violations and egregious human rights violations that reveal disturbing echoes of the violence meted out to "racial enemies" and "enemies of the people."

At the beginning of the three parts, an overview provides the arguments for the subsequent chapters. The epilogue outlines some of the worst consequences of the Gothic mode—the demonization of the other, the double or a sinister duality, psychic vampirism, the obsession with bloodlines—when the belligerents on the Eastern Front during World War II exemplified evil incarnate. The work ultimately looks to the present and questions whether the Obama administration's policies on national security issues and domestic politics can be viewed through the prism of a Gothic sensibility.

Familiarity with the more cultural–historical *That Line of Darkness: The Shadow of Dracula and the Great War,* with its abundance of references to Gothic novels and films, is valuable. This synoptic study, Volume Two, is primarily historically grounded, punctuated with allusions to Gothic conventions and therefore can be read independently

INTRODUCTION

The Gothic Spirit in the Nation State

Gothic is a mode—perhaps the mode—of unofficial history.

~ David Punter, *Literature of Terror*

The Gothic conventions and tropes discussed in *That Line of Darkness: The Shadow of Dracula and the Great War* require further commentary to smoothly transition from the Gothic texts to historical monographs that are enlisted in this work. The insights also provided by literary theorists and philosophers are valuable as a bridge between literature and the so-called real world.

Gothic texts frequently chart the trajectory of individuals who suppress or lack the capacity to empathize with others. Similarly, when individuals in the larger world succumb to an ideological virus, neither experience nor reality can disrupt their single-minded quest to achieve utopia. Their narrative often includes sanctioning the emotional humiliation and the physical assault upon those they consider non-persons. When intended victims are regarded as vermin or parasites that must be eliminated, moral restraints to cold-blooded violence are atrophied, if not abandoned.[1]

In Gothic fiction ethical codes "operate at best in distorted forms."[2] The same can be said of totalitarian states and the militant Islamists. In a chapter from *The Dictators* titled, "The Moral Universe of Dictatorship," Richard Overy argues that the Nazis and the Stalinists adopted an extreme moral relativism that subsumed individual conscience into the collective will, one that was driven solely by ideological imperatives. Just as moral elites like the church and the law were co-opted or destroyed by Nazi and Soviet ideology, the original meaning of the Quran is lost, even repudiated by the actions of militant Islamists.

Paranoia is a hallmark of Gothic fiction: the reader is uncertain about whether the fears of the characters are based on reality. In the underlying ideologies of both totalitarian states and militant Islamist groups, paranoia is a palpable force. Their irrational delusions—that a racially immaculate community will defeat a global Jewish conspiracy to subvert German civilization; that history will vindicate the virtuous proletariat over the exploitative bourgeoisie; and that since the West has waged war against Muslims, all acts of violence are justified—are the source from which their need for total manipulation of their subjects springs. The attributes assigned to enemies (real and imaginary) often reflect more about the mindset of those who would destroy them.[3]

The Gothic motif of doubling is a useful frame through which to examine the concept of evil—the willingness and intent to inflict deliberate harm on innocent human beings. This topic, however, is usually avoided by historians.[4] Sir Ian Kershaw, distinguished historian and the author of what many consider the definitive biography of Hitler, never mentions the word evil. This avoidance derives from a number of understandable reasons starting with the conviction that it is the function of historians to explain and not to judge. Evil is considered a theological concept beyond their purview. It is also often associated with the monstrous and therefore places individuals in a realm where they become unaccountable for their actions. Finally, its careless and simplistic use since 9/11 when it was bandied about without nuance—we are good, they are evil—to mute or bludgeon any critical responses (who can be against combating evil?) would act as a deterrent for historians to explore its sources and its nature in specific historical contexts.

Social psychologists and philosophers, however, are willing to confront evil head-on. Moral philosopher, Susan Neiman suggests that we abandon our attempt to foreclose the discussion about good vs. evil provided we recognize that anyone is capable of participating in it, as Victorian author, Robert Louis Stevenson, astutely explores in *The Strange Case of Dr. Jekyll and Mr. Hyde.* Neiman draws upon the experiments of social scientists Stanley Milgram and Philip Zimbardo to support her argument. Milgram demonstrated that sixty-five percent of his subjects were willing to obey fully the experimenter's commands and inflict 450 volt electric shocks despite the emotional upset many experienced (often covered over by nervous laughter at what they [wrongly] thought were the screams of their victims in another room) provided they did not need to assume personal responsibility. Philip Zimbardo randomly divided a group of healthy young men into two groups: guards and prisoners. The men rapidly became either brutal sadists or abject dehumanized prisoners, so quickly, in fact, that

Zimbardo cut short his experiment.* He observed that the right circumstances can awaken in anyone the impulse that delights in cruelty and concluded that sadism, as "the province only of deviants and despots—of Them but not Us,"—is an illusion.[5] Zimbardo's insight echoes the Gothic convention of doubling and serves as a sober reminder that in certain ways we resemble the enemy we wish to destroy.

Believing that evil takes on many forms and cannot be reduced to a single essence, Neiman suggests that only by a careful case-by-case analysis can we recognize that a line has been crossed from *awful to evil*. She notes that evil often results from brutal insensitivity rather than demonic malice. Insensitivity is accompanied by shamelessness, indifference or a lack of awareness that certain actions could lead to disgrace. The only way to stop the further erosion of shame is to return to the language of good and evil provided it is not caricatured or externalized as something only others do: "The idea of evil is neither demonizing nor Manichean." The acknowledgment that certain actions are indeed evil can offset the danger of desensitizing us or providing alibis: roughing up prisoners may be bad but cannot be compared with the evil acts perpetrated by our enemy or certain actions, however repugnant, can be defended in the name of patriotism and service to country or excused given the circumstances. If we are to avoid these alibis, Neiman suggests that the more we understand how people are drawn into evil actions the more power we have to do things differently.[6]

Neiman avoids any discussion of Nazism. She acknowledges, however, that without Nazism, the Holocaust—which she characterizes as the "gold standard" for evil—would not have been possible. As a Jewish witness to the radical evil of Nazi Germany in a German prison and as a refugee in Nazi-occupied France before her daring escape, political philosopher, Hannah Arendt, did tackle the meaning of Nazism and, to a lesser extent, Stalinism. She contended that the aim of totalitarianism exceeded that of

---

* During the first half of the powerful 2001 film, *Das Experiment*, the interchange between guards and prisoners replicates the sadism and humiliation that Zimbardo observed but, then as the situation careens completely out of control and various forms of violence and brutality occur, we are left wondering if those horrors might have happened if Zimbardo had not aborted his experiment.

8

political domination over others to a "system in which men were superfluous." From the leaders to the functionaries in the camps, they were mere instruments of their respective ideologies. In her words, "absolute evil could no longer be understood and explained by the evil motives of self-interest, greed, covetous, resentment, thirst for power, and cowardice."[7]

That Line of Darkness: The Gothic from Lenin to bin Laden explores the spectrum of evil that ranged from the camps in Germany and the Soviet Union to the forms it took in the regimes' echelons of power, the social elites, activists, informers, bystanders, and even in some of its victims. The first two parts of the book where radical evil abundantly abounds contrasts with part three which deals with modern America and the quieter, more insidious forms of evil committed by individuals who might not set out with the intent harm but either excuse it or are indifferent to it. The boundary between the two paradigms outlined by Neiman and Arendt, however, is by no means impermeable. When mockery, disdain and cruelty dwell within individuals and groups, those forces can be readily released with or without official state sanction. Under these circumstances, the impermissible becomes possible and human beings cross the line into darkness, especially when the ends are cited to justify the means. With the caveat that the state must protect itself and its citizens from those who would do it harm, the judgements expressed in this book part company with those who endorse, rationalize or condone the infliction of pain, humiliation—or worse—on the *other* whether in police states or open, relatively liberal, democratic societies.

Gothic Threads

From the ashes of World War I emerged the chimera that it was possible to create a conflict-free body politic if one pursued an ongoing campaign to redeem or eliminate divisive and obstreperous elements. In the struggle between conflicting ideologies or to maintain unity within one, the state often found it necessary to destroy the "monster [that] dwells at the gate of difference." As a result, any opposition was transformed into the *other*.[8] The Soviet Union committed itself to building a workers' paradise by reshaping the environment to influence behaviour, while Germany's Third Reich harnessed pseudo-science to justify the breeding of a racially pure *Volk*. Both regimes believed they could create a "gardening state," a concept formulated by the Polish sociologist, Zygmunt Bauman, in which it was possible to create an ideal social order by transforming society as if it were into a garden. The metaphor of the garden expresses the belief that to create an ideal society, one must cut the unfit human weeds so that a "better world—more efficient, more beautiful more moral—could be established." In the quest for ideological purity, every policy decision became an aesthetic enterprise.[9] In one sense, this pursuit of beauty and this leavening of the ideological content was an inverse of the Gothic; instead of displacing cultural anxieties into a terrifying narrative, both the Soviets and the Nazis attempted to camouflage terror by packaging through the arts, rituals and public policies a wholesome, cleansed version of reality. By uprooting entrepreneurial peasants to labour colonies and camps, the communists trumpeted hard labour as a prophylactic that would eradicate the residues (or weeds) of capitalist consciousness and rehabilitate parasites into productive, happy workers. In Nazi Germany while medical–scientific officials quietly terminated tainted bloodlines, the regime established maternity homes for women of impeccable Aryan lineage to turn out physically superior specimens of the master race. The attempt to engineer these utopian visions of perfectionism and messianism predictably created a dark dystopian reality.

The process can be better understood if it is placed in a Gothic frame. Highly stereotyped villains that inspired terror as ghosts, monsters and vampires are strikingly similar to the official biological-hygienic boilerplate that Germany and the Soviet Union used to demonize and justify the extermination of the purported subhuman *other*[10] The "racial polluters" who spread their "cholera germs," the contaminating "vampires" and "blood-suckers," and the networks of "terrorists" or "pests" in the pay of hostile foreign powers demonstrate a common ground of dehumanizing rhetoric. This language, suggestive of the forces of barbarism and attributed to others, in reality, described the regimes themselves who savaged the lives of their enemies. When language became decoupled from reality, a terrible tumult often ensued, one that could be characterized as Gothic. In his scathing indictment of Soviet rule, Alexander Yakovlev, the architect of perestroika (or restructuring) during the regime's twilight years, compared the system in which he had once played a prominent part to a site of Gothic horror. His excavation of its history required him "to descend step by step down seventy years of Bolshevik rule into a dungeon strewn with human bones and reeking of dried blood."[11] By his death in 2005, Yakovlev's interpretation had become unacceptable to the apparatchiks around Vladimir Putin and, as the epigraph at the outset indicates, relegated to "unofficial history."

The Gothic convention of fearing the past which is pitted against the modern, the barbaric against the civilized, and crudity against elegance, is applicable to Marxism–Leninism.[12] Its adherents contended that the remnants of the savage past in the form of class enemies from rapacious bourgeois exploiters, to recalcitrant peasants and superstitious priests threatened progress and modernity and, therefore, had to be destroyed. By contrast Nazi mythology, propagated during the Weimar era after the Great War, claimed that a pristine pre-modern past percolating in the soil was contaminated by a cosmopolitan cluster of decadent (often Jewish) capitalists and foreign-inspired communists. The National Socialist narrative described how their malevolent presence permeated the atmosphere with a toxic miasma that required a fumigator, as it were, to purify the *Volk*. Whether the past was idealized or demonized, the German *Volk* and Soviet Communism defined themselves by constructing a mythic, monstrous *other*. This notion allowed their citizens to see themselves as something entirely different, something healthy and sacred. The propagandists and Party functionaries were given the task of producing the rhetoric and the imagery to persuade their respective constituencies into believing that ideological purity and unflinching loyalty were necessary preconditions for protecting them from those who would suck the life blood out of the state.

The transgressive allure of the Gothic to both attract and horrify were exemplified in both regimes. Stalin combined a phantasmagorical sense of reality with an unbounded capacity for terror. He convinced millions of starry-eyed Party cadres during the heady days of collectivization and industrialization. At the same time, he installed paralyzing fear during the Great Terror of 1937–38 as Bolshevik grandees and non-Russian ethnic groups, especially those close to international borders, were mutated into enemies of the people. Similarly, Hitler's charisma captivated ideological and self-serving members of the elites and the wider public. But his and other potentates' provocations aroused revulsion and fear.

Hitler's semi-autobiographical *Mein Kampf* and Julius Streicher's infamous weekly tabloid, *Der Stürmer* (*The Stormer*), were both steeped in vampiric bombast about the powerful Jew who fed off Aryans and endangered German blood with the putrefaction of miscegenation.

The crude imagery and inflammatory writings produced a dark Gothic hue of power-hungry predators who voraciously fed on their victims' blood. Invoking ideology—the inexorable laws of nature, "unfit races," or history, a "dying class"—Stalin and his psychic clone, Hitler, transgressed all the civilized norms in pursuit of their grandiose schemes. Even before Hitler came to power, Stalin demonstrated his revulsion toward democratic parties by ordering the German Communist Party (KPD) to cooperate with the Nazi Party and to disparage the Socialist Party (SPD) as "social fascists." The leaders' kindred spirits and psychopathology outweighed their avowed animosity for each other's ideology and peoples. Their psychic makeup starkly reveals how one served as the alter ego or doppelganger for the other: as ideologues, they were incapable of nuanced thinking and the public's adoration fuelled their narcissistic self-aggrandizement. Each bore a grudging admiration for the methods employed by the other to eliminate any threat to his personal power, and used the other as a model for his own murderous actions against "subhuman" ethnic groups and classes. They developed a lethal synergy as each used the other as a bogeyman to win supporters while they turned Europe into a charnel continent.[13]

The Gothic convention of doubling operated just as powerfully within the Soviet Union. Once considered the heir to Lenin and steeped in blood himself, Leon Trotsky was the recipient of Stalin's visceral hatred. Stalin's obsession with him in part grew out of a murderous jealousy for his more charismatic, albeit not smarter, rival, and in part, because he believed that Trotsky, even in exile, posed a genuine threat. In Richard Lourie's fictional recreation of the Soviet dictator, *The Autobiography of Joseph Stalin*, he imagines the two men as existing in each other's image: Stalin's determination to write his own autobiography before Trotsky in Mexican exile could publish his biography of Stalin, becomes such a relentless fixation that the Soviet dictator virtually ignores the much greater threat emanating from his shadow in Germany.[14] Beyond the novel, but in the Gothic spirit, even before Trotsky's assassination, Stalin turned his *bête noire* into a spectre or non-person. As though he had never existed, Stalin employed an air-brushing technique, cutting Trotsky out of all photographs and deleting any print reference to him, a practice which he replicated with his Leninist colleagues, after he had ordered their deaths. Trotsky's ghostly appearance haunted the Soviet landscape: anyone offering a less-than-damning comment about him risked being dispatched to the Gulag or to his death. The fate of Trotsky exemplified the porous line between perpetrators and victims since the former often became victims of the "meat grinder." A loyal Stalinist could look at himself in the mirror and see his enemy.

Beneath the bracing promises of a thousand-year Reich and a workers' paradise resided the genetic and class laboratories whose purpose was to surgically cut the "cancerous growths" from the healthy body politic. The interrogators at Gestapo headquarters in Berlin and their counterparts in the subterranean bowels of the Lubyanka in Moscow displayed no qualms about torturing and killing their victims. Indeed, these settings were far more terrifying than Gothic tropes of haunted houses and crumbling castles. Granted that Marxism held out the one-time only prospect of redemption,* the security organs, camp administrators and guards stripped victims of their humanity and turned them into the undead of "walking corpses" to make it easier to kill them or let them die. Primo Levi, an Auschwitz survivor described the "anonymous mass" in more graphic terms as "non-men who march and toil in silence, the divine spark dead in them, already too empty to suffer. One hesitates to call them living; one hesitates to call their death, death."[15] Not surprisingly, the newsreel images of emaciated survivors from the camps of World War II evoke the Gothic conceit of the undead. Their haggard appearance eerily resembles the rodent-like cinematic vampire in the 1922 *Nosferatu: A Symphony of Horrors*.

In both countries, since large numbers of people were seduced by these destructive ideologies that demanded the purging of the "unclean," opportunities for material gratification and power abounded, not only for the perpetrators of evil but for bystanders who often became instruments of terror. Complicity occurs

---

* If an individual was arrested as an enemy of the people and sent to the camps, he may have been released if he was considered rehabilitated. If he was re-arrested, he would likely be shot.

at least in part because of psychic or emotional vampirism: the draining of the life out of one party and the reinvigoration of the other. Perpetrators, as well as the complicitous could be depleted. The burly Reich Minister, Hermann Göring, exemplifies the former: "It is not I who live, but the Führer who lives in me," while the visual record of ecstatic followers bonding with a numinous Hitler reveals the latter.[16] The public persona of Hitler, enlivened by the oxygen of his audiences, executes his well-honed skills on them; they appear hypnotized—swept along on a wave of rapture and a sense of euphoria. These feelings were further massaged by such rituals as the annual Party Rally, holidays and festivals expedited with Wagnerian pyrotechnics, as well as film and other visual arts that communicated the illusion of benign change. Concurrent with the sledgehammer deployment of terror in the Soviet Union, Stalin and his inner circle similarly enthralled millions by using Marxist ideology and sleight of hand. He too beguiled his subjects and receptive international guests into believing that the U.S.S.R. was advancing humanity toward abundance and harmony. Officials staged tours of manicured Potemkin villages,† directors churned out escapist and kitsch films, and writers produced socialist tractor-and-factory realist novels. The public image of Stalin was that of an unpretentious, avuncular figure who guided this transformation. Images of full-throated approbation of marchers genuflecting in the direction of Stalin may appear less spontaneous than the adoring crowds in Germany that palpitated over Hitler. Yet, like the magnetism of Nazism, the real power of Stalinism resided, as one Soviet historian remarked, "in the Stalinism that entered into all of us."[17] Psychic vampirism, that nurtured the megalomania of Stalin and "emptied [the] souls and brains" of his victims, complements the blood-letting from brute force. This combination provided greater assurance that the messages promulgated by the state synchronized with the public's reality.[18]

Fittingly, the Gothic narrative purports that a vampire can only

---

† Since the eighteenth century when Gregory Potemkin attempted to impress Catherine the Great, the Russians increasingly mastered the technique of an elaborate political stagecraft for impressing foreigners and its own people.

enter a dwelling house if it is invited.‡ Both regimes received un-critical support that depended as much on the collusion of the state's citizenry as on its capacity to rewire the public's internal system, stripping it of its capacity for independent thought. The psychiatrist, Robert Jay Lifton, described this process as "load-ing the language," a technique whereby the most complex issues are "compressed into brief highly reductive, definitive-sounding phrases, easily memorized and easily expressed."[19] Germans from all walks of life, disgusted by the political deadlock, class warfare, and the moral and cultural decadence of the Weimar years, en-dorsed the National Socialist notion of a German racial commu-nity and its promise of unity and solidarity. Moreover, both states successfully enlisted support from members of the intellectual and cultural elites to provide a benign sheen that would conceal their darker realities. The creative writer and journalist, Maxim Gorky, and a passel of socialist–realist artists in the Soviet Union, the in-ternationally recognized philosopher, Martin Heidegger, and the documentary filmmaker, Leni Riefenstahl in Nazi Germany en-hanced the credibility of their respective states. They crossed a moral line by lending their various services to regimes whose goals were to expunge free inquiry and the creative spark within individuals and substitute ideological groupthink.

The police agencies instilled fear among the citizenry in the Third Reich, and Joseph Goebbels' masterful propaganda manip-ulation should not be minimized. But Israeli philosopher, Avishai Margalit, suggests there is a difference between the German and Soviet public's complicity. He argues that Germans embraced a "radically evil" ideology that was a "conscious attack on the idea of shared humanity," and in practice willingly participated in the war against racial outsiders. Given that the major institutions—the mili-tary, the judiciary, the police, the bureaucracy and the churches—were co-opted, a large majority of Germans supported the Third

---

‡ In the electrifying one-man play *Adolf* by Pip Utton performed at the annual Fringe Festival at Edinburgh, Utton, who chillingly plays Hitler, pulls a remarkable stunt on his audience in the last fifteen minutes. He sheds his makeup and Hitler persona to seemingly portray him-self, a right-wing figure who parades current prejudices that everyone has heard before returning to inhabit his role as the Führer. He fixes his gaze on the audience, pointing out that he has never really left and asks: "When I come knocking at your door will you let me in?"

Reich because they believed that Hitler had rejuvenated Germany by restoring national pride and a public wholesomeness, and by eliminating the Bolshevik threat within the country. In the Soviet Union, however, the issue of the public's complicity is more complex: the formidable surveillance, the regime's specific targets *and* the random threat of the terror, namely that anyone, regardless of his loyalties, could be dispatched to the meat grinder. As a result, Margalit suggests that vast numbers were terrorized and "coerced into evil by stupefying fear."[20] Nonetheless, the Soviet leadership effectively persuaded the minority of true believers and the larger number of opportunists to dispense with "bourgeois morality" and excise the weeds from the garden. That was the price for realizing the dream of a non-exploitative classless society and a cross-cultural brotherhood.

The pervasiveness of the Gothic mode shows that its power can extend beyond the murderous states of Europe. It resonates with the fears, anxieties and desires that percolated and festered in America after 1945, and has permeated the culture in recent times. Joseph Conrad's allegorical *Heart of Darkness* (1902) effectively provides a bridge from the horrors inflicted by two totalitarian states to those perpetrated by a relatively liberal democratic state. Mr. Kurtz is a charismatic agent of an ivory company who succumbs to the dangers of the jungle. His bizarre behaviour and lack of "restraint" mirror the "primitive" beings he endeavours to civilize. The novel and the fate of the central character could be read as a cautionary warning about the dangers of venturing into unknown lands regardless of the motives.

Just as dystopian conditions exposed the harsh underbelly of Soviet and Nazi ideals, the shadow side of the American collective psyche contradicted its national dream as a just, humane and open society. A thread connecting the tyranny of police states, where both civilians and combatants demonized the *other* to that of a relatively liberal America is how demonization of the *other* during the Cold War extended to combatants. Although removing any vestige of the enemy's humanity had long been a product of war, it had been primarily designed to enlist support among civilians, not part of the training of soldiers. But since the military undertook a study of the willingness of soldiers to kill revealed that up to eighty percent of the soldiers in World War II refused to fire their weapons on exposed enemies, the Americans changed their boot-camp training. It includes a verbal "deification of killing" to wash away the human image from the recruits' mind and to underscore the message that the soldiers' main function was to kill. Unsurprisingly with this indoctrination, the firing rates increased to over one-half in Korea and between ninety and ninety-five percent in Vietnam.[21] After September 11, the Bush administration and complicit media combined fear with dehumanization to exploit that tragedy to further its policy agendas. The desensitization and conditioning that trained soldiers for war after 1945 bore a bitter fruit in the amorphous "War against Terror." Ratcheting up the politics of fear in the name of national security disfigured American life during the Cold War and the Bush years.

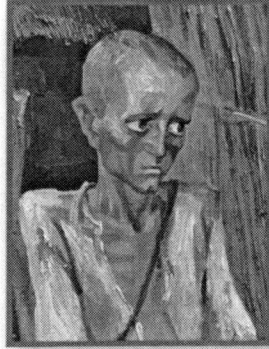

PART ONE
Modernism and Primitivism
in the Soviet Union

The contact with pure unmitigated savagery, with primitive nature and primitive man, brings sudden aIn a century or two, or in a millennium, people will live in a new way, a happier way. We won't be there to see it — but it's why we live, why we work. It's why we suffer. We're creating it. That's the purpose of our existence. The only happiness we can know is to work toward that goal.

~ Anton Chekhov, *Three Sisters*

If the intellectuals in the plays of Chekhov who spent all their time guessing what would happen in twenty, thirty, or forty years had been told that in forty years interrogation by torture would be practiced in Russia; that prisoners would have their skulls squeezed within iron rings; that a human being would be lowered into an acid bath; that a ramrod heated over a primus stove would be thrust up their anal canal [the 'secret brand']; that a man's genitals would be slowly crushed beneath the toe of a jackboot; and that, in the luckiest possible circumstances, prisoners would be tortured by being kept from sleeping for a week, by thirst, and by being beaten to a bloody pulp, not one of Chekhov's plays would have gotten to its end because all the heroes would have gone off to insane asylums.

~ Alexander Solzhenitsyn, *The Gulag Archipelago*

Background and Overview

> The Iron Heel is here. I had hoped for a peace-
> ful victory at the ballot-box. I was wrong....
> We shall be robbed of our few remaining
> liberties; the Iron Heel will walk upon our
> faces; nothing remains but a bloody revo-
> lution of the working class. Of course, we
> will win, but I shudder to think of it.
>
> —*The Iron Heel*
> Jack London

The Gothic Landscape in the Age of Nicholas II

In 1898, Peter Rachkovksy, the sinister head of the tsarist security service (Okhrana) for outside Russia, cobbled together
an infamous forgery, destined to become a notorious conspir-
acy-theory text. Although Jewish global conspiracy theories had a
long pedigree in Russia, Germany and France, none could match
the influence and staying power of the *Protocols of the Elders of
Zion*. Without actually mentioning Zionism, they purport to be
the minutes of twenty-four sessions of Jewish elders that outline
how they would foment economic and social disorder, and establish a blueprint for the Jewish takeover of the world. It is shamelessly plagiarized from two sources: a polemic, *Dialogue in Hell
between Montesquieu and Machiavelli,* by Maurice Joly, who was
himself influenced by earlier fiction, and an obscure 1868 melodramatic, anti-Semitic potboiler, *Biarritz,* by a Prussian agent provocateur, Herman Goedsche. In the former, Joly, who never refers

to the Jews, intended his satire as an indictment of the despotism of Napoleon III and the Catholic Church. In the latter, Goedsche includes a chapter about the princes of the twelve tribes of Israel who creepily assemble before midnight in the Prague cemetery to meet with the Devil. When both are folded into the *Protocols*— large portions of the cynical voice of Joly's Machiavelli are directly lifted—the pastiche constitutes a secular, updated version of the medieval trope of the diabolical Jew in league with the Devil, bent upon ruling and ruining mankind.

In a Gothic setting, a cabal of rabbis outlines activities designed to undermine the indebted governments of Europe. The instruments of liberalism—the free press, the justice system, the banks and the stock markets—are to be marshalled to destroy the aristocracy, discredit the military class and undermine the Christian Church.[1] Driven by an unquenchable hatred for Gentiles, Jewish elders insulate themselves in the universities and in the press with the goal of turning their enemies into "unthinking submissive beasts." Surreptitiously, they destabilize European monarchies by encouraging parliaments and numerous political parties to engage in frivolous exchange while transforming republican presidents into their puppets. Democratic governments are reduced to props for the tyranny to which the elders aspire. Before these diabolical Jews could attain their goal, so it went, the elders had to topple their most formidable opponent in Russia. In collusion with indigenous economic modernizers, they targeted traditional Russian elites: the aristocracy and the Church. Landowners were to be ruined by taxation and the promotion of heavy industry, the traditional Orthodox Christian faith eroded by encouraging luxury and depravity. With the arrival of the messianic age, the Jews would rule Christendom, supported by a ruthless police force and a "Super-Government" with the power "to subdue all the nations of the world." This catastrophic scenario could only be prevented if Gentiles defended themselves by persecuting Jews. Ironically, this reactionary hoax turned Joly's defence of liberalism into an endorsement of the "majestic inflexibility" of Russian autocracy.[2] Within a few years, this virulent anti-Semitic screed assumed the imprimatur of truth as its peddlers incited murderous pogroms in Russia and ramped up hatred elsewhere over the next century and beyond to the extent that the *Protocols* are still considered

22

authentic in some parts of the world.[*]

The initial purpose of the *Protocols* was to prop up the old aristocratic order and convince Tsar Nicholas II that the modernization of Russia was a Jewish conspiracy whose aim was to control the world. Agents within the Okhrana and reactionary elements at the Tsarist court believed that this document would convince the Tsar to abandon the liberal reforms recommended by his close advisor, the enlightened Sergei Witte, and at the same time, discredit the Jews. The *Protocols* were privately circulated in Russia, but it was in the revolutionary upheaval of 1905 that they became public and were used to justify the vicious pogroms directed against Jews.

The *Protocols* might have exercised a limited appeal in Russia because Russian Jews were poor and lived in overcrowded ghettoes. They were not the stereotypically chameleon-like Jew of the document. But when their publication coincided with a humiliating war with Japan culminating in the Russians losing almost their entire Baltic Fleet in May 1905, a scapegoat was needed. Although conservatives blamed liberals and Jews to explain how an allegedly robust European power could be defeated by inferior "knock-kneed weaklings," whom Tsar Nicholas II had dismissed as a "puny kind of monkey," the Russian debacle was, in fact, the result of untrained conscripts, inadequate supplies and, above all, incompetent leadership.[3] Yet according to the Judeophobic newspapers, since Jews had provided financial support for the Japanese they therefore had collaborated with the enemy. Pamphlets reinforced this message and overlaid it with vampiric and blood libel associations that referred to Jews as "the enemy in our midst" who "drink our children's blood" and "poison our youth with foul and pernicious ideas and overthrow the pillars of our Holy State and faith."[4] Although an American-Jewish banker did provide loans to the Japanese, bigots ignored evidence that the Jewish Rothschild family had financially subsidized the Russian war effort and that a disproportionately large number of Jews (thirty thousand) had served in Manchuria. Despite the scapegoating, the tsarist government could not escape responsibility for this debacle that might have cost Nicholas his throne had it not been for those loyal troops

---

[*]   For a fictional rendering of the fetid moral milieu and the loathsome characters who fabricated the *Protocols*, see *The Prague Cemetery* by Umberto Eco trans. Richard Dixon (Boston: Houghton Mifflin Harcourt, 2011).

who escaped being sent to the East.[5] The military disgrace and the maritime catastrophe fuelled the populace's grief, anger and shame and led to a spate of work stoppages, a national railway strike, the assassination of a key state official, and the mutiny on the battleship *Potemkin*.

The most dramatic and brutal response from the state occurred on January 9, 1905. Mounted detachments of the army fired on unarmed demonstrators at a peaceful labour protest leaving two hundred people dead. In the subsequent panic, horsemen trampled those who fell or had been wounded. The demonstrators were there to meet with the deliberately absent Tsar to request shorter workdays and trade-union rights. This incident became known as Bloody Sunday.

The dead did not even receive the dignity of funerals; officials carted the bodies from the hospitals before their families could claim them. Under armed guard, they were then transported by rail to a site two hours from the city, and dumped unceremoniously in a mass grave to ensure that their funerals did not serve as an occasion for public demonstration against the government. And so ordinary workers began to lose faith in the Tsar as a man of God who would listen to them. The government had given prior warning to the hospitals to expect casualties, but rather than taking some responsibility for this massacre, Nicholas listened to advisors who had no difficulty persuading him that foreign agents had been responsible. After lecturing a handpicked "reliable" group of workers on how they had been deceived by "foreign revolutionaries," he piously promised to "forgive them of their sins" because he believed in their "unshakeable devotion to him."[6]

The massacre sparked worker and peasant protests and strikes throughout the year culminating in an autumn general strike in Moscow and St. Petersburg that forced the Tsar, on the advice of Sergei Witte, to begrudgingly offer political concessions: the granting of civil liberties, nominal power to a legislative duma that would, for the first time, give people a political voice through representation, and a constitution that would limit the power of state agents such as the police and civil servants. This agreement, dubbed the October Manifesto, provoked a fanatical backlash against liberals and Jews by powerful ultraconservative elements, including the Tsar himself, who read the *Protocols* as confirmation of their blinkered worldview. Acting as if this fantasy were "prophetic," the Tsar, state officials, unenlightened members of the clergy and agents of the state offered moral, financial and legal support to groups who would thwart the plans of the "conspiratorial Jews." The most influential organization was the reactionary Union of Russian People (URP). Its membership included minor officials in the civil service and the police whose exercise of arbitrary power was threatened by economic and social changes arising from industrialism, capitalism and the creation of liberal institutions taking place in 1905. In defence of tsarist absolutism, the Russian Orthodox Church and traditional hierarchical distinctions, the Union spouted a toxic mélange of xenophobia, hatred of the intelligentsia, anti-liberalism and anti-socialism that coalesced into a virulent anti-Semitism. Invoking traditional religious imagery, it believed that a "legion of devils has entered the gigantic body of Russia and shakes it into convulsions, torments it, and mutilates it....The name of this legion is *Jew*" who needed to be exorcised from the body politic.[7] In a speech delivered to members of the URP, one of their spokesmen left no doubt as to what should be done: "The Holy Russian cause is the extermination of the rebels—Death to the rebels and the Jews."[8] This inflammatory message provided the fuse for the Black Hundreds to trigger a savage assault on Jews. They were a motley crew of proto-fascist goons comprised of uprooted peasants driven into the cities to perform casual work and of local artisans and shopkeepers threatened by the emergence of large capitalist enterprises and Jewish competition. Under the guise of patriotism, carrying portraits of the Tsar, and armed with knives and knuckle-busters, they attacked the Jewish quarters in the cities, wreaking human and material destruction: murder, torture, gang rape, mutilation and burning. At least six hundred and fifty pogroms occurred between the signing of the Manifesto in 1905 and September 1906.[9] The central authorities, fearing mass antigovernment rebellion and a decline of foreign investment, ordered local police forces to subdue these pogroms and arrest the perpetrators. But the poorly trained police forces were no match for these murderous thugs, and some national and local officials and police remained hostile to prosecuting them. Indeed, the police often organized or participated in the vicious attacks and used their own printing press in St. Petersburg to accuse the Christ killers of ruining the country and to urge the people "to tear them to pieces and kill them."[10] The worst attacks occurred in the fast-growing, industrializing city of Odessa, in which the most prosperous Jews coexisted with the most destitute. Eight hundred Jews were murdered, five thousand wounded and one hundred thousand rendered homeless.

The 1968 film, The Fixer, *based on Bernard Malamud's novel is loosely drawn upon the Beilis case. The novel and the film explore a handyman's attempt to maintain his dignity in the face of the virulent anti-Semitism he experiences in tsarist Russia. In the opening scene, shown above, the Cossacks launch a pogrom on the Jewish ghetto, wreaking death and destruction on what and whomever they find.*

Attempts to prosecute the organizers and perpetuators were stonewalled at the highest levels. Sergei Witte, one of the Tsar's most successful ministers, lost his political influence when Nicholas refused to support the findings of his official investigation into the pogroms. His support for Jewish entrepreneurial skills and his vehement opposition to the Union, the political wing of the Black Hundreds, further alienated the Tsar making him more vulnerable to the ultranationalists' vicious attacks. Witte's efforts to modernize Russia by encouraging liberalism, attracting foreign investment and establishing stock markets rendered him an unnamed enemy in the *Protocols*, thereby an assassination target.

Another barometer of the Union's power and its collusion with the tsarist government was the financial support it received from the Minister of the Interior. It also obtained the assurance that any gang member could apply for a pardon if he was convicted of participating in a pogrom.

Nicholas and his wife Alexandra, a German princess and granddaughter of Queen Victoria, bore a visceral hatred toward Jews. Nicholas became a fanatical supporter of the Black Hundreds, believing that they were a paragon of justice for all men. Like them, he believed that the Jews had largely inspired the 1905 revolution, and that the pogroms were their just punishment. Impervious to the evidence that Jews constituted a small portion of what he called revolutionaries, an epithet applied to anyone who challenged his absolute rule, he wrote to his mother that "because nine-tenths of the troublemakers are Jews, the whole anger of the people turned against them."[11] While he was endorsing the *Protocols* in right-wing newspapers, and ordering a sermon with ample quotations from the pamphlet to be presented from the pulpit in all three hundred and sixty-eight Moscow churches, his powerful Prime Minister, Pyotr Stolypin, called for an investigation of the authenticity of the document. When his investigators concluded that it was a forgery, Nicholas reluctantly ordered that the *Protocols* be dropped, stating that he could not "defend a pure cause by dirty methods." Regardless of its fanciful authenticity and dubious provenance, the royal couple's anti-Semitism did not abate. Their hostility was rooted in both ethnicity and religion; for them the Jews were a sect that sought to undermine the Empire. At a more fundamental level, Nicholas inhabited a worldview that regarded Jews as pathogens, and held that the removal of the Jews could safeguard Russia against modernity.[12]

In the years before the outbreak of the First World War, with paranoia firmly embedded in the body politic, the state ruthlessly cracked down on any activity it perceived to be insurrectionary, contributing to a culture of violence. Public hangings were the most common punishment. During the revolutionary years of 1905–1907 alone, more than fifteen thousand deaths occurred because of terrorist assassinations, government reprisals, pogroms, violent street battles and peasant revolt. The intelligentsia was no longer confident that education and science could transform and redeem society. The anti-tsarist popular writer, Maxim Gorky, a despised and anathematized target of the Black Hundreds, forced to decamp to Finland, wrote to a friend in July 1905 that the revolution "is giving birth to real barbarism, just like those that ravaged Rome." By the 1910s hooliganism appeared to constitute a threat to civilization itself as some members of the poor were regarded as impervious to the uplifting values of civilized society and therefore beyond redemption.[13] Gorky's musings about the violent tendencies in Russian society proved prescient for the Great War and the subsequent upheavals—experiences that would further confirm his worst fears about the descent into barbarism.

Even before the benchmark year of 1914, an explosive criminal case confirmed the state's willingness to mobilize public opinion against Jews, intellectuals and the liberal left. Mendel Beiliss, a clerk in a Jewish-owned factory was charged with the murder and mutilation of a thirteen-year-old boy on the outskirts of Kiev in 1911. At the boy's funeral, Black Hundreds distributed literature to the mourners proclaiming that this was a ritual murder by the Jews. These accusations merged with another canard: rapacious Jewish sex traders from the area of the Russian Pale near Poland were involved in transporting innocent non-Jewish girls across national borders for the purpose of selling them into sexual slavery. Taken together, these fantasies rendered it plausible for people who had long been manipulated into scapegoating the Jews into believing the charge of ritual murder.[14]

In the Beiliss trial, the prosecution's attempt to demonstrate a ritual murder had been committed backfired. The "expert" witnesses, used to establish that this type of crime was integral to Judaism, were exposed by the press as disreputable. One was a defrocked priest who claimed that behind their human exterior, Jews were "ghouls, vampires and fiends." No orthodox priests could be found to corroborate this assertion. Even the medical experts could not agree that the body had been drained of blood for ritual purposes.[15] The jury acknowledged that a ritual murder may have indeed taken place, though not by the accused, and Beiliss was acquitted. In the meantime, the chief investigator for the Kiev Police Department refused to participate in this charade, was fired and continued privately, with the help of former colleagues, to investigate the case which eventually led to the discovery that the killers were professional criminals, one of them a friend of the murdered boy's family.

Both the prosecution and the Tsar could find solace in the support they received from the Roman Catholic press who fanned the fears arising from the Beiliss blood libel. In the Vatican newspaper, a priest continued to express faith in the widespread existence of ritual murder. Despite the verdict, he would argue as late as 1914, that the ghastly attack was the handiwork of a people "who wanted to extract the blood. Now of such people one race alone is known." In the following month, the same priest wrote that Jews drink blood all the time and that they consider it a "drink like milk."[16] This sensational quasi-show trial served as a harbinger for one of the most salient features of the future Soviet State. Unlike its tsarist predecessor, it would act in a much more efficient and ruthless manner to achieve its desired results.

On the cusp of World War I, this notorious case highlighted the collision between modernism—the embryonic forces of liberalism that stressed the rule of law, civil and political rights and respect for individual rights—and the sclerotic, medieval despotism symbolized by the Tsar and most officials in his government. Nicholas's cynical ploy that a conviction would rally the conservative peasantry, who associated the left with Jews, and would deliver a final devastating blow to the cultural and political aspirations of the intelligentsia, not only failed, but his decision to exploit an atavistic impulse and resurrect the blood libel caused the international prestige of the imperial state to suffer. *The Daily News* of London wrote that "the acquittal of Beiliss was the most crushing blow to Russia since the Russo–Japanese War."[17] In a sense, the Bolsheviks were right. Russia under the tsars was mired in a primeval past, but Bolshevik fanaticism and indifference to human life ensured that the Soviet Union would remain wedded to that spirit.

The Central Argument

If the war in 1904–05 precipitated the 1905 Revolution that led the Tsar to concede an elected duma and a constitution, his actions in the Great War precluded any possibility of maintaining his position and permitting his heir to continue the family dynasty. The devastation of that war catalyzed the violent end of the Romanov dynasty, creating the conditions for the Soviet experiment, whose birth, and for most of its duration, heralded the triumph of terror and demagogy over humanism and the rule of law. On one level, the Bolsheviks, through their Marxist blueprint, did attempt to engineer a seismic shift from the tsarist past to the technological and cultural modernism of the twentieth century. Despite their full-throttled drive toward modernity and their fear and disdain for the primitive past, it can be argued that Soviet leaders fanned atavistic impulses that mobilized their most zealous supporters to relive that darkness in the form of class and ethnic pogroms. Under Lenin and Stalin, the Soviet Union realized some of the tsarist regime's worst anti-modernist features: authoritarianism undergirded by omnipotent secret police, antipathy towards the peasantry, endemic anti-Semitism, and a willingness to dispense terror against both Russians and non-Russians. Nonetheless, the communists mustered an unwavering allegiance both at home and abroad because their powerful messianic ideology either explained away the darker realities as "the laws of history" or blinded the naive to its monstrous consequences.

Three hundred years of authoritarian Romanov rule had bequeathed a scarred human landscape. While the culture of violence and the iconic worship of god-like tsar figures had been cornerstones of the Russian experience, the Great War empowered a new breed of ruthless ideologues. The German government helped to facilitate this shift when, in order to drive its enemy out of the war, it financed Lenin's Bolsheviks and arranged for Lenin to be parachuted into Russia in 1917 after the abdication of Nicholas II. This momentous decision was analogous, in Winston Churchill's words, to "the same way you might send a phial containing a culture of typhoid or of cholera to be poured into the water supply of a great city."[18] The pandemic of Bolshevism broke out after Lenin, desperate to exercise power, ordered the storming of the Winter Palace in October of that year. In the maelstrom arising out of the Russian war experience, the Bolsheviks hijacked the revolutionary impulse from the other socialist parties and set in motion their radically utopian vision. Emboldened by what Bolsheviks declaimed as the scientific laws of history, their leaders justified the violence deployed against counter-revolutionaries as a necessary means to establish a classless modernist state. Armed with Marxian dialectics, they promised to liberate Russia and ultimately the rest of humanity from the scourge of exploitative capitalism. As the disciplined vanguard of a one-party state, they promised they would guide the masses toward a benevolent, egalitarian communism in which the economic and social benefits of a technologically advanced society would be fairly and widely distributed. They heralded communism as the inevitable triumph of a society higher on the evolutionary ladder. Beneath the benign sheen of ideological rhetoric, however, the Bolsheviks exercised power in a manner that was more repressive than tsarism and more brutally competent than the brief experiment in parliamentary government.

While the Bolsheviks cannot be held responsible for the military losses and the massive dislocation caused by the war, they were liable for brazenly exploiting the weaknesses and instability of the February 1917 Provisional Government. During the four years that followed their seizure of power in October of that year, ten million people disappeared into the cauldron of a vicious civil war and famine within Russia and the territories that comprised the former Russian Empire, roughly the same number that perished on all sides in the Great War. The violence cheapened the regard for human life and accentuated the culture of killing by a people already brutalized by war. The enemies of the Reds, who failed abysmally to articulate a compelling alternative political and social vision to tsarism, were equally culpable for their unrelenting bloodletting, but they proved to be no match for the systematic Red terror that included Lenin's order to murder the entire royal family in a cramped cellar in the Urals. In lieu of a public trial that would have provided the appearance of due process, the executions were carried out in secret without photographs and public official sanction. As a consequence, the Bolsheviks unwittingly planted the seeds of rumours that enabled myths to thrive. Among them were reported sightings of the Tsar or members of his family; others were Gothic narratives, one being about the head of Nicholas being transported to Moscow where the Kremlin leaders could revel at their prize, another that the murders were part of a bizarre Jewish blood ritual.[19] Myths and rumours were likely more comforting than the harsh reality instituted by the Bolsheviks. Refurbished institutions exercising arbitrary terror—hostage taking, the persecution of members from rival political parties and the clergy, the rule of law supplanted by Party fiats, the exorbitant requisitioning of grain at gunpoint and in 1918 the opening of concentration camps—fuelled the creation of a Leviathan police state under Lenin.

The Bolshevik leaders with their incendiary bombast against "class enemies" set the tone for the release of primitive impulses that Stalin exploited. When the ailing Lenin died in 1924, the morbidly suspicious and obsessively vindictive Stalin, the General Secretary of the Party, successfully played off factions within the ruling elite to emerge by the end of the decade as its unrivalled leader. Garnering popular support in the cities and among rank-and-file Party members, if not among his colleagues in the Politburo, Stalin launched at breakneck speed the policies of state-planned industrialization and forced collectivization. He was convinced that the state would eliminate the market from the economy and acquire exclusive control through the creation of large, technologically efficient, agricultural factories that would, in turn, finance heavy industry. The increased output from the countryside would provide the capital for the purchase from the West of the sinews for industrial production. In the process, the Party and the cultural bureaucrats attempted to inculcate a proletarian consciousness among the peasantry, whom Karl Marx, a harbinger of modernism, had once maligned as "the class that represents barbarism within civilization."[20] When a socialist consciousness was firmly anchored among workers and the "backward" peasantry, Stalin assured his subjects that the U.S.S.R. would "catch and overtake the West." In addition to feeding the cities and the Red Army, the surplus capital would permit him to increase industrial production exponentially thus providing the necessary military security for an "imperialist war" against capitalist enemies.

In pursuit of these goals, Stalin inaugurated his first Five-Year Plan that set output targets so excessively high that it required the destruction of individual farming and traditional peasant culture. In the spirit of Leninism, he expedited his all-out war using the organs of state and Party against a rural, class enemy—a "domestic other."[21] Fully apprised of the outcome, he was blithely indifferent to the staggering cost in human misery: executions, the forced and brutal exile of its more enterprising peasants and a catastrophic, man-made famine. Blaming overzealous local officials, he could not acknowledge his part in the existence of a disabled economy rampant throughout the countryside.

To inspire support and dissociate himself from failures, Stalin resorted to jiggery-pokery making it possible for citizens to be blind to their realities so that they could deny or at least rationalize

what their common sense told them. In an important way, his success was assured because of his ability to morph his persona from
a smiling Comrade Stalin into the malevolent backroom predator,
who plotted against his enemies and capriciously approved the
execution of tens of thousands. That the public was more likely
to believe the former incarnation rather than the latter attests to
the cult of personality built around the "Marxist gardener...tend-
ing the vine of Communism."[22] His benevolent presence was
manufactured by agit-prop writers, filmmakers and visual artists
who churned out products in the procrustean genre of Socialist
Realism. Ordinary people whose lives generally remained desperate responded enthusiastically to the roseate, indeed phantasmagorical, vision of their country created by popular films, posters
and books even when it contradicted their own experience. Part
of this extraordinary seduction resided in a will-o'-the-wisp dream
that the idyllic Potemkin villages, the portrayal of life in popular
culture and in the arts, not as it currently existed, but as it would
be in the near future, would become their reality. Motivated by an
ideology that was sanctioned by a "scientific" view of history that
attacked the past, scanted the present and assured a paradisiacal
future of prosperity and humanity, millions responded positively
to Stalin's challenge of radical surgery that would accelerate the
transition toward modernity and communism.

When setbacks occurred because of inefficient central planning
and unrealistic quota expectations, Stalin seized upon scapegoats
both to explain these failures and to mobilize public support by
inflating fears that the multinational state was threatened by subversives. Kulaks, the moniker applied to the more entrepreneurial peasants, were vilified as saboteurs; engineers and specialists
as wreckers. In response to the real threat posed by a militaristic
Japan and by Nazi Germany, and his fear that the Old Bolsheviks
would become fifth columnists—secret sympathizers of the enemy—Stalin concocted a fantasy of treason against Party members,
the "double-dealers masked as Bolsheviks," who insulated themselves within the political elite, the military and security organs.

However much Stalin regarded himself as a philosopher and
interpreter of Marxism–Leninism, ideology and power were inextricably interlocked. Paradoxically, as ideology became the pro-
peller to drive a backward people into a modern industrial society, by the late 1930s Stalin increasingly identified himself with

the sixteenth-century Tsar, the sadistic and mentally unstable Ivan IV (commonly known as Ivan the Terrible), not merely the historical Ivan, but a cinematic representation of his forbear that reflected his own idealized self. Looking to a prototype who acted ruthlessly and decisively, he could justify the all-out liquidation of his internal enemies in order to unite the country against its external foes. Institutionalized terror became the lifeblood of the system and enemies more valuable than friends to the maintenance of power. The motives of the "little Stalins" within his camarilla and cadres below them—political ambition, vengeance, personal perks and life-and-death control over others—could now be safely cloaked and rationalized as necessary means for unmasking enemies and performing invaluable service to the Party.

Accordingly, the true believers/opportunists accepted the state's malevolent features: an all-out war against a recalcitrant Soviet peasantry as a necessary precondition for historical progress, a massive industrialization program, and the elimination of or forced exile of "class enemies" and "enemies of the people" who sabotaged the state's achievements. A web of terror coalesced into arrest quotas, brutal interrogation, bone-crushing torture, swift execution or deportation of "former persons" to internal exile in the inhospitable terrain and the life-in-death experience awaiting them in the remote sites of Siberia, the Far North and Kazakhstan of the Gulag[*]—a network of prisons, forced labour camps and special settlements. Its overlapping purposes

---

[*]   The term Gulag was first popularized in the Western world by Nobel Prize-winning author, Alexander Solzhenitsyn, a one-time committed true believer and war veteran, who was dispatched to the camps after the discovery of private letters that obliquely mocked Stalin. As a result of the publication of his first novel, *One Day in the Life of Ivan Denisovich*, and the letters and memoirs he received from others who spent time in the camps, he wrote a monumental and searing indictment of a regime that sanctioned the network of brutal labour camps that crisscrossed the Soviet Union. By turns autobiographical, oral history and a slashing polemic, the three volumes constitute a sprawling tour de force that exposed the gap between the ideological progressive promises and the inhumane realities from the time of Lenin to that of Brezhnev in the 1970s. Forced into exile on the foreign publication of the first volume, most of the time in a small town in Vermont, he and his family returned to his native land after the collapse of Communism where he died in August 2008 almost irrelevant to Russians unwilling to excavate their blood-drenched past.

were punitive, economic and rehabilitative; an individual could be deemed redeemed through gruelling labour and a coerced transformed consciousness, or be destroyed.[23] To supplement the political indoctrination and the brutal re-education process within the camps, writers were commandeered to package the Gulag to the public as a venue for the "reforging" of class enemies into productive socialist citizens.

Yet a caveat is in order: it is important to acknowledge that the so-called "politicals," convicted under Article 58 as enemies of the people, were a small minority of the prisoners. They were regarded as counter-revolutionaries and the most dangerous and least amenable to redemption. Vast numbers were criminals—both those that would have been considered criminal in any society and those that were persecuted for the pettiest of crimes—kulaks, citizens from other countries and national minorities. The latter were executed or incarcerated in large numbers because of a stringent campaign of ethnic cleansing and purges directed against ethnic minorities, not merely because they represented a current threat but because they might be so in the future, particularly as the possibility of war loomed. As devastatingly brutal as the police state had functioned under Lenin, its pervasiveness under Stalin torqued up the level of fear and repression. Moreover, the random and pre-emptive nature of Stalin's terror ensured that anyone, regardless of his or her loyalties, could be relocated to this dark underworld.

By the Great Terror of the late 1930s, with the ubiquitous after-midnight knock on the door, visceral fear and venal opportunism primed the base instincts of ordinary people. To ensure their complicity in the crimes of the state, the Party insisted upon vigilance from the public that required its cooperation in a witch-hunting mania through the denunciation of others. Replicating the Gothic fascination with family destruction, the state penetrated into private life, even the lives of the privileged Kremlin courtiers and Stalin's own family. As a result, the tissue of friendship and family ties was frayed if not ripped apart. If cannibalism was a tragic consequence of a deliberately engineered Holodomor (death by hunger) in 1932–33, it also served as a terrifying metaphor for a system in which millions vanished into the maw of its meat grinder.

Ironically, Stalin's purges bolstered his support among the rank-and-file members. He added a dimension that Lenin had not considered, much less expedited—the physical liquidation of Party members from the revolutionary era who were then replaced with workers from mainly working class and peasant backgrounds, and who acknowledged their good fortune by becoming Stalin's sycophantic devotees. This new breed of fanatical cadres justified the rigged show trials and devouring terror as grim reminders that an encircled state had to protect itself from its enemies. With self-serving malice, they welcomed the Stalinist revolution that fed on the reviled bosses, bourgeois specialists and enemies of the people since the successive waves of terror facilitated opportunities for them to climb the increasingly bloody pole of the Party hierarchy and enjoy the increased income and perks that accrued with their newly acquired power. As former comrades were unmasked and devolved into the less-than-human reptilian enemies of the people accused of imaginary political crimes, Stalin enticed his privileged Party lieutenants into a complicit acceleration of victims delivered to his killing machine.

Though Lenin was more capable of rethinking his ideological stances, the lines of continuity between Lenin and Stalin outweigh the differences. Lenin was no well-meaning revolutionary who reluctantly employed terror merely as a defensive necessity during the civil war. On the contrary, he embedded the cancer of police terror into the DNA of the Soviet state at its creation through illiberal institutions and the murderous actions of its agents against class enemies. Add the sheer power of his personality: a monumental indifference to human suffering and an abiding contempt for any expression of political difference, and the toxic ingredients for repression were firmly ensconced. Rather than Stalin deforming the Leninist revolution, it was Lenin who bequeathed a well functioning police state to his successor, who in turn embraced and built upon its most truculent components.

Despite these conditions, from 1917 the Soviets inspired public support from among the one hundred thousand foreigners who visited the county during the 1920s and 1930s. Although legions of visitors expressed scepticism, others, particularly public luminaries, after touring through showcase sites (schools, factories, collectives and jails) that appeared to be solutions to the problems the Soviets had inherited from the past, extolled the regime for being a revolutionary modernizer. These fellow-travellers[*] were receptive to the message that the regime was offering a compelling alternative to the boom-and-bust cycle of capitalism, and to the aggressive nationalism and virulent racism of Nazi Germany. Those among them who entertained private anxieties and suspicions of mendacity about the human costs still offered public support for the Soviet experiment. They wanted to believe that the imperfections that remained were a temporary flicker en route toward the radiant future, rather than appreciate that the costs of this social engineering—the economic devastation, social dislocation and political terror—could be safely concealed beneath a public sheen: sculpted, spotless and not really of this world.

In stark contrast to the naive and, even worse, politically gimlet-eyed, opportunistic foreigners and home-grown apologists were the voices that bore witness to the barbarity of the regime. The memoirs and oral accounts of those who were victimized by the soul-sucking Soviet "corrective labour camps," that included apostate Party loyalists, exposed the yawning chasm between its progressive rhetoric and the inhumane reality of its rule.

---

[*]   This term was invented by Leon Trotsky to pejoratively describe literary figures in the Soviet Union who cooperated with the Party but refused to join it. Soviet officials preferred "friends of the Soviet Union" to characterize foreign intellectuals who publicly heaped praise on the Soviet Union. Michael David-Fox, *Showcasing the Great Experiment: Cultural Diplomacy and Western Visitors to the Soviet Union, 1921–1941* (Oxford: Oxford University Press, 2012), 208.

The Fanatical Spirit of the Revolution

> Revolutions are produced by men of action,
> one-sided fanatics, geniuses of self-limitation.
> In a few hours or days they overturn the old or-
> der. The upheavals last for weeks, for years at
> the most, and then for decades, for centuries,
> people bow down to the spirit of limitation that
> led to the upheavals as to something sacred.
>
> —*Doctor Zhivago*
> Boris Pasternak

The Collapse of the Romanovs

The outbreak of war became an unmitigated disaster for Nicholas II, the Russian people and the minorities residing in the vast Russian Empire. Like other belligerents, its multi-ethnic people initially welcomed the war with feelings of intense adulation toward the Tsar; feelings that soon dissipated because of poor leadership, and primitive, inadequate weaponry. The influence at the court of the charismatic peasant, Grigori Rasputin, caused further harm, turning respect for the Tsar and Tsarina into contempt and ridicule. But it was systemic factors such as food distribution that ultimately destroyed the support the regime needed to survive.

The German military juggernaut in 1915 forced the Russian armies to retreat from Galicia and Poland. These debacles not only damaged troop morale but they also contributed to the fall of the regime when loyalty to the monarchy began to fade with the resignation of the military commander, the Grand Duke Nicholai

Mikhailovich, the uncle of the Tsar. It was devastating for the soldiers to see how easily the land they had fought for could slip away and to learn about the destruction of military stores of food and supplies. Soldiers expressed their bitterness by openly addressing the incompetence of their commanders. It became increasingly common to speak of "many traitors and spies in the high command of our army" and to wonder "what kind of tsar would surround himself with thieves and cheats."[1]

The situation was exacerbated after Nicholas, despite strong opposition from within his own government, made the catastrophic decision, on September 1, 1915, to become supreme military commander. By taking over this position when military prestige and its fortunes were at their nadir, he hastened his own demise. Besides having no military experience beyond the parade ground, he could not communicate with soldiers despite his fantasy that he shared a spiritual union with them. Possibly more damaging to his reputation was his subsequent decision to delegate his wife to fill the void of power at Petrograd. The Tsarina in turn entrusted this authority to the disreputable and inordinate influence of Rasputin who became the virtual ruler of Russia. Any trace of the aura associated with the Tsar evaporated with Rasputin's presence in Petrograd as his surrogates enveloped the royal palace in incompetence leaving outsiders to revel in salacious gossip and accusations of treason.

Even without the baleful influence of Rasputin, the German-born Tsarina would have experienced insurmountable difficulty in asserting positive influence over the Russian people at this time. Since Alexandra's marriage to Nicholas, her haughty demeanour, coupled with her penchant to withdraw in disdain from court, had alienated her natural allies. With four daughters and no male heir, her desperation drove her to consult with a motley group of mystics, and "holy fools" whose physical or mental disabilities were considered proof of their extraordinary powers.[2] The birth of a son temporarily provided her with joyful relief. But with the knowledge that Alexis had inherited haemophilia and consequently required vigilant protection, her reclusive behaviour, and tendencies to searchfordivine intervention, became more pronounced. Her vulnerability and need for spiritual sustenance permitted the last of a long line of magus's, the peasant Rasputin from the wilds of Siberia, to inveigle his way into the inner circle of the royal family.

The emergence of this interloper in November 1905 proved to be a decisive factor in sealing the fate of the dynasty already reeling from its disastrous war with Japan and an insurrectionary challenge to its autocracy. After Rasputin successfully controlled the prolonged internal bleeding in the joints of the young heir, he gained the confidence of the child and perhaps more important, the devotion of his distraught mother. All previous medical attempts had failed to ease Alexis's excruciating pain. Using a combination of hypnotism, magnetic eyes and a confident, relaxed manner, Rasputin successfully ministered to the heir, and once in his thrall persuaded the Tsarina that he was divinely inspired and sent by God to save her son. Given that her husband also believed that he was God's choice to rule the Russian people and thereby his mirror image, she was more susceptible to his machinations. This psychic vampirism assured him easy access to the court and the confidence of the Tsarina. Although Nicholas received from his Ministers and from Okhrana agents scathing reports about Rasputin's dissolute behaviour, he would brook no discussion about banishing the "holy man" from the court. In this "family matter," it was more important to consider the health of his son, allay the anxieties of his wife, and tolerate the antics of "Our Friend" than to listen to advisors who suggested that the semiliterate peasant besmirched the reputation of the court and alienated his most loyal supporters. For a conservative individual on matters of family and morality, it must have been very disquieting for Nicholas to hear reports (even if he refused to read them) about Rasputin's lapses into states of drunken stupor and his infamous debauchery in the city. Rasputin, who was likely a secret devotee of the orgiastic rites of the forbidden Khlyst sect, preached that only immersion in sin, especially of a sexual nature, could drive sin away because it led to suffering and suffering to holiness. The result was that hundreds of gullible women surrendered sexually to him in part because of his charisma but more in the misguided hope of achieving redemption. At the same time, he exercised a psychological influence on dissatisfied, rich women by soothing physical aches and emotional stresses with the touch of his hand. In a rare unguarded moment, Nicholas revealed Alexandra's deepening disturbance and the emotional control that she possessed over the Tsar: "Better one Rasputin than ten fits of hysterics every day."[3]

Rasputin's influence became a malignant threat to the throne during the Great War, particularly after Nicholas left Court to command the Army. Not only did he become the confidante of the Empress who wished to exercise power in her own right, but his influence exacerbated political instability and fed the gossip mill damaging the reputation of the dynasty. Given the secrecy surrounding the heir's illness and that no reputed reason was given for Rasputin's attendance at the court, the tabloid press reported that the Empress was his lover. That in turn fed rumours that the spineless, degenerate Emperor had shared his wife with the drunken, dirty rogue Rasputin. The most fantastic stories appeared in ambassadors' reports. Among them was that foreigners, criminals and traitors and possibly his own wife plied the hen-pecked husband with drink and narcotics.[4] Yet the sorcerer exploited Alexandra's dependence upon him by amassing the power to appoint and purge ministers, civil servants and bishops, anyone, in short, whose interests were in opposition to the will of the Tsar or Tsarina. He basked in this power by ensuring the dismissal of any official who attempted to thwart him. Whether he or Nicholas made the decision, the appointment of a known German supporter, Boris Stürmer, as Prime Minister in 1916, was widely attributed to the self-styled mystic. Not only was Stürmer an old, corrupt politician, but the choice was politically obtuse considering his sympathies and his German-sounding name at a time when the capital was rife with rumours of German spies skulking the corridors of power and that a pro-German court camarilla was sabotaging the war effort.

German agents were already spreading stories that the debauched German Tsarina was a spy feeding military secrets to the drunken peasant that were passed on to his surrounding scoundrels who then sold them to German intelligence. Rumours had become so distorted by the time they reached the front, demoralized soldiers were prepared to believe that the Germans had paid Stürmer to starve the peasants to death and that the Empress was supporting all the "spying Germans." How could they keep fighting as long as the Germans were "ruling Russia"? It was not difficult to ascertain the identity of who was the focus for this discontent. "Dark Forces" became the code word to describe Rasputin. Even the Tsar sensed the potential harm that Rasputin might unwittingly unleash when he warned his wife in his letters not to pass on to

"Our Friend" any information that he was confiding to her.

In the snake-pit of intrigue and gossip circulating in St. Petersburg, the Tsarina herself continued to be the target of outrageous scandal. It was reputed that she shared her bed with the incorrigible satyr and her lady-in-waiting, a tableau that was a symptom of the hatred she inspired. Alexandra's "sexual corruption" had become a metaphor for the diseased condition of the tsarist regime and the scuttlebutt contributed to discrediting the monarchy as it teetered toward its demise.[5] Just as the Romanovs traditionally scapegoated Jews, the public, angered by military defeat and incompetence, fastened on Rasputin and the court. No longer revered as godlike, the royal couple had become contemptible and risible.

Historians generally agree that the allegations against Alexandra and Rasputin were false. Given that most of her early life was spent in England and that she had jettisoned any German (and English) ties many years before, the notion that Alexandra was involved in a German cabal is preposterous. Her abiding contempt for the 1905 constitution that placed limits on the Tsar's power was indicative of her devotion to her adopted motherland and its autocracy. Rasputin was never a German agent but his power rendered him susceptible to bribes, gifts and sexual favours. He may have contributed to these perceptions through careless contacts in his concurrent life, the seamy demimonde of Petrograd (renamed during the war to expunge the German connotation of St Petersburg). Through his liaisons with aristocratic women, he associated with individuals who may have had contact with German agents. If there were any substance to the rumours, it derived from Alexandra's and Rasputin's increasing opposition to the war. Even before hostilities began, Rasputin sent a telegram to the Tsar imploring him not to "permit the mad to triumph and destroy themselves and the nation....[Otherwise] everything drowns in great bloodshed." By September 1916, Alexandra's letters to her husband revealed her desperation that unless he "stop this useless slaughter" at all costs, an inevitable uprising would occur as Rasputin had prophesied.[6]

His contemporaries viewed Rasputin as exercising extraordinary power. He knew that the widely held perception earned him a myriad of enemies, especially among monarchists who regarded him as a charlatan. He presciently warned that should any harm occur to him, the Tsar and the country would perish. When he had visions of a river of blood and of fire and smoke, these premonitions were "an uncanny and rationally inexplicable foreboding of what, in fact, would occur."[7] When an attempt to suborn him through bribery to leave Petrograd backfired after he informed the Tsarina, a shrewd move that enhanced his prestige with her, his enemies at the court decided to murder him. A coterie of court hangers-on, that included a nephew, a cousin of the Tsar and a duma deputy, finally dispatched him in late December 1916. Almost as if he possessed a preternatural presence, it took diluted wine laced with arsenic, several gun shots and a drowning in the icy waters off Petrograd to end his life.

But is this widely repeated, fantastical account true? According to Richard Cullen, a former British Police Commander, the official account is a tissue of lies to obscure the reality that British intelligence officers were instrumental in Rasputin's demise. Drawing upon forensic evidence from the Russian State Archive, a key letter from British intelligence, Russian sources that have not been translated and the findings of a prominent British pathologist, Cullen has written a radically revisionist account of the murder. He argues that British Secret Intelligence Service (SIS) was terrified that Rasputin would persuade the Tsar to make a separate peace treaty with Germany, and that one of its agents, Oswald Rayner, drawing upon his friendship with one of the conspirators, Felix Yusupov, was instrumental in the brutal torture and murder of Rasputin. The Tsarina's confident was not poisoned or drowned, but viciously beaten with a cosh and shot at point blank range. The cover story of the conspirators was of "saving Mother Russia" but, according to Cullen, it was designed to conceal the role of the SIS. Historians have largely drawn from the memoirs and diaries of the conspirators whom Cullen calls inveterate liars. The Tsar, however, always believed that the British were involved, even correctly describing the key player as "Yusupov's Oxford University friend," and questioned the British Ambassador about it. His Russian assassins deluded themselves into believing that with Rasputin's death, the Tsar would reclaim his plummeting prestige.[8]

The death of Rasputin, however, changed nothing except that he could no longer be the lightening rod for the allegations of tsarist incompetence. The assassins believed that the Tsarina would have a breakdown and be committed to an institution but despite her grief and failing health, she demonstrated a surprisingly strong will to rule.* What the supporters of the monarchy had not counted upon was the deteriorating psychological state of the Tsar. The mutinies and food riots, as well as his awareness of the gossip about Rasputin that continued to swirl around his family, released in him the impulse to retreat within, convincing outsiders that he was becoming mentally unstable. But this collapse of nerve was merely an extension of what the unprepossessing Nicholas had always done to conceal his distaste for politics, avoid hearing un-

Photo by the author.

The Livadia Palace was not only the summer home of the Nicholas II and his family but the site of the February 1945 Yalta Conference in which American President Franklin Roosevelt was and is still castigated for surrendering Eastern Europe to Stalin. This mistaken view fails to take into account that Stalin reneged on a promise to agree to free elections and that Soviet troops were already on the ground throughout what became the Soviet zone.

pleasant news or unwelcome suggestions: dissociate behind a passive exterior and a vague distant gaze. His more pronounced withdrawal into paralyzed passivity was a sign that he had given up on life itself and his future actions would be conducted as though he

---

* It is significant that at the Livadia Palace, among all the photos of the family, there is not a single one of Rasputin. One of the most revealing photographs shows a downcast Alexandra in what appears to be a wheelchair, after the death of Rasputin.

was an automaton resigned to the inevitable. More than ever he relied upon his fatalistic spirituality. His actions seemed to confirm the perception of one of his socialist adversaries who commented that Nicholas met adversity with "a kind of stubborn passivity, as if he wished to escape from life....He seemed not a man but a poor copy of one."[9]

By now Nicholas realized that his coronation oath that he would bequeath the throne to his heir, taken twenty-two years earlier, would be broken. When he signed the abdication document after having forfeited the support of his leading generals, he lapsed into a state of shock. After the initial humiliation, however, he seemed relieved, fortified by the prospect that he could live out the rest of his life in the country. But his diary accounts revealed, as they always did, the triviality of life and the vacuity of his mind without any awareness of the danger he and his family faced. Any allowance for intuition, reflection or flexibility had always been difficult; now when he most needed these resources, their absence likely contributed to the murder of the royal family.

In February 1917 the tsarist system under the Romanovs collapsed. Personalities aside, the systemic weaknesses in Russia were so severe that not even inspired leadership could have overcome them. Food distribution as opposed to production was one of the thorniest difficulties, and would plague the Tsar's successors. With the mobilization of peasant soldiers, large estates were badly affected by the war. In an attempt to pre-empt peasant seizure of their lands, landowners co-opted the wealthier peasants but they were more interested in producing for their own needs than marketing their crops to the city, a problem that would be faced by later Provisional and Bolshevik governments. These peasants ate well during the war; their cattle were better fed than were some workers in the cities. The tsarist government, like later governments, waged economic war on them through a system of price fixing and later compulsory requisition of the peasant's seed and produce. The low prices the state offered only encouraged peasants to withhold even more. Short of adopting terror as the Bolsheviks later did, the requisitions failed to induce the peasants to part with their crops; only soldiers who could trade away their coats or army boots and black marketers managed to persuade them to unload their produce. These problems were intensified by the government's decision to pay for the war by printing more roubles which fuelled inflation. Except for skilled armament workers, the real wages of most urban workers, who were performing unskilled work or of petty officials on fixed salaries, could not keep up with inflation. Even the skilled workers resented the war profiteering of their employers, a condition that was likely to cement their class solidarity with other workers.

These difficulties ultimately played out in the urban queues as women spent forty hours a week standing in line for bread provisions after their ten-hour shifts in factories. During the coldest winter of the third year of the war, blizzards and Arctic frosts brought the railways to a halt. The breakdown of the transport system starved Petrograd of regular food and fuel. Desperation drove the rumour mill; speculators and capitalists, who in the wartime atmosphere meant German or Jewish merchants, were deliberately withholding stocks. On February 23, 1917, the weather turned mild and people swarmed onto the streets to demand bread. By the afternoon, one-hundred thousand workers had come out on strike. Cossack soldiers, who usually repressed these outbursts with ruthlessness, for some inexplicable reason were not provided with their whips. Within two days, the city was virtually shutdown and the demonstrations had acquired a political character with calls for the end of the war and the overthrow of the autocracy. Although demonstrators clashed with the police, the soldiers stationed in the Petrograd garrison generally sided with the people. Any final hope that the Tsar harboured of retaining his position was shattered when he ordered the forcible repression of the crowds, a replay of what his military commander had done in 1905. But this time his commanding general did not have the nerve for such an undertaking. Nor did most of the soldiers who after one bloody encounter, refused to obey orders and fire upon their own people.

The February Revolution in 1917 was not bloodless, as it is often characterized. Anger was directed towards the monarchy and the institutions that sustained it: the police, the courts and the civil service. Opponents of the Tsar freed prisoners, often making no distinction between a political prisoner and a criminal. They tore down symbols and emblems of the old regime—tsarist statutes, imperial double-headed eagles, portraits of Nicholas II. Arsonists burned the Petrograd courthouse that housed the records of the tsarist secret service. The release of criminals and the presence of mutinying soldiers cast a dark shadow over the festive days of February. Street spectacles degenerated into hooliganism and riotous orgies as armed, drunken gangs smashed and looted stores, wine shops and particularly the underground stocks of the Winter Palace. The violence became more akin to a bacchanalia turning sour as the mobs revelled in wanton destruction and sheer brutality. In part, this bloodlust was the release of hatred which had been repressed for decades, but it was also inspired by the unbridled license of criminals to act out their psychopathic impulses. To arbitrarily execute a particularly cruel officer or to mete out rough justice on the street to a particularly corrupt official was perhaps understandable. It was unconscionable for mobs to break into the houses of the "possessing classes" and rob and rape the inhabitants. Whether this blind impulsive violence represented the actions of a small minority of unskilled labourers and renegade tsarist police or a more generalized response is an issue on which historians have not reached a consensus.[10]

What is clear is that these savage acts were expressions of the raw hatred toward the propertied classes or the bourgeoisie. But if that violence conveyed class hostility, a more generalized resentment was directed towards the *burzhooi*, a derisive epithet that applied to anyone whose appearance suggested he was not a worker, peasant or soldier. Even wearing spectacles, a white starched collar or simply clean clothes was enough to stigmatize an individual.[11] The intelligentsia especially were targeted for violent assault even in the trenches. One soldier wrote that if he could return to Russia, he would "not just bash the heads of our internal enemy but would fight a war against the intelligentsia...that old windbag."[12] By the February Revolution, *burzhooi* had become an expletive for a scoundrel similar to a speculator or saboteur. When the epithet was hurled against people on the street, violence would likely follow. When the deployment of language carried such lethal consequences, it is not surprising that more people died in February than in the Bolshevik October coup.

The Relationship between
Propaganda and the Deed

The February Revolution violence was spontaneous and without any one leader. There were, however, individuals with vested interests and members of socialist parties who targeted the monarchy through their pamphlets, songs and newspapers. The language in the streets was redolent of the Gothic; its purpose was to dehumanize. In the "Workers Marseillaise," the most popular song of the February Revolution, the lyrics expressed in a crude Gothic idiom the need to exorcise the predators in order to create a just world:

> To the parasites, to the dogs, to the rich!
> Yes and to the evil vampire-Tsar!
> Kill and destroy them, the villainous swine!
> Light up the dawn of a new and better life![13]

The overthrow of the Tsar became for many a precondition for winning the Great War. The so-called German connection had sullied the Court evidenced in its treacherous Ministers and Dark Forces personified by Alexandra and Rasputin. After February 1917 with its relaxed censorship, there was a surge in anti-tsarist pamphlets that included caricatures showing the royal couple in bed with Rasputin.[14] The lascivious depiction of Alexandra as a nymphomaniac with no sense of morality had become an emblem for the diseased condition of the royal state. The association of political with sexual corruption demonstrated how debased the monarchy had become and disabused anyone of the illusions that the Tsar was a divine being. By then, even a constitutional monarch was unacceptable to most people. Some conservative deputies in the duma would have preferred that option to a republic, but did not press the matter when they encountered stiff opposition from the elected representatives in the Petrograd soviet (council). Concurrent with the defiling of the monarchy, the revolution was interpreted as a victory over the enemy within, those treasonous elements that had sabotaged the war effort, but whose defeat could now inspire a renewal, but one incompatible with a monarchy. Even the White generals during the civil war (1918–20), who wanted a reinstatement of authoritarian rule, realized it would be suicidal to support the return of a tsar. Leon Trotsky vividly reinterpreted the Greek myth of Zeus being disgorged from the throat of his father, Cronus, reflecting that "the country had so radically vomited up the monarchy that it could never crawl down the people's throat again."[15]

The socialist press targeted the capitalists as much as the monarchy for their demonology; their rhetoric fanned the flames of class conflict. One best-selling pamphlet in 1917 was called *Spiders and Flies* published by the three major socialist parties—the Bolsheviks, the Mensheviks, and Socialist Revolutionaries.[16] In this brochure, shorn of arcane economic jargon, Russia is divided into two warring zoological species:

> The spiders are the masters, the money grubbers, the exploiters, the gentry, the wealthy, and the priests, pimps and parasites of all types!...The flies are the unhappy workers who must obey all those laws the capitalist happens to think up—must obey, for the poor man has not even a crumb of bread. The spider is the factory owner earning five or six roubles every day from each of his workers and impertinently giving them a paltry wage as if it were a kindness.

One participant in the Revolution later recalled that through this pamphlet he understood how a property owner "through merciless exploitation...sucks out the juices of the toilers like a spider."[17] His reflection reveals that emotional, polemical language, acquires verisimilitude if it connects to the reader's experience. That a popular pamphlet from the extreme rightist press also used the image of the Jew as a spider that sucked the blood of the harmless flies, namely the Russian people, would suggest a close correlation between the fanatical, socialist left and the chauvinistic, xenophobic right. [18]

Two examples of agitprop that complemented this inflammatory pamphlet were posters issued in 1919, *Kapital* and *The Spider and The Flies*. The former features a corpulent, grinning capitalist or burzhooi with slightly porcine facial features that were designed to spark repulsion in the viewer. Dressed in tails with a top hat, up to his waist in gold, he has a heart of gold hanging from his watch fob. In the background stretches a spider's web. He was the perfect stereotype for the well-fed rapacious capitalist. The latter, an anti-religious poster, shows a priest with unsavoury, smug facial features enmeshed in a web and stretching to clutch in his paw a couple of peasants (flies) intending to drink their blood, as other parishioners about to be exploited, trudge into his church. The two posters linked and ultimately conflated the capitalist with the priest, both enemies of the proletariat who would never triumph until its enemies were liquidated.[19]

Despite the Marxist–Leninist belief that language must create its own reality, it is hard to establish a direct causal relationship between the power of incendiary rhetoric and inflammatory posters, and violent action. The casual labourers or anyone who did not work in the munitions factories experienced economic difficulty in coping with the rising prices of inflation. The largely illiterate peasants who burned manor homes and seized land from landowners needed no encouragement from socialist newspapers. The exhausted, demoralized soldiers who either mutinied or simply, as Lenin once said, voted with their feet by deserting, were motivated more by rumours and wartime conditions than by rhetoric that demonized the Tsar and the Provisional Government created after the February Revolution. Indeed, when Alexander Kerensky, a lawyer and member of the Duma who had ties to the Socialist Revolutionaries, was appointed Minister of War, he acquired, for a short time, iconic status with ordinary workers and soldiers because he was perceived to be one of them. The failure of the spring offensive in 1917 with huge casualities in the hundreds of thousands, and an even larger number of desertions and mutinies, consequently dimmed the aura around him.

Leaving these important empirical conditions aside, there was a loose relationship between the power of words and the violence in the streets. Gorky, a journalist and writer with national and international stature, harboured no doubts about the destructive power of language. For one who had passionately sought the overthrow of the imperial system and hoped the welcomed Revolution would ignite a spiritual and cultural rebirth, the conditions that he observed around him were an anathema to any such liberation. He increasingly became a stentorian critic of those who fostered "the dark instincts." The newspapers, instead of promoting a sense of self worth and a greater pride in work that together would "develop and strengthen a social conscience and a social morality," succeeded in eliciting people's primitive passions. Journalists peppered their accounts with epithets such as 'scum' and 'traitor' for anyone who did not agree with them. Through their invective, they "teach people enmity and hatred for each other." With vivid reptilian imagery, he observed that "the newspapers are rolling around on the streets, a tangle of venomous snakes, poisoning and frightening the average citizen with their wicked hissing." Their choice of diction provoked Gorky to compare the newspaper polemics with the psychology of mob law where people dispensed rough justice by lynching or drowning a thief. In both cases, participants would take the "greatest delight in hitting their neighbour in the "mug" or in the heart as painfully and cruelly as possible." Instead of a revolutionary rebirth, "thick fogs of detestable vulgarity" blinded people and threatened to "poison and stifle" the dream of liberty and justice.[20] His understanding of history and psychology mobilized him to challenge the destructive cycle of injustice and revenge, and, perhaps more importantly, confront the Bolshevik leaders who inflamed the primitive instincts of the plebeians.

Gorky experienced a difficult and complicated relationship with its leader Vladimir Ilyich who acquired the nom de guerre, Lenin, in 1902. Until Lenin closed down Gorky's newspaper in July 1918 when the Bolsheviks confronted a serious military threat to their power and thereby could no longer tolerate his fusillades, the writer demonstrated great courage in scourging Lenin and the coterie around him. When Lenin called for the premature seizure of power in July 1917, six hundred Bolsheviks landed in jail and Lenin went into hiding. Gorky indicted those "who arouse the dark instincts of the masses" and the "oppressive Russian stupidity" that allows itself to be so easily manipulated by the political parties. Privately, he expressed relief that the Bolsheviks had received a major setback that might prove to be fatal.[21]

Gorky's intuitions might have been accurate if unforeseen events, known as the Kornilov Affair, had not occurred. A growing power struggle between Prime Minister Kerensky and his new Commander-in-Chief, Lavr Kornilov, contributed to a colossal misunderstanding that led the Kornilov to march on Petrograd under the mistaken impression that the Prime Minister was the captive of the Bolsheviks. Kerensky, believing that Kornilov was attempting to overthrow his government, turned to the socialist parties for assistance. Bolsheviks were released from jail and armed. The coup was thwarted, but respect for Kerensky evaporated because conservatives believed that Kornilov had been undermined. Subsequently, the socialist parties moved to the left, The

Bolsheviks being the chief beneficiaries. not only had they been resuscitated, but also because of hesitations by the other parties, Lenin immediately grasped the opportunity for seizing power. On October 25 Lenin and his reluctant colleagues encountered virtually no resistance. It is almost surreal that one of the most momentous events in the twentieth century transpired with little notice. In Petrograd the factories continued to operate, the trams to run, and the restaurants and theatres to remain open. Most of the Bolshevik leaders did not know until hours before that the revolution was to occur.

The Toxic Racism of the White Terror

After the Bolsheviks seized power, the Russian Empire devolved into a state of chaos and war between the Reds and the so-called Whites. The latter were a motley group who opposed the Bolsheviks: monarchists, landlords, members of the bourgeoisie that included small shop owners, and the liberal intelligentsia. Even the socialist parties—the Mensheviks and the Socialist Revolutionaries—opposed the Bolsheviks. That they were so fractured explain in part why they lost the civil war. The catalyst for the destructive blood-letting was Lenin's decision to make peace with Germany and sign the Treaty of Brest–Litovsk. In addition to the hatred inspired by the Bolshevik dictatorship, this humiliating treaty ceded to Germany a large portion of Russian territory on its western border, including one quarter of its pre-war population and its best agricultural land. opponents despised the national humiliation provoked by the treaty and mobilized to take up arms. Their savagery was invariably preceded by rhetoric that demonized their non-Russian ethnic enemies, especially Jews. The Whites, inspired by the *Protocols*, mobilized medical and biological metaphors that underscored their anti-Semitism.

White armies were intent on destroying Bolshevik power, establishing a military dictatorship and reclaiming the former Russian Empire. They should have defeated the Reds since they controlled most of the territory of the former empire, recruited experienced generals and officers, and received limited military support from abroad. But their disdain for politicians and the parliamentary process cost them their initial advantage. When White generals urged their men to "take no prisoners" among the Bolsheviks, because

53

the "more terrible the more victories," it proved to be counter-productive given that they incurred enemies, particularly among the peasantry who constituted eighty-five percent of the population. Since the officers were sons of the old gentry and bitter about losing their birthright, their hatred against the peasantry guaranteed that any economic and social gains from the October Revolution would be rolled back.[22] Whites would dispossess peasants from the land they had legally owned before 1917 and their economic policies restricted the right of Jews to freely trade. As purveyors of terrorism, the Whites took every opportunity to inflict atrocities upon the peasantry. The peasants in turn resisted conscription into their armies contributing to the Whites' ultimate defeat. When those dragooned into enlisting deserted, indiscriminate floggings and summary executions followed, not merely of the culprits, but also of villagers who might have sheltered them.

As supporters of centralized rule, the Russian Whites made no appeal to the non-Russian minorities. Yet the Don Cossacks in the Ukraine, who had acquired special status under the Tsars if they served in the military for a lengthy period, found a common cause with the Whites in their hatred of Bolshevism, the peasantry and Jews. The Cossacks pursued their own war of ethnic cleansing by driving thousands of non-Cossacks out of their villages and murdering hundreds as Bolsheviks.[23] Anti-Semitism escalated owing to the influx of refugees fleeing the war against Germany and Austria–Hungary, and to the pressing need of a scapegoat for Russia's continuing military deterioration. Rather than target the third-rate generals and the profiteers who were bilking millions in the production of weapons and outfitting, it was convenient to blame "internal Germans" as Jewish spies.[24] Several innocent Jews were hanged for espionage while others suffered a ruthless eviction from Petrograd.

When officers in the White Army equated Jews with Bolsheviks, the rise of Bolshevism exacerbated anti-Semitism. It was true that with increasingly violent persecution under the tsars, a large number of Jews joined the Bolsheviks. Certain well-known Party luminaries were Jews, notably Trotsky, the commander of the Red Army. This greatly contributed to the apprehension that Jews were enemies of the anti-Bolshevik cause and stoked the xenophobic Black Hundreds' fantasy that the Jews were responsible for the plight of Russia. Yet the politically active represented a small minority; the vast majority of Jews toiled in economic misery and provisionally supported the Bolsheviks because they had sanctioned the peasant acquisition of land. The larger reality that most Jews were not Bolsheviks was conveniently ignored.

Traditional anti-Semitism among the White officers accelerated fears to a pathological proportion. An English journalist who spent time at a commander's quarters reported that these officers believed a "whole cataclysm had been engineered by some great and mysterious society of international Jews, who, in the pay and at the order of Germany, had seized the psychological moment and snatched the reins of government." The conspiratorial sentiment was similar to that later employed by Adolf Hitler in *Mein Kampf.* A White intelligence report from the Ukraine warned:

> It was necessary to neutralize the microbe—the Jews....As long as the Jews are allowed to do their harmful work, the front will always be in danger....Clever [Jewish] agents, under the cover of patriotism and monarchism, mix with young soldiers, and with the help of cards, women and wine they lure the debauched youth into their nets.[25]

White generals, obsessed with the fear that international Bolshevism was plotting the destruction of Orthodox Christianity, employed propaganda to portray Lenin as a demonic entity leading a Jewish-Masonic crusade and Trotsky as the monstrous "Jewish mass killer."[26] Since Trotsky realized that his Jewish background could be a propaganda liability if he served as leader of the Red Army, he initially refused to accept the position, and only did so with Lenin's persuasion.[27] Nevertheless, Trotsky's leadership allowed the White generals to indoctrinate their forces with the canard that the Bolshevik Revolution was a Jewish plot and a phase in their struggle for world domination. They exploited this propaganda windfall by ensuring that army officers possessed extracts from the bogus *Protocols.*

Convinced by the authenticity of the *Protocols,* the Whites exploited it to unleash barbarous action against the Jews. With the encouragement of local priests, Cossacks and White officers ordered pogroms against the "chosen people of the Bolsheviks" or they refused to restrain their ill-disciplined soldiers when they participated in cruelty and the wanton killing of Jews. They found a receptive audience among the Ukrainian peasants who had been subjected to a brutal requisition policy by Bolshevik commissars. These peasants recognized an opportunity to unleash their hatred on Jews, many of whom, entrusted by landlords to manage the estates, bore the brunt of peasant hostility. Ukrainian peasants, incited by Orthodox clergy and frequently joined by soldiers, targeted the Jews, long regarded as Bolshevik spies, "foreign elements" and economic exploiters; villages were burned to the ground and Jews were taken hostage or killed in reprisal for Red Terror. In some places such as Chernobyl, Cossacks herded Jews into a synagogue and then torched the site; in other locations they gang-raped pre-teen girls. One particularly horrific practice was to bury Jews up to their neck and then ride horses over their exposed heads. In these savage outbursts, which peaked in intensity and frequency in the Ukraine, all sides, including the Red Army, participated. Recent documentation indicates that at least one hundred and fifty thousand deaths and three hundred thousand injured Jewish victims can be attributed to the pogroms of the civil war era. Only the magnitude of the Shoah conducted against Jews during World War II exceeded the holocaust that occurred during the Russian civil war.[28] Had the Whites prevailed, the Jewish population in Russia would have been decimated.

White Russians who fled Russia after the triumph of the Bolsheviks brought copies of the *Protocols* to Germany. Its distribution resulted in the revitalization of anti-Semitism through the myth of Judeo-Bolshevism. Without the Russian Revolution and the civil war, the *Protocols* would have remained an obscure document, its influence limited to a few Russian fanatics. After 1919, they achieved worldwide infamy especially in Western Europe, Great Britain, convincing even Winston Churchill, and In the United States where Henry Ford promoted them to a receptive right-wing American audience.

The Ideological Zealotry of the Red Terror

From the outset, the Bolsheviks established the prototype of the totalitarian regime in the twentieth century. They deployed a biological-hygienic boilerplate to demonize enemies, crushed any form of dissent, and dismantled political institutions and values associated with the "sham" democracy. The Party mobilized popular anger to further its ideological agenda and sought to subsume all individuality under their ideology. With the formation of an omnipotent police institution to unleash terror against alleged enemies of the regime, and the creation of concentration camps, a totalitarian regime was firmly established.

Before the October coup, Gorky had presciently and bitterly lamented how the "lies and filth of politics...will [poison] us with anger, hate and revenge." The Bolshevik Party had been extraordinarily adept at mobilizing widespread anger against both the monarchy and the Provisional Government. Once the Party was in power, Gorky excoriated it because of its willingness to exterminate anyone who did not embrace its ideological doctrines or whose class background was suspect. Its agents arrested opposition members, closed down the "bourgeois newspapers," and both encouraged and legitimized murder, demonstrating that Bolsheviks were no different from their tsarist predecessors—but far more ruthless. When they ordered soldiers to shoot unarmed demonstrators protesting the delayed opening of the Constituent Assembly because the Bolsheviks lost the November elections to the Socialist Revolutionaries, Gorky underscored the similarity between Bolshevik actions and the Bloody Sunday massacre of 1905. The presence of "red flags everywhere" was not a deterrent. A Lenin-sponsored resolution failed to pass, so he ordered the closure of the Assembly after one day. He denounced and arrested opponents, notably the Cadets—constitutional liberals who promoted political but not social reform—as counter-revolutionaries who "cold-bloodedly dishonour[ed] the revolution and dishonour[ed] the working class by forcing it to organize bloody slaughter."[29]

Lenin deemed parliamentary democracy and the rule of law archaic relics of the past that had no place in this revolution. Bolshevik power was not based upon popular sovereignty, but on the conviction that the movement of history toward a socialist future was on its side If Lenin saw himself wielding power to forge a new society untrammelled by law, Gorky portrayed him as a misguided scientist manipulating the masses as if they were pliable ore in his experiments. Lenin, who never lived among workers and peasants and had no empathy for their aspirations, regarded them less as human beings than as the raw material for his socialist vision. Even when he allowed the peasantry to seize land from the nobility, the Church and the Crown during the October Revolution, he was motivated more by a tactical reason: winning their support not redressing economic injustices, as subsequent events abundantly demonstrated. Gorky suggested that Lenin's elitist contempt for others mirrored the nobility's disdain and that his lack of morality also corresponded to its attitudes. Gorky's perception was credible given that Lenin's father rose to be a provincial director of schools and consequently acquired the rank of hereditary noble. Lenin had self-trained to become a lawyer but never held a job in his life. He was principally a professional revolutionary living apart from society supported by Party funds and the income from his mother's estate until her death in 1916. He was a "cold-blooded trickster who spare[d] neither the honour nor the life of the proletariat."[30]

While Lenin's contempt extended to the peasants, peasants equated vampires with the nobility, the lineage from which Lenin was associated. He was simply projecting upon them the insensitivity he exuded when he lived off the income of his estates, and insisted on prompt rent payments indifferent to the pleas from hungry peasants who worked his land. Rarely did Lenin muster the same degree of hatred toward the nobility that he bore toward the bourgeoisie, priests and peasants. In a similar vein through their posters, the Bolsheviks pandered to popular Gothic superstitions—faith in witches, sorcerers and monsters—with their call to "Purge the Unclean," in the sense of ritual cleansing.[31] As a demonic class species, kulaks deserved their fate. In response to kulak uprisings, Lenin's language exuded an inflammatory intensity: hang "no fewer than one hundred known kulaks," seize hostages and all the grain from the "bloodsucker kulaks." Yet in fairness to Lenin, as he became increasingly disillusioned with putting poor peasants in charge of collective farms, he toned down his rhetoric admitting in December 1920 that "we got carried away with the struggle against the kulak and lost all sense of measure."[32]

Gorky never joined the Bolshevik Party. Though he had known Bolshevik leaders and supported their ideas for many years, he was determined to retain his political independence. He viewed Lenin and Trotsky (who had recently become an official Party member) as dangerous demagogues, who had been "poisoned with the filthy venom of power." They endorsed the macho swaggering, gun-toting People's Commissars, who without scruples, arrested, and murdered anyone who did not support them. When the Commissars shouted about "the necessity of fighting the bourgeois and the ignorant masses [took] this as a direct call to murder," they were implementing Lenin's admonitions. Gorky contended that as a "slave to dogma," Lenin's "demagogy snuff[ed] out the embryo of...social conscience and spill[ed] a torrent of Russian blood" that would ultimately result in "a prolonged disillusionment with the very idea of socialism." [33]

Gorky's prognostication was wishful thinking. For Bolshevik ideologues, Marxism was not merely a faith but a science that heralded the development of communism. Unlike socialism that inspired the woolly-headed romantic dreamers of the past, Marxism followed precise demonstrable historical laws that the Bolshevik Party, renamed Communist in 1918, interpreted as general truths. Their version of history decreed that the October Revolution was irreversible; the inevitable transformation of Russian society into a workers' paradise would occur as long as the proletarian dictatorship, presided over by an elite vanguard as its guide, was protected from bourgeois or counter-revolutionary sabotage. This epochal change justified any means: the crushing of enemies, destruction of historical institutions, manipulation and lies. For its followers, all crimes, excesses and mistakes committed by the Party were the necessary price for fulfilling its historical destiny. However vehemently they were convinced that history favoured their efforts, the believers also had to accept that the Party elite were vessels for the repositories of truth and that no deviance was permitted. Any divergence from this secular theocracy was heretical, even treasonous because it could undermine the Party's lofty mission. The evangelical undertaking included the promise of universality, that is, that the historical experiment the Party was creating would spread to the West and to the rest of the world; it would become the avant-garde of humanity. That utopian belief was the premise behind the creation of the "Third International" wherein the Party endeavoured to extend its tentacles throughout the world through communist parties created in its image.[34] Without that faith, the Party could not sustain the loyalty of it adherents. The dehumanizing propaganda rallied the faithful and mobilized them into action, but that in and of itself would never have succeeded without the faith of the ideology: the conviction that from the dialectical conflict between capitalism and socialism would emerge the earthly salvation of Communism. This faith armoured the believers against "bourgeois humanism" and justified the enormous sacrifices and deprivation that they endured. The same was exacted from the refractory masses, in whose name they were changing the world, at times through the committing of cruelties and the shedding of blood.

The Bolshevik faith demanded an extensive psychological investment. In receiving this from its followers, it was rendered impervious to rational discourse even when based upon empirical evidence. That faith required from its members, in the interests of the Party, an unquestioning obedience and acceptance of its ideological certainties, unequivocal support for Lenin in the war to end privilege and a readiness to place public commitments above their own and their family's well being. Escalating the campaign against the *burzhooi*, Lenin exploited deep-rooted class resentments through his decree of "looting the looters" and sanctioning spontaneous acts of plunder and retribution. Any action from the confiscation of jewellery and dark fur coats or the imposition of punitive taxes, to the taking of hostages until debts were paid, was permissible, indeed popular, with a large number of, in Gorky's words, "ordinary people." Lenin endorsed the atavistic blood lust to avenge some ancient grudge: a neighbour with a vendetta to pursue, or a debtor who wished to liquidate a creditor.

Courtesy of Photofest

In Sergei Eisenstein's 1928 October, *his take on the 1917 Revolution, a look-a-like Lenin is given reverential treatment as his audience glows in his presence. By contrast, after Trotsky was exiled to Alma Ata in Central Asia, Stalin ordered all references to Trotsky deleted. The storming of the Winter Palace had in reality been a prosaic affair but, in Eisenstein's staging of the event, there were more casualties prompting an elderly porter who had been sweeping up the broken glass to comment, "Your people were much more careful the first time they took the palace."*

Yet Lenin was astute enough to realize he needed a loyal and merciless security police, one with power "totally unlimited by any laws, absolutely unrestrained by regulations and based directly on the use of force." Accordingly, the omnipotent Cheka was created in December 1917, and was awarded extra-judicial status at Lenin's behest to arrest, often at night, to investigate and to pass sentence, which invariably meant execution, displacement to concentration camps or involuntary exile. To ensure its brutality and to allay his feeling that Russians were too soft, Lenin pressed for the Cheka recruitment of "hard people" among non-Russians. Poles, Jews and Latvians, whose backgrounds would have instilled in them anti-Russian or anti-White sentiments, were better motivated to apply the harsh measures.[35]

Lenin's decision to appoint the fanatical Polish nobleman, Felix Dzerzhinsky, as head of the Cheka is a case in point. Aptly described by a biographer of Solzhenitsyn as a "bureaucrat of torture, thin-faced, goatee-bearded El Greco of terror," Dzerzhinsky converted the unswerving, intense religious zeal of a child into an ascetic, militant Marxist revolutionary.[36] The abiding faith in his secular religion fortified him during the two decades since 1898 that he spent either in the underground or in prison where he was frequently subjected to torture with methods he later applied to others. His prison experience turned him into a zealot. Even after he was released, he continued to subsist on the mint tea and bread that had sustained him in prison while working often late at night in an unheated room. Family considerations were secondary to the cause—Dzerzhinsky entrusted his son to a working class family where "it is easiest to preserve and enrich one's soul."[37] In the prison diaries he wrote around the beginning of the century, Dzerzhinsky articulated the philosophy that would serve as the fundamental requirement of any future Cheka recruit and loyal Party member: "Life is such that it rules out sentiment, and woe to the man who lacks the strength to overcome his feelings." A hatred for class enemies of the revolution impregnated his soul, and, according to Isaac Steinberg, Commissar of Justice, Dzerzhinsky took refuge in narcotics to deaden his conscience.[38] Like Lenin, he passionately believed that terror in any form—dismemberment with axes, slow-boiling or burning, crucifixion—was justified in the name of the ideology he served.

Similar to a medieval inquisitor who condemned a heretic to the flames, Dzerzhinsky ordered the arrest and arbitrary execution of anyone that threatened the victory of the "oppressed" proletariat.

He left the often en masse executions to underlings, "hard men without pity" that were prepared "to sacrifice everything for the Revolution."[39] Since his mandate was to search out and liquidate all counter-revolutionaries, his first and perhaps only question of a suspect was to inquire into their class origins. In chilling language in a letter he wrote to his wife, he was determined to steel himself so that he could be "as pitiless as a loyal watchdog as [he tore] the enemy apart."[40] Although some Bolshevik leaders feebly complained about the absence of due process, Lenin afforded Dzerzhinsky and the security force untrammelled freedom to arbitrarily confiscate private property, arrest, torture and execute without concerning themselves with the "nitpicking legalism." Lenin defended the Cheka "unjustly accused of excesses by a few unrealistic intellectuals."[41] They were "spineless drooling" liberals and humanitarians who protected those whom Lenin condemned as enemies: "And we need to catch and destroy active counterrevolutionaries. The rest is clear"—meaning that the "terror must be legalized" and its sphere of application as broad as possible.[42] Better that nine innocent people die rather than one genuine counterrevolutionary escapes punishment, a belief that would calcify into an unquestioning dogma. With its power to conduct prophylactic terror, the Cheka became awash in the bloody froth of its victims.

With a combination of anger and despair, and the realization that he would be the target of hostile criticism for his "betrayal of the working class," Gorky condemned the "bloody butcheries, pogroms [and] arrests of people who are not guilty of anything."[43] To his sorrow and increasing pessimism, the disheartened Gorky believed that it was the people who confiscated Church and noble property and dispensed justice in the streets through lynching, shooting and drowning. Their actions undermined his faith in the potential redemption of the Russian people. One of the most perceptive historians of the Revolutionary period, Orlando Figes, has confirmed Gorky's perceptions:

> For, however much one may condemn it, and however hard it is to admit, there is no doubt that the Terror stuck a deep chord in the Russian civil war mentality, and that it had a strange mass appeal. The slogan 'Death to the Bourgeoisie!' written on the walls of the

Cheka interrogation rooms, was also the slogan of the street. People even called their daughters Terrora.[44]

The Bolsheviks' ability to mobilize primitive impulses made it easier to destroy any remaining vestiges of the rule of law. In November 1917, Lenin liquidated the entire legal system including almost all of the courts and the professionals who served in that system. The following March, he replaced local courts with "People's Courts" where its judges tried persons charged with "counterrevolutionary crimes" and were guided by the dictates of "revolutionary conscience." These courts empowered ordinary people with no legal knowledge or experience to try cases. Since their outcome was usually dictated by class considerations, one look at the hands of the accused could determine guilt or innocence. Still, the judges disappointed Lenin because they were reluctant to pass the death sentence with the zeal he would have desired; in 1918 in 4,483 cases, they meted out only fourteen death penalties.[45] Lenin did not, however, rely on the courts alone as he demanded by the summer of 1918 that more punitive actions were necessary.

The systematic use of terror was always a core component of the Bolshevik arsenal. As early as 1906, Lenin acknowledged that the masses needed to be organized for a "ruthless war of extermination."[46] Without minimizing the dynamics of a fierce civil war in a life and death struggle against counter-revolutionary White and foreign armies, peasant rebels called Greens and national minorities in the border regions, Lenin exploited that confrontation to accelerate a campaign of terror. Their seizure of power was predicated on the assumption that terror was an indispensable instrument in maintaining and wielding power. Lenin's inflammatory rhetoric "war to the death against the rich, the idlers and the parasites" accelerated violence in the countryside. In December 1917, he conjured up entomological metaphors by exhorting each town and village to find their own way of "cleansing the Russian land of all vermin, of scoundrel fleas, the bedbug rich and so on." He then amplified his sulphurous volley with specific suggestions: prison, cleaning latrines, wearing yellow tickets after they have served their time so that the population could maintain surveillance. Finally, he recommended shooting every ten idlers.[47] Lenin's exterminatory rhetoric, even when it was not carried out in reality,

63

served to strengthen the belief of his enemies during the civil war that defeat would likely mean their death.

Any attempt to restrain coercion was scotched by Lenin and his potentates. In February 1918 when Trotsky introduced a decree supported by Lenin that execution be dispensed "on the spot" to a broad and undefined category of villains, the apprehensive Isaac Steinberg, Lenin's Commissar of Justice, objected that such a drastic measure would pervert justice and initiate revolutionary terror. When Lenin expressed unbending opposition, Steinberg proposed in jest that the Ministry be renamed the "Commissariat for Social Extermination." Lenin retorted, "Well put...that's exactly what it should be...but we can't say that." Steinberg later commented that the "soil of revolutionary Russia was poisoned in that period."[48] Six months later when an attempt was made on Lenin's life, the poison metastasised as a hardened Lenin embraced an all-out dictatorship that would ruthlessly eliminate the Revolution's enemies. Punishment and intimidation became its modus operandi to ensure that the population was cowed into submission. Zinoviev, the Party boss of Petrograd, accelerated the exclusionary message when, addressing a gathering of Communists, he made no attempt to conceal the meaning of the Red Terror: "We must carry along with us 90 million out of the 100 million of Soviet Russia's inhabitants. As for the rest, we have nothing to say to them. They must be annihilated."[49]

After the attempt on Lenin's life, the Cheka was reorganized to take pre-emptive action against enemies of the people with no obligations to consult with the police and the courts. Within the first year, sixty-three hundred non-Bolsheviks were executed without trial. Gorky believed that the social revolution had "given full play to the evil and brutal instincts" that had accumulated within the ordinary person under the Romanov dynasty, resulting in the extermination of those who were from a different class or who expressed dissent.[50] Because he oscillated in his relationship with Lenin—embracing him and the Bolshevik cause after the assassination attempt yet needling him after the arrest of hundreds of intellectuals—Lenin seized upon Gorky's poor health from a perforated lung to persuade him to go into exile. Gorky's penchant for blaming the victimized masses for the violence and underestimating the radical utopian goals of the Communist leadership, as well as their willingness to use whatever means were necessary to achieve them, proved years later to be a deciding factor in his fatal decision to return to Russia.

In the meantime, Gorky's fears of the revolution unleashing the most primitive behaviour proved accurate. As Red Army commander, Trotsky and his arch rival Stalin mirrored each other by displaying no compunction regarding the shedding of blood. Trotsky ordered the execution of Red army officers who had permitted unauthorized retreats and of political commissars for disobedience or cowardice. In 1921, on the naval base in the Gulf of Finland the Kronstadt, he also ruthlessly suppressed a rebellion of sailors who believed the Bolsheviks had betrayed the egalitarian spirit of the October Revolution; over twenty-five hundred sailors were summarily executed. On the southern front, Stalin torched villages in order to intimidate neighbouring ones from resisting the demands of the Red army and he was prepared to sink a barge and drown all the sacked former imperial officers since he believed they were sabotaging the Red cause, had Moscow not intervened to contravene the order. The Bolshevik Reds exercised a policy of revolutionary fervour as they routinely executed captured Whites. In an effort to eliminate Cossacks, one local Bolshevik leader called for "an indiscriminate policy of mass extermination" that led to the execution of more than eight thousand Cossacks over one month in 1919. If they found a child of a condemned man, he would be seized and dispatched with the parting salvo: "You can follow your damned daddy."[51]

The terror could strike anyone denounced as a counter-revolutionary, but particularly individuals whose background included either wealth or privilege or who had connections with the old regime. The seizing and execution of hostages for reprisals for potential future attacks on the Bolsheviks was a consistent thread of the Terror. A person could be arrested simply by being near the scene of a "bourgeois provocation" [a crime] or being a relative of a "bourgeois counter-revolutionary." While awaiting the interrogation that would determine his or her life, a person endured the loathsome putrid conditions of overcrowded cells, no sanitation, grossly inadequate food, water and heat, and the risk of typhus. They would be subjected to physical or psychological torture, which included a fake execution using a gun with blanks, being buried alive or confined in a coffin with another corpse.[52] The Cheka introduced what was to become a signature form of interrogation during the later Stalinist era, the conveyor belt. An "enemy of the people" would stand on cold or hot floors for days leading to swelling in the feet and legs and be deprived of sleep through uninterrupted harassment by rotating investigators.

A person could be executed or capriciously released, the latter outcome sometimes abetted with a generous bribe, or he could be astoundingly lucky to encounter a rescuer who still retained the residue of some decent human impulses. The socialist revolutionary, Pitirim Sorokin, a teacher (and later Harvard professor of sociology) recounted how during his imprisonment, he witnessed many men and women who were taken away for execution, (and in one case a fake execution). He was himself miraculously saved when one of his former admiring students, now a Chekist, intervened with Lenin. Although grateful, he could not restrain his fear and hatred toward the Bolsheviks:

> Every night we hear the rattles of trucks bearing new
> victims. Every night we hear the rifle fire of execution,
> and often some of us hear from the ditches, where the
> bodies are flung, faint groans and cries of those who
> did not die at once under the guns. People living near
> those places begin to move away. They cannot sleep.

In his diary, he grimly invokes Gothic tropes: "this voracious monster, the Revolution, cannot live without drinking human blood."[53]

Those spared from execution, including women, children and old people, would be dispatched to a concentration camp. They were primarily in Lenin's words, the politically "unreliable elements," incarcerated not for wrongful behaviour but for who they were. Inmates contended with an inhospitable terrain of Arctic cold, swampy, mosquito-infested summers, the sadism of the guards, and the horror of collective punishment: any attempt to escape would guarantee the execution of others. By 1923, three hundred camps were established housing seventy thousand inmates.[54] By the time he died, Lenin had built the foundations of the Soviet state, enabling his heir to construct an edifice that he would have approved and one that remained intact for over seven decades.

The War against the Countryside

> The Kingdom of darkness...is nothing else
> but a confederacy of deceivers that to ob-
> tain domination over men in this present
> world, endeavour by dark and erroneous
> doctrines, to extinguish in them the light
>
> —*Leviathan*
> Thomas Hobbes

Conflict Within the Party

During his last year before paralysis reduced him to a spectral presence, Lenin harboured grave misgivings about a "rude" Stalin who had directed verbal obscenities at his (Lenin's) wife Krupskaya. Demanding an apology that never occurred before he suffered a severe heart attack from which he never recovered, Lenin nonetheless dictated shortly before his death in January, 1924, a testament in which he praised Trotsky as the "most able individual in the current Central Committee," distinguished "by his outstanding abilities." He also recommended that Stalin be dismissed from his Party position (not from the Central Committee or the Party itself) and be replaced with someone "more patient, more loyal, more courteous and more attentive to comrades, less capricious, etc." One of his biographers believes that he likely would have removed Stalin from the position of General Secretary if he had not been ill. His testament was a belated effort to halt Stalin.[1] That he was not dislodged from his position and influence can be attributed largely to the suspicions of Stalin's colleagues about Trotsky's Menshevik background, his co-option of tsarist generals into the Red Army during the civil war and the perception that Trotsky was a "Bonaparte figure" who might use the armed forces to undermine Bolshevik objectives.[2] Stalin's capacity for exploiting these fears by forging temporary alliances with men he would later liquidate not only marginalized Trotsky but enabled him to carry out the hard spirit of Leninism.

That spirit in the early 1920s was much more evident in Lenin's rhetoric than in reality. To save the revolution and prevent a catastrophic famine from deepening in 1921, Lenin adopted state capitalism, the New Economic Policy (NEP). This volte-face allowed a degree of private enterprise including the right of peasants and the bourgeoisie (Nepman) to market their own goods while state industry was required to adopt "capitalist methods." Equally important was his recognition that peasants could not be coerced to join collective farms. Through incentives that included education, electrification, equipment, and medical supplies he could effect a socialist transformation in the farming communities.

Lenin's initial belief that peasants would voluntarily join cooperatives was belied by their innate conservatism that would eventually pit them against Party ideologues. Despite a good harvest in the fall of 1927, low state prices forced a calamitous decline in grain marketing and a severe food shortage in the winter of 1927–28. Peasants increasingly held back a larger proportion of their produce for their own consumption, animal feed and distilling grain into vodka prompting fears of a "kulak strike." The debate on whether to continue with NEP or embrace a more radical position now acquired greater urgency. Moderates, like the more cautious Nikolai Bukharin, who opposed forcing the pace of socialism on the peasantry, attempted to enlist peasant support with an offer of increased prices. Unlike Trotsky, Stalin had once been supportive of the NEP, but seized a competitive advantage in exploiting Bukharin's position. The Party, which faced the prospect of hunger in the cities, responded to Stalin's manifesto for a crash collectivization that would establish agricultural factories and end private farming. When Stalin reintroduced the hard spirit of Leninism by the end of the decade, the temporary respite in the war against the peasantry during the NEP came to an abrupt end, as a nightmare engulfed the countryside.

Through his position as General Secretary, Stalin was ideally situated to succeed Lenin as he had seeded his minions into the bureaucracy. But in the late 1920s, since he was only first among equals, he had to call upon his iron resolve and persuade his colleagues in the upper Party echelon. To glom onto supreme power, Stalin isolated and disgraced colleagues who exercised any political independence by exploiting their failures, including their capacity to underrate him, and by playing them off against each other. Then he could destroy them politically and later complete the job by eliminating them physically. With Lenin's former friends and associates stripped of their power and having surrounded himself with craven underlings, Stalin was in a position to convince the Party faithful that his agricultural and industrial policies were essential preconditions for the nation's modernization; only a modern society could provide military security against an "imperialist" attack. Without these fundamental changes, the Soviet Union, with its backward and superstitious peasantry, remained wedded to the pre-industrial past, one that left it marooned in a hostile capitalist world.

Stalin was largely accelerating Lenin's policies under War Communism (1918-1921). As Marxists, Bolsheviks could only articulate opposition or difference in class terms. With a distorting ideological lens, they distinguished the exploitative kulaks from other peasants. Embarrassed by the spectacle of putting poor peasants in charge of collectives, Lenin rejected this binary division and placed his hopes on the middle peasants even though he recognized that kulaks were the most prosperous because they were the most industrious and literate. Yet Bolshevik rhetoric after his death never appreciated the cohesiveness of rural communities—that almost all peasants were united in their belief that they should retain a fair share of the grain that they had toiled to produce. Distrusting the peasantry because of their potential power to control the food supply, Bolsheviks designated as kulak, denoting an inhuman enemy of the people, anyone they perceived to be a rural capitalist or to be resisting requisitioning.[3]

When stripped of their humanity, kulaks became the target of vicious verbal attacks and subsequent murderous deeds, similar to those experienced by the racial enemies of the Nazis. Kulaks were "avaricious, bloated and bestial," similar to spiders, leeches and vampires who sucked the blood out of working people. The application of Gothic rhetoric to the more enterprising peasants, "sated and self-satisfied, their money-boxes stuffed...obstinately deaf and indifferent to the starving workers and peasant poor," was anchored as much in fantasy as in objective reality.[4] This metaphorical language was partially apt because the greatest killer of the peasants during the civil war was the louse. Typhus struck at bedraggled bodies already weakened by famine. But it was also a chimera to demean peasants as inferior and unproductive, a smear that fed the prejudices of the town and urban populations.

Firmly ensconced as Lenin's heir, Stalin advanced the proposition that class warfare must intensify to assure greater progress toward socialism. To create a society free of exploitation and private gain, the state had to begin "eliminating the kulaks as a class" of capitalist exploiters who, by withholding grain or employing hired labour, prevented the Soviet Union from becoming a modern industrialized society. The target could be any peasant who, as beneficiary of the NEP, having worked hard to improve his family's lot, profited so that he now possessed a modest amount of property. Stalin's goal of "the liquidation of the kulaks as a class" was a cover for the destruction of capitalist farmers. In reality, he was waging a war of conquest against an enemy whom he believed he had the right to "plunder" and from whom he had the right to demand "tribute." Portrayed as an ape hoarding grain, a kulak was not human but a beast.[5] In January 1928 without the approval of the Politburo, Stalin pre-empted opposition from members, notably the cultivated and cosmopolitan Bukharin whose ideological commitment was suspect. He personally assembled armed squads in west Siberia and the Urals to collect the quotas set for grain, and arrest and dispatch to labour camps, hundreds of thousands of "malicious kulaks" then return to Moscow within a month with wagons of grain seized from "hoarders."[6]

Stalin's belligerence and inflexible dogmatism horrified Bukharin. He believed that the General Secretary's policy of scorched-earth collectivization would lead to an uprising that could only be drowned in blood. Bukharin believed that peasant backwardness was "not his 'guilt' but his misfortune" and that the Bolsheviks were not "vivisectionists, who...operate on the living organism with a knife." Privately, Bukharin later compared the violence of the revolutionary period to the war against the peasantry in the years 1930–32: "We executed people, but we also risked our lives in the process. In the later period, however we were conducting a mass annihilation of completely defenceless men, together with their wives and children." By 1929 Stalin had isolated Bukharin and mustered sufficient support to expel him from the Politburo for having "slandered the Party with demagogic accusations." When Bukharin reminded Stalin of their friendship, the latter responded in his typically brusque manner: "I think all this moaning and wailing isn't worth a brass farthing." In both substance and rhetoric, Stalin established the prototypical response for Party officials when he contemptuously dismissed appeals for fairness, justice or decency, notions that smacked of "rotten liberalism." As a result, he successfully deprived Bukharin of power and a forum to air his views (against collectivization) at the summit of decision making. Desperate to regain the Party's good graces, Bukharin managed to deliver a bellicose speech before the senior party faithful in December 1930. In the midst of raucous laughter, he called for the crushing of the kulaks and the closing of Party ranks in the struggle against class enemies.[7] It was beyond the point where he could prevent his expulsion from the Politburo.

Stalin had already succeeded in expelling Trotsky from the Party in 1927 and secured his exile in 1929, ostensibly on ideological grounds. Denounced by Trotsky as "the grave digger of the proletarian revolution" by refusing to continue the goal for permanent revolution abroad, Stalin advanced the need to pursue socialism in one country, a position that appealed to Russian nationalism.[8] Ironically, Trotsky had been one of the most vocal critics of the New Economic Policy, and had called for the suppression of the peasantry and a plan for intensive industrial development. In adopting Trotsky's policies while concurrently repudiating him and his alleged and real supporters, Stalin was like a vampire who sucked up his rival's will before disposing of him. On a psychic level, he was designating the more gifted Trotsky as his hated *other* or doppelganger. In this way, he could deflect onto Trotsky all the criticism that was directed at these programs and remain in his mind an unblemished figure.

As he finessed his former rivals out of power, Stalin rallied the Party by pandering to their latent hostility toward the peasantry whom they perceived as petty bourgeoisie only interested in individual land ownership. Moreover, his crude either-or mindset, which reduced people and issues to rigid dualities of right/wrong, for us/against us, was much more persuasive with the younger, less educated rank-and-file Party members than his more sophisticated cosmopolitan colleagues who excelled at the subtlety of the elaborate Marxian dialectic.[9] The Party militants, along with the security police, Red Army commanders and members of the youthful Komsomol rallied behind Stalin. To them he was the "man of steel" who had reinvigorated the robust vision of Bolshevism that had atrophied under the NEP. By his decisive action in West Siberia and the Urals, he demonstrated that he possessed the mettle to enforce a radical transformation in the countryside that would extract grain from a recalcitrant peasantry to feed the cities and export abroad.

War Against the Kulaks

By 1929, as General Secretary of the Party, Stalin's authority was indisputable. With his approval, the central authorities recruited twenty-five thousand shock troops from the urban proletariat to facilitate the rural metamorphosis. They were to educate, entice, and ultimately coerce the one hundred and twenty-five million peasants—"the dark people"—to join the collective and factory-like state farms. The Party cadres were thrilled to resurrect the martial spirit of Leninist War Communism with its manifesto of building a new socialist Russia by blazing a trail of modernization through the primitive rural sector. Fired with revolutionary élan for the collectivist cause, they sought to eliminate the personal ownership of land, tools and livestock. The result would be a collective property held de facto by the state. These urban interlopers fanned out into the countryside to find it enmeshed in a paroxysm of violence. Already deployed to dispossess the kulaks from their land were the demobilized Red Army soldiers, internal security service (OGPU changed in 1934 to NKVD) and thousands of Party and government officials. They were joined, in the scathing words of Alexander Solzhenitsyn, by "local good-for-nothings" who, "like raging beasts...[abandon] all humane principles" They humiliated peasants, forcing them to crawl and bark like dogs, and they routinely raped women. In order to immunize the poorer peasants against the virus of entrepreneurialism, these Party cadres harassed and meted out physical violence to compel them to abandon their private huts and land that they had acquired during the Revolution and to sign up to enter the collective farm. Even those who were not driven by venal motives or sadism to condemn their victims as subhuman were convinced that historical progress required the elimination of what Gorky called the "zoological individualism of the peasantry and its almost total lack of 'social feelings.'" The price of industrial progress translated into brutal, but necessary, means of eliminating independent peasants with their primitive strip farming and ignorance of machinery. The thousands who had been recruited from factories were intended to serve in the vanguard of this revolution. In their capacity as collective farm chairmen and administrators, they imposed on the peasantry the factory methods of work discipline—starting bells, payment based on piece rates and orderly meetings—and they were required to be ruthless. One Bolshevik leader told a meeting of Party organizers that they must dispense with "rotten liberalism" and "bourgeois humanitarianism" because "it's war—it's them or us." Stalin also deployed the military trope when he compared the all-out war to eliminate a class to a military assault with its "offensive along the whole front." In his novel *Virgin Soil Upturned*, Soviet writer Mikhail Sholokhov captured the zealotry of the true believer who combines ideological duty with a primitive bloodlust: "give me thousands of old men, children, women....And tell me they got to be done away with....For the sake of the Revolution, I'd do it with a machine gun...everyone of them."[10] Stalin applauded the novel for its "honesty."

The cleansing of the kulaks was meant to serve as a deterrent to other peasants who might resist entering a collective. In an orgy of state-sanctioned looting, agents confiscated everything they possessed and deported families designated as kulaks, particularly the most efficient farmers. But the epithet kulak became so elastic that village priests, outspoken Red Army veterans or peasants who opposed collectivism, regardless of their economic assets, could be candidates for "dekulakization." Zinoviev dismissed a kulak as "any peasant who has enough to eat."[11] The epithet was so plastic that anyone who opposed the regime could be stigmatized, enabling firebrands to burn their homes, destroy family icons and turn over any livestock to the collective. In an attempt to fan class war in the villages, a government decree stipulated that the confiscated property of kulaks would be the initial contribution funds for poor peasants and hired hands that joined collective farms. Supposedly, this measure would provide the material incentive to assist the security service in the process of dekulakization when they evicted kulaks from their homes, placed them on carts and took them to detention centers. Sometimes families were separated in the process. Some kulaks gave their children away to other peasants, believing that they had a better chance of survival. Given that in the packed cattle trains between fifteen and twenty per cent of the infants and children that were ill died on route, the parents' decision to leave their children was not entirely misplaced. The cruelty visited on these individuals is poignantly illustrated in this 1988 recollection of one woman who bitterly recalled how she and her husband

> had their own firewood, a plowed field, and a good broken-in stallion. But then the government came along and dekulaked us. Do you know what it means—to be 'dekulakized'? If you were a good farmer you got dekulakized—that is, you had everything taken away from you. They took everything away from us—everything—down to the last crumb, including the house. Just the kids and myself were left. My husband was taken away in a black raven. We had ten children. Five of them died while my husband was gone.[12]

In Stalin's Manichaean world, one was either for collectivization or against it. If, like the vignette offered above, a peasant was a productive farmer, he was ipso facto a class exploiter and an incorrigible parasite who blocked progress by remaining chained to the backward past with its primitive farming and open market ethos.

There is no single image that encompasses the kulak but the Soviet representation was comparable to the Nazi portrayal of the powerful and dangerous and subhuman Jew. Stalin and other Bolshevik leaders loathed the peasantry with the same irrational frenzy with which the Nazis hated the Jews. Since the kulak loomed not only as a symbol of rapacious capitalism, but of the failure of socialism to take root in the countryside, he was stigmatized as evil incarnate. They were routinely dehumanized as lice, vermin and blood suckers who would destroy loyal communists given the opportunity. By this worldview, it made sense to arrest kulaks who resisted collectivization or had hidden grain, and for the security police to shoot the heads of households, especially those who had fought on the White side during the civil war. The workers' brigades conducted a merciless campaign that resulted in a staggering loss of life. At least thirty thousand "counterrevolutionary kulak activists" were shot out of hand while their dependents were ethnically cleansed from their villages and one hundred thousand of the arrested ended up in the Gulag. According to Soviet archives, almost two million kulaks and family members were deported en masse in 1930 and 1931 to be "re-educated" through "honest labour."[13] To avoid this fate, some ten million people, mostly young single males abandoned their status as peasants and decamped to the cities and industrial centers leaving their farms forever. What happened to the kulaks bears out the current research that when a group is targeted for demonization, there are few inhibitions about destroying it in a manner similar to that which occurred in Nazi Germany.

Vassily Grossman, the Soviet journalist who reported on the Nazi Holocaust, drew an explicit parallel with the kulak ordeal in his last 1961 novel, *Everything Flows*. Based upon personal experience, Grossman's work demonstrates that one of the tragic consequences of dekulakization and collectivization was the breakdown of normal human relations in the community where, in an atmosphere of mistrust and fear, neighbours would spy on and, ultimately, betray one another. In the novel, a former Party activist during the post-Stalinist era regretfully recounts her own complicity by being silent during the deportation of kulaks and in the subsequent famine. She had been numbed by the constant barrage on the radio, in newspapers and at Party meetings and had begun to believe that kulaks were parasites who killed children and deserved to be liquidated. Others were less ideologically indoctrinated. In a frenzy of spite, some peasants took advantage of the official enemy designation to satisfy their personal agendas. Grossman labels them as Judas IV, Philistines who were devoted to acquiring material objects and satisfying the grievances that festered within themselves. They took advantage of the State's passion for unmasking enemies by settling old scores and freely denouncing other peasants for having hired help during the harvest. As a result, those peasants, along with their families would be driven out of the village. Motivated solely by self-interest, the denouncers stole clothes or boots from the victims. Along with Party activists, inoculated with the ideological virus, they vented spasms of hatred on fellow villagers that inevitably followed the dehumanization of a targeted group:

> They'd convinced themselves that the kulaks were evil, that
> it was best not even to touch them....Everything about the

> kulaks was vile—they were vile in themselves, they had no
> souls, and they stank and they were full of sexual diseases,
> and worse of all they were enemies of the people....They
> were not even human beings...some kind of beasts....

To eliminate them through a "nation-wide pogrom," the police and activists packed the "criminal kulaks" on sealed empty
"death trains"—the beginning of a six-week trip to special settlements while onlookers would shout: "Curses on you." Grossman's
weary narrator, who has spent almost thirty years in the Gulag,
renders the most telling judgment. Linking the Jewish Holocaust
with dekulakization, he notes that when the executioner cannot
see the humanity in his victim, he cuts a large perforation in his
moral fabric and ceases to be human himself; "he is his own executioner" while "his victim remains a human being forever." But
even Grossman is reluctant to judge Judas IV given their poverty,
lack of education and encouragement from the state.[14]

Some of the factory workers, along with students who belonged
to the Komsomol and had been recruited to assist in the implementation of collectivization, attempted to retain their humanity
while they observed or participated in this process of social engineering. They were often critical of rural officials for their speed
and insensitivity to the human misery that accompanied such a
task. A few of them achieved some success when they tried to
accommodate peasant traditions within the framework of collectivization and not transform the countryside along industrial
lines. Local rural officials, who resented their interference and
felt threatened by their presence, treated the workers with contempt. In the eyes of local officials, these workers were careerists
whose purpose was to launch intrigues against them. An executive Soviet official voiced the prevailing attitude in telling some of
them: "Go to the Devil. We do not need you. Go back to the city."
Hostility from local officials, several assaults upon and killings of
helpless peasants prompted worker desertions. They returned to
their factory jobs disgusted with what they had witnessed. One
reported that "there are too many injustices, it is not collectivization, it is pillage." One Komsomol who had been sent to "learn
some toughness" had allegedly gone soft and committed suicide,
while another expressed publicly her grief for the uprooted: "we
are no longer people. We are animals."[15] Such honest sentiments
suggest that not every cadre had been thoroughly indoctrinated

into believing that kulaks were not human beings.

When the kulaks reached their destination in the Kazakhstan, the Urals, Northern Territory, and especially Siberia, they lived among the free population in special settlements with appalling conditions in harsh, undeveloped terrain. Women were often separated from their husbands, and as many as two thousand women and children were packed into unheated churches or moved to overcrowded dwellings, one hundred and fifty in each. Living in filth with lice, susceptible to typhus, the survivors had to eke a living from the land. With little food and no medicine, staggering numbers succumbed to starvation, disease or cold in the extremely inhospitable climate of the Arctic tundra where temperatures could reach minus fifty degrees. The conditions were so dreadful that kulaks elicited sympathy at their plight from citizens in local communities. One letter complained that "'big time" criminals have it better than they, and these people...are being punished even though they are completely innocent." Yet families utilizing peasant ingenuity did survive, one by drinking cattle blood, while other families managed to escape and return to their villages. The plight of the men shipped to prison camps was equally if not more horrific; they often froze or starved to death because the prisoners had to build their own barracks and organize the distribution of food with insufficient rations.[16]

At the same time, the kulaks were defined in Marxist terms by one's relationship to the means of production. As this was a condition that could be changed, they, and especially their children, were candidates for redemption. Authorities gave special attention to turning kulaks and their offspring into honest citizens with a socialist consciousness. As the Soviet Union approached what it declared as a socialist state in 1936, restrictions on kulaks eased and broad amnesties were extended to former kulaks. But the Marxist belief in the malleability of human nature—that individuals could change under propitious environmental circumstances—clashed with the Stalinist suspicion that individuals concealed their true nature under an agreeable façade, that they mouthed the right words while hiding their darker more belligerent intentions. That suspicion would spill over during the Great Terror (1937–1938) when former kulaks were targeted by the security organs in and outside the Gulag.[17]

The agents of modernity increasingly mirrored in their

fanaticism the proto-fascist thugs in the tsarist past. The Party cadres' undifferentiated violence against peasants was reminiscent of the Black Hundred pogroms in its dehumanization of the enemy. Like its predecessor, this onslaught was not only economic but also religious and cultural; zealous cadres systematically desecrated and closed not only synagogues but also churches and mosques in order to instil atheism. They publicly destroyed icons, closed the market and disbanded the peasant councils, all of which had provided cohesion for the community. The church bell, a talismanic symbol of village solidarity and autonomy, was melted down for the industrial drive of the first Five-Year Plan. The authority figures, priests and the village elite, who had articulated the community's opposition, were arrested, shot, deported or simply disappeared into the maw of the Gulag.[18] Although its goals and magnitudes were vastly different, the Stalinist march toward modernity and socialism tapped into irrational and primitive impulses similar to those with which the Black Hundreds in tsarist Russia had scapegoated the Jews during their fruitless efforts to resist the pull toward modernity.

The Kingdom of Darkness

In this all-out war, peasants cut back on their sown acreage and the grain they marketed, destroyed their property, and drank their home-brewed vodka before they would turn it over to a collective farm. They objected to being deprived of their freedom, more than of their property and possessions. This was an apocalyptic struggle. As one Polish peasant living in the Ukraine explained to his son his reason for refusing to enter a collective, "I did not want to sell my soul to the devil." When a priest sermonized on the end of the world because the Antichrist had come to earth, he was arrested and a large demonstration of peasants appeared to denounce the proceedings. Peasants banded together and resisted the designation kulaks. In doing so they defied both the class analysis of local officials and Communists in Moscow and the attempts by the Party to fan class war. Villagers denied the social stratification of kulaks and poor peasants by stating that "we are all labourers here" and demonstrated remarkable bravery by voting against the expulsion of kulaks. On one occasion they demonstrated with rakes and pitchforks and installed peasants in

their own homes while demanding the liquidation of the collective farm and refusing to destroy a kulak home.[19] The most widely reported, and from the state's perspective, the most irrational,
self-destructive form of insanity was the slaughter of livestock, an
action that could only have been inspired by counter-revolutionary agents such as kulaks and priests. The fifty-percent decline in
livestock from 1929 to the famine of 1933 administered a near-fatal
blow to the collective farm system. The increased tempo of arrests, executions and deportations failed to halt what one historian has labelled "peasant luddism."[20]

Due to the cataclysmic dislocation caused by massive deportations and tenacious peasant rebelliousness, Stalin, in March 1930,
issued his "Dizziness from Success" decree, a temporary and partial retreat from forced collectivization. In it Stalin accused zealous
officials of violating the voluntary character of collectivization by
forcing people to join them with threats of military force, depriving
them of irrigated water and manufactured goods. The letter was
a sign that Soviet power at the top feared violent confrontations
with peasants when villagers vastly outnumbered local officials.
In an egregious misrepresentation of the policy, Stalin accused local officials of being "our accursed enemies." He poured contempt
on those who would stoop to removing church bells and lectured
them on racing ahead of the masses "because to race ahead is to
lose the masses and isolate yourself."[21] By blaming local officials,
Stalin camouflaged his role in initiating the war against the countryside. In fact the article, by suggesting a moratorium, aroused such
consternation among officials that they tried to prevent peasants
from reading it. The letter demoralized many of them because its
decrees denounced actions that they believed were in the spirit
of collectivization as launched by Moscow. Buffeted by pressures
from central command, criticized by urban workers and humiliated by the peasantry, many were purged from their offices in an
atmosphere of recrimination and suspicion. Others refused to retreat, believing that persuasion was useless and accused Moscow
of "playing into the hands of the kulaks," but they too were fired,
expelled from the Party or criminally prosecuted.[22]

Stalin's appearance of accommodation on collectivization only
concealed his murderous form of social engineering: that of cleansing the Soviet Union of all class enemies and social undesirables.
In a gesture of monumental cynicism, he sent one of his Party

officials to transmit the hard-line instructions by word of mouth to local authorities. The decree was simply a tactical withdrawal to protect his vaunted persona and regroup for a renewed assault upon a refractory peasantry. The attempt to blame local officials for excesses revealed how far Stalin would go to protect his carefully-constructed image of a beneficent avuncular figure. When his true character deviated from the official script—wise, caring, man-of-the-people—he projected onto others, in this case, local officials, the tumultuous fallout of what he himself had created.

Emboldened by Stalin's decree, the peasants accelerated their opposition to collectivization. Villages registered protests in the belief that Stalin and the Central Committee, who had also issued a decree against excesses, were behind them. Opposition spiralled into riots, acts of arson and massive protests throughout the countryside, especially among ethnic minorities in Byelorussia, and the Volga Germans and Chechnyans in the Caucasus region. The Kazakhs of Kazakhstan were not peasants but a nomadic people who objected to grain growing because it was an unworthy activity and because the land needed extensive irrigation. They protested by gathering their animals and migrating to China or to a mountainous Soviet republic where a nomadic lifestyle was still permitted.[23] In grain-growing areas, the violence was usually sparked by the peasant seizure of socialized livestock in order to dismantle a collective or prevent one from being organized, or in defence of a church or protection of kulaks. The protests opened the floodgates for a massive exit of nine million households from the collectives, many of them brandishing copies of Stalin's article, especially in those grain-producing areas where resistance had been most vehement.[24] Yet the peasant victory was pyrrhic; peasants who returned to their homes could not reclaim their livestock and equipment, and their taxes doubled and then tripled, giving most of them no alternative but to return to the collective.

The recalcitrance and animosity of the peasantry prompted Stalin's pungent ideological statement in 1931; the Soviet Union had only ten years to do what the West had done in a hundred years. Unless the Soviet people put an end to their backwardness in the shortest possible time, they would lose their independence. In *The Second Day*, a novel published in 1934, a character paraphrases Stalin's rationale for the acceleration of history if the socialist fatherland is to overcome its backwardness:

What did you dream of? Goodness? Sympathy? Pity? You had a weakness—pity for the misfortunate....But it's a throwback, that's all....Instead of pity we have class solidarity. We're annihilating class not an individual. Of course, a few of the hoi polloi perish in the process, but does that matter? A sight more used to perish before—look at the statistics. What matters is for us to overtake America.[25]

These sentiments encapsulated the Marxist–Leninist ideology for ferociously destroying a huge swath of the rural population. They could disguise their actions in progressive rhetoric, that the old beliefs would quail and melt before the onrush of modernity, and that the collectivist mentality would encourage the development of the highest human qualities. Peeping through, however, were the rags of brutality and savage passions. By taking refuge in the gauzy notion of class and the all-embracing idea of forging the New Soviet Person, true believers could deaden their conscience and avert their eyes from the consequences of treating human beings as less-than-human. Fired by a toxic brew of a utopian creed and a hair-trigger sensibility, they avowed that they were transforming the peasants into socialists, expunging selfish individualism, and inculcating the need for personal sacrifice for the greater good of the collective where agricultural production based on scientific methods would soar. These sentiments clearly revealed that the social engineering to the radiant future was only possible if the detached, "Bolshevik firmness" replaced bourgeois emotions of compassion.

That feat required jettisoning conventional morality, which obstructed a higher morality by impeding the progress of humanity. In the class struggle, hardness served to eradicate the "evil of philanthropy" and other "abominations" of bourgeois society. These true believers had no time for what Trotsky had once called the "papist-Quaker babble about the sanctity of life." That the official version of Stalin's greatness positively impacted some citizens is evident from diaries of the period. They attest to moments of rapture experienced by individuals who celebrate collectivization and technical progress. In one entry from 1933, the author acknowledges that without the October Revolution he would "have remained a half-animal," that he became "ideological[ly] hardened" and that he was willing to "confront any difficulties and bear any sacrifice." Years after Stalin was dead, one of his close associates could rationalize all cruelty as the destruction of the superfluous since "all acts that further history and socialism are moral acts."[26] The price for this emotional anaesthesia and repudiation of human values was ordinary human civility and empathy. There are many instances of sheer sadism documented in the memoirs of the period since compassion was officially dismissed as rotten liberalism. Nadezhda Mandelstam whose husband died in 1938 in a transit camp en route to Siberia muses ruefully that "kindness was an old fashioned, vanished quality, and its exponents were as extinct as the mammoth."[27]

In a memoir of expiation, a former activist and collectivizer, Lev Kopelev, documents the dearth of humanity in those seized by the rapture of absolutism. He ashamedly reveals how he participated in the forced collectivization, and while his innate generosity of spirit spared him from the worst excesses of his peers, he unflinchingly exposes the cruelty he doled out as affirmation of his illusions:

> With the others, I emptied out the old folks' storage chests,
> stopping my ears to the children's crying and women's wails.
> For I was convinced...that in the days to come the people
> would be better off for it; that their distress and suffering
> were the result of their own ignorance or the machinations of
> the class enemy; that those who sent me—and I myself—knew
> better than the peasants how they should live, and what they
> should sow and what they should plow.[28]

A remorseful Kopelev describes the anguish, despair and anger of ordinary people as he and his comrades extracted from them even family mementos to fulfil their quota for the state. With the benefit of hindsight and pained by his scalding conscience, he acknowledges how the blinding faith of a messianic ideology provided a cocoon from which to justify the extortion and dispense with human decency in the name of a higher abstract cause:

> It was excruciating to see and hear all of this. And even
> worse to take part in it.... And I persuaded myself, explain-
> ing to myself. I must not give in to debilitating pity. We were
> releasing historical destiny. We were performing our revolu-
> tionary duty. We were obtaining grain for the socialist father-
> land. For the five-year plan...some sort of rationalistic fanati-
> cism overcame my doubts, my pangs of conscience and sim-
> ple feelings of sympathy, pity and shame.[29]

Once the idea of historical transformation, the promise of a better future, and the infallibility of Party doctrine had securely inhabited his mind, his conscience and capacity for reflection atrophied. Equally important, he could cauterize troubling feelings by fixating upon the Party line that substituted the future for the present. In this way, he could ignore the suffering of the peasantry wrought by excessive procurement targets.

The economic results of collectivization were catastrophic. Few collectives even possessed the promised tractors to replace the slaughtered horses or those that died from hunger or neglect when they were rounded up from individual farmers and placed on collective farms. Given that the criterion for choosing the manager to run the collectives was loyalty to the Party rather than agricultural expertise, it follows that these enterprises were poorly operated. The most significant factor in the plummeting of agricultural production was the deportation of kulaks, the most energetic and successful of the peasants. Those left behind who had lived and worked on the collective lost their sense of pride and independence. They regarded their condition as labourers worse than serfdom because the state restricted their movement, took most of their crops and paid absurdly low prices in kind. Instead of the leap forward promised by Stalin, they believed they had retreated into the past. In response to the regime's determination to achieve their procurement targets, they resorted to passive resistance by working as little as they could and feigning incomprehension.[30] That sullen attitude pitted them against a suspicious Stalin, who was convinced that the peasantry was hiding grain. He demanded that the target levels be enforced, and those local officials who attempted to reduce the deliveries or ease the peasants' lot were purged as "kulak sympathizers." As the state resolved to extract all sources of value from the countryside including taxes, grain levies, milk, vegetables and livestock, refusal to work became in itself an act of "quiet sabotage." It also became an effective way of conserving energy and of expressing their hatred toward the Soviet state.

In the Ukraine and among the Volga Germans, the promise of tractors had not materialized and with the decline of draft animals the quotas set in the "internal colony" were impossible to fulfil. The authorities rationalized that the "kulak spirit" remained, and the obstreperous peasants cleverly hid the grain. They instructed local party officials, the militia and security police, to cart away the entire seed fund and all the flour and bread that could be found leaving the peasants totally bereft. Then when women were driven to desperation by the sight of their children starving, they roamed the countryside at night to cut off with scissors stalks of grain. The punitive laws, against anyone who stole a pound of potatoes or a handful of apples, explain why peasants formed the vast majority of prisoners in the Soviet camps during the 1930s.[31]

In an effort to destroy the peasants who had resisted collectivization, Stalin responded with a brutal, draconian decree to end the "sabotage." Those who stole state collective-farm property would be branded enemies of the people and either shot or, in mitigating circumstances, sentenced to a prison camp. In the first months after its proclamation in August 1932, tens of thousands of people were found guilty of "counter-revolutionary theft." Of that number an estimated five thousand were sentenced to death and many more were given ten-year sentences. A woman was given this sentence for picking ten onions from collective land. An extended stay in a prison camp virtually guaranteed a slow death. According to one historian, the average life expectancy of those sent between 1929-34 was two years and ninety percent of those dispatched to the camps before the World War II perished. In further vengeance, Stalin specifically prohibited amnesty in all cases.[32]

To deter peasants from seeking assistance in the cities, internal passports, once an instrument of the Tsar, were reissued to peasants to ensure they remained on the collective or larger state farms. On all the highways, blockades were installed to restrain starving peasants from crossing into Romania or Poland, or entering Russia proper if they were from the Ukraine. If they evaded the border patrols and did acquire bread from Leningrad or Moscow where it was available, it was confiscated at the border.

The primary target for Stalin's antipathy was the Ukraine. By 1931 he set out to punish the intransigent Ukrainians and to destroy their embryonic nationalism. Throughout the 1920s, this ethnic group had accommodated themselves to the Soviet regime because cultural nationalism, consistent with the ideas of Lenin, was allowed to flourish; for example, by 1929, ninety-seven percent of Ukrainian children received instruction in their native language.[33] Convinced that Ukrainian nationalism was an enemy, the Georgian-born Stalin, as a proponent of Russification or forced assimilation, abruptly terminated this cultural pluralism. He ordered a savage assault on those who believed that language was the essential vehicle for bringing the soul of a culture into the material realm. He purged the intelligentsia, many of whom were former political figures of extinct parties, through arrests followed by both show trials and closed trials that concluded with execution or deportation to penal camps. By 1933, Ukrainian jails and concentration camps held ninety thousand people. This decapitation of the spokesmen of Ukrainian nationalism was a prelude to the famine with its destruction of the peasantry, the submission of the people and the purge of local communist officials.[34]

The Holodomor: Death by Hunger

Although a terrifying famine hit Kazakhstan and Russia itself from 1932 to 1933, the worst effects were experienced in Soviet Ukraine. It was the direct result of Stalin's Five-Year Plan that brought industrial development to the Soviet Union along with the chaos of collectivization, brutal repression and a political culture in which peasants were regarded as "sub-human brutes." Forced collectivization in Kazakhstan was ideologically motivated—to convert nomads into a grain-growing people—and it resulted in a terrible famine. Although it had not been imposed to punish the people, one-third of the population died. By late 1932, two million pounds of grain were earmarked for the stricken area. The famine also did not extend into most of Russia proper, only to the grain-growing areas of the Caucasus in the south, or into the other Republics where there was sufficient food and the means to deliver it in order to sustain life. But the Holodomor in the multinational Ukrainian republic with its Poles, Germans and Jews was deliberately designed to engineer mass deaths. Only in the Ukraine did Party officials impose administrative decrees that guaranteed that millions would die. If peasants could not pay the grain quota, they had to pay a tax in meat which meant that their livestock would be confiscated. They were also required to pay fifteen times the grain tax if they could not meet the original tax, which meant they would be deprived of everything. When districts were unable to reach their procurement targets, they were blockaded; no one could leave and no products, including seed, were allowed in.[35]

In Varlam Shalamov's *Kolyma Tales*, a character's description of

This powerful 1999 painting, one of a series of four monumental panels, is by Ukrainian artist, Nina Marchenko, who personally suffered hardship during the Soviet era. She intended her work to commemorate the suffering in 1932-1933, especially its effect on women and children.

Children of Holodomor
Nina Marchenko, Kyiv, Ukraine
From the collection: Holodomor through the Eyes of Ukrainian Artists
Founder and Trustee:: Morgan Williams

his experience in the largest and most desolate prison camp in the far north as "Auschwitz without the ovens" could equally apply to the fate of the Ukrainian people. Since the procurement targets were hopelessly unrealistic, local food brigades raided houses for any scrap of food, leaving the residents to starve. In a scene that might have been culled from a Gothic horror thriller, it was reported that some brutal brigadiers insisted on carting the dying as well as the dead to a cemetery to save them a trip. Consequently, young children and old people lay in mass graves alive for days descending into a twilight life, a waking death.[36] One survivor testified in 1988 that he saw a child sucking at the breast of his dead mother when a sanitary truck appeared and threw the live child into the truck with the mother. Another survivor told a researcher that "Stalin reduced people to such a condition that they lost their reason, their conscience and sense of mercy."[37]

In such gruesome circumstances, human beings devolved to their most primitive state, clinging to life when starvation had turned them into tortured gargoyles, and survival depended on ingenuity and luck. Except for the urban proletariat who did not starve, and local Party officials, the famine was the worst horror ever experienced by its people, including the devastation of World War II. In a memoir of his childhood in the Ukraine, Miron Dolot relates how he and his brother hid potatoes and grain in several places in a sand dune adjoining the woods, and how trips there in the night to find these "treasures" were among his unforgettable experiences, as they could mean the difference between life and death. But he also grimly remembers how some emaciated villagers were "reduced to skeletons, with their skin hanging greyish-yellow and loose over the bones. Their faces looked like rubber masks with large, immobile eyes," that rendered them incapable of speaking and reduced to crying. Some of the most desperate "suffered from hallucinations of food, of something to bite into and chew...they were ready to sink their teeth into anything, even into their own hands and arms, or into the flesh of others."[38] Those who succumbed to cannibalism were either burned or beaten to death by neighbours or rounded up and shot. Like Nazi officials who were to relegate Jews to squalid ghettoes, "cannibals" confirmed for local Party officials that these "parasites" were sub-human. In a sense, they tragically fitted this epithet as one observer noted that when the human being died, the wild beast emerged with "a human face but the eyes of a wolf."[39] Large swathes of the landscape were pockmarked with the dead because the "walking corpses" were too weak to bury them. One expatriate American who travelled by train to a village found only one person alive, a woman who had gone mad. The houses contained only corpses, upon which rats were feeding. One dark-humoured sign that had been placed on a grave and that revealed bitter sarcasm read: ""I LOVE STALIN, BURY HIM HERE AS SOON AS POSSIBLE."[40] Given the grotesque disconnect between state economics and unfathomable human misery, that sentiment cannot have been unique. The famine and cannibalism that stalked the countryside were deliberately manufactured on Stalin's orders and fuelled by his paranoia-laced sadism.

While this Holodomor was turning villages into "cemeteries of the hard school," the Soviet government compounded its criminal culpability through nefarious economic and administrative decisions. In 1931 it blithely exported five million tons of grain to earn foreign currency for turbines, assembly lines and mining machinery, as well as for financing international Communist Parties.[41] On the domestic front, it did not ship all the food to the cities but filled warehouses and granaries guarded by security police who did not hesitate to kill desperate peasants willing to storm these facilities. The existence of local Ukrainian granaries that could be made available to the public in emergencies demonstrated that the famine was an instrument of state terror. When military personnel guarded stored grain until it rotted, it was a statement to the local peasantry that the regime had sentenced them to death by starvation. There is some anecdotal evidence that the famine was deployed as a weapon in the war against the peasantry. "For the record" one Ukrainian official told the commissar and metallurgist, Victor Kravchenko, who later defected to the West:

> A ruthless struggle is going on between the peasantry and our regime. It's a struggle to the death. This year was a test of our strength and our endurance. It took a famine to show them who is master here. It has cost millions of lives, but the collective farm system is here to stay. We've won the war.[42]

Perhaps the most monstrous criminal act by Soviet officials was to deny the very existence of a famine. By contrast, the 1921–22 famine was grudgingly acknowledged and both internal and external help could be solicited. But with a mailed fist, Stalin conducted in 1932–33 an unprecedented war against the Ukrainians that included what Pasternak called in *Doctor Zhivago*, the "inhuman reign of fiction" (in an earlier translation, "the inhuman power of the lie").[43] Stalin categorically forbade the famine to be reported, the word "starvation" was even banned, leaving the plight of the affected peasantry shrouded in silence.

But the disavowal produced powerful psychological effects on sensitive observers. When Pasternak visited the famine areas, he was so devastated that he fell ill and could not write for a year.[44] One Party official in the Ukraine reported the famine to Stalin whose derisive response was to berate him for fabricating a fairy tale saying that he should leave his post and become a writer who can "concoct fables and fools will read them." Stalin was no fool and toured the Russia's lower Volga in August 1933 to witness the devastation he created and still registered no regret. When Mikhail Sholokhov, the author of *The Virgin Soil Upturned*, attempted to relay to Stalin the full dimensions of the horror, Stalin's reply was to dismiss contemptuously the "esteemed reapers" as "saboteurs." Peasants were using hunger as a weapon, allowing their children to die so as to embarrass Stalin and besmirch the image of collectivization. Consistent with his dark and cynical outlook on reality, he earlier remarked that "full conformity of views can be achieved only at the cemetery."[45]

To ensure that Stalin's word received official legal sanction, it became a criminal offence to even mention the famine. The historian Robert Conquest provides evidence that certain individuals did receive the death penalty if they blamed the famine on officials.[46] Accordingly, any official reportage approximated what Orwell called doublespeak in *Nineteen Eighty-Four*, since language evaded and misrepresented reality to a degree that it was turned upside down. One anonymous report that appeared in *Pravda* contrasted the western Ukraine under Polish control where no one died with Soviet controlled Ukraine. "Need we contrast the pitiable hovels of western Ukrainian peasants with the bright, clean, new city that sprang up with the electrification of the left bank of the Dnieper?"[47] The news blackout was so effective that in the late 1990s, a writer who had lived a privileged life in Moscow in the early 1930s said that he was completely unaware that there was a famine in the south.[48] Given the passport system, the lack of reportage and the presence of roadblocks to prevent the visibly starving from entering the cities, his ignorance is understandable.

When Arthur Koestler, the journalist, and at the time a member of the German Communist Party, travelled through the Ukraine during the frigid winter of 1932–33, he felt scant sympathy for starving people, considering them "enemies of the people who preferred begging to work." His knee-jerk conditioning reflected the official "blanket of silence" that covered the country with regard to the famine, epidemics and the dying out of whole villages. Privately, some officials acknowledged the deaths as "unfortunate" but could justify them as the necessary means to achieving the "glorious future," a view that corresponded with his own position at the time. Koestler later noted that "the trains were lined with begging peasants with swollen hands and feet, the women holding up to the carriage windows horrible infants with enormous wobbling heads, sticklike limbs, swollen, pointed bellies." At the time he could justify these conditions as the "heritage of the past" or "the backwardness of the Russian people." Anything he liked, he registered as "the seeds of the future."[49]

After Koestler left the Party and became a vehement Anti-Communist, he was able to write in vivid detail ten and twenty years later what he had seen. He had gained insight into how he had succumbed to the totalitarian temptation by rationalizing terrible suffering.[50] He described the effect of dividing his official position from his personal experience as "a feeling of dreamlike unreality." He was also honest enough to recognize in hindsight that the "elastic shock absorbers of (his) Party training" jolted to attention when he observed suffering that surprised and bewildered him: "I had eyes to see and a mind conditioned to explain away what they saw. This 'inner censor' is more reliable and effective than any official censorship." Through this "sorting machine," he could endure the depression he experienced in Russia and remain a Communist until April 1938 when he resigned from the German Communist Party after his experience in Spain. He saw that GPU agents who were more preoccupied with executing any opponent of Franco who was not an orthodox Stalinist than in defeating Fascism in Spain, a perception that has been confirmed with the recent excavation and publication of Soviet documents.[51]

Historians estimate that the death toll from this man-made famine ranged from three and one-third million in the Ukraine alone to about six million overall in the Soviet Union including about three hundred thousand during deportations. The Holodomor was in the scathing judgment of biographer, Robert Tucker, a monstrous crime against humanity. Historians generally agree that the number of deaths due to the famine is comparable to the number of Jews murdered by Hitler—astonishing given that until recently, it rarely registered a blip on the historical radar of a public sensitive to other horrors perpetrated in the twentieth century. It was not until 1988 that the impact and the method that produced the famine appeared in Soviet publications. By their calculations among the peasantry about ten million died between 1930 and 1933.[52] Since the collapse of Communism, further, largely symbolic, changes have occurred. Although spokesmen in Russia denied any criminal responsibility—even harsh critics of Stalinism as different as Solzhenitsyn and Mikhail Gorbachev, whose own family suffered from the famine, have contended that the controversy was more political than historical—the Ukrainian parliament in November 2006 passed a bill declaring the Holodomor a genocide.[53] By December 1, 2007, fifteen countries had already passed similar resolutions. Yet one of the first decisions of the newly elected pro-Russian President, Viktor Yanukovich, in February 2010 was to delete the Holodomor from the national agenda, a move that suggests that national elections in the Ukraine are ruled as much by history as by politics. Whether this tragedy constitutes genocide among historians is at present a matter of dispute. Donald Rayfield concludes that the famine constituted an act of genocide against the Ukrainian people since Stalin purchased fifty thousand tonnes of grain from Canada to save the Siberian peasants but did nothing to alleviate the suffering of the Ukrainian rural population. Hiroaki Kuromiya, however, stops short of declaring it an act of genocide arguing that Stalin used the famine as a collective form of punishment to teach the Ukrainians a lesson against ever opting for Ukrainian nationalism.[54]

The famine bequeathed further tragic consequences when Germans invaded in 1941 and millions welcomed them and participated in atrocities against Jewish civilians. Since they could not conceive that Comrade Stalin could ever order mass murder against them, the Ukrainians believed that a Jewish conspiracy was responsible. Allotting this preposterous theory a kernel of credibility was the fact that the Commissar for agriculture was

Lazar Kaganovich who was of Jewish extraction.[55]

While conspiracy theories were bruited about, the inner censor silenced Koestler and other sensitive observers. Letters, rumours and some famine victims did reach railway stations, but given the political climate, it was not possible for individuals to speak out as long as they remained in the Soviet Union. But their silence is also a testament to the awesome power of Marxist–Leninism to grip and control the mind of even the most perceptive individuals requiring them to deny or contort the evidence of their senses so that they could reconcile Soviet practices with Marxist theory. In 1938 Stalin assisted the comrades by publishing the official history of the Soviet Union. In his surreal version, collectivization was entirely a voluntary decision of peasants "who would come in great numbers to the state farms to watch the operation of the tractor stations, admire their performance and then resolve: 'Let's join the collective farm.' "[56] Nothing was said of the human suffering, much less the inefficiency of state farms where agricultural production plummeted to pre-revolutionary levels so that even in the post-Stalinist era, the U.S.S.R. needed to import grain from the United States. Yet that seductive ideology did wield its influence on Soviet citizens and foreigners, bolstered by the cult of Stalin and its transmission through Socialist Realism in the printed word and the arts, the focus of the next chapter.

The Spirit of Socialist Realism

To us, to you, Caesar, father of the
Romans, dearest and best of men!

> *—The Master & Margarita*
> Mikhail Bulgakov

The Shame of Gorky

The distinguished cultural historian, Modris Eksteins reminds us that "the beautiful lie is, however, also the essence of kitsch. Kitsch is a form of make-believe, a form of deception. It is the alternative to a daily reality that would otherwise be a spiritual vacuum."[1] Perhaps nowhere is this insight more applicable than to the Soviet Union during the 1930s with the creation of a Stalinist cult and the implementation of Socialist Realism, the genre that exemplified the revolutionary Marxist–Leninist fantasy of expressing itself in the printed word, film and the visual arts. Its pervasiveness was so all-encompassing that it seduced not only Soviet citizens but a thicket of foreigners who were enthralled by the Soviet experiment. Yet it was possible to penetrate the smoke and mirrors of the official culture to recognize the deprivation, the emptiness or the ghastly realities, and either make accommodations with the regime or to speak out against those conditions, albeit from outside the country. Although the Russian writer Maxim Gorky had demonstrated courage during revolutionary times, it was conspicuously absent during the Stalinist era as he increasingly compromised himself in order to embrace the rigid prescriptions of socialist realism.

In Gorky's early literary output, he was unabashedly critical of reality. His heroes were loners who pined for the revolution that they would help to create. His fictional writings became part of the Soviet canon. But his own ambivalence about the course of the revolution and his differences with Lenin and hostility toward other Bolsheviks drove him into self-imposed exile. Between 1928 and 1932, Gorky made lengthy periodic trips to the Soviet Union before repairing to his homeland for good, believing that he could reconcile the tension between his earlier humanist critical writing and that of a Stalinist cultural bureaucrat.

Stalin needed Gorky as an ally to unite the Party and attract the international support that would accrue if the renowned world famous artist, the first proletarian writer, stamped his imprimatur on the policies that he had implemented. In other words, Stalin expected Gorky to serve the Revolution and work for him. He anticipated that Gorky would compose a hagiographical biography to commemorate his life just as he had for Lenin. The repatriation of Gorky was given such high priority that Stalin assigned the Commissar of State Security, Genrich Yagoda, responsibility for luring home from Italy the ambivalent writer, who, although he abhorred Italian Fascism, likely viewed with misgivings the direction that Stalin was taking the country. With intelligence and financial resources at his disposal, Yagoda planted informers around Gorky, bribed his secretary and daughter-in-law, and made cash available to Gorky himself as enticements.[2]

When Gorky declared his decision to visit Russia in 1928, he received letters in Sorrento from Soviet citizens warning him about the state of Russia since his departure. One writer asserted that it had descended into cannibalism. In another letter, he was cautioned to be wary of the Potemkin villages where foreigners "only see the external, calm side of our culture, only observing what they are shown." When Gorky did return, he ignored the warnings and dismissed his correspondents as "mechanical citizens." As he saw it, his mission was to counteract the arrogant assertions of cultural superiority among Westerners and defend the Soviet system that forged "new people" through labour. If Gorky had any suspicions about the authenticity of the carefully staged tours and receptions orchestrated by Stalin during his visits or the policies the regime had instituted, the much celebrated prodigal son never publicly expressed them. In the meantime, as Gorky vacationed with Stalin and his second wife Nadya and travelled between the Soviet Union and Sorrento Italy, his public statements revealed him to be a fervent apologist for the regime. Unleashing his life-long hatred toward the kulaks, Gorky parroted the Party position on collectivization by writing in *Pravda*: "When the enemy does not surrender, he must be exterminated." He also endorsed the Stalinist line about industrial saboteurs by writing an agitprop melodrama about a show trial of wreckers because he was "pretty shaken by these skilfully organized acts of sabotage."[3] Although his literary work allowed him

This photograph of the young humanist revolutionary and dramatist, whose plays are still staged internationally, presents a stark contrast with the Gorky who in his last years became the obsequious stooge for Stalin.

to recreate a past in which criticism had been desirable, the erstwhile independent thinker became the cat's paw of Stalin when he prostituted his journalistic writing to demonize the regime's enemies.

Gorky conceived that his more important role was to underscore the Soviet achievement in the reforging of criminals into productive citizens. With the power to reach an international audience and as an honoured guest, in 1929 he was able to visit the Special Purpose Camp (SLON) and write what turned out to be a sycophantic essay "Solovki" about the rehabilitative nature of the labour camps. In tsarist times SLON had been both a monastery and a prison on a string of small islands in the White Sea near the Arctic Circle. Created by Lenin in 1920 to incarcerate civil war POWs, the camp's population expanded from ten thousand in 1927 to seventy-one thousand in 1931, the new inmates mainly "half-animal kulaks." Lenin established the prototype for the labour camps by placing them under the control of the security police who proceeded to institute the practice of feeding prisoners according to their work output (thereby assuring that the weak would die of starvation and exposure while the strong would build the infrastructure of the state). This inhumane practice was ostensibly introduced in order to operate the camps on a profitable basis as part of the planned economy, but if measured by its production output, it was an economic strategy that failed miserably.[4]

The camp became notorious for its random executions and sadistic treatment of prisoners. The guards bound prisoners naked to posts for days where they were tormented by clouds of mosquitoes in summer. They devised punishments that could cripple a prisoner, one by forcing an individual to sit on a pole for eighteen consecutive hours. To impress (and delude) the credulous Gorky, the authorities spruced up the camp by painting the walls, providing the prisoners with new uniforms and allowing wives and husbands on this occasion to spend time together. To showcase the positive in a milieu where "new men" were created, Gorky had to gloss over its base features (that he must have seen), underscore its philosophy and be highly selective. SLON is "not Dostoevsky's 'house of the dead' because there one is being taught life, literacy, and labour." He highlighted the farm where animals were bred for fur amid the island's natural beauties and emphasized the potential rehabilitation of the adolescent criminals in their separate camp. He was able to present the extra rations for productive workers as a positive feature because he ignored the flip side of those who failed to fulfil work norms. He employed euphemisms: prisoners were "islanders." Through a sleight of hand, he conveyed how the promotion of the criminal population with power over the others was a progressive feature of the camp. Unable or unwilling to peer through the Potemkin façade, Gorky wrote about the "interesting" talks with prisoners with whom he spent only a few minutes—when he was able to escape from his handlers— the "clean barracks and big windows," the "excellent" punishment cells, and the impressive cultural events he witnessed: a concert, the museum, the library and the newspapers. He was more fortunate than most of the prisoners who were so exhausted by the day's work that they had no time for cultural activities. He never even saw the vast majority of the political prisoners who had been removed to another part of the island. In an early prototype of Socialist Realism, Gorky was not writing about the camp's current reality but as it should be.[5]

By contrast, Solzhenitsyn attempted to capture the real horror of SLON. With a combination of withering contempt and howling pain, he related that when Gorky visited the Children's Colony it was scrubbed for his visit and it appeared that every child had his own cot and mattress. One young boy cornered him and spoke to him alone for about forty-five minutes about the falseness of every-thing he was seeing and the various tortures used in the camp. Gorky was moved to tears, but when he left, he wrote in a guest book specifically prepared for him, rapturous impressions of the administrators. As soon as Gorky departed, the boy was shot, and Gorky never referred publicly to the exchange, even in the safety of Sorrento. By his deception and outright lies, a prisoner present during Gorky's visit charged that the writer had "morally justified the extermination of millions of people in the camps."[6]

For personal gain and out of vanity, Gorky diminished himself by genuflecting before Stalin. In contrast to the direct and cour-ageous letters he had once written to Lenin, whom he genuine-ly respected, his private letters to Stalin expose an obsequious courtier: "Who would take your place, in case these scoundrels would succeed to kill you?"[7] Out of a combination of conviction and ignoble opportunism, (he had already been garlanded with the Order of Lenin, provided with a palace and a dacha and had places named after him) Gorky took up Stalin's challenge that writ-ers could assist in "the engineering of human souls" to transform the consciousness of the Soviet people. It was a top priority be-cause as Stalin remarked "the production of souls was more im-portant than that of tanks."[8]

This artistic form, defined as Socialist Realism, required writers to be transmission belts for Party policy with fawning hosannas that trumpeted the glorious achievements of the Soviet Union and its hallowed leader. Any trace of ambiguity, irony, inner conflict or deviation from the canonized version of history was expunged and replaced by a coarse flatness of two-dimensional heroic types and thoroughly depraved villains. In the formulaic, melodramatic, Socialist-Realism fiction, the hero overcomes difficulties, acquires a socialist consciousness through an awareness of the class strug-gle and the need for vigilance; he is never prone to introspection that may cast doubt on this worldview. The genre was didactic be-cause writers were required to reinforce the Party line and edu-cate the proletariat about the future socialist state, whether in fac-tories or on collective farms. In no way could they attempt, even in a disguised form, to provide an accurate or critical portrait of current society but only one that its citizens would be inspired to emulate. The official de rigueur of Socialist Realism in fiction, the visual arts and films demanded that the mood be optimistic and upbeat and the content accessible. When one Party official declared "our films must be 100 percent ideologically correct and 100 percent commercially viable," it applied to the other art forms as well.[9] Any experimentation in form or style was prohibited. In both the visual arts and in literature, and to lesser extent film, artists eschewed all forms of modernism, including the brief experiment in independent creativity expressed during the revolutionary era, and hearkened back to nineteenth-century naturalism inflected with the new Soviet idiom. Any work that was abstract or did not engage the masses to identify with the heroes or to be repelled by the villains, or in a musical piece to feel the emotional epiphanies, would be reviled as formalism, an aesthetic judgment that could be tantamount to a death sentence. The fundamental principle underpinning Socialist Realism was that human beings were fundamentally good if they were freed from oppression even if it meant that readers and viewers were required to negate the evidence they experienced daily. Arguably the regime retained the support it did because this benign vision of reality, in which the present folded into the future, penetrated vast pockets of society because of its ceaseless representation in novels, films and the plastic arts. Speaking in 1934 before Soviet writers, Gorky contrasted the new official doctrine, whose goal was the creative development of the individual that would transform the world into "a beautiful dwelling place for mankind, united into a single family," with critical realism which in "criticizing everything...asserted nothing." By contrast, he contended that "true realism" required adding "wishes and possibilities," in effect a conflation of fact and fiction.[10] The latter quality was more starkly showcased as Gorky veered into a grey, even dark, zone when he championed Soviet engineering "accomplishments" and their value in rehabilitating labour.

Gorky's most egregious expression of self-abasement and intellectual prostitution before the regime was his role in the celebration of Stalin's two-hundred-kilometre White Sea–Baltic canal. Although he had been at the site, he edited, wrote and was the driving force behind White Sea Canal (also known as Belomor), a 1934 six hundred-page paean to the Stalinist security force and the re-habilitative transformation of miscreants into productive citizens. The reality behind the grotesque deception could not have been starker. The security force, the OGPU, arrested the most capable engineers as saboteurs and wreckers in order to coerce them to draw up the plans for the canal. Once that task was completed, construction began with slave labour that operated on the premise that forced labour was an enlightening and beneficial activity. The Bolsheviks were convinced in the late 1920s and early 1930s that criminality was a residue of the capitalist system where the value of labour had been degraded, a condition that could be cured with discipline and exertion. Under socialism, work, a positive attitude, and a political awareness would transform the convicts into true citizens, cleansed of impurities. It would eradicate their socially harmful thoughts and behaviour, would conquer the beast within themselves, and would render them socially hygienic.[11]

The OGPU security police offered one hundred and thirty writers a feted steamship tour of the site to inspire them to become troubadours for "Stalin's canal." Some did out of genuine conviction. Aleksei Simonov, the son of a former princess, who refashioned himself as an engineer and proletarian writer, recalled in his memoirs, "the White Sea Canal was not just about the construction of a canal, but a humanitarian school for the reconstruction of bad people into good, of common criminals into builders of the Five-Year Plan." Others recognized that they were receiving a sanitized version, one recalling in 1989 that they were seeing "Potemkin Villages" given that the writers had been restricted to interviewing guards and selected criminals, as opposed to political prisoners.[12] Whether motivated by fear, opportunism or belief, the thirty-six writers who participated in the writing of White Sea Canal complied both in substance and style with lock-step ideological correctness. Gorky and his cohorts resorted to chicanery to present a Pollyannish view that human beings could be "reforged" through a demanding labour regimen, uplifting cultural activities, and a propaganda campaign aimed at cleansing the body and language of the "canal workers."

The writers ignored the harsh realities that slave labourers suffered while building this gigantic infrastructure. No one could question either the guilt or sentence of the inmates. Nor would they expose their appalling living and working conditions. The prisoners were stripped of their warm clothes, forced to endure the Arctic elements and make-do with whatever shelter they could find. The quality of the diet was tied to fulfilling their production norms under the most dreadful conditions. Instead of being the recipients of the state-of-the-art technology heralded throughout the Soviet Union, between 1931 and 1933 tens of thousands of former kulaks and wreckers used the most primitive tools, pick axes and shovels on rocky soil, boulders and swamps to hack out a canal in twenty months from the frozen waste. Small wonder that of the three hundred thousand slave labourers dispatched to build the Baltic–White Sea canal, more than twenty five thousand died.[13] Yet according to Gorky, once the writers were acquainted with the ideological purpose behind building the canal, they became "charged up," convinced that productive labour offered redemption to kulaks, the "idolaters of private property." In the spirit of Socialist Realism, he exulted, "a mood is going to appear in literature which will push it ahead and put in on the level of our greatest deeds." Solzhenitsyn, who quoted Gorky from *White Sea Canal*, placed the passage in italics to underscore his derision for the writer and the project, understandably given the conditions and the propaganda about a canal which turned out to be useless in that its depth in some places was no more than six feet. With a phantasmagorical bravado, the writers not only fudged the human price, but with Orwellian doublespeak, they reported that only one person died during construction and that was the result of an accident. They did not consider worthy of mention those who died because they failed to fulfil their work norms. But they did highlight that the camp newspaper was open to national subscriptions and that attempts, albeit unsuccessful, had been made to clean up the vulgar language of the professional criminal population. Moreover, over twelve thousand prisoners had been released on completion of the canal "as people who were entirely reformed" and that almost sixty thousand had had their sentences reduced. That the book was read not only in the Soviet Union but translated into English attested to a belief among progressives that the Soviet approach to penal labour was in the vanguard of prisoner rehabilitation. This flurry of enthusiasm and openness did not last long as the authorities shut down any public discussion about the camps by the mid-1930s; nor was it embraced by some of the former inmates.[14]

Despite its promotion as official history, *White Sea Canal* was, not surprisingly, more akin to iconic Socialist Realist fiction. Recreating history with a "you are there" impression, the story of the canal became one of action, melodrama, stock characters, setbacks and ultimate triumph. Consider in this passage the presence of a treasonous villain who looked like a loyal communist:

> Someone has gone quickly through the station. Looking around, he runs into the bathroom and, holding his pants with one hand, writes on the wall, "Watch out, bolshevik, a white-guardist [sic] was here and soon all of you will get the rope." He signs it with a cross and draws a swastika on the wall. No one would recognize this person. He looks like a typical citizen. He could start working in a factory or go to Moscow. Tomorrow you may meet him on the streets of Moscow....There he is—walking past the Kremlin, looking at Lenin's Mausoleum.

Without a trace of irony, the writer compared the security force to athletic heroes:

> Everywhere the profile of the chekist is the same. His appearance already speaks of discipline, of self-control and a firm hand with those around him, of vigilance and fortitude....This is a system where all the muscles are trained, as if before a competition, to fulfil the orders of the Party.[15]

The period was the early thirties, but the language of "white-guardist" and "chekist" suggested again a time warp with current fears of enemy encirclement (largely manufactured) more apropos of the civil war era. The blending of emotionally charged epithets from that period when the Bolshevik survival was at stake with the contemporary tropes, "swastika" and "Lenin's Mausoleum," was a deliberate attempt to blur historical epochs. If time were not linear, greater authenticity could be given to the fantasy that only the vigilance of the secret service and the omniscient eye of Stalin were thwarting a takeover by hostile forces. If it were a matter of economic development, history moved at a rapid pace; but when the state had to wage war on its internal enemies, history retreated to a more reassuring time when the battle lines were clearly drawn between survival and collapse of the regime.

Before permanently leaving Italy in May 1933 to assume his unofficial position as head of Russian culture, Gorky continued his role as propagandist for Stalin's regime. In the second edition of his biography of Lenin initially published in 1924, Gorky tailored his revisions to reflect the rewriting of history occurring in the Soviet Union by deleting laudatory comments on Trotsky and positive statements on Jews. His experience on returning to his homeland, however, was not what he had hoped. Informers for the NKVD, who surrounded him in his "gilded cage" of palatial dwellings in Moscow and the Crimea, vetted prospective visitors. Moreover, his love of literature pitted him against the regime that published mediocre writers who obsequiously conformed to the dictates of Socialist Realism. Stalin was outraged when Gorky found excuses not to write a sycophantic biography comparable to the one he had written of Lenin. Gorky must have suspected foul play when his son, Maxim, died under suspicious circumstances. Furthermore, the arrest and murder of old Bolsheviks whom he respected, the growing cult of Stalin, and the denial of a personal exit visa were troubling signs of a totalitarian regime, worse than that of Mussolini's authoritarian Italy. His denial about its realities when he was living in the safety of exile until 1933—he denounced as "legends" any reports of famine, forced labour and terror—and his public statements and writings afterwards have besmirched his posthumous reputation. The Stalinist regime shamelessly exploited him when it turned him into an iconic figure, but his craving for fame, money and power, and his willingness to prostitute himself by "speaking Bolshevik" and surrendering his artistic integrity, only demonstrated his vulnerability to being seduced by Stalin's Mephistopheles. His acquiescence to playing the part of Faust only succeeded in reinforcing Stalin's narcissism. Many Soviet writers—Pasternak, Babel, Bulgakov, Mandelstam to name a few—also made their pact with the Devil either by apologizing for, writing obsequious odes or pleading with Stalin; they did it to survive. With the advantages of hindsight, historians should be wary of judging these individuals through the prism of a moral laboratory where the standards of ethical hygiene are higher than in real life. But the case of Gorky is different because he possessed real choices denied to the others. He could have remained in Italy and at least kept his head beneath the parapet. His biographers do not even hint that fear for himself or for his family entered into his calculation to return to the Soviet Union.[16] Given the international reach of Stalin's secret police, there were no guarantees. It was much easier, however, to eliminate him when he lived in Soviet Russia, a possibility that Gorky appears not to have entertained in 1933. Yet when he died in 1936 from tuberculosis, speculation remains that he was poisoned on Stalin's orders.

The Cynic and Fellow-Travellers

Perhaps the most important text in the creation of the Stalinist cult was a basic primer on Marxism, *History of the Communist Party of the Soviet Union: Short Course* (1938). The purpose of the Party's basic ideological text, produced by Stalin himself, was to assist the faithful to "feel the Bolshevik way of thinking." As an imaginary version of Stalin's life, a rewriting of Soviet history, and a reduction of Marxist and Leninist theory to crude simplistic dogma, the *Short Course* was a melodramatic potboiler rife with cardboard cut-out villains and two heroic figures: Lenin, and Stalin himself. Anyone, who had displayed signs of independence or, for whatever reason, had incurred his endemic suspicion and hostility, as had Bukharin and Trotsky, was caricatured as treacherous. When he alluded to the 1938 show trial of Bukharin and colleagues, he praised the Soviet people for its approval of the extermination of the "White Guard insects."[17] Stalin's nostalgic use of a civil war metaphor illustrated the siege mentality of being surrounded by enemies bent on destroying him just as he and fellow Bolsheviks had faced a no-holds-barred struggle for survival twenty years earlier. Stalin also rearranged historical and contemporary reality for the purpose of blackening the reputation of his rival, the "fascist Trotsky," and smudging over differences between Lenin and himself. In his 1946 visceral indictment of the Soviet system, Victor Kravchenko, one-time Party member, engineer, director of large factories, and during World War II, a Commissar of Armaments who defected near its end, correctly asserted that Stalin "deliberately stood history on its head, expunge[d] events and invent[ed] facts....It was a bold, specious, conscienceless fiction."[18] Granted, Stalin could be flexible over strategies, organization and slogans; those used in one historical situation could not be automatically put into place in every situation. Communists would have to adapt to changing circumstances but the basic doctrines would remain infallible.

Because Stalin's *Short Course* on Marxist–Leninist ideology was

the sole basis of political education and a precondition for graduation from higher educational institutions, students either took it as
a serious canon to absorb and launch their careers or swallowed
their disdain and parroted it on appropriate occasions to impress
others. Former Gulag prisoner, Janusz Bardach attested to the awesome power that it exerted on all students regardless of the discipline they were studying. He recalled that as a medical student in
Moscow in the late 1940s, all students were required to regurgitate
large chunks of Stalin's primer and, without any questions or class
discussion, each student was expected to recite the passage that
immediately followed what the previous student had expressed by
rote. The course and the professor terrified the students because if
they failed it, they "would be considered politically unreliable and
would therefore be suspected of anti-Soviet thinking or activity."[19]
For reasons of self-preservation, opportunism or genuine commitment, students accepted its ideological message. According to one
Soviet author, "The Communist ideology was not something external, and imposed by force, but lodged itself deep in our minds and
thoughts. The Soviet way of life came to seem natural to us and
indestructible."[20]

An American foreign journalist also contributed to the stardust
that enveloped Stalin. A purveyor of egregious falsehoods and disingenuous press reports, Walter Duranty was the *New York Times*
correspondent and the longest-serving bureau chief in the Soviet
Union. Motivated by a desire to maintain a sybaritic lifestyle in
Moscow that included jaunts to Berlin, Paris and New York City,
the ebullient, bon vivant Duranty curried favour with Soviet officials. He wrote articles that were so enthusiastic about the Soviet
experiment that he secured interviews with Stalin. Duranty's subsequent dispatches earned him the Pulitzer Prize and worldwide
fame. In his last interview with Stalin, the dictator thanked him
for his accurate reporting, understandable praise since the scribe
dismissed reports of mass starvation as "malignant propaganda."
Duranty's adage—"Russians may be hungry and short of clothes
and comfort. But you can't make an omelette without breaking
eggs"—encapsulated the appalling rationale for collectivization
rendering him Stalin's favourite reporter.[21] His cynicism that was
only surpassed by the mendacity of his dispatches that epitomized the base compromises he forged with the Soviet regime. The
price of his sycophantic Faustian bargain was the suspension of

his critical faculties and his willingness to wear official blinders. He had already endorsed the Soviet version of the wrecker trials (sabotaging the economy) and later uncritically accepted the confessions of the accused at the show trials as prima facie evidence of their guilt. "It is unthinkable that Stalin and...the Court Martial would have sentenced their friends to death unless the proofs of guilt were overwhelming." On collectivization and the famine, he was adamant that the country had experienced only "serious food shortages" and "no actual starvation, but there is widespread mortality from diseases due to malnutrition." In another article, he noted that any talk of famine was "a sheer absurdity." When he personally witnessed the suffering of kulaks in 1930, he minimized it by declaring that he had seen much worse on the trains of wounded soldiers returning from the front during the Great War. When he attested to the "heavy loss of life" in the famine, in true Stalinist fashion he breezily remarked that "a few million dead Russians" were unimportant given the "sweeping historical changes" occurring in the country.[22]

Duranty's capacity for dissembling was not evidence of stupidity or naiveté on his part; he submitted to the British Embassy an accurate account of the Ukraine "bled white" and estimated a death count of ten million in the Soviet Union in the previous year. Unlike foreign travellers who were either manipulated or self-deluded because of their ideological predilections, Duranty had a penetrating eye for what was happening. But he had no wish to jeopardize his craving for celebrity as the dean of western correspondents in Moscow. With his apartment doubling as a salon for all visiting luminaries, he basked in the comfort of a luxurious lifestyle with a chauffeur, a cook and a maid.

Duranty's half truths and outright lies demonstrated bad faith by placing amoral pragmatism and cowardly opportunism above journalistic integrity. Malcolm Muggeridge, a fellow journalist, who witnessed first hand the horrors of famine and smuggled incisive pieces out of the Soviet Union, suggested that Duranty was attracted to the sheer ruthlessness and power that Stalin wielded, and that he identified with the powerful men who counted in the Kremlin, not with the people. Celebrity and power are not mutually exclusive, and together they contributed to Duranty writing glowing reports on Stalin and his terrorist regime. Whereas Muggeridge had written that the famine was "one of the most monstrous crimes in history," except for his submission to the British Embassy, Duranty never even suggested there was a famine because he would have lost his press accreditation and visa since all journalists had to submit their dispatches to the Soviet censor.[23] But he might have made a difference to Western perceptions. Given the prestigious venue that published his articles and the cachet Duranty wielded, he might have inhibited other observers from being so easily deluded by surface appearances. As his biographer comments: "Had Duranty, a Pulitzer Prize-winner at the peak of his celebrity, spoken out loud and clear in the pages of the *New York Times,* the world could not have ignored him" as it did others like Muggeridge and "events might have taken a different turn."[24]

A postscript for Duranty occurred in April 2003, when a Pulitzer subcommittee, with the support of Ukrainians worldwide, urged the withdrawal of Duranty's award because the reporter deliberately ignored the devastating famine. In November of that year the Board decided not to revoke the prize because they found according to Associated Press reports, "no clear and convincing evidence of deliberate deception."

If the craven opportunism of Duranty merits unequivocal condemnation, the role played by the fellow-travellers who did not join the Communist Party but made pilgrimages to the Soviet Union during the 1930s is more complicated. Some visitors were openly suspicious of Soviet boasting when they visited a "run-down, muddy farm at which they could find not a single person at work," prompting their host to later write, "I did not know where to hide from shame." Complaints ranging from "everything was in deplorable condition" "indescribable" waste "paralysis in the fields" could be found in Soviet files.[25] Others, mostly public figures, were deceived in part because of the adulation they received or because of an ideological predisposition for the Soviet experiment. Unlike some of the German and English communists, who reported that conditions in the prison they visited were worse than ordinary prisons back home, the vast majority of intellectuals had never been inside a prison, a factory or been present at an industrial work site in their own country.[26] These fellow-travellers saw what they were expected to see and were either oblivious to reality, accepted the explanation that anything "bad" was a residue of tsarism, or could rationalize the brutal means employed to achieve the communist paradise. Although they could diagnose the economic and social ills in their own country with laser-like clarity, they failed miserably to penetrate the carapace of state-managed aesthetics when they flocked to the Soviet Union. Given that his hosts sheltered him from harsh realities, supplied him with lavish meals at a time of severe rationing in urban areas and hid the appalling hunger in the countryside, the Irish dramatist, George Bernard Shaw's dismissal of the famine as "poppycock" is understandable but contemptible. When the French Radical Party leader, Eduard Herriot, who had signed a non-aggression pact with the Soviets in 1932, visited the Soviet Union, the Ukraine was writhing from the Holodomor. Yet upon his return, he remarked that he

> crossed the Ukraine. So! I assure you that it looked like a garden in full yield. You tell me that this land is reputed to be going through a depression right now? I cannot speak of what I have not seen. And heaven knows I made them take me to afflicted areas. All I witnessed, however, was prosperity.[27]

On the surface, this statement could be read as a bare-faced lie or a paean of praise by one who was breathtakingly credulous, but the truth, however, is more complicated.

Had foreign visitors possessed deeper insight into the machinations of how Russians deceived outsiders and their own citizens, or if they did not have an alternative agenda, they might not have been so easily bamboozled by official rhetoric and blinded to reality. The day before Herriot arrived, the entire population was required to work from 2:00 A.M. cleaning the streets and decorating the houses. Food distribution centres were closed; queues were prohibited. Homeless children, beggars and starving people disappeared. Shop windows were filled with food but the purchase of it was prohibited. The hotel where he stayed was refurbished, and what he saw—a tractor factory, a model children's settlement and collective—and the sumptuous banquets he enjoyed with Party leaders and later with workers at a collective farm were carefully prearranged.[28] With his itinerary prettified and carefully orchestrated, with anything problematic screened from view, he witnessed no evidence of a famine. Given his ideological perspective and that his priority was to establish French diplomatic relations with the Soviet Union, Herriot had no reason to find evidence.

Neither was the famine witnessed by George Bernard Shaw

who celebrated with great fanfare his seventy-fifth birthday in the Soviet Union. As an influential member of the British Fabian society, Shaw's early political orientation was Marxist. By the 1930s, he had become enamoured with the cult of the great man of action who knew how to organize society—Mussolini, Hitler and Stalin. Like the German philosopher, Martin Heidegger, Shaw harboured fantasies of being what Michael David-Fox calls "a prophet behind the throne." Shaw considered himself merely a "professional talker" but contended that only "action" from a strong man could save the world. In his view, the flawed and barely competent public officials in the West timidly undertook to redress the economic and social problems of the Great Depression. For years he had disdained parliamentary democracy where the voters' only options were to choose between Tweedle-dum and Tweedle-dee. Until the Great War, Shaw had retained his belief in "gradual modifications of existing systems." The stupidity and carnage arising from that war had contributed to his volte-face about the pace of change. When he looked at the British House of Commons, he cynically saw what a contemporary described as "hard-faced men who look as if they had done very well out of the war." They presided over a backward county in contrast to the Soviets who were forging a superior society. The latter knew how to build an efficient socialist state creating an egalitarian society by combining enlightened dictatorship with a society of producer–consumers. If that entailed a "judicious [liquidation of] a handful of exploiters and speculators to make the world safe for honest men," it could be justified in utilitarian terms. When Shaw* wrote his polemic *Rationalization of*

---

* The simplistic and wrong-headed views of conservative commentator–TV host Glenn Beck, who portrays Shaw as the architect of the Nazi gas chambers, deserve a response. Like most religious and political fundamentalists, Beck has no appreciation of irony and satire, at which Shaw was a master. The dramatist did spout a lot of outrageous nonsense, some of it cited above, and some of it recorded, that has now surfaced on YouTube. What Beck also does not understand is that Shaw was a provocateur who delighted in shocking his audiences, not unlike Beck himself. Shaw published provocative statements in the prefaces of his plays, but he kept his polemics separate from his art, often giving the strongest arguments to the characters with whom he most disagreed. In this way, he was similar to the composer, Richard Wagner, of whom Shaw was a devotee, and different from Martin Heidegger whose politics were interwoven into his philosophy.

Russia, he referred to "weeding the garden"—"our question is not, to kill or not to kill, but how to select the right people to kill"—by arguing that anyone who resisted collectivization must be "liquidated as vermin" as this was "inevitable and irremediable under the stern morality of Communism." He also normalized Stalinist extermination by placing it in an historical context with references to Cromwell's atrocities in Ireland and the North American treatment of the indigenous population.[29]

In 1932 Sydney and Beatrice Webb, war-horses of the British Labour Party and veterans of the Fabian movement, journeyed to the Soviet Union in search of the Promised Land. Like other fellow-travellers who conducted pilgrimages to that country on "fact-finding tours," the Webbs witnessed sights of happy children, a model factory, prison and state farm. Their trip and subsequent writings illustrated how the regime shrewdly and cynically exploited myopic foreigners so that they would serve to universalize the Soviet Union's values and advertise its appeal to liberal Westerners. Because the Webbs could not speak Russian, they were dependent on their guides and the material supplied to them. The three-week trip was a confirmation of a priori faith; therefore, it was easy to suspend critical judgment and fit what they saw into preconceived moulds—Sydney's fascination with the Soviet blueprint to transform society and Beatrice's deep admiration for its "commitment to universal brotherhood." In the spirit of the authors of *The White Sea Canal,* they highlighted a showplace prison with its pleasant countryside and unlocked gates, and then extrapolated from this experience that prisons were more humane in the Soviet Union than in the West.

Nonetheless, the Webbs, especially Beatrice, were not completely naïve and wilfully blind. Her niece was married to Malcolm Muggeridge and his revelations about the famine in the *Manchester Guardian* unnerved her. In her diary, she confided that there is "some fire behind this smoke of Malcolm's queerly malicious but sincerely felt denunciation of Soviet Communism." She added, "What makes me uncomfortable is that we have no evidence to the contrary." As her doubts increased, she could only attribute the violent purges within the Party to the country's "dark side."*

---

* In a similar manner, the American writer, Theodore Dreiser's, public writings were fulsome in their praise for the Soviet Union, but in his conversations with his guide and in his diary, he defends the

Yet in their published works, the Webbs denied the famine and attributed "a partial failure of crops" to peasant "sabotage" that regrettably necessitated kulak "liquidation." They acknowledged the vast system of labour camps that had existed on the islands of the North Sea where "every form of cruelty and torment" had been perpetrated: beatings, tortures and killings. But they reported disingenuously that such inhumane treatment had ceased to exist because of international outcry. The manner in which they contorted their evidence into a Procrustean bed was evident in their analysis of the waves of terror. They denounced summary trials as abhorrent and then, like Shaw, exonerated the Communists of any culpability by normalizing Soviet violence by placing it in the context of history. The Soviets had accomplished in fifteen years what had taken four centuries in the West through violent religious, economic and ethnic persecutions. Their logic only reinforced the impression that the Soviet Union was trapped in its violent, atavistic past, a past that the Bolsheviks were committed to extinguishing. The rapturous encomiums of Western pilgrims like the Webbs puzzled the writer, Gennady Andreev-Khomiakov, because for eight years he had been "dragged through all the circles of the labour-camp hell" before being released from a Siberian prison camp. He wondered whether there was an evil in the West, unknown to Russians that eclipsed their own squalor. He did not understand that fellow-travellers' praise for the Soviet experiment was a combination of naivety, dishonesty and bad faith. Even Beatrice, in her diary, acknowledged that their massive undertaking was "an illegitimate venture—neither our equipment nor our opportunities suffice." Her worse fears were confirmed after the book's publications with the 1938 Moscow trials and the news of the Nazi–Soviet pact that she characterized as a "day of holy terror."[30] By this time, she must have recognized that she and her husband had been manipulated by Kremlin officials and turned into what Lenin once disdained as useful idiots.

---

superiority of the American system and does offer astute, if disparaging, judgments about his hosts. For example, he compared Soviet education and ideology to the rigid Catholicism of his youth and attributed the gray uniformity he saw around him to "enforced equality." This disparity might be explained by his cautious support for the Soviet experiment which contrasts with his disdain for Russian backwardness. David-Fox, *Showcasing the Great Experiment*, 127-141.

It is hard to take seriously the Webbs' impressions because they could not distinguish form from substance, the mellifluous rhetoric from the shabby and ghastly reality. It never occurred to them that anything they read or collected might have been false; they accepted all documents and comments from Soviet officials at face value. For example, in their discussion of the 1936 constitution that guaranteed citizens a panoply of civil rights, the Webbs accurately point out that there was nothing in it that resembled the office of dictator or that indicated government being the will of one person. What eluded them was that the letter of the constitution bore little resemblance to reality, that what they were witnessing was a deceptive mirage. Ironically, Stalin's constitution made the rehabilitation of prisoners more difficult since the Soviet Union was officially a socialist state; one's antisocial behaviour could no longer be excused on the grounds that he was a victim of capitalist exploitation. Within a year as the Great Terror engulfed most of the Soviet Union—some Russian provincial backwaters were relatively unscathed—the constitution was only a cynical smokescreen that concealed the murderous nature of the regime. The Webbs' credulity is staggering since they neither inquired what was behind the Potemkin village façade nor cited the works of authors critical of the Soviet Union like Bertrand Russell or Victor Serge.[31] The latter acquired considerable experience living there, and had spent three years in Stalin's prisons. As idealists and as foreigners, they could not see what Bukharin did—Stalin was a master of deceit who was using public discussions of the "most democratic" constitution as a subterfuge to conceal his efforts to transform the Soviet regime into a fascistic one. Even though the Webbs allowed caveats such as "the use of terror" and "elaborately staged show trials," their rose-tinted spectacles contributed to an egregious distortion of perception.[32]

Several reasons could be offered to explain the skewed judgments of the enthusiastic, sometimes rapturous, fellow-travellers to the Soviet Union from Britain, Western Europe and the thousands from all walks of life from the United States who went there to work and live (and die).[33] In general, when Westerners travelled to a foreign environment, they had pictures in their heads of what they expected to see. Those with a pragmatic outcome welcomed the prospects of work and benefits when America was mired in unemployment. The more ideologically-inclined welcomed the comforting certitudes of Marxism. They believed they would bear witness to a transformative society, which, although experiencing growing pains, was well on its way to achieving universal brotherhood for everyone and freedom from exploitation and oppression. If they regarded the Soviet Union as a fertile testing ground in the noble social experiment of engineering a new man in a classless society, they were more predisposed to accept without question what their guides and interpreters were saying even when the evidence of their senses often belied the robotic spiel of their hosts. As a young reporter, Muggeridge was always amazed at the

> spectacle of [foreign visitors] travelling with radiant optimism through a famished countryside, wandering in happy bands about squalid, over-crowded towns, listening with unshakeable faith to the fatuous patter of carefully trained and indoctrinated guides, repeating like schoolchildren a multiplication table, the bogus statistics and mindless slogans endlessly intoned to them.[34]

Impressionable visitors to the Soviet Union during the 1930s who did not speak the language were vulnerable to being manipulated by the carefully crafted tours of the Potemkin villages that their hosts excelled in showcasing.

Yet this picture of naive fellow-travellers is complicated by the experiences of the African–American singer and actor, Paul Robeson, who had understandable reasons to embrace the Soviet Union. Unlike in America where he experienced racism that intensified after he attempted to push for anti–lynching legislation, he was enthusiastically welcomed everywhere during his visits to the Soviet Union between 1934 and 1938, and again in 1949. He spoke Russian fluently, loved its folk culture and emotionally identified with an internationalist homeland. During the Cold War in the late 1940s, he faced government harassment and public hostility arising from his leftist political activism and his controversial positive public statements about the U.S.S.R. During his 1949 visit in which Soviet newspapers were filled with virulent outbursts against "cosmopolitanism and Zionism," he noticed the disappearance of Jewish friends and insisted on meeting with his friend, the poet, Itsk Ferrer. Privately in a hotel room, Robeson did meet with Ferrer, who had been brought from his cell in the Lubyanka prison, and through sign language and scraps of paper Robeson became aware of the terrible purge against Jews, including the murder of his friend, the actor Solomon Mikhoels. He did sing a concert that night where he acknowledged Ferrer (who was executed three years later) and announced that he "mourned the premature death" of Mikhoels. As a tribute to these men, he sang in Russian the Yiddish song of the Jewish partisans who had fought in the Warsaw Ghetto uprising. When Robeson returned to America, he never spoke publicly about his meeting with Ferrer believing it would only shore up "war hysteria" against the Soviet Union.[35] Controversy remains around Robeson's refusal to condemn Stalinism, but the allegation of his naivety about the Soviet Union surely pales when compared with that of the Webbs. Despite being a propagandist for the great experiment, he is a much more sympathetic figure than Shaw with his harsh utilitarianism.

The myopia of fellow–travellers also resulted from an inability to gauge totally unfamiliar phenomena. At the beginning of the 1930s, it would have been inconceivable to them and without precedent in modern history that a state would be willing to kill, deport and enslave its own people. Never before had a Party exercised such awesome power over its subjects that it could propagate falsehoods that squeezed out any other reality.[36] Lenin and the early Bolsheviks had not possessed that kind of power. Mussolini in Fascist Italy, for all its brutality, had to contend with the power of the Vatican, and was forced to conclude a treaty of rapprochement. From our present day vantage point, we have become familiar with the kind of state terror and ethnic cleansing that Hitler and other modern dictators have been willing to perpetrate on their own citizens. The brutal collectivization and man–made famine of the early 1930s were so alien and unfamiliar to Western experience that it was hard to recognize them as barbaric acts. True, the apparent breakdown and moral bankruptcy of capitalism in the 1930s during the Great Depression and the growing revulsion toward German Nazism contributed to the illusions that travellers acquired about the Soviet Union. Even Arthur Koestler, who was deeply troubled by scenes of deprivation witnessed during his year-long trip there and whose confidence was shaken by the huge disparity between communist theory and reality, could put those doubts aside when confronted with the immediate threat to freedom posed by Nazi Germany. Hitler was responsible for his "second honeymoon with the Party," an example of how the repression of one dictator served the interests of the other.[37]

Stalin skilfully exploited Western fears about fascism by refurbishing his regime with a humanistic patina. At a time when people were disappearing into the Gulag or being shot in the back of the head, Stalin was able to camouflage the terror with his constitutional undertaking. In his interview with an American journalist-executive in March 1936, he stated that the new constitution would be "the most democratic of all the constitutions in the world."[38] Given the steady barrage of boilerplate rhetoric directed at Soviet citizens, it is not surprising that the cult of Stalin enthralled a devoted following of clenched-fist cheerleaders. But it is astonishing that Stalin could persuade so many Westerners—among them the French who elected a Popular Front government (a coalition of left-leaning democrats and Communists)—to rally behind the Soviet Union as the bastion of anti–fascism at a time when the regime was inflicting unprecedented state violence on its citizens that in the 1930s vastly exceeded that of Nazi Germany.[39] That he could dignify barbarism with the aura of progress attested to the success of public relations that were conducted through the Comintern (the international communist movement), the secrecy under which the regime's crimes were carried out and the skill of manipulating reality through Potemkin villages. The greater visibility of the Third Reich with its belligerent nationalism, open contempt for democracy, and undisguised racism did impair the Western public's awareness because it served as a distraction to what was happening in the Soviet Union. The lithograph, *The Sleep of Reason Produces Monsters* by the early nineteenth–century Spanish painter Francisco Goya, acquires a timeless resonance when we reflect on the nightmarish state beneath the glossy veneer of Socialist Realism that so enraptured the credulous. In it, a frock–coated figure, perhaps a scholar, slumps over a plinth lost in sleep and the sky swarms with mutants and bats with cats' eyes. By way of contrast, the clear–headed George Orwell recognized the toxic consequences of crossing a moral Rubicon when "efforts to regenerate society *by violent means* [led] to the cellars of the OGPU, Lenin to Stalin."[40]

Orwell was not alone in peering through the polished exterior showcased for the outside world. The French author, André Gide, a fellow–traveller with impeccable credentials, underwent a stark reversal in his thinking. Prior to his visit, he had endorsed communism as the solution to the world's ills and regarded the First Five-Year Plan as the perfect antithesis to capitalist disorder and the emergence of reason into history. During his 1936 visit, he too noted the sweetness of the children, the politeness of the workers, the eagerness to please and receive approbation but he also discerned the lack of curiosity about the outside world. Underneath this seeming accommodation, he recognized the loss of freedom and stark inequalities that Communism was supposedly to address.* Instead of a revolutionary society, he saw conformity, acquiescence and, to an embarrassing degree, a quasi-mystical worship of Stalin, with his ubiquitous busts and portraits.

Gide began the process of shedding his own illusions when he travelled through Gori, the birthplace of Stalin. He thought it courteous to send a cordial telegram to Stalin. When he showed it to his translators, they demanded that he add more adulatory epithets—remarkable, outstanding, great and even genius—as if to impute to him preternatural wisdom. He understood that he had no choice but to accept as he had no control over the translation.[41] What he and other travellers did not fathom was that their hosts experienced fear and insecurity about them, regarding what they might say and ask, for example, about the poverty or the number of street urchins. These visitors had no idea that a Soviet agency, established to deal with non-Party cultural and intellectual figures, trained their guides. Awkward questions could be best answered by focusing on the future and what the country would become in the socialist utopia rather than dwelling on current problems, a tenet that was comparable to the aesthetic doctrine of Socialist Realism. At the time, Gide did not appreciate that the unctuousness embedded in the script protected his guides from betraying an indiscretion or lapsing into spontaneous but dangerous comments.[42] He was correct when he ruefully reflected that these kinds of obsequious dithyrambs of hero worship only widened an unbridgeable gap between Stalin and the rest of society. But he did not sufficiently appreciate that this society was an isolated one of closed boundaries. What Soviet citizens did hear about the outside world was only the authorized perspective fed to them by their newspapers like, as reported to Gide, the brutal treatment of

---

* On his trip he was regularly feted with sumptuous meals but whenever, he was able to escape his handlers, he witnessed the appalling poverty of ordinary workers.

French school children. Andreev–Khomiakov understood that, although discontent with the system was everywhere, the majority who did not possess access to forbidden books "had no criteria on which to arrive at independent judgments."[43]

The cult of Stalin effectively masked for most subjects and foreigners any understanding of the real operations of power in the Soviet Union. Nevertheless, Gide had accurately already reached the conclusion that the general population in this society was less free and more terrorized—that the smallest infractions would result in the most severe penalties—more than in Hitler's Germany of the 1930s.[44]

Socialist Realism in Films and the Visual Arts

The printed word alone could not emotionally penetrate the psyche of the masses. Film, photography and the plastic arts were mobilized to present a view of reality that conformed to Stalin's wishes. After theatre, film became for Stalin the most important and favourite art form. No film script ever escaped his attention because of its potential for manipulating reality. Stalin vetted documentary films on the civil war era that revealed his close relationship with Lenin and his heroic role in the struggle against the Whites. In a scene from one of them, he is portrayed disregarding an order from Trotsky to retreat; instead, he mobilizes a bold attack and appears on the battlefield impervious to danger watching his soldiers dislodge Whites from their position. One of the great directors of agitprop, Sergei Eisenstein, reedited his documentary *October* on direct orders from Stalin to delete any references to Trotsky who had been expelled from the Party six months earlier. The film itself was a fanciful recreation of the Revolution as a mass uprising against a "Napoleonic" Kerensky in conformity with how the Party elite wanted it remembered by posterity. Five thousand veterans of the civil war, recruited to participate in the storming of the Winter Palace, used live ammunition wounding several people. In reality, only a few hundred sailors and Red Guards had taken part in the original, less violent assault.[45]

By the end of the First Five-Year Plan, Stalin commissioned films celebrating life that depicted peasants leaping, dancing and bellowing songs against vast backdrops of wheat, a cornucopia

Courtesy of Photofest.

Lyubov Orlova shown here in The Radiant Path *(1940) was the greatest Soviet star of popular cinema in the 1930s. She was a leading actress in musical comedies and a role model for audiences, showing how with pluck, personality and effort it was possible for a person from humble background to rise above one's lot in life. Two generations later when her films were shown on television, Orlova remained an inspiration for young women.*

of food and material prosperity. Although audiences enjoyed the ebullient comedies and upbeat musicals that possessed both entertainment and correct ideological value, these fantasies were in stark contrast to their daily lives. In *The Radiant Path*, an unpretentious woman, through dint of study and hard work rises from a humble maid, a weaver in the textile industry to become a heroic shock worker (one who vastly exceeded the work production norms) who can run scores of looms simultaneously. Along the way, she becomes an engineer, travels to Moscow to receive a medal from President Kalinin and marries a clean–cut engineer. Behind the choreographed work scenes and the sprightly songs which Stalin helped to write resided the optimistic message that work was an honour and individuals could overcome difficulties and become stars. With a little more effort, sacrifice and the courage to unmask wreckers—in *Radiant* the villain is an ex-kulak who sets fire to a warehouse—paradise was just around the corner. With the promise of a bright future which audiences swallowed with trusting naiveté, this sort of kitsch, which represented a "skilful Stalinization of Hollywood style" enjoyed extraordinary popularity with Soviet audiences.[46] Endeared to her Slavic blond beauty and her winsome wholesomeness, fans wrote letters of appreciation to the star actress, Lyubov Orlova. Escapist entertainment, a balm to their troubled lives in these grim years, encouraged them to believe a better life was possible.

Like the producers of Socialist–Realist films, graphic artists contributed to the rearrangement of reality. In keeping with Stalin's imperative that life was to be joyful, even if the reality of their lives was bleak, posters were produced that showcased the idyllic joys of the collective. In 1934, a poster (a printing of sixty thousand) shows a well–groomed, happy, handsome man, his attractive smiling wife and their happy, plump toddler who is clapping his hands in tune with the music coming from the gramophone. In the background, the viewer sees an electric light and a shelf of books that include the works of Gorky, Lenin and Stalin and technical books on agriculture. The poster contains a plethora of messages. With the difficult process of collectivization over, exemplar workers can expect the accoutrements of the good life in a pastoral setting: music, material benefits, culture, and the time to study to become more skilled in order to be a good Bolshevik. In addition it urges rural men and women to put priority on personal hygiene and attire. Implicit for women is the message that they need to invest their energies in reproduction as well as in production.[47]

Plastic artists and photographers as well participated in rewriting history: a common motif was the aggrandizement of Stalin's leadership during the revolutionary era. In a steel engraving in 1936, a confident Stalin stands in front of a huge map pointing out to a rapt Lenin how the counterrevolutionary White Armies will be routed.[48] Trotsky, who actually did mastermind the defeat of the White armies, has been effectively outmanoeuvred by his double, Stalin. As one of the commanders of the southern front responsible for procuring food when the Germans and Whites occupied most of the fertile regions, Stalin had played a more substantial role in the Red victory than historians have accorded him. But he did not possess the charisma that Trotsky exuded. A turn of history's wheel inverted the officially enforced status of Trotsky from a saviour—whose portrait was even engraved on teacups—to a monstrous criminal, who belatedly was exposed as the master plotter of a powerful cabal to overthrow Stalin. In order to sanctify this view of history and justify that he was the rightful and sole heir to Lenin, Stalin required his official biographer and artists—photographers, sculptors and painters—to doctor their relationship and to communicate why he was a worthy successor. Stalin's iconic status or apotheosis, implying he was not only heir of Lenin but of the Russian Tsars, Peter the Great and Ivan the Terrible, was the central motif of his official biography written by the fellow traveller French writer, Henri Barbusse. In a famous painting of Lenin arriving at the Finland Station in Petrograd, Stalin is inserted alighting from the train behind him. In a sculpture, the aged Lenin sits, looking up and touching the arm of a confident, standing Stalin as he gives his heir some last parting advice.

No visual artist could ever reproduce Stalin's diminutive height of five feet three inches, his pockmarked face or his withered arm. In photo historian David King's fascinating book, *The Commissar Vanishes*, there is a photo of a preternaturally–youthful Stalin, his dark hair salted with grey and facial skin airbrushed of wrinkles. A 1924 photograph was substantially retouched in 1939 to coincide with his sixtieth birthday so that his "skin has been positively pancaked, his hair and moustache are now as smooth as a matinee idol's, and the glint in his eye is all that remains of the original." Any casual observer would conclude that the 1939 copy shows a younger man than the 1924 original. Despite the vigilance of the censors, occasionally a visual representation illuminating a psychological truth escaped. There is a remarkable photomontage that juxtaposes a smooth–faced Stalin at Lenin's bier, ostensibly to highlight his grief at Lenin's funeral and solidify his role as the rightful heir. Stalin looks out at the viewer, a hovering spectre, a sinister vampire, redolent of decay with a touch of necrophilia.[49] But by 1939 when this photomontage was done, almost anyone who might have regarded Stalin as a sinister figure had been physically eliminated.

The hagiography of Stalin was accompanied not only by the physical eradication of opponents, but also by a visual obliteration of their pictorial existence as though they had never lived. Group photographs that included old Bolsheviks who had been physically purged would be redacted so that by the end of the

1930s Stalin was virtually alone in these photographs. In an ironical twist of fate, many of the contributors and the leaders glorified in *White Sea Canal* were themselves purged within a few years. Copies were removed from public libraries and many owners destroyed theirs since it was dangerous to possess the book. All of Trotsky's books were removed from libraries, and paintings and photographs where he was often seen, alongside Lenin, were expunged from public memory before an NKVD agent assassinated him with an ice axe on August 22, 1940 in Mexico. One of the most famous photographs taken of the revolutionary era is one of Lenin addressing the troops outside of the Bolshoi theatre in 1920. On the steps to the right, Trotsky can be clearly seen. After 1927 when Trotsky was expelled from the Party, his image no longer appears.[50] The blatant manipulation of the historical and contemporary record was a cynical ploy to demonstrate how will-o'-the-wisp any effort was to search for a reality independent of the whims and fantasies of one man. Reality kept changing and crystallized into what Stalin decreed.

The 1930s were hard years with corruption, shortages and accusations of saboteurs. The power of Socialist Realism was that it allowed countless individuals to rationalize the deprivations and the political tumult as temporary imperfections. One way to rationalize was to surrender to the illusion of the Potemkin village that existed as a form of deception to inspire the Soviet masses. This cheerful, upbeat portrait of Soviet life that was screened in the kitsch movies and bleated in newspapers and speeches was, if not life in the present, reality in the future.[51] The only way that the sacrifices, material deprivation and suffering could be justified was to believe that the present was a mere way station on the way to the promised paradise in the near future. Evidence that the future as a tangible reality resonated can be derived from the comments offered to researchers in the Harvard Project after World War II. Among the émigrés interviewed, one betrayed a lingering affection for the regime: "I thought that all the difficulties were concerned with the sacrifices which were necessary for the building of socialism and that after a socialist society was constructed, life would be better."[52] Sacrifices could be borne as long as the Soviet people believed that Communism could transform their reality.

Despite the hostility from pockets of the public, especially among the peasantry and non-Russians, Stalin did succeed in creating a community of the faithful, a society that cherished him as a benevolent, wise father figure. By 1939, the eighty percent of current Party members who had joined since the mid–1930s were both beholden to Stalin and wedded psychologically and ideologically to Soviet achievements.[53] Those who participated in the building of the "beautiful pavilions" that grace the Moscow subway revered him. During the 1930s a generation came of age that valued political conformity and was reluctant to question authority.

Whether for reasons of ignorance, idealism or rationalization, the beliefs of these people can be understood more than the fellow-travellers in the West during the 1930s who, having nothing to fear, maligned Gide for his "betrayal" after he published his pamphlet repudiating Communism and the "dictatorship of the Soviet bureaucracy." The following year, Gide responded to his critics with a postscript where he incorporated the Moscow trials into his account. In evocative prose, he laments and indicts the injustice and the hypocrisy:

> I see these victims, I hear them, I feel them around me. Last night their stifled cries awoke me; today their silence dictates these lines. No one is intervening in their favour. All the right-wing journals use them, moreover, to stir up the regime they execrate; those who hold the idea of justice and liberty...have said nothing, are saying nothing; and around them the immense proletarian crowd, blinded.[54]

Gide's condemnation of the political right and the left in the West, and his compassion for the victims of the Great Terror distinguished him from so many others who should have known better. But like the Party cadres and the larger public in the Soviet Union, they too were captivated or blinded by the power of ideology, or immobilized by its handmaiden, the apparatus of terror that was harnessed supposedly to protect the state. Stalin's waves of terror, his reasons for them, his timing and choreography of them, and how he used others to dissociate himself and ensure the complicity of both Party potentates and the wider public are the focus for the next chapter.

Stalin Cannibalizes the Party

> We resembled the great Inquisitors in that we
> persecuted the seeds of evil not only in man's
> deeds, but in their thoughts. We admitted no
> private sphere, not even inside a man's skull.
>
> —*Darkness at Noon*
> Arthur Koestler

The Dynamics of the Show Trial

Stalin needed scaegoats to explain the faltering economy that resulted from the mismanaged, rapid industrialization and ferocious civil war in the countryside. From 1928 he elaborated upon the judicial masque established by Lenin during the Revolutionary era. In 1922 Lenin had established a precedent for deploying show trials as a vehicle for eliminating enemies of Bolshevism. He issued a secret polemic (published in full in 1990 for the first time by a Soviet publication): "the more members of the reactionary bourgeoisie and clergy we shoot the better." Yet Lenin's intemperate language against enemies of the people did not always result in lethal outcomes. The estimations by some historians that eight thousand were executed after show trials are belied by documents that indicate numbers as low as forty-four, excluding those who were summarily executed.[1] Stalin turned show trials into a ritual that was to feature writ large on the Soviet political and psychic landscape during the 1930s. Unlike Lenin, he utilized them as political theatre to purge rivals within his own Party, many of whom were opposed to his policies. His motives

and obsessions were also more complex than his predecessor's—
he longed to turn around his sagging popularity and to accelerate
policy goals. The trials also possessed for Stalin a psychological
dimension: to satisfy a compulsion for revenge and to displace his
guilt onto the victim. In the process, Stalin set a tone of top-down
terror that would drench his minions in blood and implicate large
sectors of the public in his web of sadism and terror.

In 1928 Stalin choreographed his first show trial for public consumption so as to advance his political agenda. He conceived it as
an inquisition into the soul of the accused whose hidden beliefs
could be exposed through public confession in a venue replete
with theatrics that concurrently satisfied his compulsion to replay
and avenge old hatreds.[2] In the so-called Shakhty trial (named after the mining town of the same name), over fifty engineers and
technicians, including three German citizens, were charged with
sabotage. They were mostly men of the old intelligentsia accused
of arson and of causing explosions and deliberate flooding of the
mines. The conspirators were alleged to be acting in the interests
of foreign intelligence as well as of the former mine owners living
in exile. Stalin fabricated this conspiracy to convince the people
that the capitalist world, specifically Britain, France and Japan,
was hostile toward the U.S.S.R. as evidenced by its willingness to
support those enemies within. Stalin unleashed his fertile suspicions on the public by mobilizing a crisis atmosphere: "We have internal enemies. We have external enemies. This must not be forgotten."[3] Through rapid modernization and nation building, the state
would be strong, but only if vigilance was exercised against those
class enemies, the "bourgeois specialists," who would sabotage
its goals. In this and later trials, Stalin required the manufacture
of enemies to justify the sacrifices exacted upon the population.

Stalin's belligerence during the Shakhty trial was reflected by
the press. An editorial in *Pravda* set the tone for the sham trials
that followed in the 1930s: the allusion to a toxic underworld residue from the civil war, the dehumanizing imagery and the association of contagious disease with betrayal, were underscored:

> It shines a clear light on the secret back rooms and the
> 'underside' of our construction, on the criminal labyrinth
> in which the white monarchist reptiles have arisen who are
> spreading fire and poison on the proletarian milieus infecting
> Soviet air with the miasma of treason.[4]

Nonetheless, the overheated rhetoric was designed exclusively for domestic consumption since the execution of foreigners could disrupt relations with European Powers whose technical expertise was essential. As a result only five of the accused were executed, forty-four were sent to prison and the three Germans were acquitted.

In keeping with the ideological shift away from a global revolution and toward Stalin's commitment to "socialism in one country," the trial was designed to promote xenophobia, national chauvinism and a heightened conspiratorial mindset. It conveyed to the public that it was essential to pursue revolutionary policies. The purpose behind Stalin's machinations at this time was to publicly parade scapegoats for the state's technical and economic failures. He set out to undermine his rivals in the Politburo and replace experts with younger underlings even if their technical skills did not equal their ideological enthusiasm. In this and subsequent judicial travesties in the early 1930s, the charge was usually "wrecking" and the men accused were both foreign and home-grown experts: engineers, economists and managers.

The show trial of technical experts dubbed the Industrial Party was staged in November 1930 after Stalin's policy failures led to a bankrupt economy. When over a billion roubles went into circulation, the paper money was virtually useless. Silver coins were hoarded, resulting in a steep decline in the standard of living and an economy based on bartering. Stalin was largely blamed while the more cautious Bukharin's popularity increased. In response the dictator linked the coin crisis to an industrial plot by "class enemies" and ordered his security service to fabricate a case against "bourgeois specialist wreckers" who had played a prominent role during the NEP. His plan was to link the "silver speculators" to the rightists and foreign anti-Soviet organizations.[5] By suggesting that "terrorist organizations" were responsible for the financial crisis, the increasing number of machines breaking down and industrial accidents (rising from unrealistically high quotas), Stalin sought to repress dissent within the Party by intimidating any expert who might be tempted to question the speed or accuracy of projects for his mandated industrialization. That five of the eight on trial, who initially were sentenced to death, had their sentences commuted, suggests that Stalin's real targets were not technical experts, as they were useful, something he publicly admitted one year later.

The treatment of the accused in the Shakhty and Industrial Party trials and the rituals in the press and court also set a pattern for later show trials: the accused were physically and mentally coerced to confess participation in a conspiracy with members in the central government. They were subjected to unrelenting conveyor belt interrogations: sleep deprivation by round-the-clock investigators, thirst accentuated by salty food, verbal and physical abuse, standing for hours and solitary confinement in malodorous cells. In later trials, these methods were supplemented with much more physical torture and death threats to family members. Once the accused appeared in court, they were expected to recite, as if performing in a theatrical venue, memorized lines of a grovelling confession to outrageous charges. Stripped of their dignity, they would incriminate others who would subsequently share the same fate.

Self-abasement and a preordained punishment were not sufficient. The state demanded a humiliating public ritual at the expense of its victims to demonstrate an overarching power by having the state prosecutor deliver his scripted denunciations of the accused. Andrei Vyshinsky, who was later to become infamous for his hysterical tirades demanding the death penalty while performing in the starring role, made his debut in the Shakhty case in the relatively minor role of an opportunistic judge seeking to elevate himself to star status. In his limited role, the judge only read out the sentence that he had not written. The insipid words from the supporting cast, the defence, were barely distinguishable from the case presented by the prosecutor. In the famous Moscow trials of the late 1930s, most of the defendants waived their right to a lawyer. Like the later trials, only confessions were presented as evidence. But in the Shakhty imperfectly stage-managed judicial melodrama, only ten of the defendants openly confessed and implicated each other while the rest maintained their innocence. One of the accused attempted to retract his confession, but after a night with his interrogators, relented and reaffirmed his guilt. Another defendant mysteriously "committed suicide." In the public trials during the late 1930s, those who did not confess to the false charges were shot.

The coercion applied during this prototypical pageant facilitated a dangerous process; it that allowed the security organs to dispense with investigative techniques and convert criminal charges into confessions of guilt without any political interference. Any intervention was interpreted as support for criminals and an attack on the state. In this way Stalin was able to pre-empt the grandees, Lenin's former colleagues, from challenging procedures that he had updated not only from his tsarist predecessors but also from the early Bolsheviks.[6] Their failure to foresee these trials as a potent instrument to eliminate rivals proved to be a fatal oversight. Perhaps his colleagues really believed that Lenin's injunction to fellow Bolsheviks to "let no blood flow between you" would never be transgressed.[7] Nonetheless, they also recognized that the Party devoured their existence; even family relations were to be given scant consideration. By 1936 Stalin's confidence in the effectiveness of the show trial would be mobilized against the very men who had countenanced it against others, and family members bore more than their share of suffering.

Stalin's compulsion for show trials suggests he was also driven by inner psychic pressures; no facet of this ritual escaped his careful surveillance. In a propaganda rant during the Shakhty trial, the twelve-year-old son of one of the accused rose from his seat to repudiate his father by renouncing his name and demanding the death penalty. This scene repeated by sons was a ritual that perhaps allowed Stalin to vicariously re-enact his rage toward his own father for repeatedly beating his son, seriously injuring his left arm leaving it two inches shorter than the right. Stalin's testimony against him in 1890 resulted in his father being sentenced to prison.[8] But the ceremonial re-enactment of destroying his father did not suffice to appease Stalin's psychic needs. In his emotional speech in 1931 about the desperate need of the Soviet Union to catch up with advanced countries, he repeatedly invoked the metaphor of "beating" as a warning to a once weak and backward Russia. It was a metaphor that also resonated with personal memories: when the abused boy, identifying with his aggressor, became the unrivalled dictator, he could administer the beatings.

Equipped with a formidable memory and a psyche that perceived any personal slight or alternative viewpoint as a grievance, Stalin craved vengeance against a growing list of real and fictitious enemies. As early as 1923, he candidly articulated to Lev Kamenev, one of his later victims, his predatory sadism in extinguishing his prey: "The greatest delight is to pick out one's enemy, prepare all the details of the blow, to slake one's thirst for a cruel revenge and then go home to bed."[9] On occasion the drama either on stage or behind the scenes became a combination of the accused besmirching themselves with demeaning confessions and cat-and-mouse games that Stalin played with his victims; he promised and then reneged on assurances to save their lives. The courtroom with its legalistic gloss provided an ideal venue for him to satisfy his obsession with having others confess to crimes either that he had committed or were a product of his suspicious mentality.

At the same time, the ritual required the active participation of the public and the complicity of his colleagues. Emotionally aroused into fever frenzy, the public reinforced the base impulses that underpinned the mock trials. Thus he provided a venue and the rhetoric to legitimatize, for others, the use of the courtroom to avenge their grievances. The outlandish confessions would also reinforce his need to rearrange reality; metaphysics supplemented psychology. Whether he actually believed the confessions to be true is irrelevant. When he later heard the confessions of erstwhile colleagues, accused of treason and spying for fascist regimes, it is unlikely he believed their statements conformed to empirical reality. But in his conspiratorial inner world, the fear of treason and of being overthrown by foreign powers always lurked. Expiation could only occur if the trial was staged as a melodrama: a clash between innocent victims and "double dealing" masked traitors who were stopped before they could do irreparable damage only because of the vigilance of the state. Since his former Kremlin coterie were professional revolutionaries, they knew that the Party had the only real claim on their lives and that the unquestioning acceptance of it was de rigueur, that personal considerations were inconsequential, even if they meant the annihilation of the self. Consequently, Stalin promoted fawning sycophants who were dependent exclusively on his patronage: cars, chauffeurs, flats and dachas. His goodwill could, along with their lives and the lives of their families, be removed if he believed them to be no longer useful or if they offended his idiosyncratic personality. Their unquestioning allegiance enabled him to nurture the idealized and omnipotent image that he cultivated of himself as the "universal genius."[10] As impresario, skulking in the shadows and hovering menacingly in spirit if not in physical presence around the courtroom performers, his control over every facet of the show trial against vulnerable foreigners and technical specialists would serve him well when he proceeded against his more formidable colleagues.

The Old Bolsheviks Devolve into Former Persons

When Stalin deployed the show trial to ensnare high-ranking officials who had been close associates of Lenin, it was clear that he and his minions feared that their own unpopularity within the Party could be a pretext to oust them from power. As early as 1932, a number of senior grandees, disturbed by the bleeding of the countryside through collectivization and famine, produced what became known as the "Riutin platform," named for N. N. Riutin, a former district Party Secretary, who had been expelled from the party in 1930. Written for a secret meeting of his group, his courageous and heretical lengthy manifesto personally attacked Stalin and the apparatus that he had created around himself. Riutin compared Stalin's theoretical writings to a "heap of dung," and declared that his policies of rapid industrialization and forced collectivization had resulted in "an unprecedented quagmire," crimes that had caused mass impoverishment while "killing the cause of socialism." Most damning was his call for the "removal of the dictator" Stalin by force.[11] Stalin understood removal as assassination, and he quickly decided on a pre-emptive strike. An advocate of the death penalty, Stalin was not yet powerful enough within the Politburo to impose his will. Riutin received ten years in prison. Stalin later considered him a candidate for a show trial, but when Riutin refused to admit guilt or sign a deposition, Stalin changed his mind and ordered his enemy to be shot. To ensure that no one in the family could seek revenge, Stalin ordered that Riutin's two sons be killed and his wife be tortured to death in 1947. Stalin remembered anyone who supported Riutin and marked them out for death in the future when it was convenient.

In December 1934 Sergei Kirov, an ethnic Russian and the Leningrad Party leader, was murdered, likely on Stalin's orders. It was an epochal event that provided Stalin with the pretext to accelerate his war against his own people, including members of the Communist Party. The assassination became a benchmark for a personal witch-hunt against "anti-party groups" that sucked the nation into a vortex of terror by initiating waves of nocturnal arrests, interrogations followed by either immediate execution or a lingering death in the camps. Seven million Soviet citizens died between 1934 and 1941. During the Seventh Party Congress in early 1934, several provincial delegates approached Kirov with a proposal that he replace Stalin, a curious choice since he was a loyal Stalinist who was more of a local administrator than a participant in high level politics. Despite the fact that he had informed Stalin about these discussions, Kirov knew his fate was sealed. In actuality, he had likely doomed himself three years earlier when he opposed Riutin's execution, even though Kirov himself in that report had been named as a Stalinist "scoundrel."[12] After Kirov's murder, Stalin launched a pogrom against the population of Leningrad, particularly the old intelligentsia and Party members who had expressed criticism of Party policies. Through mass roundups and executions, he endeavoured to eradicate the oppositionist spirit of the city once and for all. An impassioned witness vividly attested to the indiscriminate nature of the terror that not only assaulted the people of Leningrad in 1934 but also dogged Soviet citizens at different intervals until Stalin's death:

> The future enemies of the people stood without moving,
> awaiting the blow of the terrible Antichrist brand. They
> sensed blood, like bulls in a slaughterhouse, they sensed it,
> but the enemy of the people brand kills without selection,
> anyone at all—and they all stood there, obediently like bulls
> waiting for the blow. How can you run if you know you're
> not guilty? How do you behave during interrogations? And
> people died, in a nightmare, confessing to unheard of crimes:
> espionage, terror, sabotage. And they vanished without a
> trace, and after them were sent their wives and children, entire families.[13]

After the brutal collectivization and dekulakization, Stalin permitted a temporary respite before launching the Great Terror of 1937–38. He increasingly distrusted the old guard whom he accused of abuse of power, losing its revolutionary zeal and deteriorating into "petit bourgeois" self-complacency. What the Party needed was the promotion of a younger generation of energetic leaders who were not tainted by the violence of collectivization. Better to destroy his disgruntled former comrades before they could unite and topple him.[14] When the NKVD arrested vast numbers of men and women in "mass operations" who were subsequently shot or disappeared into the Gulag camps, the regime attempted to distract their friends, family members and colleagues, and the public with show trials of old Bolsheviks who, although innocent of the improbable charges, were steeped in the blood of other crimes they had committed.

The first of the public show trials of former high-ranking original Bolsheviks began in 1936. The accused were two acolytes and friends of Lenin, the erstwhile party bosses of Moscow and Leningrad, Lev Kamenev and Gregorii Zinoviev respectively. Already convicted of moral responsibility in the murder of Kirov, they had been given lengthy prison terms. They were recalled, and along with others, accused of planning a fascist coup to eliminate Stalin and his top associates. Before they even came to trial, Stalin ordered the press to coordinate a "death to the traitors" campaign that included "spontaneous" petitions from hundreds of worker organizations demanding the death penalty. Brandishing his credentials as a bona fide Stalinist with a killer instinct, Nikita Khrushchev, before during and after the Moscow trials, aroused Party workers into a frenzy of hatred with venomous speeches on the "rightist deviationist heretics" and brayed for the execution of the "mercenary fascist dogs."[15]

The chants of the workers and even the death of erstwhile potentates were, however, bagatelles compared with Stalin's compulsive need for confessions. It was as if they would somehow expiate his crimes and reorder reality. When important persons did not cooperate and confess their crimes, Stalin became restless and was unable to sleep. Why order the NKVD to "give them the works until they come crawling to you on their bellies with confessions in their teeth" unless the former seminarian believed that their words could purge *his* sin?[16] What better way of accomplishing this goal than to attribute his crimes to old Bolsheviks who already had blood on their hands? Zinoviev, for example, had ordered without trial the execution of five hundred rebels who had participated in the Kronstadt rebellion. Among the sea of lies that were issued during the show trials, there were kernels of truth.

Yet his obsession with confessions is complicated because he was convinced that the Party and society were full of people hostile to him; there were "two-facers" and "spies" everywhere, and the confession was *proof* that he was right. If his fear of chimerical enemies, aligning themselves with foreign powers to overthrow him was a product of his paranoia, he *was* correct in his assessment that some Party members were not supportive of his policies. They were opposed to the persecution of the kulaks, the "over-industrialization" that created in the words of Bukharin at his trial, "enormous factories" that resembled "voracious monsters that would devour everything and deprive the broad masses of the means of consumption." They were also hypocritical in their displays of personal affection. He knew that Bukharin, Zinoviev and Kamenev had betrayed their genuine opinions on telephones tapped by the security police, who turned over the recordings to Stalin. The show trial with its confessions and public humiliations was his best instrument for destroying his enemies and ensuring that they could never become martyrs.[17]

The trials further provided an opportunity for Stalin to indulge his sadism by offering assurances he had no intention of keeping. Before their trial, Stalin promised Kamenev and Zinoviev that their lives would be spared if they publicly demeaned themselves by confessing to these outlandish charges. They, along with fourteen other defendants, all reduced to shabby husks when they appeared in court, duly complied, although Kamenev deviated from the script to plead for his children. Stalin predictably reneged on his word. After the reptilian prosecutor Vyshinsky had demanded that "the mad dogs be shot," the judges ordered their executions. The defendants were returned to their cells and were shocked shortly after midnight when the executioner appeared accompanied by witnesses. Zinoviev in particular was incredulous, not realizing that Stalin had been toying with them. Later Stalin would derive great pleasure from hearing one of the witnesses to Zinoviev's execution mimic the desperate pleas to spare his life.[18]

In the following year, Stalin authorized the use of torture against the military elite whom he feared posed a threat to him. In a note to the head of the NKVD, Yezhov, Stalin wrote, "Can't this gentleman be made to tell his dirty deeds? Where is he—in a prison or a hotel?"[19] The license to torture allowed special treatment to elicit the "dirty deeds" of the leadership of the Red Army, the only force in the Soviet Union that might have stopped Stalin. Trumped-up charges of treason by colluding with the Nazis were levied against Marshal Tukhachevsky and fifteen of the top military commanders. After being beaten with rubber truncheons or iron rods, Tukhachevsky confessed to being a German agent in league with

Bukharin to seize power. The Soviet Union's most talented general, along with the other military commanders, were quickly convicted by their forced confessions in a closed court martial and immediately executed. Not content to destroy the very upper echelons of the armed services, Stalin discharged about one quarter of the officials for political reasons, many of whom were shot or disappeared into the Gulag camps. By the time Stalin decapitated the military, he had become an absolute dictator where his word was law. Historian Robert Service has characterized these actions as the "statesmanship of the madhouse," mad because if the purpose of Stalin's Five-Year Plans was to strengthen the state, the violent assaults on the military leadership vitiated national security.[20] But in Stalin's mind this purge of senior officers was necessary to pre-empt a possible military coup.

Although military and political factors had been primarily responsible for their deaths, the implication of sexual debauchery contributed to the downfall of Marshall Tukhachevsky, the "Red Bonaparte," and his senior colleagues. Sexual liaisons in themselves were not punishable—Stalin's security chiefs, Yezhov and particularly Beria were notorious sexual predators—but if anyone lost Stalin's confidence, sex, or what V. M. Molotov called "the weak spot...women," could be used against the politically disgraced.[21] Stalin never trusted the power of sexuality: the sexual freedom of the early 1920s shocked him and kissing in films, including a passionate kiss in the 1945 release of *Ivan the Terrible, Part One*, had to be excised. Perhaps more important than priggish puritanism was his fear that women could know too much, that within their circles lurked the fear of duplicity and treason. Bourgeois morality was a bulwark against dangerous gossip. To the suspicious Stalin, who saw conspiracies everywhere, a single verbal slip or a sexual indiscretion was sufficient grounds for execution or banishment to the camps.

Stalin's orchestration of the show trials of old Bolsheviks coincided with the cultural emphasis on the need to look smart. But in the cyclonic madness of the Great Terror when official discourse fed on the fear that there were traitors in their midst, civilized appearance and behaviour were packaged as fragile membranes that could mask all-out bestiality. Stalin nurtured this fear by pointing out that the new saboteurs were "mostly part people...[that] cringe before our people, extol the people, bow before them in order to win their trust."[22] External manifestations of civility elicited paranoia and an obsession with 'unmasking,' as summed up in this portrayal revealed in a 1938 Komsomol periodical:

> The image of the hooligan has changed! The enemy is dressed according to the latest fashion. He is gallant. He dances nicely, speaks beautifully. He knows how to enchant women. But if you delve into such a person, you will uncover his beastly interior.[23]

The trope of the subhuman creature pervaded the Great Purge Trial in March 1938. The sycophantic prosecutor, Vyshinsky, poured out a torrent of abuse on the contagious political "leper," Nikolai Bukharin, and other disgraced members of the Party elite. In that ghoulish scenario, the twenty-one defendants played out their roles by confessing to ludicrous charges of murder, treason, wrecking and espionage that included participation in a fascist conspiracy to dismember the Soviet State and murder Stalin and his liege men. The courtroom spectators responded in "appropriate 'hiss-the-villain' style. One journalist sitting in the hall reported that he wanted to jump and grab the accused by the throats." In a riveting first-hand account of this Moscow show trial, the British diplomat, Fitzroy Maclean, recalled that the Soviet members of this audience could be not only excited and edified, but "horrified, and perhaps even terrified, by a spectacle which would partake at once both of the medieval morality play and of the modern gangster film."

In this melodrama, a special damnation was reserved for the black-impostor Bukharin. Dubbed the "double dealer" *par excellence* who wore a mask to conceal his hatred toward the Party, his "verbal poison" constituted a "slander" on the virtuous community. Behind this venom resided Stalin's personal hatred for what Bukharin encapsulated and what he (Stalin) could never possess. Bukharin was a brilliant theoretician who was genuinely popular, and perhaps most importantly, had been close to Lenin. Moreover, there had been a fundamental political difference when Bukharin promoted the NEP as an alternative to Stalin's forced collectivization. Out of sheer perversity, Stalin ensured that Bukharin was indicted for attempting to murder Lenin in 1918. In exile, Trotsky wrote "Super-Borgia in the Kremlin" in which he outlined a much more plausible scenario in which Stalin may have poisoned Lenin.

Maclean provided an atmospheric description to Trotsky's article by observing that Stalin, "the Supreme Puppet Master...[while] peering out from behind the black glass of a small window" illuminated at one point by "a clumsily directed arc-light," watched the proceedings.[24]

Courtesy of Photofest

The 1943 film, Mission to Moscow, *is based on the memoir of the same name by Ambassador Joseph Davies. The film was made at the urging of the President Franklin Roosevelt who wanted to cement the American-Soviet alliance during the war. Unfortunately, both memoir and film offer a blinkered view of the Soviet Union during the Great Terror. In the scene depicted above, the 1938 Moscow trial of disgraced Bolsheviks looks more like an American trial where due process is accorded than the histrionics of a show trial in which the verdict and sentence have been predetermined.*

The courtroom was packed with a younger generation of Party men, Stalin's minions, who were prepared to feast on the humiliation of a grandee. But Bukharin did not allow them that satisfaction. Retaining his personal dignity and fully aware that he and his co-defendants were, in Arthur Koestler's memorial phrase, "dead men on furlough," he was defiant.[25] With uncommon courage, Bukharin dared to deviate from the script on several occasions once by demolishing the accusation when he cross-examined state witnesses "their faces grey and corpse-like." In order

135

to save his family, his strategy was to accept personal responsibility for the entire criminal indictment while denying with logic and clarity the absurdity of its specific charges. Presenting himself as a theoretician rather than a common criminal, he sought to indict Stalin's regime by showing that its charges were political falsifications. To the seething annoyance of the prosecutor, Vyshinsky, he argued that the Communists on trial were not counter-revolutionaries, but the revolution's true followers with a different vision of the Soviet future.[26]

Undeterred, Stalin's star performer, the hyperventilating Vyshinsky adhered to his script by reviling the condemned at the docket as the monstrous *other*. The accused were the "scum of humanity," "the most perverted of criminals," and a "foul-smelling heap of human garbage." As if he were an actor in a Gothic horror movie, Vyshinsky hysterically reminded his audience that when their masks were ripped off, their "bestial countenance" was revealed. They ["had] lost the appearance of human beings....Our country only asks one thing: that these filthy dogs, these accursed reptiles, be wiped out." In the words of *Pravda*, "honest folks" cannot live among "contemptible vermin," but Vyshinsky offered a balm of purification:

> Time will pass. The graves of the hateful traitors will grow
> over with weeds and thistle; they will be covered with the
> eternal contempt of honest soviet citizens. But over us,
> over our happy country, our sun will shine with its lumin-
> ous rays as bright and as joyous [as] before. Over the road
> cleared of the last scum and filth of the past, we, our people,
> with our beloved leader and teacher, the great Stalin, at our
> head, will march as before onwards and onwards toward
> Communism. [27]

The culmination of these macabre theatrics, its biological and hygienic references to "vermin" and "filth," in stark contrast to its cloying sentimentality toward Stalin and his virtuous followers, was the predetermined execution of Bukharin and his co-defendants. Through self-abasing confessions, the accused would be subsequently shamed and humiliated as "vermin" and "filth." They became the necessary scapegoats who drew evil into themselves so that their subsequent sacrificial death served to purge society of its "evil spirits."[28] These 1930s show trials were replicated in the post-war Stalinist satellite states.

The 1970 Costa Gavra film *The Confession* brilliantly depicts a detailed examination of a Stalinist show trial from arrest to sentence. Based on the book written by a participant who survived the ordeal, the film charts his travails in the 1952 so-called Slansky trial, named after one of the defendants who had been General Secretary of the Party in Czechoslovakia, a Soviet satellite state. Unlike the Moscow show trials of the 1930s, the Slansky trial did not allow Western observers into the court despite its being broadcast live. Similar to the Moscow trials, the accused in *The Confession* are eminent Party members subjected to the conveyor method of interminable interrogation and sleep deprivation until they confess their guilt for imaginary crimes, including treason. They are coached by their lawyers as they are required to memorize their lines before they appear at trial.

The show trials of wreckers and the old Bolsheviks between 1936 and 1938, a large percentage of whom was Jewish, demonstrates the veiled anti-Semitism present in Stalinist Soviet Union in the 1930s. The alleged mastermind conspirator was the Jewish Trotsky who was tried in absentia in 1936. In a show trial during the fall of 1930 when Stalin shifted the blame for the disastrous harvest after collectivization to wreckers, the accused had Jewish sounding names; the next day *Pravda* published a wrecker with a hooked nose struck by lightening.[29] In post-war Stalinist Czechoslovakia, however, there was a substantial difference. The film pointedly indicates that eleven out of the fourteen accused are Jewish, underlining how anti-Semitism after 1948 had become official policy.

The show trials and execution of former Party heavyweights were only the most visible element of the mass psychosis that destroyed the lives of millions when class enemies merged with enemies of the people. During the Great Terror, one and one-half million people were arrested on political grounds; hundreds of thousands were shot and the population of the labour camps increased by half a million. One sign of the massive haemorrhaging that pulverized the Party was that more than one-half of the two-thousand delegates of the 1934 Congress had been arrested by the 1939 Party Congress. Once an individual was expelled, his liquidation would inevitably follow, given that his guilt was *a priori*, regardless of the empirical evidence.

In addition to eliminating rivals, Stalin implicated his inner circle to guarantee absolute control over them. He spent hours signing execution decrees for thousands of people personally unknown to him, as well as for former loyal Party members, retaining his power of life and death over others. A dash beside a name could save one person's life. At the same time, Stalin did not hesitate to sign an order for forty-eight thousand executions by quota. On November 12, 1938, he and Molotov signed three thousand one hundred and sixty-seven executions.[30] To deepen the blood bond with his gaggle of sycophants, Stalin insisted that they share the task of assigning quotas for the repression of targeted groups and approving death sentences. As the "Soviet political counterpart of Al Capone," he took pleasure in encouraging not only senior Politburo members but up-and-coming thugs to demolish their rivals by employing a vivid Gothic metaphor: "the sharper the teeth the better."[31] The Politburo complied with relish by adding a scrawl of curses after the name of a doomed individual in order to impress the boss. A refusal by anyone in his inner circle would have led to stigmatization as another enemy of the people followed by a swift death for him and his family.

Khrushchev demonstrated his zealotry by exceeding his Moscow quota of 50,000 in 1947 when he ordered the shooting of 55,741. A year later in the Ukraine he again surpassed his quota by arresting over 106,000 people in order to root out the "hidden Enemies."[32] He would have also earned approval from his mentor at a Moscow Party conference by inciting rank-and-file members, already crazed with fear, to denounce each other. Drawing upon the familiar, masked double-dealer image, he must have panicked his audience with his outburst of demagoguery:

> This is a struggle with the man who sits next to you, who
> hails our successes and our party's achievements, while at
> the same time squeezing the revolver in his pocket, choosing
> the moment to put a bullet into you the same way they did
> into Sergei Mironovich Kirov.[33]

The willingness of Stalin's minions to sign death quotas made them not only culpable of mass murder but complicit in accelerating the level of tension in a bloodlust miasma. Their actions also allowed Stalin to unload his dirty work onto them, enabling him to see himself as unstained and aloof from the terrifying killing machine around him. When Khrushchev raised with Stalin the possibility of innocent people being persecuted, the *Vozhd* (the leader) attempted to sandbag his gullible acolyte: "I know what you mean; there are these kinds of perversions. They're gathering evidence against me too." Stalin was being disingenuous. In June 1937, he acknowledged that if five percent of those arrested turned out to be actual enemies, "that would be a good result."[34] Stalin never missed an opportunity to send up a smokescreen of deception around the use of terror and his role in directing it.

Stalin's most hated and feared enemy, Leon Trotsky, intuitively understood Stalin's machinations. Shortly before his 1940 assassination, Trotsky revealed Stalin's capacity to project onto others crimes that he had committed: "With his monstrous trials, Stalin... disclosed his secret laboratory; he forced one hundred and fifty people to confess to crimes they never committed. But the totality of these confessions turned into Stalin's own confession."[35] All of Stalin's former Kremlin colleagues, including Trotsky, became doppelgangers to be sacrificially purged so that Stalin could embody and project Soviet power. But Trotsky did not grasp the full meaning of Stalin's blood bonding. Like those who had signed death warrants, Trotsky had shed blood and been complicitous in the crimes of others. As a committed revolutionary, he consistently supported the use of systematic terror against opponents of the Soviet state.

Although specific groups were targeted, the random nature of the terror ensured that no one was safe. Because the security forces had quotas to fulfil, anyone could be arbitrarily dragooned into what Solzhenitsyn has dubbed "the sewage disposal system." In his 1970 sanitized memoirs in which he redacted his own zealotry, Khrushchev recalled the rationale of security officials who worked out elaborate tortures to extract confessions when he was Stalin's viceroy in the Ukraine: "If I don't do this, then others will do it to me; better I do it than have it done to me."[36] But terror has a way of folding back on itself. The interrogators frequently became its victims—after a purge at the top some security officials recognizing their fate preferred the quick suicide. They too endured the beatings with truncheons and the lashes of whips that they had once administered, followed by a swift execution or deportation to the Gulag. There they might be protected by the NKVD or singled out by prisoners for retribution.

An example of this role reversal was the new Commissar for

State Security, the bestial Nikolai Yezhov. At the apogee of his power when he presided over the NKVD bailiwick between 1936 and 1938, the dwarfish Yezhov worked with a savage glee as he "played midget Faust to the Kremlin Mephistopheles."[37] With an ideological zealotry to match his psychopathic mentality, his mandate was the "total crushing of the enemy." With no qualms about fulfilling quotas and manufacturing evidence, he was responsible in 1937 for the arrest of one million people in the Party alone; 353,074 were shot outright while the others were dispatched to the Gulag.[38] He even had a special abattoir built near the torture chambers of the Lubyanka for carrying out executions. The far wall of the killing room was built of logs, and there was a sloping floor making it easier to wash away the fluids. One day Khrushchev asked him why his shirt was covered with blood. He proudly replied that it was blood of the enemies of the Revolution. But the pressure of "living a vampiric nocturnal existence of drinking and torture," which included the liquidation of NKVD protégés, took its toll. He consoled himself by indulging in bisexual orgies that the prim Stalin noted with displeasure. More damaging were the indications that his efficiency deteriorated because he was often, in the words of Stalin, "dead drunk."[39]

Once an individual's trust and usefulness to Stalin began to erode, in short order he would lose his power, liberty and frequently his life. By symbolizing the "awful stench of Stalinism," Yezhov became a candidate to be sacrificially served up when Stalin wanted to burnish his image as the Beloved Leader and demonstrate that he was reining in the security forces for their excesses.[40] And that he did in late 1938. As a gesture toward winding down the Great Terror, Stalin arranged for Yezhov to be charged for the arrest of innocent people and his involvement in a plot to kill the Soviet leader. Given his experience with the deception of other prisoners, he refused the offer of Lavrenti Beria, his successor, that Stalin would spare his life if he confessed at his trial to being a spy for the Polish, Japanese and British governments. Although spared the torture that he had so indiscriminately meted out to others, Yezhov harboured no illusions about his fate. Not surprisingly, as he was hauled into the same abattoir where he had dispatched so many, this now-sobbing sadist showed less courage than many of his victims.

The purge of NKVD chiefs proved politically useful to Stalin. In a move similar to his "Dizzy with Success" letter, Stalin exculpated himself from the purges: "Yezhov was a rat; he killed too many innocent people. We killed him for that."[41] Stalin could have made the same comment about Yezhov's predecessor, Genrikh Yagoda, who had already been charged and executed for the murders of Kirov and (allegedly) Gorky in the Bukharin trial earlier in 1938. Stalin's purpose in eliminating Yezhov was significant because the subsequent release of 327,000 people from the Gulag labour camps restored many people's faith in the justice system; the "Yezhov terror" was an aberration that had been corrected once Stalin understood the abuses that had occurred.[42]

Stalin's actions reinforced a widespread belief that there were dangerous conspiracies against the State and its leadership. After all, a people that had been isolated by a lack of information from sources independent of Party organs and bombarded by a steady diet of xenophobia and paranoia would experience an increase in fear and insecurity. When they witnessed the arrest and disappearance of friends and relatives, people deluded themselves into thinking that their friends had committed a heinous crime. Alternately, they believed that Stalin was unaware of these miscarriages of justice and that everything could be redressed if they could directly appeal to him over the head of the NKVD.

The memoirs of those who survived the suffering and inhumanity of the camp experience reveal that many victims firmly believed that Stalin was unaware of NKVD actions. For instance, when the teenaged Polish Jew, Janusz Bardach was court-martialed for accidentally rolling his tank, he was sentenced to be executed and forced to dig his grave. Fortuitously, his sentence was commuted to a ten-year stay in the camps. In his memoir, Bardach reveals that that like so many others in the camps, he initially believed that if Stalin only knew what the NKVD was doing, "the false accusations, arrests, interrogations, and executions would be stopped and many prisoners including [him] would be released." These delusions were lemming-like re-enactments of the belief that it was the Tsar's ministers, but not the Tsar who were responsible for people's misfortunes. Stalin encouraged this perception by ordering periodic purges of NKVD chiefs, officers and their men. Stalin himself succumbed to this illusion in June 1941 when German planes were strafing Ukrainian cities and German troops crossed the border he persisted in the belief that these actions were a "provocation" by German officers and that "Hitler simply does not know it."[43]

The historical impulse to trust the Tsar demonstrates to a large extent how the benighted past could leach into the present. Trotsky invoked the medieval witch trials, to question what was more probable: women confessing to unleashing disease after consorting with the Devil, or the Moscow defendants slandering themselves. He implied that in both situations the defendants faced the "red-hot poker of the Inquisition."[44] In her diary memoir, Olga Freidenberg, a cousin of Boris Pasternak, reflected on how the terror blighted not only physical lives but corroded their souls:

> No one who has [not] lived in the Stalin era can appreciate the horror of our uncertain position. A person's life was poisoned secretly, invisibly, as witches and sorcerers were hounded in the Dark Ages. Something mysterious was accumulating under the earth and coming to a boil. A person felt at the mercy of an inescapable force aimed at him and certain to crush him.[45]

Given her determination to pursue an independent course as a Greek scholar at the University in St Petersburg and her refusal to toe the Party line, she was fortunate that her perceptive (and courageous) reflections eluded prying eyes. The NKVD never discovered her diary.

Collusion with the Terror among Ordinary People

Most people did not possess the insight of Freidenberg. They did not appreciate that the unlimited scope and arbitrariness of the Terror left no one safe from being denounced as an enemy of the people. Perhaps for reasons of self-protection, so many dissociated and remained blithely unaware until it personally affected them or a member of their family. Even the Komsomol subscribed to the illusion that the trials were directed at the Party panjandrum, and could not penetrate as far down as their lives. The belief—that they could not be arrested because they were "good"—is supported by both the recollections of elderly survivors in the 1990s and in the memoirs.[46] According to the autobiography of a former Party member, Victor Kravchenko, "the population at large...was pretty indifferent to what seemed to them a family quarrel amongst their new masters." But he also remarks that "if anyone in Russia honestly believed in the fantastic 'confessions,' I for one did not meet him." He acerbically adds that he encountered credulity only when he came in contact with foreigners "in particular 'liberal' Americans [who] had swallowed the macabre hoax, hook, line and sinker."[47]

Indifference to the awful plight of others easily bled into repellent clichés about Jews during the terrible purges of the 1930s. In Leningrad and Moscow, where the largest number of Jews were located, deeply engrained stereotypes circulated in tales that associated Jews with state power and corruption. Because Jews composed a large segment of the intelligentsia and occupied (or had occupied before their purging) plenipotentiary positions in the inner circle with Stalin, they were understandably identified as part of the ruling elite. That perception was reinforced after the murder of Kirov when complaints were heard that "the murder of Kirov was carried out with the intention of reducing the number of Russians in government and increasing the number of Jews."[48] From the experience of the Jewish Nadezhda Mandelstam, these coarse anti-Semitic, or to be more precise, anti-intellectual feelings emanated from those who had acquired a Stalinist education and not from ordinary workers and collective farmers.[49] In any case, despite Lenin's official prohibitions, anti-Semitism increasingly became a symptom of the constant need to find enemies to explain the failures of a secular evangelical doctrine. Unsurprisingly, the ghost of the *Protocols* reappeared with the belief that Jews were driven by power and greedy for world domination. Since many prominent defenders in the show trials were Jewish and because the spirit of the über-demon Trotsky hovered over them, the association of the Jew with the traitor remained etched in the minds of ordinary Russians, a fear that Stalin would later exploit after the end of Second World War.[50] By stoking the fires of traditional Russian nationalism and xenophobia, Stalin would transmute enemies of the people and "terrorists" into "rootless cosmopolites," the codeword for primarily Jews, but also ethnic groups such as the Tatars in the Ukraine, for allegedly not showing sufficient patriotism to the U.S.S.R.

This Manichaean worldview, as it suited both political and psychological needs—a polarized world divided into exploiters and exploited revolutionaries and counter-revolutionaries—had been fanned by the Communist Party since the Revolution. The Party's absolute power could be best maintained if it could convince the public that enemies constantly threatened the promised future, even if those evil forces shifted in a kaleidoscopic rubric: shake the container and new fragments appear. The Nationalist Socialist regime that had been portrayed as their most lethal enemy, morphed into fellow comrades after the Nazi–Soviet pact of 1939. Psychologically, the "us–them" partition permitted the people to take comfort in the illusion that they were innocent, honest workers. They were the Party members, the new bourgeoisie, engineers and technical workers, Jews and the "rotten intelligentsia." The stagnant economy of the mid-to-late 1930s and the punitive labour decrees fed resentment toward these privileged apparatchiks. Since Stalin directed the most visible component of the Terror against the Party apparatus, and because ordinary people felt they were excluded from power, there was ample opportunity for workers to lash out against members of the new aristocracy whom they believed deserved their comeuppance. Those who wielded power did not work; they were dishonest, corrupt and morally degenerate because they drank the blood of ordinary people by depriving them of what was rightfully theirs. Instead, the bosses issued decrees and had a lot more money and privileges than workers. If some individuals questioned the veracity of the show trials, others responded with indifference. The stereotype of the honest, innocent worker and the corrupt leadership made working people more vulnerable to the official boilerplate on wreckers and sabotage within the Party.[51]

The anger was anchored in a certain reality as the apparatchiks did enjoy a privileged lifestyle. Such perks included special closed shops stocked with food and goods that were not available to ordinary Soviet citizens. That was the case with the family of Elena Bonner (the future wife of Andrei Sakharov) who enjoyed these perks because her step-father was a "big boss" in the Comintern, (the international Communist movement) and her mother was a committed Party member until they were arrested in 1937. In her childhood memories, she could find no hint of malfeasance to justify either her father's execution or her mother's eight-year time in the camps. In fact, Bonner remembers her parents, who rarely had days off, as frequently being away on business and conscientiously working for the Party and a better future for the people, albeit at the cost of emotional restraint towards their daughter.[52]

The Terror elicited a degree of popular support because it fed on base human impulses masquerading as righteous anger. The lack of privacy with families sharing common facilities in cramped apartments was a major source of tension, although the communal housing did serve the Soviet system's need for mutual surveillance and the self-policing of the population. Motivated by a desire for more space or simply sheer maliciousness, neighbours denounced others to the authorities as enemies of the people or someone with "bourgeois inclinations." When the targeted were evicted from their flats, those who remained enjoyed improved housing. For those evicted, the press mobilized the metaphors of social hygiene to impugn their patriotism and strip them of their humanity. *Pravda* referred ritualistically to them as "predatory beast[s]," "base traitors and deserters," "scoundrels" and "refuse... [who] have lost the appearance of human beings." In the words of one reviewer, "these frenzied attacks had the formulaic quality of a morality play featuring an apocalyptic struggle between good and evil."[53]

The trouble with the "us–them" mental construct was that it permitted ordinary people to deny that they were participating in the terror that devoured those around them; instead it encouraged them to don the mask of self-righteous innocence and gloat in *schadenfreude*. This Stalinist mindset operated in a milieu of repression that encouraged mindless support and duplicity that was manifest when the Moscow show trials were replicated throughout the Republics. Throughout the countryside in 1937, show trials of local officials and chairmen of communes were conducted. In contrast to the trials held in Moscow where the accused were charged with heinous political crimes with rigged evidence based upon phantasmagorical confessions, the accused outside of Moscow faced allegations of economic crimes that included abuse of authority. The allegations were corroborated by peasants themselves on the witness stand. In this melodrama, villainous bosses cruelly exploited virtuous peasants, but the reality was often more complex. Although many of those officials charged were local peasants themselves, and the position of chairman was hotly contested among village factions, none of this ever surfaced in the trials. Often officials possessed little education, no qualifications, were dissolute and treated the peasants in a manner similar to the tyrannical landlords.[54] The desire for revenge would manifest itself during the sentencing process. When the prosecutor and the judge often settled on sentences ranging from a few months to ten years, in the tumult of the courtroom, the peasants would often call for the death penalty. Co-opting the bombastic, shop-worn phrases that acquired widespread currency during the Moscow trials, they brayed for blood, demanding that the litany of enemies of the people, "terrorists and Trotskyites" be "given what they deserve."[55] Tatyana Tolstaya, herself a descendant of the illustrious Leo Tolstoy, understood this collusion: "Without popular support, Stalin and his cannibals wouldn't have lasted so long. The 'executioner' genius expressed itself in his ability to feel and direct the evil forces slumbering in the people."[56] Participation in the public ritual of denunciation during a show trial was a sure method of burnishing one's credentials as a "little Stalinist."

Stalin's Historical Model

By 1938 Stalin's purpose in staging the trials extended beyond unmasking the double-dealers among the *nomenklatura*. He then sought to exaggerate the presence of his internal enemies as fifth columnists and to link them to foreign powers like Japan and Germany that did pose external threats. By heightening the climate of fear, he could justify a pre-emptive strike to eliminate class and ethnic enemies at home and then turn them into non-persons. He wanted to ramp up public fears about the danger of war by alerting citizens to take greater responsibility in rooting out enemy agents among ostensibly loyal citizens. An individual might have some vulnerability either in his own life or that of his family, which if exposed, could taint him and his relatives. By this logic, an individual's only defence was to be vigilant against the transgressions of others. On a deeper level, the darkness resided within the individual. In the words of one worker, "the enemy...is dressed in the same overalls as us." The Austrian Communist, Ernst Fischer, who was in Moscow in the 1930s to cover the trials, recognized thirty years later that the source of the hysteria resided in resentfulness:

Vigilance! Are you blind? Can't you see the enemy? Anyone

may be the enemy unless you know him inside out. Vigilance
became a matter of competition. Haven't you discovered
an enemy yet? You mean to say your organization's the
only one without an enemy? How strange, how suspect....
And then, how is it he's got a flat and I haven't, when flats
are hard to come by? That he's got a good job and I haven't?
That he enjoys the chief's confidence and I don't. Vigilance
also required one to be on guard against any failing within
oneself.[57]

Vigilance invariably entailed denunciation and the practice had
a long pedigree in Russia dating at least back to the sixteenth century. The arbitrary and violent rule of Ivan the Terrible became a
model for Stalin because, in his mind, Ivan was unquestionably
resolute, ruthless and wise. The Muscovite warrior-king, Ivan IV,
whose struggle against the boyars and his conquest of foreign territory, bore similarities to Stalin's own purge of Party members and
the expansion of the Soviet Union under the Nazi–Soviet pact. He
modelled the NKVD after Ivan's secret police, and after the Terror
of 1937–38 his alter ego was used to justify his own murderous policies. Stalin compared his Terror to Ivan's massacre of the boyars:

Who's going to remember all this riffraff in ten or twenty
years time? No one. Who remembers the names now of the
boyars Ivan the Terrible got rid of? No one....The people had
to know he was getting rid of all of his enemies. In the end,
they all got what they deserved.[58]

Stalin also admired Ivan because he protected Russia from foreign encroachment and because, in pursuit of this goal, Ivan had
waged war on a treasonable aristocracy. Clearly, Stalin perceived
striking similarities between the mid-sixteenth century and his
own time, but the Tsar's weaknesses—agonizing over certain murders and allowing some noble families to remain alive—he would
not repeat. An obsession with treasonous conspiracies in the service of foreign powers and the subsequent chilling rationalization
for murder were integral components in Stalin's character struc-
ture, given that he felt little if any empathy for others. By the fall of
1938, however, when it appeared that it would not be long before
the entire population could be incarcerated, Stalin retreated and
informed the NKVD that it could not arrest people solely on the
basis of unsubstantiated denunciations.[59]

Nonetheless, Stalin was interested in providing his subjects with an historical model that would serve as a prototype that justified his actions. He commissioned the great Soviet director, Sergei Eisenstein, who had distinguished himself with *Battleship Potemkin* (1925)—a film that became emblematic of the struggle against tsarism—to make a sympathetic movie about the sixteenth-century tsar as a model for Russian nationalism, whose military engagements extended the country's borders. *Ivan the Terrible Part One*, which opened in 1945, received Stalin's approval because of its portrayal of the Russian people who beg Ivan to return and rule over them. The film reinforced Stalin's conviction that the people needed a tsar to rule over them. *Part Two* incurred difficulties—and did not open until 1958—because of Stalin's displeasure. Dismissing it as a "nightmare," he objected to the portrayal of the secret police as hooded bodyguards resembling the Ku-Klux-Klan instead of "a progressive army." Worse was the "irresolute-like Hamlet" depiction of Ivan who spent too much time in prayer and repentance, although Stalin believed the historical Ivan shared the weaknesses of his cinematic counterpart. What he surely must have detested was Ivan's capacity for mercy to his enemies. Unlike Stalin's fabricated enemies of the people, Ivan confronted real treachery from not only the boyars, but the Church and even from his own family who foolishly planned to replace him with an addled-brain prince. Stalin had no objections to the executions shown provided the reasons for Ivan's "cruelty" were explained, and that, in the words of Molotov, "the wisdom of statesmanship [was] depicted."

Stalin's Foreign Minister objected to the Gothic tone that suffused the film. The "cellars and enclosed spaces" and the "fascination with shadows" only "distracted from the action," comments that reflected the psychological reality of Stalin's own regime as much as that of his forbear.[60] What most likely disturbed this grandee was the similarity between Eisenstein's dark, claustrophobic court with its mildly homo-erotic atmosphere and the conspiratorial intrigue in the Kremlin in which Ivan was compared to Yezhov. In addition, the hedonistic decadence of Ivan's court with his loyal lieutenants dancing, dressing up as monks and giving themselves over to mime shows eerily resembled the de rigueur all-night stag dinners over which Stalin presided. These evenings often deteriorated into bizarre farting competitions, homoerotic close dancing and boorish drinking bouts so that Stalin could "loosen [the] tongues" and find out "who was thinking what." The purpose of gross adolescent antics was to humiliate a rival: Khrushchev, for example, never forgot the sting he felt when Beria, to the guffaws of everyone else, pinned a piece of paper on the back of his overcoat on which was the written the word "prick."[61]

Photo by the author

Since Stalin did not enjoy his official quarters in the Kremlin, he acquired a number of dachas. One of his favourite summer homes was located in Sochi on the Black Sea.

The Family of "Enemies of the People"

Whistle-blowing may initially have been inspired by civic-minded motives such as exposing bureaucratic abuse and the pursuit of justice. Some convinced themselves that in informing they were motivated by ideological commitment and the pursuit of justice, while others were clearly driven by personal malice, fear and self-preservation or a combination of these forces. By the late 1930s when the frenzied milieu of conspiracy and spy mania had engulfed society, the taint of being identified as an enemy of the people spread through "plague bearers" and infected not only a specific target but also members of their family. Stalin encapsulated this thought, if not the metaphor, when he warned if any Bolshevik deviated from the Party

149

line: "We will destroy each and every enemy...we will destroy all his kin, his family....Anyone who by his deeds or *thoughts, yes his thoughts,* threatens the unity of the socialist state."[62] No one was safe from Stalin's suspicion.

As Stalin's former comrades were extinguished, the NKVD made every effort to destroy or remove from society members of their families. They were guilty by blood and association as Stalin believed that the designation, *enemy of the people,* was a genetic disease. If one member was guilty, the others could be as well, and children could inherit the same suspicious genes. If Kamenev believed that a full confession would spare his family, his faith was tragically misplaced. Not only had Zinoviev shamelessly denounced him, but Kamenev, along with his family, was also doomed through his association with his brother-in-law Trotsky. Both Kamenov's wife and elder son were shot; the younger son Glebov eluded the security organ's grasp because an official changed his name when he was put into an orphanage. In 1945 the sixteen-year-old, Glebov, was allowed to go to Leningrad to study, but one year before graduation he was arrested, convicted of being an aesthete and sentenced to ten years, a term that was cut short at Stalin's death. His real crime was that he was the son of an original Bolshevik; in Stalin's mind, a son would avenge his father's death, and that possibility had to be aborted.[63]

Similarly, spouses were singled out for punishment and sent to special camps for "wives of traitors to the motherland." Bonner's mother and Anna Larina, the widow of Bukharin, were relatively fortunate to survive the camps. Larina was condemned to twenty years including prisons, camps and Siberian exile and even endured the horror of a mock execution. Wives, who were not arrested, were evicted from their apartments along with children, and forced to fend for themselves. If they also lost their jobs, they could only regain them and protect the rest of the family from stigma if they divorced (for the small fee of three roubles) and denounced their condemned husbands. Thousands of women, however, did not disown their husbands, and it may have been the knowledge that someone was waiting for them that helped so many men survive.[64]

The children of those persecuted endured the pressure to denounce their parents. The logic behind this insidious practice was that if a family member wanted to survive, he or she had to be prepared to bury their feelings toward the condemned or risk the consequences. One student who refused to denounce her parents was given a ten-year sentence in Kolyma, one of the worst of Stalin's penal colonies in northeast Siberia. Elena Bonner was luckier on two accounts. When the organizer of a Komsomol meeting proposed that she repudiate her parents as traitors, she refused. She was not sentenced to a camp or sent to an orphanage but was adopted by relatives. Yet the power of communist ideology could be effective in shredding family ties. After her father was arrested, Bonner remembers her younger brother saying in a private exchange: "Look what those enemies of the people are like. Some of them even pretend to be fathers."[65] Regardless of whether they disowned their parents, almost a million children were raised in orphanages, breeding grounds for disease and criminality. Some offspring did not see their mothers for twenty years—if both parties were lucky enough to survive. Because of their weak familial links, orphanages were predictably recruiting grounds for Soviet collectivist institutions. Children of the parents condemned as enemies of the people often felt ashamed, a feeling that only lifted when they joined the Pioneers and experienced pride as valued Soviet citizens. As they grew older and became a Komsomol, they relinquished their family traditions and came to regard Stalin as a paternal figure of authority and love. Not only would they never question the arrests of "spies" and "terrorists" or any of Stalin's decisions: the offspring of parents with a "spoiled biography" became the most fanatical informers.[66]

The "godfather" of these children extended the purge to his own family and members of his entourage. After the November 1932 suicide of his second wife Nadya, Stalin nursed grievances toward the family members he believed were responsible for her death and who had witnessed his grief and vulnerability. By the Terror of the late 1930s, the boundary between private and public life had dissolved and the time was ripe for settling personal scores with political overtones. He struck out against his two brothers-in-law, one of whom had given the gun to Nadya with which she had killed herself. The other was a member of the NKVD, now in Stalin's mind, a breeding ground for spies. Both of them perished. Among his many victims were members of his first wife's family, the husbands of his sisters-in-law and eventually his two sisters-in-law, one of whom had gone mad in prison.

Family members were always at risk because of the potential for loose talk that could blemish Stalin's character. His callous attitude toward in-laws extended to the families of his closest Kremlin retinue. He frequently became agitated about the private lives of married couples among his powerful magnates because their commitment to each other could undermine their "marriage to the Party." He believed that wives of his lieutenants "especially women of ideas" could be spies; indeed he became "obsessed with wives knowing too much."[67] As part of his strategy to maintain the unswerving allegiance of his entourage, Stalin often ordered that the wives of Politburo members be arrested, including the Jewish wife of his trusted Foreign Minister, Molotov—part of his growing post-war, anti-Semitic campaign. Unlike other political wives, Polina ran a perfume business, showed a dangerous mark of independence by meeting the future Israeli leader, Golda Meir, on her trip to Moscow in 1948, and initiated contacts with Jews later designated as enemies of the people. She spent five years in exile and was allowed to return only after the death of Stalin—unlike her two sisters and brother who died in prison. For one who had been embittered since his wife's death, it did not bother Stalin that the spouses of his inner circle or his own family members were among the casualties of the Party's struggle.[68]

Stalin could rationalize his actions by proclaiming that *he* was making heavy sacrifices in order to enhance the security of the country, a view that his underlings endorsed. Molotov remained unrepentant years after the dictator's death. In his conversation with Soviet journalist, Felix Chuev, Molotov acknowledged that some mistakes and "excesses" were made owing to the work of renegade elements within the security agencies. Yet Molotov justified the Terror because its victims, especially the military officers, were guilty not necessarily of an overt treasonous act, but of what they might do in the event of a Nazi invasion. By destroying a "fifth column," Stalin helped to secure a Soviet victory over the Germans. Molotov's rationale even extended to defending the elimination of the wives and children of the purged victims in order to avoid any future trouble.[69] As one of the last Stalinists, Molotov refused to admit that innocent human beings, ethnic groups and former kulaks, not the political and military elites, had been the real victims of the meat grinder.

The Shadow Cast over Former Persons

> At the moment of your arrest you already
> feel halfway vanished. In prison you're a
> former person and already dead. In camp
> you're almost sure you're never been born.
>
> *—House of Meetings*
> Martin Amis

The hurricane of Stalinism penetrated every level of society decimating ethnic and national groups, friendships and families. After the brutality in the countryside, followed by the repression after Kirov's murder, Stalin permitted a temporary respite before launching the Great Terror of 1937–38. In an atmosphere rife with the bacillus of suspicion, where newspapers published cases that led to the unmasking of foreign spies, ownership of such innocuous items as a typewriter or binoculars could be fatal. The anticipation of war increased the fear that suffused day-to-day life. Anything a person did or represented could activate the NKVD to arrest, or in the social hygienic language of the times, to "smoke out and destroy the nests of Trotskyist-fascist bugs."[1] A complaint against authorities, work violation, denunciation by someone for personal reasons, having the same name as a prominent enemy of the people, or contact with relatives abroad could precipitate an arrest and drive the juggernaut of repression. To have an unusual surname or a desirable apartment was sufficient justification for the NKVD to fulfil their arrest quotas. That organ was known to produce counterfeit confessions after indiscriminately shooting innocent people. A NKVD officer who wrote "everyone is a traitor until he proved the contrary by exposing someone else as

153

an enemy" encapsulated the paranoid, surreal atmosphere. During the Great Terror, nearly three quarters of the people arrested were sentenced to death. About one million were executed.[2]

As the international situation worsened, Stalin prepared for the "wholesale liquidation" of "anti-Soviet elements." He authorized in 1937 mass operations against any class, social group or ethnic minority that in his mind constituted a potential threat to national security. His first priority was to address the problem of former kulaks. Although these "former persons" had spent five years in special settlements or labour camps, had their civil rights restored and were allowed to return home, reports surfaced alleging that embittered kulaks had resumed their hostile acts toward the Soviet state, indicating that they were immune to socialist corrective measures. In response, Stalin ordered NKVD operatives to arrest "endemic enemies," that also included priests and "criminals," and to execute the "most hostile." The NKVD chief, Nikolai Yezhov, authorized the immediate execution of 70,000 and the deportation of 186,500. But local NKVD branches felt free to interpret "anti-Soviet elements" and exceeded the quota issued from Moscow five times by executing 386,798. Execution was the preferred method over deportation; kulaks were too "dangerous" for the Gulag. The "kulak operation" was carried out in secret as no one, including the accused, was told the sentence before it was carried out. In the Marxist lexicon, redemption was not offered twice. Maxim Gorky reinforced the Party line by indicating that the "dictatorship of the proletariat" only kills "when it is not possible to eradicate the ancient habit of feeding on human flesh and blood."[3] The reality was that Stalin, his subordinates and the security organs, fed on human flesh.

Stalin believed that he was surrounded by both external as well as internal enemies. He therefore embarked on a "mass operations" campaign to eliminate any group that he and his potentates believed threatened the unity of the Soviet Union. Counterrevolutionary national contingents would constitute a fifth column if a war were to occur: these subversives and defeatists would reveal their true colours and would sabotage the motherland's capacity to defend itself. Stalin hated foreigners and was convinced that hostile states were sending agents into the ethnic colonies within the Soviet Union to incite wrecking campaigns and espionage. He believed that the non-Russian nationals would be receptive to recruitment by foreign intelligence agencies. In response he authorized large scale national operations that involved deportations and executions against potential "spies" among the Poles, Germans, Finns, Koreans, Mongolians and Chinese. Ethnic Poles living in Soviet Belarus, Soviet Ukraine or around Leningrad were the most persecuted group in Europe in the late 1930s, second only to the kulaks in the number of people executed in this pre-war period. Stalin ordered the NKVD to eradicate "this Polish filth," which was interpreted by one officer of the security police as to "destroy the Poles entirely." After looking up Polish names in the telephone book and watching who attended Roman Catholic services on December 25, over 140,000 were arrested for espionage: seventy percent of them were executed; the rest were deported to the camps. Incarceration was not enough; some of the camps became death camps as Moscow ordered the NKVD to execute 10,000 prisoners in the camps; non-Russians were especially vulnerable. In 1937 and 1938 the kulak and national operations claimed 633,955 lives, more than ninety percent of the total of lives claimed during the Great Terror. These people were secretly shot, buried in pits and, until recently, forgotten. To conceal their deaths, their families were told that they had been sentenced to ten years without the right of correspondence.[4]

Stalin and his apparatchiks also snared Americans, who had migrated for mainly economic reasons to the Soviet Union, into the Terror's tentacles. It did not take long for the thousands, lured by the sham of Soviet propaganda, abetted by George Bernard Shaw's effusive lecture on American national radio and the lies published by Walter Duranty in the *New York Times*—lots of jobs, no layoffs, plenty of food—to discover the ugly realities beneath the purported rosy exterior. Although initially lionized by the Soviet Union, and even allowed to form their own baseball teams, the idealism of Americans quickly melted in the face of poverty, lawlessness and terror. When they surrendered their passports on arrival, they unknowingly became Soviet citizens. Since Stalin feared these Americans might spread agitation among the Soviet population, or worse, would educate their fellow-countrymen about the true state of affairs in the U.S.S.R. if permitted to leave, he gave strict orders that these foreigners would not be allowed to return. Only a few were lucky enough to depart before the curtain came down for decades. When they sought help from the

American Embassy they were arrested and disappeared into the maw of Stalin's meat grinder. There they were abused by professional criminals at the behest of the guards and exposed to elements that rendered survival next to impossible. George Kennan, who was embassy secretary during the Terror, recognized that American citizens were at the "mercy of the Soviet authorities," and that a publicity campaign might assist them. But none was forthcoming since he received no support, especially from his boss, the American Ambassador, Joseph Davies, who was too enthralled by Stalin to use his power to support trapped Americans. Even when Davies returned briefly to America he publicly celebrated Soviet achievements refusing to mention the screams and volleys of gunfire that awoke his wife in Moscow. As a result, only a handful of them returned to America decades later. The historian of the Americans abandoned in the Soviet Union, Tim Tzouliadis, rightly understands that Davies did not possess the courage of an Oskar Schlinder or Raoul Wallenberg:

> someone willing to lend sanctuary, to hand out passports, to speak to the President, and to kick up a very loud and very public fuss in a time of peril. Someone in short, who might hold a protective hand over [American citizens] when their lives were so evidently endangered.[5]

The Americans were among the "politicals," who crossed over into the Stygian underworld that began with their arrests under Article 58 promulgated in 1926. Those charged under this provision were frequently deemed the most serious of criminals, counter-revolutionaries, often more politically aware individuals, and were subjected to much harsher incarceration. Brutal interrogation procedures from savage beatings to the excruciating "methods of active investigation" resulted in the execution of "former persons" or being hauled off to the inhospitable terrain of the life-in-death experience awaiting them in the Gulag. Among a sprawling network of thousands of prisons, labour camps, special settlements and special camps, Kolyma, "the land of white death" in the Arctic Circle, was the epicentre of Stalin's burial grounds. It is estimated that in Kolyma five hundred thousand of the over nine-hundred thousand prisoners died, either as a result of shooting or starvation.[6] Those fortunate enough to be rescued from the outdoor work or the lethal gold mines had at least a chance to survive their sentence before returning to the mainland. "Ghosts" who returned from the "other side"—sometimes called the zone—were warned to never speak about their harrowing experiences in the torture chambers of the Lubyanka labyrinth or the degradation of the camps. Mute with terror, aged, often broken in body or spirit and traumatized, individuals lived with their recurring fear. Some remained steadfast in their ideological beliefs and cleaved to the Party line. Others refused to take solace in illusions and found the courage to challenge hoary dogmas, official mendacities and bear witness on behalf of those who lost their lives.

"Have You Come to Arrest Me?"[7]

The failure to inform on others became a capital offence because it suggested complicity. For many Soviet citizens, as well as Americans working in the Soviet Union, this sparked the descent into lunacy; seized by fear, inspired by the unsavoury impulse to redress old grudges, or out of personal or professional jealousy, many denounced others to pre-empt a similar action toward themselves. They condemned friends, acquaintances, fellow workers, bosses and strangers, sometimes with tearful regret, sometimes with righteous indignation and, most often, to save their own skin. When the political émigré, Thomas Sgovio, was released after spending eight and a half years in the camps, he reconnected with his sweetheart, a Lucy Flaxman, who informed on him leading to his incarceration two days later and another seven years in the Gulag. Given the "anti-cosmopolitan campaign" against foreigners of the early Cold War, Sgovio was not surprised by his rearrest recognizing that the vampiric Stalin "felt hungry again." Sgovio did not know that Flaxman had informed on him until he was shown a copy of his NKVD file in 1996. Given that she had confessed to him in 1949 that she had been spared the camps by becoming an informer, he was not surprised by her betrayal but understood: "It was a frightening time for everyone."[8]

A close or even casual connection with a disgraced individual, such as the "Judas Trotsky," was sufficient to be vulnerable to the treasonous charge of enemy of the people. Eugenia Ginzburg's comfortable life as a university history professor and editor was abruptly shattered when she was accused of terrorism for failing to denounce a fellow professor for his reputed Trotskyism, though she had no awareness of this allegation.[9] In this maelstrom, omission or "insufficient vigilantism" as well as commission could rip the fabric of family ties.

A careless remark returned to haunt individuals, even years later. Suzanne Rosenberg reveals in her memoir that after her husband was arrested for anti-Soviet agitation and sympathy for Zionism in 1949, she became a pariah, was arrested and convicted in 1950 on the baseless charge of espionage. Despite being a loyal Party member, who had long avoided conversations on political topics, her fate was sealed when the interrogator asked her if she once went "around saying that Moscow toilets were dirty?"[10] Fifteen years earlier, she had been an Intourist guide for the future Prime Minister of Great Britain, Clement Atlee, and was embarrassed when after lunch he needed a washroom. She had to direct him to reeking open holes in the ground with raised platforms, later complaining to fellow guides about the filthy conditions of Moscow's toilets. That admission led her to provide another piece of evidence, that her interrogator did not know—that she once accompanied a visitor into the American embassy. Even authorized contact with foreigners required the utmost care; unauthorized associations could be tantamount to a death sentence.

The state's omnipotent power to conduct invasive domestic espionage against its own citizens fuelled denunciations and midnight arrests and left a corrosive scar across the fabric of Soviet society. Elderly survivors often refer in memoirs or interviews to packing a suitcase, keeping bread on hand, sleeping in their clothes in case "they" came for a specific individual or needing to fulfil a quota. Sometimes the fear of arrest that invariably occurred in the middle of the night was visceral. One man recalls how his father "would stay awake—waiting for the sound of a car engine....I could smell his fear, his nervous sweating, and feel his body shaking though I could barely see him in the dark."[11] If a spouse was taken away one night, the partner was expected to suppress any feelings of fear and grief, smile and behave as though nothing untoward had happened. When colleagues saw "former persons" still arriving at work, their looks communicated, "What! Are you still among the living?"[12] Since the Terror often blurred the boundaries between life and death, a Gothic convention became a terrible reality for fear-filled inhabitants in the Soviet Union, especially those in the large cities.

The Terror also dissolved the distinction between public and private life. Parents could not openly discuss their feelings within the home lest they let slip an incriminating remark that a child could inadvertently pass on at school to a teacher. An expression of private opinion to another person, or to oneself in a diary could be construed as evidence of terrorism or of counter-revolutionary crimes warranting the death penalty or a lengthy term in prison or the labour camps. Fear became so embedded in people's psyche that one writer observed that "many have learned to keep completely silent...as if they were lying in a grave."[13]

Distrust and suspicion were contagious because anyone could be an informer in the toxic atmosphere. These feelings were captured in an exchange between a naïve Janusz Bardach, and a Soviet military officer. Imbued with the ideals of social justice espoused by the Communist Party, Bardach had greeted the 1939 Red Army entrance into Poland under the terms of the Nazi–Soviet pact as a welcome alternative to the Nazi German invasion. But the unbridled brutality of the NKVD officers, who raped, murdered and confiscated the property and valuables of his family and neighbours, soon disabused him of his illusions. When he approached the commanding officer and raised the issue of trust, the Soviet official curtly replied: "Janusz, you know what Comrade Stalin says about trust? Trust and check. Don't trust anyone, not even yourself. This is how we must live when surrounded by enemies. You must always be on guard, even with your own family."[14]

Even more dangerous was contact with foreigners since Stalin believed that any association contaminated a Soviet subject. The author, Isaac Babel's relationship with Western writers and supporters of Trotsky led to his arrest and execution in 1940 for being a French spy under the control of the novelist and politician André Malraux. In a powerful memoir, Nadezhda Mandelstam reports that when she and her husband, Osip, were on the run after his release from prison, they had solicited Babel's help. She was astonished that he was living in a house populated by foreigners. Babel's pursuit of danger and his insatiable curiosity also drove him to establish contacts with militia men, a euphemism for what she termed Chekists, including at that time its head, Yezhov, because he yearned "to have a sniff and see what it smells like." Later his fear understandably led him to remark, "today a man only talks freely with his wife at night with the blankets pulled over his head."[15]

The nature of such a conversation was risky for Suzanne Rosenberg. After she and her lover Victor attended a film in 1936 that portrayed a wise and benevolent Peter the Great and downplayed the terror of his time, neither of them felt comfortable sharing their feelings about the film: "[We] dared not trust one another with our thoughts, lest at some future date, perhaps under torture, they might be wrested from us as 'evidence.' " Shortly after this date, Victor was arrested never to be seen again. Years later when Rosenberg was released prematurely following Stalin's death in 1953, after three years in prison camps, "a captive animal kicked about and tormented," she cautioned a colleague about the presence of informers even in her communal living quarters. Her colleague had just returned from a visit to the United States and was lavishing praise on American democracy. When she blurted out that she had once informed upon another friend who was subsequently sent to the camps never to return, Rosenberg reported feeling sick with the shock of the confession.[16] With the benefit of hindsight and safely ensconced in the West, Rosenberg cannot permit herself to reflect on this exchange or the larger question of how informing constituted personal betrayal and undermined the fabric of human relationships.

Paralyzing fear demobilized people preventing them from taking action that could result in disastrous recriminations. Arrest for the vast majority resulted in death by midnight executions in the basement of NKVD headquarters or in a secluded forest after being transported there in vans dubbed the Black Marias. For others, death came slowly in a prison or labour camp. Before sentence was passed, everyone was subjected to a gruelling interrogation in the charnel house of the Lubyanka. The brilliant theatre director, Vsevolod Meyerhold, was likely arrested because he publicly refused to accept the doctrine of Socialist Realism. Instead of directing his actors to deliver their lines in the acceptable highly emotional manner, he encouraged them to be calm and cool so that the audience could think about what they were hearing. Tragically, any expression of creative independence was tantamount to treason. Sometime during his interrogation, he wrote a letter to the Soviet government that was relegated to the KGB archives for years until it became accessible during the glasnost era of the late 1980s. The letter recounts how he was repeatedly bludgeoned by his interrogators and ended with his wish for the release of death.

He was a frail, sick 65-year-old man at the time of his arrest in 1939, and he describes in chilling detail how confessions were extorted in an eighteen-hour ordeal:

> I was made to lie face down and then beaten on the soles of my feet and my spine with a rubber strap. They sat me down on a chair and beat my feet from above, with considerable force....For the next few days, when those parts of my legs were covered with extensive internal haemorrhaging, they again beat the red-blue-and-yellow bruises with the strap and the pain was so intense that it felt as if boiling hot water was being poured on these sensitive areas. I howled and wept from the pain. They beat my back with the same rubber strap and punched my face, swinging their fists from a great height.

Besides the excruciating physical pain, his interrogators claimed that he eventually accepted that his punishment was "what I deserve!"[17] He was executed February 2, 1940. Likely Meyerhold experienced the guilt of implicating others. During an interrogation when individuals were confronted with the names of people who allegedly denounced them, they were coerced into implicating them by including them in their conspiracy. Whether certain individuals named actually did denounce can never be certain since the investigator could fudge the record.

Outside these walls, the loose lips of informers, whether motivated by fear, material advantage or ideological zeal resulted in the deaths or the life-in-death of the camps for hundreds of thousands. Their actions betrayed their complicity with and support for a regime that had no regard for human life. Nadezhda Mandelstam assessed their immeasurable value to a murderous system: "the more people [that] could be implicated and compromised, the more traitors, informants and police spies there were, the greater number of people supporting the regime and longing for it to last thousands of years."[18]

The Ninth Circle

When he was in his absolutist communist phase in the 1930s, Arthur Koestler had reviled André Gide for tarnishing the Soviet Union in his writings. After he abandoned his faith, however, as a result of both personal experiences in

Spain and disillusionment with the 1939 Nazi–Soviet Pact, Koestler became an outspoken anti-communist. He went on to praise Gide for his honest portrayal of the Soviet Union. In his 1940 master-piece, *Darkness at Noon*, Koestler attempted to understand how he had been suborned by the logic of an ideology and how that iron faith had been based on a lie. Set in the Soviet Union of 1938 (though the country is never named) during the Moscow trials, the novel recounts the solitary confinement and harsh interrogation of Rubashov, a fictional version of Nikolai Bukharin and an incarnation of Koestler's former zealotry. An old guard revolutionary and veteran of fascist jails, he is arrested for treason and for an attempt on "No. 1's life" by the government that he once helped to create. While he knows he is innocent of the imaginary charges against him, he cannot shake the nagging doubt that the Party is always infallible: "History knows her way. She makes no mistakes."[19] While in jail, he reflects that the more the Party tries to build the utopia as dictated by reason and logic, the more repression is needed. Loyal Party members become schooled in deception and murder. His first interrogator assures him that in order to advance history and the cause of humanity "a collective aim justifies all means... and demands that the individual should in every way be subordinated and sacrificed to the community." This meant "tearing off the old skin of mankind and giving it a new one." After devoutly committing to the "collective aim" for forty years, Rubashov is in the process of disavowing the Marxist–Leninist premise that history is a science:

> I see the flayed body of this generation: but I see no trace of the new skin. We all thought one could treat history like one experiments in physics. The difference is that in physics one can repeat the experiment a thousand times, but in history only once.[20]

Privately, he adds, it is wrong to justify terror based on the "laws of history." The revolution faltered because it lacked "ethical ballast" and caused severe suffering to human beings. He realizes that he has blindly accepted the sophist notion that good is only what serves the Party and advances history; he realizes that the individual is incapable of distinguishing between good and evil. Still, as his last service to the Party, he is willing to acknowledge his "crimes" and debase himself in a public trial with a confession of guilt.

Similar to Koestler's fictional protagonist, Eugenia Ginzburg was a high-ranking provincial Party functionary whose incarceration enabled her to re-evaluate her former ideological beliefs. Unlike Koester's protagonist, she repudiated the belief that the ends justified the means. She emphasizes the evil that was visited on the millions who were swept into the bowels of police headquarters for interrogation and execution, or into the vortex of the Gulag's dehumanizing brutality and, for many, premature death. Her journey into hell has all the earmarks of a Gothic horror. Like Kafka's fictional Joseph K., who is informed by telephone that his case will be briefly examined the following Sunday, the tissue of lies began when Ginzburg was summoned to make a brief appearance at NKVD headquarters. Although Kafka's imagination in *The Trial* created the labyrinthine menace and its bureaucracy of terror in the ordeal of Joseph K. that ended with his death "like a dog," he could never have conceived of the range and depth of the Stalinist terror with its steamroller of cruelties. For Ginzburg, it lasted eighteen years before she was allowed to return home. Her descent into this subterranean world began with the conveyor interrogation of seven days without sleep in which the "special prison light" and the "perpetual twilight" of a masked window gave the illusion of being entombed alive.[21] A conviction for being a Trotskyist and for participating in a terrorist counter-revolutionary organization, followed by a ten-year sentence of solitary confinement, reinforced the illusion of a premature burial. She was confronted by former close friends who, out of fear, had willingly signed statements confirming that Ginzburg was a subversive counter-revolutionary. She served over a year in solitary (with one other prisoner because the prisons were so crowded), that involved the compulsory scourge of five-day spells in underground glacial punishment cells with rats crawling across her face. In retrospect, her time spent in prison appeared idyllic compared to what she would experience when her sentence was commuted to forced labour. As one of her browbeating interrogators boasted, the justification for this treatment was that condemned enemies of the people were not human beings; as a consequence, "we're allowed to do what we like with them."[22]

When political prisoners left the interior, their journey toward a new life tested their physical and emotional mettle in ways that prison with its attendant horrors rarely had. Prisoners shipped north or east on the Trans-Siberian Railway had to survive the four to six-week journey in extreme cold or heat in overcrowded pestilent cattle cars or an enclosed so-called "Stolypin wagon," where the guards observed them at all times. They were limited to three hundred grams a day of dry bread, suffered raging thirst that was exacerbated by a diet of salted fish. They endured the indignity of having to relieve themselves among strangers. Arriving in overcrowded transit camps in a weakened physical state, they were vulnerable to the typhus epidemics that razed the camps. Those who could work were assigned to hard labour at a stone quarry or in the forest felling trees. Survival then depended upon fulfilling work quotas.

Worse was their first encounter with the tattooed criminal population, with its own strict code of rules, who had been treated with indulgence since the time of Lenin. Solzhenitsyn labeled these criminals as the "camp storm troopers" who were given extra rations, did not work, exacted a tribute from the rest of the zeks (inmates) but were lauded by the Communist apparatus. He contended that Gorky had celebrated thieves at the White Sea canal site by shouting out from the rostrum to the roaring approval of the criminals: "After all, any capitalist steals more than all of you combined."[23] Professional criminals were perceived as "socially close" to the vanguard of the proletariat while the non-violent political offenders, who constituted a minority of prisoners in the Gulag, were regarded as "socially dangerous."[24] With relative impunity, these thugs preyed upon the political prisoners by robbing them of their belongings and food. With the complicity of the authorities, they had license to kill politicals who resisted their demands for food or clothing, a practice that terrorized them unless they made alliances with other criminals or banded together. Two Americans, Thomas Sgovio and Victor Herman, survived their Gulag ordeal partly because of exceptional luck and partly because criminals took a liking to them, earning their respect, the former because he could regale them with stories about American gangsters, the latter because as a trained boxer he was capable of physically defending himself. The Polish Jew, Bardach used his story-telling ability and his mastery of the crudities of the criminal argot to earn respect and protection from other criminals.[25]

The transit ordeal was followed by a gruelling one-week trip of unimaginable horror to Kolyma on a "death ship." Comparable to the ships that once transported slaves from Africa, three to four thousand prisoners were confined in the filthy, fetid hold. In these dungeons, armed with knives, razors and spikes, the criminal population, "tattooed demons who seem to have been vomited up from the underworld," terrorized the politicals by committing gang rape and murder, again with impunity.[26] Ginsburg's powerful description of these ghastly predators recalls the horror of H. G. Wells' novellas featuring Morlocks and the Beast People:

> Down through the hatchway poured another few hundred human beings, if that is the right name for these appalling creatures, the dregs of the criminal world: murderers, sadists, and experts of every kind of sexual perversion....The fetid air reverberated to their shrieks, their fantastic obscenities, their caterwauling and peals of laughter.[27]

Either out of indifference or fear of the criminals, the guards rarely intervened. Bad weather conditions only worsened their misery. Heavy seas and storms often meant that the exhausted, enfeebled prisoners lay in their own vomit and excrement, the living and the dying shared the same plank-platform with the dead. One survivor recalled, "Anyone who has seen Dante's hell would say that it was nothing beside what went on in that ship."[28] But this inferno was merely a prelude to the poet's ninth circle where the worst sinners, the betrayers, were consigned, frozen in ice, mute and immobile, a terrible but apt metaphor for Kolyma.

In the northeast corner of the Soviet Union, Kolyma epitomized the non-luminous world of the Gothic. The largest and most desolate of the Stalin-era concentration camp complexes was located in the coldest inhabited region on earth stretching a thousand miles from the Arctic Ocean to the Sea of Okhotsk. On this netherworld of taiga where nearly a third of the prisoners died each year, inmates contended with unventilated gold mines, fourteen-hour shifts and the constant threat of starvation and disease—from typhus to tuberculosis or scurvy. They could also be hosed down and left to freeze in the cold or shot on either the whim of a guard or for a violation of a camp regulation such as stealing a newspaper. On arrival at the northern port of Magadan which served as an entry point for a vast network of camps, the prisoners were subjected to a ritual similar to that at Auschwitz when Dr. Mengele would arbitrarily decide who would be provided with a temporary reprieve from certain death. In this bone-chilling wasteland,

NKVD officials would adjudicate who would survive by determining the nature of their work. Unlike the Nazi Holocaust, there is little evidence that the weak among them were deliberately shot upon arrival; many were allowed time to "fatten up" before being allocated for exhausting labour. Ginzburg was among those who spent time in hospital recovering from the ordeal of the agonizing journey that took them to Kolyma.

A sea-change in the treatment of zeks worsened during the Great Terror as political prisoners convicted under Article 58 were worked to death under dreadful working conditions and reduced rations, if they were not executed. The majority of them assigned to the stone quarries or the mines faced a virtual death sentence unless luck transferred them to inside work. Within two years of digging for gold or working without fur coats and felt boots in this necropolis of ice when temperatures fell to -50°F while subsisting on a starvation diet, almost everyone succumbed to disease. Perhaps the most terrible was pellagra, "the disease of despair," which resulted from a severe niacin and protein deficiency and was characterized by skin eruptions, and digestive and nervous system disturbances. A survivor, Lev Razgon, described the afflicted as "indifferent, without the will to live, corpse-like figures covered by a taut grey skin [who] sat on the board beds and calmly waited for death."[29] That outcome frequently happened unless there was direct intervention. Razgon recalls a dispute between an administrator whose only concern was work productivity and a doctor who wanted to save two hundred and forty-six pellagra victims by providing them with a "bonus meal" of a little runny porridge that would enable them to survive but to be fit for only light work. The administrator vetoed the proposal insisting that these rations would only be given to those who could work in the forest. Within a month all of them were dead.[30] Given the diseases that destroyed prisoners who were commandeered for heavy physical labour, it is not surprising to read of the desperate measures to which they would resort to avoid this work: there are harrowing accounts of prisoners who would ingest glass or, despite the severe punishment of a longer sentence, mutilate themselves. A survivor etched a vivid image of the undead as "robots, their grey-yellow faces rimmed with lice and bleeding cold tears. They ate in silence, standing packed together, seeing no one."[31] Since men were largely assigned to this life-destroying work, women were more likely to survive in the camps. In their final days, many "goners," who looked like wraiths, were returned to the mainland in order to reduce the statistical numbers who died in that Arctic zone.

Men convicted as counter-revolutionaries under Article 58 were worked to extinction by guards, ravaged by insects and tormented and threatened with homosexual attacks from the criminal population. Technically, Bardach was not a political because he was sentenced for wartime treason. Yet he was lumped with them and assigned brutal manual labour. In his memoir, he perceptively commented that the "intent wasn't simply to extract as much labour as possible but to force the prisoners to devolve into animals."[32] He could have added that they were fed starvation rations as a result of drastic cuts after the German invasion in 1941 and faced the possibility of execution since the authorities considered some so-called counter-revolutionaries too dangerous to live. Even if the zeks satisfied the requirements of the Plan, their diet was drawn primarily from flour, so they largely subsisted on bread. Survival was most difficult during the war years when famine, lice-born typhus epidemics, and overcrowding exacerbated the suffering and the death rate spiralled to 600,000 in 1941–43 alone.[33] Consequently, after spending eight months toiling at the mine's surface, Bardach was debilitated by scurvy and night blindness, and only survived because of a truck accident. He assisted in taking the injured to a hospital where, despite no prior medical education, he inveigled the authorities into giving him a job as medical assistant. Extreme inclement conditions ratcheted up the odds against survival; breathing was painful at -25ºF and prisoners were lost in snowstorms, their bodies to be found in the spring. At Kolyma, Sgovio would not have survived working in the gold mines and outside on infrastructure projects if not for his artistic skills that enabled him to work as a painter of propaganda posters. Ginzburg had to cut trees and hack away at the permanently frozen earth with a pick and shovel at -40ºF subsisting on a meagre ration. Similar to the story of Sgovio, she was rescued by a physician who arranged for her transfer to indoor work, even though the duration of that kind of work depended upon the whim of the commandants.

The devastation of the inmates' life in Kolyma where they suffered severe frostbite, malnutrition, cruelty and indifference was cast in stark relief to the rose-coloured experience of foreign dignitaries. The American Vice President, Henry Wallace, and

Professor Owen Lattimore visited the site in 1944 and were duly impressed, given the Potemkin village treatment which conveyed the image that this was a cheerful Russian Klondike full of happy gold miners. A photograph shows Wallace shaking hands with a well fed, shaven prisoner, one of the criminal elite. The watch-towers were razed, the stores were laden with goods, and all prisoners were kept out of sight for the three-day duration of their visit. When Wallace was shown a farm, the best in the area, fake girl swineherds, who were in fact NKVD office staff, replaced the prisoners for the occasion.[34] The Americans' idealized impression of sturdy criminals rehabilitating themselves presented a stark, surreal contrast to the real prisoners who were the focus of indifference and sadism from the camp officials and their criminal overseers. The Americans failed to distinguish the small minority of political prisoners from the peasants, usually former kulaks or workers who violated labour discipline, and the criminals, some of whom were exceedingly dangerous and who posed as much danger as the guards. Needless to say, no English speaker such as Thomas Sgovio was allowed close to the American visitors. That the Wallace party, including military officials, could be so easily deluded can be explained in part by the fact that they perceived Soviet Russia as a valiant wartime ally. Although Wallace was later reviled by Congress and the public for his naivety during the fraught atmosphere of the Red Scare, his views during wartime were no different than members of Roosevelt's administration, notably his closest advisor, Harry Hopkins, and much of the mainstream media. Hopkins was one of the key policy makers in the Soviet Lend Lease program that shipped fifteen million tons of materials to the Soviet Union, some of it food and machinery, that arrived at the wharves of Magadan and was unloaded by Gulag labour.[35] Moreover, the death ships that escorted the convicts to Magadan were retrofitted in American harbours. Yet during the war, *Life* magazine vividly portrayed an upbeat view of a wartime ally "with photos of graceful ballerinas, gallant soldiers, and cheerful tractor drivers." The popular periodical even designated Lenin "perhaps the greatest man of modern times" and the NKVD as "a national police similar to the FBI."[36] At least Wallace publicly apologized for being deceived by the Soviet organs later during the Korean War when he became convinced of the Soviet Union's malignant global intentions.

Yet when the U.S.S.R. had been an ally during the war years, many liberal Americans could not fathom that an ideology that purported to be progressive could simultaneously prompt its adherents to behave so callously towards its own citizens. In the second volume of her searing memoirs, *Within the Whirlwind*, Ginzburg provides a striking example of this dynamic when she described the director of a state farm for convicts. After being informed that a particular building was empty because leakage in the roof had caused the bulls to become ill, he ordered that the women be lodged there. There was no point in risking the lives of the bulls; the women were expendable and ranked below the animals because they were enemies of the people. Without bitterness, Ginzburg stoically assesses him, a trained philosopher but an ideologue inoculated against empathy: "He was not a sadist. He derived no satisfaction from our sufferings. He was simply oblivious to them, because in the most sincere way imaginable he did not regard us as human." As with other guards and commandants she observes, he discarded the old fashioned concept of morality and replaced it with "the infallibility of dogmas and quotations he had learned by heart" and which enabled him to manage an efficient farm and fulfil the plan without being troubled by a bad conscience. He never doubted the hierarchy of the world or its accepted rituals with the Great One at the top and prisoners on the lowest rungs. If some prisoners died as a result of the fury of the elements, he could easily replace the "wastage" with new penal recruits confirming his high tolerance for casual indifference. Another survivor told a researcher in the late 1990s that inmates learned that they were "nothing" and "you will die here. You are dust."[37]

Despite the subjugation and cruelty of the Soviet prison system, Ginzburg rightly believes it did not display the undisguised brutality of the Nazi extermination camps. (There was nothing comparable in the German netherworld to the twenty percent of the Gulag population that was released each year even though the death rate was huge, and reforged Soviet prisoners could earn an early release through their labour productivity until 1938 when Stalin stopped it.)[38] But she found that the camps' more subtle effects could be as deadly. As a children's nurse for the offspring of the occasional liaisons, she acknowledged that whereas in a Nazi camp the children would be instantly put to death, she observed the de rigueur lack of empathy for the children of the damned led to a prolonged death in the Gulag. Although they were fed and cleaned, camp regulations prohibited nurses from attending to their emotional or intellectual needs so that the children were never held, comforted or talked to. Many could only express themselves through inarticulate howls and mimicry. Whether these children survived is uncertain, but tens of thousands of adolescents, culled from orphaned street children and from the offspring of enemies of the people, did languish in camps both with adults and in separate colonies. Their experience of deprivation and exposure to criminals who both offered protection and a model for behaviour contributed to their own developing criminality. Lev Razgon recalls that all child prisoners devolved to a more primitive state as evidenced when they "displayed a frightening and incorrigibly vengeful cruelty without restraint or responsibility.... There was nothing human left in these children and it was impossible to imagine that they might return to the normal world and become ordinary human beings again."[39] They became feral, atavistic creatures who became part of the criminal underworld after their experience in the Gulag.

Evil Will Never Conquer[*]

In March 1953 a million Gulag prisoners were released after the death of Stalin. While this did signify a desire to end the terror, the process became increasingly complicated as an anxious public forced Khrushchev to gyrate from a liberal to more conservative stance. Only twenty-two percent of the Gulag prisoners were serving sentences for "counter-revolutionary" crimes and most of the first amnesty wave was from the criminal population, therefore violent crime increased.[40] The public became increasingly fearful of these enemies of the state even though Khrushchev, in his famous 1956 Secret Speech to the Twentieth Party Congress, derided the term because it had allowed Stalin a "formula" for seeing "spies" and "enemies" everywhere. Yet based on letters to the

---

[*] "But if what is human in beings is not destroyed even now, then evil will never conquer."

—Vasily Grossman, *Life and Fate*, trans. Robert Chandler (London: Collins, Harvill, 1985), 410.

authorities retrieved from the archives, Khrushchev's initial focus on re-education and urging the public to find "the man" behind the criminal was greeted with more scepticism and resistance than support. Many were offended by the coarseness of the camp argot fearing its harmful effect on young people, and some officials regarded rehabilitation as "something rotten" and the rehabilitated as "unclean." One official likely spoke for many when he warned a reformed zek: "The mark was removed but the stain remained." Consequently, in response to the growing hostility within the Party and to appease public anxiety, Khrushchev's effort to liberalize the criminal justice system in the late 1950s was abandoned. His call to weed out the "hooligans" and "parasites" contributed to the blurring of criminals and political counter-revolutionaries, both of whom were regarded with suspicion. Party members, many of whom remained Stalinists, and the public feared the return of angry alienated ex-zeks who might rail against the political system. Indeed, to identify with American capitalism appeared as threatening to Soviet society as the spike in rapes and murders.[41]

Although some gradually entered the state bureaucracy and a few were invited into Khrushchev's inner circle, the conflation of criminals and political prisoners, that actually began in the Gulag itself during the post-war era, likely contributed to the terrible treatment of the non-criminal population. When they returned home from the camps, colonies and from internal exile, thousands were like spectral presences: prematurely aged, suffering from chronic illnesses and unrecognizable to family members, some so depleted that they died shortly afterwards. Others refused to talk about their experiences and did not publicly until the relatively liberal climate of the late 1980s. According to one scholar, many suffered from "concentration camp syndrome" in which regular sleep was made difficult by the fear of the dreaded midnight knock on the door, leading to their being rearrested and sent back "there," and by nightmares and traumatic daydreams.[42] Regarded with suspicion and shunned by neighbours and colleagues, their post-traumatic stress was not acknowledged. No apology was offered. They were stigmatized as Gulag returnees and faced discrimination in housing and employment unless they were able to obtain rehabilitation certificates, an often lengthy, Kafkaesque, bureaucratic procedure. Others were unable to shake off the camp culture becoming emotionally cold, resorting to coarse language and being cruel toward family members. Most of the returnees were incapable of personal reflection preferring the less painful option of accepting external structures. As a coping mechanism one woman adopted a position of "uncritical acceptance" toward everything she heard from the Soviet regime. Many sought and were grateful to be re-admitted to the Party, partly for pragmatic reasons because they received the benefits of a pension or reinstatement in their profession and social status. Life was certainly easier with a rehabilitation certificate or a Party card since an individual was readmitted into Soviet society and not required to give details of his stigmatized history.

Party membership also allowed returnees to believe again in Party positions such as recognizing Stalin's triumphalist role in the Great Patriotic War often celebrated in books, films and ceremonies. Even after Khrushchev's denunciation of the cult of Stalin, returnees or their relatives, despite their suffering, adopted a nostalgic outlook toward Stalin: to them, he won the war, he provided the basic necessities of life and the order and discipline that was currently lacking in current Russian society.[43] Other survivors took a more nuanced position but adhered to the ideology that they had embraced when they were young. Some of the survivors of the camps who spoke to historian Catherine Merridale in 1997 still exonerated the revolution and its goals. They attributed the violence they had endured to the "corruption, sadism and weakness of individuals." Indeed, some of them still believed in their own guilt, or that the system was not mad but that an error had been made in their specific case.[44] Even the elderly survivors who deposited their memoirs or told their stories to the Memorial Society, still believed in the Communist ideals that gave their life meaning, even when a parent was arrested and executed during the Great Terror. One survivor of the camps contended that what enabled him to survive on "the other side" was his "unflinching, inextinguishable belief in our Leninist Party and its humanist principles."[45] Perhaps there is some truth in what Stalin once said to a foreign journalist who, when asked if the regime survived on terror, replied that what sustained the regime was the people's belief in the communist cause, in salvation and that the laws of history were on their side.[46] They also could not jettison Stalin who came to embody the organizing touchstone, that of Soviet power and the system that gave meaning to their lives. Rejecting Stalin would be like repudiating religion and leaving the people nothing to believe in.

Yet there is a counter narrative to this embrace of Stalinism, one that is told by a small minority that challenged the spectre of Stalin. Rather than relying on a secular belief, certain individuals have reflected on what it meant to live in a society rent by hypocrisy and lies. The American journalist, Adam Hochschild, relates the moving story of Susanna Pechuro who, along with five other intelligent teenagers in the early 1950s, recognized with remarkable clarity the truth behind the Stalinist façade and quixotically resolved to challenge it. Objecting to the censoring of their poetry on the grounds that a mournful mood was not worthy of Soviet youth, they decided to inform themselves about their society. Using the resources of their ringleader's library—extraordinary as it contained banned authors and a copy of Lenin's will that warned the Party about Stalin—they concluded that they lived in a Bonapartist regime. They saw that the promises of the revolution were not being realized, that collective farming was merely the reimposition of serfdom, and distributed two leaflets to that effect. In 1951 after a former teacher reported them to the secret police, they were all arrested, three were executed and the others were sent to prison camps. Pechuro was the only one still alive in the 1990s.

Pechuro was interrogated for more than a year during which she was allowed little sleep. While her sentence stretched into five years in prisons and labour camps, she believed her survival was a result of two serendipitous factors. The first was that inept police work had missed a copy of the leaflet in her parents' apartment when she was arrested. Investigators were more proficient at manufacturing confessions for imaginary crimes than in recognizing the evidence of real ones. Secondly, she was the beneficiary of an interrogation by a NKVD officer who remembered her as a little girl playing in the yard of the same apartment building where he lived. His modus operandi was to spread out on a table documents that summarized other interrogations which showed the extent of police knowledge of her case. She could answer questions without implicating someone who was not included in that summary. She estimated that she saved twenty other people from being arrested while his display of courage resulted in his arrest.

When interviewed by Hochschild in 1990, Pechuro insisted that not only did she and her group know what was going on, but despite their denials, citizens of her parents' generation "really saw everything. It was easier for them to persuade themselves that they weren't seeing—then they were relieved of any obligation to do anything." There is some truth in her assertion that people knew what was happening, in the same way that Germans knew when Jews were dispossessed of their homes and shipped east. She revealed that her elderly father had lamented: "To think that I've spent my life being cheated. That I still believed—at a time when you understood everything. And I, a grownup believed. My life has been spent in lies."[47] His self-reproach is a reminder of how people perceived themselves. What they may not have understood was that their unequivocal acceptance of the official version was a necessary defence mechanism that had helped them to survive. Hochschild wondered why her story had not been the subject of books and films similar to those about the courageous White Rose movement, a youthful group of anti-Nazi protesters who in 1943 had distributed leaflets in Munich and who had paid with their lives, and were the subject of two films. He ruefully understood that if her story were turned into a film, it would reproach others who did nothing.

The regrets of Pechuro's father appear to echo the 1979 death-bed memoirs of the onetime Stalinist poet, Konstantine Simonov:

> To be honest about those times, it is not only Stalin that you cannot forgive, but you yourself. It is not that you did something bad—maybe you did nothing wrong, at least not on the face of it—but that you became accustomed to evil. The events that took place in 1937–38 now appear extraordinary, diabolical, but to you, then a young man of 22, or 24, they became a kind of norm, almost ordinary. You lived in the midst of these times, blind and deaf to everything, you saw and heard nothing when people all around you were shot and killed, when people all around you disappeared.[48]

But unlike Pechuro's father, Simonov was a powerful commissar and his belated regrets seem a tad self-serving.

Like Pechuro, Eugenia Ginzburg refused to devolve and shed her humanity. She survived her (longer) ordeal in the Gulag so that she could bear witness and challenge the ideological underpinnings beneath the terror. Besides a strong constitution, empathy and luck, what contributed to Ginzburg's survival was her indomitable spirit that she nourished through her love of poetry. The capacity to create her own poems and recite memorized poetry not only nurtured her spiritual resilience but likely saved her life. Poetry, the "lighted candles," helped sustain her when she endured punishment cells, the raging thirst on the train and the blizzard-lashed marches in Kolyma when there was so much madness, indifference and sadism around her. But it also enabled her to remain rooted in reality when many of the platitudes about communism that she had parroted for years "lost their sparkle...under the blows of the inhuman machine that descended upon us."[49]

The poetry likely sharpened Ginzburg's moral compass and deepened her reservoir of compassion. Her refusal to betray or steal food from anyone, and her capacity to offer solace to the sick and dying often, though not always, elicited generous impulses from other prisoners and the guards. For example, when she was sent out on a seventy kilometres march to a lime quarry to join hardened criminals because she had offended a narrow-minded and vindictive female commandant, she was given extra clothing and food from the guards. At the halfway point, another commandant allowed her food and rest, an expression of humanity that would have been inconceivable in a Nazi camp. For almost a month at this "isle of the damned," she had to break stones, live with psychopaths and fend off would-be rapists. But owing to the intervention of friends, she was transferred to another worksite as a medical assistant which saved her life. Like so many ex-zeks she described the kinship that developed among prisoners as sincere and enduring human relationships, bonds that distinguished the prisoners from "them" (the camp administrators).

Ginzburg's remarkable belief in the goodness of people is a sharp contrast to the "human to wolf" motif that suffuses Bardach's experience. While Ginzburg was afforded such experiences as falling in love with a German doctor in the camps, Bardach, before he worked in the hospital, graphically describes the sadism and cruelty from both the guards and the criminal population that he witnessed and experienced, including a vicious attack that nearly killed him after he attempted to escape from a train car. Although he did befriend some criminals—something that afforded him some protection from others—it was only in another inmate, a political he could trust, that Bardach found proof that he didn't have to "become a beast to survive in this human wilderness."[50] Had he not had this experience of compassion and therefore retained his own humanity, he surely would not have lasted very long as a medical assistant. He survived with luck and a strong constitution to eventually become a celebrated plastic surgeon and professor of medicine in America.

Ginzburg's ultimate purpose in writing her memoirs was to explain how her eighteen years in perdition was the price, not for the preposterous crimes with which she was charged, but for her unthinking acceptance of Party dogma and practices before she was arrested. Prior to her arrest in 1937, she never had the slightest doubt about the Party line and was prepared to dedicate her life to it. She had not shared the growing idealization of Stalin but, as a Party activist, she had "fervently supported the policies of industrializing the country and collectivizing the land."[51] Because of her erstwhile commitment, she felt that she carried a heavy share of blame for all the innocent victims before the time of her arrest. She loathed her previous life:

> When you can't sleep, the knowledge that you did not directly take part in murders and betrayals is no consolation. After all, the assassin is not he who struck the blow, but whoever supported evil, no matter how: by thoughtless repetition of dangerous political theories; by silently raising his right hand; by faint-heartedly writing half-truths. Mea culpa...and it occurs to me more and more frequently that even eighteen years of hell on earth is insufficient expiation of guilt.[52]

Her determination to avoid alibis and any form of ideological sophistry distinguished her from other accounts of participants. People such as the one-time Party activist, Lev Kopelev, and above all, the Western apologists who, with nothing to risk, shamelessly peddled Stalinist distortions and lies which harmed others directly through their participation in Stalinist horrors or indirectly by giving support to the regime. She lived to bear witness to the barbarism and nightmarish undead world of interrogation and terror. Like Solzhenitsyn, who was once a fervent Communist Party member, she shed her prior "magnificent illusions."

That integrity also infused Susanna Pechuro's conversations with foreign journalists. Unlike Ginzburg, however, she was not seduced by the sirens of Marxist–Leninism. Although she could never become a teacher because of her camp certificate, she worked in a university library that enabled her to speak with students. Most prisoners were expected to sign documents that forbade them to speak about their prison and camp experience, but

Pechuro refused and, as she told journalist, Anne Applebaum, in 1998, she has "been talking about it ever since."[53] She has consistently remained a human-rights activist, opposing the death penalty, and has been a volunteer for the Memorial Society. Since its formation in 1988 with branches throughout the country, the Memorial Society commemorates the millions of Soviet citizens who either spent time (or for many ended their lives) in the Gulag or were victims of the firing squads. Even though it is more of a grieving agency and does not call for justice through the law courts, it existed in a country with little public memory of these terrors and the system that made them possible. We can be grateful that Memorial is a repository for the recollections of these former Soviet citizens and a lodestar for Western scholars.

Pechuro was reluctant to speak about her personal suffering preferring to refer to her work for Memorial and to her role as an advocate for human rights, even though it has not earned her much popular support. That was not the case with Bardach who was a victim of both the Stalinist and Nazi horrors. After spending five years in prisons and camps, he discovered that the Nazis were responsible for the murder of his parents and his wife. His grief and the attendant emotional turmoil of reliving the camp experience, where violence, sadism and indifference had been commonplace, unhinged him in ways that have been rarely documented in the memoirs of Gulag returnees. Living in Moscow and no longer having to concentrate on sheer survival, Bardach would wake up at night with a "sucking piercing nauseating feeling of hunger" with his "jaws stiff and aching form chewing in [his] sleep." He was plagued with nightmares about death, corpses and his murdered family. His fear of filling out application forms, on which, by necessity, he had to lie leaving him vulnerable to being exposed and re-arrested, was well founded but debilitating. His terror prompted his brother, who was a military attaché at the Polish embassy in Moscow and who arranged for his early release from the Gulag, to warn him to "shed [his] prisoner's skin" if he expected to have a normal life and decent job.[54] The advice made sense but for Bardach there was the additional burden that he had survived whereas his family had not. With his brother's encouragement, he enrolled at a Moscow medical school, and it was there that he discovered his passion for reconstructive surgery. Despite difficulties with physics and chemistry, he graduated with a prestigious Red

Diploma that enabled him to pursue graduate studies. Granted a travel visa, he visited Poland where he returned to his home and to the forest where his loved ones were among the 24,000 Jews murdered. It was the beginning of his healing process that continued when he spoke to friends who had survived the Holocaust. Even though he was expected to praise the "Great Leader" and tout the obligatory Party line, something that had been de rigueur in his studies, Bardach courageously disabused his Polish friends of any illusions that they nurtured about Soviet intentions in Poland for social justice. He openly told them about the camps, the secret police and the realities of life in Moscow. His medical training was shadowed by another wave of impending terror, xenophobic and anti-Semitic, which rendered him exceedingly vulnerable to being purged as a foreigner, a Jew and a doctor. Moreover, his personal happiness was put in jeopardy when he fell in love with a Soviet citizen when Soviet law prohibited marriage with foreigners. Deus ex machina arrived for Bardach when Stalin died, a potentially massive purge came to an abrupt end and the law was altered allowing him to marry and pursue a professional career in Poland. Bardach managed to achieve a balance between paying lip service to Stalinist rituals and harbouring no doubts about its realities, including living with the presence of anti-Semitism in Poland.

The Past Is Never Dead*

In the mid-1980s, Mikhail Gorbachev, the last General Secretary of the Soviet Union and the grandson of Gulag prisoners, set out to reform and modernize the system with the belief that Stalinism had perverted the spirit of Leninism. Under the new watchwords of glasnost and perestroika, Gorbachev encouraged artists and historians to fill in the "blank spots" of history and not be guided by "rose-coloured glasses." One of the most impressive achievements was the film, *Repentance*, a surrealistic allegory of Stalinist terror inspired by real events in Georgia. A man was unjustly imprisoned and released, his life destroyed. When he returned home he dug up the grave of the man responsible for sending him to prison, took out the corpse and stood it up against a wall. He would not allow the dead man to rest. In the film, a

---

* It's not even past. William Faulkner, 1951

woman, whose parents died in the camps because of her father's opposition to the government using a medieval church as a scientific laboratory, reprises the scene by digging up the corpse of a deranged provincial mayor who was responsible for the death of her father. The son of the despotic Varlan is no better; he rationalizes to his own son the actions of his father: "what are a few lives when the well-being of millions is at stake?" The woman will not forget, nor will she let anyone around her forget. The film is about the necessity of memory and not allowing the evils of the past to be repeated. Gorbachev allowed the film to be shown, blandly noting that "History must be seen for what it is." His friend, Alexander Yakovlev, expressed his admiration in starker, visceral language: the film "smash(ed) like a sledgehammer the system of lies, hypocrisy and violence."[55] When *Repentance* was commercially released in 1987, it attracted huge audiences, especially among the intelligentsia, many finding it a cathartic experience.

The long-term impact of the film is harder to gauge. By the beginning of the twenty-first century, the horrors of Stalinism had receded into grey oblivion and the children of the glasnost generation turned their attention to consumerism and pop culture. Art films like *Repentance* were not well received by a public weary of more terrible historic revelations. The public was much more receptive to blockbuster action thrillers like the gritty 2004 *Night Watch* that features a band of warriors endowed with supernatural powers battling vampires and witches to protect the world from the forces of darkness.

Any notion of a public reckoning with the Soviet past and reconciliation was scotched by Vladimir Putin. After his election in 2000 he reversed perestroika and steered the country back toward authoritarianism. He initiated a campaign to end the "blackening" of Soviet history by what one Kremlin propagandist has called "smearing the Motherland with filth" and to resurrect Stalin as a "strong leader" who resorted to "harsh methods" for "justifiable ends." Putin virtually rehabilitated Stalin whose "mistakes," he contended were not substantially different than those committed by Western leaders. Textbooks were censored and the reputations of historians, who insisted on dwelling on Stalin's crimes, were impugned for their lack of patriotism. Putin even reinstated symbolic features of the Stalinist regime notably the melody of the Soviet anthem, albeit with different words. Yet Putin had a lot of public support. One professor noted that "any attempt to dig into the past evokes irritation" because it clashes with the fundamental Russian goal of teaching history—to garner support for a strong

The image of a couple buried alive is from a dream sequence in the 1984 landmark Georgian film, Repentance. *In her dream, she and her husband attempt to flee the Stalinist mayor, Varlam, who pursues them in a car along with knights on horses. Her dream is precognitive since he is arrested and sentenced to ten years without the right to correspondence, meaning that he will be executed. Before her own arrest, she believes that he is buried alive in the camps.*

state. Unfortunately, the price for this myopia is the absence of accountability and the rule of law, and the low value attached to human life. It is no surprise that a television poll in 2008 revealed that Stalin was the third most popular leader in Russian history (after the medieval hero, Alexander Nevsky, a symbol of defiance against the West and the patron saint of the FSB, the successor of the KGB, and Stolypin).[56]

On December 4, 2008, the fledgling neo-Stalinism of the Brezhnev years (1964–1982) resurfaced. Masked men forced their way into Memorial Society offices in St Petersburg confiscating the hard drives that contained the entire archive of Memorial and the Virtual Museum.[57] Granted a court found that the search and the confiscation contained "procedural violations" and the hard drives were returned. But the authorities had sent their message: we will do anything we can to hamper you. The writing and teaching of history has become intensely politicized in the Russian Federation as anything considered contentious is in danger of slipping down Orwell's memory hole. Writing before this theft of valuable historical documents, historian Catherine Merridale expressed at least a partial truth: "collective amnesia suits the current leadership." According to a 2007 study, the public appears to be in agreement. Although the vast majority believed that the repression of "1937" could not be justified, many young and affluent saw no reason for raking over the past and, unlike the perestroika generation, did not believe that the government should engage in an act of national repentance.[58]

Nonetheless, Putin did undertake gestures that challenge the view that he was an unequivocal apologist for creeping Stalinism by eliminating any public expression that acknowledges its dark past. During the seventieth anniversary of the Great Terror, he personally presented an award to Solzhenitsyn, who did more than anyone to publicize the Gulag. A former KGB career officer, Putin also attended a commemoration to the victims at a NKVD killing field, the first Soviet or Russian leader to do so. Perhaps it is not surprising that a Gulag survivor and a former KGB officer should reach an accommodation since according to historian Steven Barnes:

> Solzhenitsyn, despite his radical hatred toward the
> Bolsheviks, himself operates in the same ethos imaging a
> contaminated society—sure enough contaminated by the
> Bolsheviks themselves as opposed to the class enemy, but
> contaminated nevertheless. 'What kind of disastrous path
> lies ahead of us if we do not have the chance to purge our-
> selves of that putrefaction rotting inside our body?'

Solzhenitsyn's biological trope and a foaming indignant style— "We have a duty to seek them all out and bring them all to trial [and for them to confess] 'Yes, I was an executioner and a murderer' "—is redolent not only of exclamatory language of the show trials but also reveals the degree to which he internalized the Stalinist political theatre of his youth. In Gothic terms, he became the double or the mirror image of that which he most despised.

And Putin embodied the split that exists in his nation regarding Stalinism: about one-half views Stalin as a "wise leader," while the other half regards him as an "inhuman tyrant."[59] Given that Putin has long-term tsarist ambitions, it is no wonder that in a 2011 interview with *Der Spiegel* Gorbachev accused Putin and his United Russia Party of pulling Russia back into the past.

Ambivalence is embedded in the psyche of the majority of the victims of Stalinist repression. Post-traumatic stress and "talking cures" did not sit well with Russian sensibilities. As all interviewees in the 1990s told Merridale, who suggested that talk therapy might have helped ease their suffering: "Dear girl, this isn't your England." Conditioned to repress their emotions and silence grievances, citizens during the Soviet era sealed off their private pain from their public lives by joining in the rituals that celebrated the "collective struggle for human liberation" through work, songs and marches. Some knew that the boilerplate of historical destiny was improbable and had to be taken with a degree of irony. For others, however, their personal identity was connected with the pride they acquired after rebuilding their country despite their own or their parents' suffering. For both groups it felt invigorating to be part of the collective effort. Cognitive therapy, not psychotherapy, was more relevant for Soviet citizens. Through an act of will, "happiness" could be engineered but it would take effort. Even if you did not feel like it, forcing yourself to smile would be the first step.[60]

The implosion of the Soviet Union, the tidal wave of free-market reforms that created hyper-inflation, wiped out savings and jobs, and created a cohort of billionaires during the chaotic Yeltsin years soon disillusioned Russians about freedom, capitalism and democracy. In this climate, some clung to nostalgia for a time when, despite the perversities and cruelties of the system, the vast majority shared a common purpose. There was no serious attempt at a moral reckoning to make officials of the Soviet regime accountable— as in Czechoslovakia when *lustration* deprived senior Party officials of the right to re-enter the government for five years. Instead, Vladimir Putin, who, as a former KGB officer, would have been ineligible to hold public office under a Russian version of *lustration*, offered political stability and used the revenue from oil and natural gas to lift the people out of extreme poverty.

In a culture where moral reflection was discouraged and little public space was available to honour the victims of the Soviet regime, a work of art like *Repentance* had briefly allowed Soviet citizens a window for a collective cathartic experience, an occasion for "the return of memory" without the further opportunity for working it through. This experience would not have been possible without Gorbachev's effort to resuscitate a comatose superpower. Once Stalinism was excavated and scrutinized, the corrupt and cruel system created by Lenin lay nakedly exposed, unwilling or incapable of healing itself. Ironically, Gorbachev's attempt to re-energize the Soviet Union sent the behemoth into its grave, a death that Putin proclaimed as the greatest geopolitical catastrophe of the twentieth century. Yet he has been the chief beneficiary of that collapse, a formidable presence for twelve years as of 2012, who amassed huge wealth and great power, regardless of his formal position, more akin to a tsar who regarded the state as a master rather than a servant of the people. Despite opposition from urban middle-class professionals and feminist rock musicians who object to his authoritarianism and crony capitalism, as the newly elected President in March 2012, he is not likely to initiate the necessary structural changes to strengthen democratic institutions.

PART TWO

Racial Purity:
Fantasies and Realities in Germany

There awakens within him a doubly strong yearning for a Leader to take him tenderly and lightly by the hand, to set things in order and show him the way;...the Leader to build the house anew that the dead may come to life again, and who himself has risen again from the multitude of the dead; the Healer who by his own actions will give meaning to the incomprehensible events of the age, so that Time can begin anew.

~ Hermann Broch, *The Sleepwalkers*

If Hitler were the adored and cursed personification of nothing, in whom there was nothing to restrain him for anything at all, his true face could not be revealed in a literary mirror...since there was no face. In that case he was more comparable with Count Dracula, a vampire feeding on human blood: one of the 'undead.'

~ Harry Mulisch, *Siegfried*

Overview

Midway through the journey of our
life, I found myself within a dark wood,
for the right way had been lost.

—Divine Comedy
Dante

The fantastic, chimerical *Protocols of the Elders of Zion* infiltrated the European *Zeitgeist* and fuelled the trend to slander and scapegoat the Jews for the suffering and disorder attendant upon the Great War. Initially utilized by the White Russian armies during the civil war, the 1919 German translation of this fabrication ensured the accessibility of the *Protocols* for deployment by pan-German nationalists. The latter used the postwar revolution in Hungary and abortive attempts in Germany as evidence of a sinister conspiracy by the Jewish elders to plot revolution and world domination. The qualities attributed to Jews—their control of public opinion, their desire to exploit economic chaos and their hatred and need for revenge—expressed precisely the intent and language of the anti-Semitic nationalists who appropriated the *Protocols*. They had no doubt that Jewish economic power and cultural influence could wreak devastating havoc on the German people by creating a "universal economic crisis" and massive unemployment, and as a result of "blood poisoning," they had the power to unleash a world war.

For many Russian refugees, particularly sympathizers of the White cause in the civil war who were uprooted from their native land and fled west after the Bolshevik Revolution, the widely believed *Protocols* provided a prophetic description of the Jewish

187

plan for worldwide hegemony. One of those refugees, Alfred Rosenberg, of Baltic German descent, read this document and had his worldview crystallized: that a vast subterranean conspiracy organized by Jews was responsible for the disintegration of the Russian Empire. In his commentary on this "horror-comic," Rosenberg embellished the theme that the war had resulted from the machinations of the Jews and that they had been its sole beneficiaries.[1] Developments that unfolded in the tumultuous chaos of post-war Germany provided further confirmation. When radical Socialists with the support of workers acquired power in Bavaria and created a two-week, Soviet-style government whose leaders in both experiments were largely Jewish, there was sufficient "evidence" for these allegations.

Rosenberg, who also served as liaison between Russian émigrés and ultra-nationalist Germans, arrived in Munich with a copy of the *Protocols* in his suitcase. There he joined the rabidly anti-Semitic racist Thule Society, named after the legendary kingdom of Nordic mythology. Their members were drawn from the nobility and the professions, and they were required to prove they descended from three generations of Aryan blood. Ostensibly a scholarly organization that read old Germanic literature and promoted Nordic folklore to foster ethnic nationalism, it participated in extremist politics, with many of its ideas taking root in the German Workers Party in 1919, the forerunner of the National–Socialist Party. Through the Thule Society, where he was often a guest, Adolf Hitler became acquainted with the *Protocols*. As Hitler astutely recognized, it was not a pamphlet at all, but a secret textbook outlining strategies and tactics for world domination. In other words, it provided the pretext, the rhetoric and the inspiration for Hitler to launch a pre-emptive attack upon the Jews. The German author of the first important biography of Hitler, *Der Führer: Hitler's Rise to Power*, Konrad Heiden, a former Munich journalist who reported on the fledgling dictator's early speeches, recognized that Hitler "would become the 'king' and 'ruler' of the world prophesied in the *Protocol*."[2] The conspiratorial fantasy encapsulated a malevolent spirit that fed paranoia and embittered rage, a mentality that embraced chauvinistic nationalism and toxic racism—cancerous tissues that incubated before metastasizing into the collective psyche of the German people.

Perhaps not surprisingly, the appointment of Hitler as Chancellor of Germany in January 1933 was greeted with elation by large sectors of the German population who in the previous summer had supplied sufficient electoral support to enable the National Socialists to constitute the largest contingent in the Reichstag. Even though the unpopular Weimar Republic (named after the city where the Constituent Assembly first met) provided a degree of political and economic stability for most of its existence, any residual support for it evaporated after the economic dislocations that occurred following the Wall Street collapse in October 1929. What the Nazis offered were not merely political or economic remedies but something more fundamental: the promise of a national rebirth, a purified and racially regenerated state with "hereditarily healthy," physically fit and politically reliable Germans, after years of inertia, decadence and decay.[3] Despite the subversion of the rule of law and the arbitrary exercise of police terror, the regime enjoyed vast popular support because it offered a community identity and a sense of purpose, as well as economic and social recovery, enabling the population to subordinate individual interests to the *Volk*—the ethnic racial community—and to accommodate their language and behaviour to the "new order" even if that meant violating traditional Christian values.[4] One of Hitler's biographers opined that if the Führer (strong leader) had died in 1938, he would have been recognized as one of the greatest German statesmen, "the consummator of German history."[5] It is not uncommon for this opinion to be echoed by contemporaries who lived through what was for them a congenial period. The wife of a prominent German historian told an interviewer that "eighty percent lived positively and productively throughout the time....We also had good years. We had *wonderful* years."[6] That sentiment is shared by others, who even during the prosperous post-war period in West Germany, remember "how much better it all was in Hitler's day" because they "believed in something" that took them out of their narrowed lives.[7] Undoubtedly, the nostalgic haze, that envelops the recollections of some individuals for at least the first half of the Third Reich's duration, renders them incapable of recognizing the malfeasance that disfigured the regime from start to finish. Indeed, if National Socialism could be decoupled from the Holocaust, generic fascism would acquire greater respectability, and Hitler's regime would serve as an inspiration for large numbers of people and states craving national revival, order and convenient scapegoats.

Courtesy of Photofest

In the 2009 disturbing German film, White Ribbon, *beneath the placid exterior of a village in northern Germany before the Great War, vandalism and abuse occur. In the pastor's home within this hierarchical community, the children are severely disciplined and forced to wear the humiliating white ribbon until their father is convinced that they have been cleansed. The children are obsequious but the school teacher, who narrates these events from the perspective of old age, is convinced that they have been abusing other children.*

Based on an ethos of self-love and other-hate, membership in the German *Volk* did not include genetic or allegedly racially inferior peoples.[8] That ethos is rooted in part on a crude version of Darwinism—a world of predators or victims—that is captured in Michael Haneke's 2009 austere but powerful film, *The White Ribbon*. Set in a small village in northern Germany in the year before the Great War, it reveals how in a hierarchical, authoritarian community, paternal authorities abuse their children. They in turn, the film suggests, (the details are rarely revealed) become agents of violence when two vulnerable young boys, one with a handicap, are scapegoated and viciously beaten. Smarting from humiliation and wearing an embittered sense of victimhood, coupled with an obsequious manner before authority figures, these children, too young to participate in the horrors of the coming war, potentially carry a romanticized version of it into adulthood and support for the aggressive militarism of National Socialism.

Nazism also derived its authority from the pseudo-science of race that overlapped and then replaced traditional Judeophobia.

The alleged dangers of miscegenation and the strengthening of the German *Volk* laced the prose of Richard Wagner. That the German dictator was enthralled by Wagner's musical dramas is well known, but whether he understood them is less certain, especially the vast four-part *Ring of the Nibelung*, given its philosophical and aesthetic complexity. Nevertheless, Teutonic folklore and myth in Wagner's musical output did fuel Hitler's fantasies of himself guided by providence to lead the charge toward a brave new world. Wagner's stage designs also inspired the pageantry and Party regalia prominently displayed during the Third Reich and the choreographing of the pyrotechnic rituals organized by the Minister for Propaganda and Popular Enlightenment, Joseph Goebbels, and Hitler's master builder and protégé, Albert Speer. If Wagner seduced Hitler, the latter intoxicated the maestro's daughter-in-law, Winifred, who, by elevating the Hitler–Wagner connection, turned the composer into a posthumous accomplice of the regime.

More importantly, the National Socialist movement proved to be a compelling magnet, a Mephistopheles, so to speak, to the professional elites. Given their pre-existing political convictions, it was not difficult to co-opt members of the intelligentsia with financial inducements and prestige. They succumbed to the illusion that they were being anointed the *übermensch* (the superior men) of a national revival for a healthier society, which rendered them politically naïve and opportunistic. Through lucrative research programs, professionals elevated mere folk prejudice into an advanced "sound science." They disdained the bizarre seminal absorption fantasy peddled as science by popular culture, guttersnipe journalism and in *Mein Kampf* that the Jews had the capacity to poison permanently the blood of a German woman through a single sexual experience. But their own research into diseases and the harmful effects of race mixing was not substantially more sophisticated. Because they shared a broad sympathy with goals of the Third Reich, that of detoxifying the *Volk* of pollutants from without and within, physicians and scientists believed that the panaceas for arresting national decline and the dilution of German blood could be found through enforced racial hygiene. They instituted biological terror to root out anyone who endangered the genetic heritage of healthy Germans by supporting and implementing arbitrary procedures that resulted in sterilization and "mercy killing" against alleged genetic and racial inferiors.

They were assisted by American eugenicists who, obsessed with the fear of miscegenation between blacks and whites, provided financial, technological and ideological support to their German colleagues. Regardless of whether German scientists endorsed the National Socialist creed that blood was the essence of race, or even participated in the later atrocities, they were the enablers of evil. Their work, hidden beneath the carapace of supposedly scientific objectivity, legitimatized the Reich's exclusionary agenda, namely that disease and evil were inborn in non-Aryan races and could only be corrected by the most extreme measures.

Hitler's obsession with engineering a racially immaculate Aryan-only national community by promoting and fanning ethnic hatred remained the *sine qua non* of National Socialism and rendered political and economic grievances after 1918 peripheral to his *raison d'être*. True, Hitler exploited public fears of international Bolshevism and disorder in the streets and received vast support for his decision to crush political opposition, starting with a foreign-inspired Communist Party and continued with his decision to purge his own party when it represented a threat. By addressing these fears, he soothed the psychological stress in millions of Germans who believed their world was disintegrating and that anarchy would engulf them. After he consolidated power and enabled Germans to believe that the decadent and humiliating past was behind them, Hitler was free to implement his utopian vision of an ethnically cleansed, expansionist Germany in need of *Lebensraum* (living space) for ethnic Germans, those with a verifiable healthy pedigree. That dream turned into a nightmare for those excluded from the national community: political dissidents, homosexuals, "social outsiders" (those incapable of earning a living), the handicapped, and the "inferior races."

Whether the Nazi propaganda machine was effective in persuading German citizenry to endorse the genocidal hatred of Hitler and the die-hard fanatics is debatable; a more convincing argument can be made that it was most successful at trading on semi-dormant hostility rather than shaping new attitudes.[9] Those who regarded Jews as "un-German" allowed the Nazi virulence to cascade over them and willingly accepted the canard that the Jews exercised too much economic and cultural influence and deserved their déclassé status. Some Germans did harbour sympathy for individual Jews and were horrified by acts of violence toward them; however, the broad mass either through indifference or compliance remained culpable to the fate of Jews in general and that of other so-called lesser breeds that either did not fit in or failed to satisfy the prescribed political, social or racial criteria of the new *Volk*. Regardless, a staple of the Nazi worldview vilified Jews as not only leering pornographic *Untermenschen* (subhuman) degenerates who also posed a formidable power—over-intellectual, "over-evolved cosmopolitan sophisticates effortlessly controlling the infrastructure of the modern world"—rendering them a potent enemy that threatened to suck the oxygen out of the Aryan race.[10] This penchant to project the darkest impulses of the Nazis onto the Jews, thereby elevating them into a powerful doppelganger, congealed into substantive political and economic measures to deprive Jews of citizenship and to drive them out of the community, culminating in the vicious pogrom of *Kristallnacht* in November 1938.

Along with the thuggish behaviour and systematic violence of the ideological zealots of the police and paramilitary forces, the politics of exclusion could never have occurred to the degree it did without the complicity of ordinary Germans. For law-abiding Germans weary of crime, the regime was effectively able to mobilize vast popular support for its draconian law-and-order program. Even without state coercion, individuals were willing to denounce neighbours, colleagues and even family members for both patriotic and opportunistic reasons, a characteristic that revealed how their consciousness was impregnated with fascism. Having yearned for a saviour to lead the *Volk* out of its political and economic disarray, they were willing to accept the harsh conditions meted out because they believed they could materially benefit from the persecution of others, were doing their patriotic duty, or accepted the assumption that the *other* was inherently criminal.

A malignant spirit alone cannot explain the popular appeal that Hitler and National Socialism exerted over vast pockets of the German people. The seductive side of this Janus-faced movement that enthralled its citizenry can be explained in part by an improvement in their material circumstances. Self-interest was supplemented by a shrewd design to package the National Socialists less as a political party and more as a religious revival that offered the German people a unity they craved and a spiritual solace that would eliminate the turbulence that had shrouded their recent past. Portrayed as a canonized being in film and at rallies, notably Leni Riefenstahl's, *Triumph of the Will*, Hitler successfully communicated the mystical notion that the German people were a unique racial entity with the power to create mankind anew. A powerful current coursed through the *Volk* that involved a special relationship to the land, and Hitler could best express the deepest aspirations that resided in German hearts. Even before he was given power, he harnessed that energy by cultivating an emotional bond with the masses by offering them a vision of a nation reborn, one which would change their spirit, their way of thinking and acting. That millions were "working toward the Fuhrer" without explicit orders from above meant that they had internalized the ethos of the Third Reich, something a purely coercive regime could not have achieved.[11]

If a minority uncritically endorsed the ideology of the National Socialists, a majority accepted the regime because Hitler exploited the seductive energies of ceremony and ritual through the camera-ready staging of gigantic extravaganzas and by adroit use of the audio-visual spaces to create a common culture.[12] From film to German genre art, the media offered a radical, utopian vision of health and authenticity, of a community in touch with its roots devoid of the blemish of cultural Modernism that exemplified and exuded degeneration and cosmopolitanism. Through the efforts of the exceptionally ruthless and skilful Goebbels, film was used to aestheticize politics with threadbare propaganda while simultaneously anesthetising the citizens to the violence that was directed against designated targets.

The willingness of the elites and the wider public to accept a "just us" (Aryan) society produced an illiberal public culture predicated on ethnic purity and the erasure of moral obligations toward non-Germans. By encouraging civic engagement through participation in Nazi ceremonies, the regime rendered a public not supportive of the fanaticism of Party insiders and street ruffians vulnerable to collaboration with a colossal evil. A starting point for understanding the relationship between ideology and aesthetics is to revisit the controversy over whether the anti-Semitism of Richard Wagner tainted his art, given that both his prose and musical dramas were (mis)appropriated *after* his death to buttress the ideological content and style of the Third Reich. It is arguable that unlike Martin Heidegger, whose philosophy was interwoven with his politics, and Leni Riefenstahl whose art is inseparable from her politics, who actively embraced the new regime—and are the subjects of subsequent chapters—Wagner, despite his personal demons, should not be judged by the same ethical standards.

The Art and Influence of
Richard Wagner

A man perceived as a terrible man
can produce beautiful and ultimately healing works of art.

> —*Wagner: The Terrible Man
> and His Truthful Art*
> M. Owen Lee

Many consider Richard Wagner's art to be tainted by his associations with the ideology of the Third Reich. Hitler maintained a genuine passion for the music of Wagner and the composer's visceral anti-Semitism is well-known. Even though that epithet was not coined until 1879, Wagner's hostility toward Jews was increasingly based, not on religious but on ethnic and cultural differences. He gradually moved toward "scientific racism"—an individual was defined by his race endowed with a distinct physiognomy and unchangeable character traits. His bile, however, was frequently muddled as he oscillated between Judeophobia—traditional religious prejudice that purports redemption to be possible through conversion—and a racist mindset. The major historical challenge is to assess whether Wagner's anti-Semitic theoretical writings infected his artistic oeuvre, notably his magnus opus, *Der Ring des Nibelungen*, and whether the art itself contributed to the racist ideology of National Socialism. Looking for universal acceptance by ensuring that his art would not be compromised by crude propaganda, Wagner strove to keep his anti-Jewish obsession separate from his art.[1] Hitler deeply admired Wagner's music, but there is little evidence that he plumbed the composer's writings to reinforce his ideology, and, as we will see, for good reason.

The issues are not merely academic considering that an informal ban on his music still exists in Israel. Self–censorship arguably falsifies history because it implicitly assigns historical responsibility to Wagner for the Nazi atrocities from *Kristallnacht* to the Shoah (the Hebrew word for catastrophe). Although it is neither a specific reason for the ban nor an assertion that has been substantiated, the allegation that his music was used to accompany Jews into the gas chambers has fuelled antagonism toward Wagner. Yet the historical record is unequivocal that the Nazis explicitly forbade his music to be played in the camps.[2] This decision is understandable given that the ideas and techniques in the *Ring* were antithetical to the crude worldview of the Nazis. Apart from Hitler, the potentates were surreptitiously hostile to Wagner, even as they selectively appropriated his art when it served their purposes.

Wagner's Anti-Semitic Prose

Wagner's theoretical writings and private pronouncements in personal letters and in the diary entries (1869–1883) of his second wife, Cosima, were threaded with a torrent of rage against specific targets. Yet even in these forums, his musings were often inconsistent. Powerful, visceral emotions constituted the animating force in Wagner's life. As early as 1850, he had written his friend, the composer and brilliant pianist (and his future father-in-law) Franz Liszt that he "harboured a long suppressed resentment against this Jewish business and this resentment is as necessary to my nature as gall is to blood." This hostility extended to Wagner's frequent rants against the French and the Roman Catholic Church, especially the Jesuits.[3]

Odious references to Jews did infuse a small but significant percentage of Wagner's voluminous prose, particularly the scurrilous pamphlet, *Judaism in Music*. First published in 1850 under a pseudonym and republished in 1869 under his real name, *Judaism* maligns Jews as "repugnant in appearance" and portrays their traditional worship as "nonsensical gurgling, yodeling and cackling." Their Yiddish–German accent—a "creaking, squeaking, buzzing snuffle"—assured that they could never properly speak the language of their adopted country.[4] He regarded language as the expression of the nation's soul; therefore, the Jewish reputed inability to master it prevented them from expressing true passion and creating authentic music. Furthermore, he believed that because they conceived of every aspect of life in commercial terms, they were responsible for the evils of capitalism. He was wilfully ignorant to the larger historical reality that the Jewish people had been excluded from the traditional guilds and unable to own land.

The primary targets of Wagner's venom, however, were the Jewish artists, poets and specifically musical composers. That animus was rooted in his over two-year Paris experience when, as a struggling young composer, he envied the commercial success of the composer, Giacomo Meyerbeer. Wagner believed that he had demeaned himself by obsequiously asking his older colleague for money. In high dudgeon, he lashed out at Meyerbeer specifically, and Jewish artists generally, as a "swarming colony of worms in the dead body of art."[5] As they could not access the unconscious cultural traditions of the country in which they resided, they were incapable of producing original art; at best they could mimic and parody the art of Gentiles. Even a gifted composer like Felix Mendelssohn, while producing diverting work, could never delve deeper than his conscious intentions.[6] This specious logic was absurd given that Wagner freely borrowed musical ideas from Mendelssohn and even admitted in private that the composer was a genius. The first edition of *Judaism* did not create much controversy because its readers recognized that it was purely a polemic against Jewish artists.

In the 1869 edition of *Judaism*, Wagner repeated his rant that Jews had infected art and therefore accelerated the "decay in our culture," but then proceeded to malign his Jewish contemporaries. In a new preface and afterward, he denounced an alleged conspiracy in the "Jewish press" against his works. Wagner's decision to then participate in the chauvinistic backlash against the Emancipation Decree that had enabled Jews to enter into the professions, contributed to its tumultuous reception in which audiences hissed at performances and attendance declined. He contended that Jews were an alien nation within a nation, that Germany had been invaded, leaving itself vulnerable to extensive Jewish influence in finance, journalism and the arts even though Jews constituted only one and a quarter percent of the population. Wagner raised the possibility of the "violent ejection of the destructive foreign element," although he publicly deemed the proposal impractical; in private he considered it more seriously. In his essay, he preferred assimilation, an option later ignored by commentators who sought to arrogate Wagner for a racially defined, militant *Volk*. But mere assimilation was not sufficient given a private remark from a diary entry by Cosima on April 7, 1873. In response to someone who suggested that the answer to the Jewish presence lay in intermarriage, Wagner stated that "the Germans would cease to exist, since the fair German blood is not strong enough to resist this 'alkali.' " Jews needed to repudiate their Judaism while Germans needed to develop themselves. He emphasized in italics the effort required by Gentiles: "*when we ourselves were redeemed as true human beings.*" If successful, it could result "in such a way that...it shall ripen toward to a higher evolution of our nobler human qualities" and a major transformation of humankind.[7] Unfortunately, this reference to Jewish and German redemption is nebulous and could not erase the spiteful remarks that preceded it, ensuring that its publication would be greeted with protests, and not only from Jews.

Yet the increasing anti-Semitism and nationalist sentiments during the 1870s rendered Wagner's views more palatable. Given the turbulent economic climate, to suggest that Jews were economic exploiters of the German people would not have been considered outrageous. Previously written in 1865 to proselytize his most important patron, King Ludwig of Bavaria, Wagner in 1878 published "What Is German" in the journal *Bayreuther Blätter* (*Bayreuth Journal*). In it he opined that Jewish intrusion had sullied the *Volk*; he warned that they had already gained control of Polish and Hungarian industry and trade. In Germany, Jews were "representatives of the 'un-German' utilitarian principle, [and] as the profiteers of capitalism: 'The Jew seized these advantages and the Jewish banker nourishes his enormous wealth on the crippled and declining national prosperity.' "[8] The medieval blood libel had morphed into the money libel.

In his final years, Wagner became increasingly fanatical. He was convinced that racial pollution resulted from miscegenation, and that crackpot theories such as vivisection, a practice allegedly sanctioned by the Jewish God, Jehovah, and meat-eating degenerated the state of Europeans in general and Germans in particular. In one diatribe after another, he repeated variations of this palpable nonsense. The once pure Aryan race that descended from the hero-gods Hercules and Siegfried with its pure-blood strain devolved as their blood has been mixed with that of "one-time cannibals now trained to be the business leaders of society."[9] Blood united Germans just as did language and culture. To breed outside it was to surrender one's genetic heritage and its superior essence. In an 1881 diary entry, Cosima recorded that Wagner blamed women for the pollution of German vitality: "In the mingling of the races, the blood of nobler males is ruined by the baser female element." In his essay, "Artwork of the Future" he wrote that the blood of the Jews threatens the vitality of the *Volk*; they are like vampires who "suck their life's blood from the wasted strength of the *Volk*."[10] In one of his final essays entitled "Know Yourself," he revisited the emancipation question when he argued that giving full citizenship to Jews would be comparable to the situation in Mexico where "blacks were given *carte blanche* to consider themselves white."[11] They and coloured people descended from apes, and through the centuries drained the Aryans of the purity of their blood. Without this blood, the inferior peoples would achieve nothing. Their only hope would be partaking of the blood of Christ through communion—an option that illustrated Wagner's confusion over religion and race. This could not occur through the hated international Catholic Church, however, as he regarded it as not much different from Judaism. Both were insidious foreign influences that vitiated the German *Volk*. By this time, except in the musical sphere where he could still attain greatness, Wagner's mind had eddied into whirlpools of madness rendering him incapable of calm reflection.

As abhorrent as Wagner's notions appear to a post-Holocaust world, they must be examined in their socio–historical context. The *Zeitgeist* of the latter half of the nineteenth century indulged, even encouraged, racist attitudes. Underpinning them were the new pseudo-sciences that asserted Jews were a race with immutable qualities that dictated that a Jew could never become a German. In the words of one pamphleteer: "The conversion to Christianity could no more transform the Jews into Germans than the skin of blacks could be turned into white." Accordingly, "even the most honest Jew, under the influence of his blood" was the "carrier of Semite morality" that contaminated the vital forces of German society, threatening it with degeneracy and death.[12]

Because these modern social theorists reinforced their writings with the new pseudo-scientific language of the "Semitic" cranium and haunch-formation, they impressed the more sophisticated who would have been embarrassed by the traditionalists who labelled Jews as "Christ killers." Wagner was both a product and a contributor to the times that pulsed with anti-Semitism. Racism was a toxin that infected Wagner's psyche but a purely reductive response—to equate his polemics with his art—would be short sighted. Paradoxically, the bigotry expressed in Wagner's writings would be relegated to an historical footnote if he had never written any music. The anti-Semitism of other artists like Frederick Chopin or Liszt has not diminished their popular appeal. They did not write anti-Semitic essays.

Wagner's Aesthetic and Political Philosophy

If definitions of race and notions of blood purity provide a divisive backdrop for an emerging nation, Wagner's enduring music dramas burnish in the foreground. A great artist can never be exculpated or excused for peddling hatred even in the spirit of German Romanticism where he was regarded (or regarded himself) as an *artist.* It should be stressed that Wagner's manic energy primarily was expended on his aesthetic output. He implemented his conviction that the so-called eternal German truths, characterized by an inner unchanging substance, could be reinterpreted to provide meaning for contemporary audiences when set to music. Furthermore, his passion for a Teutonic Christianity, albeit stripped of its Jewish origins, with the themes of sin, repentance and salvation, suffused *Lohengrin* and *Parsifal.* Both are based upon the myth of the Holy Grail, a talisman with magical properties that could cure mortal wounds and illnesses.[13] Because the Grail was visible only to a knight with a pure heart, Wagner imaginatively portrayed the psyche of an individual blessed with that state of mind. He intuitively recognized the need to set aside his base feelings and reveal a better self in his music that was regrettably absent from his life and some of his prose. Working within the Romantic tradition that appealed to his turbulent emotions, he conveyed primitive urges not only through complex characters and hauntingly sensual music, but also through the grandiosity of its palette, a distillation of grief, compassion and eroticism.

Underlying all his work was the conviction that art should transform, not reflect, consciousness and leave no part of his audience's lives unchanged.

Wagner tried to separate his corrosive polemics from his art. In one of his essays, "Know Thyself," he appears to indict merchant Jews when he refers to the Nibelung's ring as a "pocket book." Yet, in addition to writing the musical scores and librettos, he wrote voluminous pages explaining them, their plots and the characters; there is not a single comment that could be construed as anti-Semitic. He explicitly repudiated the idea that Jews should appear or be represented on stage because their general appearance was unsuitable for aesthetic purposes.[14] The sentiment is repellent but it does suggest that his distasteful characters were not meant to be representative of Jews but expressions of human flaws. He might have constructed characters who could be interpreted as resembling Jews but the evidence is sparse that Wagner's contemporary audiences, or those during the Third Reich recognized anti-Semitic messages. In his own time, Jews were among the most enthusiastic supporters of his music, if not his prose. And surely, the bored rank-and-file Nazis who were later dragooned into attending the Bayreuth summer festivals would have been aroused from their stupor if they had identified anti-Semitic allusions.[15]

Wagner's racism is complicated by other considerations. He was personally fond of a number of Jews, often treating them badly, but he equally reviled Gentiles who did not provide the undivided loyalty and support he demanded. Many Jews, including conductors, singers, stage designers, and orchestra players, gladly entered into his personal orbit. They endured his tirades, slights and condescension because they recognized that his artistic genius created sublime music within a unique operatic form. They understood that great gifts and paranoia could coexist in the same person. One possible reason for this curious phenomenon is that his themes of "alienation, perpetual wandering, false accusation, a race chosen of the gods despised by everyone else, racial suffering, the longing for homeland, the need for redemption" reveal that he unconsciously identified Jews with Germans.[16] Whatever his tangled and obsessive feelings toward Jews, which included envy and jealousy of their hardiness and intelligence, Wagner recognized that art took priority over his own festering hatreds and the art required him to choose artists with talent. In vain, he tried to persuade one of his conductors to renounce his ancestral heritage and convert to Christianity in order to take communion with him. Redemption was possible by the acceptance of Christianity and through art, which he believed was essentially a religious experience. According to Cosima, he remarked on February 14, 1881, that the Gospels, not racial strength, were what really mattered and later on December 17, "races are done for; all that can make an impact is...the blood of Christ."[17] The impulse to proselytize worthy Jews distinguishes Wagner from the more biologically-based racism that abounded in anti-Semitic vitriol, especially after his death.

Wagner's ambivalence toward individual Jews was replicated in his complex, twelve-year relationship with Friedrich Nietzsche. The philosopher's journey from intense admiration to profound disappointment in Wagner and his music following a painful break in 1876 made him an excoriating, but perceptive critic. Concurrently, he recognized Wagner as the "great benefactor" of his life. Even before Nietzsche left Bayreuth, he inveighed against Wagner's crass commercialism. The "old magician" that provided the "purest radiant happiness" had morphed into a showman for the Philistines: "the Wagnerian had become master over Wagner" for the "the whole idle riff-raff of Europe" who attended the festival and "could go in and out of Wagner's house as if it were a sporting event." Nietzsche recognized that Wagner's ingratiating public persona mirrored what he had years earlier despised in the French commercial opera composer, Meyerbeer. When Nietzsche distanced himself from the aura of chauvinism surrounding Bayreuth, he also became repelled by Wagner's anti-Semitism and the "sickness and unreason" of Teutonic nationalism associated with the place. But in a private letter written shortly after Wagner's death, his deeper feelings toward his former mentor emerged, "Wagner was by far the *fullest* human being I have ever known, and in *this* respect I have had to forgo a great deal for six years. But something like a deadly offence came between us."[18] In his remaining books, he would attempt to resolve his conflicted feelings toward his former mentor. By the time he wrote his last and most autobiographical work *Ecce Homo*, he had decidedly acknowledged that Richard Wagner had nourished him intellectually and emotionally and was the most important connection he had experienced with a German.

Both Wagner and Nietzsche initially supported German nationalism. Wagner believed, in tandem with his art, that the unification of the German states could be an instrument to achieve greatness and to bind the people together. Nineteenth-century nationalism was a liberal inclusive movement before it became tainted with militarism and chauvinism. Wagner was therefore continuing a tradition of artists, such as Verdi in the 1850s and 1860s, whose operas were suffused with the ideals of liberty and nationhood to further the cause of Italian nationalism.

Wagner's support for German nationalism was rooted in his impassioned belief in the fusion of art and politics, or more precisely, that politics should be the handmaiden of his art. As the Royal *Kapellmeister*, the young Wagner had been frustrated by the unwillingness of the king of Saxony, his employer, to stage an innovative music drama that presented a redemptive message. His disappointment in 1849 fuelled his revolutionary, anarchist period when Wagner challenged the monarchist state at the barricades in Dresden. He proclaimed its destruction was necessary to release Germans from the shackles of a bourgeois, mercantile society that sprang from money-worship and the commercialization of art. Its abysmal debacle drove Wagner into a fifteen-year exile to avoid a potential capital punishment charge for treason. Yet in an unjust world, he still believed that the artist should put his art at the service of revolutionaries who prepared the way for overthrowing tyranny and installing "a righteous world."[19]

If Wagner's dream of a marriage between art and politics had been scuttled, his passionate belief that the ancient legends of the *Volk* could be revitalized found expression in his musical dramas. They exemplified his philosophy of *Gesamkunstwerk*. Translated as total artwork, it is a synthesis of the poetic, visual, musical and dramatic elements. Through a collective aesthetic experience, that was as much mystical as it was artistic, he believed that the German people could experience, through art, a spiritual rebirth that could transcend the malaise of modern culture with its money worship and its bondage to property and capitalism. He offered spiritual redemption, a theme that informs almost his entire oeuvre, as an alternative to traditional opera that was, in his opinion, more primed for frothy entertainment. Nowhere do the disappointments of his forays into politics and the importance of mining myth reveal themselves more powerfully than in his incomparable *The Ring of the Nibelung.*

Wagner began to write the libretto of the *Ring* in the aftermath of the abortive 1848 Revolution. He originally conceived the work as an allegory for the pernicious effects of capitalism and the destructive power of money, symbolized by the gold ring. Early interpreters such as Bernard Shaw furnished critical credence to this view—the oppressed Nibelung in *The Rhinegold* did resemble the workers who toiled in endless misery in the factories and mines. But by the time Wagner was composing the last act of *Siegfried* in 1869, he had lost the fiery spirit of the 1848–49 revolution and in exile had read Arthur Schopenhauer. Consequently, he moved from class relationships to metaphysical issues about renunciation of the world and will.

Schopenhauer harboured a profound distaste for all revolutionary turmoil and instead advocated a withdrawal from the realm of public affairs. He believed that the world was a place of unfathomable suffering and that human misery could not be alleviated through political change but only through philosophy and art, especially music. Forced to re-evaluate his philosophy because of his abiding intellectual and artistic debt to Schopenhauer, Wagner elevated art above the new gods of science, technology and progress, and valued intuition and the irrational above reason. Whatever his conviction about the role of art when he wrote the libretto for the *Ring*, he gradually understood that his "artistic intuitions [were] working in opposition to his consciously held opinions."[20] Armed by a richer understanding about the role of the art, Wagner was inspired to complete the musical score and assign a greater significance to the music than he had previously because it possessed a deeper capacity for expressing his ideas.

With the defeat of France, (and the removal of Paris as the leader of global culture), Wagner briefly celebrated German unification under the leadership of Prussia. Hoping to curry favour with the Chancellor Otto von Bismarck for an official position in the new Germany, he offered to compose a tub-thumping, patriotic march. When it was first performed in May 1871 with the Emperor and Empress in attendance and with himself conducting, Wagner believed that the alliance between artist and monarch had been achieved. With the chorus in the audience that was encouraged to participate, the setting achieved in miniature the "holy trinity" that Wagner had envisioned constituted national unity.[21] Alas, this minor tableau never converted to a canvas writ large in the new German Empire; there would be no partnership between culture and politics. In this authoritarian state, the artist could never achieve equal billing with the state's most powerful politician.

Wagner's dashed hopes and growing disillusionment with Bismarck ended his brief rapprochement with the state and reinforced within him Schopenhauer's view that an individual could expect nothing from the external political world. With his monumental narcissism, it was inconceivable to Wagner that the "Iron Chancellor" would never place the resources of the state at the disposal of a strutting musical genius. Although they met briefly, Bismarck was not interested in elevating art into an integral part of the new German state, or in being a patron of artists. Wagner's dream of forging the "holy trinity" and providing free concerts to the people never materialized. He received neither state funds, nor support from "bourgeois intellectuals." In his subsequent frustration, he considered immigrating to America. The failure of the government and the elites to underwrite his musical dramas signified for Wagner their decadence and moral collapse. Bitterness toward Bismarck reanimated other old hatreds and dovetailed with the growing, new biologically based, anti-Semitism. For his part, in keeping with the spirit of realpolitik, Bismarck would only act if German national interests were at stake. In 1888 only five years after Wagner's death, Bismarck did offer financial assistance to Bayreuth at the request of Cosima, because he was concerned about maintaining loyalty to the national state and the goodwill of Bavarians.

After Wagner's death his widow Cosima, who had been a paragon of devotion to her older husband, set out to preserve his legacy. She proclaimed herself as the authoritative keeper of the Wagnerian shrine. She believed that Wagner's music dramas, especially his epic masterpiece, the fifteen-hour tetralogy, *Ring*, with its authentic recreation of old Norse and Germanic legends, illustrated how an ancient, stalwart Aryan people who offered the gift of civilization, had been damaged by miscegenation. In his theoretical writings Wagner lashed out at Jews collectively and individually, blaming them for his own misfortunes although he was privately willing to admit some responsibility for what had happened to him. After his death, his intransigent views were trumpeted while his ambivalent positions were expunged from the public record by an increasingly anti-Semitic Cosima. Given that she detected "Jewish revenge" behind any critical press reports while abhorring Jewish faces and beards, it never would have occurred to her that the toxicity in her late husband's theoretical works would diminish his stature.[22] But she was acutely aware that his personal peccadilloes—the creditors he swindled and the friends he exploited, particularly one of his conductors and her former husband, from whom Wagner co-opted his wife—might present awkward difficulties. To prevent this contingency and burnish his posthumous image, she strove to recover all his correspondence, and to burn anything incriminating. Indeed, because she believed that she alone understood her husband's will—she even continued the practice of enlisting Jewish conductors overriding opposition from Bayreuth insiders—Bayreuth became, under her autocratic direction, the quasi-religious Mecca of both the Wagnerian cult and *Volkisch* nationalism.

The beginning of the Wagner cult occurred after the *Festspielhaus* (festival house), specifically designed for performances of the *Ring*, opened in 1876 in the northern Bavarian town of Bayreuth. This venue showcased the musical dramas of Wagner, especially during the annual summer festival. The *Bayreuther Blätter*, its official monthly magazine was distributed to its patrons. Founded in 1878 to provide interpretations and a celebration of Wagner's works, the magazine initially focused on art and philosophy, avoiding politics for its first five years. After Wagner's death, like the festival itself which became a vital centre for the dissemination of *Volkisch* Messianism, the content of the magazine became more overtly political and racist. It subsequently served as an ideological banner on behalf of proto-Nazism and later National Socialism itself until its final issues in 1938. The magazine increasingly published a malodorous bouquet of racist, xenophobic, anti-democratic ravings. According to the historian of the Bayreuth Festival: "It would be difficult to find anywhere in the Western world in the late nineteenth century, even in the darkest quarters of the French right, a publication so poisonous, so hate-filled, so spiritually demented."[23] Wagner had passionately believed that art could ennoble man, yet his art was prostituted for political purposes. The summer musical spectacles, accompanied by the publicists' paraphernalia, were yoked to the political indoctrination of the social elite.

Doubling and Mirroring in the *Ring*

Whether Wagner's deeply felt antipathy for Jews infused and found endorsement in his music dramas has been a hotly contested issue among scholars. Some have argued that Wagner's pernicious anti-Semitism infected and imbued them with the spirit of proto-Nazism through the inclusion of Jewish negative stereotypes. One scholar has suggested that the "hooknosed dwarf Alberich who renounced love and beauty out of greed for gold, [became] the symbol of antinatural, antispiritual Jew."[24] By contrast, the heroic qualities of the Volsungs are exemplified by the full robust voice of the racially pure, guileless, albeit easily duped, Siegfried. The premise behind this argument is that the *Ring* is an anti-Semitic allegory in which the Nibelung, a race of dwarves, represents the malignant, contaminated *other* whose very existence threatens the more ennobling human Volsungs and the gods. By treating Wagner's musical dramas as essentially plays that are sung with no musical intrinsic value, Paul Lawrence Rose dismisses the music as "a distillate of Wagner's own personality" permeated with "shameful cruelty and hatred."[25] To assess the aesthetic worth of an artist's creations based on his personality and prejudices is reductive. His single-minded attempt to collapse anti-Semitic history, Wagner's polemics and art into genocide strips away all ambiguities and nuances. If the music was nothing more than the expression of "violent hatred," it would not have been taken seriously. Rose's flawed treatment of Wagner is amplified by Joachim Kohler in his provocatively titled, *Wagner's Hitler*, in which he argues that Wagner was the primary inspiration for Hitler's ideas and program of genocide. Similarly, albeit with an appreciation of the musical dramas, Marc A. Wiener attempts to demonstrate how Wagner's racial theories are integrated into his artistic works. He argues that his repellent views are expressed through bodily form, gesture and in the music. He plausibly links Wagner's belief that Jewish artists were only capable of imitative art and the smithery of Mime—as his name implies—he is skilled only at copying whereas it took an artist like Siegfried to reforge the superior sword "Nothung." Ultimately, he fails to provide persuasive evidence for his assertion that audiences "would have been sensitive and receptive to the racist implications of Wagner's material." True, during the Nazi era, the directors at Bayreuth did portray Mime and Alberich as *Untermenschen* (subhuman), but their interpretation is not reflective of evidence of Wagner's intentions.[26] That Wagner transposed his political and racial views into his art is troubling but it does not convince; it is too one-dimensional and speculative.

Regardless, these views have enjoyed a long pedigree expressed both in a more crude ideological manner by Nazi apologists and insightfully by Wagner's critics in the 1930s. Revisionist biographers selectively cited from Wagner's writings and his life to demonstrate that he was an avatar of the Third Reich even suggesting that he should be posthumously inducted into the Party. At the same time, the avowedly anti Nazi, exiled German philosopher, Theodor W. Adorno, in 1937–38 was appalled by the anti-Semitism not only in his prose but in selected art works. As he memorably phrased it, "all the rejects of Wagner's works are caricatures of Jews."[27]

The alternative and more persuasive interpretation is that the differences among the gods, dwarves and human beings are more apparent than real. Rather than the *Ring* endorsing a racial hierarchy, its flawed characters double and mirror each other and are not exemplifiers of hoary cultural stereotypes or any modish pseudo-scientific racial traits. If the Nibelung are Jews, they are portrayed "as pathetically downtrodden workers, the very image of the misery for which Jewish capitalism is responsible."[28] If the tyrannical "sulphurous dwarf,"—in the words of one of the Rhinemaidens—Alberich, represents inferior racial stock, it is he who mercilessly uses slave labour and forces Wotan, the king of the race of gods, into unsavoury deals that undermine the latter's dream of humanizing the world. Alberich's megalomaniacal obsession with power and longing for vengeance are qualities that most resemble those of Hitler. From the outset, Hitler could only view the world and therefore the *Ring* as a conflict between the noble—the dragon-slayer Siegfried—and the base as exemplified by the verminous Nibelungs. This schematic conflict does not operate in the musical drama despite Rose's assertion that Alberich is the "abhorrent Jewish counterpoint of Wotan."[29]

The Romantic motif of the doppelganger is woven throughout *The Ring*. Ostensibly, enemies are the antithesis of each other, but below the surface their similarities emerge. The god, Wotan, bestrides the world from the glittering mountaintop of Valhalla. The power-lusting, cunning Alberich, who dwells in the subterranean depths, *appears* to serve as a foil for him. Wotan's authority "to rule the world" is supposedly based on the rule of law for benevolent ends while Alberich craves untrammelled power. Yet although Wotan claims to operate through consent, we are informed that the corruption of power set in even before the musical drama began when Wotan fashioned his spear from the once "lush and thick" world-ash tree's sacred branches which then "withered." This corrosion allows Wagner to portray the different manifestations of power through the sky god and the dwarf; in the libretto, Wotan calls himself "Light Alberich" as opposed to "Black Alberich." Whether Wotan is revealing a moment of self-awareness or self-deceit is open to question.

What is undeniable, however, is that beneath their personas both are covetous, manipulative and treacherous. After the giants seize Wotan's life-sustaining sister-in-law—her golden apples maintain the gods' vitality—as payment for building Valhalla, Wotan enlists his duplicitous minister, Loge, to finagle an alternative payment that would secure her release. Together they kidnap Alberich and demand as a price for his freedom that he surrender the gold, including the ring, which purportedly confers power but in reality wreaks havoc. Craving revenge, the dwarf puts an imprecation on the possessor of the ring; its wearer will find no pleasure from the wealth and will experience sudden death, a curse that drives the narrative of the tetralogy until its suttee-like conclusion. In exchange for his sister-in-law, Wotan offers the giants the booty of the Rhinemaidens, reluctantly including the ring. Despite previously witnessing a demonstration of the curse's power, notwithstanding his contract with the three Rhinemaidens that he would never acquire the gold, Wotan calculates how to keep the ring from Alberich.

His capacity for ruthlessness and mendacity aside, Wotan is a more complex character. He admits that he has been "heedlessly deceitful" when he violated his own conviction that honouring contracts provides the order essential to tame the world in its Hobbesian malevolence, spite and brutishness.[30] He is internally torn between love that confers a meaningful life and the need to maintain the laws and contracts that ensure social order. At one point, he attempts to replace the rule of law with the rule of love, but sadly recognizes that he would have no basis for ensuring that others obeyed him. Wotan reluctantly approves the death of his mortal son, Siegmund, in order to honour the marriage contract after Siegmund has absconded with another man's wife. Their union also violates the law against incest as the couple are twins separated at an early age. Wotan understands that his son is not a free agent but a proxy for the gods, an instrument of his will. If Siegmund were allowed to live out his life with his wife, Sieglinde, it will besmirch his own reputation as the upholder of contracts and bargains and undermine the foundation of his power.

Alberich is more one-dimensional, avaricious and obsessed with world domination. Unwilling to acknowledge the rule of law, he steals the gold from the Rhinemaidens; as he later says to Wotan, "the law of the jungle" is the only law. His theft which darkens the Rhine mirrors Wotan's blight upon nature when he sullied the ash tree. During Alberich's failed attempt to seduce one of the cavorting Rhinemaidens, they reveal to him that only one who renounces love can acquire the gold: a condition that he willingly accepts in order to possess the wealth and power that rivals that of the gods. His unabashed greed drives him to become a merciless tyrant who enslaves his fellow dwarves, coercing them with a whip, day and night, so that they can fashion more treasures from the gold. He can without any misgivings gloat over the death of his brother, Mime, because an obstacle has been removed in his quest for the ring.

In the first two musical dramas, *Das Rheingold* and *Die Walkure*, Wotan is willing to finagle his power base through squalid arrangements that he professes to despise; by *Siegfried* he has shed his illusions. Schopenhauer's concept of the denial of the will is clearly evident in Wotan's quasi-Buddhist detachment—"Let what I have built/ fall apart/ I renounce my work"—in atonement for his ruthless greed. He appears resigned to his death and the disappearance of the race of the gods. Acting more like a comrade-in-arms than an avowed enemy, he encounters Alberich outside the lair of the giant Fafner. He advises Alberich on the difficulties of acquiring the treasure to the point of ironically offering assistance. Despite their apparent differences, Wagner reinforces the idea that one is the double of the other: musically the leitmotif associated with the building of his fortress Valhalla, from which the deceitful and corrupt Wotan could maintain order, and the motif associated with the ring forged by Alberich to rule the world, has the same musical chord sequence.

The apparent contrast between the heroic Siegfried and the double-dealing dwarf, Mime, also dissolve under examination. Consistent with the importance of authenticity and the value Romanticism placed on resoluteness and vitality, Wagner insisted that care be exercised on stage to ensure that the archetypes never slip into stereotypes, commenting that despite his ugliness, he "felt every sympathy for Alberich" and that there "must be nothing approaching caricature" in his browbeaten brother Mime.[31] Regardless, some historians cite Wagner's schematic polarity between the dark dwarf and the blond proto-German hero as being stereotypical caricatures of German and Jew that influenced Hitler. For example, Joachim Köhler contends:

> The vicious caricature of Mime, through which Wagner set out to make the racial characteristics of the Jew perversely explicit, was accepted by his disciple in Landsberg (where Hitler served his prison term for his abortive *putsch*) at face value. To him the 'unclean and shameless' Jews lived in the filth and grime of the squalid Nibelung hovels like those he had seen in performances of the *Ring* in Vienna.

According to Köhler, Hitler regarded the cunning Mime as a personification of everything he hated about Jews: "They pretend to be respectable, even amiable citizens but are merely concealing their sordid selfishness, and no trick is too shabby for them to play in their pursuit of their secret aim."[32] Even Owen Lee, one of Wagner's most sympathetic critics, suggests that Siegfried's killing of Mime represents the most distasteful, anti-Semitic moment in the Ring despite Mime's intention to murder Siegfried.[33] A case for self defence seems much stronger.

The insidious Mime is a complex character: already abused by his older brother and filled with frustration, he incessantly whines about ingratitude and refuses to explain to Siegfried the adolescent's origins. It is not surprising that Siegfried prefers to spend his time with the beasts of the forest rather than with his hapless guardian. Mime has raised the orphan Siegfried in primitive isolation without any civilizing influences, as he promised the infant's mother, Sieglinde, who died in childbirth. His motive, however, is base. He believes that one day he will recover the ring and the gold for himself by seducing the young warrior into slaying the giant Fafner who has transformed himself into a dragon that guards the treasure. Wagner's portrayal of a shambling dwarf intent on acquiring power and wealth allowed audiences to see Mime as a trope for Jews. But did they? Cosima's diaries, which contained detailed comments on this musical drama, make no reference to the Jewish subtext. Surely, it strengthens the case that her husband attempted, even if he did not entirely succeed, to keep his anti-Semitic obsession out of his art.

Similarly, Siegfried is not an inspiring character. His crude adolescent pranks are by turns brash and belligerent as he bullies and manhandles the nerdish Mime. The hero of the myth is endowed with authentic courage. He enters into battle as an underdog and overcomes his fears. As a child of nature, Siegfried never learned to fear. He appears invulnerable, and with his invincible sword, slays the dragon without appreciating the risk he is taking. When the dragon's hot blood spills into his mouth, its taste momentarily unleashes his intuitive power. He understands the warbling of the Forest Bird that serves as his inner voice. The bird warns him of Mime's sinister intent. It enables him to distinguish between the fawning language of love (expressed mainly in the music) and his guardian's murderous thoughts (expressed mainly in the libretto) as Mime offers him a sleeping potion after which he plans to behead him. The ingestion of blood also releases in Siegfried a blood-lust that leads to his killing Mime, albeit followed by a pang of regret since the act leaves him alone. If Siegfried's attitude toward Mime did reflect Wagner's attitude toward Jews as critics have suggested, Siegfried's brutish behaviour is less heroic and more indicative of the proto-fascist superman: an impulsive man of action who "thinks with his blood," living only for the present.

Wagner's deployment of the doppelganger to reveal different facets of the same personality can extend to the artist himself. If "it is possible to see the various characters of the *Ring* as multifarious aspects of a single personality"—that being the artist's personality, it follows that the different characters Wagner dramatized on stage possessed attributes of his own character, whether he was aware of it or not. If "the Jew in the mirror was the negative image of an unfulfilled personality," one expects to recognize similarities between the composer and the dwarf Mime.[34] On a physical level, with his "oversized head perched on a small excitable body," the antithesis of the heroic Nordic Siegfried, Wagner resembles Mime. When Wagner complained that Jews were beset with a "prickling unrest" and lacked a "noble calm," he could be expressing dissatisfaction with his own hyperactive personality. If the character of Mime was designed to suggest Philistine materialism, it was no secret that Wagner coveted wealth and frequently indulged himself. And the dwarf's penchant for scheming demonstrates the "virtuoso's arsenal of techniques for flattery and dissimulation."[35] Moreover, given Wagner's outbursts of anger and tears stemming from feelings of impotence or artistic insecurity, it is plausible that the race of Nibelung, especially Mime, who constantly bemoans his fate, could symbolize an obstacle to personal growth. It is tempting yet speculative to characterize the outcast Nibelung as Wagner's own double.

Wagner craved recognition and artistic power. Endowed with a megalomaniac temperament, his passion to dominate everyone around him was a force of nature. As the diaries of Cosima reveal, he expressed a fierce hostility toward anyone who frustrated him.[36] Those who resisted his vampiric compulsion to sponge off friends or patrons incurred his enmity. With the possible exception of his immediate family, who still had to subordinate their needs to his monomaniacal compulsions, he could feel benevolent only toward those who were completely subservient to him and who gave him unqualified approval. From the diaries, the reader can imagine Cosima sitting at the Master's feet, being a selfless handmaiden for his portentous pronouncements, and in total agreement, recording them in order to fulfil one of her roles—the amanuensis of his life. His sentiments reveal a fanatical reservoir of hatred that was targeted against a gallery of real and imaginary enemies. But his rants did not constitute the complete Wagner. Otherwise, he could not have composed some of the most marvellous music ever written. Mining his own unconscious, Wagner plumbed some of the darker aspects of his psyche and sublimated them into his art.

The Jewish-born Gustave Mahler recognized Wagner's genius. He even incurred the admiration of the young Hitler for his "perfection" in conducting Wagner's operatic works in Vienna. Mahler believed that Wagner intended to malign Jews, both musically and textually in his (Wagner's) portrayal of the kvetching Mime, but, according to Mahler, "for God's sake, it must not be exaggerated and overdone." He tellingly adds that "it would be pure lunacy" to incite the Viennese audience, a remark that suggests both that traces of Wagner's anti-Semitism may have spilled into the work, albeit peripherally, *and* that Mahler had no illusions about the anti-Semitism of the Germanic peoples.[37]

The Meaning of the *Ring*

The *Ring* is the largest operatic work of art in the Western repertoire. It took twenty-six years to complete and is rich in psychological depth. Its central idea—the conflict between power and love—is seamlessly interwoven into the music and the libretto. Hitler would have been indifferent to the psychological complexity of this magisterial work of art, particularly the idea of the doppelganger. Passionate about architecture, he was fascinated by the stage designs. He was also interested in the performances and most of all he derived a visceral emotional resonance from the heroics: Siegfried's slaying of the dragon, the pageantry surrounding the death of Siegfried, and Brünnhilde riding into the fire that will consume a polluted world and incinerate the gods.

Hitler's admiration for Siegfried notwithstanding, the dragon slayer possesses little capacity for acquiring insight except in the moments just before his death. Gauche and naïve to a fault, Siegfried is an easy mark for the machinations of Hagen. He explains to Siegfried the power of the Tarnhelm, the ring's companion device that enables the wearer to change his form and instantly transport anywhere. Having quaffed a magic potion that erases his memory of his relationship with Brünnhilde, Siegfried dons the helmet and morphs into Gunter, his recently acquired blood brother, who desires Brünnhilde as his wife. In the guise of Gunter as a night intruder, Siegfried forcibly retrieves the ring that he had previously given her as a symbol of his love. The potion appears to be an artificial device inserted by Wagner to further the narrative. Nonetheless, it has been persuasively argued that Siegfried's lack of inner strength and maturity rendered him easily susceptible to outside corrupting influences and that he would have had difficulty sustaining an exclusive erotic relationship. The potion merely accelerated that which would have occurred anyway.[38] Despite the frequent references in the music and by other characters to his purported heroism, he casts a pale shadow when compared to the strength of character of his father Siegmund, who was willing to forgo the joys of immortal life in Valhalla for the sake of his love, the "tired and sorrowful" Sieglinde.

The exploration of the human condition and the emergence of consciousness became the overriding, if unconscious, goal of Wagner's art. If Siegfried is a callow rube, Brünnhilde grows in stature from a fierce Valkyrie warrior devoted to her father Wotan, to a vulnerable woman capable of a wide range of experiences that culminates in the acquisition of wisdom and authority. When moved by Siegmund's love for Sieglinde to disobey Wotan's command that Siegmund be killed, she is intuitively honouring her father's deepest wishes, as he, after venting his anger, acknowledges. When she loses her divine Valkyrie status as punishment and is awakened by Siegfried, she struggles as a mortal woman with the diminution of her powers, including her intuitive wisdom, but is awakened to the possibility of erotic love. Driven to fury when to all appearances Siegfried has profaned their love, she is complicit in his murder by revealing to Hagen Siegfried's only vulnerability. In her rage, she reprises Siegfried's earlier susceptibility to the sinister Hagen. Yet on seeing the murdered body of Siegfried, Brünnhilde assumes authority over the chaos around her, realizing that private ecstasy has no place in a debased world. She removes from his finger the ring that had earlier symbolized for her enduring love, one so unsullied (or so she believed at the time) that she resisted the blandishments of her Valkyrie sister to return it to the Rhinemaidens and possibly save Wotan and the gods from extinction. With circumstances radically different, she recognizes the need for reconciliation between nature and society and that the ring be returned to its rightful owners. In an act of affirmation and a renewal of her love for Siegfried, she commands that a funeral pyre be built for him and ignited. As the flames consume the hall, they billow upward to Valhalla, where under Wotan's command a fire that destroys the fortress is lit. Originally, Wagner intended that the ending should be a paean to love and its redemptive power. As finally dramatized, Brünnhilde's sacrificial act can be interpreted as merely being the instrument of Wotan's will (again) to purge a world of intrigue and deceit. Yet she recognizes that only in its destruction can she honour her father's wishes, and vindicate her own life and her love for Siegfried.[39]

Wagner contended that ancestral myths were the repository of truths about humanity that remain fluid. Disillusioned with politics as the means to resolve human problems, he looked to myths as a vehicle to portray the complexities of life. The *Ring* tetralogy is a cosmic drama that evolves from the primeval innocence at the beginning to the destruction of a benighted world ending with a return to primeval innocence. Corruption metastasizes from the first wrong-doing: Wotan's exploitation of the natural world. The ensuing events, set in motion in *The Rhinegold*, destroy the tissues that bind succeeding generations. Although Wotan holds the instruments of coercive power to enforce the world's rules, he is contaminated by his unscrupulous actions and, in due time, recognizes his own destructive impulses, his guilt and the limitations of his power. In the end, Wotan comprehends that the world of the gods and humans must be destroyed if there is to be a transformation. The *Ring* is Wagner's meditation on the decline of Western civilization. Yet the final moments of the orchestral score reveal him to be a cautious optimist. The fire and flood that wipe the slate clean, including the petty Gibichungs, re-establish the primordial state of natural and human simplicity with the potential for renewal.

The *Ring* offers a commentary on modern life with its corruption of human relationships along with its hopes for a better world. When the Scottish Opera Company performed the full cycle at the 2003 Edinburgh Festival under Tim Albery's stage direction, it stripped away much of the mythological trappings to present a thrilling rendition in modern dress that focused on human interaction. An urban concrete jungle—seedy hotel rooms, flophouses, a kitschy nightclub and a sleek high-rise apartment—replaces Wagner's romantic forests. Even Valhalla is transformed into a precarious skyscraper. One of the most memorable scenes occurs when Siegfried, looking out of place in a shirt and tie, appears at a modish plush apartment belonging to the oleaginous but insecure Günter, the social-climbing ruler of the supposedly nobler Gibichungs. His half-brother, Hagen, provides Siegfried with an aphrodisiac that arouses his sexual feelings toward Gunter's sister, Gutrune. Later during the hunt, Hagen offers the unsuspecting Siegfried another drink that restores his memory of loving Brünnhilde: hearing this, the others assume Siegfried knowingly betrayed her, which to their minds justifies Hagen's decision to stab him in the back. These vignettes have universal resonance and illustrate what Alex Ross contends is the significance of Wagner for our times, that myth is a "magnifying mirror for the average, desperate modern soul."[40]

Wagner and the Third Reich

In his art, Wagner ponders a question with which the Romantics wrestled: whether human beings can find a better way to relate; creating social harmony that precludes the need for external authority. Little could he have imagined that his dream of "social harmony," his utopian vision of a just new world, would descend into a nightmarish dystopian reality. Indeed, it would be engineered ironically by one of his most passionate admirers, who acknowledged in 1924 that the Master had "forged the sword" with which the National Socialists fought. In our time, the great-grandson of the composer, Gottfried Wagner believes that a strong connection exists between Wagner's anti-Semitism and the Holocaust and has speculated that the style of Hitler's *Mein Kampf* was consciously Wagnerian. Alex Ross tested this hypothesis and did find similarities in style. Conceding that certain phrases circulated throughout anti-Semitic literature, he concludes "it is likely that Hitler first encountered them in his youthful study of Wagner's writings."[41] Yet Hitler only displayed an enthusiasm for his music and never mined Wagner's biography or his theoretical works to justify his hatred of or to legitimatize Nazi policy toward the Jews. Any careful reading of them would reveal too much equivocation and ambivalence on the Jewish question. The Master had Jewish friends and conversion was always an option, and both were anathema to Hitler.[42]

That did not stop Nazi ideologues from misappropriating both Nietzsche and Wagner to bolster their agendas. When Nietzsche succumbed to madness in his last ten years, his sister Elizabeth, whom he had dismissed as a "vengeful anti-Semitic goose," reconfigured her brother's ambiguous beliefs to conform to her own racist and nationalist sentiments. She wrote a self-serving biography and re-edited his *Will to Power* to package him as a nationalist, proto-Fascist visionary.[43] A measure of her success was that in her dotage she became a sort of dowager empress to the Nazi movement. To gain an intellectual pedigree for his movement, Hitler visited her for the purpose of being photographed before the bust of a resolute Nietzsche. Later, with his photographer present, he attended Elizabeth's funeral in 1935. Likewise, it was easier for the Nazis to exploit for propaganda purposes the anti-Semitism in Wagner's prose, often accompanied by his music. His writings,

In his 1942 Wagner, *Arthur Szyk places the composer at the piano creating Wotan, who is emblematic of the forces of destruction epitomized by the Nazis and their allies. Because of Wagner's well-known anti-Semitism and Szyk's background as an American of Polish-Jewish descent with family members who perished in the Shoah, his view is understandable. This is a not uncommon but questionable perspective.*

which included a desire for a ban on any public expression of the Jewish religion and a recommendation for their expulsion from Germany, signified how a selective reading of his most racist and xenophobic prose could be effectively utilized. They were insidiously incorporated into the battering ram of hate, the 1940 film, *The Eternal Jew*, in which he is quoted as stating that "the Jew was a demon who was behind the corruption of mankind."

None of this manipulation of Wagner's work should obscure the fact that, of the Nazis, only Hitler cherished Wagner's music; the paladins around him were almost uniformly hostile to Wagner, preferring Beethoven. Unsurprisingly, since its central message was one of compassion, *Parsifal* was condemned as "ideologically unacceptable" while the Nazi potentate, Rosenberg, condemned the *Ring* as neither heroic nor Germanic. He understood better than Hitler that the *Ring* is not a celebration of power, but a commentary on how greed and corruption inevitably destroy the world of the gods. By 1942 there were no further productions of it during the Third Reich: the Nazis correctly intuited that a grand epic about the crumbling of power structures could foreshadow their own demise. As Heinz Tietjen, the general manager at Bayreuth during the Nazi era—and who made himself invisible whenever Hitler appeared—remembered after the war:

> Germany believed and believes still in a 'Hitler Bayreuth'
> that never was. The Party tolerated Hitler's enthusiasm, but
> fought, openly or covertly, those who, like me, were devoted to his works—the people around Rosenberg openly, those
> around Goebbels covertly.[44]

Official opposition to Wagner reflected public opinion. German audiences during the Reich did not find his music accessible, fewer of his musical dramas were staged and the Hitler Youth movement shunned his music. Songs glorifying Hitler were a vastly more popular vehicle for civic engagement.

Wagner would have vehemently opposed a police state that misappropriated, for its zealous ideological purposes, his *Die Meistersinger von Nürnberg* (*The Mastersingers of Nuremberg*): it was intended as a celebration of a self-governing city in old Germany. In a lengthy radio address, Joseph Goebbels, the Minister of Propaganda, seized upon the final scene of *The Mastersingers*, misquoting lines from the final chorus, to promote his strident nationalistic message, declaring the work to be "the incarnation of our nationhood." The writer Thomas Mann was disturbed by this politicization and considered it "nothing but demagogy" to wrench Wagner's libretto out of context and "ascribe [to it] a contemporary meaning.[45] The decision to perform selections or the entire work at rituals like torch-light parades and the Nuremberg rallies from 1935 further illustrates Mann's misgivings.

If Hitler's imagination had grasped the ideas presented in the *Ring*, he might have entertained second thoughts about giving free rein to his insatiable will to power. If anything, the musical drama is a devastating critique of the true nature of power, showing it to be counterproductive to the life of true feeling and the strength of love. In an act of life mirroring art, like the final conflagration in *Götterdämmerung* (*Twilight of the Gods*), during the final days of the Third Reich, Hitler ordered a scorched-earth policy to destroy the entire infrastructure of Germany. Given his fascination for fire—according to Goebbels, he was "deeply impressed by photos of London burning"—it is fitting that the self-immolation of Brünnhilde in the final scene from the *Ring* was among Hitler's favourites. According to the composer's daughter-in-law, Winifred Wagner, Hitler wanted to hear only *Twilight of the Gods* in the final years of the war. He preferred a nation of sacrificial victims to one of surrender and would have been happy to see the entire German people die with him on his self-made pyre. Shortly before becoming chancellor, he reportedly said, if defeated, "we shall never capitulate—no never....We may be defeated, but if we are, we shall drag the world with us—a world in flames."[46] The credit for Germany not being consumed by an apocalyptic conflagration belongs to the architect, Albert Speer, Hitler's protégé, and by then his Minister of Armaments who loathed a self-destructive spectacle. No longer willing to submit to Hitler's spell, he daringly contravened the Führer's orders, but only after he had ingratiated himself with Hitler. Since he had designed Germania, the Führer's Valhalla, Speer was the only member of Hitler's entourage who could have circumvented his authority without incurring his rage and provoking accusations of treason.

Both Hitler's volcanic rages and pathetic self-pity are brilliantly conveyed by the Swiss-German actor, Bruno Ganz, in the 2005 German film, *The Downfall*. It charts the last days of the Führer barricaded inside the transitional world of the Bunker, what Speer in his memoir fittingly dubbed the "Isle of the Departed," beneath Berlin, while the final battle with the Red Army was raging above. Through his shambolic physical mannerisms, hunched over with his injured left hand fluttering behind his back—David Denby describes him as "a would-be Siegfried who has collapsed into Alberich"—Ganz exudes Hitler's deformed fantasies and a psychotic disconnection from the devastation on the ground.[47] He contemptuously dismisses the German people as unworthy of life because they have lost the war, screams at generals for lying and betraying him, and after hearing of the defections of Herman Goring and Heinrich Himmler, he demands their immediate executions. But he tearfully laments Speer's refusal to obey his order to destroy Germany's infrastructure and stay with him to the end. Life may be a refraction of art but not always a reflection: the last concert of the Third Reich, performed on April 12, 1945 as Russian tanks pulverized Berlin shifting its landmarks under the dunes of rubble, was the conclusion to *Twilight of the Gods*.

Wagner's intention to demonstrate the transcendental power of German art would remain long after its political and military power faded into mist. He explicitly stated that "true art is the highest freedom, and only the highest freedom can bring her forth from out herself."[48] Wagner still harboured few illusions. He wrote as early as 1854 that "the world was evil....It belonged to Alberich," and it is the dwarf's spirit of vengeance that percolates in the latent civil war of the Weimar years and surfaces in 1933.[49] Had Wagner lived into the 1930s, it is unlikely he would have exalted a regime that regimented the arts and prescribed thought, given that he despised Bismarck as a tyrant akin to Robespierre. Regardless, Wagner was surely right on one score: that art would outlast politics. Hitler and the Third Reich have been relegated to the dustbins of history yet the art of Wagner thrives in opera houses throughout the world.

Coda: Bayreuth Fantasies

During the Weimar years (1918–1933), the ultra-nationalists at Bayreuth looked for a saviour who would rescue the festival from financial near-ruin and Germany from chaos. Their search helped to launch Hitler into politics. Virtually unknown, he needed connections and respectability beyond the uncouth lot of his fellow ex-veterans and the rest of the motley crew that joined his fledgling Nazi Party. Deeply misguided, infatuated and credulous, Wagner's family supported him with emotional support in his time of crisis, which Hitler never forgot.

Siegfried, Richard and Cosima Wagner's only son, a prolific yet mediocre composer and conductor, presided over the second generation of the Wagnerian dynasty. As a conservative nationalist, he dismissed Weimar as weak and chaotic, he agreed on the need "for a strong man to take charge." Believing that Germany was wedged between a decadent West and an aggressive Soviet power, the Bayreuth circle placed their hopes in some form of radical German nationalism. He was a rapturous devotee of the young Hitler: at the time of the 1923 *putsch*, he wrote, "Thank God there were still German men."[50] Within a couple of years, he distanced himself from the *Volkisch* ferocious anti-Semitism of National Socialism, recognizing that Jews were stalwart supporters of the Festival. He also cooled to Hitler, annoyed that the future "saviour of Germany" was usurping his own family position. Siegfried increasingly feared the growing influence of the brown-shirted movement. He resented the intrusion of ideology into aesthetics and the subordination of art to politics when, for example, the *Festspielhaus* itself became the site of demonstrations and the meeting place of, at that time, the illegal National Socialist Party. When the Bayreuth Festival reopened in 1924, the first since the beginning of the war, with a performance of *The Mastersingers of Nuremberg*, politics invaded art. In the final scene when the generous cobbler, Hans Sachs, proclaims the virtues of holy German art and the audience leapt to its feet, enthusiastically singing three verses from the national anthem, *Deutschland über Alles*, traditional Wagnerians, including Siegfried, were displeased. Furthermore, Siegfried recruited talented Jewish artists for the festival much to the chagrin of Hitler who witnessed "racial desecration" when a Jew performed the role of Wotan in the *Ring*.[51]

In contrast, Siegfried's ambitious wife, Winifred, the newest and soon to be the most influential member of the Wagner clan was thrilled when aesthetics and politics melded. This allowed her to live in a fantasy realm, one for whom her personal history had made her particularly vulnerable. Raised in an emotionally arid British orphanage from her second to her ninth year, Winifred Williams was adopted by a German couple—she a distant relative of Winifred's English mother and he an aging pianist, a former student of Liszt and a devotee of Wagner. They provided her with a sense of belonging that she had never experienced before and sparked in her a love for Wagner's music. At seventeen she met Siegfried at Bayreuth and a year later she was married to him, her senior by over twenty years, in effect repeating the pattern of his parents' marriage. As the newcomer into this coterie, she learned to negotiate the tangled emotional pathways to the increasingly frail and reclusive matriarch, Cosima, who insisted that parts of the house remain exactly as they had been from the moment Richard had died in 1883. Moreover, she endured slights from her venomous sisters-in-law who resented her very existence. She consolidated her position, however, by presenting Siegfried with four children, thereby marginalizing her in-laws and ensconcing herself as the "saviour of the dynasty."[52] But she never forgot the early humiliations she experienced at the hands of her arrogant relations—painful encounters, that would have reawakened earlier memories and reinforced the emotional armour that had insulated her as an eighteen-year-old Cinderella and as an orphan. She was largely left to fend for herself, given Siegfried's avoidance of confrontation, his penchant for working in his bachelor cottage during the day and his predilection for indulging his homosexual proclivities. Yet she was either wilfully blind or unconcerned since her compensation was being married to the son of the Master. One indication of her indifference toward her husband may be gleaned from Goebbels, who regarded Siegfried as spineless. In a diary entry about a dinner party at Wahnfried in 1926, he noted: "She put her sorrows to me. Siegfried is so limp."[53] Whether she was talking about his milquetoast temperament or sexuality is unclear. She recognized that her adopted country had become a sanctuary for her, and like him she longed for a knight, not an elderly, distant husband. When she met Hitler in Bayreuth in 1923, she intuitively realized that she had found her saviour. She was fanatically attracted to him and invited him to come the next day to Wahnfried.

Hitler's pilgrimage to the Wagnerian dynasty home permitted him to strengthen his ties with the coterie of Wagner's devotees. After meeting Cosima, he was given the grand tour of the sacred halls and grounds of the place that included the ultimate shrine, Wagner's gravesite. There, with tears in his eyes, he pronounced the composer the greatest German of all time, identifying his own early struggles with the adversity experienced by Wagner. He could also relate to the heroics of the Teutonic knight Lohengrin and the Roman tribune in *Rienzi* who sought to restore the Empire to its earlier unsullied values. The choreography of the serried ranks of triumphant marchers on stage in *Rienzi* provided Hitler with the model that he transplanted to the open-air arena at the annual Nuremberg rallies.[54] Equally important was the powerful alliance and dalliance that he established with Winifred, who perceived him to be a kindred spirit, an outsider who needed salvation as much as she had. The redeeming role of the woman, which had been inculcated in her as part of her Wagnerian upbringing, was reflected in the nickname, Senta, given her by her stepfather after the heroine who attempts that task in *The Flying Dutchman*, became her part after she met Hitler. Once she inhabited that persona, she could live out the fantasy convinced that Hitler was "rescuing Germany and Bayreuth from the powers of darkness, from the Bolsheviks and the old Wagnerians."[55] Because decorum made sexual fulfilment impossible, even after her husband's death, Winifred sublimated desire into a "heroically idealized 'loyalty' and 'unbreakable friendship.' " According to her granddaughter, Nike Wagner:

> The fact that Winifred still raved about Hitler's blue eyes fifty years after meeting him, and her boast that she would have loved to welcome him as a dear friend if only he could have stepped through her door again, clearly reveals her fixation on Hitler's person: a fixation that went beyond all critical reason and political judgment.[56]

As late as 1975, four years before her death, she reiterated in a five-hour television interview her feelings of affection for Hitler leaving little doubt that she valued loyalty above all else. In the 1920s, the test of her desire to extend the fantasy beyond the confines of Wahnfried was not long in coming.

Five weeks after receiving his benediction from the Wagner family, Hitler, exploiting public anger provoked by the mega-inflation which wiped out savings, launched his abortive *putsch* on Munich. He hoped it would lead to a march on Berlin, much as Mussolini had done in 1922. Its failure, owing to the lack of police and army support, did not deter Winifred, who witnessed the proceedings, from writing an open letter endorsing Hitler. She wrote that he should be commended for his willingness to sacrifice his life "for the ideal of a purified, united Germany" and for having the courage to open the "eyes of the working class to the internal enemy and the danger of Marxism." After the arrest of the *putsch* conspirators, Winifred collected food for the families of these men. As idealism and heroism had been part of her Berlin upbringing, she now believed during the 1920s that they applied not only to Wagnerian drama but to the world around her. In spite of her later rationalization of herself as an "unpolitical person," her attendance at Party meetings, her financial support for the families of arrested *putschists,* and later, her ability to keep the theatre free from Party control, attested to her involvement in politics.[57]

In gratitude, Hitler acted out the role as the gallant knight Lohengrin for her and the Wagner family. After her physically and emotionally absent husband died in 1930, Winifred became the powerful mistress of Wahnfried. She jettisoned the remains of the pre-war cosmopolitan atmosphere at Bayreuth and was able to transform the festival into the cultural flagship of the Third Reich brimming with *Volkisch*, messianic fervour, largely because of Hitler. He saved the festival by conferring upon it money and prestige, and exempted it from taxation that enabled it to continue even during the war years until 1944. That the Bayreuth festival was largely unconstrained by National Socialist control after 1933 depended solely on the personal relationship between Hitler and Winifred, not Nazi forbearance. Unique among cultural institutions after 1933, the festival retained a relative degree of independence—there were no swastikas decorating the auditorium—a mark of Hitler's undiminished affection for Winifred.

On a personal level, she continued to offer Hitler emotional sustenance and maintained the illusion that he belonged to a distinguished family. She encouraged Hitler to visit, to stay at a house on the grounds, to become a surrogate father; he responded by helping to put the children to bed by telling them stories and by allowing them to call him by his nickname Wolf. Whenever he drove from Munich to Berlin, he would stop at Villa Wahnfried, spend the night there, returning in the morning "strangely elated" and even "blissful"* as recorded by Speer giving rise to speculation

---

*   In *Winnie and Wolf* (London: Random House Group, 2007), A. N. Wilson weaves his fictional rendering of Hitler and Winifred Wagner around the conceit that they had a liaison and produced a child. From

that Hitler was having an affair with Winifred.[58] Whatever the exact relationship between Hitler and Winifred, it conferred privileges on the children: when they became bored with the Hitler Youth Movement, they were allowed to quit. Later during the war years, he exempted his favourite "nephew," Wieland, from military service so that he could pursue his musical studies. This is why Winifred said in retrospect that "I will love him with gratitude, because he literally tended the flowerbeds here in Bayreuth and helped me in every way."[59]

Winifred's capacity to maintain an unreconstructed world-view and ignore the consequences of Hitler's speeches and policies resided largely in her ability to perpetuate a fantasy. On the one hand, there was the private world of Wahnfried and the person of Adolf Hitler who was a part of this inner sanctified world. Then there was the outside world of petty politics, the Party, the Streichers who may have done terrible things to the Jews, which might involve the dark side of the Führer, but none of this touched any of the family. This internal split precluded her acquiring any insight that might blemish the reputation of her unique saviour. Whenever evidence of Nazi horror appeared, such as the images of mass carnage at Buchenwald, she dismissed it as American propaganda or as the work of "them." Winifred developed the capacity to provide water-tight compartmentalisations: "And anything that is dark about him, I know that it exists, but for me, it doesn't exist because I don't know that part....That will perhaps remain incomprehensible forever."[60] The price for her myopia was that "Hitler's court theatre," as Thomas Mann aptly phrased it, probably did more to disfigure Wagner's posthumous reputation than the venomous prejudices that the Master had paraded in his lifetime.

---

the vantage point of the early 1960s, his unnamed narrator writes a memoir of that relationship to the adult daughter living in America. Although there is no empirical evidence of an intimate relationship, Wilson tantalizingly suggests that H feared his demons while his doppelganger, Uncle Wolf, found the solace and family affection that he craved enabling him to be a "normal" human being whenever he visited the palatial Wagner home in Bayreuth.

The Culture of Blood Treason

I realize now the whole purpose of my life
has been to bring down that accursed race.

> —*The Prague Cemetery*
> Umberto Eco

The Seminal Absorption Fantasy

The post-war atmosphere in the twenties bristled with sensibilities coarsened by the war and with the inability of Germans to recognize that they had been defeated in the field. When personal frustrations and disappointments coalesced with the collective trauma of military defeat, the irrational personal neurosis fed on and contaminated the body politic to create a psychotic entity. The war hardened the anti-Semitism of Artur Dinter, a now-forgotten writer of racist novels. Stock anti-Semitic stereotypes—the Jewish hunger for money and lust for Aryan women—fuelled his writing. These tropes corroded the minds of Hitler, his alter ego Julius Streicher and his minion Heinrich Himmler who was obsessed with creating a racial aristocracy.

In 1919 Dinter published a crude potboiler, *Sin against the Blood*. It is the story of a young Aryan scientist who, through his personal unhappiness, learns about the so-called laws of race and the diabolical machinations of the Jewish conspiracy. He leaves his first wife, the "polluted" daughter of a Jewish press baron after she gives birth to sons, one of whom is described as "dark-skinned... scarcely human...[with] deep dark eyes...under long dark eyelashes...[and] a squashed flat nose like an ape's." His second wife, a blond, blue-eyed Aryan German gives birth to a child with pronounced Jewish features: "curly black hair, dark skin, dark eyes" simply because years earlier she once slept with a Jewish army officer. The German scientist learns from a "medical friend" that one "crossing" is sufficient to pollute, irredeemably, the blood of an Aryan woman. In desperation, his wife's deepening depression drives her to kill the child and commit suicide. He comes to understand that his tragic circumstances are a punishment for "sinning against the holy blood of his race," and that he is a victim of a larger Jewish conspiracy to pollute the blood of Germans. The protagonist, after killing the Jewish officer who had dishonoured his wife, conducts his own defence. He warns listeners at the trial: "If the German *Volk* does not succeed in shaking off and rendering harmless...the Jewish vampire, which it has unsuspectingly nourished with its heartblood, then it will be destroyed in the foreseeable future." Acquitted, he enlists and is killed on Christmas day 1914, fulfilling his wish "to die for the holy Fatherland."[1] Dinter's phantasmagorical novel voices the murky implications drawn from biology.

Although Dinter does not purport to have written a Gothic novel, his emphasis on the bloodline and its potential to be irreversibly contaminated by a poisoned one surely renders it one. Through genetic impregnation, the Jew's sperm would ensure that the woman would forever transmit his hereditary characteristics to children regardless of the seeds implanted by future men. Most significant about this seminal absorption fantasy is how it attributes awesome power to a Jewish man. By Dinter's logic, the main character's all-embracing zealotry is an act of heroism; he rallies his fellow Germans to destroy the "Jewish vampire [that] was systematically corrupt[ing] and poison[ing] the German Volk."[2]

Dinter's novel resonated with a throng of true believers, steeped in racial purity and a rabid anti-Semitism. In the sulphurous postwar era, amid the confusion of economic and political upheaval, he vividly rendered the horror of racial defilement. The language of parasitology was now used to designate the Jew as no longer human. He was a parasite, who literally lived off his host, the German people and a carrier of infection, germs, bacillus, and microbes, which attack the organism and poison it.[3] One extreme nationalist referred to Jews as explicitly vampiric:

230

> Of course any Jew loves the German people. It draws him
> to itself in its very being, its spiritual nature, the physicality
> of its daughters and sons. He seeks to restore himself with
> blood that is virginal and fresh....What moves us to flee from
> Jewry, no matter how much love we may harbour for individ-
> ual Jews, is the repugnance we feel in the face of degeneracy
> personified.[4]

The phenomenal commercial success of Dinter's novel enabled him to endorse solutions that included restriction of Jewish immigration, exclusion of Jews from the professions and nullification of their equal civil rights—proposals that became official policy during the Third Reich. Dinter's public speaking propelled his meteoric rise in the Nazi movement. He heightened fears about blood contamination, permitting the legitimacy of radical solutions that called for removal, if not extermination, of aliens from within Germany's midst. In doing so, he set the histrionic tone for other more notorious and better known personalities to transmit this dangerous bile to massively larger numbers over the next twenty-five years through the Weimar years and the Third Reich. Nonetheless, his ideological fundamentalism earned him an expulsion from the Nazi Party due to his criticism of Hitler's accommodation with the "Jewish–Roman papal church" even going so far as to characterize the Führer as one of the "traitors" who had embraced the "liberal–bourgeois capitalist front."[5]

Pornographic Obsessions of the Psychic Twins

One of the most odious voices on the extreme nationalist right was the fanatically vociferous Julius Streicher. In 1923 he first published the illustrated weekly *Der Stürmer* based on the policy of fostering a splenetic hatred of the Jews. Possessed of limited intelligence and imagination, the former elementary schoolteacher unashamedly expended through every possible venue his demagogic energy to vilify and demean Jews as the bogeymen to blame for Germany's misfortunes. Until he antagonized powerful grandees within the Party, Streicher flourished both as a rabble-rousing, popular public speaker and as an unscrupulous journalist in drawing a *cordon sanitaire* around Jews as either the reincarnation of the devil or his minions. With no scruples about fabricating or distorting evidence, he published repellent cartoons and demeaning photographs that depicted Jews as short, fat, unshaven and endowed with animal-like facial features. It was not sufficient to malign them as financially dishonest and politically treacherous: they were satanic, ritual child murderers. On May 1, 1934, *Der Stürmer* published its notorious special issue on Jewish ritual killing. On the front page was a grotesque drawing of two hideous-looking Jews, one of them brandishing a bloodstained knife, holding a vessel to collect the blood streaming from the naked bodies of sweet-looking children that they had just murdered. In his extraordinary diaries that span the entire Third Reich, Victor Klemperer, a converted Protestant but defined as a Jew by the Nazis, noted in an entry of March, 1938, that "*Der Stürmer* has dug up its usual ritual murderer." He mordantly added, "I would truly not be surprised if next I would find the body of a child in the garden."[6] Streicher also revelled in using his hate-clotted tabloid, *Der Stürmer*, to attack Jews as lascivious sex offenders who craved the racial pollution of German women and the destruction of their race. It was common to see graphics of a leering, reptilian, "Jewish looking" boss in his private office attempting to defile a blond Aryan maiden.

Streicher also published illustrated children's books; one of the more insidious examples of this genre is *The Poisoned Mushroom* (1938). The storybook begins innocently enough by distinguishing edible from poisonous mushrooms. It soon, however, segues into a malicious portrayal of Jews as the Devil in human form, hideous hook-nosed poisoners. The child learns it is the duty of Germans to save humanity from destruction.

In addition to a pathological hatred, powerful sexual fears motivated Streicher to reduce the racial question for domination of the female sex to a war between Aryan and Jewish men. He outlandishly proposed that Jews celebrated the desecration of Gentile women as a holy act, and that a Jewish wife approved of her husband's actions since his unfaithfulness was "a deed pleasing to God, not adultery." Repeatedly, his broadsheet echoed his friend, Artur Dinter's, fantastical notion by warning that once an Aryan woman bedded with a Jew, it was enough to "poison her blood forever...[that] the Jew employs every device of the seductive art in an attempt to dishonour German girls at the earliest possible age." In language that carries the trademarks of a Gothic novel in which a decent girl is turned into a vampire, Streicher describes her as irreversibly polluted by the "dragon seed." She could never bear

Aryan children and her progeny were inexorably condemned to be bastards and murderers. This contamination would also alter the mother's appearance and character so that she would cease to be German. When the "indescribable glow of sweetness" disappeared and as her speech became "monotonous," she "looked dead and empty," the inexorable sign that her soul "had become Jewish."[7] Besides being repellent, these astonishing sentiments are eerily akin to vampirism as described by one critic: "the vampire's power to make its victim resemble itself is a very real mutation of the once human victim."[8] Streicher even proposed that a drooling predator could seduce vulnerable German women and cause this "mutation." Besides the allurement of money, the Jew in Svengalian-like fashion could hypnotize and captivate women by a mysterious devilish power, that, if need be, could be supplemented by drugs, alcohol or, as a final resort, through violence.

But even a cursory review of Streicher's life demonstrates that *he* was the psychopathic satyr. When he was appointed *Gauleiter* (regional boss) of Franconia (the region around Nuremberg), he amassed sufficient power to intimidate alleged purveyors of degeneration in Germany. He humiliated German girls who had been friendly with Jews by clipping their hair and forced Jewish prisoners to eat befouled grass. Hitler's first biographer perceptively commented that Streicher "ecstatically wallowed in filth and made libertinism his religion."[9] He harboured no illusions that everyone, even some Nazi supporters, would appreciate the racist paranoia that drenched the pages of his salacious gutter rag. Despite criticisms that rained down on him from Nazi paladins, who believed him to be an embarrassment to them both for his outlandishness and his corruption, Streicher was protected by Hitler for many years; he valued Streicher's loyalty, even praising him in *Mein Kampf.* At times through his speeches, Streicher was able to reach audiences that, under other circumstances, might have recoiled in horror or derisively dismissed this coarse brute as a grotesque joke. In private he was a licentious predator and vicious bully who wielded a whip on his enemies. The leering, sexually obsessed Jew that he frequently conjured up was a reflection of his own conduct. All photographs of Streicher, whose squat stature, shaven head and convulsed features epitomize the antithesis of the blue-eyed, blond Nordic specimen, capture the caricatured double of Jews portrayed in his tabloid. He was not impervious to this connection as he allegedly once said "You have to have a good dose of Jewish blood in your veins to hate that race properly."[10] By treating women as sex objects, his description of defiled German women would apply more to *his* victims than to so-called "race polluters."

The image of the Jew—sensual, deceitfully clever, and greedy for power—echoes how chauvinists have traditionally regarded women. Forced to submit to the authoritarian control of their fathers, German sons grew to despise their mothers for their weakness, likely because they failed to protect their sons from their fathers but were forced to repress these feelings. It is theoretically possible that as adults, these men harboured repressed early feelings towards women as they simultaneously desired them, and found in Jews a substitute hate object.[11] Even though we possess little relevant knowledge of his early life, Streicher's behaviour revealed an egregious contempt for women in concert with Jews. Regardless of its psychological source, his malignant hatred gave his life a sense of purpose that was tragically destructive. The effect of his rhetoric was to desensitize his readers to the plight of Jews, whether they participated in an active persecutory role against them or were merely indifferent to their fate. His conservative rural readers would have been more shocked by the obscenities he laced throughout his newspaper than by its racial virulence.

A similar, prurient tone and apocalyptic message of racially defiled women exude from inflammatory passages in *Mein Kampf* when Hitler stoked the fires of racial corruption. His obsessive fixation, from which he never deviated, focused on the preservation of the Aryan race. He remained implacable about racial purity: it was an essential precondition for German greatness. Racial mixing was entirely responsible for the collapse of all past civilizations: "*Blood sin and desecration of the race are the original sin in this world and the end of humanity which surrenders to it.*" When the blood, with its magical properties, was not preserved in its pure form, as evinced by the flood of social ills—syphilis, tuberculosis and hereditary diseases resulting in cripples and cretins—then nature wreaked its vengeance. Because nature "has little love for bastards," it meted out punishment to the *Volk* manifested by Germany's lack of will power and a feeble constitution. In his mind, this miscegenation would inexorably result in the extinction of the

Aryan race and everything that constituted beauty and achievement. Along with former Quartermaster-General Erich Ludendorff, Hitler believed that the *Volk* organism had been infected with the Jewish bacillus. Both employed sexual imagery to describe its assault on the German body: rape, castration and the victim of syphilis. To safeguard the *Volk*, Hitler invoked the gardening metaphor to "prune off the wild shoots and tear out the weeds." [12]

Sexuality in the service of the *Volk* and his manic fear of syphilis developed into obsessions for Hitler. During the 1920s, he seemed to be gripped by the fantastical notion that the precious liquid of blood was being irretrievably diluted and contaminated by Jewish pimps, pornographers and rapists. Whenever he referred to the idea, his diction was permeated with hatred: "Systematically, these black parasites of the nation defile our inexperienced young blond girls and thereby destroy something which can no longer be replaced in this world." In one notorious passage, he launched into an apoplectic fit when he conjured the lurid image of the black-haired Jewish youth lurking for hours "with satanic joy in his face" spying on the "unsuspecting girl whom he defiles with his blood, thus stealing her from her people." Expounding on the importance of physical beauty in young women as the primary basis for dating, he exploded into a hysterical and ugly tirade on "bow-legged, repulsive Jewish bastards," who seduced hundreds of thousands of German girls. The most explicit allusion to the seminal absorption or crossover belief occurred when he reviled the male Jew, who "poisons the blood of others, but preserves his own." When racial treason was committed, "the bastards, however, take after the Jewish side." [13] He was most explicit when he inflamed the fears of his conservative Bavarian audiences toward Jews and whetted their hostility toward that "sinful Babylon Berlin" by pandering to their prurient impulses (something he would accuse the Jews of doing) with his shrill rant on sexual pollution. In one night in Berlin, the epicentre of sexual unshackling and decadence, "Jew-boy after Jew-boy with a German girl on his arm,...thousands and thousands of our blood are annihilated forever in an instant and that child and grandchild are lost to us." As if to demonstrate that the political and economic convulsions endured by Germans after World War were ephemeral to the more pressing apocalyptic danger, he added, "we can break the peace treaty...but once the blood is poisoned it can no longer be changed. It remains and multiplies and presses us lower from year to year." Degeneration could only be reversed if the lascivious Jew paid the ultimate price: "Every Jew who is caught with a blond girl should be...[strung up!"][14]

The majority of his early, embittered audiences who heard Hitler's visceral reductionist message and observed his theatrics responded with delirious pandemonium. But there were exceptions. Although not specifically addressing the theme of sexual defilement, the dramatist Carl Zuckmayer recalls being in small towns of rural Bavaria and remembering the puffed-up pub orator working the beery crowd with his high-pitched demagogy:

> For people like us the man was a howling dervish. But he
> knew how to whip those crowds jammed closely in a dense
> cloud of cigarette smoke and wurst vapours—not by argu-
> ments but by the fanaticism of his manner, the roaring and
> screeching, interlarded with middle-class oratory, and espe-
> cially for the hypnotic power of his repetitions, delivered in
> a certain infectious rhythm. He would draw up a catalogue
> of existing evils and imaginary abuses, and after listing them
> in higher and higher crescendo, he screamed the rhetor-
> ical question into the beer-hall crowd: 'And whose fault is
> it?' following up with the sharply metrical reply: 'It's all/ the
> fault/ of the Jews!' The beer mugs would swiftly take up the
> beat, crashing down on the wooden tables, and thousands of
> voices, shrill and female or beer-bellied basses, repeated the
> imbecilic line for a quarter of a hour.

Zuckmayer concludes that many of Hitler's supporters were crude, limited, pigheaded bumpkins, who believed that Jews and Marxists were "superdiabolical bloodsuckers and monsters as portrayed in the propaganda."[15] His semi-literate followers would be most susceptible to accepting the theory of seminal absorption that Hitler in his early days as a backroom orator was so adept at communicating.

All that Hitler wrote and spoke about the reputed sexual procliv-ities of the Jews was the product of a far deeper motive than polit-ical ambition. Though he might have received crude bombast and vicarious sexual gratification at these meetings, his words were expressions of the lubricous impulses of his own overwrought fan-tasy world; it was simply projected onto the Jews. In an ever-recur-ring nightmare, Hitler dreamed that "the cruelly chained naked Germanic woman is approached by a lurking, black-haired Jewish butcher, while he himself, a cowardly, inhibited, ever-failing St. George does not set the maiden free but leaves her to the 'dragon.' " It may be that the dream provided Hitler with "the rationalization of the hatred and vengeance aroused by such humiliating dreams," but the rhetorical question should be asked: *who* was the "black-haired butcher" who is about to ravage a vulnerable Germany?[16]

Hitler and Julius Streicher in 1938 at Munich during a remembrance for the 1923 attempted putsch. Through his stridently anti-Semitic tabloid, Der Sturmer, *Streicher represented the doppelganger for Hitler when the German dictator felt he needed to tamp down his own virulent views and present himself as a statesman and unifier of the German people.*

Streicher, whose fantasy world was similar to that of the supportive Hitler, squalidly publicized this dream, which reveals the psychic connection between Hitler and his *bête noire*, the Jews. Both men, who prided themselves on their overpowering virility, believed that women yearned for domination by a man. Hitler was never able to develop an intimate relationship with a woman. He appeared to avoid relationships—he proclaimed that he could not wed because he was already married to Germany—and completely dismiss women "[as] only the passive part" of a marriage, an institution that he frequently sentimentalized. His opposition to the "so-called equal rights to women" because "vis-à-vis both man and society...she will necessarily be inferior" reveals not only his paternalism but also his fear of intelligent, independent women. Both men fully endorsed the sentiments of Gottfried Feder, one of Hitler's earliest friends in the German Workers' Party who penned these misogynist lines:

> The Jew has stolen woman as a wife from us....We, the younger generations, have to march forth and slay the dragon, in order that we may win back the holiest thing in the world: the wife who is both servant and slave.[17]

Despite a monkish persona, Hitler indulged his private fantasies by revelling in the sensuous paintings of voluptuous female nudes by the *fin-de-siècle* Munich painter Franz von Stuck. With such provocative titles as *Sin* and *Medusa*, the artist featured femme fatales, feline and predatory, that included women coiled around snakes. Later when Hitler acquired power, he commissioned his favourite contemporary painter, Adolf Ziegler, (known throughout the art world as the Reich master of pubic hair) to paint a series of curvaceous female nudes that included the allegorical kitsch *Judgment of Paris*. The emotional turbulence stirred by the combination of sexuality and his obsessive fear of the "Jewish poisoners,"—"eternal bloodsucker" and "typical parasite,"—remained central to Hitler's anti-Semitism in the 1920s. In his febrile fantasy world, the sexual promiscuity of Jews was responsible for the "Jewish disease—both syphilis and prostitution. That virus caused "civilized peoples [to] degenerate and gradually perish," rendering them vulnerable to the Jewish tyranny of Bolshevism.[18] As Hitler gravitated to the levers of power, he was shrewd enough to push his sexual agitation to the deepest recesses of his mind. In suppressing the pornographic side of his racism, he allowed his doppelganger Streicher to represent "the true, unmasked face of primitive hatred that [he] harboured."[19]

The inflammatory rhetoric that fulminated against "Jewish race polluters" had generally been confined during the 1920s to the underbrush of hardcore Workers' Party zealots. Hitler's belief in blood pollution formed the cornerstone of one of the three 1935 Nuremberg Laws, the "Law for the Protection of German Blood and German Honour." The other two proclaimed the colours of the flag and limited citizenship to people of "Germanic blood." The Nuremberg Laws criminalized intermarriage, forbade extramarital sexual relations between Germans and Jews, "gypsies" and blacks, and denied Aryan women under the age of forty-five the right to be employed in a Jewish household. The seminal absorption theory had mutated into grim, overtly racist, decrees that received widespread support not only from hard-line activists: the general German population, also hoped that the appearance of legality would lance the random intimidation and violence toward Jews in the streets. The vast majority had been opposed to these disorders not for humanitarian reasons but for economic self-interest; they supported the ends of removing Jews from economic life but not the means because it hurt business and they feared international repercussions. Now discrimination and social ostracism acquired more cachet with the imprimatur of legality.

These laws served as the centrepiece of the regime's official race hatred that placed Jews beyond the pale of "Germanness" as they were turned into pariahs. When the philologist, Victor Klemperer, attended a national convention of literary scholars, he lamented that "not one of all my Romance Language colleagues called on me; I am like a plague corpse."[20] Moreover, the laws frequently carried harsh legal consequences, including capital punishment for "racial treason," with no possibility of redress. Even a quietly heroic action could be stigmatized as a criminal offence. When a Jewish physician recognized that his Aryan patient needed a blood transfusion and donated his own blood, the doctor was sent to a concentration camp for defiling the blood of the German race.[21] Judges, influenced by pressure from the Justice Ministry, interpreted the law so broadly that "race defilement" could include any contact, friendly feelings or being by happenstance in the same place at the wrong time. A Jewish man in 1938 was arrested for being on the same elevator as an Aryan woman even though he was already there when she entered. Jewish women could be accused of seducing "innocent German-blooded" sexual partners. In the tradition of the vamped femme fatale, but virulently updated to suggest that she was panting for Germanic sperm, one woman was accused of being a "sex crazed, morally degenerate, Jew-woman, who with her unrestrained sexual desire and ruthless determination had the defendant under her strong influence."[22]

The implementation of official decrees by a compliant judiciary fortified the stereotype of the lustful Jew. They employed the already accepted notion of Jews as sexual predators and combined it in some instances with a dose of misogyny. In the Nazi pornographic imagination, the Aryan revulsion of the sight of the Jewish body conjured the fear of racial defilement. It expressed itself in the immodest behaviour of Jewish women, the sexual harassment of Jewish men, or as portrayed in a 1937 potboiler novel, a sexual assault on an Aryan woman in an open-air swimming pool. In the novel, the victimized woman reinforced the Nazi perception when she exclaims "These Jewish swine are ruining us. They are polluting our blood. And blood is the best and the only thing we have."[23] Although a minor player, Dinter contributed to these fears institutionalized in the Nuremberg laws and the public's perception of Jews as alleged economic pirates and sexual deviants. A much more significant and sinister presence was that of Heinrich Himmler who was convinced that he knew how to counteract the threat of blood pollution.

Himmler's Fantasies

Himmler's creation of a pure-blooded racial aristocracy, the SS, was one of the chief instruments for realizing the vision of racially superior bloodlines. With a passion for power and perhaps a psychological need to compensate for his own physical attributes—plump, a pince-nez set against his almost Mongolian eyes, pasty-faced, sloping-shouldered, broad-bottomed—the former chicken farmer and agronomist, turned human breeder spearheaded its implementation.[24] His disciplined SS elite were the embodiment of glamour kitsch, resplendently outfitted in black uniforms and shining boots. Frequently referred to as a knightly order, they exemplified for Himmler the most recent scions of a long lineage of Germanic nobility based upon blood rather than class.

Unlike the brawling hooliganism associated with the callow youth and occasional-potbellied, embittered veterans of the plebeian SA, Himmler's SS were subjected to stringent racial and eugenic vetting. It was crucial that they met the "objective" criteria of admission standards to this ideologically schooled elite force. An officer was required to demonstrate both an impeccable bloodline that certified his Aryan ancestry back to 1750 and a prepossessing physical specimen; even one filled tooth was enough to prohibit his admission. But a dauntingly clean pedigree and an impressive tall physique were insufficient if the candidate revealed "subjective" failings. Any detritus of countervailing moral codes that had been imbibed from Christian teachings—compassion, humility or softness—required excision if the candidate expected admission into this privileged caste. To help facilitate that process, he was exposed to an SS pamphlet that described the Jew in language that was steeped in the Gothic tradition but actually mirrored the spirit of the very men who absorbed its insidious message:

> From a biological point of view he seems completely normal.
> He has hands and feet and a sort of brain. He has eyes and
> a mouth. But, in fact, he is a completely different creature, a
> horror. He only looks human, with a human face, but his spir-
> it is lower than that of an animal. A terrible chaos runs ram-
> pant in the creature, an awful urge for destruction, primitive
> desires, unparalleled evil, a monster, subhuman.[25]

The ideological indoctrination during the lengthy novitiate involved military and labour service and the acquisition of athletic prowess. In addition, the candidate was expected to exude hardness, ruthlessness, unquestioning allegiance to the order, and a quasi-religious deification to the person of Adolf Hitler. When he fulfilled all the necessary criteria to Himmler's satisfaction, he was initiated into this elite order through a midnight torch-bearing oath-swearing ceremony.[26] Once inducted, the SS member maintained a passionate commitment to his fellow members that surpassed every other relationship. One member writes:

> Even the ties of love between man and a woman are not
> stronger than that same friendship that there was among us.
> This friendship was all. It both gave us strength and held us
> together, in a covenant of blood. It was worth living for; it was
> worth dying for. This was what gave us the physical strength
> and courage to do what others did not dare to do because
> they were too weak.[27]

However intense the camaraderie that existed among the SS members, it was de rigueur of this "new nobility" to continue the bloodline in accordance with Himmler's obsession, the creation of a pure German race. True, male bonding and the exaltation of the virile body, features which were celebrated in the monumental homoerotic sculptures, constituted part of the appeal of the Nazi movement, particularly for the SS. Himmler, however, was also one of the most vehement antagonists of homosexuality within the Party and guarded against homoeroticism collapsing into same-sex relationships by pressuring his men into becoming human breeders. To this end "in the battle for births," the propagation of a large brood was not "the private concern of the individual, but a duty towards our ancestors and *Volk*." Once accepted, (and it was for life) SS members, who wished to marry, required permission from Himmler or one of his most trusted subordinates. A potential bride was carefully screened in order to satisfy racial and genetic requirements before authorization would be granted. SS doctors were entrusted with the responsibility for assuring that she satisfied these criteria through a complete physical examination and by producing the relevant genealogical documents. Any evidence of racial taint or history of physical or mental family difficulties, or anything less than absolute allegiance to Nazi ideology, would disqualify her. If accepted, she could attend "Bride School" where she would be instructed in domestic skills and learn about health and hygiene. Once married (in a pagan ceremony) the couple would strive for a minimum of four children. The bride's highest duty was to conceive and breed thoroughbred Germans before her husband went off to battle, so that if he died, Himmler's dream of creating tall, blue-eyed productive members of the master race could still be realized. That the SS shared his dream is evident from the testimony provided by these men at the conclusion of their courses. One of them wrote about the urgency of being the progenitors of "pure-blooded children" so that they could live on through them, their grandchildren, even their descendants through countless generations: in this way, they could achieve "eternal life."[28]

In his mania for breeding an uncontaminated Aryan race, Himmler believed that his SS men should sire as many offspring as possible, but the Catholic Church's imposition of monogamy impeded that essential goal. In order to bypass the strictures of the Church and bourgeois convention, he encouraged his SS soldiers to fertilize unwed women that were racially and genetically certifiable. Hence the creation of the *Lebensborn* programme (Fount of Life) which operated midway between a maternity home and a health farm as an incubation centre for creating specimens of the master race. As an integral part of the Nazi eugenics vision, unmarried pregnant girls and SS wives could give birth to Aryan children in a healthy environment. Away from the censorious influence of priests, pampered women received the best antenatal and postnatal care available—medical, nutritional and emotional. Himmler fantasized that these women would be honoured as the progenitors of the Thousand-Year Reich, a first step taken in 1937 when unmarried mothers could confer upon themselves the title, "Frau."

Behind this sentimentality, Himmler regarded these women as factory producers for the regime's population policies; their personal happiness was of no consequence. But Himmler's fantasies bore little relationship with reality. The uneasiness about the sanctioning of illegitimacy for both religious and scientific reasons accelerated with the knowledge that approximately half of the twelve thousand children registered in *Lebensborn* homes between 1935 and 1945 were illegitimate. Moreover in a study conducted in 1939, the 115,690 married SS men had an average of only 1.1 child each, hardly numbers that would have pleased Himmler's illusions or the Reich's eugenic policies.[29]

The *Lebensborn* program also bequeathed a legacy of guilt, rejection and shame, particularly for the children of non-German Nordic women. Apart from its original intent, these homes became the site of a repugnant program during the war when the SS abducted an estimated 250,000 children regarded as racially pure from their parents in the occupied territories. They subjected them to racial examinations and Germanized and Nazified them. In the process, they were forced to forget their biological parents. If they refused or did not satisfy the genetic criteria, they were beaten and sometimes killed. If they passed and accepted the ideological training, they were raised as Aryan children and adopted by SS families. This program was given unwitting legitimacy by the physicians and social scientists whose ideas and techniques provided its scientific rationale

Eugenics and Blood Purity

> We have embarked on something gigan-
> tic beyond imagination. There are no more
> impossibilities for man now. For the first
> time we are attacking the biological struc-
> ture of the species. We have started to breed
> a new species of Homo sapiens. We are
> weeding out its streaks of bad heredity.
>
> —*Arrival and Departure*
> Arthur Koestler

The Culture of Racial Hygiene before 1933

After the Great War, the German population declined greatly as a result of both its massive war losses and territorial
scissoring imposed by the Versailles Treaty. The decline
propelled the study of eugenics; no longer a minor intellectual
movement, it became a significant force during the years of the
Weimar Republic. After the Nazis rose to power, eugenics became a
dominant component in the ideological armoury of the biomedical
experts. Indeed, it is arguable whether the Nazi revolution would
have acquired public legitimacy without the valuable research—
some of it on the cutting edge of science—and political support of
the medical profession, including psychiatrists, and distinguished
professors in the social and natural sciences. Geneticists voluntarily cemented a Faustian pact with their political masters by trans-
gressing ethical boundaries to validate the Party's racial policies
and programs. In the allegedly neutral language of science, they

participated in procedures and the ideological training of those that violated the regime's most vulnerable groups.[1]

Like their counterparts in Britain, Scandinavia and America, a growing number of eugenicists—physicians, lawyers, and scientists—were disturbed by the falling birth rate of the gifted members of society. What exercised them even more was the proliferation of individuals suffering from alcoholism, tuberculosis, mental illness and criminality; these hereditary diseases threatened to damage the Aryan germ plasma and thus posed a financial burden on society. German criminologists, for example, largely accepted the theories of their nineteenth-century Italian precursor, Cesare Lombroso—that most criminals were born with a genetic predisposition and therefore could be physically identified. Society had to protect itself through such measures as castration of sex offenders and violent young men in prison, compulsory sterilization before such an individual could reproduce himself and in some cases capital punishment.[2]

In the Weimar Republic, large numbers of the scientific elite abandoned any faith they might have once retained in democracy and in a liberal society of multiple perspectives, and any respect for individual rights by promoting Nordic supremacy and racial hygiene (eugenics). The extensive bloodletting on the battlefield during the Great War and in civilian casualties that included approximately seventy thousand asylum inmates who died (possibly deliberately) through starvation or neglect, had coarsened the sensibilities of professional health care workers. These losses were compounded by an acute sense of national grievance and the economic devastation wrought by a spectacular mega-inflation in the early 1920s and a severe Depression at the end of the decade. It followed that the search for more cost-effective measures and for preserving the hereditary endowment of the race took priority over the well-being of individuals.

Some physicians and medical students embraced the proto-Nazi ideological fervour of the paramilitary *Freikorps*. They believed that a civilized nation could succumb to the siren of Bolshevism. Among its horrors were sexual immorality followed by a spate of abortions which jeopardized the nation and the patriarchal family, as well as epidemics of venereal disease—a hotbed of germs that had to be eradicated—that would spiral into hereditary degeneration and contaminate the German blood. A number of medical trainees, who belonged to fanatical anti-Semitic fraternities, joined the reign of terror against socialists and Communists. Their actions included the cold-blood murder of unarmed leftist workers, for which a military tribunal acquitted them. The *Freikorps* experience infused their medical ideals—a commitment to enhance the German gene pool by excluding "racial inferiors" and the "biological unfit"—when they later became the leaders of Nazi medicine and science.

One of the acquitted murderers was a medical student by the name of Otmar von Verschuer. He joined the paramilitary *Freikorps* so as to apply his zealotry to causes ranging from rooting out Bolsheviks to eradicating the genes of hereditary diseases. After he specialized in genetics, he supported compulsory sterilization before Hitler came to power, deploying military language that compared chromosomes to military units carrying out manoeuvres and genes to machine gun bullets. Even before the Third Reich, he entered the grey zone of ethical science by administering tests that could be painful and potentially dangerous to twins as young as fifteen years of age not for therapeutic benefit but for research purposes.[3] At the Dahlem branch of the Kaiser Wilhelm Institute, von Verschuer cooperated in the training of physicians under the guidelines and auspices of the SS. This entailed seminars on the teaching of techniques for testing "conjugal fitness" and on sterilization assessment. By the time of the war, he had evacuated the grey zone for something much darker. This thumbnail profile of von Verschuer illustrates the relatively straight line that some physicians travelled from the *Freikorps* mentality to forced sterilization and later, to the legitimization of medical murder.

At the same time, von Verschuer's case can only be fully understood if placed in the context of the medical culture after 1918. During the Weimar years with the loss of their colonies and the decline of emigration as a potential safety valve for social problems, German physicians across a broad ideological spectrum recognized the need to establish a population policy. They were convinced that the war had depleted the population of large numbers with superior genetic heritage and left the weak, degenerate elements to reproduce disproportionately. Several took the professional initiative to sterilize patients they deemed feeble-minded or mentally ill, a category that encompassed the blind, alcoholic and those diagnosed as schizophrenic. When the Weimar government drafted a bill to legalize sterilization in 1932, its effect was to sanction a procedure that was already a de facto reality. Unsurprisingly, no profession constituted a larger representation in the Nazi Party than did medical practitioners; over one-half of them joined the Party.

Population concerns did not stop with sterilization. The publication in 1920 of a polemical tract by a lawyer and a psychiatrist entitled *Permission for the Destruction of Life Unworthy of Life* urged Germans to kill the physically and mentally disabled members of society. They argued that the *Volk* could only be strengthened by the sacrifice of "idiots." They purported this "travesty of human beings" to be an economic burden to society because they represented "a massive capital in the form of foodstuffs, clothing and heating."[4] Although some professionals were concerned about the scope for abuse and questioned the rationale for euthanasia, increasing numbers supported sterilization and euthanasia. A director of an asylum even dared to contend that people with mental handicaps had the capacity and will to enjoy life. Yet when he asked the parents of his patients about painlessly curtailing their children's lives, he was surprised that a large majority approved, in part because they would be no longer burdened with a handicapped child. Several parents even wanted to be deceived by being informed that their child had died of a particular illness.[5]

Without the benefit of any understanding of science, Hitler pontificated and dispensed crude solutions to complex social problems. As a simplistic Darwinian, he never grasped the Darwinian proposition that, as a part of nature, man was in a constant state of flux: essentially that everything could change and nothing was necessarily permanent. The *Volkisch* stress on the superiority of the eternal German verities was totally irreconcilable with evolution.[6] Hitler predictably endorsed the law of the jungle that the fittest should thrive, the weak should perish, and that any sensitivity toward the sick or fragile and the criminal was tantamount to racial suicide. He expressed a similar, and not uncommon, social Darwinist sentiment that only the healthy should sire children. When he asserted that the state "must declare unfit for propagation all who are in any way visibly sick or who have inherited a disease, and therefore can pass it on," no doubt sterilization, if not euthanasia, was in front of his mind. Hitler was explicitly warning that when his movement acquired power, it would be the state, not individuals or families in concert with their physicians that would decide on the fate of individuals whom it deemed were unlikely to make a substantial contribution to the *Volk*. Like other sentiments expressed in *Mein Kampf*, he was true to his word.[7] Perhaps Hitler intuitively sensed a greater acceptance of euthanasia, as in the course of a speech to a Nuremberg rally in 1929, when he praised ancient Sparta's policy of selective infanticide as a model for Germany and generated little opposition. In the amplification of an idea that he had already addressed in *Mein Kampf*, where the predatory instinct of Nature would destroy the weak, Hitler denounced "sentimental humanitarianism" and the "sense of charity" which he considered responsible "for maintaining the weak at the expense of the healthy." He warned that "if Germany was to get a million children a year and was to remove 700,000 to 800,000 of the weakest people, then the final result might even be an increase in strength."[8] Even though the endgame scenario of the eugenics case was sheer speculation, a threshold had been crossed.

The culture of "biological self defence" offered a compelling inducement which motivated scientists, even those who did not endorse National Socialism, to support racial hygiene. The metaphors of creatures, parasites, and "beasts in human form" that criminologists used for those they perceived as lower on the evolutionary scale gained currency among physicians and anthropologists during the Weimar years.[9] American funding from the Rockefeller Foundation enabled research into different city districts to study "hereditary psychopathic signs." The studies were surveys conducted by social scientists that would eventually form the hereditary data banks which provided details of a family's health, school records, fertility and police records. These surveys targeted those with physical or mental handicaps, "asocial" criminal types, and the racially inferior. Among them were the mulatto children, the *Mischlings*, of colonial French troops, the "Black Shame on the Rhine" stationed in the Ruhr in the early 1920s, and German mothers who were (incorrectly) branded as rape victims or prostitutes. As early as 1908, Eugen Fischer had studied the mixed-race children in the German colonies and concluded that every European nation that had assimilated the blood of "inferior races" had suffered "intellectual, spiritual and cultural decline." His recommendation: keep them alive "only as long as they are of use to us. Otherwise...extinction."[10] Because of his expertise on "hereditary pathology," and as director of the Kaiser Wilhelm Institute for Anthropology, Fischer would later play a key role in assisting the Nazis in the sterilization of the "Rhineland bastards."

Your Body Belongs to the Führer

Although a number of health professionals and academics found Hitler's anti-Semitism too radical, they welcomed the Nazi revolution because it brought them relative freedom. While the 1920s saw the imposition of regulations and restrictions on science, race scientists now possessed the support of the state to pursue their work in eugenics. The Reich increased funding to higher educational and medical institutions in 1933 after the renowned Kaiser Wilhelm Society assured the Ministry of the Interior that it would serve the Reich for racial hygiene research. The Institute for Anthropology alone, among some thirty institutes, was richly endowed with funds for a wide range of research projects that involved separating the effects of nature and nurture. They included studies on the inheritability of certain diseases, the link between miscegenation among gypsies and criminality, and studies in race crossing. By 1940 the Institute had already published over five hundred scholarly works. Twin studies, strongly advocated by the human biologist von Verschuer, were lavishly funded to demonstrate that heredity, rather than environmental flaws, was the key to human talent or imperfection. The renowned eugenicist, Fritz Lenz, a co-author of a textbook that was praised not merely in Germany but internationally, argued that environmentalism could be upheld only on ideological, not scientific grounds. He contended that those who espoused this liberal view were Jews because of their "inborn drive to assimilate, to blend in—a kind of human variant of the 'animal mimicry' common in the rest of the animal kingdom." Speaking for many of his colleagues, he wrote in 1931 that "the question of our hereditary endowment is a hundred times more important than the dispute over capitalism and socialism."[11] In the spirit of Lombroso, Lenz confidently asserted that he could assess an individual's genetic potential by their appearance: the size and shape of the forehead and a large nose demonstrated intelligence and the size of the chest showed the degree of vigour. After 1933, these ideas would be put into operation at every level of society.

In a culture that traditionally revered physicians, the new regime capitalized on this cachet by linking its ideology to appeals to the medical profession. When Deputy Leader Rudolf Hess proclaimed in 1934 that "National Socialism was nothing but applied biology," he was in effect elevating physicians to "biological soldiers," an honour that no other profession could match.[12] To ensure that physicians would jettison their traditional Judeo-Christian compassion for the individual and work toward the pruning and cultivation of the genetic stock of the future, the regime offered incentives such as career opportunities, enhanced prestige and unprecedented power. The large number of Jewish and socialist physicians purged from the profession—some already resented because they provided less expensive health care—opened up desirable positions in clinics and the universities for thousands of Aryan physicians. Doctors parlayed their expertise into appointments to high government and administrative posts where they could mandate what bloodlines—indeed, by 1939, what lives—should be terminated.

A support system that consisted of other professionals, including anthropologists and geneticists, was offered new responsibilities such as the training of physicians in "genetic and racial care." These physicians, meaning SS doctors as well as medical students and academics were enthused about the opportunity to deliver expert opinions at the Hereditary Health Courts or Higher Appeal Courts. They determined whether an individual was sufficiently physically incapacitated, feeble-minded, mentally ill or suffering from alcoholism to qualify for the surgeon's knife under the involuntary sterilization law of 1933. Eugen Fischer was a racial scientist expert and sat on the appeal court in Berlin, listening to evidence, often rooted in gossip and hearsay, on anyone that suffered from an emotional disturbance and allegedly posed a burden for the welfare system. In addition to questionable medical criteria, intelligence was assessed, and undesirable social behaviour was scrutinized to determine whether suspected individuals were "morally feeble-minded." The individual was expected to answer to the satisfaction of those who sat on these courts such "objective" questions as "Why does one learn things," "what are respect, modesty, loyalty, piety" and "what is the present form of government in Germany?" Any answer or behavioural sign that suggested deviance from the prescribed norm or a mere emotional difficulty would condemn the hapless individual to sterilization. Women were particularly susceptible if they changed sexual partners too frequently or had more than one illegitimate child. Under these dubious criteria, ninety percent of cases tried in the first three years of the law resulted in sterilization, the majority for alleged feeblemindedness. Throughout the years of the Third Reich, an estimated 360,000 people were sterilized, most involuntary. Five thousand people, mostly women, died from either complications or surgical incompetence, such as the wrong anaesthetic. Apart from those who committed suicide as a result of the operation, many of those sterilized suffered enduring trauma.[13]

Although the law did not cover the *Mischlings*, Hitler secretly ordered the sterilization of the mixed race without any protest from the medical community whatsoever. To prevent, in the words of one Nazi official, the "poisoning [of] the entire bloodstream of the race," an estimated three hundred and eighty-five such individuals were forcibly sterilized often without the benefit of anaesthesia. Using the testimonials from the Fischer team, the decision was based on their racial composition rather than any genetic defect.[14] Through this slow holocaust, Nazis and their complicit academic partners believed that the "black curse" could be eradicated. After the Nuremberg laws, which stripped Jews of their civil rights and outlawed any sexual relations between Aryans and Jews, physicians, anthropologists and geneticists expressed by word and action their support. Medical journals agreed that Judaism was "disease incarnate" because Jews were more susceptible to homosexuality, criminality, hereditary feebleness of mind and other inherited conditions. They endorsed the Blood Protection Laws that would help gird the German body against further encroachment of "foreign racial elements" and help "cleanse the body of the *Volk*." Anthropologists and physicians trained in genetics offered the regime support by sitting on the Racial Hygiene courts. There they decided the fate of thousands through their alleged expert opinion, sometimes merely on the basis of a snapshot, whether an individual was Aryan or Jewish. Such a dubious undertaking could be, by 1941, a virtual death sentence for someone designated a Jew.[15]

Despite their complicitous relationship with the regime, the medical and academic elites deluded themselves into believing that they were objective scientists. Professionals preened themselves on being a substantial cut above the "unscientific" prejudice of Streicher, the Party ideologues and the gutter vulgarity that suffused *Der Stürmer* and *Mein Kampf.* They prided themselves on their superior knowledge of theoretical link between heredity, genetics and National Socialism. When scientists argued that they were engaged in detached, value-free science, they refused to see that their methods and conclusions masked, not merely the irrational impulses of the time, but as well, their own racial, ethnic and gender biases. Also, the targets of their venom—blacks, Slavs, children of mixed marriages, women, gypsies, Jews—were never allowed a voice to refute these perceptions. Indeed, the nature of the research ensured that these objectified individuals could not articulate their own experiences. Professionals who bought into a warped ideology guaranteed that they would be as myopic or subjective as any layman. For instance, Fischer publicly proclaimed in 1933, at a time when dissidents were being rounded up, thrown into concentration camps, tortured and murdered: "I repeat: this is a peaceful, orderly revolution, a revolution under civilized conditions and without bloodshed."[16] Similarly, the psychiatrist, Alfred Hoche, one of the authors of the tract of 1920 that urged active euthanasia, was as much motivated by the grief of a son he lost in the war as he was by any consideration of scientific objectivity about the welfare of the nation. If his only son, one of the fit, could make the sacrifice, surely the unfit could. One further example: a group of German scientists subverted blood research by attempting to correlate blood type with racial characteristics to prove an individual's ethnicity could be identified through his blood type. With this flawed hypothesis, the findings that

> blood type B appeared with slight[ly] greater frequency among Eastern Europeans and Jews,...[resulting in] Nazi doctors identify[ing] it as a 'Slavic' or 'Jewish' marker befitting an inferior people heedless of the evidence that in Berlin, there was a greater incidence of type B among Aryans than among Jews.[17]

When scientists spoke about the capacity of genetically superior women to give birth several times, their cultural milieu and Nazi ideology influenced them as significantly as any objective criteria of science. For example, when Fischer suggested in the German *Dictionary of Science* that a woman could bear "an average of eight or nine children" over the course of her life, a colleague who reviewed Fischer's piece disagreed. He suggested that a woman was capable of bearing fifteen children over a thirty-year period. "Anything less than this must be considered the result of unnatural or pathological causes." This professional exchange was symptomatic of a deeply encrusted patriarchal attitude that not only ignored the woman's physical and emotional wellbeing, but also regarded feminism as pernicious, something that would promote a "birth strike"—a "black plague" threatening the race with extinction.[18] The birth rate was down during the Weimar years, contraceptives were readily available in urban areas, and there were two million more women than men. This relationship between two academics was more likely, however, a product of the widely held assumption that women were primarily vessels of reproduction.

Clearly, the elites' attitudes toward women, blacks and Jews were not apolitical or objective. Their professional writings conveyed a similar misogynous outlook to those of Hitler. In his memoirs, Hitler asserted that the main task of a girl's education was to prepare her for motherhood, not because it might enrich her life, but because it would increase and preserve the race. Early marriage would also inhibit her from being tempted into a lascivious lifestyle that would open the floodgates to pollutants contaminating the genetic bloodstream. He was even blunter in private revealing his insensitive, crude attitude. In the presence of his mistress, Eva Braun, he remarked to Albert Speer, the only man with whom Hitler maintained an emotional relationship: "A highly intelligent man should take a primitive and stupid woman. Imagine if on top of everything else I had a woman who interfered with my work! In my leisure time, I want to have peace."[19] Despite the rarefied language and the absence of prurience in their professional writings, the sentiments of the scientists toward women who refused to be cloistered breeding machines were consistent with the Nazi worldview. Similarly, they shared basic premises on racial matters.

Indeed, the scientists' overwhelming penchant toward viewing human development in terms of biological determinism readily accommodated the racist aegis dictated by Hitler. In *Mein Kampf*, he declaimed that character was something that was inborn rather than developed or acquired; neither could one change his essential character because "the man of egotistical nature is and remains so forever....The born criminal is and remains a criminal." As for those who have inferior genes like the Poles, "it is criminal lunacy to keep on drilling a born half-ape until people think they have made a lawyer out of him....For this is training exactly like that of a poodle."[20] By the same token, Hitler's appalling ignorance of Mendelian genetics and inheritance embarrassed hygienists. His belief that the "blending process" corrupted the purity of German-Aryan blood disregarded modern knowledge that a child's genes were not a blend of those of his parents.' Biologists scorned Hitler's notion of an Aryan and Germanic race and attributed his racial anti-Semitism to nineteenth-century *Volkisch* ideologues.[21]

Nonetheless, scientists embraced the notion, "Your body belongs to the Führer!" that blazoned propaganda posters and encapsulated state control of racial hygiene.[22] They were generally agreed that science should serve the *Volk* and endorsed programs that would strengthen its gene pool. To this end, scientists, physicians and public health advocates filled the interstices between sound science and direct or indirect participation in the monstrous crimes committed by the regime. When scientists established a firm link between cigarettes and lung cancer, others enthusiastically supported a variety of preventive measures that displayed the worst and the best of Nazi science: the portrayal of smoking as a Jewish, gypsy and African habit, the ban on smoking in government offices and hospitals and restrictions on tobacco advertising to ensure that smoking would not be portrayed as a glamorous activity. Besides waging a war on tobacco, they urged women to undergo regular screenings for breast and genital cancer, pioneered research to identify workplace carcinogens and approved the ban on women and children working with certain industrial chemicals. But in keeping with their commitment to the *Volk*, they expressed no misgivings when concentration camp inmates and prisoners of war worked with toxic chemicals and radiation without protective clothing. Frequently, the same men were in the vanguard of both progressive science and criminality. The virulent anti-Semitic president of Jena University, Karl Astel, simultaneously banned smoking on campus and advocated the murder of psychiatric patients. Leonardo Conti, the Reich Health Minister who championed preventive medicine and recognized the dangers in tobacco because it was addictive, actively organized Germany's "euthanasia operation."[23]

Yet even scientists committed to the *Volk*, but who did not accept racial biology, never fully grasped that their vaunted science

255

remained subordinate to the ideology of blood, For Hitler and his senior potentates, the essence of race resided in blood, not in its physical properties, but in its ineffable mystery which could not be measured. Indeed, because empirical inquiry was considered "Jewish," natural science had to be rooted in the natural spirit of the *Volk*.[24] Because they did not understand this core of National Socialism, many of these professionals did not support Hitler's rabid anti-Semitism and his rabble-rousing oratory that generated support among the lower orders where they considered psychopathy was prevalent. Like the sophisticated Berliners who rushed past *Der Stürmer*, pretending not to see, or dismissing it with contempt, they too gave a wide berth to the crude presentation and lowbrow tone that distinguished Streicher's tabloid. Similarly, when Matthias Göring, a psychotherapist, Party member and director of the Berlin Psychoanalytical Institute, and cousin to the famous Nazi grandee, required all his colleagues to read *Mein Kampf* not as a study in psychopathology but as a "scientific" text, the vast majority refused. Despite his beseeching, its coarseness and scientific ignorance repelled them.[25] Eugenicists privately speculated whether Hitler was a psychopath and questioned whether he was Nordic.

Regardless of their elitist disdain, any effort to display scientific independence was severely rebuked. When scientists wrote articles that appeared to contravene government policy, Party ideologues trawled them in and subjected them to intrusive controls. For example, the *Lebensborn* program encouraged Aryan women to be impregnated by, what Hermann Goring called, "SS stallions," in an effort to increase the genetic pool. When Fritz Lenz stigmatized illegitimate children as "predominately feeble-minded [and] psychopathic" and "an absolute evil" in a published paper, his journal editor was sharply reprimanded.[26] A fanatical Party ideologue like Himmler, who resented marriage laws and monogamy, did not tolerate scientists who criticized his pet program or his conviction that every German woman should offer to the state at least one child. Lenz's rebuff signalled the publication of fewer scientific articles and more puff pieces that lavished fulsome praise on Nazi policies. Absolute submission to Hitler and the Party was the price that self-deluded scientists paid for supporting a regime that valued ideology over conservative morality.

The scientists' predilection for conceiving any physical or

mental defect as a product of defective genes rendered them vulnerable to the Nazis' influence, notwithstanding that many of them were reluctant to join the Party. Information regarding all criminal behaviour and personal defects as inheritable, as well as the financial inducements from research grants combined with the immense prestige, enhanced income and the perks of power, could be easily manipulated to further the Party's agenda. The scientists had been grateful to exploit the opportunities granted them, including entry into the profession after the purge of Jewish physicians. There was a price to pay. The Nazi Medical Association announced their unequivocal support for a cornerstone of Nazi racism when it declared that "neither deception, nor baptism, nor name change, nor citizenship, and not even nasal surgery could help. One cannot change one's blood."[27] Physicians further compromised their profession by violating confidentiality when they reported to the health authorities anyone with a disorder that by law required sterilization. Under the veneer of academic and scientific respectability, these professionals allowed their anxieties surrounding race, crime and health to be transformed into medical and biological problems. Since they believed that it was the duty of every German doctor to support the eugenic health of the nation, they attempted to resolve these problems through their writings, teaching, participation in health courts and performing surgery.

The medical endorsement of progressive science coexisted with murderous cruelty because the regime rationalized both as necessary for restoring the nation's vitality. True, there is evidence that some physicians who supported compulsory sterilization abstained from and even opposed the medical killing programs that began in late 1939.[28] Others, however, accepted race demonology and the policies that incrementally produced the isolation, deportation *and* finally extermination of racial and genetic undesirables. When the thinking of members of these medical disciplines and research scientists became encrusted with a fanatical ideology and personal ambition, we may well ask whether their racial science was more substantive than the crazed seminal absorption fantasy propounded by Hitler and Streicher. When the majority of scientists actively supported the regime's policies, they transgressed a moral line into darkness by allowing their intellectual flummeries to be prostituted for Nazi ends. They willingly lent their authority and expertise to these infamous policies, including the gassing of eighty thousand patients of mental hospitals and the deadly medical experiments conducted in the camps, all in the name of science. In his book published shortly after World War II, author, Max Weinreich, rightly indicted "German scholarship [that] provided the ideas and techniques, which led to and justified this unparalleled slaughter."[29]

The Complicity of American Eugenicists

During the 1930s, Germany's racial policies received endorsement from American eugenicists and entrepreneurs. With callous disregard for the Reich's violation of civil and human rights, Thomas Watson, the CEO of IBM provided the data processing technology and the punch cards that assisted the regime in implementing its racial policies. In his rapacious search for profits, the American businessman facilitated the census surveys that enabled the regime to identify not only professing Jews, but also those who fit their racial definition of a Jew, those that intermarried and converted, as well as their employment and place of residence. It could then restrict the number of Jews in the academic, professional, governmental and commercial fields by individually naming them. As early as 1933, German census provided a "profession-by-profession, city-by-city, and indeed a block-by-block revelation of the Jewish presence." Not only was the technology used to discriminate against Jews and Poles, the latter being the first to be expelled in the fall of 1938, but it was pivotal to the German rearmament program and its preparation for war. A secret military report stated that the punch card system was invaluable in the redeployment of the general public, the military and the work force. According to an internal memo, "the punch card does not replace all considerations, judgments and decisions, but it makes them easier."[30] For his contribution to the Reich, Watson was awarded a medal from Hitler personally. The technology he provided was an example of the collusion between Germans and a foreign interest whose primary agenda resided in profit. Other agendas motivating Americans included strong ideological affinities, namely the fear of miscegenation, and reciprocal support for German scientists, physicians, financiers and corporations that reached up to the Führer himself.

Through public policy and financial support, the United States provided the engine room for Hitler's eugenics. Even before legal sanction was provided, American physicians ended the bloodlines of individuals they identified as defective (in some cases as a treatment for masturbation). They accomplished this through sterilization and castration of prisoners and the "feebleminded" poor because of the widespread perception that hereditary weakness posed a fundamental threat to society. American eugenicists were militant about the urgency to weed out the racially, ethnically and socially unfit—that included the epileptic and the blind—on the dubious premise that individuals with social problems or criminal histories were victims of a recessive gene. Legalized in Indiana in 1907, sterilization spread through several American states and Canadian provinces, with its implementation in California outpacing all states combined in which the ratio of blacks sterilized outstripped that of whites.

The eugenicist, amateur anthropologist and proponent of "scientific racism," Madison Grant, provided a scholarly veneer to this "most momentous" cause through his manifesto, *The Passing of the Great Race* (1916). His dire warning about the dangers of miscegenation—between the virile Nordic with his "splendid fighting and moral qualities" and the Indian or Jew would likely result in its reversion to a lower type—even earned a personal letter from Hitler who said that "the book was his Bible." That endorsement should not surprise given that Grant lamented that America was being contaminated by the "human flotsam." He felt "the weak, the broken and the mentally crippled of all races drawn from the lowest stratum of the Mediterranean basin" would sap the vigour of the Master Race. Sounding like an apologist for a totalitarian state, he scoffed at the "sentimental belief in the sanctity of human life" and argued that "nature requires(s) the obliteration of the unfit and human life is valuable only when it is of use to the community or race." Grant also warned that "Asiatics" and the "swarms of Polish Jews" would swamp America through immigration, endangering the Nordic white race. His panacea to preserve the blood of tall, blond Nordics was sterilization beginning with the "social discards" extending to "weaklings" and "perhaps ultimately to worthless race types."[31]

In 1927 the eminent jurist, Oliver Wendell Holmes delivered the Supreme Court majority decision upholding compulsory sterilization. The ruling legitimated an outlook that politicians, physicians and conservative professors had been proclaiming since the late nineteenth century. In unrestrained language that garnered full approval in Germany, he stated: "Three generations of imbeciles are enough."[32]

The man who wrote the guidelines for the sterilization law in California fully agreed. The career of Harry Laughlin, the assistant director for eugenics at the Cold Spring Harbor Laboratory, provides compelling evidence that American eugenicists served as inspiration for Nazi policy. Laughlin's stalwart support for eugenics included testimony he presented before a Congressional Committee in 1924 to prove the genetic inferiority of central and southern European peoples and Jews. His efforts influenced the 1924 Immigration Act that put stringent quotas on prospective immigrants who, he had argued, were genetically inferior, a law that determined immigration policy for forty years and one that Hitler referred to approvingly in *Mein Kampf.* Laughlin was awarded an honorary doctorate in medicine from the University of Heidelberg in the 1930s. In 1937 he and likeminded eugenicists founded the Pioneer Fund, a foundation that in its early years supported racial policy in Nazi Germany (short of extermination) and continued to offer financial grants for research into the relationship between race and intelligence. *Eugenics News* commented that "to one versed in the history of eugenics sterilization in America, the text of the German statute reads almost like the American model sterilization law."[33] Support for eugenics extended into the wider community convinced by the argument that no feebleminded person should be a parent. According to a 1937 survey conducted by *Fortune Magazine,* a majority indicated support for the extension of sterilization. The palpable increase in its popularity emboldened advocates of eugenics to extend their connection with likeminded enthusiasts' in Nazi Germany.[34]

The American eugenicists who visited Germany and listened to their German counterparts won kudos by praising Hitler for the construction of a "comprehensive racial policy of population." After absorbing without question what they heard, they returned to rhapsodize about the clarity and directness of sterilization law and how its legality was assured because "its application is entrusted to specialized courts and procedures." One of the law's most enthusiastic supporters returned with an English version of a German film endorsed by the Führer promoting sterilization.

Among the images were "four feebleminded siblings" who had cost the state "together during more than eighty years of institutionalization 153,000 marks." The film's last scene showed a man and a woman planting with the subtitle: "The farmer, who prevents the overgrowth of the weed, promotes the valuable." The film contended that Jews were susceptible to mental retardation and moral deviancy but its American promoter denied that it depicted "racial propaganda of any sort." Repeatedly, the proponents of the film defended it as an educational film about "the problem of hereditary degeneracy." Similarly, they denied that the sterilization law was a "racial purifier" promulgated by a racist regime that discriminated on the basis of race or religious belief. Even during the war when Americans continued to visit Germany, their vision was skewed. One tourist was impressed by the "amazing amount of unbiased information" pertaining to the "physical and psychological defectiveness of the Jews" that he observed at the Kaiser Wilhelm Institute. Another visited the new Hereditary Health Courts, where experts witnessed the case and decided on genetic grounds the outcome of "an apelike man with a receding forehead and flaring nostrils who had a history of homosexuality and was married to a 'Jewess' by whom he had three 'ne'er-do-well children.' "[35] The man was branded a degenerate race polluter responsible for thrusting upon society cretins, the perfect stereotype of the born criminal pioneered by Cesare Lombroso. Whether these observers were self-deluded dupes or merely bigots legitimatized by their professional respectability, they exercised a powerful influence.

Eventually, over sixty thousand were forcibly sterilized in America in the first seven decades of the twentieth century, over a quarter of them in California. Afro-Americans, Native Americans, and Latin Americans were the prime targets in the 1960s and 1970s. In the politics of immigration, race continues to be Gothicized—the demonization of non-Caucasians as the *other*—in print by right-wing polemicists and on Fox News. They pander to the fear of the proliferating racial *other* swamping the "white culture." In turn, they support a "crackdown" on suspected illegal immigrants and the tacit practice of "sundown" or whites-only communities that punctuate the American landscape. For example, Patrick Buchanan's polemic argues that America is being overrun by Third World immigrants, both legal and illegal, and that America is on the path to

"national suicide" since "white folks" are not reproducing at sufficient rate.[36]

The Bitter Fruit of the Faustian Pact

In September 1939 under the smokescreen of war, Hitler authorized the murder of five thousand physically or mentally handicapped children conducted in a Rockefeller-funded
branch of the Kaiser Wilhelm Institute. Once this threshold had
been crossed, it was followed by the killing of thousands of Polish
mental patients to provide barracks for German soldiers, and the
killing of German physically and mentally handicapped patients
with carbon monoxide gas. What had been misconceived as a concept based on science had morphed into a lethal instrument in
which Nazi eugenics claimed a scientific basis for its unique form
of racial purity. By 1941 over 100,000 had been killed, the majority German. Despite efforts by the regime to shroud these criminal
acts in secrecy, knowledge of them filtered through to the public
where the disclosures were not received with wholesale acquiescence. Clerics were the most outspoken, especially the Bishop
of Munster, August von Galen, who lashed out at the involuntary
euthanasia program in a series of sermons. He denounced the
murder of sick, poor people that the state had labelled unproductive as if they were old horses or cows about to be slaughtered. If
the regime could dispense with these people, they could follow
with the elderly or seriously wounded soldiers. The sermon resonated with many and received huge coverage with the BBC making broadcasts of it and the RAF dropping copies over Germany.
Despite the urgings of Nazi leaders to have von Galen hung, Hitler
refused, deferring a decision for the future. In order not to offend
Catholic sensibilities, he publicly retracted by ending the mass
gassings, although the practice continued through starvation or
with lethal medication in concentration camps and mental institutions. Von Galen's courage was a rare example of a bystander,
supported by relatives of the victims and some lawyers, confronting the evil of the Third Reich. A much more common practice for
German civilians was to occupy the vacated property of Jews or
for soldiers to send relatives a cache of loot pilfered from the occupied territories.

Their complicity, however, paled in comparison to the geneticists. Given that there is no evidence that gave any thought to the

Courtesy of Photofest

In the 2011 American film, The Debt, *itself a remake of the superior 2007 Israeli film of the same title, a 1960s Mossad plan to kidnap an unrepentant Nazi physician, who conducted heinous experiments in a death camp and return him to Israel for an Eichmann-like trial, goes terribly wrong. The operatives then determine "we can decide what is truth" and must live for thirty years with their decision of that day. In the scene above, the physician taunts one of his captors by telling her that "Jews do not know how to kill, only to die." In the 2007 version, "the butcher of Treblinka," boasts to one of his male captors that what he did was "in the name of science."*

unethical nature of their symbiotic relationship with their political masters during the 1930s, it is unsurprising that they became increasingly desensitized to the consequences of placing their science at the service of ideology. Both Fischer and von Verschuer had not joined the Party during the 1930s likely because they wanted to protect their international reputations; however, by 1940 both men became official Nazi members. If Fischer in his writings and public speeches referred to Jews as racially "alien to the European races," by 1941 he went further by denying that "Jewish Bolsheviks" were part of the human species. By 1944 he wrote "that it was high time [that action on the part of scientists was taken against the Jews] since the Jews have been leading not only a political but also a spiritual campaign against us for years." His protégé, the baron, von Verschuer was even more fanatical as he regarded the concentration camps and death camps and the "euthanasia" hospitals as a mother lode for the harvesting of body parts for "scientific material" that would advance his research and career opportunities and commercial profits.[37] By 1944, he acknowledged that Germany was waging a "racial war" against "World Jewry." His contribution to that war was through his experiments, training medical students in "hereditary race discipline," that included techniques to examine the suitability of potential marriages for "conjugal fitness," and mentoring sadistic killers.[38]

The most notorious product of von Verschuer's influence was his protégé and former assistant, Dr. Josef Mengele, a camp doctor and a member of the military SS. Mengele became known as the Angel of Death when he exercised absolute power over individuals' lives as soon as they arrived at Auschwitz. Mengele's predilection for cruelty extended to using Jewish and Gypsy twins as guinea pigs in his medical experiments. He sent the eyes of murdered Gypsy children, the internal organs of children and the brain specimens from others deliberately infected with typhoid to his mentor at the Institute in Berlin's fashionable suburb Dahlem in the years 1943–45. It was a collaboration that proved both scientifically worthless and morally unconscionable.

None of von Verschuer's reprehensible activities damaged his career. After the war, he airbrushed his personal biography by stating that he was "openly opposed to the National Socialist race fanaticism."[39] In 1949 a research committee exonerated him from any association with Nazism. With his whitewashed résumé, he became a lynchpin within academia as a university professor esteemed by the international academy, especially scientists on the political far right in America.

Von Verschuer was not alone. Many others were able to thrive in post-war Germany, since some physicians put on trial received light sentences. Many eluded justice altogether. Mengele—the epitome of the sadistic-omnipotence syndrome—escaped to South America where he lived undisturbed for thirty-five years.

A toxic combination of opportunism and ideology largely explains the devolution of the physician from healer to killer. Material rewards, prestige and genetic purification eclipsed the value placed on the sanctity of life enticing medical professionals to abandon their oath to avoid harming others. Starting with the coercive sterilization of the racially and genetically defective, by 1939 physicians—and not merely a few aberrant ones—partici-pated in killing the physically or mentally deficient infants and children with lethal injections. This was followed by adults "unfit for life" carried out in the gas chambers of special institutes (alto-gether about seventy thousand "euthanasia" patients). In a society that revered physicians, their involvement in eliminating the "un-worthy" gifted it a legitimacy that it might otherwise not have ac-quired. Their approval led a large portion of the public to accept it. As the war progressed, physicians worked closely with the SS and became acclimatized to conducting medical experiments (the vast majority proving to be medically useless) and killing victims from the concentration camps. Finally they lent their considerable pres-tige to the mass extermination of racial groups in the killing fields and in the camps. At Auschwitz, for instance, they participated in the selection process; they determined who would die immediate-ly and who would instead become the "living dead"—those slated to be worked to death. For the Jews who arrived frightened, con-fused and expecting to be "resettled," the physician's presence on the platform in his white coat was a deceptively reassuring sign. He appeared solicitous asking them about their health and occupation, while he was ruthlessly deciding into which line the victim would go. It was an easy decision whenever he saw the very young, old, infirm and pregnant. The bestialities that phys-icians perpetrated occurred at the extremity of a continuum that stretched for years prior to the Third Reich. During World War II a significant number of physicians violated the healing ethos and the primacy of individual life to a value peripheral to the *Volk* with its genetic and racial priorities.[40]

The Sorcerer's Apprentice

It could sometimes seem that a demon had crept into him.

—Karl Jaspers on Martin Heidegger

Without an Audience,
You're No Better than a Corpse[*]

I t would not be unusual to characterize Hitler and his underlings, especially Goebbels, as master sorcerers. They excelled
at the art of manipulation by weaving their dark spell over vast
sectors of the German population. More striking is to apply that
epithet to one outside the higher echelons of the Party leadership,
particularly to one in academia. Martin Heidegger, an internation-
ally-esteemed philosopher deserves the appellation because of
his ability to enthrall not only his own students, but generations of
scholars and philosophy readers, despite his Nazi involvement. It
is insufficient to argue that Heidegger may have been temporarily
naïve and therefore should be excused his political indiscretion,
or that there was a schizophrenic division between his politics and
his philosophy. Just as Hitler came to life when he could mesmer-
ize and drain his audiences of their critical faculties, Heidegger
seized the opportunity to feed his own Führer fantasies. Not only
during his lifetime (until May 26, 1976) but since, he bamboozled
his admirers by obfuscating and concealing his true convictions.

When Hitler acquired power, he immediately began to execute
his plans for European domination. Within a few days of being

---

[*]   Eva to Adi in *Moloch,* Directed by Alexander Sokurov (1999)

ensconced in the Chancellery in 1933, he summoned his generals and informed them that the overriding goal of German foreign policy must be the acquisition of "living space in the east, in order ruthlessly to Germanize it."[1] To achieve economic self-sufficiency and a racially pure-bred empire, the cost would eventually entail ethnic cleansing and genocide. But he intuitively understood that he needed to proceed cautiously.

Notwithstanding his bellicose foreign policy goals, Hitler remained a shrewd politician. He believed that contingency plans were essential because circumstances could require him to soft-pedal his rhetoric and alter his tactics to suit particular audiences and current needs. Hitler's grasp of people's psychology—what they wanted and what his regime could offer—enabled him to be publicly gracious and circumspect if the occasion required. For example, the more powerful he became, the more he dampened his anti-Semitism, recognizing that it could be counterproductive with the majority of Germans. Instead, he effectively targeted the failure of democracy and ridiculed its inept parliamentary system with its thirty-odd political parties. Specifically, he excoriated the political parties of the left whom he blamed for Germany's war defeat, the capitulation to the reviled Versailles Treaty, and the 1918–1919 conflict arising from the Spartacus uprising. One of the more effective actions in this respect was to associate the Social Democrats with the fear of Marxism by using the famine in the Ukraine as an indictment of how it affected ordinary lives. In a March 2, 1933 speech, Hitler proclaimed that "millions are starving in a country that should be the breadbasket for the whole world."[2]

Hitler was also adept at playing upon the cultural fears of Germans angered by the decline in moral standards exemplified by cosmopolitan Berlin. He promised to clean up the trash and filth in the hedonistic cities and to reassert Christian moral standards and family virtues. This endeared him to conservatives in rural areas and the urban middle class who believed that Weimar society and culture had degenerated from the wholesomeness of the Wilhelmine era. True, the Nationalists delivered the same message; so he assailed them for neglecting their social responsibilities to the collective. When he promised to reconcile nationalism with a socialism that transcended class conflict, he appealed to the working class. Despite his revulsion for the spiritual essence of Christianity, Hitler mollified Catholics as he emphasized his deeply religious sensibility and praised Christianity as the "foundation of our entire moral health and the germ cell of our ethnic and political body." After he assumed power, he incorporated biblical allusions into his speeches so that the effect, according to eyewitnesses, was that his rallies were more akin to a religious revivalist meeting than to a political rally.[3]

Hitler's ability to tap into popular sentiments helped generate popular support. Part of his appeal was the extraordinary, almost preternatural rapport he established with ordinary people. His repetitive repertoire was delivered in histrionic harangues: the appalling contrast between Germany's glorious past and its divisive, enfeebled present, the betrayal of the men whose lives were sacrificed by treacherous Marxists and Jews on the home front who sabotaged the war effort and capitulated to the enemy with a shameful peace. Spitting venom and wild gesticulations alone could never have afforded Hitler the rapturous symbiotic relationship with the German people. He thrived when he held an audience spellbound. Conversely, during the later war years when the military situation and security considerations precluded public appearances, Hitler "progressively deteriorated and seemed to all witnesses a 'spectral ruin.'"[4]

When he promised to unify them, to restore order and national greatness, Hitler astutely capitalized on the peoples' yearning for community and their deeply rooted desire to overcome the enervation of class, regional and political divisiveness. With speeches full of generalizations and contradictions, his arguments could be rationally refuted. His sure-handed manipulation of an audience, however, rendered discourse irrelevant. His technique was to skilfully express the nameless fears of his audience, give "the spectre a name," and then to offer them "redemption, a triumphant happy ending."[5] His bromides were deliberately impervious to reason; indeed, they were a celebration of unreason. In his memoir and speeches, he remained scathingly contemptuous of "eggheads." In 1923, he declaimed in a speech, "Today we suffer from over education...the know-it-alls are the enemies of action. What is needed is instinct and will."[6] Intuitively, he sensed that the most effective means of communicating his message was to stress form over content to ensure that the masses' prejudices would not be disturbed by reflection or education.

As a master sorcerer before and after coming to power, Hitler perceived that the German people longed for a movement that transcended politics: something only a quasi-religion could deliver. Hitler carefully honed his speeches by rehearsing them, along with body gyrations and choreographed gestures, in front of a mirror. He projected a charisma through religious rhetoric and a cadence in his speeches that seduced the German people like no traditional politician with his monotonic, rational speeches ever could.

He understood that "they [would] succumb more easily to the dominating force of a superior will."[7] This evangelist would begin with a studied silence, conveying a soft image as he spoke in a quiet voice before rising to a howling crescendo. Brimming with hatred and passion as he outlined the grievances caused by satanic and godless enemies, Hitler's peroration promised them deliverance and temporal salvation. An expatriate historian recalled how his words that ricocheted throughout a hall managed to appeal to both material and spiritual needs: "National Socialism was a promise at once of immediate melioration and of satisfaction of a deeper yearning...[where] stirrings of the German soul [could find] turbulent expression."[8] The American reporter, William Shirer, who watched the 1934 spectacles at Nuremberg, captured this sense of exhilaration and mind-numbing fanaticism when he witnessed "a mob of ten thousand hysterics who jammed the moat in front of Hitler's hotel, shouting: 'We want our Führer.' " When Hitler appeared on the balcony, the women particularly shocked Shirer as they "looked up at him as if he were a Messiah, their faces transformed into something inhuman." A couple of days later, he observed how tens of thousands of German youth, "suddenly made the German spectators go mad with joy when, without warning, they broke into a perfect goosestep." Inclined to regard the gesture as "undignified and stupid," Shirer understood for the first time "what an inner chord it strikes in the strange soul of the German people." Shirer could not comprehend that Hitler "needed the orgiastic excitement which only the ecstatic masses could give him" to lift him out of the banality of his private existence and even the boredom of daily governing (which he usually left to others). Even in private, Hitler required the rapt attention of senior Nazis and generals to listen in silence to his lengthy monologues. Shirer did appreciate, however, the other effect of this psychic vampirism:

the shedding of their individual souls and mind—with
the personal responsibilities and doubts and problems—
until under the mystic lights and at the sound of the magic
words of the Austrian they were merged completely in the
Germanic herd.[9]

Upon hearing the deafening applause at a Nuremberg rally, an Australian historian remarked "it was a definite struggle to remain rational in a horde surrounded with intense emotionalism."[10] Ordinary people recalled after the war that they experienced Hitler's speeches as though they possessed the uncanny power of a siren.* One woman remembers that as teenagers, while attending a Nazi event, "we were in a trance. We did not know what was happening to us."[11] Even his immediate circle, who exercised power on their own turf, became in his presence "insignificant and timid." In the presence of Hitler, according to Albert Speer's later recollections, "they were under his spell, blindly obedient to him and with no will of their own."[12] Hitler also understood that his Svengali-like power enabled him to transport both large and intimate audiences. He excelled at choreographing spectacles to enthral and flatter the very people that he dismissed as the masses but dubbed the master race. Every public move was cynically calculated to enhance his "masculine" power over the impressionable "feminine" masses and to scuttle every semblance of what was once a variegated or pluralistic public. As the informational content in his speeches was so slight and would have been disseminated beforehand, Hitler concentrated his energies on deepening the emotional bond between himself and his audience. Responding as if their brains were anesthetised, people became convinced that he could sweep away all their fears. He led them to believe that life was not a series of random defeats, but the result of nefarious forces arrayed against them that could be vanquished.

The effect was to transform Germany into an atavistic tribal

---

* Fritz Lang's 1933 *The Testament of Dr Mabuse* is a political allegory about a master criminal who exerts his power through his disembodied voice. From an insane asylum, and even after his death, this preternatural villain is able to exercise a hypnotic influence over his outside agents so that they can continue their criminal activities—and the psychiatrist who treats him. Near the end of the film, Mabuse's undead presence leaves the asylum suggesting that his omnipotent and malevolent spirit cannot be confined by mere institutional restraints.

When the mayor of Nuremberg presented Hitler with a print of Albrecht Durer's 1513 The Knight, Death and the Devil, *during the 1933 September Rally, the famous engraving became emblematic of Hitler's crusade against what the Nazis considered the forces of evil.*

state. Projecting the rapture of a national community united by blood, the Nazi leadership attenuated the German collective moral compass and took the first step toward segregation and genocide. At a time when members of the other political parties were either self-immolating or being persecuted, the exhilaration that the Nazis provided for ordinary people was later remembered by an expatriate anti-Nazi German journalist as, "a widespread feeling of deliverance, of liberation from democracy," its divisiveness, its banalities and its lack of élan.[13] Reviewing *Mein Kampf* in 1940, George Orwell observed that Hitler's appeal resided not in offering "comfort, safety, shorter working hours, hygiene, birth-control and in general, common sense" but in challenging Germans to embrace "struggle, danger and death."[14] With Hitler setting the tone, Nazi ideology jettisoned free thought and reasoned debate in favour of rallies and ceremonies that honoured martyrs, celebrated the warrior and projected the illusion of seductive certainties.

The infamous book burnings of May 1933 epitomized these impulses. The Nazi regime sanctioned the participation of SA storm troopers and students from thirty university cities and towns, in hurling into the flames "degenerate" books that symbolized everything the Nazis despised: pacifism, cosmopolitanism (a code word for Jew), homosexuality and satire. This cultural barbarism was no spontaneous event but the apogee of deeply rooted passionate convictions. Nazi students, who had chanted during the Weimar period, "We shit on freedom," tapped into a cultural conservatism that included among its supporters clergy and lay representatives from both the Catholic and Protestant Churches.[15] Their campaign against "trashy filth," from the banning of (tame) nudist publications to the elimination of dangerous ideas, anything associated with liberalism, modernity and the antithesis of family, nationhood and marriage, culminated in the Harmful Publications Act of 1926 that placed designated books on a prohibited index. To ensure compliance with the law, religious lay organizations encouraged its members to participate in the surveillance of bookstores, street vendors and newsstands. These actions were merely a prelude to a more dramatic state-sponsored eradication of "filth and trash" literature, the immolation of books in June 1933.[16] Participants raided bookstores and private dwellings, albeit the authorities installed a *cordon sanitaire* around research libraries, to confiscate the proscribed literature. They epitomized what

Hitler most wanted from his young followers: "a violent haughty, dauntless, cruel youth...beasts of prey" liberated from the "thousands of years of human domestication."[17] They in turn referred to their Führer as the knight in the 1513 master engraving by Albrecht Dürer, *The Knight, Death and the Devil.* It followed that the Devil was embodied in the literary expression of decadent racial and ideological enemies, from Freud to Einstein and Marx, whose ideas and representatives would be expunged from the revitalized national community. As Goebbels intoned at the Berlin *auto-da-fé* where over two thousand books at the university entrance were incinerated, Death was the passing of the Weimar Republic; the burning signified "committing the evil spirit of the past to the flames."[18] In the destruction of books, the Nazis sent a message about the medium itself. The intimate exchange between author and reader that often involved reflection was suspect because the regime stressed will, belief and the importance of blood. As Hitler said in another context, "Blood is stronger than all the paper documents."[19]

The response of the intellectual community to this act spoke volumes about their attitude toward the recent past, the life of the mind, and the German intellectual heritage. Whatever criticism or even misgivings the intelligentsia harboured about the wisdom of the book burnings was extremely muted. The university community, the majority nationalistic and living in mortal fear of Bolshevism, rejected and despised the Weimar Republic. One professor of literature unequivocally endorsed the expurgation of books when he stated, "we want a literature that idolizes the family and home, the *Volk* and blood and the whole life of pious allegiances."[20]

The Weimar era with its multi-party system and its pluralistic culture of diverse, emancipated lifestyles (single, childless or homosexual) was anathema to the mandarin caste who acquired their conservative values in the more settled era of the Wilhelmine monarchy. No doubt the vast majority of them would have endorsed Goebbels' condemnation of liberalism in the Weimar Republic as "anarchy of the spirit." At one university in Tübingen, a professor indicated that "anyone who confessed an allegiance to democracy and affirmed it, even in private, was regarded by most of the faculty as socially suspect."[21] Carl Schmitt, a distinguished legal theorist who became a stalwart apologist for the Third Reich, abhorred cultural diversity. He endorsed the book burning for destroying the "anti-German filth" regretting only that the works of non-Jewish authors, who were influenced by pernicious Jewish ideas, were exempt from the fires.[22]

The professors' authoritarianism seeped into and corroded the sensibilities of their students, who in turn believed that civic freedoms and moral relativism were destructive. The latter's distrust of democratic values is borne out in a study of German youth in 1932: "These young people have only unspeakable contempt for the 'liberal' world;...they know that compromises in matters spiritual are the beginning of all vices and lies."[23] Like their teachers, these students believed that Germany was confronted with a fundamental crisis, that democracy was a moral invertebrate. The only solution was an unquestioning allegiance to a great leader who had the spine to remove, in Hitler's words, "the canker of Democracy" and inspire educators to minimize book learning, and instead mould character and develop comradeship with fellow Aryans.[24] By minimizing "insipid intellectualism" and promoting a vision of the *Volk* purged of "impurities," the aim was to relieve the German public of any responsibility for what subsequently occurred by surrendering their capacity for thought and placing faith in their Führer. On the very day of the book burnings in Berlin, the Marxist and Expressionist playwright, Ernst Toller, captured the essence of what happens to people who succumb to the seductive belief that "reason paralyses the will, saps the spirit and destroys the basis of society." No longer capable of responsible thinking, they become susceptible to the collective delusion that

> a man would come, a leader, a Caesar, a Messiah, and perform miracles. He would assume responsibility for the future, take control of everyone's lives, banish fear, put an end to misery, create a new people, a glorious new Reich, and fulfilling a supernatural mission, change old Adam into a new man.[25]

Martin Heidegger:
The Love Affair with Unreason

Despite the official contemptuous attitude toward reason, intellectuals also repudiated the checks and balances of a democracy and embraced a preternatural, albeit secular, Messiah. Among the one-half of German philosophers who became members of the Nazi Party, was the illustrious Martin Heidegger. He too succumbed to the belief that a leader could socially engineer the new man and that he could play an instrumental role in facilitating that change. Such illusions rendered him vulnerable to the opportunism offered by the siren song of power. His affiliation with National Socialism, not only in his brief official capacity but also in his lifelong inner commitment to its spirit, rendered him a self-deluded individual, but more importantly, resulted in his worldview filtering into his philosophy. As a charismatic teacher, Heidegger captivated generations of students. He refuted the free discussion and criticism of the Enlightenment, its belief in the rights of man, in individual liberty and in democracy. He rejected with equal disdain both liberalism and Bolshevism since they were in the business of "making a people happy;" however, he considered communism more authentic and truthful than democracy.[26] Despising the German manifestation of liberalism, the Weimar Republic, he saw it as mired in mediocrity, a bickering party system and a nihilistic culture that exuded a soulless modernity. Heidegger contended that the pluralism and hedonism of the Weimar years besmirched the self-sacrificing Teutonic toughness displayed by soldiers during the Great War and by the paramilitary *Freikorps*. It disturbed him that the Great War, in which German combatants made a conscious decision "to live dangerously" and avoid the "flight from death," had hardly rippled the national consciousness. He responded by calling in 1929 for "someone capable of instilling terror into our *Dasein*" (literally being-there) and of taking the decisive action to confront the evils of modernity posed by Communism and modern technology.[27]

Given his ultra-nationalist sensibility, his exaltation of the need for sacrifice and his authoritarian temperament, it is unsurprising that Heidegger greeted National Socialism as a "great awakening." To him it was a deliverance that would reverse the liberalism and Germany's precipitous decline and allow it to be the saviour of Europe. Given that Heidegger also rejected traditional morality and logic preferring in his words the "turbulence of more original questioning," it is understandable that he embraced Hitler as a modern philosopher-king who appeared to incarnate "authenticity;" as he had distinguished himself from the masses, he would mobilize the *Volk* to transform the world.[28] According to his biographer, Heidegger was "bewitched" by Hitler and believed that "the revolution was more than politics; it was a new act in the history of Being, the beginning of a new era." Far from thinking that his country was collapsing into barbarism, the genius of Nazi revolution represented the "overturning of the entire human Being," an occasion that would "penetrate his philosophy to the core."[29]

Until recently, most scholars maintained that Heidegger's foray into politics was a disgraceful but brief aberration that in no way tarnished his academic reputation. But recently, a number of scholars have convincingly argued that his philosophy is inseparable from his politics, a position that Heidegger himself would have supported during the period of the Third Reich.[30] Indeed, he made this stunning admission to a former graduate student, the Jewish Karl Löwith, when they met in Rome in 1936. Observing that Heidegger was sporting his swastika insignia in his lapel, Löwith suggested to him that "his partisanship for National Socialism lay in the essence of his philosophy. Heidegger agreed with me without reservation."[31]

His work *Being and Time* only subtly evidences that Heidegger was by the late 1920s already a proto-Nazi. On the surface, his brand of existentialism appears to be apolitical, offering little insight into the author's 1933 submission to Hitler. Without offering any real evidence and assuming it would be self-evident to his reader, he argues that most people conform to social norms and avoid authentic choices regarding fundamental decisions such as those that give recognition to their own mortality. Instead, guided by public opinion exemplified by newspapers, they act according to their "anyone self." In this "tranquilized" state, people's opinions and pleasures are a flight from the truth about what it means to be "authentic" and thereby live in a noble and courageous manner. Their language degenerates into "idle talk" and Plato's "cave chatter." By contrast an authentic existence which Heidegger calls *Dasein* that encapsulates a "resolute and radical autonomy" individualizes and isolates us. After freeing oneself from conventional norms in order to choose, the burden of authentic resoluteness is too unbearable:

> we are never capable of stepping out on our own without
> relying somehow and to some extent on pre-existing cultural
> roles and norms....The choice is not made by the individual at
> all but is predetermined by the destiny of the *Volk* in which
> one belongs.

Given the state of Germany at the time, *Dasein* predisposed Heidegger to Nazism. He urged his fellow countrymen to open themselves to the historical possibilities that this movement offered them because "individual fates had already been determined by the Hitler revolution [and] could only consist in an unconditional submission to Hitler."[32] Authenticity is not possible for the individual since the individual or the human 'I' counts for nothing, unless he surrenders to the "community of the people." In this moment in German history, only the illiberalism of National Socialism could relieve the burden of an autonomous existence by providing a sense of belonging and relieving its people of having to think for themselves.[33]

Even before 1933, Heidegger's ideological beliefs revealed a close compatibility with official Nazi policy. Although most scholars contend that he rejected biologically-based racism, the philosopher Immanuel Faye argues that Heidegger's racism was inseparable from his conception of existence. According to Heidegger, "Race and lineage" should not be "described on the basis of an outdated liberal ideology" that was "insufficiently deep" and based on a foreign Anglo-Saxon Darwinism, but be "transposed into the existence of man." The health of a people could only be understood in racial terms. He made explicit his beliefs after Hitler came to power in 1933 when he addressed physicians: "For every people, the first warranty of its authenticity and greatness is in its blood, its soil and its physical growth," and that growth can only be assured through its "extension," by expanding its living space. In another context, he referred to the unity of the "people" as the "unity of blood and stock," linked to "race."[34] No wonder that he endorsed the Führer's ethnic nationalism about the need to purify the *Volk* from the cultural contamination of the Jews. In a private letter about the granting of scholarships in 1929, Heidegger argued that Germany needed more scholars rooted in its "soil" while complaining about the "Judaization" of intellectual life. Jews for Heidegger should be excluded and denied the privileges of native citizens because they represented a danger as a consequence of their nomadic wanderings and urban identity that never allowed them to grow roots in the homeland.[35]

There was both a linguistic and political dimension to Heidegger's belief in the superiority of the German *Volk* over other nations and in his contempt for Jews. In the tradition of German Romanticism, Heidegger believed that the German language, along with Greek, was original, and therefore privileged. For Heidegger only those who shared the language bond with the Greeks could genuinely experience the truth of Being. All others, including Jews, were merely "foreigners" ontologically, and increasingly, politically. By 1933 in private conversation he spoke of "a dangerous network of Jews" and he wrote that "Bolshevism is in fact Jewish."[36] His philosophy and politics became increasingly intertwined. Historian Peter Gay provides possibly the best and most pungent explanation for why Heidegger succumbed to the totalitarian temptation:

> Heidegger sanctioned professorial respectability to the love affair with unreason and death that dominated so many Germans in this hard time....Reason and intellect are hopelessly inadequate guides to the secret of being; had not Heidegger said that thinking is the mortal enemy of understanding?...And Heidegger's life—his isolation, his peasant-like appearance, his deliberate provincialism, his hatred of the city—seemed to confirm his philosophy, which was a disdainful rejection of modern urban rationalist civilization, an eruptive nihilism. Whatever the precise philosophical import of *Sein und Zeit* [*Being and Time*] and the works that surrounded it, Heidegger's work amounted to a denigration of Weimar, that creature of reason, and an exaltation of movements like that of the Nazis, who thought with their blood, worshipped the charismatic leader, praised and practiced murder, and hoped to stamp out reason—forever—in the drunken embrace of that life which is death. By no means all who read Heidegger were Nazis, or became Nazis because they read him....But Heidegger gave no one reason not to be a Nazi, and good reasons to be one.[37]

Just as philosophically Heidegger purported the individual should be subsumed into the national community, he believed the threat posed by the Soviet Union meant that individuals should be sacrificed for the *Volk*. Based on the impressions of a friend, who visited Heidegger at his cabin retreat in the Black Forest, the philosopher believed that only a dictator who would not shrink from imposing Draconian measures could defeat Bolshevism because *that* represented the destruction of everything of value. He supported any means—the anti-Jewish boycotts, the suppression of civil liberties by the employment of brutal police methods, including incarceration in concentration camps, and the murder of political opponents—that strengthened the blood and soil of the German race.[38] In this respect, he was no different than millions of his fellow Germans who were seduced by National Socialism, illustrating what Hannah Arendt, his former student and lover, characterized as "the alliance between the Mob and the Elite."[39] The most unsavoury thuggery could be justified to eliminate all dissent from the political left, which he reviled as the scourge of Bolshevism—precisely what the leadership was proclaiming. According to his friend and fellow philosopher, Karl Jaspers, Heidegger was "gripped by that intoxication," a force so powerful that as late as 1942 he could still speak of "the historical uniqueness" of National Socialism.[40]

"Conquering the world of educated men and scholars"*

In the hope of becoming the philosophical tribune of the Nazi movement, Heidegger joined the Party with great fanfare in a public ceremony on May 1, 1933. This was a momentous decision for Heidegger, who later stated that until this moment he had shown no interest in practical politics. Yet there is evidence that he concealed the extent of his involvement in National Socialism and that his private commitment to it dates back as far as Christmas 1931. The philosopher believed Hitler's revolution was transformational since the occasion represented the triumph of non-political politics—a collective breakout from Plato's cave. It then offered Heidegger a pivotal opportunity to implement his educational and philosophical goals that he had conceived during his political incubation of the 1920s when he was writing *Being and Time*.

Later in May, Heidegger's election to rector at Freiberg was carefully staged by National Socialists within the university. When

---

* Hugo Ott, *Martin Heidegger: A Political Life*, trans. Allan Blunden (London: HarperCollins, 1993), 169.

he delivered his infamous address amid swastika flags, '*Sieg Heil*' salutes and a robust rendition of the Horst-Wessel song, he surely appreciated that the atmosphere in the room was charged with an intensity that revealed those rare moments of authentic existence. Inspired by a contemporary biography of Herman Göring, whom he admired for embodying the essence of German manhood, Heidegger's speech was equally studded with Nazi clichés about the essential will, mission and hardness. He informed his enthusiastic audience that "we must commit all our struggle to conquering the world of educated men and scholars for the new political spirit."[41] In stark contrast to his previous views that scholarship should be free from utilitarian considerations, Heidegger now asserted that it should serve national goals. Heidegger declared that the much vaunted academic freedom (in his mind "inauthentic") was over, and would be replaced by obligations and service: work camps and military service should have equal weight with academia. Since Heidegger believed that his philosophy was the only authentic possibility for national renewal, the philosopher and his students no longer should be confined to the classroom or the library. Rather they would be dispatched to perform work and military service in order to serve the state. In contrast to the superficiality of the "literati's dishonest chatter," he revered the rural peasants' simplicity and lack of sophistication and was convinced that the "world of the intellect" must draw its strength from the sources of "blood and soil." Only then could it retain its pre-eminence. The divisiveness characterized by "political parties, classes and academic disciplines, and competing value-claims [could] only be resolved by recourse to a *total state*." Heralding deliverance from democracy and endorsing a militaristic state, Heidegger announced in a bellicose tone that "German students are on the march." Heidegger left no doubt about his conviction that the "traditional university [was] dead" and that its replacement should "reject the humanizing Christian ideas" and harness its energies to that of the *Volk*.[42]

Given his belief that the community should supplant the egoism of individualism, Heidegger's delusion that Hitler was creating an authentic Germany is explicable. But for one who had spent almost his entire adult life thinking, teaching and writing, it is disquieting how dismissive he could be of traditional philosophy and his fellow philosophers. Since he announced "the end of the philosophy" that had exalted a "thought deprived of soil and power," there was little need for most teachers.[43] During a June 1933 conversation with Karl Jaspers, a friend and colleague, Heidegger stated that it was "nonsense that there should be so many professors of philosophy, only two or three should be kept in Germany." When Heidegger was asked which ones, he tellingly remained silent.[44] Given that he regarded himself as the greatest philosopher since Heraclites, we know for certain who one of them would be. This was Heidegger's way of indicating that few who taught philosophy at university were capable of thinking about the radical questions necessary for the National Socialist revolution to remain true to its meaning.

In the following year as rector, Heidegger tried to implement the ideas expressed in his rectoral address that one scholar contends is a "condensed and concentrated expression of Heidegger's most enduring philosophical themes."[45] Inspired by Nietzsche's repudiation of academic freedom and support for a "great Führer," Heidegger formulated his educational philosophy and in a memo circulated it to the university deans:

> Since the first days of my acceptance of office, the defining
> principle and the authentic [if only gradually realizable] goal
> [of my rectorship] has been *the fundamental transformation
> of scholarly education on the basis of the forces and demands
> of the National Socialist State*....The individual counts for noth-
> ing. The fate of our *Volk* in its state counts for everything.[46]

In terms of applying this philosophy, he stated that the criteria for hiring and promotion of faculty would in part depend upon "political evaluation" of the candidate's suitability. Putting his ideas into practice, he jettisoned academic freedom and the democratic structures of the university by introducing the "Führer principle," a top-down hierarchical reorganization which would make him its virtual dictator.

Even though he did everything he could to avoid combat operations in both world wars—he served as a weatherman in meteorological service helping to prepare poison gas attacks by aligning them with favourable weather conditions—he celebrated the martial spirit and delighted in issuing military orders. His leadership style vicariously satisfied a need to experience the military life. Like others, including Carl Schmitt, who missed the frontline war experience, he revered the combat soldier and transformed him into a mythic figure. Both men counted the war hero and author, Ernst Jünger, among their friends, and hated the pacifist disillusionment of Erich Maria Remarque. Heidegger's speeches were decorated with bellicose rhetoric as he lionized the young men who fought in the Great War—who demonstrated courage under fire and a readiness to die for the *Volk*. Those that did fall in combat "died the most beautiful and greatest death" because "it dared to be the most supreme sacrifice for the fate of the *Volk*."[47]

Service to the community—through military training or simply blind loyalty to Hitler—was also an expression of heroic "resoluteness." Any sign of ambiguity signified a lack of decisiveness, an expression of inauthentic being. One scholar has provided a cogent summary of his goals:

> Heidegger wanted nothing less than, in his words, 'the complete overturning of our German existence'—beginning with the university system—so as to bring about a spiritual rebirth of the West. And with a blindness and naiveté that only a philosopher could muster, he chose to ride the tiger of Nazism to what he thought would be the greatest cultural revolution since Plato.[48]

Accordingly, he ordered a faculty member, a former naval commander, to write a military code for the faculty whereby they would be treated as an officer corps. The draft approved by Heidegger contained the following ominous sentence: "We seek to cleanse our ranks of inferior elements and thwart the forces of degeneracy in the future." No doubt he was aware of the political and racist implications of this statement. As it turned out, the code coalesced with the 1933 law to purge the Civil Service of Jews. This meant the expulsion of all Jews from the university staff though he did write a letter to the Ministry of Education in an attempt to prevent the dismissal of two "Jews of the better sort" as their "scientific standing was beyond doubt."[49] Even after his rectorship ended, as late as 1938, Heidegger, the lapsed Catholic, destroyed the careers of two Catholic students because they were insufficiently enthusiastic about National Socialism and he believed that no Catholic could ever be a genuine philosopher. On a personal level, he shamelessly informed upon and blackballed colleagues whom he believed did not embody National Socialist convictions.

Among these victims was a Nobel-prize winning chemistry professor who had expressed pacifist leanings during the Great War. Furthermore, Heidegger ended his relationship with his former mentor, the Jewish Edmund Husserl when the latter was forbidden to teach under Nazi law. Later Husserl expressed with some bitterness his feelings about his once-warm relationship with Heidegger:

> The lovely conclusion to this 'bosom friendship' between philosophers was his publicly enacted entrance into the Nazi party on May 1: very theatrical, indeed! Before that he took the initiative and broke off relations with me—soon after his appointment [at Freiburg] in fact. And over the last few years there was his anti-Semitism, which he came to express with his increasing vigour, even against the circle of his most enthusiastic students, as well as around the department. That was a hard thing to get over.[50]

Heidegger's military proclivities and assault on the traditional university similarly affected student life. In November 1933, he wrote an article in a student newspaper proclaiming that the National Socialist Revolution brings the total transformation of our German *Dasein* urging them not to "let principles and 'ideas' be the rules of [their] Being. The Führer alone is the present and future reality and its law," lines that later provoked his former student, Herbert Marcuse, to rue that they constituted a "betrayal of philosophy as such and everything it stands for."[51] Despite Heidegger's statement in his 1966 *Der Spiegel* interview that he ordered a ban on book burning, one did occur at Freiberg during the first week of May and the students planned one for June that was cancelled due to rain. Despite his later denials, he was there for the one in June and was one of the speakers who lauded the burning of books that symbolized the destruction of the un-German spirit: "Flame, announce to us, light up for us, show us the path *from which there is no turning back*."[52] Heidegger also prohibited Jewish students who had begun their doctoral dissertations with him receiving their degrees and withheld economic assistance from them and their Marxist colleagues; however, he granted them to student members of the SA and SS. The military code also mandated the obligatory use of the Nazi salute at the beginning and end of each class in which he regularly appeared in a brown shirt. With his long-time friend, Eugen Fischer, one of those responsible for the legitimization of the Nazi theories of racial hygiene, Heidegger coordinated the organization of the Department for Racial Matters directed by the SS who in turn arranged for specialists to teach courses. Attendance was compulsory as was the wearing of the SA or SS uniform in class. To ensure that students received sufficient indoctrination, he organized and supervised the creation of camps, to which students were marched from Freiberg in their uniforms so that they could, in his words, "harden [themselves] deliberately." When they were not communing with the hills of the Fatherland, they were listening to talks on race and the racial principle. Part of Heidegger's responsibility was the elimination of participants "who didn't fit in there." One indication of his attitude toward the camps was his willingness to continue as director after he left his position as rector. Interestingly given his devotion to the military ethos, when Heidegger was drafted into the reservists in 1944, he was relieved to be released from his obligations because of Fischer's intervention. [53]

Thinking his Way into Evil

H eidegger's resignation as rector in April 1934 has prompted speculation that he became disenchanted with the Party. To be sure, his military style alienated many colleagues and there is little doubt that within the Party there was a faction of petty and jealous former colleagues that was determined to prevent his being awarded a high position in the Reich. Despite his resentment toward this vicious campaign, Heidegger renewed his membership every year until 1945 and he remained unstinting in his commitment to Party ideals and his faith in Hitler, even after the military defeat of the Nazis. In retrospect, Heidegger stated that he became disillusioned with the Party after the June 1934 "Night of the Long Knives" in which thousands were murdered, but a few weeks later, he signed a declaration of allegiance to Hitler. Months later in one of his courses, he did not hesitate to assert that "the [present] state should...continue to exist beyond fifty or one hundred years." In another course he has nothing but praise for the "one and only Führer."[54]

Karl Löwith recalled that Heidegger in 1936 left no doubt about his belief in Hitler. Heidegger was convinced now, as before, that National Socialism was the right course for Germany. In one lecture, he dismissed the significance of the "external takeover" and focused on the "inner re-education of the whole *Volk* to the goal of willing/wanting its own unanimity and unity"—in short his anathema to liberalism.[55] Löwith noted how Heidegger dismissed Streicher and the *Der Stürmer* as pornography, and suggested that he (Streicher) was very different from Hitler. Heidegger did not possess the insight to recognize the psychic similarities in the two men. Löwith, however, was under no illusion. Writing in 1940 with the memory of the pogrom vividly etched in his mind, Löwith perceptively commented: "In truth, the programme of that 'pornography' was fulfilled in every last detail and became a German reality in November 1938; and nobody can deny that Streicher and Hitler were in total agreement on this matter."[56] Presumably so too was Heidegger as he never registered the slightest resistance to *Kristallnacht*.

Some scholars have argued that Heidegger during the 1930s was proposing something far more radical than the Party was prepared to accept and that its members viewed him with suspicion. Faculty members warned Nazi officials that Heidegger's belief about philosophy's role in assuring the success of the revolution could "dissolve into an aporetic [insoluble contradiction] of endless questioning" and result in paralysis. This was nihilism.[57] These misgivings were likely grounded in a combination of legitimate fears and petty jealousies, misgivings that would be received sympathetically by some Party officials. There is also no question that a Party, whose very essence was anti-intellectual, would have members who resented intellectual elitists. Additionally, Heidegger's writings are notoriously dense and, therefore, the vast majority of the members would have no real comprehension of his philosophy. Yet this disdain for him should not obscure the fact that he continued to support Hitler and the ideology of the Third Reich. In his speeches, lectures and private letters, Heidegger endorses a close relationship between his philosophy and politics. Consider also that if Heidegger were estranged from Party elites, it is hard to understand why, in 1938, a long excerpt from his rectoral address would be published in a book of documents that featured speeches by Hitler and other potentates. Heidegger was the only academic represented.[58] That said, he still harboured misgivings toward certain Party officials for misleading the Führer.

Heidegger's 1935 lectures, *An Introduction to Metaphysics*, was a defence of Nazi ideology, though some apologists have dubbed it a critique. In the work, Heidegger argues that the Party could only achieve its historical destiny and German greatness if it focused less on appearance and more on the essence of National Socialism. He warns his readers that Germany was threatened from the two great dangers of the twentieth century, American capitalism and Soviet Communism, which were "both driven by the mad rush of unbridled technology and the endless organization of the average man."[59] There was nothing to distinguish them from each other as both represented the unbridled nihilism of modern life, one preoccupied with size, speed and mass consumerism, the other based on control of economic production. Nonetheless, *Metaphysics* cautions that National Socialism could lose its way and succumb to the "same dreary technological frenzy" with a hedonistic, mindless culture if Germans abandoned the "hardness and comfortlessness of philosophy."[60] It could be diverted by the histrionics of mass rallies and banalities, signs that threatened to fritter away its revolutionary potential. In metaphysical terms, this meant the German nation would betray its historical destiny and sink into superficiality and consumerism, and intelligence would be placed at the service of utilitarianism. He pleaded that "this *Volk*...must move itself and thereby the history of the West beyond the center of their future 'happening' and *into the primordial realm of the powers of Being.*" This is the ultra-nationalist and militarist speaking. With this turgid passage, Heidegger is attempting to justify the German need for *Lebensraum* while adorning this imperialist– Fascist view with his own metaphysical idea of the history of Being.[61] He extolled the creative elite of "violent men" who stood above and outside the law "without statute and limit," who disdained everything "safe and unendangered." These "perpetrators of violence" forsake safety in order to "embrace the danger of the battle for Being." They were essential to crush the "encrusted powers of convention and everydayness" of routine; only through their violence would the German people become strong and great.[62] In oblique language, Heidegger was trying to legitimatize what Hitler would undertake a few years later when he set out to conquer Europe.

After Germany invaded and defeated France, Heidegger pulled a volte-face in his lectures on European nihilism. Since technology had contributed to *Blitzkrieg* victories for the Reich, he rhapsodized about the "machine economy". As the embodiment of a "new humanity," the victorious German army mastered the new technology in order "to establish an unconditional mastery of the earth."[63] His earlier despair about the proliferation of technology and the cult of production was forgotten. Heidegger fully endorsed the regime's passion for autobahn construction because it served not only the utilitarian need to transport large number of soldiers and weaponry, but the equally important goal to "demonstrate that technology could overcome nature, the physical world could be changed by an act of will."[64] As late as 1942 with the Holocaust underway, he firmly believed that "the Germans and they alone can save the West for its history."[65] With the defeat of Nazism, he returned to his critique of technology. When he did comment on the Holocaust during a lecture in 1949, he grotesquely trivialized it by comparing it to the problems caused by mechanized agriculture, another mere example of the abuse of technology. By then, he lamented that the Third Reich, like America and the Soviet Union, had succumbed to the perils of technology.

While the collapse of the Third Reich revealed to him the dangers, if not the barbarities of Nazism, he never abandoned his faith in National Socialism. Its outer organizational, administrative and military-political form had failed, but its ideology remained unsullied. Its collapse precipitated a dramatic reversal in his personal fortunes when a de-Nazification committee in 1945 investigated him; a process that included an evaluation from his one-time friend, Karl Jaspers. Jaspers was by no means a liberal democrat; he believed that Heidegger should continue to write, though he should not be allowed to teach. Jaspers contended that the problem was not Heidegger's opinions, but his mode of thinking that was "fundamentally unfree, dictatorial and uncommunicative." He should not teach until a "genuine rebirth" took place within him. "I think it would be quite wrong to turn such a teacher loose on the young people today, who are psychologically extremely vulnerable. First of all the young must be taught how to think for themselves."[66] Heidegger was not allowed to teach again until 1950.

During these years, there is little evidence of Heidegger undergoing a "genuine rebirth." Yet in order to reclaim his reputation, Heidegger made every effort to appear respectable. After 1945 he attempted to disassociate his philosophy from his politics. He did so by laundering his past about the extent and nature of his involvement with the Party, re-editing some of his collected writings and ensuring they were not published in his lifetime. In a set of lectures Heidegger had delivered in 1935 on Nietzsche, he deleted from the 1961 print edition (that has only become available posthumously) his contention that as long as "Europe still feels the need to cling to "democracy"...this would be its historical death."[67] When *Metaphysics* was published in 1953, he did not refer, as he had in the 1935 lectures, to "the inner truth and greatness of the National Socialist movement," but only to "this movement." If the meaning expressed in that work about his enthusiasm for the warrior ethos was not clear, Heidegger was more direct when he addressed students. In unpublished manuscripts from the period that were culled from the archives, he referred to the need to identity the enemy "who poses an essential threat to the existence of the people and its members." The most dangerous enemy was "not necessarily the outside enemy." He may not even appear to be an enemy because he "may have grafted himself onto the innermost root of the existence of the people," but he must be hunted down "with the goal of total extermination." These subtle references suggest that Heidegger had the Jews in mind. Elsewhere, in a euphoric rhapsody about the "superiority of the Fuhrer," who endows the people with the strength to provide the necessary sacrifices, he warned that the threat they face will come from "death and the devil." As the latter epithet was specifically used by Hitler to demonize Jews in *Mein Kampf*, it is unlikely that Heidegger or his audience would not have understood that allusion. In another document, he is more explicit when he asserts that "Semitic nomads" should be denied access to "German space." As Karl Löwith commented in 1946, "he [Heidegger] was a National Socialist and remained one."[68]

Despite the shifts in Heidegger's thought, certain attitudes remained consistent. Having always expressed from his Olympian perch a preference for rank and hierarchy, he could barely contain his contempt for individuals who largely lived "inauthentic" lives "guided by chatter, idle curiosity and ambiguity," believing they were incapable of determining their own destinies.[69] His chief explanation for this lamentable state of affairs was the elevation of the individual. Since the Renaissance, the individual has been "tragically" regarded as the measure of all things and the subsequent effort of the individual to "develop the personality" has led by 1933 to the "downfall of our state."[70] Human needs, ideals and interests merit no value; the individual has no criteria to judge himself because criteria are prescribed by society.

Ethics was not a part of Heidegger's philosophical repertoire; his call to free oneself from conventional restraints was encouragement to reject morality. When one of his former protégés, Herbert Marcuse, asked his views about the death of millions during the war, Heidegger revealed his bankrupt morality. All he could do was to suggest a moral equivalency between the Holocaust and the ethnic cleansing and death of Germans who were expelled from Western Polish territory by Poles, many of whom were themselves refugees from the newly-expanded Soviet territory. What happened to these Germans, as well as those from other parts of Eastern Europe, was a tragedy to be sure, but given the monstrous crimes perpetrated by the Nazis upon European Jews, Poles, Czechs and Soviets, among others, it was inevitable that in the expulsion of up to twelve million Germans to the new shrunken Germany, authorized under the Potsdam Agreement, that a certain amount of revenge would be exacted leaving an estimated two and one quarter million Germans dead. The uprooting of Germans from their homes, and their death by hunger, exposure, disease and executions, cannot be equated with the magnitude of the Nazi agenda to exterminate every Jew, to enslave those Slavs they did not murder and to expedite the Hunger Plan that entailed starving thirty million Soviet citizens. None of these foul Nazi deeds caused Heidegger to question his philosophical premises that were anchored in authoritarianism and elitism; indeed, they did not appear to disturb him.

Whatever mild criticisms he levied against a lawless and racist regime were not political but ontological. In Heidegger's veiled criticism of the Third Reich, he argued that it failed to live up to its revolutionary potential because the Party did not share his metaphysics or the quasi-mystical politics of *Dasein*. They, not him, had destroyed the "inner truth" and the "greatness" of the movement. But like Schmitt and the myriad scientists who lent the regime the prestige of their names, Heidegger was equally complicitous because he claimed he understood Nazism better than did the Nazis themselves. He believed it would be his responsibility, according to his colleague, Jaspers, to "lead the leader." Even if Jaspers' memorable phrase was hyperbolic, there is little doubt that Heidegger tenaciously harboured illusions of being the

philosophical avatar of the movement. Through the grandiosity of
his disappointments, he could only interpret the policies and practices of National Socialism as a "betrayed revolution, which to him
was a metaphysical revolution, a 'revelation of Being' on the soil
of a national community."[71] For one who had wanted the nation to
ask the hard questions, and had written on the existential themes
of responsibility and resoluteness, the unrepentant Heidegger
failed to reflect upon any possible personal malfeasance or recant
any of his positions. With wilful amnesia, he would not even ascribe responsibility for what had happened to Germany to any human agent. Instead he allotted the blame to impersonal forces. In
a lecture delivered in 1949 but not available until 1994, Heidegger
did refer to the Holocaust in ontological terms:

> Hundreds of thousands die *en masse*. Do they die? They per-
> ish. They are put down. Do they die?...They are liquated un-
> noticed in death camps. And also, without such—millions in
> China sunken in poverty perish from hunger. But to be able
> to die means to carry out death in its essence. To be able to
> die means to carry out this resolution. We can only do this if
> our essence likes the essence of death.

According to Heidegger, "no one died in a death camp because
none of those exterminated there bore within their essence the
possibility of death."[72] Heidegger's casuistry was in stark contrast
to the courage and mea culpa expressed by Jaspers. In August
1945, he delivered an address whereby he reminded his audience
that

> we did not go in the streets when our Jewish friends were led
> away, we did not scream until we were destroyed. We pre-
> ferred to stay alive, on the feeble, if logical, ground that our
> death could not have helped anyone....We are guilty of being
> alive.[73]

Heidegger could never transcend his parochial attachment to
the pre-industrial simplicities of German Romanticism and his revulsion for urbanization, industrialism and cosmopolitanism. That
attachment was in part physical; he rarely travelled and only for
short times. It was also metaphysical because he endowed the landscape and its peasants with a mystical status: "the inner relationship of my own work to the Black Forest and its people comes from

a centuries-long and irreplaceable rootedness in the Alemannian–Swabian soil."[74] Based on his writings, it is clear that German territory could only be populated by Germans, including those who had been relegated outside its borders by the "forced peace" of Versailles. There is no evidence, however, that Heidegger was as explicit in condemning the cosmopolitanism of Berlin as did one obscure Wilhelm Stapel who scathingly referred to its liberal intelligentsia as a "cesspool...the spoiler of all noble and healthy life" who exuded "saucy airs" and the "endless cackle of irony." But Heidegger's celebration of the "hard race" in its struggle against Slavs and Eastern European Jews leaves little doubt that he would likely endorse Stapel's sentiment that these inferior peoples were blighting the city with "an embarrassing mixture."[75] On linguistic grounds alone, these interlopers would disqualify as authentic Germans. Combine his reverence for the soldiers who died in combat with his indifference to civil rights and political details, the essence of Heidegger's personal brand of National Socialism did not radically deviate from the official version.

Although Heidegger eventually rejected any form of political activity and preferred instead to live in his head, his thinking never abandoned the totalitarian premise that the ends justified the means. While there is much in his ex cathedral writings that would baffle the true believers of National Socialism, there is also a cluster of assumptions and explicit statements that explain why he fully endorsed its messianic visions. The central thrust of Heidegger's thought is that we are essentially creatures of time who exist in a specific historical moment; according to his thinking, the choices he made during his time form the basis of how posterity must judge him. Seduced by delusions of power, monumental myopia and an enduring but misplaced faith in the ability of Germans to lead Europe out of nihilism, Heidegger failed to distinguish between metaphysics and the empirical realities of individuals, particularly those that the regime declared persona non grata. In 1947 he trivialized the radical evil Hitler had inflicted on the world: "Perhaps the only distinguishing feature of the present age lies in the fact that wholeness as a dimension of life is closed to us. Perhaps this is the only evil."[76] Evidently, concrete acts of evil were not worthy of his philosophical purview.

Heidegger was by no means unique in his seduction to the totalitarian temptation. In certain respects, he resembled the French philosopher, the fellow traveller, Jean-Paul Sartre, who was deeply influenced by the German apologist for National Socialism. Although their motives differed, both men displayed no compunction about supporting barbarous regimes. Sartre justified the cruelty of the Stalinist regime after World War II because of its purported benevolent social intentions, even though its primary victims were the people it claimed to benefit. Sartre also fabricated his role as a resistance fighter during that war and maintained that stance throughout his life in a manner similar to Heidegger's exaggeration of his war effort during the Great War.

A large swathe of the wider population, who would have struggled greatly with Heidegger's prose, shared his disdain for anything that smacked of liberalism or cosmopolitanism. They supported the Nazi intention to destroy un-German literature, art, theatre, music and film because they viewed cultural modernism as expressions of degeneration and decay. Cultural conservatism assisted Hitler in manipulating the *Zeitgeist* for his own purposes as he understood that the regime's ideological and racial enemies and their avant-garde artistic expression seamlessly flowed together, the living and the printed embodiment of the un-German spirit.[77] To silence his enemies, he destroyed their artistic endeavours and in 1933, removed their Jewish and "politically unreliable" creators from official state positions; therefore, he foreclosed any alternatives to a prescribed way of viewing the world. One example of his ability to mould the German intellect according to his own political agenda was a poster from an exhibition at the Essen library in 1937 that applauded the one-third decrease in book borrowings within four years as "healthy recovery—decline in indiscriminate reading." The reasons cited reveal the narrowing down of the individual's area of freedom and his private life: "return to employment, political activity for nation and state, labour service duty, military service."[78] Will and action, not reflection, were de rigueur in Hitler's Reich. According to a French journalist who did a walking tour of Germany during the late Weimar and early Third Reich, the new breed of National Socialists "didn't like intelligence, what Hitler calls 'so-called intelligence.' And wherever they encounter it, they pursue it, bind it to the stake, and deliver it to the flames."[79] The book burnings encapsulated the National Socialists' fear of cultural pluralism and the cut and thrust of the market place of ideas. This barbarism vividly illustrates that anti-intellectualism,

which dulled critical faculties and increased the potential for succumbing to trances and escaping responsibility, is a fundamental
trait of fascism. Even a man such as Martin Heidegger—a brilliant
thinker and deeply erudite—was within reach of such a powerful
and corrupting influence. The radiance he experienced during the
early days of the Third Reich cast a permanent shadow over him.
In his memoirs, Karl Jaspers recalled his own reaction to greeting
a euphoric Heidegger shortly after Hitler had been named chancellor. He "no longer trusted his [Heidegger's] transformed nature"
and felt threatened "in view of the violence in which Heidegger
now participated." We should not be surprised, therefore, by a perceptive reviewer who contended that Heidegger "did not drift into
evil, but thought his way into it."[80] That descent extended beyond
his disastrous foray into politics; it persisted throughout his life as
he continued to flog his own version of the faith, one that could
only be achieved through control and homogenization.

Aesthetics in Nazi Germany

People like to say: Revolution is beautiful, it is
only the terror arising from it which is evil. But
this is not true. The evil is already present in
the beautiful, hell is already contained in the
dream of paradise and if we wish to understand the essence of hell, we must examine the
essence of paradise from which it originated.

—The Book of Laughter and Forgetting
Milan Kundera

A palpably disingenuous feature of National Socialism was how its proponents attempted to promote its cultural products as disinterested, even apolitical. In reality, official art—by no means oblivious to aesthetic qualities—was primarily designed to express approved political and social values and to make it accessible to the public. Apart from a few egregious exceptions, the visual arts stressed the benign and the wholesome in which the ideological messages could be consciously missed; the subtlety contributed to its effectiveness. This aesthetics philosophy was successful primarily because its intended Aryan audience that benefited materially from the Reich was to a large extent receptive. As the Kundera epigraph suggests, the hellish nightmare of the Third Reich can never be fully grasped unless the "dream of paradise," that is its seductive nature, is recognized and its meaning unpacked.

Nazi efforts to secure compliancy from Aryan Germans relied heavily on appealing to economic self-interest. Economic, social and fiscal policies were designed to achieve that goal.

Unemployment vanished through its work creation programs in the form of building the autobahns and the armament industries. The poorer workers became recipients of the National Socialist Winter Aid charity. Pensions increased dramatically and workers were enrolled in a national health insurance program. Rent controls were strengthened. Family allowances and a progressive income tax were introduced, and newly married couples received substantial loans. Taxes were relatively low for all but the wealthiest Germans and corporations. By the outbreak of war, private citizens' spending power had risen to unprecedented levels. These benefits were largely possible because of deficit financing and the financial burden for tax revenues was shifted to the racial aliens. Jewish wealth was cannibalized. Later the citizens of the conquered territories were fleeced of their income, possessions and food, and were dragooned into supplying forced labour to ensure that Germans enjoyed a relatively good standard of living during the war.[1]

The increase in holiday entitlement and worker paid vacations contributed to the widespread support for the Labour Front's agency, "Strength through Joy" that offered tourism—combining pleasure with ideological content. Money confiscated from the old trade unions and other Weimar organizations enabled the government to subsidize vacations for working people. Group activities were encouraged: physical energy could be expended in swimming and hiking, diverting it from illicit sexual behaviour; those with modest incomes were able to enjoy the leisure pursuits—golf, tennis, sailing, skiing or horseback riding—which had formerly been the exclusive preserve of the rich. In order to satisfy both consumer desires and present a cross-class appeal, theatre and concert trips were arranged and even inexpensive cruises were made possible. Pleasure per se was never the Party's motivation in these athletic and cultural pursuits. Besides structuring free time, they were intended to synchronize tastes and indoctrinate travellers and recreationists with political and racial ideas. For city people to travel to other parts of Germany, especially rural areas, was the state's attempt to harmonize the different regions. If they toured abroad, they would be reminded of the superiority of German values. Even if there were snafus, like social class tensions over rowdy behaviour or racial lectures were sparsely attended, the subsidized prices allowed the more prosperous working class holiday opportunities which had never been possible and they did not hesitate to express their gratitude. More importantly, the program allowed former critics to become reconciled to the regime. Even after the Third Reich came to a devastating end, the "Strength through Joy" program was nostalgically and fondly remembered.[2] One historian has suggested that individuals not targeted for exclusion by the regime could live throughout the Reich years with rarely witnessing any evidence of a sinister state.[3] If this assessment is true, (and there is counter-evidence to suggest otherwise) certain Nazi goals were accomplished: a groundswell of support for the regime and a more cohesive *Volk*. When barbarities were inflicted on the state's supposedly less-than-human members, including confiscated property, others benefited from those who were dispossessed and ultimately driven out of the Reich. It is not surprising that the material advantages Germans acquired served as a narcotic to dull consciousness

Germans needed to fulfil certain obligations to become bona fide members of the *Volk*. After the 1935 Nuremburg laws, individuals had to secure the necessary paperwork to establish that their four grandparents were Aryan even if it meant soliciting the services of a genealogical researcher. They were also expected to participate in state rituals, and the evidence suggests that they did so voluntarily and in vast numbers, even though intimidation cannot be discounted. It is estimated that almost every German did at one time spend some time in a work, educational or community-service program. From the German Labour Front apprenticeships to the one million who participated in the annual charity drive before the war years, Germans embarked on the process of self-transformation that involved adapting their vocabulary to include the language of national integration and racial exclusiveness. The attempt to mould Germans into Aryans was an explicit goal of the Hitler Youth program that stressed physical fitness, heavy doses of indoctrination and military training. Whether the Youth leadership succeeded in the short term is uncertain. Large numbers objected to the regimentation and the lack of free time, and the incessant and crude efforts to eliminate individual consciousness. The latter was implemented by crushing civilized and sensitive behaviour and promoting comradeship in an effort to instil a coarse National Socialist sensibility. Over time the leaders' stress on heroism, struggle and competition did produce a generation of young men who were brutalized by the indoctrination. Easily prone to intimidation and violence, many were inclined to a visceral anti-Semitic and even an anti-Christian ethic. While they were alienated from their familial values, the raw material would be groomed to constitute one of the best fighting forces in the world.[4]

Economic and social well-being, along with the pride of being a member of a racial community, rendered *Volk* members more susceptible to the aesthetics of National Socialism. Officially approved films, visual arts and popular novels were explicitly designed to express the perfect Third Reich—in Hitler's words what was "eternally healthy, eternally beautiful." In this spirit, Hitler commissioned Leni Riefenstahl to translate this aesthetic into film and provided her with unstinting official support and unlimited resources. The results were the technically innovative, epic hymn to naked power, *Triumph of the Will* and the more subtle but insidious documentary on the 1936 Berlin games, *Olympia*, achievements that made the director the pre-eminent propagandist for the regime.

The Complicity of an Artist

L eni Riefenstahl was an ambitious careerist who sought to advance herself at any cost. A former dancer, she starred in a number of popular mountain films, a genre which combined the heroic striving and yearning for the ecstasy of German Romanticism with the proto-fascist sensibility that nature could cleanse the city dweller and only the healthiest would survive.[5] Prior to the Nazis coming to power, Riefenstahl made her directorial debut in a feature mountain film, *The Blue Light*. An overblown romantic fairytale about a wild-eyed witch frightening the stolid villagers, climbing up a mountain and communing with crystals above the swirling Alpine clouds, it showcased impressive images, inspired by early German Romanticism, particularly the landscape paintings of Caspar David Friedrich. Critics, however, reviled its mystical glorification of the forces of nature as sentimental kitsch. In retrospect, the scribe who denounced it as "sick at the core" was prescient because it anticipated the National Socialist ideology of blood and soil as the healing powers of nature. Reputedly outraged by the "Jewish critics," whom she dismissed as "foreigners" who did not understand German art, she sought a protector to shield her from unsympathetic reviewers and personal attacks.[6] Riefenstahl found him in Hitler, an early supporter of her film; its storyline about the sacrifice of a woman for the sake of a community was immensely appealing to the future Führer.

Even before they met, the attraction between the patron and his acolyte was mutual. During the filming of *The Blue Light* she found time to read *Mein Kampf* and "was fascinated by it." Riefenstahl heralded the author of this virulently racist tract as "the coming man" for whom she would work.[7] She heard him speak at a public rally and reveals in her self-serving memoir that she was "infected" by her sorcerer in late February 1932 from the moment she heard his address, "Fellow Germans!" She recalls a sensation that elevated her to orgasmic heights:

> I had an almost apocalyptic vision that I will never forget. It seemed as if the earth's surface was spreading out in front of me, like a hemisphere that suddenly splits apart in the middle, spewing out an enormous jet of water, so powerful that it touched the sky and shook the earth. I felt quite paralyzed.[8]

This gushing outburst toward a rabble-rouser whipping up mass hysteria in a sports stadium may have been an opening for insightful retrospective self-reflection. She might have wondered how it was possible that she separated his personality from his racist rant, that she dismissed it as campaign rhetoric, and that he would learn moderation once he was in power. Instead, almost fifty years later she would compartmentalize him in the same manner that she had always distinguished her own art from the politics swirling around her: like Winifred Wagner, she would quarantine him from the vicious excesses of the Party.

Her unremitting effort to sanitize her past and absolve herself of any responsibility for her collusion with the Nazi regime is evident in Ray Müller's 1993, *The Wonderful and Horrible Life of Leni Riefenstahl*. She conveys the impression that she had never heard of Hitler before hearing him speak. Yet according to two recent biographies, we know that she had already read *Mein Kampf*. Beyond her elaborate justifications and brittle dodginess that she expresses in Müller's film and in her autobiography, the biographies fully documented her propensity for outright lies, half truths and deceptions about her friendship with Party officials, her feigned ignorance about the state-sanctified racism of the Third

Reich, and her zeal for refuting the depth of her relationship with Hitler. Detractors—her label for what she believed were character assassins—who attempted to penetrate her obfuscations or question her veracity ended in a litigious battle that she usually won. Although she witnessed an atrocity of Jews being murdered in a Polish small town during the first days of the war, and was photographed displaying genuine distress, she later denied it by saying that "I did not see one dead person in Poland, not one soldier, not one civilian."[9] Moreover, when she was filming *Tiefland*, she employed as extras slave-labourer Gypsies, most of whom later perished in the camps. She lied, saying that she met them after the war. She also denied that she visited the camps and sued the publisher of a German magazine who published the story. She won her libel case but during the 1980s a documentary maker located a few of the extras who did survive and they testified that Riefenstahl had indeed handpicked them and had witnessed the living conditions to which they were condemned. In Müller's film she continues to deny that in *Tiefland* she used gypsies from a concentration camp. Like Martin Heidegger, another famously unrepentant apologist for the Reich who believed that metaphysics should trump ethics, Riefenstahl's words and actions indisputably revealed her to be a shameless collaborator for whom aesthetics (and personal ambition) did take priority over morality. The only regret she ever expressed was how her connection to the Third Reich harmed *herself*. For over half a century, living until one hundred and one, she sought a historical restitution, rendering her, in the words of one critic, "the ultimate 'undead' figure of post-war culture."[10]

Despite her protestations to the contrary, Riefenstahl was never the naïve artist indifferent to politics. Her first meeting with Hitler not only reinforced their mutual attraction but demonstrated how inextricably intertwined art was with politics. He greeted her effusively as a fellow artist inviting her to make films to document his goal of saving Germany after he came to power.[11] With that initial encouragement, she disported her seductive arsenal, from coyness to tantrums (something she would draw upon throughout her very long life), to nurture his support and that of any other man who could advance her ambitions. Her willingness to tolerate Hitler's sexual overtures and the percolating rumour of a liaison enabled her to achieve a degree of professional independence in an overtly misogynistic regime that maintained tight bureaucratic control over artistic production. She secured from Hitler esteem rivalled only by Winifred Wagner at Bayreuth. Yet whenever she encountered artistic interference, even from Goebbels himself, or financial pressures to compensate a former film collaborator, she could trade upon her personal relationship with the Führer and other friendships, notably the Jew-baiting publisher, Julius Streicher.

Initially, Riefenstahl had to earn the full support of her most important benefactor. Although she refused to make a film about the SA thug, Horst Wessel, she agreed to make a film about the first Nuremberg rally. The result was the technically amateurish *Victory of Faith* that, despite rapturous reviews, was withdrawn from circulation seven months later (for almost half a century), probably on the orders of Hitler because the political landscape had dramatically shifted. First, the revered President Hindenburg died, an occasion that allowed Hitler to assume absolute power by combining the positions of Chancellor and President. Secondly, in *Victory* there was considerable footage of Hitler enjoying the company of his long-time friend, the SA leader, Ernst Röhm, and images of him with the beefy homosexual suggested their relationship was central to the film. But Röhm's murder on Hitler's orders required a new film that would transform Hitler from an unruly storm trooper into a statesman and was a vehicle to apotheosize him and his mystical union with the German people. She later claimed that Hitler forced the project on her even though the evidence suggests that it was the other way around.[12] The time for dry runs and traces of familiar newsreel footage was over.

The result was Riefenstahl's operatic spectacle, *Triumph of the Will*, which became a benchmark in cinematic productions with its extraordinary breakthrough in technique. Her innovations in the use of camerawork and feature-film editing set new standards that, according to biographer Steven Bach "remain exemplary for filmmakers seven decades later." Yet he also believes that "she used her century's most powerful art form to make and propagate a vision that eased the path of a murderous dictator who fascinated her and shaped a criminal regime that she found both inspiring and personally useful."[13] The synchronicity of their relationship can be seen in the way Hitler's impresario and acolyte, Albert Speer, meticulously planned the rallies—the apogee of Wagnerian excess with their grandiose motifs of giant swastikas,

massed marchers and symbol-laden liturgy—down to the last detail—to communicate the image of a Messiah–redeemer and an embodiment of the German dictator bonding with the people. The
trio believed that this ceremony would establish a pattern that less
charismatic successors could maintain for years: the symbiotic relationship of the leader with the German community. Riefenstahl
shaped (as opposed to recorded) the 1934 Nuremberg rallies in
which scenes were rehearsed, re-filmed and rearranged to sub-
stantiate her thesis of a united Germany under the guidance of a
Führer. She thereby belied her later claim that the film was a neutral documentary of a Party rally.

Courtesy of Photofest

This scene from Leni Riefenstahl's 1935 film, Triumph of the Will, *reveals
the adulation that the German people showered upon Hitler and thereby
their complicity with the Third Reich.*

In its famous opening sequence, an unseen Wotan-like Hitler,
descends from Valhalla to approach the city from above. A silhou-
etted airplane emerges from a white bank of clouds, piercing the
clear sky over the picturesque splendour of medieval Nuremberg
with its spires and towers wrapped in mist. The plane's shadow
passes over thousands of Germans marching in geometric precision in the streets below, an apt if inadvertent metaphor for what
was transpiring in Germany. Modern technology and a rebuilt

nation are grafted onto the richness of the German past. On the soundtrack, the swelling overture of Wagner's *The Mastersingers of Nuremberg* segues into the Horst Wessel song, again the old fusing into the new. When the plane makes contact with the earth and stops, Hitler emerges in uniform, a messiah with the promise of deliverance to seduce a disorientated people. The rapturous crowd gripped by mass hysteria surges forward to greet him. In his celebratory entry into the old city, Riefenstahl uses a telescopic lens to scan the crowd. Allowing the camera to linger on shining ecstatic faces, children and young comely women, the implication is eye contact with Hitler. When Riefenstahl brilliantly edits the footage to create the illusion of a god that enthralled women, it is believable that large numbers of women "fell into ecstasies when they saw him in person, who even set up a 'Führer niche' in their living rooms with flowers and his picture, in place of the religious shrine they previously would have had."[14] As the cavalcade of cars streams through the streets, Hitler stands in the lead car while a film montage shows a rear-view of his salute, the camera panning over fountains and statues of former heroes juxtaposed with individual images of his adoring followers who line both sides of the street. This technique connects the architectural and sculptural emblems of a rich past to the vibrant present, demonstrating that the National Socialists are the true heirs of Germany's heroic legacy.

In the stadium where the ceremonies begin, on the orders of Speer, Hitler is almost always photographed from below and alone to enhance his physical stature. He appears to tower above the rest of the proceedings as though he was a numinous deity bathing the ecstatic crowds in his divine aura. In a rare moment of quiet when Hitler marches with the new more deferential leader of the SA, Viktor Lutze, and the SS potentate, Heinrich Himmler, through the cloven masses to the flames that burn in memory of martyred Nazi heroes, he is one step ahead. Unlike his earlier march in *Victory of Faith* with Röhm, he is alone, omnipotent with no rivals. Consistent with the paganism that suffused Nazi rituals throughout Germany, was the movement's quasi-worship of the dead as if they had been heroically received at Wagner's Valhalla. One of his biographers comments that whereas "life seemed to paralyze his inspiration...Hitler's talents as stage manager reached their summit when the object of the celebration was death...he could always invent impressive effects for funeral ceremonies."[15]

In another sequence, he solemnly goes among the men of the truncated SA to shake hands and touch each new flag with the old "blood flag" stained by the failed putsch of 1923. This blood ritual is a cross between a baptismal rite and a resurrection where fallen comrades are symbolically joined with the new generation of fanatical devotees. Indeed, through the liturgy of chanting, "You are not dead, you live," the young men are consecrating themselves to the movement. It is hard to escape the impression that, given the mantra about the Thousand-Year Reich, it is the cult of the dead which spiked the movement. At its core, National Socialism, with its saints and martyrs, was a political religion that embraced necrophilia rather than life.

Yet it is easy to be lulled into thinking that the film's seductive images capture a moment in time ignoring Nazi aesthetics and the ideology that underpin it. Through constant movement with mobile cameras located above the action and spectacular lighting designed by Speer that illuminates the night, the film superbly captures the kaleidoscope of human movement produced by the billowing swastika flags (a symbol of rising sun and rebirth) and swirling banners, the sounds of drums and the torchlight processions. The viewer rarely catches a glimpse of the faces of the men beneath the canapé of banners. Their individuality is submerged in the symmetrical formations of blaring bands and disciplined marches. *Triumph* also reflects Nazi aesthetics of physical perfection and heroic masculinity. The sequence of workers holding spades conveys a liturgical quality, as they chant their local region and the nature of their physical work to emphasize national unity and respect for their class. As Hitler addresses them, the camera accentuates their apple-cheeked youth and physicality; there is no hint of illness or unfitness. The symbolic purifying fire and the sacred character of the cathedral of light along with the rituals of Nazism that pervade the theatrical pageantry riveted the leaders and spectators alike.

Triumph's mesmerizing pyrotechnics papered over the political and social cracks that the Nazis sought to exclude from public view. Both Riefenstahl's film of the rallies and the official printed version that she authored—a fact she later denied—failed to depict the excessive alcoholic consumption, hooliganism and acts of vandalism, which characterized the seven-day extravaganza. Being a cosmetic exercise in covering up the blemishes of Nazi rule, any mention of mafia-style massacre of SA storm troopers that had occurred the previous June is noticeably absent. Hitler addresses the tensions by making reference to the "black shadow [that] cast itself over our movement" and vows that it will never be divided again. The film also omits any trace of the Party's anti-Semitism, an omission that Riefenstahl later cited to deny her own anti-Semitism and to justify her judgment that *Triumph* was apolitical: its message was the need for work and peace. She did not wish to admit that the airbrushing of the Party's racist agenda was de rigueur in order to present a more palatable image to Germans and the international community, in short a more effective propaganda package. Outside of Germany where it did receive limited distribution, viewers simultaneously appreciated its aesthetic merits and regarded with alarm its overweening idolatry of a dictator. The local audience, however, greeted it as a joyous pictorial paean to a healthy national community moving confidently into the future while rooted in its past. That this virtuoso and influential artefact of psychic vampirism was a box-office sensation attested to its power to achieve such aims.

If *Triumph* concealed and manipulated, the same techniques were deployed in Riefenstahl's next major film, albeit in a more nuanced manner. She had a long fascination for the beautiful physique steeled by sports and took full advantage of the opportunity to make a two-part film on the 1936 summer Olympics in Berlin. On the surface, *Olympia*, particularly the foreign version, is devoid of Nazi doctrines and less political than *Triumph*, and more in the spirit of her mountain films. Her cameras devoted loving attention to the athletic prowess and physical grace of the athletes. Riefenstahl caressed with her lens the Afro-American four gold-medal winner, Jessie Owens, in a manner that an American filmmaker, given the overt racist Jim Crow laws in America, would not have dared. That apparent willingness to defy taboo could be cited as evidence of the apolitical nature of *Olympia*.

Beneath the surface, however, Riefenstahl conformed to the Nazi credo both politically and aesthetically. To avoid any hint of racial intermingling, she did not film Caucasian children lining up for autographs from Owens and she minimized the achievements of other Afro-Americans. Nor did she photograph any Czechoslovakian athletes, as Hitler was at loggerheads with the country over the Germans in the Sudetenland, a conflict only settled when Western powers shamefully obliged Hitler's sabre rattling. But her awe for non-Aryan athletes, which included Japanese swimmers from a friendly nation, was not incompatible with her approval of the Reich's master-race aesthetic. She renders these specimens of physical perfection god-like, a theme she underscored in her prologue as the sculpture of a naked Greek discus thrower morphs into "the perfect Aryan superman," a German athlete. In the German version, there is more footage of Hitler and, the best slow-motion shots are reserved for Germans, and the narrator voice-over "often describes the games as racial and national battles" in which black runners are lining up against "the strongest representatives of the white race."[16] Her "body beautiful" ethos reflected the New Germany's "glorification of health, strength and physical perfection" of naked bodies in a natural setting, a legacy of its Romantic "Blood and Soil" ethos.[17] It celebrated the official Nazi message of "Strength through Joy" because like pleasure, beauty was not valued as an end in itself but was subtlety harnessed to an ideological agenda. Riefenstahl was only interested in filming athletes who fit her criteria of health, strength and physical beauty. The implication was that those who were not physically endowed or healthy were not welcome in the *Volk*.

Olympia was the cinematic version of a sanitized Berlin. The seemingly apolitical nature of the film mirrored official instructions from the propaganda ministry that any expressions of Nazi racism and militarism be hidden in the city itself during the staging of the games. Despite excluding German Jews and other non-Aryans from participating in the games, every effort was made to impress an international audience with a façade of an efficient, benign nation of cheerful sports-loving people. To showcase the "New Germany," Hitler camouflaged official policy, reining in his most zealous followers by temporarily prohibiting the public harassment of Jews and removing offensive anti-Semitic signs. He even ordered that copies of *Der Stürmer* remain inconspicuous when the Olympics were staged so as not to antagonize world opinion and jeopardize investment. From the evidence available, he was astonishingly effective in convincing the American press and countless tourists and dignitaries that tales of persecution were exaggerated, despite the existence of the Sachsenhausen concentration camp thirty kilometres from Berlin. Goebbels astutely packaged Germany as a vibrant society with a healthy economy that possessed a leader who posed no threat to world peace. The German version of a Russian Potemkin village during the 1936 summer Olympics that so beguiled visitors bore little relation to Hitler's military plans and the ongoing reports of persecution.[18] Beneath the glossy veneer operated a ruthless regime based on a vision articulated by Hitler in the 1920s: a racially and genetically defined national community that would expand its territorial borders regardless of the human cost, a worldview that most Germans and the international community could not grasp.

A defining element for the Potemkin mirage was the emotional appeal of National Socialist rituals that overcame reason. The kaleidoscopic array of choreographed mass rallies was stunningly effective in communicating an imposing show of strength and invulnerability to captivated audiences. Often at night, they were thinly disguised pseudo-religious festivals with their mystic symbolism and narcoleptic-inducing pageantry. The anesthetising effects of politics were not lost on the French Ambassador who witnessed the 1937 Nuremberg rally:

> The atmosphere of general enthusiasm into which the old city has been plunged is amazing and quite indescribable: the particular frenzy which has gripped hundreds of thousands of men and women, the romantic excitement and mystic ecstasy which has overtaken them like a holy rapture. An effort is produced which many find irresistible. They return home seduced and taken in, ready to serve the cause, with no idea of the dangerous reality, which is concealed beneath the deceptive pomp of the huge processions and parades.[19]

In his biography of Riefenstahl, Bach aptly quotes the distinguished German writer, Thomas Mann: "art is moral in that it awakens," but in a tragic exception to this maxim, "Leni's art lulls and deceives."[20]

The Artistic Celebration of the *Volk*

Ironically, the words Mann used to assess Riefenstahl were similar to Joseph Goebbels' artistic credo. The Propaganda Minister possessed the necessary guile to recognize that the most effective means to cloud a people's awareness was not overt demonization and the obvious lie but manipulation of the truth. Unlike Hitler, he believed that overtly heavy-handed propaganda could be counter-productive. The most effective form occurred when it was subliminally delivered "without (the audience) ever realizing that they are being saturated."[21] Like the view of Germany presented to the outside world, most of his films transmitted onto the screen a make-believe world of kitsch, a seductive alternative to daily life, masquerading as life, but wearing the mask of Death.[22] True, anti-Jewish sentiments were incorporated into the film, *Hans Westmar* (1933), in which Jewish villains from the Communist International gather in dank cellars and on shadowy street corners. Inflammatory dialogue that compares the hero's adversaries to "rats [who] avoid the light, [stage] cowardly group attacks, [murder] in the dark, and disappear back into their holes," punctuate the film.[23] But it resembles more the Hollywood spy thriller of the Cold War era than the virulent anti-Semitic films of the early 1940s. The filmmakers' agenda during the 1930s was to demean city life in the Weimar era rather than ramp up anti-Semitism.

The Nazis reviled the Modernism of the avant-garde artists and social critics of the Weimar era. They savaged it as mired in soulless corruption and anaemic mediocrity, a product of Jewish "rootless cosmopolitanism" and a "destructive" intelligentsia living in cramped, fetid apartments with small or no families. The artificial, all-devouring monster of the city was the quintessential symbol of modernism. Its decadence and infertility, epitomized by 1920s Weimar Berlin, was dismissed as a cultural and moral wasteland teeming with Jewish "speculators" and Marxist slaves who either rigged the market or nurtured the siren of communism. They were determined to purify the city of its irreverence, as exemplified by the mordantly satirical paintings and drawings of Otto Dix and George Grosz. They graphically depicted crazed sex killers and the rollicking orgies of aging prostitutes and swinish officers. The Nazis, like the potentates in all police states, had no appreciation of satire and mistook the Hogarthian form used by Grosz. They viewed his garish red paintings of the city not as exposés of the hypocrisy and bestiality in man, but yet another example of how modern art served to encouraged barbarism.

By the middle of 1930s, the cities were "cleansed" of "Jewish Bolshevism." There was no longer the need to portray the Weimar era of Jewish "swindlers" and parasitical capitalists along with heavily made up treacherous femmes fatales. Films were expected to be au courant and celebrate the vitality, economic strength and technology of the new urban Germany. Even the once "decadent"

Berlin could be a positive "central character."[24] In the production of light comedies, melodramas, musicals and historical costume pieces, Goebbels' main goals were to ensure technical competence with slick production values rivalling Hollywood conventions and to produce feel-good entertainment with soft-sell propaganda. To that end, he believed that films should largely project feelings of hope and elation—escapist entertainment that did not mirror or reflect on the realities of life in Germany. In order to exploit the popularity of American-style movies, the vast majority of German productions were designed to "aestheticize politics in order to anaesthetize the populace" even remaking popular American films to suit National Socialist needs. The result was that although ten percent of the films made during the Reich possessed substantial propaganda content, only about ten percent of those could be acknowledged to be masterpieces of film making.[25] The schlock genre, *Blut und Boden*, became a cultural staple of the Third Reich. Combining popular entertainment and alluring ideology awash in the make-believe world of nostalgic kitsch, none of its productions could be considered masterpieces.

Popular culture was the handmaiden to official Nazi policy. Fulfilling a similar function to that of Socialist Realism in the Soviet Union, the spate of accessible Blood and Soil novels and films promoted the message of the urgency to acquire land in the East to be populated by large families of genetically healthy Germans. Along with the need to safeguard racial purity, they celebrated the German-ness in the peasant's mystical relationship to the land and the male camaraderie that arose out of war. *Volkisch* writers and filmmakers revered the warrior hero, the Teutonic race and the Nordic past, in short the power of myth to stir emotions. The authors and directors of this genre gained a mass following because they appealed to traditional tastes. To a society plagued by agricultural decline and the uncertainties of growing industrialism, they offered a reassuring, accessible narrative that appealed to powerful emotional impulses.

The myth of the land was seductive to people who believed they possessed in their collective soul eternal verities. Who could better embody those spiritual truths (or fantasies) than the pious, hardworking, clean-living peasants, who remained tethered to the land and an exemplar of the race? Unlike the materialistic, "wandering Jews," they continued to live out the age-old customs and habits of the German people and find solace in the familiarity of the landscape. A representative example of this kind of mawkish kitsch can be found in the speech delivered by the heroine in the propaganda film, *The Homecoming* (1941). The beleaguered German population of Poland has been imprisoned and one German patriot has her swastika necklace ripped off and is stoned by Poles. While Germans await liberation, she soothes them with a beguiling mantra of their *Heimat (Homeland)*:

> My friends just think what it will be like when there are just Germans around us, and when you go into a shop it won't be Yiddish or Polish that you hear, but German! And it won't be just the whole village that will be German, but everything around us will be German....We'll be living on the good old warm soil of Germany....There will be a wonderful feeling in our hearts when we know that the soil in the field and our little bit of life, the rock, the waving grass, the swaying branches of the hazelnut and the trees, that all this is German.[26]

The cloying dialogue aside, heightened by the melodrama of her being shot before the Wehrmacht arrives, *The Homecoming* is a grotesque distortion of a complex reality. The tiny population of ethnic Germans was discriminated against and in 1939 approximately two thousand were killed in mass shootings or died from exhaustion from forced marches. But the Goebbels propaganda machine effectively magnified the number to fifty-eight thousand thereby exploiting the deaths to convince Germans that the invasion of Poland was just. In response, enraged ethnic Germans living in Poland created a militia killing about thirty-two thousand Poles as acts of revenge.[27]

Notwithstanding the gap between fantasy and reality, the xenophobic and anti-urban orientation of the Blood and Soil genre extolled Nordic peasant life as wholesome. It conveyed a natural state where large Aryan families with clean pedigrees rooted in the distant past lived in harmony. The paintings of the period abound with ruddy-cheeked peasants praying before a modest meal, mothers suckling their babies or attending to their children, and brawny men tilling their fields with a scythe (and nary a Socialist Realist tractor to be found). As portrayed by visual artists, their sturdy features and basic decency endowed peasants with a spirituality that inoculates them against doubt or inner turmoil and fortifies them to ward off alien forces which threaten their way of life. If paintings in the Third Reich tapped into nineteenth-century Romanticism with the landscape serving to inspire contemplation, in the contemporary *Volk*, the land represented living space for Germans with untainted pedigrees. As Hitler remarked in 1939: "Never forget that in this world the most sacred right is the right for a plot of land that one wants to cultivate by himself, and the most sacred sacrifice is the blood which one shreds for this soil."[28] Although painters attempted to capture bucolic scenes of happy blond, blue-eyed families in picturesque single-family cottages, if a viewer were to look closely at Adolf Wissel's *Farm Family from Kahlenberg*, (1939) he might wonder at a darker undercurrent. The grim-faced family members, frantically occupying themselves or staring at nothing, do not appear content; is there a sense of foreboding as they contemplate the prospect of their "sacred sacrifice" in Hitler's upcoming war?[29]

Regardless of whether any subversive message is present, Nazi officials shrewdly exploited this paean to pre-industrial kitsch while they concurrently pursued industrial modernization with their autobahn construction and motorization program. The underlying ideological message of this genre embraced a collectivist culture with personal alienation dissolving into community bonding that disavowed individual rights and democratic politics. By warning against the dangers posed by Western liberalism and cultural pluralism, artists celebrated an idyllic rural life awash in peasant virtues and the sacredness of the German soil as an antidote to the urban "asphalt culture" with its "degenerate art."[30]

The Cinematic Demonization of Jews

Nazi criticism of modern art was based on the conviction that it failed to repress the destructive instincts. As Hitler once said, "it is not the function of art to remind men of the forms taken by degeneracy." That was the preserve of Jewish art which glorified everything that was deformed and grotesque.[31] But the propaganda debacle of *Kristallnacht* of November 11, 1938 caused a volte-face in Goebbels' artistic expression. The wholesale destruction of Jewish businesses did not elicit the expected favourable response from the German public. Nazi art was forced to mirror that which was attributed to Jewish art and Goebbels supported films that overtly demonized Jews.

Although the turnabout in film productions offended Goebbels' aesthetic principles, it suited his psychological makeup. Physically, he was the mirror image of the grotesque caricatures that often appeared in Nazi hate propaganda: a malformed intellectual with a clubfoot, one leg longer than the other with a rodent-like face. Not unlike the ugly trope of the lecherous Jew, he too possessed a capacity for being a Lothario who knew how to dazzle women with quick-fire repartee, wit and compliments. (Not every woman succumbed to his charms. Martha Dodd, the daughter of the American Ambassador to Germany during the early years of the Nazi regime, had many love affairs with powerful officials including Rudolf Diels, the first Gestapo chief and Boris Winogradov, a NKVD agent. In 1939, however, she caustically dismissed Goebbels in her memoir, *Through Embassy Eyes*: "If there is any logic or objectivity in Nazi sterilization laws Dr. Goebbels would have been sterilized quite some time ago."[32]) Goebbels had maligned Jews as early as 1919, when he etched into his diary epithets like "filthy pigs," "traitors" and "vampires."[33] His analogy with the Nosferatu not only applies to its blood-sucking compulsion but also its protean capacity to change form, explaining the "Jew's" alleged omnipotence. Motifs of racial pollution and disease, the danger of cosmopolitanism, greed and financial dominance (that controlled international markets and the stock exchange) permeated German propaganda. The ability of the 'Jew' to mutate into an unrecognizable Gentile remained a powerful anti-Semitic trope.[34]

A film eerily prophetic of the Third Reich's efforts is Friedrich Murnau's 1922 silent-classic, *Nosferatu: A Symphony of Horrors*. Though not part of the regime's repertoire, it depicts the attempt to link foreigners (Bolsheviks) from the East with disease and the need for Germans to sacrifice themselves for the larger community. The vampire casts an ominously large shadow, a fitting emblem for what occurred in Germany until 1945. The vampire figure, Orlock, looks more animal than human with long predatory arms culminating in claw-like nails, a pale bald head, pronounced fangs in the middle of his mouth and bat-like ears. In keeping with the anti-Semitic *Zeitgeist*—Goebbels[*] proclaimed that Jews were "the syphilis of European peoples"—Orlock has both prominent

---

[*] In Wilson's, *Winnie and Wolf*, the unnamed narrator aptly refers to Goebbels as Nosferatu.

Semitic features and, with his facial deformities and corpse-like posture, looks both syphilitic and cadaverous.[35] With his gaunt, skeletal frame and parchment-like skin, this other-worldly vampire mirrors the hideous images of "degenerate Jews" in Streicher's *Der Stürmer*. He is also the personification of deadly disease. It was a common assumption even in medical circles that Jews were susceptible to physical and psychological illnesses. Unambiguously repellent and pitiful because of his need for blood, he not only kills on an individual level by sucking the life-blood out of his victims, but, as the embodiment of death, he also unleashes a pandemic. The earth around Nosferatu's coffin is swarming with rats, and when it is loaded onto the ship, a rat bites a workman's foot thereby igniting a plague. The entire ship's crew succumbs to the disease before the boat reaches Germany where it infects new victims in Bremen. Unlike *Dracula* and other cinematic adaptations, his victims do not turn into vampires but remain dead. While Stoker's Dracula at least energizes his female victims, Murnau's Orlock makes no attempt to seduce his victims. Instead, he uses his hypnotic power to overwhelm them before scrambling forward to claim his prey.

The association of a foreign agent—as carrier of contagion—with a dehumanized being that requires eradication, found a receptive audience. Although not intended as an anti-Semitic film, during the war years in Vichy France, art critics supportive of the fascist regime, found in *Nosferatu* a powerful image with which they could demonize Jews, even though the film does not refer to the vampire as Jewish.[36] In a scene suggestive of racial pollution, the saintly Ellen sacrifices herself in the interests of the community to Nosferatu's raw carnal lust. Within the anti-Semitic fantasy world, international Jewry was symbolically encapsulated by Murnau's representation of the Nosferatu: an evil threat to the community that could only be destroyed by idealistic, self-sacrificing Aryans, a value that is explicitly endorsed in *Mein Kampf*.

The tropes deployed by Murnau in 1922 became the raw material of Nazi propaganda. A few years later in *Mein Kampf*, Hitler associated Jews with vampires and rats. But it was Fritz Hippler's 1940 hate film, *The Eternal Jew*, which is most widely remembered for comparing Jews, crowded together in the ghetto, with rats that scurry about in packs devouring grain, carry microbial infections and spread contagious diseases. Taking its title from the familiar

Christian legend of the wandering Jew, the narrator of the faux documentary boldly announces that Jews are the source of the plague, an illness that "threatens the health of the Aryan peoples." We hear how the Jews—dirty, diseased and nomadic—are parasites living off their German host. At one point, the camera pans over a group of Jews while the voice-over narrator conflates them with rats: "Whenever rats appear, they bring ruin, by destroying mankind's goods and foodstuffs. They spread disease and plague....They are cunning, cowardly and cruel." One can imagine how the viewer is to interpret the comparison of other human beings to a dangerous pest.

Hippler's demonization of the Jew as a protean parasite that attacked and contaminated the body of the nation reinforced Nazi anti-Semitism. In *The Eternal Jew* we witness the transformation of ghetto Jews wearing caftans and yarmulkes into assimilated grinning (obviously duplicitous) European Jews shaved and in western dress. They insinuate themselves into foreign cultures as they learn the language of the host nation; barely distinguishable from their deluded hosts, they economically exploit its people. The implication is that Jews can change only their outer appearance, not their inner essence.

Actual footage was shot in the ghettos in Poland, and *Jew* maintains that what we see is normal life for Jews, something they have chosen. There is no acknowledgment that the scenes of filthy, unsanitary conditions, overcrowding and deprivation are the result of Nazi policies. Jews were humiliated, stripped of their possessions and homes in Nazi-occupied Poland before being herded into walled-up ghettos. There, in the way station en route to the extermination camps, they were to be a captive labour force subject to continual culling by disease, starvation and the spasms of random violence by their tormentors. Besides recording these scenes, the film's offensiveness is exacerbated by the demagogic commentary. The narrator informs the audience that Jews enjoy these conditions; that they are lazy, given to bartering and trading rather than engaging in actual work. Data is fabricated to support the contention that Jews were parasites and responsible for most international crime: in the hope of playing on sexual fears, the film's unseen expert asserts that Jews were responsible for ninety-eight percent of all prostitution in 1932. After arousing a visceral reaction to this portrayal, Hippler torques the level of hatred with scenes of a gruesome ritual slaughter as the sneering faces of Jewish butchers fade in.

Despite the *raison d'être* of creating a murderous anti-Semitism among the general population, *The Eternal Jew* was a box office disaster. The cinematic dissolve executed in *Jew* did not possess the narrative power that would draw in an audience. Except for a hardcore group of fanatics, the public was deeply alienated by the film and the crudity of the juxtaposition of people and rats. Reports indicated that many left "in disgust in the middle of the performance," meaning that they left before the ritual slaughter images. Victor Klemperer noted that despite all the "ballyhoo" around its opening in Dresden, "it disappeared here again after less than a week."[37]

In contrast, the lavish costume drama, *Jew Süss*, was extraordinarily lucrative. Released two months after *The Eternal Jew*, it succeeded in part because of its state-of-the-art production values including powerful acting performances. Loosely based on a 1920s novel about an eighteenth-century Jewish moneylender executed for his alleged crimes in which the Jews were scapegoats, the film instead portrays Joseph Süss-Oppenheimer as a conman, extortionist and rapist. A moneylender from the Frankfurt ghetto, Suss becomes financial advisor to the vapid Duke of Württemberg. Although the film promises to adhere to the documentary record, it blackens Süss at every opportunity in order to suit Goebbels' ideological agenda. For instance, the film suggests that Süss, in a move to enhance his power and drive a rift between the Duke and his people, initiated a crisis that enabled the Duke to acquire absolute power. In reality, Süss, caught between the Catholic Duke and the Protestant-dominated Diet, becomes the victim of a plan hatched by the Duke to increase his power without ever informing his financial advisor.

More importantly, the film feeds on existing anti-Semitic stereotypes. Uprooted and nomadic, Süss fits the image of the 'Wandering Jew' who has no homeland; it is incomprehensible to his interlocutor, the heroine, Dorothea that Süss could be at home "everywhere." Like a virus that mutates, Süss is portrayed as a "master of disguises" who, as a protean Jew can transform himself from a ghetto-bearded Jew into a smooth, cosmopolitan European courtier, possessing the guile to outfox his patron in his quest to increase his capital and seduce innocent women. He can alter his speech from that of the ghetto to that modelled on courtly discourse, returning to his original Jewish countenance where he sounds "Jewish" before his execution. In addition, one Aryan actor plays his secretary, the rabbi, butcher and even an ugly old man to suggest that nearly all Jews can be collapsed into "one unclean, coughing or cackling body [that] tries to efface Jewish humanness."[38] The Jew as vampire sucking blood out of the citizens of Württemberg is suggested by Süss's aggressive taxation that bleeds them of their wealth. Indeed, critics have drawn explicit parallels between the film and Stoker's *Dracula*.[39]

Even though *Jew Süss* operates in the historical-costume drama genre rather than the Gothic tradition, a perceptive viewer can glean the similarities. Without invoking the supernatural, the film's eponymous protagonist, Süss, whose origin is Frankfurt, is presented as a malevolent alien from the primitive "East," biologically and sexually different, an invader of the civilized "West." Both Dracula and Süss are intent on domination. The latter vows to "open the door: it may be tomorrow, it may be the day after, but it will be,"—a threat similar to the fear that the vampire will "create a new and ever-widening circle of semi-demons to batten on the helpless." The invasion is explicitly depicted in *Süss* after the financial advisor persuades his patron to allow the Jews from Frankfurt to enter the city of Stuttgart. We witness an interminably long diagonal line of bedraggled Jews entering the city to the horror of the local citizens; one spectator compares them to "locusts." Furthermore, the novel *Dracula* and the film *Süss* dramatize the fear of sexual pollution through the violation of a woman by an alien. For the original viewers familiar with the anti-Semitic warning of racial poisoning, the rape of the heroine, Dorothea, by Süss and her subsequent drowning, presumably because of the shame she experienced, is a personal tragedy that demands retribution. Not only were they convinced of the insatiable lust of the "Jew;" but this act of "racial treason" confirms his personal fate and the decree that all Jews must leave Stuttgart within three days. The judgment concludes with the statement that if their descendants maintain a separate existence from the Jews, they will avoid the sorrow and blood pollution that they have recently experienced. In contrast to the film's indictment of miscegenation, the historical Oppenheimer, albeit a womanizer was never indicted on these grounds as such evidence would have compromised many courtly women. Instead, he was convicted and hanged for Christian treachery and hypocrisy.

A striking parallel also exists between Süss and Hitler that further illustrates how the representation of "the Jew" was an expression of the Führer's doppelganger. The following account of the fictional Süss tracing his arc to power eerily resembles Hitler's historical trajectory:

> Süss preys on a conflicted state run by a weak leader, opportunistically choosing the right moment to make his move, aligning himself with a moribund order against the people's representatives, insisting on an enabling decree that grants him special powers that allow him to open the gates for his previously proscribed comrades. He proceeds quickly to eradicate opposition and creates a private militia, monitoring all movement and maintaining a specular (sic) tyranny, murdering and terrorizing an entire population.[40]

It is no wonder Hitler could astutely but privately acknowledge that "the Jew is the exact opposite of the German in every respect, yet is as closely akin to him as a blood brother."[41]

Jew Süss was a huge commercial success judging by the large numbers who saw it between 1940 and 1943. Whether this scurrilous anti-Semitic film conditioned the German population for the fate of the Jews is, however, questionable. True, audiences loved it while being "instructed" about the Jewish question. Showing the film to members of the SS and concentration camp guards did encourage the maltreatment of prisoners. According to the Strasbourg Security Police, its screening also provoked members of the audience to spontaneously leap to their feet to shout out: "Dirty pig Jew...particularly from women."[42] Yet the overriding consensus is that to a large extent its success can be attributed to the (Aryan) actor who portrays Süss. He is compellingly charismatic—much more than any of his antagonists—and we know that some members of the audience responded very warmly to him as he received "baskets of love letters from every cinema in Germany." The accomplished performances of the film's stars, the quality production values and a gripping narrative of sex and violence handled with restraint explain the film's box office popularity. The film more likely succeeded not because of its anti-Semitism but despite it. As one critic stated, "no film can make the viewer a willing executioner."[43]

That films did not make audiences more rabidly anti-Semitic should not imply that this poison failed to exercise a significant role in peoples' lives. The kind of legal apartheid recommended at the conclusion of *Süss* had already found approval through the Nuremberg Laws, even though the majority "would have drawn the line at physical maltreatment."[44] These films at best reinforced existing prejudices while a large percentage of the population remained indifferent. This argument is persuasive until the outbreak of war. In wartime anti-Semitism became more complicated since the public, bombarded with doses of anti-Jewish hatred, accepted the regime's position that Jews were responsible for causing the war. The German civilian population regarded Jews mainly as an abstraction because they were primarily preoccupied with surviving Allied bombing. The failure of *Eternal Jew* to activate the homicidal hatred that Goebbels expected might be explained by the fact that when his Party embarked on its campaign of extermination in 1941, they took precautions to keep their activities secret, albeit with limited success. By 1943 as rumours began to circulate, Goebbels publicly acknowledged that the Germans could be historically judged as "the greatest criminals." To ensure that Germans kept fighting so that they could "avoid a final moral reckoning," they "produced an intimacy of complicity" so that no one could ever claim ignorance.[45]

The trope of the protean nature of the Jew continued after 1945 in German films but with the aim of parodying and subverting the Nazi obsession with race. Agnieszka Holland's 1990 *Europa, Europa*, is based on the experience of Salomon Perel, who inhabits different personas in order to survive. A Jewish boy is seamlessly transformed into a Komsomol (the youth wing of the Communist Party) in a Soviet orphanage/school in eastern Poland, a purebred Nazi soldier and a student in the Hitler Youth movement. Solly presents the counter-image to the anti-Semitic fantasy portrayed in *Jew Suss* when a race expert proclaims that he has pronounced Aryan features.[46] In a dream sequence with the Hitler and Stalin waltzing together, Holland suggests that the murderous dictators are a doppelganger for the other.

Despite the more benign purpose of most of the cinematic productions, visual arts and the packaging of the new Germany for international approval, the Nazi agenda's primary goal was to purify. To implement its vision of engineering a superior people, it became necessary to purge the *Volk* of "all sources of physical or mental decay and all threats to the new order."[47] The Reich's blood lust underpinned by the security forces and concentration camps ensured the ideology was put into practice.

State Terror and Public Complicity

Berlin cops stopped being people when they...joined a Gothic-looking family that included the Gestapo, the SS, and the SD.

—*Prague Fatale*
Philip Kerr

Music for the Dance of Death in the 1930s

In 1931 a sensational murder trial took place when Peter Kürten was accused and convicted of murdering nine men, women and children and attempting to kill seven others. Dubbed by the press as the "Düsseldorf Vampire" because the sight of blood incited him to drink it from his victims and receive sexual gratification, the case attracted intense attention from a public already exposed to sexual violence in films, paintings and novels. The frequent depiction of gruesome murders by painters George Grosz and Otto Dix, novelist Alfred Döblin and in films such as *The Cabinet of Dr. Caligari* confirmed for diehard conservatives their hatred for avant-garde art. They believed that crime in the new democracy was being celebrated rather than fought. Despite their attempt to portray the Weimar Republic as the hotbed of decadence, the artists' portrayal of violence in Germany was no match for the mayhem inflicted on individuals during the Third Reich. During the purportedly good years of the 1930s, ideologues, sadists and ordinary "racial comrades" peeled back the "dream of paradise" patina from the public sheen. In doing so they revealed its feral instincts by infecting the nation "with a germ that causes

321

its people to treat their victims like wolves."[1]

Coincidentally, Fritz Lang's film *M* was released in the immediate aftermath of the trial. Although scripted before Kürten's arrest, it too portrays a serial killer who is more frightened by his image in the mirror than he is of the criminals in pursuit of him because their activity is threatened by the intensive police investigation of this case. They subject him to a mock trial before the police enter and apprehend him for a legal trial. *Eternal Jew* includes this clip from *M* in which the killer confesses his crimes to the city's criminals. The scene is taken out of context to suggest that *M*, directed by the Jewish Lang, exonerates the killer played by a Jewish actor, Peter Lorre, by implying that the children are to blame for their own deaths. Lorre's character is presented as proof that he, the Jewish actor, is the murderer and the film is evidence of Jewish criminality. This distortion was a metaphor for the way the Nazis manipulated the public to dehumanize enemies of the Reich. The timing of the Kürten trial, along with publicity given to the film, stimulated a passionate debate about the resumption of capital punishment. The hue and cry for the quick dispatching of this "subhuman beast" illustrated how far the public, press and the political parties had moved to the law-and-order agenda endorsed by the political right. Supporters of capital punishment resorted to the language of eugenic cleansing to justify the execution of a 'born criminal'; in the words of one journalist, Kürten epitomized the "end-point of the racial decline of a family [that] points up the terrible route taken by degeneration.".[2]

The furore surrounding such a grisly crime story is significant as a trope for the ideological purity and blood lust of the Nazis themselves. The Nazis cared little about the depravity of the Kürten case. The public's revulsion, however, enabled them to launch their law-and-order campaign and persuade the public that the elimination of unhealthy agents "hostile to life" was a necessary precondition for national renewal. The Nazis perpetrated hideous crimes they had made legal by revising the laws. With widespread popular support they discredited what they claimed to be the pernicious culture of individualism that coddled criminals and was allegedly destroying Germany in the Weimar years. In doing so they transformed the principle of retribution into a justification for a full-fledged war against "enemies" of the *Volk*. After they assumed power in January 1933, they began the purge with trade unionists and leftist politicians, followed by dissident priests and so-called "asocial elements." After 1935, the primary target shifted to the Jews, the embodiment for all that the Nazis anathematized: internationalism, Bolshevism, avant-garde art, and above all, the carriers of "blood poisoning."

Like the professors who remained silent about the book burnings, the criminologists, generally concurred with Himmler that the purpose of the security services was to "keep our blood and our people healthy" by purging those elements which threaten the race. Stigmatized individuals no longer needed to commit a crime to pose a threat; their very nature presented a danger to the *Volk*. In 1935, the Party's self-styled philosopher, Alfred Rosenberg, wrote that "punishment is...simply the weeding-out of alien types and beings foreign to our species." With their mania for order and purity, rather than the rule of law, Nazi communiqués in official speeches and newspapers left no doubt that once they assumed power, the "murderers of the people,"—far worse than real murderers—would be cleansed from the German *Volk*.[3]

Nazi sources were not the only ones that warned of an impending bloodbath. A courageous coterie of reporters and editors at the aggressively anti-Hitler *Munich Post* tried to warn Germans and the world about the criminality and bogus science that underpinned the Nazi Party. Dubbed the "poison kitchen" by an enraged Hitler, the *Post* had been exposing the gangrenous rabble of the "Hitler Party" since 1921 with streetwise investigative zeal. Hitler even successfully sued the newspaper for publishing an early poison-pen polemic, "Adolf Hitler, Traitor," that an anti-Hitler faction in his own movement had written and privately circulated, one that suggested that he was Jewish, dictatorial and questioned how he earned his living. The *Post* investigated the Party's financial corruption, its sex scandals and its secret death squad. In the two years preceding Hitler's accession, the newspaper diligently catalogued its reign of terror: shootings, stabbings, strangulations, drownings and disappearances. In 1932, it provided an exposé of how the Party planned a bloodbath, a massacre of its political enemies once in power. Remarkably, the *Post* recovered a revealing statement by Hitler about his own responsibility: "Nothing happens within the movement without my knowledge, without my approval." That would include a "secret plan" which itemized exactly how Jews would be disenfranchised and ultimately excluded

323

from German life, a document that included the euphemism "Final Solution." According to the journalist, Ron Rosenbaum, who uncovered this powerful story, these journalists from the *Post* were "enlightened police reporters covering a homicide story in the guise of a political one." In short, the "Hitler Party" was a pack of gangsters that "garbed itself in ideological belief." Despite its revelations, the *Post* was fighting a losing battle in its efforts to turn German public opinion against the Nazis. Tragically, their Cassandra-like mission to expose the Nazi capacity for evil abruptly ended in March 1933, when SA thugs burst into the *Munich Post* building and frogmarched its writers and editors to prison.[4]

Armed with knuckle-dusters and lead-filled truncheons, the brown-shirted SA—the paramilitary storm troopers—carried out their most savage beatings in the months before and after Hitler came to power. The recollections of a communist provide further confirmation of the vicious thugs who flouted the rule of law:

> Dead men were found in the surrounding forests, and no one dared to know anything about them. People disappeared without a sound, and their best friends did not have the courage to ask where they had gone. Only very rarely did a scream, a gruesome rumour...make itself heard; they were paid less notice than everyday traffic accidents.[5]

Pariahs to be Purged

Any institution or individual who challenged the Nazis encountered swift reprisal. After Pius X in 1937 condemned racism, neopagan doctrines and those who worshipped idols of the nation and state, Hitler ordered Goebbels to discredit the Catholic Church. To this end he accelerated the campaign alleging that the Church protected paedophiles and homosexuals in its midst. In a nationwide radio broadcast, Goebbels lambasted the Church, an "ulcer on the healthy body of Germany," for corrupting German youth, a sufficient reason to eliminate the confessional schools. The Gestapo used bribes and intimidation to secure charges of sexual molestation and homosexuality, ensuring that newspaper coverage of these trials was saturated with salacious details. Some convicted priests, who were investigated by the Church itself and turned over to the Gestapo, were guilty of the offences but this fact served only to fuel the Nazi propaganda machine to smear the entire institution. Of the 2,720 clergymen, primarily Catholic priests, who spent time in Dachau, the main holding centre for religious offenders, about fifty percent re-emerged.

Priests were not the collective most arrested for sexual impropriety. After the Röhm murder, the Nazis accelerated their persecution of homosexuals largely due to the image of aggressive manliness so exalted by National Socialist identity. A fine line existed, however, between approved homosocial behaviour called "comradeship" and active homosexual behaviour. The fineness of that line might explain the pathological brutality of the police and the SS who could disavow in themselves any inclination of crossing it by pulverizing suspected gay men, as well as monitoring overtly effeminate men, who constituted in reality a small minority of homosexuals. In 1935, Paragraph 175 of the German Criminal Code was amended to encompass any form of "criminal indecency" that included a touch, gesture or look. Moreover, innuendo and gossip could be admitted as evidence. Himmler and the SS were particularly militant in their homophobia; the mouse-like Himmler believed that homosexuals were pederasts who, if given the opportunity, would seduce every minor with whom they came in contact. At the same time, he maintained that they were responsible for "a deficit in the sexual balance sheet" because they failed to fulfil "their duty to procreate." The criminal police harassed and rounded up suspected homosexuals, and once in a police cell, they were subjected to such extreme pressure and indignities that some committed suicide. The fortunate ones were given a trial and usually sent to prison. In 1940 Himmler issued a decree that all those sent to prison for homosexual offences with more than one partner were to be transferred indefinitely to a concentration camp. Between ten and fifteen thousand were dispatched to the camps, wore the pink triangle and were subjected to abysmal treatment only above that of Jews. Because homosexuality was regarded as a social disease, the official goal remained "re-education," not extermination, but they were subjected to forced labour, experimental surgery and castration. The SS guards were particularly sadistic; one survivor recounts how the inmates were forced to push their wheelbarrows to sites in the camp while the SS took target practice resulting in several deaths and serious wounds. Some did survive, however, and whether they were singled out for extermination remains a matter of controversy.[24]

Members of an umbrella group excluded from the national community were the designated asocial elements. The Nazi officials deemed these individuals "parasites who had to be eradicated for the people."[25] At first, it was habitual criminals who were awarded the appellation because they had offended three times and were perceived to be the "scum of the criminal class." Soon, however, the vast majority were petty thieves, vagrants or beggars driven by severe economic insecurity, individuals who had at best performed casual work without consistent employment. In 1933 prison authorities were empowered to haul these prisoners back to court and have them retroactively sentenced to indefinite periods of confinement. Those who languished in prison contemplated suicide as preferable to being "buried alive." As bad as their tribulations were, the terror increased during the war. More convicted criminals were executed, imprisoned under appalling conditions, or sent to concentration camps. Prison officials and criminologists interpreted their recidivism as proof of their incorrigibility, and the general public would have agreed.[26] The elastic term of "asocials" was broadened to cover prostitutes and pimps or Gentile "racial polluters." Women incurred the label on the basis of their sexual behaviour or demeanour.[27] Any indication of promiscuity was interpreted as a threat to the national body because it spread fertility-destroying diseases and did not direct sexual behaviour toward population goals and promotion of family values. Hitler, who reviled the scourge of prostitution in *Mein Kampf,* ordered tens of thousands of prostitutes to be dispatched to workhouses and concentration camps since they posed a threat to his goal of a pure-blood race.

The Nazi attitude toward prostitution was in fact double-edged because these women satisfied "an urgent necessity." Indeed, the service of male sexual needs was believed at the time to discourage the incidence of homosexuality. In the interests of protecting the racial community, state authorized brothels with enforced hygienic standards were created despite resistance from religious groups and venereal disease experts who argued that red-light districts would increase the possibility of illicit behaviour. Despite the opposition and the Party's official rhetoric against prostitution, brothels continued to operate, and during the war, were further tolerated as serving the military function of rewarding hard-fighting soldiers. As for the women themselves, their ostracism from society made it "more difficult for individual women to redeem themselves in the eyes of the 'national community' and reintegrate themselves into mainstream society" during and after the war.[28]

Those without a fixed address were vulnerable to asocial classification, an estimated twenty thousand Roma were targeted. Unlike Jews, they had not benefited from emancipation, and were never admitted into civil society. Because of their "strange" language, customs and nomadic way of life, coupled with the perception that they were a source of crime and a burden on the welfare system, Roma had been a target of discrimination during the Weimar years. After 1933 harassment intensified as Nazi ideology designated them a non-Caucasian ethnic minority. They came under more intense scrutiny through "Gypsy research" and supervision when they were included with Jews as pariahs and aliens in the Nuremberg laws. They were then subjected to racial–biological examination by scientists who studied the biological determinism with the aim of detecting criminal behaviour before crime was committed. They were either sterilized or sent to concentration camps. The first major roundup occurred prior to the 1936 Olympics, ostensibly to control crime and beggary in the nation's capital. "Gypsies" were sent to a suburb of Berlin, which became a permanent camp for incarcerating entire Roma and Sinti families. Between 1935 and 1939, central authorities complied with local requests from mayors, welfare officials and the police, and several camps were established, initially without barbed wire, a condition that did not last long. There they would be dragooned into compulsory labour schemes that benefited local economies and reduced the welfare load. Considered particularly dangerous were the "mixed gypsies" even though many of them assimilated into German society. This did not prevent one writer from describing them as "Nomads...of another race, who because of their vermin, filth and stench remain foreign to us today."[29] Their real crime was their supposed contribution to blood pollution.

In April of 1938, Himmler ordered a massive nationwide roundup that resulted in the asocial being kept in "protective custody." Prior to this, social deviants could be sent directly to the camps. Now they remained a few weeks in local police prisons and then were incarcerated in camps. His mandate was to apprehend fit unemployed young men. In their zeal, however, the criminal police arrested anyone perceived to be a liability: the sick, the old, the hopelessly alcoholic, and even the gainfully employed. Not only was the operation expedited without due process, the judicial officials were informed that "now and in the future, the German police... will take care of the cleansing of the anti-social from the national community." In the camps asocials wore the black triangle which placed them near the bottom of the camp hierarchy where they could be sterilized or castrated. In camps that were located near stone quarries like Buchenwald near Weimar and Sachsenhausen north of Berlin, all could be forced into slave labour at a time of a labour shortage in the large construction projects. Conditions were ghastly: labour in the quarry brutal, the guards' maltreatment and beatings ubiquitous, rations meagre and frequently inedible, and typhus and dysentery common. Any attempt at mutiny or escape justified execution, and in the camps the guards were beyond the purview of the judicial system. Besides providing economic fodder for large-scale projects, the police sought to make the life of anyone miserable "who did not fit the image of the hard-working citizen and committed racial comrade."[30]

A Paralysis which Blighted all Human Relations*

The hard-line attitude among the police forces toward any form of criminal behaviour found a receptive audience among vast numbers of the general public. Substantial numbers of Germans from all classes had been attracted to the National Socialist Party because of its law-and-order agenda that promised to "clean up the streets" and create a conflict-free national community. With the Nazis in power, ordinary Germans supported their punitive measures as safety took precedence over the need for due process for miscreants. The ends of eliminating the enemies of the new Germany justified any necessary means. They employed the rationalization that if these minorities had acquired power, as a concentration guard noted years later, "they would have done the same things to us, and maybe worse."[31]

---

* Here was an entire nation, he now realized, that was infested with the contagion of ever-present fear. It was a kind of creeping paralysis which twisted and blighted all human relations. Thomas Wolfe, *You Can't Go Home Again*, 1934.

Unfortunately, once the public accepted cruel treatment for the least popular groups—the communists and habitual criminals—it failed to recognize the pernicious slope that eventually led to the incarceration or execution of citizens who initially supported the correction measures. Indeed, after defeat in the Soviet Union, and the attempted assassination of Hitler in July 1944, any expression of defeatism, such as expressing a desire to surrender to the Allies, waving a white flag or even listening to foreign broadcasts risked the death penalty.

Public attitudes were derived from, and to a degree conditioned by, widespread knowledge of the camps recounted in hundreds of stories slanted to reflect the regime's views. In their reports of camp visits, journalists enthused that the regime was defeating crime by re-educating the criminals through a healthy dose of military discipline and work therapy. Some garnished their reports with fanciful details of inmate life: good food, sports and reading activities. They legitimatized the camps, saying that they offered the enemies of the state "an opportunity to reflect on their shameful deeds." They portrayed the inmate leaders as hardened communists who refused to be transformed into decent Germans, and the guards as protectors of law and order who justifiably shot prisoners in "self-defence." Stories also emphasized that violence in these camps paled when contrasted with the brutal images associated with the French and Russian revolutions.[32]

The press's sanitized views of the camps' harsh realities and its uncritical reportage that conformed to the regime's race-tinged theories was particularly evident in its close-up pictures of the "sub-humans." Captions would "ask readers to notice the deformed head shape by which such people could be recognized." Pandering to public prejudices and revulsions, associations were made between the photographs of Jews and race defilement (sexual relations between Germans and Jews) to suggest that Jews were in the camps because of sex crimes. Himmler underscored the official position on the connection between racial or biological defects and crime by claiming that the concentration camp was a microcosm of this self-evident proposition: "There is no more lively demonstration of the laws of heredity and race than such a concentration camp. There are those with hydrocephalus, cross-eyed, deformed, half Jews and a whole series of racial inferior types."[33] Although the ostensible purpose of the camps was educative, his implication was that certain individuals were beyond redemption and would therefore never emerge from them.

The majority of citizens who blithely accepted arbitrary terror had not experienced direct confrontation with the various police forces. The disinformation in press stories of the concentration camps registered favourably because it was tailored to match the values and beliefs of German readers. One historian carefully studied the complicity among ordinary people for the Nazi regime, concluding that its coercive practices gained more support for the regime than it lost.[34] Some of that support likely derived from the fear of what would happen to them if they did not quietly accept Nazi practices and rituals. The Gestapo played upon and exploited the fear that private lives were not immune from the prying eyes of the state. Nonetheless, Party leaders recognized that their ideology released pre-existing impulses of hatred among the general population that had been repressed during the Weimar Republic. By extolling violence toward political dissidents and religious and cultural minorities, the regime encouraged people to act out their destructive drives through prescribed channels. The flood of offers from people who applied to the Ministry of Justice to be a public executioner demonstrates the extent to which violence had been legitimatized.[35] Hitler applauded the base instincts of people who endorsed violence when it was meted out to the unworthy. When informed of SS cruelty, Hitler foamed at the mouth and responded:

> The plain man in the street respects nothing but brutal strength and ruthlessness—women and children too for that matter. The people need wholesome fear....Why babble about brutality and be indignant about tortures? The masses want that. They need something that will give them a thrill of horror....Terror is the most effective political instrument. I shall not permit myself to be robbed of it because a lot of stupid, bourgeois mollycoddles choose to be offended by it.[36]

One criterion for assessing the merit of Hitler's rant is to examine the extent of ordinary participation in the regime's war on purported "enemies." Contrary to a once widely held assumption about its omniscience, the Gestapo was an understaffed set of detectives and bureaucrats, who did not possess the resources to conduct an effective, proactive surveillance on the majority of its

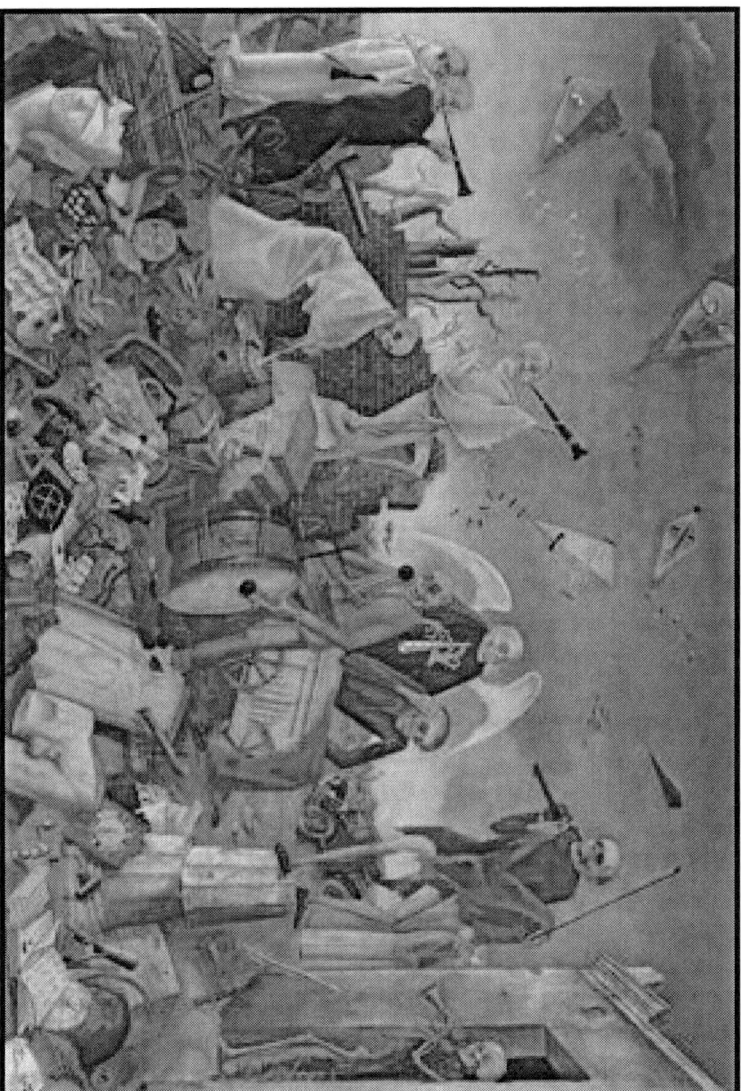

Felix Nussbaum, Music for the
Dance of Death 1944 Estate of Felix
Nussbaum/SODRAC

Felix Nussbaum's Music for
the Dance of Death *(sometimes called* Death Triumph*)
presents not only a powerful Gothic trope, but it pre-
figured his own death. While
visiting Italy when the Nazis
came to power, he never returned to his native land but
with his wife went into hiding in France and Belgium.
His internment in a camp in
France before escaping provided him with the experience to imagine the death
camps in Poland as skeletal
figures play and dance to
music in a barren wasteland.
This was his last painting
(April 1944). Shortly afterward, the two were captured
and shipped to Auschwitz.*

citizens. Its priority was targeted groups and it depended on the cooperation of the regular police and members of the Party. But it also relied on the loyalty of upstanding Germans and capitalized on their prejudices in the hope that they would denounce suspicious behaviours. In return, the Gestapo ignored or treated lightly minor offences among the citizenry, such as petty grumbling or attending swing clubs. The regime experienced little difficulty in legitimizing and mobilizing people's prejudices to further their ideological agenda. Excluding the brutal purge of the left in 1933 and its ruthlessness toward Jews after 1935, the vast majority of cases the Gestapo investigated were the result of tips from informants.

In this atmosphere, evil was everywhere and commonplace. Denunciations came from ordinary civilians who were under no legal compulsion to report individuals unless they suspected high treason. Although some were motivated by a sense of patriotic fervour or civic responsibility, for others it was more prudent to demonstrate that they belonged to a society in which the terrible cost of social exclusion was not hidden. To complement the hard reality of state repression, large numbers of citizens participated in so-called "soft terror" by denouncing the vulnerable or anyone who displayed an expression of independence or courage: those who did not possess a regular job or family, exhibit sufficient Nazi zeal, or who fraternized with Jews, forbidden since the Nuremberg laws of September 1935. A population conditioned to place a sinister interpretation on the most innocuous social interaction could easily misconstrue innocent gestures or friendliness. In one case, neighbours repeatedly denounced a woman in Würzburg from 1936 to 1941. The Gestapo took her in for questioning because she demonstrated unconventional behaviour by occasionally having a woman visitor into her place. On top of everything this strange woman "looked Jewish." For ignoring warnings, she was sent to a concentration camp in 1943 and died there. In her dossier, the Gestapo officer concluded that she was "beyond redemption."[37]

Behind the veneer of patriotism resided a cluster of mean-spirited motives—opportunism, the desire for revenge, envy and malice—that prompted individuals to denounce their neighbours and associates. If they rendered the state a service, they could anticipate that the state might reciprocate by removing a rival, an unwanted spouse or by providing some material advantage. The cancer of denunciation infected the family. Husbands incriminated wives in the hope of gaining a more favourable divorce settlement. A wife denounced her physician spouse as an abortionist after he infected her with a venereal disease contracted during an ongoing illicit affair. To redress a power imbalance and acquire some semblance of dignity, wives denounced husbands who were verbally and physically abusive toward them, and as an afterthought, noted their lack of commitment to the regime. In these cases, the authorities rarely took action against a racial and genetically fit husband unless the wife reported that her spouse suffered from a venereal disease; then personal family problems coalesced with the regime's eugenic policies. Not only did ordinary Germans willingly supply the authorities with incriminating information they also volunteered to work for the Gestapo as agents.[38] Clearly, Hitler intuitively connected with a large portion of German citizenry who had not been bullied into compliance. These people abandoned their ethical scruples for sordid personal reasons or they willingly accepted "the limits of empathy" given the priority for exercising vigilance to "weed out racial undesirables." In 1934 the German–American historian, Felix Gilbert, captured this spiritual dimension when he commented, "I don't know how to put it, but it is if a people were beginning to lose its soul."[39]

German citizens displayed few qualms about reporting Jews for racial crimes. Even before the Nuremberg laws, when sexual liaisons between Gentiles and Jews were not illegal, people reported any suspicion of them to the Gestapo with the result that a Jewish person could find himself in protective custody. Denunciations of "race defilement" became contagious and bizarre as groups of schoolgirls scoured Jewish quarters looking for cases of "open miscegenation," while members of the Nazi Women's Organization patrolled the streets with cameras to record the evidence. The historian Robert Gellately examined data from the Würzburg archive and estimates nearly sixty percent of the cases he studied began with a denunciation from people not members of the Party. He concludes: "without the active collaboration of the general population it would have been next to impossible for the Gestapo to enforce this kind of racial politics."[40] It did not, however, rely only on denunciations when it tracked Jews. The regular police and Gestapo were proactive and ruthless in resorting to entrapment or planting evidence when they targeted Jews for protective custody and concentration camps. Women would be dragooned into luring unsuspecting Jews into compromising situations and then denouncing them to the police. These individuals would then be tortured into signing confessions.[41] When the Gestapo ferreted out "racial polluters," it dispensed with even the semblance of legality.

"All Better Instincts Were Silenced"

Improvement in the economy and a dimming of the international spotlight on Germany after the 1936 Olympics allowed the Nazis to accelerate their campaign of persecuting the Jews. After the promulgation of the Nuremberg laws, race defilement became the most common charge. A Jew was four times more likely than a Gentile to have a case lodged against him based on dubious, unsubstantiated allegations. However, the persecution of Jews was carried out discreetly so as not to invite international condemnation.[42] By the late 1930s, the only hope of a Jewish person being released from a concentration camp was a commitment with the proper papers to emigrate. Hitler's decision to gorge for the first time on European real estate—the incorporation of Austria and 200,000 more Jews into the Third Reich in March 1938—set the stage for their economic strangulation and the most serious threat yet to their personal safety.

Austrians displayed a zealotry which exceeded that of Germans. A substantial number of Germans were willing to tolerate anti-Semitism, but stopped short of inflicting violence on Jews and seizing their property; the majority of Austrians lacked that restraint. Although Austria comprised only eight percent of the population of the Third Reich, its citizens constituted fourteen percent of the SS and forty percent of the special units involved in the genocidal operations during the war. These figures should not surprise given the ferocity of the anti-Semitism in March 1938 during the *Anschluss*. Among the many Austrians who deliriously welcomed the arrival of Hitler and his motorcade, thousands of Viennese took to the streets to assault, plunder and humiliate the largest Jewish population in Europe after Warsaw and Budapest. In many cases, the perpetrators were long-time neighbours who were not even Party members. Accompanied by raucous laughter and taunts of "work for the Jews," they coerced Jews of all ages and both sexes to scrub pavement with brushes on their hands and

knees. For weeks, gangs roamed Vienna streets desecrating synagogues, beating and killing at random, stealing—money, jewellery,
furs and cars—and forcing old men to perform endless callisthen-
ics and even eat grass.[43] Sensitive contemporaries experienced
these scenes with unforgettable abhorrence. In his autobiography,
Carl Zuckmayer recalls the evening of March 11, 1938 as though he
had been transplanted to a medieval pogrom, one visually evoked
by a master of horror:

> The underworld opened its gates and vomited forth the low-
> est, filthiest, most horrible demons it contained. The city was
> transformed into a nightmare painting by Hieronymus Bosch;
> phantoms and devils seemed to have crawled out of the sew-
> ers and swamps. The air was filled with an incessant screech-
> ing, horrible, piercing, hysterical cries from the throats of
> men and women who continued screaming day and night.
> People's faces vanished, were replaced by contorted masks:
> some of fear, some of cunning, some of hate-filled triumph....
> All better instincts were silenced....It was a witches' sabbath
> of the mob. All that makes for human dignity was buried.[44]

The teenager, George Clare, who also witnessed these scenes,
later recalled that the "paradox of Vienna's outburst was that it
saved thousands of Jewish lives."[45] Except for those who lost all
hope and committed suicide and the aged and the sick who could
not leave, everyone who could, fled the city and the country to
almost any destination. If German Jews had received mixed signals from the Nazi regime that life might be difficult but they could
survive if they did not antagonize the regime, Austrian Jews from
March 1938 entertained no such illusions.

The outburst of violence in Austria toward Jews provided inspiration for like-minded Germans. During the spring and summer ominous signs appeared that presaged what transpired
in November. Synagogues were burned down in Munich and
Nuremberg. Economic pressure was applied to Jews to register financial holdings worth more than five thousand Reich marks and
they were forbidden from taking valuables out of the country. As
in Vienna, Jews endured indignities and brutalities. Some were
forced to run in circles until they collapsed while others were
strapped into the seat on a roller coaster with the machine set at
high speed until they had heart attacks and lost consciousness.
Inmates at concentration camps were set to work at enlarging the

camp for new arrivals. As part of the June action to corral asocials, there were fifteen hundred Jews of whom most had previously been convicted of a minor legal infraction, five hundred for traffic violations.[46]

The pain and the humiliation visited upon Jews in early 1938 foreshadowed the whirlwind of hatred that descended upon German and Austrian Jews during *Kristallnacht*. Emboldened by his diplomatic triumph at the Munich Conference, Hitler launched a nationwide pogrom against the Jews and cavalierly disregarded any censorious world opinion. Its enormity, conducted with sheer fury, was a defining moment for Jews, who no longer sustained any illusion that they could live in countries governed by National Socialism. A foreign sanctuary became an urgent priority, regardless of cost, the perilousness of the destination, the lack of language or marketable skills.

In an effort to ingratiate himself with Hitler, who had been annoyed at his messy extramarital affair with a Czech actress, Goebbels staged with Hitler's full blessing an all-out assault on the Jews in Germany and Austria. Goebbels seized upon the early November assassination of a minor German diplomat in Paris and constructed the event as the product of an international Jewish conspiracy. It was in reality a desperate Polish Jewish teenager protesting the summary expulsion of his family along with seventeen thousand Polish Jews from Germany into Poland. After whipping Party members and the security organizations into a frenzy, he ordered a "spontaneous" reprisal to burn and raze every synagogue and trash Jewish community centres and free-standing businesses. Instructed to don civilian clothes to heighten the deceptive appearance of righteous citizen anger, members of the SA and SS vandalized homes and economic properties by smashing furniture and sporadically looting money, clothes and jewellery. Ritual degradation included herding men into exhibition sites and forcing them to exercise incessantly without food, water or toilet facilities, requiring them to read aloud from *Mein Kampf* and sing the Horst Wessel song. As buildings were torched, fire brigades assured that the conflagrations did not spread to adjacent Aryan properties. Ordinary Germans participated in the brutalities and the police were ordered not to interfere. Given the years of incessant propaganda citing that Jews were criminals, no effort was made to assist the terrorized victims. Although Hitler publicly disassociated himself from these events so as to avoid any personal criticism, Goebbels diaries clearly indicate his explicit involvement. On November 10, Goebbels penned in his diary: "he [Hitler] decides: demonstrations should be allowed to continue. The police should be withdrawn. For once the Jews should get the feel of popular anger."[47] As a consequence of that anger, approximately one hundred people were murdered during the riots, hundreds committed suicide. Although Goebbels took the heat from other Party members concerned about the licentious material damage and Germany's international reputation, Heydrich quietly ordered that males be arrested. About thirty thousand Jewish men were hauled off to concentration camps where some did not survive.

The second phase of the state-sponsored pogrom occurred when the men arrived hungry, battered and frightened at one of three concentration camps: Dachau near Munich, Buchenwald near Weimar or Sachsenhausen north of Berlin. Whatever beatings and humiliations they had previously experienced did not prepare them for the barbarism of their reception in the camps. Forced to run a gauntlet, the terrified prisoners were tripped up by guards raining iron bars, kicks, rifle butts and fists, flailing whips, shamelessly stealing everything of value. Those who fell were mutilated or murdered. Some had their eyes knocked out and skulls smashed. Prisoners in thin rags were required to stand at attention on the parade ground in below freezing temperatures for up to twenty hours without food and water. In Buchenwald, the homicidal commandant arbitrarily seized four prisoners a night and took them out to be murdered. Some were so terrified of being murdered that they committed suicide by running against the electric fences. Older men who often had World War I records were singled out for the most severe punishment. The guards being mainly youth found it intolerable that individual Jews distinguished themselves in war contrary to the indoctrination that they had received. Many of them, who had never served in war, took out their rage by seriously injuring or killing veterans.

Although murder and death abounded, these concentration camps were not the extermination depots that were created in the East a few years later. The primary purpose of this ordeal was to deliver an unequivocal message. Release from these infernos would only be forthcoming if the prisoner could guarantee that he would soon emigrate. The responsibility for liberating the men was left to their wives. They marshalled all their resources to secure an exit permit from venal officials and find a country that would grant them a visa or one that would accept them without conditions. The international condemnation of Germany, notwithstanding, most countries, unwilling to alter their inflexible quotas, restricted the entry of Jews. Visas, therefore, were difficult to obtain and took time. In addition, the women had to possess moxie in negotiating a maze of bureaucracy to secure passports, passage tickets and cash for bribes to meet officials' capricious demands. As husbands did not survive long in the camps, time was of the essence and this meant considering other options instead of waiting for a visa that might not come from prized havens like Britain or America. The only country that did not require a visa was the war-torn, chaotic, disease-ridden Shanghai. Michael J. Blumenthal recounts how his mother secured the release of his father after she had sold household furniture to pay emigration expenses to Shanghai, including a substantial bribe to acquire the necessary documents. His father, a once proud war veteran, was now a "shrunken and broken man" after six weeks in Buchenwald, reduced to a "small, pitiful figure sitting in his old living room chair, a gaunt sixty pounds lighter, embracing [others] silently and hardly able to talk." Upon release, prisoners were silent on their experience because they were warned that a word of it would mean an indefinite return to the camp. When the Blumenthals departed for Shanghai, just prior to the outbreak of war, they were part of a seventeen thousand contingent.[48]

The pogrom inflicted severe economic consequences on Jews. Demonstrating the persistence of Nazi cruelty, the regime blamed the victims for the extensive material damage inflicted on them by ordering the Jews to pay a collective fine of one billion marks. This was to be the financial part of their punishment for being part of the international Jewish conspiracy to assassinate the German diplomat in Paris. Any insurance to cover the damage of Jewish property would not be paid to the victims but instead was diverted to government coffers. Further, Göring issued a ban excluding all Jews from any business activity. The process of Aryanization continued to accelerate as the regime ordered the confiscation and selling of all Jewish businesses and property at a fraction of what they were worth. The rapacious exploitation of Jews disturbed some Gentiles. In a letter, a Munich businessman, a self described

Nazi and member of the SA, registered his shock by comparing his Aryan colleagues to "vultures swarming down, their eyes bleary, their tongues hanging out with greed, to feed upon the Jewish carcass."[49] This imagery was usually paraded in Nazi rhetoric when vilifying Jews.

In addition to driving Jews out of the Third Reich, a secondary purpose of *Kristallnacht* was the intimidation of Gentiles who might evince sympathy for the Jews' plight. Although much of the public disapproved, there were others, especially in smaller, non-Catholic communities who, succumbing to their worst instincts, joined the Party activists in taunting and beating Jews and vandalizing their homes. Some Germans, especially Catholics, felt for the first time *real* fear of being the next victim of Nazi terror, since the confiscation of Jewish property could set a precedent for the plundering of wealth from other prosperous citizens.[50] Onlookers registered shock and shame at the raw fury of the mob, its undisciplined, lawless and chaotic nature, reminiscent of a pogrom in Eastern Europe which felt out of place in civilized Germany. People were prepared to accept legal measures in the service of ethnic cleansing and the exclusion of non Aryans from national life, but the process had to be orderly and hopefully humane.[51] They were more concerned about the physical destruction and how the rest of the world might punish Germany through a worldwide boycott of its businesses rather than for the plight of the Jews. In *My Father's Country: The Story of a German Family*, Wibke Bruhns appreciates that her mother was enraged by the pogrom, that it was "a disgrace" and "cowardly" but she ruefully notes that a pertinent diary entry "contains not one word of sympathy for the afflicted Jews" because her primary concern was how the "honour of the Germans" was being "sullied by other Germans."[52] Her mother's detached indifference toward Jews was not untypical, but an example of the passive evil that made the Holocaust possible.

Still, some individuals believed that a moral transgression had occurred and that solidarity had to be shown with the victims. One courageous Swabian pastor told his congregation that the Nazi assault on the Jews would bring divine punishment; his reward was to be viciously beaten by thugs and then sent to prison. In a memoir infused with rage toward the Nazis, the historian Peter Gay remembered these times as a "nightmare" and a "collective orgy hard to believe and impossible to forget." Nonetheless, he paid tribute to his father's Gentile business associate by dedicating his book to him. Emil Busse was a courageous outspoken anti-Nazi who sheltered Gay's father when other men were being dispatched to a concentration camp. He also helped the Gay family secure documents that enabled them to board the last ship to set sail to Cuba that was not turned back to Europe, and protected the family valuables when they fled.[53] Though arrived at by a very different journey, Melita Maschmann revealed a similar perspective. Once a stalwart activist in the League of German Girls, the female wing of the Hitler Youth, her own detoxification process took over ten years. In a mea culpa memoir, she revealed how it was possible for a basically decent person to be gripped by a myopia that had rationalized these barbarities. Recalling that she slept soundly on the night of November 9, she arrived in the centre of Berlin the next morning to witness the damage. After she asked and was informed by a police officer what had happened, she ruefully remembered musing:

> For the space of a second I was clearly aware that something terrible had happened there. Something frighteningly brutal. But almost at once I switched over to accepting what had happened as something over and done with and avoiding critical reflection. I said to myself: 'The Jews are the enemies of the new Germany. Last night they had a taste of what this means. Let us hope that World Jewry, which has resolved to hinder Germany's 'new steps towards greatness,' will take the events of last night as a warning. If the Jews sow hatred against us all over the world, they must learn that we have hostages for them in our hands.

In another passage, Maschmann reveals how her upbringing imprinted upon her consciousness a Gothic trope. She believed that Jews were "wicked," possessing "an evil power, something with the attributes of a spook. One could not see it, but it was there, an active force for evil."[54]

Apart from these myriad responses—anger, fear, indifference and individual acts of kindness—most telling was the absence of any domestic or international protest that would have had negative repercussions for Germany. True, a wave of international condemnation and revulsion was issued from the press, newsreels and radio broadcasts, including an ominous comment from the *New York Times* wondering whether anything else can be done to

German Jews "short of physical extermination."[55] But these outbursts were not followed by any concerted economic or diplomatic action, much less military manoeuvres, which might have deterred Nazi barbarism toward their own people. Nor did countries like the United States and Canada raise their restrictive immigration quotas to allow more Jews to immigrate, even these nations displayed odious garden-variety anti-Semitism and xenophobic sentiments in certain government departments and among the public. Despite the failure of Goebbels' propaganda efforts to elicit a total "eliminationist" anti-Semitism among the German public, the regime was confident that it could proceed undeterred with intensifying its war against racial enemies. Klemperer ends his account of 1939 with the caustic comment: "I believe the pogroms of November 1938 made less impression on the nation than cutting the bar of chocolate for Christmas." He was not far from the truth given that, Sebastian Haffner, an Aryan opponent of the Nazis recognized in 1939 that the task of the Nazis was to "train the Germans to be persecutors of the Jews...and if possible to exterminate them."[56] With the outbreak of war in September of that year, these perceptions turned out to be powerfully prescient.

Notwithstanding the deluded true believers, Germans were not brainwashed automatons. The die-hard ideologues exploited the faith and appropriated the energy of those who yearned for a better Germany. These idealists, who joined the Party and its attendant organizations, were imbued with the spirit of selfless devotion; they were the heirs of the nineteenth-century Romantic impulses that explored whether it was possible to live in a more natural way. Disgusted or bored by the party politics of the Weimar era, the idealists welcomed the destruction of what they perceived as a corrupt system based on laws and contracts. They craved an alternative, and Hitler surfaced as the numinous vessel for their deepest aspirations. What they failed to recognize was that the kind of radical utopianism promised by the National Socialists could only be achieved by eliminating dissent. This necessitated the purging of any trace of empathy and humanity toward others who were racially or genetically different. With the steady barrage of boilerplate Nazi rhetoric and images that demonized "criminals" and "racial enemies," the presumption that "Christian principles would prevail" was myopic and in bad faith. Maschmann, the former National Socialist devotee was more astute when she mused, "that it was not the gangsters and roughnecks, but decent, intelligent and moral people who allowed themselves to be induced to acquiesce to something deeply evil and to serve it."[57] Bruhns' insightful exploration of her parents' history revealed how her father, who became a member of the SS, unquestioningly accepted the conventional wisdom of the times. Most significantly, the notion that "foreign" Jews were responsible for the "chaos" before 1933 through their control of the left wing press and the universities became a common belief which allowed Hitler to be regarded as a leader who brought "salvation" to the Germans by ending that domination.[58] Hitler and his underlings exploited this specious logic—accepted by millions—to lead the country into national psychosis, a calamitous war and unprecedented loss of life.

Evil was inherent in the seductive promise to create mankind anew by remaking the *Volk* in the image of an idolized leader with an apocalyptic ideology. When solipsistic thinking prevailed, when one's country's pride, power and suffering encompassed the only reality and the individual had no intrinsic value, the state was empowered to spread its poison and seduce the unthinking idealists and the majority who applauded its coercive instruments. This lesson should not be lost as we vault toward our own times.

PART THREE

America:
The Cold War and September 11

No doubt the attacks of September 11, 2001, played a part, revenge sweeping the nation. Kill the Islamists and two objectives were accomplished. Vengeance was sweet. They would kill no more, once they felt the full fury of righteous American anger.

~ Ward Just, *Forgetfulness*

Torture has perhaps saved some, at the expense of honour, by uncovering thirty bombs, but at the same time it aroused fifty new terrorists, who operating in some other way and in another place, will cause the death of even more innocent people. Even when accepted in the intense realism and efficacy, such a flouting of honour serves no other purpose but to degrade our country in her own eyes and abroad.

~ Albert Camus, *Preface to Algerian Reports*

14

Overview

We also have to work sort of the dark side,
if you will, spend time in the shadows.

Dick Cheney

America during the Cold War of the 1950s may appear remote from our times; however, there are palpable continuities. The psychological manipulation and treatment of prisoners during the Korean War produced a subsequent obsession with brainwashing that became a staple of the popular culture. Not as well known were the medical experiments in psychic "depatterning" (the erasure of the personality and memory) conducted by Ewen Cameron, among others, a scientist at McGill University, funded at the behest of the CIA. The hideous effects of these experiments on unsuspecting patients mirrored the public's fear of foreign and domestic Communists' ability to penetrate American institutions. Mind control, or in Gothic patois, psychic vampirism, is the unifying thread that stretches into contemporary America.

A study of 1950s America is a necessary prelude to explore how the September 11, 2001 attacks on the heart of its financial and military institutions provided the George W. Bush presidency with two irreducible convictions. First, these assaults constituted an existential threat to the country and secondly, the constitutional principles of domestic and international law could be dismissed as indicative of "pre-9/11" thinking. Resultant to the attacks that galvanized a lackadaisical "compassionate conservative" into a War President was a new direction in counterterrorism policy that prompted critics to accuse the Bush administration

345

of forsaking American principles and seriously damaging its reputation at home and abroad. In the fallout of 9/11, the administration conducted a blitzkrieg, a vampiric attack, on due process and America's cherished ideals. This was most evident in its treatment of enemy combatants and its decision to invade Iraq. In reality, Bush's administration and the unquestioning media drained much of the public of its critical faculties by trading on the fear of terrorism and marginalizing the critics. The CIA applied what it had learned from Korean prisoners of war and Cameron's experiments to its treatment of offshore prisoners of America's "War on Terror." Prisoners experienced interrogation behaviour and techniques that would not have been legally permitted on American soil. Counterterrorism policy directives bred disinformation that resulted in the radioactive occupation of Iraq, the outcome being countless dead, injured or displaced civilians, the abuse of prisoners, and the physical or psychic damage, or death of coalition soldiers. Policy makers framed the conflict as a clash of civilizations, between good and evil, one that mirrored the image purveyed by militant jihadists. Both played to constituencies who craved vengeance.

The Islamism of Osama bin Laden and al-Qaeda combined an apocalyptic ideology with a yearning for destruction. Until bin Laden's death, it remained a malignant growth within the culture of Islam. Financed by Saudi money and the drug trade in Afghanistan, the movement was fomented by the demagoguery of radical clerics, supplemented by indoctrination in training camps. An endless barrage of video and audio messages, distributed globally, preached the "narrative" that the West was waging war on Islam. This effort was assisted by the damage unleashed by Desert Storm, the war launched against Iraq in 1990–91, and the presence of foreign troops in the Middle East and later in South Asia. Militant Islamists sought to persuade their impressionable followers to do their duty as Muslims by embracing aggressive jihad[1] against the unbelievers for which they would be rewarded with the blessings of martyrdom.

Just as a Gothic lens can illuminate police states, so too can it enrich our understanding of the more recent struggles roiling democratic societies. Monsters in fictional and filmic Gothic texts stand at the border of what it means to be human and frequently challenge those boundaries even as they elicit primal fear. In contemporary political discourse they are then transformed into something horrifyingly unnatural—as if human beings were incapable of hideous and evil acts.[2] The assertion by George H. and George W. Bush that Saddam Hussein's Iraq was a "chamber of horrors" (like North Korea, Iran and Syria, among others) was well grounded. The regime did create the same sense of terror and dread that permeated the Nazi and Stalinist eras. With its "mass graves," "torture chambers" and "mansion of gloom," it possessed a Gothic dimension. To demonize Hussein as the *other*, however, as a revenant Hitler was to transport him out of the realm of power politics into a preternatural presence as the embodiment of evil and depravity. By orchestrating the politics of fear to prepare the international community for war, the Bush administration, abetted by a predominately unskeptical media, created a Gothic tableau with the "Butcher of Baghdad" superimposed on the blurred image of Osama bin Laden. The aura of ghostliness and darkness continued with tales of his lair in labyrinthine tunnels in the Tora Bora Mountains and later in the tribal territories of Pakistan. Hidden from view, he and al-Qaeda "exploit the dark recesses of sovereign states to prepare and launch their terrorist attacks." The narrative and style are reminiscent of Bram Stoker's account of Dracula's castle in Transylvania where he plots his invasion of England.[3] A deconstruction of this Gothic scenario will demonstrate the fantasy of a vampiric madman in an unholy alliance with the über terrorist.

The demonization of thugs and killers into preternatural monsters does exact a price. The first temptation is to engage in a heroic fight to hunt and exterminate them. Early presidents, notably John Quincy Adams, warned against such a crusade, arguing America "would involve herself beyond the power of extrication in all the wars of interest and intrigue, of individual avarice, envy and ambition." Adams warned that the greatest danger lies in the desire to uphold ideals and search for monsters that have desecrated countries. In doing so, America risks becoming, in his words, the "dictatress of the world" it seeks to destroy.[4] Given the misadventure that destabilized Iraq and revived al-Qaeda, Adam's sentiments convey wisdom and prescience. In other words, when politicians demonize the *other* as evil, they fail to recognize their own capacity for evil, as well as that of their citizens. The initial images from Abu Ghraib that went viral were merely the tip of the iceberg of moral transgressions, given what transpired and was not photo-graphed or was shown on offshore sites. Still, much of the public and the conservative media absolved the president and his men of any responsibility for "abuses" by scapegoating a few low level soldiers working in the Iraqi prison. The aptitude for egregious misconduct is why an understanding of doubling is so important: under the terrible pressures of war, a patriotic American soldier can become his own worst enemy. This transformation was articu-lated by a former CIA officer who reflected on the mental health of those who participated in or observed enhanced interrogation techniques. He poignantly echoed an insight from Joseph Conrad in the *Heart of Darkness*: "When you cross over that line of dark-ness, it's hard to come back. You lose your soul....You can't go to that dark place without it changing you."[5] His apprehension en-capsulates one of the fundamental truths that can be gleaned from applying the Gothic mode to the real world.

Mind Control during the Cold War

In my practice I have seen how people allowed their humanity to drain away....
Only when we have to fight to stay human
do we realize how precious it is to us.

—Invasion of the Body Snatchers (1956)

Popular culture will always draw from the well of the vampire myth, but so too does the Gothic elucidate the historical experience. *Dracula* ranked among the most popular
paperbacks during World War II. The American government even
created a special edition that was distributed free to its servicemen. Its cover sported a fused image of a vampire with that of a
Hun, one that further demonized the Nazis.[1]

More invasive psychological techniques were instituted in the
crucible of the early Cold War. This chapter provides an impres-
sionistic overview of the Korean War and its aftermath, specifically the treatment of prisoners of war, the CIA responses, including
funding the medical experiments by the scientists, and the preoccupation with brainwashing in popular culture. Both the CIA
techniques and Ewen Cameron's experiments yielded destructive effects that resonated personally and politically long after the
Cold War ended. Gothic filters knit together the threads of fear
and the dynamics of what used to be called "brainwashing"—still
considered a viable concept by some scholars[2]—that connect the
Cold War with "the global war on terror." The lens of psychic vampirism can illuminate the process of mind control that occurs in
various ways: patients are used as guinea pigs; a toxic ideology
is fed to impressionable followers; in an open society large numbers of citizens in the grip of fear are vulnerable to deception; and

interrogators apply techniques that threaten to breakdown the detainees' sense of self. This assault on the self, ranging from coercive manipulation to mass persuasion, robs victims of agency and will-power (at least temporarily) leaving independent thought a rarity. Doubling explicates how antagonists devoted to radically opposing ideologies, in reality, begin to mirror one another.

The successful war against Nazism was scarcely over when the fear of nuclear annihilation gripped the minds of North Americans and Europeans. The instantaneous destruction of Hiroshima shocked the world with the realization that mankind possessed the means to destroy itself. The wartime alliance between the United States and the Soviet Union dissolved into suspicion, hostility and mutual recrimination when the latter extended its empire into Eastern Europe and developed atomic weaponry. At the dawn of the nuclear age, in 1948, essayist E. B. White presciently captured America's vulnerability, particularly its cities: "A single flight of planes no bigger than a wedge of geese can quickly end this island fantasy, burn the towers, crumble the bridges, turn the underground passages into lethal chambers, cremate the millions."[3] For over four decades, generalized anxiety both consciously and unconsciously permeated the flash points of the Cold War: the insidious influence of McCarthyism in America, a nuclear standoff over Cuba, and vicious proxy wars in Africa, South East Asia and Central America. The Cold War between the two superpowers inspired fear universally because the spectre of a nuclear holocaust in response to a crisis was a stark possibility.

Controversies Surrounding an Unknown War

Although the fear that shadowed the Cold War has recently dissolved into the mist of history, it is instructive to recall an early flashpoint, the Korean War (1950–1953), because echoes of that war reverberated during the Vietnam War and more recently in the war against terrorists. It is important to understand that the brutal occupation by the Japanese of Korea between 1910 and 1945 gave rise to guerrilla warfare beginning in 1931, then to raging military combat between North and South Korea from 1950 to 1953, a conflict that has resonated over the years as a hot war simmered into a war of nerves. After the Japanese were defeated in 1945, the Americans established a three-year military occupation before relinquishing power to Syngman Rhee and a generation of Koreans in the police and military who had once served the interests of Japanese imperialism. His dictatorship with American complicity claimed upward of 100,000 lives in large part because of the widespread and indiscriminate butchery against poor peasants who revolted against landlord appropriations and the burden of government taxes. Walter Sullivan, a correspondent of *The New York Times* wrote in early 1950 that parts of South Korea "are darkened today by a cloud of terror that is probably unparalleled in the world"—and this occurred before the beginning of the Korean War.[4] In June 1950 the Soviet-sponsored North Korean government dispatched troops across the 38th parallel into South Korea as part of that ongoing war.

Under pressure from domestic anti-communist zealotry, especially after allegations that his administration was responsible for the "loss" of China to the Communists, President Harry Truman, under the aegis of the United Nations, ordered American air power and ground troops to Korea. During the war, the American Air Force rained destruction on North Korea with large conventional bombs and napalm that destroyed its entire infrastructure, driving the survivors to live and work underground in caves complete with hospitals, schools and factories. The United States dropped more bombs on Korea than it did in the entire Pacific theatre during the Second World War. When U.N. soldiers—the vast majority American—retreated, overwhelmed by the number of Chinese soldiers who entered the war, they resorted to a scorched-earth policy of torching small cities before the enemy reached them.

Terrible atrocities occurred on both sides: prisoners and the wounded were executed on the spot without any due process. The North Koreans and Chinese executed an estimated 30,000 people. The South Korean authorities and auxiliary right-wing youth squads executed around 100,000 people suspected of sympathizing or collaborating with the enemy. American soldiers frequently witnessed the summary execution of North Korean POWs. In a single massacre during the first week of July 1950, the South Korean police authorities killed at least four thousand people while American officers stood by and photographed the slaughter. American generals and journalists dehumanized Koreans as "apes," "gooks," and "a shade above the beast"; therefore, it was easier for American combatants from the air and on the ground to follow orders to fire upon civilians, leaving two hundred and fifty dead. This incident was publicly told for the first time in 1999 when the Associated Press printed a series of articles based on the recollections of survivors and veterans detailing the atrocity. The media reaction varied from portraying it as an isolated incident, neutralizing its impact by emphasizing that both parties killed civilians, to denying the story because one of the veterans cited in the articles could not have been on site at that time. Yet over the years more evidence has surfaced which clearly indicates that senior officers did order the killing of civilians, a decision that has affected even the perpetrators. One American soldier, Art Hunter, was haunted by nightmares for fifty years "imagining the faces of two old people, a man and a woman, hovering above his bed."[5]

Four million died in the Korean War, at least fifty percent were civilians. When what Truman referred to as a "police action"—because he had U.N. approval—concluded with an unsatisfactory stalemate, (but no peace treaty) the conflagration had razed almost the entire Korean peninsula. The insurgency and the subsequent war were tragic for the Korean people.

Horrific as it was, this war had the potential to be far worse. When the Chinese Red Army crossed the Yalu River bordering on North Korea, Truman came under pressure from the United Nations commander, General Douglas MacArthur, to escalate the war with nuclear weapons that would create in MacArthur's words, "a belt of radioactive cobalt." Had Truman authorized their deployment, the Soviet Union's Chinese ally would have urged Stalin to respond, aggravating his fear of a nuclear war with America. Indeed, notwithstanding his pathological suspicion and xenophobia, Stalin wanted to avoid war with America to the extent that he was willing to accept American occupation of North Korea even though it bordered both the Soviet Union and China.[6] Truman did not act but his successor, President Eisenhower, threatened the North Korean and Chinese governments with atomic weapons if they did not reach a resolution. All parties in this war agreed to a stalemate rather than risk a wider war.

The Korean War had domestic repercussions since Truman had no alternative but to fire General MacArthur for insubordination. The president was particularly incensed by the general's conversations with foreign diplomats from Spain, Portugal and Brazil who subsequently relayed his thoughts to their own governments; the remarks were intercepted and decrypted by the National Security Agency (NSA). Among those comments, MacArthur expressed his hope that intervention by China would provide the excuse for an all-out nuclear war that would destroy Communist China.[7]

Truman predictably faced political fallout from alienated conservatives. Blind to the consequences of a nuclear attack on Communist China, they regarded Truman as a spineless appeaser who was so afraid of victory that he would be willing "to murder American boys." William Jenner, one of MacArthur's supporters in the Senate, used the belligerent rhetoric redolent of the extreme political right in Weimar Germany to suggest that MacArthur was the martyred Siegfried to the treacherous Hagen, the President himself. The senator charged that the government was "in the hands of a secret inner coterie which is directed by the Soviet Union." Indulging in over-the-top paranoia, he asserted that Truman should be impeached to "find out who is the secret invisible government which has so cleverly led our country to destruction."[8] MacArthur's dismissal, the widespread American belief that America was militarily unprepared for the Korean War—in 1951 Gallop reported that seventy-three percent of Americans held this opinion—and the rising American casualties in Korea (over thirty-six thousand dead by the armistice) contributed to the President's growing unpopularity and further fuelled the toxic politics of McCarthyism.[9] Truman chose not to seek another term in 1952. During this period, critics of the Korean War, save for those who spoke from a hard-right perspective, risked being maligned as Communist sympathizers.

Anti-communism in America inveigled itself into the collective American psyche during the Cold War. At no time was it more visceral, irrational and destructive than when Joseph McCarthy carved his malevolent niche into American politics in the early 1950s. His demagoguery appealed to primitive impulses in the American mind that condoned the abuse of power and due process if it could uncover moles in the State Department. His targets were disparaged as "Communists and queers" or "egg-sucking liberals."[10] In reality, he cared little about communism or espionage—these issues served only to bolster his sagging popularity. Even before McCarthy's emergence to national prominence, Truman retooled his predecessor Franklin Roosevelt's national loyalty programme to screen prospective candidates who would work in areas of national security to ensure they had no history of sabotage or sedition. Truman considered the loyalty programme an effort to control the growing anti-communist hysteria by striking a balance between protecting both national security and constitutional liberties. Yet his Congressional critics, J. Edgar Hoover and the FBI, and even his own Justice Department were primarily intent on ferreting out what they called subversives. The loyalty programme careened out of Truman's control as it was extended beyond employment involving national security. The Loyalty Review Board relied on unverified information, and the accused, although they could secure a hearing with a lawyer present, could not confront their accusers. Truman was particularly concerned about the zealotry of Hoover, who deceived the president into authorizing wiretaps. According to the president's White House counsel, Clark Clifford, Truman was "afraid of a Gestapo" looming within the FBI. Those fears were heightened in 1950 when McCarthy recklessly claimed, without evidence, that government employees were Communists or agents of the Soviet Union. Both McCarthy's grandstanding and the covert activities of his secret sharer, Hoover, exaggerated the threat of domestic communism. The FBI chief was able to take advantage of Truman's loyalty programme by investigating any federal employee whenever "derogatory information" appeared in his file. Its "politically conservative standards of evidence" resulted in thousands of government workers losing their jobs.[11] This number does not include the hundreds of professors or individuals dismissed and blacklisted from the media and film industries. Although the repression of this era can in no way be compared to that which occurred in the Soviet Union, American violation of constitutional liberties was a precursor for what occurred over one-half century later after 9/11.

This dark notion of the ends justifying the means was etched into popular culture. As a cultural bellwether of his times, Mickey Spillane understood that American sensibilities had changed as a result of the war and that Americans were not averse to the portrayal of violence in their fiction. As a result, Spillane created a series of best selling potboilers featuring Mike Hammer, the cynical private detective who has no scruples about ruthlessly dispatching his enemies. His exulting in the extermination of Communists— "I shot them in cold blood and enjoyed every minute of it....They were Commies....They were red sons-of-bitches who should have died long ago"—gives voice to an era that interpreted difference or calls for social justice as treason. Given the zealotry of their commitment to Party and nation, that conformity always took priority over diversity in the expression of opinion. Since both suppressed and punished dissent, it can be said that American Communists and anti-communists were mirror images of each other.[12]

The fear and loathing of communism did not inspire much support for repatriated American prisoners of war when hundreds of returnees accused each other of collaborating with the enemy. Yet there was little understanding of the physical and psychological depredations POWs suffered and the unique nature of their prison-camp experience. During the first year of captivity, they endured starvation, filthy living conditions, extreme cold and death marches where their guards shot anyone who could not keep in line. Three thousand of the seven thousand POWs died in the first six months alone. Their North Korean and Chinese captors launched an ideological assault on their minds with the goal of gaining their allegiance or at least using them as pawns in a wider propaganda war. Compelled to listen to lectures, undertake compulsory readings, write autobiographies, and sit on "peace committees," the prisoners faced relentless pressure to cooperate. They were subjected to beatings, the threat of execution, the removal of their meagre rations and being dispatched to the horrors of the "Caves." These were holes in the ground where POWs turned into "living skeletons or walking corpses, with their eyes bulging, just like bullfrogs" before dying.[13] Given these conditions, in which over forty percent died, prisoners succumbed to signing a "peace petition" or a statement declaring the U.S. the aggressor in the war and some were forced to regurgitate a prepared public pronouncement criticizing their government. As a result, military spokesmen and journalists maligned veterans as weak-willed and malleable in the enemy's manipulations. They became scapegoats for America's inconclusive war that claimed over thirty thousand American lives and left another ninety-eight thousand wounded. Experts considered the court-martial of fourteen repatriated POWs an example of personal inadequacies and by extrapolation, of national deficiencies operating in American society.

One of the most prominent and influential spokespersons of this ilk was the journalist, Eugene Kinkead. He wrote an alarmist account alleging that one out of every three prisoners collaborated.

He excoriated the "sad and singular" record of POWs for the low escape rate, the high mortality rate in the camps—many lacked the will to live because they suffered from "giveupitis"—and for the scale of their collaboration. Describing their treatment as "a highly novel blend of leniency and pressure," Kinkead asserted that death rate "was not due to Communist mistreatment [but]... [to] the ignorance or the callousness of the prisoners themselves." Ignoring the responsibility of the Chinese for their barbaric treatment of the prisoners, his real target was the permissiveness and "softness" in American culture: the lack of physical fitness, religious adherence, childhood training and the poor quality of education. The latter was unlikely to change given teachers' fear of the red list and the stress of providing the "right answers" rather than the "excesses of a permanently open mind." These conditions were the presumed source for the lack of discipline and mental toughness* that rendered prisoners vulnerable to the skilful machinations of Chinese interrogators and contributed to the high number of deaths in the camps.[14]

In this debilitated condition, the emaciated POWs were believed to have been brainwashed. Coined by the partisan journalist and CIA operative, Edward Hunter, whose writings during the 1950s enjoyed wide currency, brainwashing was applied by malevolent masters in Red China intent on "mind murder." They had short-circuited the synapses of American prisoners of war and cleansed their minds, turning each of them into "a living puppet—a human robot—without the atrocity of being visible from the outside." John Foster Dulles, who was to become Secretary of State in the Eisenhower administrations, admitted to being strongly influenced by Hunter's writings. His greatest fear was the total erasure of thoughts followed by the creation of "new brain processes" in which individuals "so conditioned can only repeat thoughts that have been implanted in their minds by suggestions from outside."[15]

In addition to the shame of some POWs' alleged collaboration, twenty-one Americans refused repatriation. An editorial in the *New York Times* opined that their decision offered "living proof that Communist brainwashing does work on some people." Two

---

* Popular culture, especially Western films, spoke to these fears. The immensely popular *High Noon* portrays Gary Cooper as the epitome of manliness who, alone among the spineless cowards around him, is willing to confront the dangerous invaders.

men changed their minds and did return after they were assured there would be no retribution, only to be arrested, court-martialed and imprisoned. (All but one ultimately returned home.) The defectors who journeyed to China were vilified in the press as homosexuals, spineless, "garden-variety quitters," and "pathetic men" who "lacked guts" and "knuckled under." In varying degrees, these weaknesses were applied to the POWs as a group. Rather than being the product of brainwashing, the evidence, however, suggests that the twenty-one prisoners-of-war who refused repatriation arrived at their decision rationally. They had come from broken homes, possessed limited education or grew up in extreme poverty; affluent America offered them few opportunities. Some were angry at America for prolonging the war and one POW feared retribution for his collaboration in a prison camp. His fear is understandable when one considers the revulsion and summary justice meted out to a "*chink-lover*, [a] *squealer* and a *rat.*"[16]

Racial discrimination in America was a crucial factor in the decision of three black POWs, an explanation that was dismissed at the time as propaganda. American magazines proudly noted that Communist propagandists could find only three black soldiers to exploit. A *U.S. News and World Report* comment, "American Negro soldiers did not swallow the Communist line on racial equality," implied that racial discrimination did not exist in America. In 1991 one of the Afro-American veterans turned the brainwashing rationale on its head: "Brainwashed? The Chinese unbrainwashed me. The Negro had his mind brainwashed long before Korea. If he stayed in his place, he was a good nigger."[17] His insight challenged the conventional wisdom of the media, the general public and political officials who excoriated former Korean War prisoners by erroneously classifying them as brainwashed. As one of the former prisoners, who had suffered severe frost bite and an infection from a battlefield wound remarked, "those American [psychiatrists] weren't interested in a damn thing except did we collaborate."[18]

The fantasy that POWs were generally brainwashed persisted as the CIA studied Stalin's show trials. After the publication of Arthur Koestler's *Darkness at Noon*, there was greater understanding about how Soviet interrogators exploited the residual loyalty to the regime to produce convincing false confessions from prisoners who had once belonged to the political elite. But the show trial confessions of the avowed anti-communist, Cardinal Mindzsenty of Hungary, and that of an American businessman, Robert Vogeler, in 1949 convinced the CIA that they had been drugged or hypnotised. The organization became obsessed with means to manipulate the human mind so that secrets could be extracted and then erased leaving the individual with no memory of what he had revealed. It employed drugs, including sodium pentothal, chemicals and torture to wring out confessions from suspected double agents in secret prisons in Germany, Japan and the Panama Canal Zone. Richard Helms, one of the CIA officers in charge of "overseas interrogations" once said that a foreign agent could not be trusted "unless you own him body and soul." At a retreat, an army civilian employee, Frank Olson, was sprayed with LSD and then subjected to an intense interrogation for the next two days because he had violated his Army and CIA oath. According to H.P. Albarelli, who conducted a thorough ten-year examination of the case, the biochemist Olson was murdered in 1953, not driven to suicide by depression as the official cover story originally asserted, because he had talked to the "wrong people" about a secret experiment conducted by a Special Operations Division of which he had been a member. The SOD had sprayed a town, Pont-St-Esprit in southern France, with a substance that caused mass psychosis inducing terrifying hallucinations and epileptic convulsions as a result of which at least four people died. In 1975 President Ford met with the Olson family to offer an official apology on behalf of the CIA for drugging Frank with LSD after Dick Cheney wrote a memorandum to his boss, the White House chief of staff, Donald Rumsfeld, indicating that a settlement and an apology would forestall any trial or hearing that might require the release of more incriminating documents. The apology was a way of covering up the murder. Albarelli asserts that when two men, one an assassin contracted by the CIA, attempted to remove him from his hotel room, the frightened Olson resisted and was "pitched" through the closed window.[19]

The CIA sought other explanations for the apparent collaboration among American POWs. At the agency's behest, two distinguished neurologists issued a report that flatly denied the existence of brainwashing in North Korean and Chinese POW camps: the Chinese did not resort to hypnosis, drugs or technology to alter the minds or personalities of the prisoners. Instead, they found that the Chinese aim had been indoctrination by subjecting the prisoners to the obligatory study of Marx and Mao. Its psychological warriors sought "to replace the prisoner's 'internal milieu' with their own external milieu [whereby they] became willing not only to say but to *be* [sic] what their captors wished."[20] Yet as an expression of the prisoners' resistance, in 1952 four hundred sergeants went on a hunger strike against compulsory indoctrination sessions throughout the camps; as a result, the Chinese backed down and "self-study" sessions became voluntary.[21] The North Koreans and Chinese also resorted to Stalinist procedures and psychological stress. Prisoners endured sleep and food deprivation, extreme physical discomfort, isolation cells, verbal abuse, beatings and torture. Worse was the constant fear of being executed, given that almost eight thousand military personnel were summarily executed as prisoners of the North Koreans or their Chinese allies.[22]

Intense psychological pressure was derived from the humiliating group self-criticism sessions. Failure to cooperate could mean lack of food or medical care and the real possibility of dying. But the fear of succumbing to malnourishment, untreated wounds, and the physical abuse and psychological coercion weighed heavily on prisoners of war. Many of them became vulnerable to making gestures or statements that they likely did not believe in. The current consensus is that one out of ten prisoners signed a peace petition or delivered a radio confession of alleged American misdeeds, the most sensational being their government's purported deployment of biological warfare in Korea. Although most historians have concluded that accusations of biological weapons have not been substantiated, at the time their confessions convinced public opinion in Europe, provoking large demonstrations, and diminished America's moral reputation.[23]

Similarly, social scientists debunked the notion of character weaknesses and brain washing. Albert D. Biderman, who studied the POWs for the army, offered the most penetrating critique that exposed Kinkead's polemical theory. By comparing POWs with those from other wars, he concluded that they did not act any differently from the Americans in Korea. His investigation documented the coercion and the torture that POWs endured, procedures that Kinkead trivialized in his tirade. Biderman suggests that methods, notably standing in extreme cold for a prolonged period of time or long hours of isolation, may have toughened American resistance to "playing along" and offering false confessions. When he examined air force personnel, he concluded that these forms of coercion did not convert these men into Communists, fellow travellers or collaborators. Likewise, Robert J. Lifton, who served as an Air Force psychiatrist in Japan and Korea, noted that the stance of parroting Chinese propaganda quickly disappeared once they were en route home. As he found no evidence of permanent change in thinking and beliefs, he rejected the term brainwashing.[24]

Popular Culture Mirrors Reality

If brainwashing was understood as something akin to preternatural control of thought, it is more reminiscent of *fin-de-siècle* Gothic novels than the realities of POWs' experience. While the Gothic villain often exercises mind control over his victims, some veterans *freely* decided not to return home while others chose to malign the lack of patriotism of their fellow inmates. In stark contrast, "brainwashing" was more redolent of the science fiction films of the time. The 1956 *The Invasion of the Body Snatchers* portrays an alien race from outer space that lands on earth, first merging with plants, and then proceeding to take over a human being. When a huge pod is deposited on an individual's premise, it splits opens revealing a featureless body which slowly begins to acquire the shape and features of that individual. When his consciousness is at its weakest during sleep, the pod takes possession. The original body decomposes and is disposed of by the double who acquires an exact physical replication of that individual possessing his identity, knowledge and memory, but bereft of his humanity. As emotionless automatons, these pod people are incapable of love and are convinced that they have been "reborn into an untroubled world." It is no accident that the most memorable and, in retrospect, most cited line occurs toward the film's end when the doctor who has resisted falling asleep runs onto a freeway yelling at heedless drivers: "They're here already! You're next!" Although the script is apolitical, the subtext is suffused with contemporary fears of expansionist, international communism. Susan Sontag perceptively suggests that science fiction films are "the vampire fantasy in a new dress" since an individual could be turned into the "automatized servant or agent of...alien powers."[25] *Invasion* could also be interpreted as the chilling effects of conformity and passivity that McCarthyism at home generated. Both

One of the most terrifying moments in Don Siegel's 1956 Invasion of the Body Snatchers *occurs when Miles, a local town doctor, who along with his fiancée, Becky have been attempting to escape the "pod people," stop to rest in a cave. He leaves her inspect a nearby farm where more pods are located. When he returns, she has fallen asleep; when she awakes after he kisses her, he realizes to his horror that she has become one of them, an emotionless automaton, incapable of love*

interpretations suggest that eternal vigilance is necessary if the citizen is to protect his identity and his country. As an allegory, the film provides a faint echo of the conformity and vigilance demanded under Stalin.

Security does have its attractions. The 2007 film, *The Invasion,* the fourth adaptation of the 1954 Jack Finney novel contains a couple of innovative applications. Unlike the earlier versions where pod people replace human beings, the film plays upon our fear of disease and people are taken over not by pod duplicates but by the spores themselves. After they pass from person to person in the form of a spew of green bile and enter the blood stream, the spores attack and replace the human cells while people are in REM sleep. The benefit of this sedated conformity is that there is greater global harmony. In the background, television monitors reveal individuals such as G.W. Bush and Venezuela's mercurial Hugo Chavez shaking hands, and peace erupting in the most unlikely places. While the dramatic foreground focuses on a few heroic types who resist the transition into a disengaged automaton, this tantalizing ambiguity that suggests a potential upside to a world of less violent people is left unexplored.

America's cultural fixation on brainwashing was given new life in Richard Condon's 1959 novel and in its 1962 film adaptation, *The Manchurian Candidate*. The book played upon the fear that brainwashing could be permanent, that minds could be altered forever. Film director, John Frankenheimer, who depicts POWs with minds "not only washed but dry-cleaned," credited Kinkead's *In Every War but One* as a seminal influence. Critics praised the film as a cultural artefact that exposed the anxieties of the time. Former Korean POWs, on the other hand, reviled it as a heavy-handed treatment that stigmatized them. Historian Bruce Cumings acknowledges that *Candidate* was the one "Korean film of lasting significance, but it mostly reinforces stereotypes about Asian Communists and what the war was about."[26] It also played into the paranoia of Senator Jenner (discussed above) and his ilk that the American government was controlled by agents from Moscow.

In *The* Manchurian *Candidate*, an unpopular officer, Raymond Shaw, is programmed to be an agent of the Kremlin and a guiltless political assassin. He then returns home as a decorated war hero and his men are conditioned to remember their commander as "the bravest, kindest, warmest, most wonderful human being" ever known. The film both lampoons McCarthyism and appears to vindicate early Cold War fears about Communists in the corridors of power. Yet the film does not dramatize that the American government was "riddled" with Communists even though that allegation was made by the senator from Wisconsin. Joseph McCarthy posed a genuine threat to civil liberties and did inspire fear. The senator in *Manchurian* is modelled on McCarthy but the character is a drunken buffoon whose baseless charges about Communists in government could hardly frighten audiences. He is merely a pawn under the control of his manipulative wife, the top Soviet agent in America, and the mother and operator of Shaw, who is determined to climb to the pinnacle of power by ensuring that her husband becomes president of the United States.* She, not the hapless McCarthyite figure, and the savvy Communists, having mastered mind control, are the real villains of the piece. They include scientists from the Pavlov Institute who use post-hypnotic suggestion, sensory deprivation and drugs to programme a GI to become a perfect assassin, to robotically kill on command without mercy and to lack the capacity for memory. When his reflex is triggered by the queen of diamonds, his vacant stare is similar to the lifeless eyes of the pod people in *The Invasion of the Body Snatchers*.[27]

The malevolent sophistication attributed to the Communist scientists in the *Manchurian Candidate* mirrored the determination of the CIA to manufacture a "Manchurian candidate" of its own.[28] They funded the aggressively invasive procedures of behavioural scientists, among them, the internationally prominent psychiatrist and former president of the American Psychiatric Association, Dr. Ewen Cameron. As the director of Montreal's prestigious Allan Memorial Institute from 1953 to 1963, he treated patients afflicted with relatively minor anxiety, postpartum depression and alcoholism by regressing them to a near vegetative infantile state—a tabula rasa—before remaking them. Instead of treatment, Cameron's experiments on human guinea pigs for his scientific research have the hallmarks of a ghoulish Gothic thriller.

Cameron's research was inspired by the role he played as a scientific expert in Germany at the end of the war. Having attended Nuremburg in 1945 to deliver his professional opinion about the fitness of Rudolf Hess to stand trial, he listened to the magnitude of the Nazi crimes. He concluded that a "psychological epidemic" had occurred as a result of "mass manipulation" by a charismatic

---

* Angela Lansbury's portrayal of "Mother" as "an incestuously-inclined monster" of an "emotionally stunted son" exemplifies for some what critic, Philip Wylie, reviled as "Momism," the overbearing mother who renders her son dependent and unable to withstand the pressures of captivity.

leader and could occur again if society were not mentally healthy.[29] The role of psychiatry was to ensure the development of individuals able to withstand the pressures of modern life. Unfortunately, Cameron did not witness the second round of Nuremburg trials that tried physicians who willingly implemented Hitler's biomedical vision to eliminate what they perceived to be bad genes threatening the health of the *Volk*. He would have heard the accused citing in their defence similar American non-therapeutic experiments conducted on prisoners. This defence did not exonerate German physicians, several of whom were sentenced to death.*

After this trial, American jurists drew up the Nuremburg Code that consisted of ten principles. They included putting the onus on physicians to receive informed consent from their patients/ subjects, to ensure that these people had freely volunteered for the experiment, and that physicians desist from further experimentation if they have reasonable grounds for believing that continuation of the experiment would result in injury, disability or death of the subject. American physicians believed that the Code was appropriate to "barbarians" but not to them. For many scientists who conducted biomedical research, the Code was either ignored or paid loose lip service. Two examples will suffice. For forty years from 1932 to 1972, the American Public Health Service conducted the Tuskegee Study to examine how syphilis was "different" in blacks. To that end, physicians exploited and abused four hundred uneducated Afro-American sharecroppers by subjecting them to painful procedures and denying them effective treatment. Maligned by one physician as "a notoriously syphilis-soaked race," as though the disease was unique to their race, these men believed they were suffering from "bad blood." Neither they nor their families were informed of the true nature of their illness, and despite assurances to the contrary, they were given placebos and denied penicillin. On a project that turned out to have no scientific value, medical journals published reports about the monitoring of the course of the disease and the results of subsequent autopsies. The *Los Angeles Times* editorialized in 1972 that this experiment was only possible "because the doctors obviously

---

* Kurt Blome, who admitted to injecting plague vaccines into concentration camp victims, was acquitted owing to the intervention of the Americans. They were interested in recruiting him to work in their biological and chemical weapons programme.

did not regard their subjects as completely human." Like the patients of the Tuskegee Study, the prisoners who volunteered at the Holmesburg Prison in Philadelphia County between 1951 and 1974 were unlettered, poor and uninformed about the nature and the risks of the experiments in which they participated. For a small fee, inmates offered "a piece of their skin" to test commercial products that caused illness, lesions and skin discolorations. Others were exposed to highly dangerous photo-toxic drugs, ultraviolet rays and radioactive isotopes, and were left with permanent memory loss and seriously impaired cognitive ability. Given this broader medical context, Cameron's experiments on human subjects for advancing scientific knowledge were hardly exceptional. He even believed that he was adhering to the Nuremburg Code since everyone who came to the Allan Memorial did so voluntarily, could leave at anytime and signed a voluntary consent form. But Cameron's belief that scientific experts should develop methods for controlling citizens, and decide who should govern and parent contained the potential for repeating the totalitarianism of Nazi Germany. His authoritarian inclinations and lack of empathy toward easily manipulated personalities increasingly mirrored the enemy he most despised.[30]

Cameron's egotism and hatred of totalitarianism rendered him susceptible to the unsavoury financial inducement of the CIA. The Agency laundered funds to hospitals for covert mind-control research through a front organization in order to learn about the techniques it believed operated behind the Iron Curtain. Cameron received financial support for research enabling him to turn in part[*] the institute into one resembling a terrifying house of horror, a setting that could have been ripped from the pages of a Gothic novel. In the renovated basement, he built an Isolation Chamber in which he "soundproofed the room, piped in white noise, turned off the lights, and put dark goggles and 'rubber eardrums' on each patient." Incidentally, his patients were never informed of the treatment beforehand and the risks involved. To ensure that no patient escaped, Cameron administered to some patients the drug curare, a South African arrow poison which creates paralysis, turning them into prisoners of their own body.[31] In what he believed was

---

[*] It should be pointed out that about the same time, Dr. Wilder Penfield was doing his pioneering work in neurosurgery at the same institute

cutting-edge therapy, Cameron instituted a technique he called "depatterning" or wiping the human mind clean of all thought. To this end, Cameron used frequent and high voltage electroshock therapy, sensory deprivation and a battery of drugs that included sedatives and LSD. Once he rendered a person's mind blank, he proceeded to implant new patterns of "healthy" behaviour with a technique he called "psychic driving." After being drugged with a "sleep cocktail," the patients spent almost a month in a coma listening to taped messages sixteen hours a day, initially piped through a loud speaker in their darkened rooms and eventually relayed through earphones. In his zeal to endow his patients with new and healthy personalities, he "depatterned" about two hundred individuals and administered "psychic driving" to over one hundred.

Over a seven-year period with support from the CIA, Cameron conducted various experiments in sensory deprivation. In one horrific experiment a woman was confined to a specially built isolation "box" for thirty-five days to destroy any sense of time and place. Rather than therapy for a psychiatric disorder, these extreme measures were comparable to a prisoner enduring torture—a realization Cameron himself arrived at. In an interview in 1955, he recognized the similarities between his patients and POWs facing interrogation stating that they "like the prisoners of the Communists tended to resist [treatment] and had to be broken down."[32] Instead of concern about his patients' well-being, his interests lay in designing techniques for influencing human behaviour. By working in this manner for a "higher cause," be it advancing science or winning the Cold War, Cameron mirrored the Nazi doctors he abhorred; he too regarded his patients as "laboratory animals to be exploited in the search for the cure to mental illness."[33] As an ideologue, his sadism under the guise of treatment was an unconscionable abuse of power in the doctor and patient relationship.

Cameron's results were a disaster with irreversible consequences for the patients, ravaging their lives. Psychiatrist, Harvey Weinstein, recounts that his father, a once successful business man who suffered anxiety attacks, was referred to Cameron for treatment during which he devolved "from man to animal to pitiable creature."[34] Although Weinstein does not make a direct connection, it is possible that his father's anxiety attacks were related to his experience as an infant in 1907 Romania; during a pogrom when he began to cry threatening the family's existence, his mother stuffed a scarf into his mouth. After three years of institutional degradation, suffering from serious memory loss, lethargy and confusion, he was discharged, incapable of functioning. Another patient endured six months of Cameron's repeated use of electroshock therapy, multiple drugs and an eighty-six day drug-induced sleep. She emerged with no recoverable memory of her first twenty-six years, unable to read or write, or recognize her husband and children, and had to be toilet trained. Yet since then with courage and determination, she has rebuilt her shattered life.[35] Another patient, who suffers severe back pain and memory problems about events since her release, told journalist, Naomi Klein, that she continually has flashbacks and "electric dreams" in which she receives "visits from the Eminent Monster." As if she was a character from a science-fiction horror film from the period, she hears "people screaming, moaning, groaning, people saying no, no, no" and that she had a "peculiar feeling in the head: Like I had a blob, not a head."[36] These three examples represent a sampling of Cameron's patients who endured a plethora of life-long problems. Given these iatrogenic outcomes, it is apt to describe Cameron's patients as the living dead while under his control.

His grandiosity is redolent of the same primal fears evoked by the protagonists in Gothic classics: *Frankenstein*, *Dr. Jekyll and Mr. Hyde* and *The Island of Doctor Moreau*. Like Cameron, they are scientists who, in pursuit of a higher cause, violate accepted ethical norms and cause disruptive acts of violence. They become the doppelganger of their creations; Cameron was the double of the Nazi scientists he despised. Like Cameron, they manifest little compassion toward their subjects. They are destroyed by their hubris; Cameron's posthumous reputation has surely been sullied.

Cameron's descent into the dark side of psychiatry was in part an inspiration for a 1963 CIA interrogation manual used during the Cold War. It claimed that if its medical, chemical and electrical techniques were used properly, they could destroy (a subject's) capacity for resistance and extract information.[37] His experiments and the CIA handbook anticipated the treatment of enemy combatants in the twenty-first century. What he began as psychiatric research into brainwashing contributed to a scientific rationale and a refinement of techniques for administering torture.

The POWs' apparent breakdown of military discipline motivated American authorities to develop a programme that mirrored the methods deployed by Soviet, Chinese and North Korean Communists. Among the Korean-war pilots, who confessed to planning biological warfare raids in North Korea, was Marine Colonel, Frank Schwable. This bogus confession was offered and later recorded for global consumption after he endured physical and mental degradation during which North Koreans confined him to a punishment cave naked and unbathed, and a full-frontal assault on his psyche. Unlike other captives, he was not indoctrinated but was the victim of "menticide," a process that was designed to break a prisoner so that his "mind is completely devoid of will power."[38] A later U.S. military board of inquiry decided that Schwable had only three choices: to sign, to die or go insane. Schwable's brutal treatment—he was also excoriated by prominent Americans as a coward and a traitor—prompted the military to establish SERE (Survival, Evasion, Resistance, Escape): a secret programme in which military psychologists devised techniques of mock torture. They subjected Air Force pilots and later Special Forces to "waterboarding, sleep deprivation, isolation and bombardment with agonizing sounds, sexual and religious humiliation, and temperature extremes." The aim was to prepare men in the event that they were captured, thus preventing them from producing false propaganda for their captors. Devised as a defensive programme after 9/11, SERE became an offensive weapon for the CIA to apply these "enhanced" interrogation techniques on terrorist suspects at offshore sites.[39]

The interrogation that occurred under the aegis of James Mitchell is similar to the machinations that occurred in Cameron's sleep rooms. A former military psychologist and after the terrorist attacks, a CIA contractor, Mitchell also regarded his subjects as less-than-human and could justify his actions as good science, serving a higher cause. He believed that suspects should be treated "like a dog" with the intent of breaking their will through the application of electric shock treatments.[40] It is hard to fathom these actions that we associate with a police state or the realm of science fiction with those scientists who conducted experiments on human guinea pigs or inflicted pain upon them à la Mengele. Cameron recalls the mad eugenicist in H. G. Wells' *The Island of Doctor Moreau* in which the physician is willing to inflict as much

pain as necessary on the animals in surgery to achieve his goals.*
Both Cameron's "depatterning" of patients and Mitchell's zeal to
"break" prisoners were similar to the ordeal of Frank Schwable
and less like other POWs who were not "brainwashed." Their
physical and psychological conditions rendered them vulnerable
to being manipulated by their captors. Schwable was depleted of
his will power, became a propaganda tool for the Communists and
a victim of psychic vampirism. Cameron and Mitchell mirror the
Chinese interrogator who did wash Schwable's mind.

These invasive assaults recall the sci-fi cult film *The Invasion of
the Body Snatchers*. The two major characters, Miles and Becky, attempt to escape the "plague zone," preserve their humanity and
warn others that this "illness" must be contained. But they cannot escape the need for sleep and when Miles leaves Becky for
a few minutes and returns, he sees her napping. When he kisses
her awake, as the life flickers out of her eyes, he is aghast that she
has mutated into a soulless *other* entity. One critic aptly describes
the replicant Becky as having "the classic appearance of the vam-
pirized female."[41] Becky, like Lucy in Bram Stoker's *Dracula*, lost
her humanity in her slumber. When Miles laments that the girl he
loved has become "an inhumane enemy," he is referring to the invasion of her mind, a form of control so insidious that its supporters promise a utopian vision of a pain-free existence, but it leaves a
person without guilt or conscience. The film, however, should not
be regarded as a direct parallel to the treatment of POWs. Apart
from a minority of prisoners who collaborated in order to secure
more favourable treatment, the majority did not contaminate their
fellow prisoners or import a foreign ideology into America. But
their parlous record left some commentators wondering whether the softness of a consumer society would encourage citizens
to yield to what Orwell called in *Nineteen Eighty Four* "the boot

---

* Stalin was so intrigued by Wells' classic that, according to recently declassified documents, in 1926 he ordered a scientist to produce a
super-warrior, half man, half beast who would be insensitive to pain
and unbeatable on the battlefield. The experiments were inevitably a
failure and the disgraced scientist received a five-year sentence in jail
that was later commuted to exile. Similarly, Nazi authorities doled out
a stimulant, pervitin—known today as crystal meth—for the purpose
of rendering soldiers capable of performing superhuman feats on the
battlefield. Some, however, became hopelessly addicted and resembled
an army of zombies rather than an effective fighting force.

stamping on the human face" to gain the security of the emotionless pod people.[42] An amorphous fear of a foreign attack during the Cold War became much more immediate and visceral in the twenty-first century when America experienced a direct attack from stateless actors.

The Psychic Power of Militant Islamism

Passionate hatred can give meaning and
purpose to an empty life. Thus people
haunted by the purposelessness of their
lives try to find a new content not only
by dedicating themselves to a holy cause
but by nursing a fanatical grievance.

—*True Believer*
Eric Hoffer

The Manchurian Candidate is a fictional microcosm for what
has happened to many impressionable young Muslim
men by the manipulation of firebrand imams who led the
faithful in prayer. That deceit was reinforced at al-Qaeda training
camps where recruits were inculcated with a hatred for the West
because of its alleged war against the Muslims. That hatred derived from religious authorities, Middle Eastern politics and the
legacy of European racism. Among Muslims who practised Islam,
a sizable number were Islamists who strove to create an Islamic
state; among those activists were a fringe movement of zealots
who willingly embraced the ideology and methods of al-Qaeda.
Whether they were graduates of secular schools or madrassas
(religious schools), the messages these young men frequently received were a grotesque distortion of the Quran. In part those
messages reflected the radical ideology that derived from an obscure Egyptian, Sayyid Qutb, who inspired the al-Qaeda leadership; whether a direct link can be made between his thought and
that organization remains controversial.

Sayyid Qutb, the spiritual father of modern jihadism, began

his journey to ideological certainty in Egypt and on his trip to America. Poet, civil servant and literary critic, he grew up in British-dominated Egypt where his hostility toward the Egyptian monarchy and "collaborators" shaped his early nationalism. His experience living under the humiliating sting of colonial contempt drove him to take an increasing interest in social and political issues, especially regarding Egyptian independence and a more equitable distribution of the nation's wealth. To detour his political discontent, the Ministry of Education sent him to America during the late 1940s to study American curricula and pedagogy for primary and secondary-school students. His two-year sojourn reinforced his belief that American materialism was anathema to Islamic religiosity. Even the large number of churches in Greeley Colorado was interpreted by Qutb as more a sign of competitive consumerism than of spirituality. Appalled by its popular culture, racism and what he perceived as lasciviousness—this was the time of the Kinsey Report which he read and commented upon—his experience left him with a lifelong disdain for the West, its secularism and moral decay. American women, in particular, both fascinated and repelled him. His simultaneous attraction, "an enchanting nymph" and disgust, "you can smell her burning body," not only disturbed him but inspired legions of young men, including Mohammed Atta, to radical Islamism as it reinforced their fear of sexually provocative women.[1] As he idealized women, Qutb never met a woman who possessed sufficient moral purity, and therefore, remained a bachelor.

If Qutb's experience in America solidified his preconceptions about the West, the rise of Zionism and the disastrous Arab defeat by the Israelis in the 1948–49 war fuelled his long standing animus toward the Jews. In one sense, the Jews or the Zionists (which he conflated), were merely another example of the corrupted Manichean *other*—the British, French, Americans and the sycophantic Egyptian elites—that set "the enemies of Islam" apart from spiritual Muslims. In another sense, his antipathy toward Jews was different than the others—a deeply rooted product derived from his reading of the Quran. He compared the seventh-century troubled relationship between the Prophet and the Jews with the Zionists in Palestine. In his 1950 *Our Struggle with the Jews*, he portrayed modern Muslims as the victims of the "same Jewish machinations and double-dealing which discomfited the

Early Muslims." He depicted Jews as conspiratorial and obsessed with destroying Islam. Considering Qutb's thesis that the Jews had waged war by committing "unprecedented abominations" against Islam since its inception, historian Jeffrey Herf argues that Qutb's animus toward the Jews was comparable to the hatred harboured by the Nazis. He also suggests that Qutb's screed was remarkably like the Arab harangues broadcast in wartime Berlin and speculates that Qutb might have listened to them. Qutb's declaration that Jews were engaged in a "Crusader–Zionist" war strongly suggests a stark continuity with modern terrorism.[2] In other areas of his thought, he is more ambiguous.

Qutb's time in prison radicalized him and clarified his ideological convictions. He resigned from the ministry and in 1953 joined the Muslim Brotherhood—an organization founded in 1908 with the express purpose of establishing Sharia law in Muslim societies. It had been outlawed in 1954 after an assassination attempt on Gamal Abdul Nasser, the secular Arab nationalist leader of Egypt. Members of the Brotherhood were arrested; some were executed while others received long-term prison sentences. Qutb spent almost a decade in prison, maltreated and tortured, and was only released because of his frail health. The authorities did not want a potential martyr to enflame further violence. Within a year, he was rearrested on charges of subversion against Nasser's increasingly repressive government and subsequently hanged after he refused to recant. Throughout his years in prison, he distilled his experiences into his writings, which were smuggled out to friends and family who found a publisher for *Milestones*, his most uncompromising statement. It would become an internationally influential manifesto of the Islamic revolution.

Qutb was perplexed at the practice of Muslims torturing other Muslims and arrived at the conclusion that his jailers, who served Nasser's nationalist and avowedly anti-imperialist regime (and one that he initially had supported), could not be true Muslims. He concluded that Muslim society generally had degenerated into *jahili*, "ignorance of God's truth." The "rubbish heap of the West," with its secular values had emasculated Islamic societies. Under the leadership of Nasser, this viral influence was becoming an "evil and dirty materialism" that threatened to "exterminate" Islam.[3] The only way to discard Western contaminants of selfish individualism that prevailed over the common good was through a theocracy wherein ultra-conservative Islamic values would pervade every aspect of life and restore God's sovereignty on earth. To that end, he reactivated the concept of jihad and transformed it from the idea of conflict against a specific target into an "eternal revolution" against anyone who had usurped God's sovereignty. The refusal of Nasser to make Sharia the law of the country rendered his authority illegitimate. Rejecting advocacy politics, an activism that he had once engaged, he now considered it ineffective in a regime that was prepared to destroy its critics. To prepare for the global struggle against *jahili*, a noble "vanguard" of true Muslims should allow Islam to inform every facet of their personal, social and political lives. These true believers should avoid playing the "political game," remove themselves from corrupting influences within their environment and imbue their fellow Muslims with an Islamic consciousness. In this way, society could be rebuilt from the bottom up. In the year he spent out of prison, Qutb, inspired by Islamic scripture and pragmatism, cautioned his followers against launching an attack against the Nasser regime given its strength. Such an aggressive action could entail disastrous consequences for the movement. He, however, did not rule out the need for military training and the stockpiling of weapons against the day when Nasser's forces might move to crush the movement as they had in 1954.[4] He never, however, advocated the excommunication of "faux" Muslims who pay lip service to Islam but never integrate it into their lives; nor did he brand individuals as "unbelievers" or endorse indiscriminate violence against civilians. According to those closest to him and his biographer, Qutb, despite his hostility toward the West, never supported waging war against Britain or the United States. Nor would he have endorsed a transnational organization like al-Qaeda.[5]

The future leaders of al-Qaeda cherry picked Qutb's ideas and implemented them in a manner that raises questions about whether a direct connection can be made between his ideas and the ideology and methods practised by al-Qaeda.[6] Ayman al-Zawahiri, a cerebral Egyptian doctor was imprisoned during the early 1980s after the assassination of Egyptian President, Anwar Sadat. Like Qutb, torture further radicalized al-Zawahiri, but he went further than Qutb by embracing the apocalyptic credo, that only violence can change history.* Al-Zawahiri, who had studied directly under Qutb's brother, Mohammed, in Egypt, praised Qutb as "the most prominent theoretician of the fundamentalist movements" but defended violence as the means to restore dignity to humiliated Muslims.[7] Mohammed Qutb, after becoming a university professor in Saudi Arabia during the early 1970s, was also responsible for introducing his brother's radical ideas to a wealthy Saudi-born socialite, Osama bin Laden, who would become his most famous protégé. During the Afghan war, Osama parlayed his money and his willingness to sacrifice comfort for the cause into becoming a formidable presence in the jihadist struggle. He set up a "training base" in 1988 to prepare recruits to remove the Soviet presence from Asian states. Until 1995 he had been reluctant to support the killing of Muslims and refused to provide financial support for domestic jihads against Egypt and Algeria, the "near enemy." The latter was part of a larger goal—to install theocracies in secular Muslim states, most notably Saudi Arabia, and restore the Islamic caliphate** rule that would unite Muslims.

The invasion of Iraq in 1991 and the presence of American troops in Saudi Arabia radicalized bin Laden. "The far enemy" —the United States—had long propped up Middle-Eastern conservative regimes by providing them with financial and military largess. A crucial turning point in bin Laden's life occurred after Saddam Hussein invaded Kuwait in 1990 and his offer to deploy his army from the Afghan war to defend Saudi Arabia was rejected . Bin Laden was especially outraged that the House of Saud invited American troops, including women, to profane its sacred soil. He openly declared war against the Saudi royal family, accusing the king of being an "apostate"; the American military presence was proof that the U.S. was intent on establishing hegemony over the Arab and Muslim world. As a result, bin Laden established the transnational organization, al-Qaeda, which became

---

*   Others who emerged from the Egyptian torture chambers abandoned armed struggle and sought an Islamic state through non-violent political persuasion.

**   This title was originally bestowed upon the successors of Prophet Muhammad but later was used by medieval Muslim kings. The caliphate existed throughout the Ottoman Empire until it was abolished in 1922 by Kemal Atatürk, who proclaimed Turkey a republic the following year.

fully operational by 1998. Al-Zawahiri, whose priority had been the removal of the secular Egyptian state, not waging war against the "far enemy," was desperately short of finances and reluctantly joined with bin Laden. The two of them conceived of al-Qaeda as the elite vanguard of the Islamist movement. They adopted a top-down chain of command in which bin Laden became a cynosure for the disaffected while acting as a medieval ideologue and exercising absolute power. In 2001 its membership peaked at ten thousand members, all of whom had sworn a personal oath of allegiance to bin Laden. By this time, he had authorized the killing of civilians, including Muslims.[8]

As an implacable ideologue, bin Laden never let reality interfere with his narrative that the West inflicted only misery and humiliation on Muslims. He could never acknowledge America's decision to end its large scale military presence in Saudi Arabia by September 2003. He hypocritically protested the continuing violence against Muslim civilians from Israel to Iraq stating that "attacks against American civilians [were] necessary so that they [could] 'taste the bitter fruit' that Muslims have long tasted." Yet until the sectarian war in Iraq, he appeared indifferent to the much greater number of civilian Muslims killed by al-Qaeda. Nor did he take any interest in the protection of Muslim lives when NATO bombing prevented the Serbs from unleashing further terror against Bosnian Muslims during the 1990s or when the major international assistance was given to Indonesian Muslims during the 2004 tsunami.[9] Instead, Muslims purported humiliation could only be avenged by global jihad. Al-Qaeda surfaced as a revenant of the European totalitarian states of the twentieth century that had supposedly been consigned to their graves. Like the Bolsheviks and the Nazis whose illiberalism, cult-like worship of its leaders and deft propaganda seduced millions among the young, bin Laden's charisma inspired the disaffected and gave purpose to their inchoate feelings.

Although they were reared elsewhere, the September 11 highjackers acquired a cosmopolitan outlook and received a quality education in the West. More importantly, they were united by a sense of displacement. Despite the accomplishments of those who gravitated to Hamburg Germany, and the beneficiaries of perhaps the most liberal asylum policy in the world, these young men felt marginalized by what they perceived as the materialistic culture around them. At the mosque, they were not only enthralled by the message of the mullahs who preached the glories of the jihad against the Soviet Union but they also acquired a sense of kinship for fellow Muslims. They also were infused with a sense of identity and purpose that would send them to an al-Qaeda training camp in Afghanistan where their fevered imaginations would be exploited and channelled into a nihilistic creed. Once informed that they were chosen to be martyrs, these men relinquished all facets of their previous lives, including their rational capacity, and reincarnated themselves with a single consuming *raison d'être.*

Courtesy of Photofest

Abu Jandal, the nom de plume for Nasser al-Bahri, a former bodyguard for bin Laden is the compelling subject for the 2010 documentary The Oath. *A lapsed jihadist, who was visually captured on film attending one of its training camps in 2000 and heard bin Laden speak, Abu Jandal in this film drives a cab in Yemen to support his son. He still believes in armed aggression against the enemies of Islam but was shocked by the attacks of 9/11—he personally knew all nineteen attackers—and opposes the targeting of civilians*

According to "Mohammed Atta's Testament," a document named after the purported leader of the hijackers who flew the commandeered airliners on September 11, 2001, these true believers were programmed to "listen and obey" all instructions.[10]

This was the message communicated in the West: Islamists were indoctrinated terrorists. What the Western media overlooked or minimized was that the vast majority of Arabs and Muslims were appalled by the attacks. The candle-lit vigils and the vehement denunciation among more moderate jihadists throughout the Middle East attest to this. They regarded the deliberate killing of civilians as a stain upon Islam and as un-Islamic, and feared that bin Laden's actions would lead to the demonization of Islam. Scholars and mainstream Islamists lambasted bin Laden for his "catastrophic leadership" and his underestimation of American resilience. In contrast to the fifty thousand Muslims who flocked to Afghanistan after the Soviet invasion in 1979, bin Laden's call to arms after 9/11 encountered an almost deafening silence. Indeed, some of his most severe critics were already serving life imprisonment terms for their part in the 1981 assassination of Sadat. They contended that jihad was only one duty of Islam, that it was a means and not an end—the attacks had only brought suffering to Muslims and had forfeited public support—that American "interests" rather than a "Crusaders" mentality motivated its involvement in international affairs, that bin Laden had sacrificed what Islam had always practised, that of peaceful coexistence, and that the crimes were un-Islamic; not only were the victims civilians but the bombers had been guests in America. They nearly dubbed bin Laden and Zawahiri apostates for believing their views could override those of the Prophet. Even the Taliban Amir, Mullah Omar, who had "ordered" bin Laden to refrain from attacking America, and was not informed of it when they did, rightly perceived them as a calamity for his country. Still, he tenaciously refused to turn over bin Laden to the Americans or a third party.[11] Among these reactions, the West focused only on Omar's decision and did not hear the torrent of criticism that was levelled at bin Laden and al-Qaeda. Americans' preference for wanting to hear that "they hate us" mirrored what the most militant Islamists told their followers.

The "terror narrative" delivered by Western media failed to provide the historical context of American support for the mujahedeen movement during the Afghan war against the Soviet Union during the 1980s, and instead focused on the words and images of a small minority who undeniably welcomed the attacks and promoted a violent extremist version of Islamism. An Islamic cleric who celebrated these perpetrators as "the magnificent nineteen" did typify some imams and unscrupulous warlords who sought to inspire a new generation of jihadists. A large number emerged from the madrassas in the Middle East and South Asia. This institution had acquired a distinguished pedigree for educating future Islamic scholars and clerics. During the Cold War, however, when the Americans, obsessed with defeating its ideological enemy, "sup[ped] with the devil of jihadism," some of these schools with American approval devolved into recruitment centers to produce mujahedeen to fight the Soviet Goliath in Afghanistan.[12] After the latter's humiliating withdrawal in 1989 and America's loss of interest in the country, some imams in South Asia shared ideological values with radical militant groups, notably the Taliban. From a minority of madrassas—the terror narrative emphasized the madrassa role—they bred a fresh supply of young "fighters" imbued with global jihad fervour; these men were convinced that if they could defeat the Soviets, they could repeat their success with America. After the September 11 attacks, hundreds of madrassas opened in Pakistan funded by puritanically rigid Wahabi groups in the Gulf Arab states and by Pakistani citizens. In an effort to appease the Americans, then-President Musharraf attempted to introduce a modern curriculum of science, math and history into these hotbeds of fanaticism but this endeavour was shelved after Islamic parties opposed them. These political parties even denied the existence of al-Qaeda and purported that the CIA and Israel were responsible for the attacks on New York and Washington.[13]

This type of fantasy bore some similarity to the misperception in the West that all madrassas were merely recruiting centers for jihadism: institutions where children from poor and deprived areas were limited to learning how to handle firearms and rote-learning the Quran. Yet the curriculum in some madrassas was much broader. Certain wealthier parents, who sent children to public and private schools, often enrolled one child in a religious school in order to expose them to that worldview. Most tellingly, some of the militants, who had a high degree of literacy, were educated in government schools.

Still, there is some substance to the opinion that the young were being indoctrinated with hatred toward anyone who was not a devout Muslim. One nineteen-year-old Afghan who travelled to Pakistan acknowledged that his teachers told them it was their duty to fight for their country and religion against the unbelievers and the hypocrites in government. Since all of his friends had joined, he "didn't want to be left behind." This view was echoed by some of the best educated students in Pakistan.[14] They were expected to kill civilians, a transgression of Islam, and therefore the instructors inflated their enemy by turning them into monsters. The process is another example of "loading the language" with the "thought-terminating cliché."[15] In a minority of madrassas and in the al-Qaeda training camps, the indoctrinators preyed upon the credulity of their young charges by instilling in them the belief that "*we* are distinct from *them*...an evil enemy who...is waging a 'new Crusade' against the lands of Islam." This enemy is monstrous and only understands, in the words of bin Laden's deputy, Zawahiri, "brutality arrogance, and disregard for all taboos and customs." Yet it was the Taliban that burned schools and killed teachers who taught literacy to young girls.[16] Despite the jihadist rhetoric about defending Islam, religion was subordinated to power and the possession of the souls of the vulnerable.

Similarly, radical imams throughout the Muslim world and Western Europe inflamed their followers with hatred toward Jews, women and modern secularism. No wonder that Mohammed Atta, the al-Qaeda operational commander of the September 11 attacks, loathed New York's cosmopolitanism and regarded it as the epicentre of Jewish power. Imams spread conspiracy theories about 9/11 regarding how Jews who worked in the Trade Centre were forewarned about the attacks. They turned a blind eye to self-immolation, honour killings and the forced marriages of pubescent girls, while construing women's rights as an enticement to imitate the shameless impertinence of Western women. They condoned the Taliban's barbarous treatment of women—its forced veiling of women in public, its whipping and stoning of women and its virtual endorsement of rape—even though they are explicit violations of Quranic verses.[17] They ignored or denied the genocidal violence that Arab Muslims inflicted on dark-skinned African Muslims in Darfur and the sectarian violence between Shiites and Sunnis in Iraq which killed far more Muslims than did the Western forces. To justify their attacks, they used sophistry to blur the distinction between martyrdom and suicide when the latter is categorically prohibited in the Quran. While taking grievous offence at any comment, image or artistic presentation that allegedly besmirched

Islam, these ideological zealots hurled rhetorical violence against Christians and Jews. Even moderate Muslims became increasingly marginalized, as apostates—a codeword for a death threat—if they challenged the worldview of the Islamic militants. A typical ploy was to portray themselves as innocent victims and never the perpetrators of violence. In a 2007 audio message, bin Laden exemplified this technique by taunting Europeans when he suggested that the only reason for the West to continue "this unjust war" was that [Afghans] are Muslims and Western aggression "illustrates the extent of the Crusaders' hatred of Islam and its people."[18] Like the spokesmen for Germany's National Socialism, radical Islamists demonized their enemies, donned the mantle of victimhood and wove racism into their ideology.

Islamo-tribalists exploited the 2005–06 Danish cartoon tempest in which the Prophet was portrayed as a terrorist, parlaying anger into irrational rage. Mobs burned embassies, ugly marches demanded beheadings and nearly two hundred and fifty people were killed in riots in the Muslim world. The hysteria was to be expected as four of the cartoons used the physiognomy of the Prophet in ways similar to the racist attributes of Nazi iconography when it demonized Jews. What surprised was the response of some Muslims to the destruction that occurred during the riots: their outrage over that exceeded their own anger at the cartoons themselves because it appeared to reinforce the stereotype that Islam was a violent religion. They would have been further disturbed had they known that the imams of Denmark, who led the global censorship campaign, were complicitous to that violence. They took to Cairo three false extremely offensive cartoons, one of Mohammed being sodomized by a dog, another, the prophet as a pedophile, along with the original twelve Danish cartoons. Although there was a note attached to the dossier that the three false cartoons, which may have originated from a right-wing U.S. website, were not printed in the Danish newspaper, it appears that few Middle East leaders and Muslims internationally took notice. It was expediently easier to lump all the cartoons together, condemn the publication as hate speech and attempt to exceed one another in indignation. The occasion was utilized to "reinforce their often shaky religious credentials" while remaining silent about the mullah who offered a huge bribe for the assassination of the cartoonist. [19]

In the diaspora communities in Western Europe and Great Britain, jihad provided a compelling focus for susceptible, often lost, second-generation Muslims. As part of his inquiry into the tensions and resentments in Amsterdam after the murders of a conservative politician, Pim Fortuyn, and a controversial film director, Theo van Gogh, the Dutch-born scholar, Ian Buruma describes a large cohort of frustrated, ghettoized, largely underemployed, Islamic young men. They became disorientated by the liberal culture of their adopted country with its bewildering temptations of casual sex, drugs and racy entertainment. When their fantasies of sex with "easy" European women were dashed, compounded by contretemps with police and local authorities, they angrily rejected secular "Westernized" culture. They covered their humiliation and rage of "being mentally disappeared" by retreating into tribal honour and religious rectitude in search of a new purpose to their lives.[20]

Geert Wilders, the provocative far-right Dutch politician, is the mirror image of these alienated youth. Regarding Islam as an ideology rather than a religion, his short 2008 film, *Fitna (Strife)* juxtaposes Quranic verses and Islamist extremism with stills from the Madrid and London bombings. The film's virulent anti-Islamism bears an uncanny resemblance to the message and tone of the venom expressed toward Jews in Hitler's *Mein Kampf.* Wilders' apocalyptic rants about the growing Islamist threat resulted in anti-hate criminal charges. Vindicated by the judge, who considered his offensive comments part of legitimate debate, he pursued his campaign to ban mosque construction and the sale of the Quran.

The rancid detritus of European racism mirrored a large swathe of the population in the Middle East: the media and public endorsed conspiracy theories about the absolute power of the Jews over world affairs. Newspapers frequently featured caricatures of Jews with fangs and exaggerated hooked noses. School textbooks from Jordan, Pakistan and Saudi Arabia portrayed Jews as "Allah's curse," steeped in usury, sexual exhibitionism and prostitution, and equated Jews with apes. Christian infidels were demonized as swine. The Saudis exported an English version of the Quran to North Americans where derogatory references to Jews (and Christians) were inserted not only into the notes but into the text itself. Incidentally, a Saudi version of the Quran was found in the home of the convicted Times Square bomber. The *Protocols* also contributed to deforming people's judgements. Its allure as a weapon of mass deception is explicable as this counterfeit clearly provides a blueprint for the creation of an authoritarian police state. This fantasy often appeals to individuals and groups who feel themselves to be either powerless or in the grip of an all-encompassing ideology without the resources to establish an omnipotent political entity in either a secular or theocratic form. The focus on the Jews and their alleged power is merely a symbol of what the power they really covet for themselves. The *Protocols* were mobilized to explain the defeat of the Arab armies in 1948. As a secret society, Jews controlled the U.N., the U.S.A. and the U.S.S.R. Without that power, surely they would have won.[21] The 2003 Egyptian television series broadcast of the *Protocols of Zion* unveiled, among other outrageous assertions, the canard that the sperm of Jews is superior to that of Gentiles (the flip side of the Nazi propaganda). The *Protocols* were also cited in the Hamas Charter as evidence of the Zionist expansionist designs for Arab lands from the Nile to the Euphrates. *Mein Kampf* remains a best seller in the Middle East. The President of Iran, Mahmoud Ahmadinejad, elevated Holocaust denial to statecraft when he called it "a myth." Considering that bin Laden demonized the West as a "world of contaminants" in need of purification, and given that al-Qaeda's rhetoric was similar to Nazi rhetoric, it follows that a thick strand of Middle-Eastern culture was receptive to that message: Jews exaggerate the Holocaust to rationalize their abusive treatment of Palestinians.

This perniciousness extended to America. According to Marc Levin's 2005 documentary, *Protocols of Zion*, the book was popular even in New York with cassettes and CDs also available. His film clearly shows how the *Protocols* remained the über-text for modern anti-Semites in America: neo-Nazis, Muslim extremists, Christian fundamentalists and reprobates that bloviated on talk radio and in the streets. In an attempt to counteract his outrageous hoax and reach a wider audience than would a serious academic study, Will Eisner, used his mastery of the medium to write *The Plot*, a 2005 comic book history of the *Protocols*. In the Foreword, he expressed his desire that his book would contribute to driving "yet another nail in the coffin of this terrifying vampire-like fraud."[22]

Nonetheless, Islamist zealots successfully preached the

pathologies of hatred against the *other* and the appeal of a purified, global Islamism. Imams adeptly preyed on these young men and women, harvesting their self-hatred and channelling their energy into born-again jihadists as Armageddon's special agents. Deploying incendiary rhetoric and proficient with the new digital technology, the mullahs and imams hijacked history and Quranic scripture with their cut-and-paste brand of Islam. Militant Islamist clerics persisted in enticing male youth into martyrdom with the promise of seventy-two virgins, even though they knew its scriptural provenance was dubious. The idea was popularized during the 1980s Iran–Iraq war as a means to recruit Iranian men who would most likely die in the war. The Quran did promise male residents in heaven would have the company of young maidens; moderates interpreted this passage as a metaphor for satisfactions inconceivable on earth.[23] Imams ignored these subtleties as they lured their charges into embracing the culture of death with the apocalyptic message that a world without infidels would eliminate injustice, suffering and pain.

Anger drove young Muslims to terrorism, provided the right ingredients were available to channel their emotions. Just as the totalitarian top-down model cannot fully explain the popular appeal of Bolshevism and National Socialism, support for jihad terrorism was frequently a bottom-up process in which young men were as likely to be recruited in informal social settings, notably mosques and chat rooms, where bonding can occur. Isolated from the outside world, they lived in tightly-knit cells with their new "family," surrounded by a small circle of groupthink friends. According to a former militant, in this state of isolation, "people in 'real life' became very distant. They became barely human any more." Islamist websites, tapes and DVDs that condemn Europe as a "land of unbelief" incited the faithful to defy its laws and follow Sharia law.[24] When recruits watched videos, showing Muslims as victims of violence followed by the dehumanization of the infidel perpetrators having their throats cut, they possessed no conscience or felt any empathy for their future targets. Their behaviour exemplified the research of scientist, Simon Baron-Cohen, who contends that certain genes are associated with empathy. But if the "empathy circuit" in the brain is damaged and shuts off, the result can cause someone to behave callously or cruelly toward others.[25] Among those (that would also include the Madrid, Bali, and Mumbai terrorists) who vindicated Baron-Cohen's thesis were the Beeston bomb-ers, responsible for the July 2007 attacks on the London subway and a double-decker bus that killed fifty-two people. They bonded and primed themselves by watching videos of atrocities against Muslims in Iraq, Palestine and Chechnya; its effect was to eradicate any vestige of empathy they might have possessed for their future victims. One of these bombers was trained in a Pakistani camp. Instructors taught battlefield and civilian skills needed to carry out attacks and provided them with the discipline with further ideological training. Their apocalyptic nihilism was inspired by bin Laden's adept ability to tap into their humiliation and angst, and enflamed by the Western presence in Afghanistan and Iraq.

Gothic Undertones in the War on Terror

The horror! The horror!

> —*The Heart of Darkness*
> Joseph Conrad,

Mirroring, Irony and False Assumptions

If evil is a presence in contemporary life for so many, because of the cruelties inflicted either upon themselves or on others, their most pronounced penchant has been to demonize the *other* and to underestimate or justify their own capacity for evil. This trait is particularly true of ideologically-driven believers who possess a Manichean worldview wherein the world is divided between the forces of light and darkness; in aligning themselves with the good, an external devil appears to be the source of all evil. Its proponents call this perspective "clarity," a position that frequently blinds them to the complexities and messiness of realities on the ground and exonerates them of any responsibility for their own misguided if not reprehensible actions. But if the princes of darkness do represent our more atavistic side, the potential for becoming creatures of the night increases when these primitive impulses are released. Even ostensibly good intentions can career into legitimatizing the violence in destructive behaviour or produce the blowback of unanticipated consequences. When this happens, light elides into darkness. This chapter examines how the Gothic convention of mirroring and doubling applies to the adversarial relationship between the Bush administration and Osama bin Laden and al-Qaeda—that despite the vast differences between them, they needed and sustained each other. The analysis dovetails three perspectives. First explored is the cultural divide in America between those who adhered to the official position and the skeptics who rejected binary thinking. Then there is an empirical analysis of the failures in Afghanistan after the American invasion toppled the Taliban. Finally, supplementing both is an impressionist Gothic account of how the American government and media conjured bin Laden.

Recent history provides abundant evidence that people can surrender their humanity when seduced by ideology or overtaken by fear, and that human beings are susceptible to the dehumanizing consequences of war. The suicide jihadists, who crashed the hijacked jets into American landmarks on September 11, 2001, never posed an existential threat to America despite the human carnage and the financial setbacks. Although the conflict became a long-term struggle with stateless assassins, the attacks signalled a tectonic shift on the geopolitical landscape. Armed with righteous anger, tempered not by reason or evidence, the administration of G. W. Bush allowed emotions and a preconceived agenda to dictate foreign policy, one that rendered it vulnerable to disconnecting from reality. Instead of publicly articulating a carefully recalibrated need for greater security, which would entail compromises on civil liberties and greater power for the state, the Bush–Cheney administration employed deceit, secrecy and the culture of fear that came to define the next seven years. Perhaps the greatest threat that radical Islamists posed to the American way of life was its capacity to sow fear. Yet officials and their supporters in the media, among them the former editor of *Commentary*, Norman Podhoretz, argued that America was fighting World War IV with "Islamofascism." Not only did this implicit comparison minimize the danger posed by totalitarian regimes during the World War II and the Cold War, the comparison inflated the power of these nihilists granting them the status they wanted—that al-Qaeda was an equal adversary.[1] In this state of war, the Bush administration shrivelled, even reversed, constitutional guarantees by trampling on civil liberties and the shredding of the rule of law.

Bush's decision to politicize a heinous criminal act transformed bin Laden into his psychic double, his shadow, by endowing him with a political mystique. In this surrealistic titanic "clash of civilizations," each viewed the *other* through a moralistic lens. Both were deeply religious, fortified by their faith and inoculated against any form of doubt or uncertainty. They shared a Manichean vision of the world. Both believed that they were inspired by God and regarded themselves as "His righteous and wrathful agent."[2] As if he were following a script written by al-Qaeda, Bush inadvertently uttered the emotionally-loaded epithet 'crusade' shortly after September 11 when he associated it with the "war against terror." This holy war dichotomy suffused the Oval Office throughout the Iraq War. When Secretary of Defence, Donald Rumsfeld, personally delivered to Bush top secret intelligence updates during the war, the cover sheets showed pictures of tanks and troops with exhortatory passages from the Bible. One was a photo of tanks rumbling under the crossed-swords archway in Baghdad accompanied by the quotation: "Open the gates that the righteous nation may enter / The nation that keeps faith."[3] This expression of rapture politics was explicitly designed to manipulate a president who delighted in quoting scripture. That he believed God spoke through him is evident from a remark he made after the invasion to the Palestinian leader, Mahmoud Abbas: "God told me to strike at al-Qaeda and I struck them, and then he instructed me to strike at Saddam, which I did."[4] His swift displacement of the culpability of 9/11 from bin Laden to Saddam Hussein was possible because he genuinely believed that his mission was to eliminate the "axis of evil."

Alas, Bush was not a devotee of the American theologian, Reinhold Niebuhr. During the Korean War, Niebuhr warned against American "dreams of managing history" born out of overweening pride since "virtues [can] turn into vices when too complacently relied upon." America was vulnerable to "the temptation of claiming God too simply as the sanctifier of whatever [it] most fervently desire[s]." His warning about communism also applies to Islamic radicalism: "the evils against which we contend are frequently fruits of illusions, the fruits of illusions which are similar to our own."[5] Both Bush and bin Laden were intent on radically altering the Middle East. Events in 2011 suggested that the region might indeed be dramatically changing, but whatever the transformation, it would not result from the machinations of either the United States or al-Qaeda. Niebuhr's perceptive and prescient reflections should be heeded by those who pontificate about American exceptionalism—the belief that America, from its earliest history, has an obligation to bring light, civilization and democracy to the world. The proponents of this worldview might heed the cautionary warning depicted in Joseph Conrad's *Heart of Darkness*. A man endowed with "immense talent" is convinced he can bring civilization to the natives, but overreaches, does more harm than good and succumbs to madness.

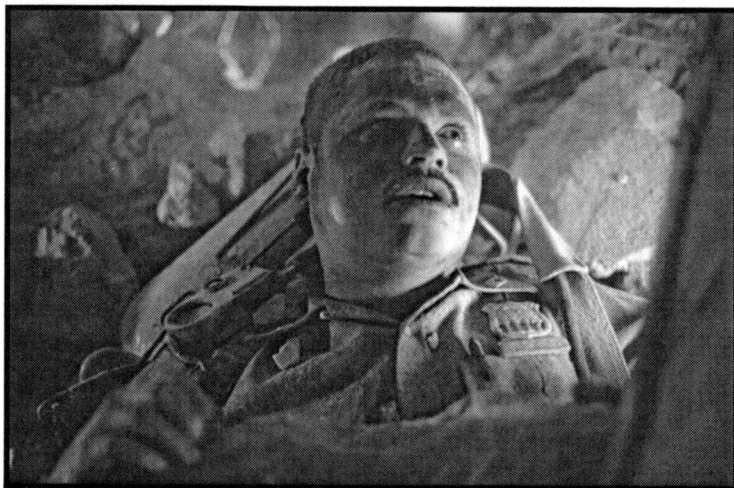

Courtesy of Photofest

Amid the burning skyscrapers and the plumes of smoke on 9/11, Oliver Stone's 2006 World Trade Center *narrows his focus to a team of Port Authority police officers who arrive at the site to assist the victims of the first strike only to be buried alive beneath the collapsing masonry and twisted metal. The image of these men entombed in the dark waiting to be rescued (not all of them survive) is a Gothic trope for our time.*

The *other*, Osama bin Laden, the Pied Piper of the suicide bomber and regarded in the West as the Prince of Darkness, displayed a similar sanctimonious outlook. He invoked the "grace of God almighty" to require every Muslim in the name of Allah, to kill the "Crusader" and the Jews. He too possessed a Manichean vision of a conflict between the "forces of faith" against "the evil forces of materialism."[6] Yet he revealed a crusader's mindset in his self-perception as an instrument of God's will and had no scruples about the indiscriminate killing of Muslims who did not share his fundamentalist brand of Islamism. Nor did he have any intention of compromising his theocratic vision that would implement Sharia law under a restored caliphate throughout the Islamic world and beyond, regardless of tribal, ethnic or national objections. He deployed terror in order to create an atmosphere of insecurity, fear and hysteria, and to solicit an overreaction; in both instances he succeeded. Not only did America become bogged down in two major wars, but its war on terrorism became widely perceived throughout the Islamic world as a war on Islam. To his credit, however, Bush attempted to distinguish between them by appearing publicly with Muslim and Arab spokesmen and declaring that the enemy was not Islam but fanatical Islamists. Yet since Bush and bin Laden were convinced that they had embarked on an apocalyptic struggle to eliminate the face of evil, each believed that his mission justified any means used to achieve it. As one became doppelganger for the other, each shared the same fundamentalist certainty, invoking a sense of self-righteous piety while projecting existential evil onto his enemy, and utilizing the media to further paranoia.

The rhetoric and strategic decisions made by Bush and members of his administration reveal stark similarities with those employed by bin Laden. There is a common loss of perspective that accompanies faith-based thinking and arrogant self-righteousness. Bush's dichotomous "either you are with us or with the terrorists" left no opportunity for a nuanced understanding of the conflict. Moreover, the Western presence and support for autocratic regimes in the Middle East contributed to the murderous fury of the Islamists. Any challenge to the official assumptions and policies was perceived as unpatriotic anti-Americanism. For Bush and his ideological supporters, the enemy was *purely* evil and the *only* response was an overwhelming military response. This binary thinking precluded any consideration for the context in which terrorism emerged or even curiosity about the nature of the enemy in this conflict between states and non-state actors. Had there been a wider perspective, Deputy Secretary of Defence, Paul Wolfowitz, might not have so cavalierly dismissed bin Laden before 9/11 as "this little terrorist in Afghanistan."[7] According to counterterrorism expert, Richard Clarke, Wolfowitz spoke for Bush's inner circle when he said that the 9/11 operation was too sophisticated for a terrorist group alone to execute; it could only be carried out with a state sponsor, namely Iraq.[8]

Bin Laden first came to public attention in 1996 when he declared war on America. Two years later al-Qaeda launched assaults on American embassies in East Africa. Saddened though the public may have been about those attacks, it was merely terrible foreign news. Bin Laden had not yet seared its consciousness. Nonetheless, for five years he had been goading America into attacking Afghanistan. With a hubris that matched that of the Bush administration, he believed his brand of jihadism would reprise the success the mujahedeen had experienced in their decade-long struggle with the Soviet Union in the 1980s. Since he regarded America as a paper tiger, it would pull its troops out of Muslim countries as it did in Somali in 1993 or launch a few ineffective cruise missiles as Clinton had ordered in 1998 against Sudan and Afghanistan. In the short term, it was a serious miscalculation on bin Laden's part, since the bulk of al-Qaeda was destroyed in December 2001 when Bush ordered a counterterrorism assault to punish the Taliban for allowing bin Laden's organization to train terrorists in Afghanistan. Ironically, by attacking Iraq, the Americans did fight the type of war and counterinsurgency al-Qaeda wanted which enraged Muslims and inspired a new cluster of militants. Bin Laden admitted that it was "easy for us to provoke and bait this administration."[9] Fundamentalists on both sides of the ideological divide fell into reflections of each other; American neoconservatives and evangelical Christians needed bin Laden and the Islamists to sustain public support for their "war on terror." Bin Laden, however, needed Bush to revitalize his brand of jihadism after the debacle it experienced in Afghanistan.

The Cultural War after 9/11

The implication that the American government's rhetoric and actions in any way mirrored those of their attackers is totally alien, indeed anti-American to a public woefully uninformed about global issues. The responsibility for the population's ignorance resided in part with the media. Apart from PBS, television reduced the time devoted to world affairs and pandered to a celebrity culture exemplified by so-called "reality" shows. After that September morning, the major networks fanned the flames of fear that Americans felt by incessantly replaying the telegenic collapse of the Twin Towers and the raw terror on peoples' faces. Dazed news anchors eagerly told audiences how to feel and how they themselves felt. By way of contrast, television reports from the British and Spanish media after the subway attacks in London and the train attacks in Madrid, while not ignoring the carnage, reported spontaneous acts of calmness and a defiance not to be cowed into fear by these terrorist acts.[10] Being patriots before journalists, the American media did not muster the skepticism to question an administration whose focus on news management was to parlay a national panic into partisan political gains.

The Bush administration was also responsible for hyping fear and ignoring geo-political realities. Given that the President's personal popularity soared after the attacks, it is not surprising that Karl Rove, the engineer of Bush's political victories and a master at leveraging fear into power, indicated in 2003 that the war on terror would be central to Bush's re-election. In lieu of a forthright public conversation on the political roots of terrorism or sensible advice about realistic risks, members of the Bush administration inflamed fears with official alarmism using colour-coded alerts based on vague intelligence.[11] In addition, they inflected their speeches with a Gothic coloration. Officials described the global terrorist as a religious fanatic who relished the sensual rush of death in anticipation of his reward beyond the grave. Bush spoke of "sleeper cells" living in the country awaiting orders, often from outlaw regimes, awakening to carry out their horrific deeds like "ticking time bombs." When he declared that "terrorists try to operate in the shadows," and labelled them "parasites," he was portraying radical militants (and by extension Muslims in general) as vampiric creatures.[12] He never suggested that terrorism was even partially rooted in the bone-deep distrust of Western and Russian foreign policies in Islamic venues—Palestine, Somalia, Chechnya, Kashmir and Lebanon—and in American support for authoritarian Islamic regimes in the Middle East, notably Saudi Arabia and Egypt.[13] Nor did he mention that terrorism grew out of years of stagnation and repression in the Arab world that fostered despair, humiliation and religious extremism. America, for reasons of strategic interest, "stability" or access to oil, was an ally of these autocracies, and in the case of Egypt, a financial supporter. Had Bush done so, Americans would at least have understood how its country had become the "far enemy."

The internal cultural divide that bedevilled America reduced

the country's awareness about geopolitical realities. The 2007 publication of the crude polemic *The Enemy at Home* by the conservative provocateur, Dinesh D'Souza, widened the chasm. It claimed
that the cultural left, the *other*—the liberal media, the universities,
liberal Democrats in Washington, Hollywood and liberal organizations—were responsible for the attacks of September 11. D'Souza
argued that the cultural left enraged the terrorists because they
embodied the atheistic and anti-patriarchal values Islamists feared
having imposed on them. D'Souza could be interpreted to be reviling his own "near enemy,"—the cultural left—to the extent that he
ignored bin Laden's attack on his own "near enemy"—the traditional conservative states in the Middle East that D'Souza held in such
high esteem. No wonder he expressed his own admiration for the
"dignified fellow in the long robe" and asserted that American religious conservatives would have more in common with traditional
Muslims than with leftists, an admission that suggests these two
fundamentalist groups mirror each other.[14]

When D'Souza strayed into foreign policy, he appeared unaware of the work of Peter Bergen. Along with fellow journalists
Steve Coll and Lawrence Wright, Bergen is a recognized authority
on bin Laden. Writing before September 11, he contended that the
militant Islamist's war with America was the result of U.S. policies
in the world, not its democratic institutions or its cultural values
exemplified by the simplistic slogan: "They hate our freedoms."
Bin Laden's hostility toward America was political not cultural. He
did not decry the pernicious effects of Hollywood movies, pornography—pornographic videos were found at his compound in
Abbottabad—and to drugs or alcohol in the West, except for a brief
reference in his 2002 open letter to Americans.

In his earlier more important 1996 manifesto, bin Laden issued
his *fatwa* that it was the duty of every Muslim to "kill the Americans
and their allies—civilians and military" because of their intrusive
and oppressive policies in the Middle East. These policies included America's unconditional support for the interloper, Israel, and
the corrupt regimes in Egypt and Saudi Arabia. His most compelling argument (or propaganda ploy) was the ongoing bombing and
imposition of economic sanctions on Iraq after the 1990–91 first
Gulf War that, according to UNICEF, killed an estimated 500,000
children under the age of five. This tragedy in part transpired because Iraq was prohibited from importing the parts necessary to

repair the electrical and water purification system that had been deliberately targeted during the 1991 war. In response, bin Laden targeted symbols of U.S. military and economic power: U.S. embassies, military installations and warships.[15] But those assaults were at the periphery of Americans' awareness. When they left huge suppurating sores on its homeland on that September morning, Americans wholeheartedly accepted Bush's contention that "no act of ours invited the rage of the killers."[16] Believing that America was a force for good in the world, they consoled themselves into thinking the strikes were unprovoked. They were prompted by evil Islamists who hate America for its values, institutions and its economic prosperity.

When Susan Sontag challenged this naïve belief in an article published in *The New Yorker* shortly after the Twin Towers collapsed, she was buried under an avalanche of abuse from all sides of the political spectrum. She lashed out at the "self-righteous drivel and outright deceptions being peddled by public figures and TV commentators." They failed in their duty to inform the public that those who perpetrated the "monstrous dose of reality" on American soil were not motivated by their hatred of "civilization" or "the free world" but were opposed to "specific American alliances and actions." She pungently added that "a few shreds of historical awareness might help us to understand what has just happened and what may continue to happen."[17] Even though her logic was sound and grounded in historical reality, critics reviled her for "unusual stupidity" and "moral vacuity." Due to her timing and apparent insensitivity to the rawness of the public's grief, she was perceived to be excusing, or worse, justifying, the attacks. A year later, former mayor Ed Koch was predicting that "Susan Sontag will occupy the Ninth Circle of Hell." In truth, she suggested that the attacks were the blowback or unintended consequences of past military and economic policies in the Muslim world.[18] Predictably, her message that Americans were ignoring political realities was dismissed as sanctioning a moral equivalence between foreign policy decisions and the mass murder of innocents. But as philosopher, Susan Neiman, reminds us if we are to understand the application of evil and not be drawn into it, we need to start, not stop, thinking.[19]

The denigration of Sontag extended to other women (but interestingly not to acidic male critics, notably Paul Krugman of the

New York Times), such as writers, Barbara Kingsolver and Katha Pollitt, who questioned the chest-thumping nationalist call to arms. The terrorist attacks unleashed a tidal wave of repressed rage against "feminists" who were not only outrageously pilloried in the media for being bitches, morons and traitors but also subjected to vile personal threats via email or telephone. In an echo of the militant masculinity trumpeted in the Cold War, hawkish columnists reviled the women's movement as a treacherous "fifth column on the war on terror," responsible for men going "soft" and turning America into a "nanny state." Mark Steyn warned that if the nation were to prevail in the coming war, the "grief counsellors" who drool about 'healing' and 'closure' should be silenced "until the guys have stopped firing," sentiments reminiscent of those expressed by the radical firebrand, General Jack Ripper in the 1964 film *Dr. Strangelove*. He was itching to attack the Soviet Union for putting fluoride in the water that would "sap and impurify all our precious body fluids" (a satirical swipe at the extreme right-wing John Birch society). These macho pundits declaimed that the country badly needed the testosterone-powered "culture of the warrior" to wreak vengeance on its enemies and rescue in Rambo-like fashion vulnerable women such as Private Jessica Lynch. In 2003 the Central Command Media Centre in Doha, Qatar deliberately fabricated a triumphal, pre-packaged saga of an American heroine, who shot her way out of an ambush, was wounded and beaten by Iraqi soldiers, before being rescued by American troops. In reality, she had been in a motor-vehicle accident and her life had been saved by Iraqi medical personnel. But the media spin prevailed and she became the subject of a hagiographical book and film. Lynch later told *Time* magazine that she was aware of the symbolic role she had played in the media.[20]

Reeling from the magnitude and ferocity of the attacks, most Americans were willing to place their faith in the steely-eye ethos encapsulated by the president. He assumed a "trust-me" stance that promised "we will smoke him out" and said that the assault was an act of war rather than a vicious crime perpetrated by crazed fanatics. With his macho resolve, Bush presided over warroom sessions with a "commander's grip" while enhancing presidential power and privilege; most of the Foxified media exultantly or meekly acquiesced. To question America's historical and current role in the Middle East was delegitimized as unpatriotic and effeminate. Alternatively, going to war and "kicking ass" was the correct and masculine response.[21]

Initially, attempts were made to censor anyone who attempted to question the conventional pieties about the 9/11 cataclysm. Conservatives issued an all-points bulletin on the Internet and in print reviling as subversive any university lecturer—college campuses were often the only places where the U.S. response to terrorism was seriously analyzed and debated—who registered the mildest form of dissent, tarring them as supporters of suicide terrorists. In this "culture of retribution," Walter Isaacson, the president of CNN warned, "If you get on the wrong side of public opinion, you are going to get into trouble."[22] In the visual arts, the American public inveighed against any image that they found disturbing. On September 12 some newspapers published a photograph of a falling man who likely jumped from the Trade Centre; the reaction was so vehemently hostile, the photograph was not shown again. Similarly, the nude sculpture *A Tumbling Woman* by Eric Fischl was draped and removed from the Rockefeller Centre because it offended public sensibilities.

When the Iraq war turned sour, the political ground shifted. Sontag's denunciation of the "sanctimonious reality-concealing rhetoric" of government officials and news anchors in retrospect appears not as callous but prescient: two knowledgeable students of terrorism substantiated her message. Michael Scheuer and Richard Clarke, who worked in intelligence and counter-terrorism, supported Sontag's argument that the root causes of the attacks reside in foreign policy decisions. Scheuer, the former head of the CIA's bin Laden unit, argued that any attempt to explain the appeal of terrorism and then counteract it by ignoring geopolitical realities would be self defeating. His central thesis is that "the greatest danger for Americans confronting the radical Islamist threat is to believe—at the urging of U.S. leaders—that Muslims attack us for what we are and what we think rather than what we do." Richard Clarke agreed that Bush's approach was substantially different from his recent predecessors who had undertaken a more global perspective:

> Bush might have tried to build a world consensus and address the root causes, while using the moment to force what had been lethargic or doubting governments to arrest known terrorists and close front organizations. One can imagine

> trying one more time to force an Israeli–Palestinian settle-
> ment, going to Saudi Arabia and addressing the Muslim
> people in a moving appeal for religious tolerance, pushing
> hard for a security arrangement between India and Pakistan
> to create a nuclear-free zone, and stabilizing Pakistan. Such
> efforts may or may not have succeeded, but one thing we
> know that they would not have done is inflame Islamic opin-
> ion and further radicalize Muslim youth into a heightened
> hatred of America in the way that invading Iraq has done.[23]

Perhaps most destructive to Bush's argument for why America was attacked occurred when the Pentagon released a report three years after the attacks. The authors explicitly stated that "the Muslims do not hate our freedoms" but rather our policies.[*] Similar to critics such as Clarke and Scheuer, the report itemized grievances that had been largely ignored in America: the invasions of Afghanistan and Iraq; support for dictatorships in Egypt, Saudi Arabia and Jordan, and America's one-sided support for Israel.[24]

The press also became less mute in its criticisms of the Bush administration. Still, outside of academic studies, there was little analysis of how foreign policies contributed to the attacks of 9/11. Had Americans been more aware of the presence of seven hundred and twenty-five American bases around the world, they might have had a greater appreciation of why people in the developing world were angry with Americans. As indicated in the previous chapter, the presence of American troops in Saudi Arabia was a tipping point for bin Laden's zealotry. It is significant that by the fall of 2003 the Bush administration quietly and wisely removed five thousand troops from Saudi Arabia, a tacit admission that their presence did evoke hostility from a major ally in the region. Another possible reason for invading Iraq was to build bases there; some of the ones that were subsequently built were designed to be permanent. Still, an understanding does not mean excusing the deliberate murder of roughly three thousand civilians even though the allegation of moral equivalence was frequently hurled against critics of the Bush administration. Fortunately, the media became more skeptical due to the growing fear that America and the world

---

[*]   Even bin Laden mocked Bush's argument by videotaping a message: "Contrary to Bush's claims that we hate freedom. If that were true, then let him explain why we do not attack Sweden." Bergen, *Manhunt*, 64.

were not safer because of the strategic and moral disaster to invade Iraq. These unanticipated developments have challenged Americans to be more receptive to a counter-narrative than was possible in the two-year traumatic aftermath of the 9/11 calamity.

The Consequences of the Gothic Impulse in South Asia

The September 11 attacks led directly to an aerial bombardment over Afghanistan, the destruction of the al-Qaeda sanctuary and the upending of the Taliban regime. For five years since 1996, the neo-medieval thugs had run the country as a vast concentration camp enslaving the female population. Although a few thousand American troops were deployed to Afghanistan, the fighting was left primarily to their generously bribed allies, the Afghan United Front, an amalgam of anti-Taliban guerrillas constituted primarily from the ethnic Tajiks who dwelled in the centre and north of the country. Within weeks, these warriors, assisted by elite Special Forces operations and methodical intelligence gathering, routed the Taliban by November 2011 and inflicted devastating damage on al-Qaeda by killing or capturing almost eighty percent of its members and closing its sanctuaries. This vacuum left the warlords on the CIA payroll in a more powerful position. Among them was the notorious General Abdul Rashid Dostum, allegedly responsible for the mass execution of two thousand Taliban prisoners in 1997 and whose troops killed three hundred prisoners in November 2001.

The human cost was high: air strikes alone between October 2001 and November 2003 accounted for between three thousand and three thousand six hundred civilian deaths. This number was augmented by starvation, exposure and disease.[25] The high number of civilian casualties was a result of the decision to deploy a "light footprint" with relatively few troops because it was difficult to acquire accurate intelligence. Coalition forces often had to depend upon information from individuals, motivated more by seeking revenge on rival militias than routing out the Taliban. In one instance, Americans responded to rumours that Taliban leaders would be attending a wedding party in late June of 2002 in the village of Deh Rawood and a raid was planned. This rumour was discovered to be just that—a rumour—and an Afghan wedding party was obliterated by American air fighters. They pulverized the area leaving forty eight dead, one hundred and seventeen wounded and surviving family members filled with hatred toward Americans.[26]

Instead of prematurely proclaiming victory, had the Bush administration fought the war against al-Qaeda and the Taliban with more commitment and resources, the war could have been over. Bush, Cheney and General Tommy Franks knew that bin Laden was hiding in the Tora Bora caves, yet Franks was reluctant to put in harm's way the four-thousand Marines who had landed in the Afghan theatre of war. When ground commanders requested and were denied the deployment of eight hundred soldiers to seal off the area and smoke out bin Laden and Aymen al-Zawahiri, it was widely cited as the most serious mistake of the war. Only three dozen Special Forces troops were committed to this area, a vast labyrinth of caves refurbished and modernized by the Americans during the 1980s, allowing the elusive bin Laden, and the al-Qaeda leadership to slither away to the tribal regions that form a buffer zone between Afghanistan and Pakistan.

Bin Laden's escape only reinforced his image as an ineffable shadowy figure, a malevolent wizard with preternatural power. He increasingly became less a man and more a ghost, recognizable primarily through his cryptic recorded messages, video clips and wanted-dead-or-alive posters. Years earlier, Soviet conscript soldiers had called the CIA-supplied Afghan rebels *dukhi* or ghosts because they could never grapple with them. The mujahedeen remained ghosts after the Soviets departed as they morphed into the Taliban and al-Qaeda.[27] The latter organization, which had been on life support after the American invasion of Afghanistan, nonetheless subsequently mutated into a global franchise movement, decentralized, utopian and bent on an apocalyptic agenda. Its new-generation adherents viewed the world as a contest between the "sons of light" and the "sons of darkness." As for bin Laden, living in a constricted world in his compound in Pakistan, he was more than a spiritual guru. He was a player in the global terror network plotting attacks and making decisions. Because he took his image so seriously—he once said that ninety percent of his battle was fought in the media—he continued to release videotapes, one a parody of a presidential address from the Oval Office, filmed at his Abbottabad lair.[28]

The remnant Taliban was also able to make a strategic

withdrawal to Pakistan. Given sanctuary by Pakistan's intelligence force, the ISI, it melted into the supportive tribal areas, regrouped, and inspired by the subsequent Islamist resurgence in Iraq, as a reconstituted Taliban, launched a lethal insurgency in Afghanistan in 2005. Despite its mistakes of 2002, had the U.S. remained committed to a long-range agenda of nation building and crippling the narcotics trade instead of siphoning its war machine to Iraq, Afghanistan might have evolved differently. But due to its ideological aversion to "Clintonian" nation building, the Bush administration spent less money per capita in Afghanistan on reconstruction than had any other post-World War II administration.[29]

Exhausted by years of civil war and conflict, the Afghan people by 2002 were initially receptive to international aid and effective government. But the Bush administration squandered that opportunity by empowering warlords to pursue a counterterrorism approach and turned a blind eye to the cronyism, corruption and the narco trade at all levels of government. In winning his first presidential election victory October 2004, Hamid Karzai provided the post-medieval government of Afghanistan with a patina of international legitimacy that brought promises of financial support, even though that election may have been tainted.[30] Regrettably, in one of the world's poorest countries, most of the funds (along with drug money) flowed to corrupt, unaccountable government officials, among them members of the President's family who lived in palatial homes. Observers close to the scene contended that Karzai did little to end the criminality, the vastly profitable drug trade, and the political malfeasance: warlords terrorized the local population by raping women, kidnapping individuals and forcing family members to pay a ransom. Locals were forced to bribe officials so that they could travel on the roads in some degree of safety. Karzai co-opted into his government a number of notorious warlords who operated drug gangs and were suspected of committing heinous war crimes. Although it appears counter-intuitive and contrary to Rumsfeld's press releases, Pakistani author, Ahmed Rashid, suggests that the Defence Secretary regarded the drug trade as a social issue unconnected to fighting terrorism, did not support efforts by the State Department under Powell to intercept convoys of drug traffickers and overruled a Department official who sought to eradicate the crop through ground spraying. Yet it was drug money that financed a rejuvenated al-Qaeda and Taliban, the reopening of their training camps and the purchase of newer and better weapons. Rashid argued that drug money was largely responsible for the failure to rebuild the economy and establish a stable government based on the rule of law, and that Rumsfeld was out of touch with the realities on the ground.[31] The combination of a cavalier official attitude toward endemic graft, a sullied police force and brutal treatment by unaccountable, largely Tajik officials, and American and NATO counterproductive search-and-destroy tactics and air strikes, alienated the Afghan people, particularly in the more volatile southern provinces.

The Afghanis disaffection with their own government extended to the Westerners. After the 2001 fall of the Taliban, the CIA empowered these officials, in many cases the same warlords whose corrupt and repressive actions drove the Afghan people to support the Taliban in the early 1990s. Limited Western efforts during the Bush years to provide sufficient incentives to grow alternative crops—the southern province of Helmand produced three-quarters of the world's heroin controlled by the neo-Taliban—did not disrupt the narco-economy where the cultivation of the opium poppy remained entrenched. Hundreds of thousands of poppy farmers received only one fifth of the profit generated, while the rest went to the traffickers who used it to bribe government officials and fund the resurgence movement. Aerial bombing that killed civilians and burned the poppy fields of impoverished farmers, leaving them deeper in debt and their families destitute, only intensified their resentment toward coalition forces and receptivity to joining the Taliban. Yet its moralistic blandishments and brutality undercut further potential support when they terrorized locals into fearing retaliation as the price for cooperating with NATO troops.[32]

In this political minefield, Pakistan became the fulcrum around which American and NATO policy turned. As the ostensible ally of the United States in its war against terror, it was awarded by the Bush administration a hefty bribe of which ninety percent flowed to the military. Unsurprisingly, the quasi-military state was riven by internal pressures. The ISI, its intelligence agency and officials within the Pakistani military gelded the state by aiding the insurgency in Afghanistan against NATO troops sanctioned by the United Nations. Myopically, they ginned up a non-existent threat with India, by providing support to international terrorist attacks

at Mumbai in 2008 while mainly ignoring the aggressive encroachment by the indigenous Taliban, which, akin to Frankenstein's
creature, remained beyond the control of its creator. Violence increased in Afghanistan and Pakistan because the relatively small
but semi-autonomous tribal regions increasingly came under the
authority of radicalized warlords and imams. They in turn murdered pro-government Pashtun tribal chiefs to ensure the continuation of a porous border with Afghanistan and a sanctuary for
al-Qaeda. While then President Pervez Musharraf was willing to
accommodate the Americans and hunt down al-Qaeda operatives,
he ignored or placated the neo-Taliban whose militancy and fanaticism were regarded by the growing secular urban middle class
and even by religious conservatives as a frightening fringe movement capable of wreaking havoc in Pakistan through assassinations and suicide bombers.*

The difficulties worsened when law and order collapsed in much
of Pakistan's tribal areas where kidnappings for ransom abounded,
leaving the provincial government powerless. The Taliban leader's
declaration that democracy and civil society were all "systems of
infidels" and its offer of sanctuary to al-Qaeda belatedly revealed
to the political and military elites as well as to the wider public the
true malignant face of these religious extremists. Most disturbing
was the Taliban's avowed goal of extending its influence through
violence—it slit the throats of local opposition leaders, hanged men
for the offence of drinking, and shot burqa-clad women for supposed promiscuity, filming it for widespread distribution. As a result
of widespread revulsion over widely circulated video images of
the Taliban flogging a seventeen year old and al-Qaeda's bombing
of the Marriot hotel in Islamabad, the new civilian President, Asif
Ali Zardari, widower of Benazir Bhutto, ordered the deployment of
over thirty thousand troops into the tribal regions. This mandated
that one and one-half million civilians be uprooted, but ended the
reign of terror.[33] Yet Zardari, who regarded himself as a strong ally
of America, was powerless to control the military and the ISI, who

---

* After an unsuccessful suicide bombing that killed over one hundred
and forty people the day she returned from exile, militant Islamists succeeded on December 27, 2007 in assassinating Benazir Bhutto. Hovering
like a ghost over the election campaign, she secured a posthumous victory in the February, 2008 election when her Party scored a resounding
defeat over Musharraf's party.

played a balancing act between supporting America and providing covert support to the Taliban. This was a delicate problem not only for Pakistan but also for America given that it, in effect, created the problem by funding and training the mujahedeen during the 1980s, then abandoning the region after the defeat of the Soviets until 9/11. Considered one of the most dangerous countries in the world, the fear of Pakistan imploding from a civil war and losing control over its nuclear weapons remained. The global community could not minimize the dangers posed by its volatility given that the tribal territories *and* its cities remained a safe haven for the insurgents and, as it turned out, Bin Laden himself.

Owing to Bush's failed policies in Pakistan and Afghanistan, NATO troops were locked in a life-and-death struggle, particularly in the more dangerous southern provinces where the Pashtun tribes predominated and remained allies of the insurgency. Additionally, they possessed a motley alliance of Taliban, foreign and domestic mercenaries, drug lords and private militias. The vast majority of the reconstituted Taliban were not ideological zealots. Some were manipulated foreign fighters from Pakistan or were pressured to join once the Taliban seized an area. Some were opportunists who were offered more money to kill foreigners than they could earn as civilians, particularly after the Americans destroyed their poppy fields. Although Western air strikes since 2004 from radio-controlled unmanned drones degraded al-Qaeda and neo-Taliban in Afghanistan, and especially in the tribal areas of Pakistan, the death of civilians was a major factor that fuelled the insurgency and the demand for a blood tribute.[*] The Taliban's primary goal was to expel foreign intruders and protect their traditional way of life. They did not, however, see themselves as part of a global jihad and remain vastly ignorant about the outside world.

Simultaneously, NATO troops attempted to engage the Afghans in rebuilding their shattered civil society. This counterinsurgency posed many challenges—soldiers, for example, suffered more casualties from suicide bombers and lethal roadside bombs (IEDs)

---

[*]   In David Ignatius' engrossing 2011 thriller, *Blood Money* (New York: W.W. Norton), he imagines how it would feel to survive a drone attack while watching his family members eviscerated. He creates a computer scientist who lives in the modern world, yet is bound by the tribal code of honour that perpetuates the cycle of violence by demanding a blood tribute to avenge murdered relatives.

than from direct enemy fire. The obstacles raised a heated debate about the role of NATO in those countries that have participated in combat operations. Having spent eight years in Afghanistan, Sarah Chayes was critical of the Americans for not having a plan after the fall of the Taliban government and for their support for the warlords, corruption and torture. In her 2006 book, *The Punishment of Virtue*, she, however, contended that the NATO presence, particularly the Canadian soldiers in Kandahar, was welcomed by the locals. Her perceptions were borne out by a 2005 BBC/ABC poll that revealed a high level of support for foreign troops provided they deliver on their promise to help midwife a more secure and prosperous country. That recovery required foreign support directed more toward economic development and depended upon NATO officials to run interference for the locals by pressuring the warlords to become more accountable. Outsiders should shun offensive combat, exercise restraint and emphasize efforts to improve Afghan living conditions and self governance.[34] The alternative view was that nation building was only possible if the military degraded the capacity of the Taliban to inflict terror on the local population, at least until the Afghan army could assume full military responsibility for defending its country.

As conditions in Afghanistan worsened, critics generally agreed that this grave state of affairs could have been avoided. Indeed, by the end of the Bush years hardly anyone believed that a military defeat over the Taliban was possible and the Taliban's strength was greater than at any point since they abandoned Kabul seven years earlier. The White House's pivotal decision to invade Iraq enabled the resurrection of both al-Qaeda and the Taliban who fed off the blood (so to speak) of Muslims and Westerners alike. Not surprisingly, European NATO members were reluctant to send troops to the more dangerous south: they viewed the post 2003 Afghanistan war as an extension of the Iraq war they had vehemently opposed.

Iraq: The Disconnect between Fantasy and Reality

And now what will become of us
without the barbarians? Those
people were a kind of solution.

— *"Waiting for the Barbarians"*
Constantine Cavafy

If Conrad's *Heart of Darkness* inspired Francis Ford Coppola to create his 1979 hallucinatory film *Apocalypse Now* as an allegory for the Vietnam War, it is tempting to speculate whether a future filmmaker's imagination would engage a similar exploration of the Bush administration's reasons for and conduct of the almost nine-year Second Gulf War. The journalist, Pepe Escobar, labelling them warrior–intellectuals and trained killers, compared Kurtz and Captain Willard from *Apocalypse Now* to the fired General McChrystal, who once headed a killing squad in Iraq.[1]

Failing to win broad international support for his belief that Iraq posed an apocalyptic threat to the world in March 2003, an insufficiently informed George W. Bush launched a preventive and ill-conceived America-led war, one based on false premises, that dispatched troops into the Mesopotamian heart of darkness. Despite opposition from several current and retired generals,* professional diplomats in the State Department and substantial CIA personnel, his administration turned on the fulcrum of fear and the popular impulse for revenge by successfully exploiting the September 11

---

* Among the distinguished retired generals were Norman Schwarzkopf, Anthony Zinni and Wesley Clark.

Courtesy of Photofest

Joseph Conrad's Heart of Darkness *can be perceived as emblematic of the American experience in Iraq but the novella is often overshadowed by its most famous 1979 adaptation, Francis Ford Coppola's film on Vietnam,* Apocalypse Now. *Although punctuated by visual pyrotechnics—one being the pulsating Wagner helicopter scene—the quiet moments between Kurtz, a decorated hero, who has gone rogue and established a jungle sanctuary in enemy territory, and his would-be assassin, Willard, who comes to increasingly mirror Kurtz, remain the most resonant. When the latter tells the former that "you need to have men who are moral, who at the same time are able to utilize their primordial instincts to kill without feeling, without passion, without judgement," we are reminded not only of what Kurtz calls "the horror, the horror" that prevailed in Vietnam and Iraq, but also of Himmler who in 1943 informed SS officers in Posen, Poland that they were "moral."*

tragedy. It subordinated national security to politics and pursued an agenda—regime change in Iraq—which had been a top priority for the neoconservatives since 1997 when they signed a manifesto calling for Saddam Hussein's removal and the forceful imposition of American values. The war harvested tragic consequences for the Iraqi people when post-Saddam Iraq descended into chaos, eviscerated by a Sunni–Shia civil war made worse by an influx of al-Qaeda militants and a prolonged occupation.

Employing imperial hubris and the talent for "electrifying large crowds," Conrad's Kurtz possessed "immense plans" for "humanizing, improving, instructing" the lot of the Congolese natives before ruthlessly exploiting them and turning himself into an object of worship. Charlie Marlow, sent by his company to check out what has happened to Kurtz, sets out binary distinctions—virtue and greed, civilization and savagery, the self and the *other*—all of which dissolve over the course of the novella. Coppola's Colonel Kurtz was a decorated war hero before becoming a renegade who leads Montognard tribesmen on killing missions and has made himself an object of worship. Captain Willard, ordered to "terminate with extreme prejudice" the deranged Kurtz, increasingly comes to mirror his madness. These scenarios are echoed in the Americans' invasion of Iraq, who like Kurtz, were convinced that "by the simple exercise of our will we can exert a power for good practically unbounded," and in the Americans' actions in post-Saddam Iraq when they attempted to impose a political and economic neo-conservative blueprint on the Iraqis, as indifferent to their welfare as Hussein had been. So too, Kurtz's in his madness is a metaphorical microcosm for those soldiers who mistreated *hajis* (pejorative military slang for Iraqis), as well as for the thousands of emotionally and physiologically damaged American soldiers who returned from Iraq. The two situations are not exactly analogous but if the novel and the film are regarded as allegories in a manner similar to that in which George Orwell's *Animal Farm* is an extended metaphor on the attractions and pitfalls of revolution, Conrad's prophetic tale, to a much larger extent than Coppola's film, should serve as a cautionary warning for how idealism can slide into monstrosity.[2]

The Drumbeat for War

In the first year of his watch, Bush repudiated the multilateral approach of his predecessors and withdrew America from its international treaties. Locked into a Cold War mentality against hostile states, he was preoccupied with ballistic missile defence. Despite warnings from the outgoing administration, explicit messages from Ahmed Shah Massoud, the warlord who presented the most formidable and viable alternative to the Taliban and al-Qaeda, from the Taliban foreign minister and from the CIA, Bush appeared insouciant about the blight of terrorism.[3] As a result, he, like Clinton before him, ignored the operational plan prepared by counterterrorism expert, Richard Clarke, who recommended that the U.S. should hit back at Osama bin Laden after he orchestrated the attack on the U.S. Navy cruiser, USS *Cole,* which killed seventeen crewmen. Despite the more than forty daily briefings Bush received between January and September, the administration's sleepwalking state persisted. The first meeting to discuss the security threat of al-Qaeda occurred on September 4, one week before the attacks. His Secretary of Defence, Donald Rumsfeld, was adamant about resisting NSA (National Security Agency) interceptions of telephone conversations by al-Qaeda operatives, calling them a "hoax," messages that had terrified Clarke and CIA head, George Tenet, convincing them that an attack was coming and "going to be the big one." When the NSA and CIA confirmed that the terrorist destruction on September 11 was the handiwork of al-Qaeda, Rumsfeld refused to believe the news and ordered Pentagon officials to prepare plans for retaliatory attacks on Iraq. Even after that "day in hell," as one retired NSA intelligence officer later dubbed it, this rogue-state mindset continued. Within twenty-four hours during the first meeting of the cabinet, Rumsfeld and others advocated "getting" Iraq because it offered better targets than Afghanistan while Bush pressured Clarke to make a connection between the attacks and Saddam Hussein.[4]

After the toppling of the Taliban, the neo-conservatives prepared the ground for an invasion of Iraq that they believed would stabilize the Middle East (and safeguard American interests). Despite their hidebound loathing for the United Nations, the Bush administration attempted to provide a patina of legitimacy for its invasion by getting the approval of a United Nations Security Council resolution to allow U.N. inspectors to return to Iraq. America soon encountered opposition from France and Germany over the limited time allowed for the inspectors to carry out their duties. Having repeatedly experienced the devastation of war on their soil, Europeans were understandably suspicious of turning diplomacy into a crusade. They contended that insufficient evidence existed that Saddam Hussein posed a dangerous and imminent threat until the U.N. inspectors had completed their work. Moreover, they believed the goal of building democracy would be more elusive and bloodier than the Americans anticipated. That they were right on all three positions did not deter American pundits from becoming intoxicated with self-exultation and a finger-in-your-eye attitude toward the French.[5]

War hawks in the Pentagon and the Vice President's office, cherry picked data from various sources that resulted in, what military historian, Max Hastings, called, "the greatest failure of western intelligence in modern times," to support their case for war. It misrepresented Iraq as endowed with a huge cache of Weapons of Mass Destruction (WMDs) and a programme that was within a year of producing a nuclear weapon. Vice President, Dick Cheney, articulated in a November 2001 briefing that if there was a "one percent chance" of truth in any suggestion or allegation, it must be considered true and justified a response. Even though access to secure oil was a primary motivation behind the invasion, as later acknowledged by Paul Wolfowitz, then Assistant Secretary of Defence, Bush terrified the American public into believing that only a war could prevent Hussein's misuse of WMDs.[6] To inflate Hussein as the *other*, a monster ruling over a "rogue state" that "possesses weapons of terror" hidden "in the dark" that threatened America with "a mushroom cloud" in the lead up to the 2003 war, ignored historical realities. His regime was much more hideously powerful during the 1980s when he was America's "friend" (during the Iran–Iraq war) and the recipient of food aid and military technology that enabled him in part to conduct state terrorism against his own Kurdish people. In addition to relying on collective amnesia, the administration exaggerated Hussein's nuclear capabilities, given that the U.N. inspectors destroyed his nuclear programme in the early 1990s. It also ignored German intelligence warnings that the CIA's principal informant on Iraq's supposed biological weapons, whom the Germans held in custody, was a fraud and known to be a pathological liar.

Worse was the willingness of the administration to distort pre-war intelligence to support its case for war. When Saddam Hussein's last foreign minister, Naji Sabri, himself a spy for French intelligence, reported through an intermediary that Iraq did not possess WMDs, the C.I.A. rewrote the report into a false assertion that Sabri had substantiated suspicions about an active biological and nuclear programme. Similarly, Tahir Jalil Habbush, Saddam's last intelligence chief, insisted in conversations with British intelligence in Amman, Jordan, that Hussein had abandoned his weapons programme but would not admit it publicly. FBI agent George Piro, who was assigned the task of interrogating Saddam Hussein after his capture, confirmed Habbush's testimony on a *60 Minutes* CBS report January 27, 2008. Saddam admitted to him that he was willing to foster the illusion that he possessed WMDs because he feared an attack not from the United States but from Iran whom he rightly feared wanted to exact revenge on him for starting the eight-year Iraq–Iran war. The administration, however, deep-sixed Habbush's intelligence.[7] Weapons inspectors would have apprised the world of Hussein's nonexistent nuclear, biological and chemical capabilities had they been allowed to finish their work. When the respected arms expert, David Kay, reported to Congress in 2004 that "We were almost all wrong," he was only confirming what Mohamed ElBaradei of the International Atomic Energy Agency was already publicly saying before March 2003: there was "no evidence" of an Iraqi nuclear programme. With its fixation on Iraq, the administration lost its moral compass.

The second rationale for an invasion of Iraq, given the alleged connection between Saddam Hussein and al-Qaeda, was to punish the perpetrators of the 9/11 attacks. The degree to which the Bush administration would go to fabricate an airtight connection between al-Qaeda and Iraq was revealed by journalist Ron Suskind in *The Way of the World*. According to Suskind, the White House instructed the C.I.A. to forge a letter, backdated to July, 2001, purportedly from security chief Habbush to Saddam himself stating that the hijacker, Mohammed Atta, had completed a training course in Iraq and secondly that Iraqi intelligence had received shipments of uranium ore from Niger with al-Qaeda's support, a cache that would assist Saddam to develop an atom bomb. This letter was published in a conservative British newspaper and was subsequently extolled by hawkish American journalists. That the document was a forgery there is little doubt given that two former C.I.A. agents admitted that they were personally charged with carrying out this deception.[8] At the time of writing, however, no one has substantiated that the White House issued this order. At the time, Richard Clarke, who served as the counterterrorist coordinator in both Republican and Democratic administrations, attempted to inform the President and his cadre of acolytes that no operational links existed between Iraq and al-Qaeda. Given that Iraq posed a bogus international threat, he contended that a war to topple Saddam Hussein would be perilously irrelevant to tracking down al-Qaeda operatives. Clarke's views were disregarded because the Bush–Cheney–Rumsfeld axis had already decided to invade. According to the Downing Street memo that surfaced in the spring of 2005, as early as the summer of 2002, Bush was committed to military action and planned on justifying the invasion by linking terrorism with WMDs by "fixing" the "intelligence and facts."[9] This document clearly contradicted the Bush stance that he was misled by the intelligence services. On the contrary, the memo reveals that the administration was deceiving the country by manipulating what at best was ambiguous intelligence data to support their arguments for war. It took the July 2004 bipartisan 9/11 commission to reject the administration's rationale and reinforce Clarke's conclusions: "We have seen no evidence [the contacts] ever developed into a collaborative operational relationship. Nor have we seen evidence indicating that Iraq cooperated with al-Qaeda in developing or carrying out any attacks against the United States."[10] Further confirmation was provided in April 2007 when the Pentagon released documents that clearly debunked any such connection. Saddam Hussein in the *60 Minutes* interview with George Piro told him that he regarded bin Laden as a "fanatic" and an enemy of Iraq. Likewise, bin Laden regarded the Iraqi dictator with disdain as a "secular socialist."

At the time, its sophistry was delivered by Secretary of State, Colin Powell, at the U.N., a speech that ultimately cast a "blot" on the illustrious record of public service by one of the most respected members of the administration. When Powell, who combined the military gravitas of MacArthur and the political leanings of Truman, appeared before the U.N. Security Council on February 5, 2003 to deliver his dog-and-pony show, he was widely praised for his commanding performance, in part because he exuded sincerity by expressing what he believed to be true. It turns out that these commentators were wrong. On his way to the U.N., he met with British Foreign Affairs Secretary, Jack Straw, and, according to a report that appeared in the British *Guardian*, Powell expressed angry reservations about the veracity of the allegations in his speech that would present the case for war and that the material approved by the Pentagon would not pass a reality test. A few days later the British Foreign Office admitted that many of the details in their Iraqi file that Powell heavily drew upon for his

presentation were lifted from a twelve-year-old doctoral disserta-
tion. These misgivings were reinforced a year later in an interview
between author, James Bamford, and senior officials at the State
Department when the latter expressed how aghast they were at
the prepared script that Powell had been ordered to deliver, calling it "bullshit—it was unsourced, a lot of it just out of the newspapers," especially the material that Powell had termed the "garbage on terrorism" that linked al-Qaeda to Iraq. Powell endured
three rehearsals before officials from the White House to ensure
his compliance with the party line, which, as a good soldier taking
his orders, he did. Powell's refusal to participate in groupthink resulted in his being ignored and politically emasculated by the time
America went to war in the spring of 2003.[11]

Despite the false arguments, torqued intelligence and trumped-
up evidence, the allegation that Hussein had turned Iraq into a
"chamber of horrors" was anchored in reality, particularly before
1991. The Iraqi born architect turned writer, Kanan Makiya, paint-
ed a horrifying tableau of a totalitarian Iraqi society that existed
before the first Gulf War. The high level of state-sponsored violence
that liquidated real and imagined opposition bore striking similarities with Stalin's Great Terror in 1937–38. The cult of Hussein
presided over an extensive network of spies and informers, layers of secret police, a bureaucracy and the Baath Party itself that
collectively cultivated an "all embracing atmosphere of fear." The
regime inculcated "distrust, suspicion, conspiratorialism and betrayal," values that sanctioned secrecy, torture, show trials, public
confession and executions, even a rape room in prisons. Poisons
that gradually took hold were dispensed through soft drinks to
suspects or relatives of escapees during what otherwise was an
ordinary interrogation. The time between the dreaded knock on
the door and a body being sealed in a box could take one hour.
The Iraqi public became complicitous to the regime's crimes by
immersing themselves in state functions and rituals, becoming
informers or by being sucked into the agencies of terror: the secret police, army and militia. Even children were co-opted to inform upon their parents and not speak to foreigners.[12] Moreover,
there is no doubt that Hussein was a psychopathic mass murderer,
the genocidal killing of 100,000 Kurds in 1988 and the murder of
300,000 Shiites after the First Gulf War were among his most criminal acts. Iraqi society had the aura of a vast concentration camp.

After Hussein's attack on Kuwait in 1990, writers in frightened Arab states, portrayed the Iraqi dictator as a Gothic monster. At a Cairo book fair, Makiya noticed a copy of *The War between Islam and the Devil* with a cover image of Hussein with Dracula-like fangs protruding from his mouth and blood dripping from a dagger pointed at the Kaaba in Mecca. Makiya recognized that Arab writers were demonizing and scapegoating a brutish dictator as if he alone were to blame for everything that had gone wrong in the Arab world in the previous twenty years.[13] Nonetheless, if there was ever a case to be made for an international humanitarian intervention, it would have been in 1991.

In his preparation for the First Gulf War (Desert Storm) in order to secure access to energy reserves of the Persian Gulf, the administration of George H. W. Bush also demonized Hussein by drawing false analogies with World War II. Attempting to mobilize public support in America and at the United Nations Security Council for the purpose of raising an international force to expel Iraq from Kuwait, the Citizens for a Free Kuwait hired the public relations firm, Hill and Knowlton (H&K), to publicize their cause. Chosen because its executives had close relationships with powerful members of the Republican Party, H&K manufactured and polished an expensive ad campaign to convince politicians, diplomats and the public that Saddam Hussein was the ghost of Adolf Hitler and that his soldiers resorted to ghastly atrocities when they entered Kuwait. The centrepiece of its dog-and-pony show was an emotional video delivery by a fifteen-year-old girl named Nayirah, who tearfully spoke about how she witnessed Iraqi soldiers taking fifteen babies out of their incubators. The clip was repeatedly shown and picked up by politicians, including the President himself, to inflame public passions against Hussein's Iraq. What was not known was that Nayirah was the daughter of Kuwait's ambassador to the United States, and that the baby incubator story was a fabrication. Babies likely did die during the invasion when large numbers of Kuwait's doctors and nurses stopped working and fled the country in panic but not in the manner portrayed by H&K. Like the hyped-atrocity stories about Belgian children that enraged millions during the Great War, the incubator-baby deception was so persuasive that it temporarily hoodwinked even the usually more cautious Amnesty International (A.I.) into accepting the story. President Bush cynically invoked the NGO when he played the Hitler card by portraying Hussein as a clone of Hitler, cynical because he had ignored A. I.'s past attempts to publicize Hussein's flagrant human rights violations and the President later refused to meet with its representatives when they became concerned about abuses in the newly liberated Kuwait. It was not necessary to exaggerate or misrepresent horror when Hussein not only presided over a murderous regime but clearly disregarded the U.N. Charter by violating the territorial integrity of Kuwait. But for Bush senior to make the *casus belli* on the violation of international law would not have been an easy sell to the opinion makers and the American public given their long standing disdain for it whenever it challenged American policies.

Under different circumstances in 2003, Hussein still posed a threat, but only to his own people. His military power a shadow of what it once was, he was a "tin pot" dictator presiding over a state reeling from the destruction of much of its infrastructure by American air power during the First Gulf War and the subsequent U.N. mandated sanctions. The Bush administration, who wanted "to finish the job" in the count-down to the 2003 war, excluded a more nuanced portrait of a weakened Saddam Hussein from its carefully crafted message told to the American people. Also ignored were America's strategic interests in the Persian Gulf that included its need for easy access to oil, especially after Hussein in the mid 1990s hinted that he planned to open up his oil fields to French and Russian oil companies that could exclude American multinationals such as Halliburton Industries in which Cheney had been CEO. Following below the radar was an unguarded statement made by a former Secretary of State, James Baker, who explicitly admitted that oil was the reason why America went to war.[14]

Instead, the administration cast the Iraqi dictator as the epitome of evil and Iraq as another Third Reich. Bush and his allies made every effort to equate Hussein with the pure evil embodied by Hitler and every attempt to negotiate as equivalent to the failed appeasement policies of the 1930s. Rumsfeld invoked the analogy when he was questioned whether the administration had sufficient evidence of Hussein's intentions. He testily lambasted the European powers in the 1930s for appeasing Hitler and not taking aggressive actions against him, actions that would have saved millions of lives given that the German dictator had already stated his intentions in *Mein Kampf*. The Bush administration official,

Richard Perle, appeared on "Meet the Press" to compare the visits by United Nations weapons inspectors to Iraq with the infamous 1944 visit by Red Cross officials to the Nazis' Theresienstadt ghetto where the performances of the prisoners' orchestra served as an emollient to persuade the visitors that the Jews were not so badly treated.[15] When it was reduced to eliminating evil of this magnitude, the choice for policy makers appeared to be an easy one, both politically and morally. The problem, however, with invoking the Munich analogy and appeasement polices of the 1930s was that they concealed more than they revealed. Although both Hitler and Saddam were brutal dictators and committed aggression against their neighbours and their own people, Hitler had presided over the most powerful military–industrial complex in Europe while Saddam in 2003 could only project an image of power.[16] Nonetheless, the strategy of demonizing Hussein effectively neutralized Democrats in Congress and the Senate and, fearful that they could be cast in the role of being an ally of evil, an appeaser or unpatriotic, most joined the Republicans in authorizing the president to use military force in Iraq.

In this carefully calibrated climate of fear, the Bush strategy also persuaded the public that Hussein was a mirror image of bin Laden and that they were in Bush's words "different faces of the same evil."[17] A majority of the American electorate accepted the erroneous messages promulgated by Bush and the war hawks in his administration. In a CNN/USA *Today* Gallop poll in August 2002, eighty-six percent of those surveyed believed that Hussein had "plans to attack the United States." According to the Pew Research Centre for People and the Press in October 2002, sixty-six percent of Americans believed that Saddam Hussein was involved in the September 11 attacks and seventy-nine percent believed that the Iraqi dictator currently possessed—or was close to possessing— nuclear weapons. By March 2003 polls showed that fifty-three to seventy percent of Americans believed that Hussein was personally behind the attacks and fifty percent thought the hijackers were Iraqis. Two weeks before the 2004 election after the Senate Intelligence Committee Report on Iraqi weapons of mass destruction made clear that there were no such weapons, and despite the massive coverage about the failure to find them, three Bush supporters out of four believed that Iraq had either weapons of mass destruction or a "major programme" to develop them; the same percentage believed that Iraq was directly or indirectly involved in the Twin Tower attacks. As late as 2005, the same percentage continued to believe that the Iraqi dictator and the jihadists supported each other. These distortions and flights from reality illustrate how a steady diet of misinformation that inspired excessive fear reduced the capacity to reason and the inclination to confirm the facts that they had been given.[18]

These unsettling figures demonstrate that the politics of faith and Karl Rove's well oiled propaganda machine suppressed the

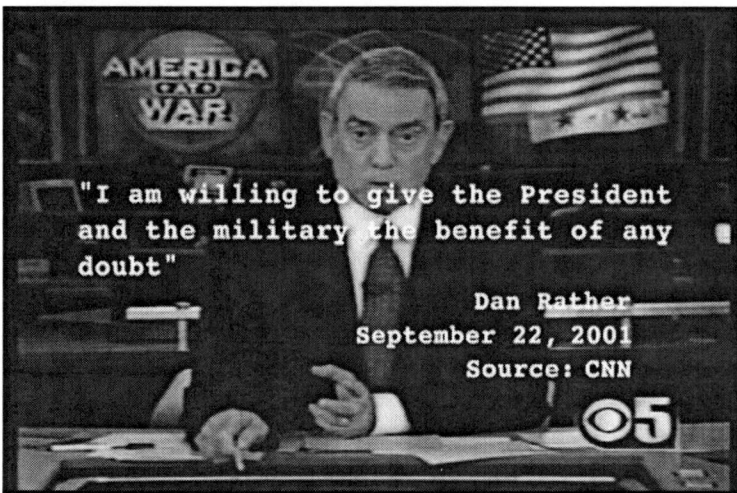

Courtesy of Photofest

CBS anchor Dan Rather's comments, shown here in the 2004 documentary Weapons of Deception, *reflected America's ostentatious patriotism (and grief) in the days following the 9/11 attacks. By the time of the Iraq war, however, he recovered his journalist's scepticism. He indicted the Bush administration for its belief that the public does not need to know, that what the administration and media spin says is more about covering the backside of the architects of the war. Such an attitude, he contended, was harmful to a democracy. By exalting the leader, America was in danger of becoming a miniature version of a totalitarian state.*

realities about the non-existent WMDS and the phantom Hussein–bin-Laden connection. When an advisor in the Bush administration informed a reporter that "We are an empire now, and when we act, we create our own reality," he was revealing the psychic vampirism that the Bush team was able to exercise over the American people.[19] Its deceptive spin and a complicit corporate media in pursuit of higher ratings combined to whip up a jingoistic war fever to broadcast a public receptive to the official version: a dastardly state actor, especially one demonized for over twelve years as the incarnation of Hitler, was surely responsible for the crimes perpetuated on September 11 and constituted an imminent threat to America. These fears were exploited during the 2004 election campaign when the proverbial soccer moms turned into security moms and voted for Bush. No doubt they heeded Cheney's preposterous assertion that a Kerry victory would increase the probability of a terrorist attack, another example of the administration's (successful) fear-mongering that contributed to Kerry's defeat.

Part of the administration's success in convincing so many that the war on Iraq would make America safer was its capacity for engineering a phantasmagorical assault on reality. It created fictional stories when a cast of fake reporters on the government payroll appeared with administration officials on television complaining about media bias. It organized prefabricated town hall meetings that involved rehearsals the night before in order to ensure that nobody deviated from script. It depended on the willingness of the Pentagon to pay over twenty-five million dollars to a public relations firm to place more than one thousand upbeat articles in the Iraqis press, secretly written by American military personnel. A supine Congress and the scourge of hyper-patriotic journalism also abetted Bush in what Rumsfeld called the "perception management" of that alternative reality.[20] The public relations campaign was also a mini version of what transpires in a totalitarian state.

In addition to receiving an echo chamber on most talk radio and the stridently partisan Fox News, the White House's "slick product," disinformation aimed to evoke a combination of fear and patriotism, was endorsed by a narcoleptic and groupthink press who acted more like cheerleaders and stenographers than journalists. With few exceptions until no WMDs were ever discovered, columnists, editorialists and reporters either pressured the administration to invade Iraq or cowered before it by peddling 'official truths.' Unsurprisingly, Fox News, the network with its high decibel conservatives was the "most fear-soaked television channel."[21] A clangourous tabloid press and bloggers with a lynch-mob mentality, the "patriot press," branded the mildest skepticism as

"American bashing, pessimism and anti-war agitation." and co-opted liberals, leaving the public either ill-informed or outright deluded.[22] Even the flagship liberal *New York Times* was spooked because it failed miserably to probe the Bush administration's war justifications and post-war planning. It forced the resignation of Chris Hedges, a Pulitzer Prize winner and a fifteen-year foreign correspondent at the *Times*, by reprimanding him for publicly speaking out against the Iraq war at a college graduation ceremony (where he was booed off the stage). By contrast, the paper deferred to one of its stars, the Pulitzer-prize-winning journalist, Judith Miller who wrote a series of exclusives about Hussein's WMD programme—which turned out to be stunningly inaccurate. She fed fears about an Iraqi nuclear build-up by relying on self-serving defectors, administration voices and the disinformation provided by an Iraqi exile, Ahmed Chalabi, a conman who entertained fantasies of becoming the prime minister in a post-Saddam Iraq. Chalabi, who at one time had close contacts with the Vice President, the CIA and top civilian officials in the Pentagon, used funds provided by the State Department to plant at least one hundred and eight stories in the foreign press that Hussein possessed WMDs and had support from the al-Qaeda terrorists. With perhaps some hyperbole, columnist Frank Rich, whose own critical faculties remained unblemished during this period, opined that "the salesmanship was so merciless that one half of the country was brainwashed into believing that the 9/11 hijackers had been Iraqis."[23]

No wonder the public accepted the official position that regime change in Iraq was necessary to save its people from a tyrant. Yet with two of his pillars for selling the war gradually cut out from underneath him, Bush focused on the third, that the war achieved its purpose by liberating the Iraqi people from a cruel dictatorship. A fourth belated impetus for war was the promotion of democracy in Iraq as a model for the region, a rationale which was more a fantasy and an ex post facto or retroactive justification for American actions in Iraq. The removal of the tyrannical regime in itself was a minor component of the Bush rhetoric when he promoted the need for liberating the Iraqis from their "nightmare world" of "torture chambers and poison labs." Tunnel-visioned ideologues naively believed that American troops would be welcomed by Iraqis "grateful and dancing in the street" as liberators and there would be a clean and easy transition to a legitimate post-war government without a major effort at reconstruction and its attendant social spending. But American actions after the invasion, as we will discuss, suggest that the administration feared true democracy and really wanted a regime friendly to American interests.[24] The Pentagon neglected to construct a post-war strategy for putting in place the building blocks of a civil society that are a prerequisite for a genuine democracy: the rule of law, due process, an independent judiciary and respect for pluralism. Instead, Bush, Cheney and company focused attention on marketing the invasion through scare tactics by torquing up the danger Saddam Hussein posed to American national security. No one in the administration considered the possibility of an insurgency. Paul Craig Roberts, who once served in the Reagan administration, provided in March 2005 a succinct summary of the assumptions and promises that guided the Bush administration even as they began to unravel when they clashed with the realities on the ground in Iraq:

> Delusion has settled over America. Washington cannot tell fact from fantasy....The Bush administration is the first government in history to initiate a war based entirely on fantasy—fantasy about nonexistent "weapons of mass destruction," fantasy about nonexistent "terrorist links," fantasy about "liberating" a people from their culture, fantasy about a "cakewalk" invasion, fantasy about America's omnipotence.[25]

Although Roberts did have the advantage of hindsight, experts on the Middle East expressed similar sentiments before the invasion to British Prime Minister, Tony Blair. (Bush never invited to the White House scholars who would have provided an alternative view.) George Joffe from Cambridge University informed Blair that "Iraq was a very complicated society, there are tremendous intercommunal resentments, and don't imagine you will be welcomed." Furthermore, since Saddam had virtually destroyed civil society, there were no independent organized forces that could serve as allies for the coalition. Unsurprisingly, Blair preferred to focus on the "uniquely evil" Saddam and ignoring these cautionary warnings, joined the American coalition, a catastrophic association that cast a shadow on his historical legacy even though he defiantly affirmed his position in the November 2009 Iraq inquiry on Britain's role in that unpopular war.[26]

A fundamental error of the Bush administration was that its

strategic thinking was frozen in a Cold War mode. By focusing on a rogue state, it underestimated the danger posed by stateless criminal groups who wage asymmetrical warfare. Despite all the administration's talk about how the world had changed since the twin towers collapsed, the mindset of the war's architects, primarily Cheney and Rumsfeld, was locked into the Cold War assumptions of September 10. They were convinced that hostile dictatorships were the major threat to American security and that with its military power the U.S. could successfully invade states and topple regimes as a demonstration to other hostile powers what could happen if they defied American authority. A free-standing bin Laden would never have constituted a serious security risk unless tethered to a state actor like Hussein. Worse, the administration could never deviate from its ideological rigidities regardless of the briefings from career diplomats and the American intelligence services.[27]

Had the neo-conservative ideologues not been so gung-ho and impervious to empirical evidence, they would have recognized that Hussein's secular, nationalist regime was hated by bin Laden who regarded him as "a thief and an apostate."[28] The primary aim of these puritanical Wahhabi Islamists had been to topple secular, even religiously conservative, Islamic governments, with the purpose of eventually creating a modern caliphate—a theocratic Muslim super state. Bin Laden acknowledged in the video he released shortly after September 11 that the secular Turkish leader, Kemal Atatürk's, elimination in 1924 of the caliphate was a cataclysmic event since it triggered a decline of Islam as a powerful force in the Arab world and ushered in an era of humiliation and disgrace. Given the differences between Shiites and Sunnis, secular and theocratic, Arab and Persian, and the widespread revulsion to Taliban-like regimes, the revival of a caliphate ringing the north of Africa and the Middle East is a delusional fantasy, one that mirrored the American illusion that it could transform the Arab world into democracies.

The Bush administration was not entirely wrong in its belief that a stateless terrorist organization could benefit from state allies; it focused on the wrong state, Iraq instead of Saudi Arabia and Pakistan. In the summer of 2002, a congressional hearing chaired by Democratic Senator Bob Graham found evidence that a Saudi government spy had funnelled over forty thousand dollars to two of the hijackers in San Diego. Yet when the committee's report detailed the possible links between the hijackers and a state sponsor, in Graham's words "our supposed friend and ally Saudi Arabia," Bush ordered that these pages be redacted.[29] Moreover, a linkage between al-Qaeda and Pakistan was virtually ignored. Bin Laden and al-Zawahiri met with an increasingly radicalized Pakistani nuclear scientist, Sultan Bashiruddin Mahmood, in August 2001, a fact not widely known amid the welter of distortions and fabrications. Ironically, the American-led invasion of Iraq that toppled Saddam Hussein's regime was a gift to al-Qaeda.[30] It distracted American military and intelligence establishments from maintaining a single-minded focus on these über-terrorists, helped to reconstitute it after its manpower and infrastructure losses in Afghanistan, and allowed al-Qaeda to establish a foothold in Iraq and wreak murderous violence.

Yet this baleful development enabled Bush to connect the war in Iraq with the war on terrorism by making the former the central front on the latter. By staying the course in Iraq, America did not have to fight the terrorists at home, and his truculence resonated with large numbers of Americans, even those who were critical of the war's execution. Until a couple of speeches he delivered in March and September in 2006, Bush repeatedly conflated the al-Qaeda that launched the September 11 attacks with its Iraqi incarnation even though the 9/11 Commission Report in 2004 rejected that assumption.* He ignored the realities that the presence of al-Qaeda and other foreign jihadists in Iraq was a result of the 2003 invasion—they arrived in Iraq about eighteen months after the Americans—that their numbers remained infinitesimally low, about five percent of the insurgents, and that Iraq had become a breeding ground for jihadists' "sacred rage" at American actions during the occupation. This development was acknowledged by then CIA Director Porter Goss when in February 2005 he warned Congress that "Islamist extremists (were) exploiting the Iraqi

---

* At least on one occasion, as revealed in Eugene Jarecki's compelling 2005 documentary, *Why We Fought,* Bush let it slip that there was no evidence that Iraq was behind the September 11 attacks. Still, that message did not penetrate to the evangelicals who, on the eve of the November 2006 Congressional elections, steadfastly continued to believe that the insurgents in Iraq attacked first on 9/11 and that America is safer as long as the war continues in Iraq.

conflict to recruit new anti-U.S. jihadists" and those "who survive (would) leave Iraq experienced and focused on urban terrorism."[31]

Goss was refreshingly transparent. The nature of terrorism did change after the U.S. chased al-Qaeda out of Afghanistan in late 2001. The organization metastasized on a global scare into spontaneously generated cells or affiliates. Its tactics were learned from a digital world and from "on-the-job training" in Iraq that became an incubation centre for terrorism; these included roadside bombs, landmines and suicide bombings, to be deployed, among other places, in Afghanistan. The number of al-Qaeda terrorist attacks increased after 2001; they averaged more than ten major attacks per year between 2002 and 2006, and that excluded Afghanistan and Iraq.[32] Those attacks spilled over into the West as home-grown terrorists conspired against their adopted country ensuring that the "global war on terror" made the world a more dangerous place. Meantime, American administrators in Iraq were attempting to impose its vision of a free market economy on the country fuelling outrage among its citizens.

Free Market Fundamentalism

Predictably, the fantasy of imposing a Western-style democracy clashed with the messy realities on the ground. American soldiers failed to provide security by stopping the massive looting of Iraq's hospitals and cultural institutions, even though American archaeologists had forewarned Rumsfeld that pillage would occur unless steps were taken to protect these venerable sites.[33] Given that American personnel protected the Oil and Interior ministries and failed to provide clean water and electricity, they aroused suspicions among ordinary Iraqis that their well-being was not an American priority. Rumsfeld's negligently flippant, "stuff happens," followed by a barrage of ridicule, only underscored official American indifference if not contempt.

Rumsfeld's disregard for the Iraqi people was replicated by Paul Bremer, the American viceroy who presided over the Coalition Governing Administration (CPA) in the new Iraq. According to Australian scholars, CPA was a euphemism that in reality signalled death and destruction and increasingly presided over a police state.[34] Bremer defanged the democratic process by handpicking members of the Iraqi Governing Council, cancelling local elections and nixing a constituent assembly if he believed that the wrong people, unsympathetic to the Americans, would acquire power. Besides not sealing the borders or securing Saddam's arms cache, in May 2003 Bremer disbanded the Iraqi army and expelled all members of the Baath Party from government, the competent along with the criminal, thereby creating a pool of four hundred and fifty thousand new recruits for what became a ballooning insurgency, which began with the devastating attack on U.N. personnel in July of that year. A combination of the failure to provide security and build infrastructure, betrayal of the promise of democracy and the willingness to create an army of resentful unemployed proved to be a toxic cocktail.

Bremer accelerated Iraqi hostility to the imperial-like occupation by enacting an ideological neo-liberal blueprint for privatizing and hollowing out the state. In part his decision to disband the army and the public service was motivated by a desire to purge Hussein loyalists from the public payroll. Yet Bremer made no secret of his hostility to the "Stalinist economy" and the urgency of privatizing and deregulating Iraq. An arrogant and inept CPA, largely staffed by ideological cronies of the Bush administration with no expertise in the language, religion and culture of the Iraqis, remained in its insular and privileged bubble in the Green Zone in Baghdad, dubbed the "Versailles on the Tigris." Its members were too busy working on schemes to privatize every aspect of life in Iraq to pay any attention to the daily realities of Iraqi lives. Civilian contractors made little effort to restore the electricity outside the Green Zone, leaving Iraqis without power for twelve hours a day when temperatures soared in the summer to one hundred and thirty degrees prompting riots in the south of the country and nostalgia for the days of the former dictator, who at least provided basic services.[35]

The gutting of the public sector through the privatization of state factories and the elimination of publicly-funded workers that included doctors, nurses, teachers and engineers meant that hundreds of thousands of employees lost their jobs and were forced to fend for themselves in a state of Wild-West lawlessness. Although the CPA enjoyed state-of-the-art health care in their city state in the Green Zone, Iraqis had to cope with war-ravaged, unsanitary medical facilities. Instead of working to shore up the public health system which had provided free care for young children with illnesses such as diarrhoea, CPA decided to privatize the distribution of drugs. Bremer also decreed that the borders would be open to unrestricted imports, that the Iraq Central Bank could not provide loans to the state-run factories, and that they in turn were prohibited from acquiring emergency generators. Farmers also suffered from these neo-liberal polices when the Bremer regime discontinued the state policy of free insecticide for date trees thereby requiring farmers to hire private services. When they were unable to do so, the trees became infested damaging what had been a lucrative crop for farmers. Over the objections of the State Department, the U.S. military began to spray the trees convinced that the devastation of the date industry was "fuelling the insurgency."[36]

Nonetheless, Iraqi hostility deepened when the people were generally excluded from the reconstruction of their country given that over forty percent of the population was unemployed. Instead of buying local supplies and building materials, Americans imported them at a much higher price. When Iraqi businesses inevitably went bankrupt and saw their shops bought at a fraction of their value, angry local merchants financed the insurgency. American companies frequently did not hire skilled local technicians because foreign workers were cheaper. Perhaps worse was the failure of American companies that were the recipients of lucrative government contracts and enjoyed legal immunity from Iraqi and American law, to deliver on their promise to provide services: clean drinking water, adequate sanitation facilities to hospitals and electricity to homes. The work that was carried out was often done in a perfunctory or negligent manner. The CPA awarded a substantial financial contract to KBR, (formerly Kellogg, Brown and Root) a subsidiary of the highly influential Halliburton, to install electrical wiring in thousands of buildings, work that was so shoddy that an American soldier died from electrocution. When these companies departed with their huge profits, jobs uncompleted or ineptly done, fraud and other scams rampant, the Iraqi public united in vehement opposition to the Americans. It understood that the American decision to impose a neo-conservative experiment of social engineering on the Iraqi people and its decision to give lucrative contracts to government-connected U.S. companies served American not Iraqi interests. Ahmad Chalabi, who once had been the poster boy of the neo-conservatives, viewed the American economic experiment with bitterness: "an utterly corrupt reconstruction program that oversaw one of the biggest financial crimes in history, which has left average Iraqis with little water, power, health care, education or even food." Fittingly, historian, John Dower dubbed the privatization mania "free-market jihad fundamentalism."[37]

Bremer's preoccupation with creating a new constitution was also not in the interests of the Iraqi people. Hardly a priority given the more immediate problems when the 1970 constitution, ignored by Hussein, was acceptable, it was an effort to ensure that his changes—the imposition of a flat tax, the right of foreign companies to own 100% of the assets and their right to take out of the country all of the profits—could not be revoked by future Iraqi governments. The cumulative effect of the CPA ideological agenda was the citizens' repudiation of secular government. An Oxford Research International poll found that whereas the majority of Iraqis wanted a secular government in February 2004, six months later when the occupation took a more violent turn, seventy percent of Iraqis wanted Islamic law to be the basis of the state.[38] Not surprising since the once noble pronouncements of liberating Iraq veiled total self-interest and rapacious greed. This narrative of Bremer's role in Iraq has resonance with *The Heart of Darkness* when the station manager of the company informs Marlow: "Mr Kurtz has done more harm than good for the Company" because he failed to exercise caution and "did not see the time was not ripe for vigorous action."[39]

The Descent into Madness

A vaunted war of liberation turned into a nasty occupation and a resurgent resistance. In the run-up to the 2003 invasion, the willingness of the Bush Administration to consistently fan public fear and anger by conflating the "House of Hussein" with the "incorporeal presence" of bin Laden—the president insisted that Hussein planned to employ al-Qaeda as his own "foreign army" against the West and his vice president insisted that there was "overwhelming evidence of a link"—turned out to be a serious miscalculation. American soldiers, who absorbed the subliminal message that the war against Iraq was retaliation for Saddam's role in the September 11 attacks, treated Iraqi citizens more as terrorists to be punished than as a people to be liberated. Less than one-half of the soldiers believed that civilians "should be treated with dignity and respect. When American troops admitted to abusing Iraqi detainees, a common response was "retribution for September 11, 2001."[40]

In the PBS *Frontline* documentary, "Wounded Platoon" (May 18, 2010), two veterans, who are currently serving prison sentences for serious crimes after they returned to America, admitted to killing unarmed Iraqi civilians. It did not matter whether they were civilians or insurgents, the *hajis* were "all guilty" and "not people to us." They were the primitive and primeval *other*. Their callousness is reminiscent of Conrad's megalomaniacal Kurtz who writes in his journal, "Exterminate the brutes," then commits "unspeakable rites" by planting his victims' heads on pikes.[41] Although the soldiers' testimony should be treated cautiously and not representative of the conduct of all American solders, it does provide insight into the state of mind of some soldiers damaged by multiple tours in Iraq and suffering from post-traumatic stress or brain injury.

Regardless, soldiers meted out brutal punishment that came with a warning that civilians would also be attacked if they sheltered insurgents. The violence at Falluja is a case in point. In April 2003 soldiers opened fire on protestors, killing a dozen and wounding seventy-five. A year later in response to the murder and mutilation of four "civilian" and "humanitarian" contractors (who turned out to be members of Blackwater, the largest private army in the world), despite the condemnation of the murders by most Iraqis, the Bush administration ordered a full-out Marine attack on Fallujah. Lt. Colonel Gareth Brandl of the U.S. Marines, whose troops stormed the city and treated it as a free-fire zone, spoke of the Iraqis in apocalyptic terms: "The enemy has got a face. He's called Satan. And we're going to destroy him."[42] Serving soldiers told Human Rights Watch that they had the power to administer beatings to detainees and order demanding physical exertion without food, water and sleep "sometimes to the point of unconsciousness," in order that they would be so "demoralized that they [would] want to cooperate."[43] The media networks followed suit by braying for blood regardless of the human cost. On Fox News, the sabre-rattling Bill O'Reilly, without any trace of irony or awareness of the implications of what he was saying, called for a "final solution" and to "knock the place down" since Americans were not going to "win the hearts and minds" of the citizens of Fallujah. Instead of a target of demonization, he contended that Saddam Hussein should serve as a model for Americans to emulate by ruling Iraqis through fear.[44] Assisted by Blackwater operatives, the American military's subsequent attacks on the city that year appeared to take to heart O'Reilly's message. The aerial and ground assaults resulted in six hundred civilian deaths and the displacement of hundreds of thousands. The accusations of American war crimes included the deployment of the chemical white phosphorous, skittish soldiers firing indiscriminately into unarmed crowds of child demonstrators, the deliberate targeting of ambulances, using Iraqis as human shields, attacking hospitals, massacring civilians and, in defiance of international law, the deployment of collective punishment. Most Americans were woefully under-informed about these activities in Fallujah because the vast majority of journalists were embedded with the American military. According to correspondent, Patrick Cockburn, the public was unaware that out of a population of 300,000 the guerrillas numbered about 400. "But by assaulting a whole city, as if it were Verdun or Stalingrad, the U.S. Marines...managed to turn it into a nationalist symbol." The city was physically and economically devastated and resentment toward America remained unabated. The American promise to rebuild the city has not been carried out; it still lacks basic services and the signs for recovery remain dim. The human cost is immeasurable given the huge increase in cancers, brain tumours and birth defects.[45]

The mayhem at Fallujah was not a one off. Shootings at checkpoints, summary executions of detainees, massacres of civilians and rape/murders combined with the murderous sectarian violence among Iraqis, turned the country into a near disintegrating condition. The 2005 massacre at Haditha, in which marines opened fire on twenty-four unarmed men women and children, further damaged the relationship between the Iraqi public and coalition forces, stiffening resistance to the American occupation. Vicious Sunni–Shia internecine warfare resulted in a barrage of suicide attacks, kidnappings, torture and sectarian death squads that slit throats or used electric power drills. Thirty-five hundred civilian deaths in July 2006 alone and, according to a military database, over six thousand "significant acts" of violence during May

2007 undermined a fractious and increasingly dysfunctional government on life support and the efforts by NGOs to build a civil society.[46] Instead of the CPA building a "corporate utopia," the country became a "ghoulish dystopia where going to a simple business meeting could get you lynched, burned alive or beheaded."[47] One estimate is that although Saddam killed five hundred thousand during his nearly thirty-year reign of terror, the death of Iraqis that date back to the economic sanctions by American and British forces is more than double that number. According to one observer in 2007, the numbers were, relative to its population, roughly two September 11 massacres per week. Even though the sectarian warfare was responsible for much of the violence, Iraqis believed that most of the deaths could be attributed to American actions.[48] When, for example, the military failed to deliver on promises to protect local leaders and civilians recruited to inform on insurgents or to act as translators (paid less than ten dollars a day), and then abandoned them to meet a grisly fate as collaborators, the Americans were held responsible.

Stepping Back from the Brink

By 2006 Iraq threatened to implode. To avert that debacle, the stabilization of Iraq, rather than its democratization, became the American goal. A new approach was needed and what became known as the "surge" was adopted. It succeeded insofar as the level of violence dramatically decreased. American officials and the media celebrated it as an "extraordinary achievement." What is not sufficiently appreciated is that the reduction in the spiral of violence had as much if not more to do with timing and conditions within Iraq and throughout the region than American efforts to win the hearts and minds of Iraqis. The bloodshed that threatened to tear Iraq apart, especially within Baghdad itself, had largely played itself out by the time the Americans changed their strategy. The violent fragmentation of the Shiite militias and their extortion demands on the Iraqi people had alienated their original supporters forcing its leader al-Sadr to call a truce. Having supplied military assistance to the Shiites, Iran recognized that the chaos descending upon Iraq would not be in its best interests and decided that no group would receive high-power weaponry. Increasingly alarmed about the potential domestic blowback,

Syria and Saudi Arabia made efforts to restrict their citizens from crossing the border into Iraq. Indeed, the respected journalist, Jason Burke, has suggested that if the surge had been attempted six months earlier, it likely would have failed.

The American military leadership's success resided in taking advantage of these conditions. Bush deployed an additional thirty thousand U.S. troops. This time a concerted effort was made to protect civilians by walking among the population and by moving the military out of their heavily fortified bases into small outposts. Americans co-opted 100,000 insurgent Sunnis into tribal militias and paid them three hundred dollars a month. It was an astute decision given the Sunni revulsion toward their former allies in al-Qaeda for the mayhem they had inflicted upon the Iraqi people. The effort to radically change conditions within the prisons paid further dividends. In addition to isolating hardcore militants, the military leadership recognized that the vast majority of prisoners could be susceptible to the influence of clerics who focused on the basic tenets of Islam and of psychologists, both of whom promoted tolerance and peace.[49] Even so, not every commentator regarded the years since 2007 in positive terms. Andrew Bacevich, historian and a former army officer who served in Vietnam and in the first Gulf War, observed that the 2010 pullout of American troops was really a cosmetic exercise that concealed a much darker reality: "The surge, now remembered as an epic feat of arms, functions chiefly as a smokescreen, obscuring a vast panorama of recklessness, miscalculation and waste that politicians, generals, and sundry warmongers are eager to forget."[50] Bacevich was correct in his assessment that the political, economic and human costs bequeathed a fraught legacy for Iraq and America.

Iraqi political, social and economic problems, including the ownership of oil and the division of its revenues, along with ethnic and religious tensions, have not fundamentally changed. Indeed, the demons of sectarianism oscillated between lying dormant and unleashing violence—bombings, targeted shootings and kidnapping for ransom—that threaten to unravel the state's fragile stability. The ethnic cleansing of Baghdad neighbourhoods and the threats issued by the militias who carry them out continued. Women were at greater risk than they were under Saddam, the victims of rape, kidnapping and honour killing; because of harassment and fear, women suspended their education. By September 2007, 4.6 million people, one of every seven Iraqis, had been uprooted from their home and contributed to the largest migration of people in the Middle East since the founding of Israel in 1948. Among them, as of the summer of 2011, was the mass exodus of an estimated forty percent of the Iraqi professional classes, who had not returned because of poor services such as the lack of potable water, electricity and security. Less than half of the doctors who were present at the beginning of the occupation remained.[51] Iraqis resented the occupation, the abuses committed and the raids sanctioned even as they recognized that they needed, but did not receive, American protection. As of 2008, "occupation forces could not deliver electricity, water, or jobs—or even safe passage to the next neighbourhood."[52] In 2011 when the Iraqis arose in protest against their own government for its inability to provide these basic services, Iraqi government forces fired on them.

With the American pullout, there was the belief that a fragile Iraq would have a stable government with consensual, pluralistic politics because it had a parliament, oil production had increased and the level of insurgency had dropped considerably. At the same time, some American military analysts believed that the government was incompetent, corrupt and "riddled with sectarianism." Some feared that it could become an Iranian proxy even though Iraqis did not want a theocratic state or its national sovereignty compromised, or that Iraq could be exploited by other regional powers like Turkey and Saudi Arabia. More likely, Iraq could be ruled by "younger tougher versions" of Saddam Hussein who in the interests of keeping a lid on the smouldering sectarianism would not be concerned about the either the media or collateral damage.[53] In 2012 Prime Minister, Nouri al-Maliki, who shares the resentments and suspicions of the Shiite majority, appeared determined to exacerbate sectarian tensions that could undermine confidence in the state, encourage its people to look to their ethnic or tribal unit to protect them and precipitate a civil war.

Arabs outside of Iraq were also not optimistic. In a 2008 poll conducted by the University of Maryland and an assortment of institutes in the Middle East, eighty-one percent of Arabs believed that Iraq was currently worse off than it had been under Saddam Hussein, that "Iraq will remain unstable and spread instability in the region," and that America "will continue to dominate Iraq long after the transfer of power to the Iraqis."[54] Even writer, Kanan

Makiya, considered by some Americans to be the conscience of Iraq and who welcomed the invasion, in March 2008 expressed his regrets about post-Saddam Iraq, including the self-centeredness and sectarianism of the government. Perhaps most importantly, he acknowledged that he had underestimated how thirty years of extreme dictatorship would affect Iraqis. Their mutual distrust and fear would take a long time to shift into taking initiative and assuming responsibility.[55]

Unlike Iraqis, the vast majority of Americans did bear any burden from the war since Bush made it clear that he was not requiring that the sacrifice be shared. Because the war, estimated at one trillion dollars, was not financed through taxation—indeed, Bush cut taxes—but by borrowing from overseas creditors, most Americans, until the 2008 recession crisis, were shielded from the economic fallout. Most of the physical and emotional sacrifices were borne by American soldiers, who were thrust into the cauldron of urban guerrilla warfare in which they were neither trained nor prepared. After almost nine years of war, forty-five hundred American soldiers had died, and an estimated thirty-two thousand were wounded. Among the casualty numbers were the permanently disabled (and shamefully treated) veterans and the large percentage of soldiers who were the psychic flotsam of the war, notably the record number of suicides. In April 2008, the Rand Corporation released a study that indicated 300,000 troops from Iraq and Afghanistan, about one-fifth of those that served, were suffering from post-traumatic stress disorder, their condition worsened by lengthy and multiple deployments. Outbursts of anger, insomnia, nightmares and the inability to concentrate were among the most common symptoms. The study also estimated that another 320,000 sustained a possible traumatic brain injury (TBI) as a result of multiple concussions from roadside bombs that severely impair their judgment when they are in stressful situations. A "ticking bomb inside the soldiers" contributed to the violence directed at others and themselves. As of January 2008, the *New York Times* reported one hundred and twenty-one cases of veterans charged with murder. As "Wounded Platoon" reveals, soldiers in combat zones were provided with antidepressants, sleep medications, uppers and downers that likely fed their alcohol and drug addictions when they returned home. Frequently prone to violence, they were often discharged from the army either before

433

or after committing criminal acts. Few received psychiatric treatment. The record number of suicides[56] occurred in part because the military culture attaches stigma to those who seek help. Suicides could also be attributed to the guilt and the pain soldiers experienced after they returned to civilian life as they endeavoured to deal with the enormity of the abuse/cruelty/torture they had inflicted on Iraqis. Joshua Philips comments: "they were hurting people, and they lost their humanity when they were doing it." One particular tragedy (not in Philip's book) was eerily resonant of "Strange Meeting" by the Great War poet, Wilfred Owen; a veteran committed suicide because he was convinced that he was being haunted by the ghost of the Iraqi man he killed.[57] We will never know to what extent these suicides were the result of the moral and legal lines that were transgressed as a result of American counterterrorism, the subject of the next chapter. We do know that both detainees and perpetrators were scarred by the experience and that America's reputation was diminished.

That Line of Darkness

It does not sadden me that we should
note the horrible barbarity in a practice
such as theirs. What saddens me is that,
while judging correctly of their wrong-
doings, we should be so blind to our own.

—*"On the Cannibals"*
Montaigne

The Gloves Are Coming off Gentlemen[*]

Middle Eastern opinion was enflamed in the spring of 2004 by revelations of sadistic maltreatment of Iraqi detainees including torture and murder at Abu Ghraib prison near Baghdad. The detention site became universally notorious after the release of a sample of the eighteen-hundred photographs that showed the taunting and sexual humiliation of thousands of detainees. Initially and falsely dismissed as an aberration by a few "bad apples," rather than a "bad barrel" that pressured soldiers to gather intelligence by any means necessary, the infamous images turned out to be merely the visible tip of systemic abuse/cruelty/ torture in prisons and detainment centres in Afghanistan, Iraq, the Caribbean, and at secret CIA sites. Even though some of this degradation occurred prior to official sanction—for example, two Afghans were beaten to death—the treatment of most detainees

---

[*]   The gloves are coming off gentlemen regarding these detainees.
Email from U.S. Command in Baghdad 2003.

was a logical extension of policy decisions initiated by Bush and Cheney and implemented by senior officials in the administration and commanders on the ground in detention sites. As a result, America forfeited the high moral ground and polarized its citizens: some were shamed by America's use of state terror while others, driven by a combination of vengeance, hostility and fear of Arabs, Muslims and foreigners—in short, the incorrigible *other*—defiantly defended detainee treatment and interrogation procedures.

As early as the evening of September 11, 2001, Bush informed his counterterrorism staff that wide latitude would be given for retribution, saying that "any barriers in your way, they are gone." With a coarseness of language that captured his dismissive attitude toward treaties and the rule of law, he brushed aside any mention of legal restraint: "I don't care what the international lawyers say, we are going to kick some ass."[1] The most important decision was to declare that detainees or Persons Under Control (PUC) were enemy combatants and not prisoners of war. As enemy combatants, they could be deprived of the "quaint" constraints of humane treatment and due process—notice of a charge, access to lawyers and impartial courts, opportunity to present a defence—required by the "obsolete" Geneva Conventions. Bush decided that al-Qaeda and the Taliban did not merit prisoner-of-war status even though the latter were fighting on behalf of their country, Afghanistan. Since these groups allegedly did not honour the Geneva Conventions, especially the provisions about respecting civilians, American forces were under no obligation to abide by the Conventions. Detainees would also be deprived, in the words of the philosopher Giorgio Agamben, of "the status of persons charged with a crime according to American law." Accordingly, they were "removed from the law and from judicial oversight." White House, Harvard-educated lawyer, John Woo, supplied the legal rationale for the repudiation of the Conventions, the Convention against Torture, the Eighth Amendment and the Uniform Code of Military Justice: interrogators could inflict pain short of organ failure, impairment of bodily function and death, and they need not worry about legal prosecution.[2]

The torture memos provided political support and legal justification for the actions of rank and file soldiers in offshore prison sites and secret "black sites." Even before their circulation, low-level grunts operated in the law-free zones of Kafkaesque random terror, depravity and humiliation.[3] Unrestrained by international and American law, military personnel, hampered by limited training and without support from a responsible chain of command, denied detainees the most basic humane treatment and the most rudimentary due process. Worse, they allowed their base instincts to become dominant. As a result, they crossed a moral threshold that not only diminished—and in a few cases destroyed (through suicide)—these young Americans but also the country they served.

In early 2002 two Afghans, Mullah Habibullah and a taxi driver known as Dilawar were taken into custody at Bagram Air Base and beaten to death. Habibullah, who was wrongly accused of links to a Taliban commander, died in his cell after six days of violent beatings. Dilawar was arrested because he had an electrical device in his car, and the Americans were looking for a rocket launcher. He was suspended from a grated ceiling by his wrists with only his toes touching the floor, subjected to sleep deprivation, and kicked and kneed in the lower legs. Soldiers laughed when they heard his anguished cries. Five days of this unrelieved torment that included peroneal strikes—hitting a prisoner on the lateral side of the thigh—led to his death. An autopsy described his legs as "pulpified," and that had he lived, his legs would have required amputation. Ironically, according to Alex Gibney's 2007 award-winning documentary, *Taxi to the Dark Side*, it turns out that the paid informant who delivered Dilawar to the Americans was the bomber they were looking for. Thanks to the diligent investigative reporting by *New York Times* reporters, some of the individuals involved in the homicide of Dilawar and Habibullah were tried and convicted. The atmosphere of sadism captured in the film strongly suggests that the torture, if not sanctioned by their superiors, was condoned; no officer was punished. According to journalist Joshua Philip's more recent investigation, in 2002 there were one hundred and twenty-eight cases in which Afghans were seriously abused with the same techniques used on Dilawar and Habibullah at a time when American casualties were quite low.[4]

The provenance of this appalling treatment (whether intentional or not) was Stalin's NKVD and the Chinese Communists' treatment of prisoners of war during the Korean War to obtain confessions. Americans adopted those "coercive management techniques" at their military base in Guantánamo Bay, Cuba (Gitmo), where almost six hundred and fifty "non-uniformed combatants" were housed.

Rumsfeld wrongly referred to them as "the worst of the worse." According to former CIA operative, Michael Scheuer, less than ten percent were high-value prisoners with potentially valuable information; the rest were foot soldiers who "knew absolutely nothing about terrorism" and were simply caught in the trawl for suspects.[5] Scheuer's assessment is not surprising given that according to the Pentagon's own figures, eighty-six percent of those turned over to Gitmo occurred after bounties of between three thousand and twenty five thousand dollars were offered to anyone in Afghanistan and Pakistan for information about terrorists. Once interned, according to one detainee, Jamal Al Harith, they were informed by guards: "You have no rights here." Even the dogs with air-conditioned kennels and grassy space to exercise had more rights.[6]

Consider what happened to two of the individuals who were not even foot soldiers but in the wrong place at the wrong time and were turned over to American authorities. One detainee was a Turkish–German resident, Murat Kurnaz who, while visiting Pakistan to study the Quran, was kidnapped by Pakistani authorities and sold to the Americans for a three-thousand dollar bounty. Kurnaz spent two hellish months in a secret prison in Kandahar where he was constantly beaten, subjected to extreme cold, nudity, electric shock treatment and, perhaps most disturbing, being hoisted up on chains and hung for days from a ceiling, monitored by a doctor every few hours to ensure his survival. Moazzam Begg, a British Pakistani Muslim, a law student and a witness to the murder of Dilawar was incarcerated at Bagram, Kandahar and then Guantanamo, where, without ever appearing before a tribunal, he spent over a year and a half in solitary confinement with no natural light. During that time, he was subjected to harsh interrogation and threatened with execution. His captors believed that he was a trained assassin who bankrolled suicide missions because of his empathy with Muslims suffering in Bosnia, Chechnya and Afghanistan and his activism in battle zones. These actions were interpreted as evidence of his support for terrorism. After three years, following intense British pressure over the objections of the Pentagon, he was released.

Begg subsequently wrote a memoir of his experience in captivity that revealed his humanity, on occasion his humour, and his insight into his fellow prisoners, his guards and interrogators. He specifically condemned the murder of civilians, clearly not supporting the ideas of some detainees who defended the September 11 attacks. Despite his treatment, he did not become consumed by bitterness toward his captors. He was capable of differentiating the frightened, untrained and the juvenile from the sadistic, and, most surprisingly, in those adversarial circumstances, he began to like some of them, particularly and strangely for a Muslim male, a few of the female guards who shared human conversations with him.[7] Although Begg's and Kurnaz's memoirs are subjective and unverifiable, when triangulated together with independent evidence, an outside observer detects a pattern of consistency with regard to the brutal detention conditions and interrogation, even though the specific experiences vary in their details. Begg, for example, did not experience sexual abuse but he was aware that others did.

Like Begg, Kurnaz was airlifted in shackles, under excruciatingly painful conditions, his body completely covered, to the Guantánamo Naval Base in Cuba. Images of bound and shacked men dressed in orange jumpsuits, on their knees, heads bowed, under armed guard in narrow enclosures behind barbed wire were merely the most visible facet of the incarceration that these men, the living dead, experienced. Kurnaz endured almost five nightmarish years of humiliation—the defilement of the Quran and the sexual provocation from female guards probably most upset him—even though after six months the Americans knew he was innocent. After three years, because of a Supreme Court decision, he saw a lawyer for the first time. Through his efforts and the intervention of German Chancellor, Angela Merkel, who personally spoke with President Bush, Kurnaz was released. In an emaciated condition, he weighed one hundred and thirty pounds.[8] His treatment at Gitmo had been sanctioned by the Defence Secretary.

Rumsfeld endorsed a litany of enhanced interrogation techniques, a euphemism for torture used to diminish the horror of inhuman acts, perpetrated on detainees like Kurnaz and Begg. They included being chained hands and feet in a fetal position requiring them to defile themselves and spend thirty days in solitary confinement, but in reality much longer which threatened to drive inmates into madness. Kurnaz spent a year in solitary confinement in total darkness either in a cooler or an oven because he refused to confess. His captors' sadism continued with exposure to prolonged unbearable noise, snarling dogs (especially terrifying given that in Muslim culture, dogs are regarded as vermin), hooding, and the staging of mock executions. Their families were also threatened with murder or sexual assault. Perhaps the most common technique was sleep deprivation, through the "frequent flyer programme" in which Kurnaz and others were moved from cell to cell every few hours, and. At one point, Kurnaz endured three weeks without sleep.

One of the most widely reported and controversial measures was the twenty-hour interrogation that involved multiple sessions with waterboarding, a water torture, sometimes inaccurately described as simulated drowning but in reality it is controlled drowning. This notorious practice was committed by American troops as far back as the Philippine war (1899–1902) and as recently as 1983 was prosecuted as a crime by the Justice Department. Although President Theodore Roosevelt referred to it as the "Filipino" or "Chinese" water torture, it was a common practice during the Spanish Inquisition, employed by the Nazis and then by the Chinese on American POWs during the Korean War.[9] Extensive media coverage about waterboarding, which the CIA admitted had been administered to three terrorist suspects, paradoxically distorted the torture debate. Acknowledging that the technique was used, albeit rarely, gave the impression that this applied to all torture, therefore, the more frequently used enhanced interrogation methods discussed above and below were relegated to the shadows or minimized.[10]

Other techniques to break the "barbarians" involved "walling," (slamming prisoners against walls, taking care not to break their necks), stripping and humiliating them sexually, and standing them for more than forty hours with arms shackled above the head. One man was tortured to death by hanging him from his arms to slowly dislocate the shoulders, a method first used during the Inquisition known as the *strappado*. The CIA operative later admitted that he received no useful information from this detainee.[11] Prisoners were also denied access to a bathroom after having been subjected to force-fed liquids, and were put in a "tiny coffin box" with threats to bury them alive in order to "break" them, a replication of procedures that the CIA had used earlier in its "dirty war" in South Vietnam.[12] One former guard referred to other guards as "psychotics," who were able "to do things to people that they had always dreamed of." Former World War II veteran, Samuel Hynes, asserted that when "absolute power confronts absolute powerlessness," it becomes "Battlefield Gothic except that there is no battlefield and no battle." Since prisoners' names were withheld and their relatives had no idea that they were even alive, the inmates were akin to the undead. They were the forced disappeared.[13]

In light of the Bush administration's determination to sanction hyper-aggressive methods for detainees, what transpired at Abu Ghraib was predictable. When an Army team from Guantánamo arrived at Abu Ghraib, its chief, Major General Geoffrey Miller told General Janis Karpinski, who had the unenviable job of presiding over the Iraqi prisons, that interrogation would involve ending the soft treatment by "taking the gloves off" and treating the prisoners "like dogs." He added that "if...they believe that they're different from dogs, you have effectively lost control of your interrogation from the very start....And it works. This is what we do down at Guantánamo Bay." (Kurnaz had noticed a deterioration of the treatment for detainees when Miller took over at Gitmo. Interrogations became more frequent, more brutal and lengthier, and sleep deprivation more common.) At Abu Ghraib, Miller's get-tough message was also communicated to Lieutenant General Ricardo Sanchez, the chief commanding officer in Iraq. In September 2003, Sanchez set out interrogation procedures that reached Rumsfeld through Miller, methods which would "create fear, disorient detainees and capture shock," the same techniques that had been deployed at Gitmo to dehumanize the detainees and make it easier for their captors to abuse and intimidate them.[14]

During the American occupation, some 120,000 Iraqi men, women and teenagers were picked up at random, in military sweeps, at different times, primarily to humiliate, shame and inflict pain on them and only secondarily for interrogation. The coercion began when troops entered houses after dark; without any explanation, they rousted individuals from their beds, hooded them, and tied flexi-cuffs behind their back—so tight that it caused skin lesions—before herding them away. At Abu Ghraib, about thirty-two kilometres from Baghdad, insurgents launched mortar and rocket-propelled grenade attacks into the prison. The Military Police (MP) came under pressure from Military Intelligence to "soften up" detainees lest the blood of dead Americans would be on them. The MPs responded aggressively as they threatened the detainees with dogs, kicked, punched and beat them with hard objects, forced them to squat or stand shackled for hours, deprived them of sleep— as long as ninety-six hours and subjected them to electroshock.[15] Yet between seventy and ninety percent of the persons taken to this bedlam that swelled to ten thousand were arrested by mistake. A two-star general told Congress in 2006 that "probably 99 percent were guilty of absolutely nothing" and added "but the way we treated them, the way we abused them, turned them against the effort in Iraq forever."[16] This egregious maltreatment of detainees that had largely escaped public scrutiny changed in April 2004 when CBS broadcasted an exposé on *60 Minutes II*.

Graphic and indelible photographs of flagrantly abused prisoners at Abu-Ghraib went viral, intensifying Muslim anger worldwide, stoking the insurgency and deeply embarrassing the Bush administration. A hooded man standing on a box with electrodes attached to his body in a mock execution ceremony, naked men smeared with feces stacked in a pyramid, American military officials, both men and women posing with naked prisoners, sometimes with snarling dogs, and a female MP, Sabrina Harman, grinning beside an ice-packed corpse of a man who died from a "stress" position were tableaux more representative of a ghastly Gothic Hollywood B production or a quasi-Bosch-like vision of medieval hell than of deeds perpetrated by twenty-first century American military, CIA and private contractors. Unfortunately, the *60 Minutes II* programme conveyed the impression that this horrific maltreatment was an aberration carried out by, in the words of Secretary of Defense, Donald Rumsfeld's damage control cover story, "some kids got out of control" rather than, as Seymour Hersh documents, the result of a systemic pattern of torture approved by Rumsfeld, to apply physical coercion and sexual humiliation on Iraqi prisoners. The rules were: "Grab whom you must and do what you want."[17] The images, however, carried greater weight with mainstream journalists and the public, who saw (or wanted to see) the perpetrators as isolated examples, not representative of something systemically deformed in the military. Apparently it did not occur to the public that the trophy photographs of the perpetrators, alongside their helpless captives that were emailed home to friends and loved ones, transpired because the soldiers' believed that they enjoyed official support from the chain of command.* That myopia enabled the Bush administration to deflect responsibility and scapegoat a few rogue servicemen and women while permitting the political and military leadership to maintain the status quo and ensure that no visual evidence of other misconduct would resurface.

The released images that became emblematic of an increasingly discredited war, however, were misleading and never revealed the worst atrocities. Not shown but later reported was the pouring of phosphoric acid and the sodomization of detainees with a baton. No one saw electric shocks administered or that some men were so badly beaten that they were hospitalized for months. Neither were there images of unarmed men killed by nervous guards, children incarcerated higgledy-piggledy with thousands of other prisoners in conditions of horrible squalor, or women who were allegedly raped. Nor did they expose what happened to the "ghost detainees," because, as high ranking officials reportedly in possession of valuable information, there was no official record of them being detained. Indeed, the bigger picture of the military culture of violence in its treatment of detainees was occluded from the public.[18]

Military authorities ordered medics to disregard the Hippocratic Oath for individuals held in custody. Medics were required to participate in the interrogation that involved, as one soldier recalled, "repeatedly lashing a detainee's back which was covered with third degree burns" and to withhold or dispense medical care with deliberate sloppiness by refusing to change gloves or sanitize the equipment. One former medic, who was by no means the worst, later reflected that he had become "a monster" as "he was drawn in by the power of aggression" and "the level of blood thirst it triggered."[19] Anyone who dared to register a protest was considered delusional and threatened with dishonourable discharge, exposed

---

* This argument is not incompatible with the revelation that Sabrina Harman, one of the MPs who was charged, did write in a letter to her partner, Kelly Bryant, in October, 2003, that she took pictures as a whistle blower and as a way to protect herself. The document was entered in evidence at her court martial but the government's position was that the letter only applied to her state of mind at the time and did not constitute evidence of whistle blowing. Indeed, as soldiers told sociologist, Ryan Ashley Caldwell, the Army was "killing two birds with one stone" by prosecuting Harman: it could expel her for her abuse of detainees and for her sexual orientation. *Fallgirls: Gender and the Framing of Torture at Abu Ghraib* (Surrey: Ashgate, 2012), 111, 45.

to the anger and retribution of fellow soldiers, or cashiered out of the military. When Major-General Antonio Taguba investigated the conduct of the Military Police, he was shocked at the "extremely graphic evidence," that consisted of over one thousand images and nearly one hundred video files. His report was uncompromisingly direct—"this systemic and illegal abuse was intentionally perpetrated"—and ignored while he was sidelined, soon to retire.[20]

Among the estimated ninety-eight detainees who died while under American custody after 2002 at Abu Ghraib were a former Iraqi Air Force General and four men who were killed on November 24, 2003, for protesting prison conditions. They were beaten in the presence of a CIA officer who led them, with sledgehammer handles by a paramilitary squad of Iraqis, the Scorpions, organized by the CIA. It is as if the small sample of garish brutality photographed and made public at the time, though embarrassing to the government, was a distraction from the far greater crimes perpetrated by soldiers and CIA operatives hidden from public exposure. None of the hapless low-level grunts captured on camera and turned into sinister scapegoats to receive a dishonourable discharge or serve time were above the level of sergeant. By contrast no senior officer was prosecuted; Karpinski was reprimanded and demoted, succeeded ironically by Miller, while Sanchez was forced to retire. No one has been convicted for the murder of detainees.

What happened at Abu Ghraib and Guantánamo constituted merely the visible tip of a global archipelago of detention centers and secret CIA-run "black sites" that operated beyond the rule of law and outside public transparency. At one time they housed roughly fourteen thousand detainees beyond American borders. At least nine countries, many of them fledgling democracies with histories as police states, were financially rewarded for secretly interrogating prisoners in medieval-like dungeons. In two detention centres in Afghanistan known as the "Salt Pitch" and the "Dark Prison," prisoners were kept in tiny pitch black cells and fed once a day. Extreme sensory deprivation was applied and some were put in hot metal shipping containers for twenty-four hours, deprived of food, sleep and water followed by blasts with strobe lights and heavy metal music. Or prisoners could be exposed to extreme cold as when a CIA supervisor ordered that an unidentified prisoner be stripped naked and chained to a concrete floor overnight in a freezer. The prisoner froze to death while the supervisor was reportedly promoted. Detainees endured one of the most painful "stress positions," a technique mastered by the Communists, in which they were required to stand naked on their tiptoes with arms extended out and up over their heads with shackles on their wrists and ankles for up to eight hours a day. This torture was repeated daily for two to three months. Some were kept in tiny boxes for up to a week. In his testimony to the U.S. Congressional Hearing, Maher Arar, the Canadian who was rendered to Syria by American authorities, described his cell as a "grave...three feet wide, six feet deep and seven feet high." Although the International Red Cross released a report on fourteen detainees from these sites, no images have emerged.[21]

The mistreatment of detainees reached back to the late Clinton years when the CIA was able to circumvent the law. As an alternative to the legal but cumbersome process of extradition, Michael Scheuer, at the time a key operative in the CIA, created, in 1996, the extraordinary rendition programme—suspects were outsourced to a third party beyond the rule of law and American constitutional guarantees—a process that did not require judicial approval. In that period, the CIA apprehended only individuals that had been convicted in absentia; after September 11, even this safeguard was removed. Agents masked and totally dressed in black, overpowered suspected terrorists and transported them, blindfolded and drugged in a jumpsuit, to the torture chambers of cooperative countries, notably Uzbekistan, Egypt and Jordan. Egypt's security service was notorious for its torture of prisoners who were stripped naked, blindfolded, beaten with rods, whips and subjected to electric shocks and sexual assaults. Between September 2001 and February 2008, there were fifty-three documented cases of extraordinary rendition. Nineteen have not been heard from since they disappeared.[22] Among the renditioned were individuals whose names were mistakenly confused by the CIA and, as a result, innocent civilians were kidnapped. Khalid el Masri, a German was seized at the Macedonian–Serbian border, injected with drugs and flown to a secret prison in Afghanistan where he was beaten, thrown into a filthy cell and given putrid water to drink. The CIA soon recognized they had the wrong man but held him for five more months. When he returned home to Germany, having lost fifty pounds, airport authorities did not believe that he was the man pictured on the passport.

During the Bush years, individuals suspected of terrorism continued to exist in a Kafkaesque twilight zone where they could be detained indefinitely, and the Americans and the British could carry out torture by proxy. In the nod-and-wink outsourcing to sites largely hidden from the outside world, the prisoners, most of them indoctrinated Taliban foot soldiers who knew little, were not only denied the protection of POWs but were at the mercy of individuals who displayed no qualms about resorting to the most extreme brutal measures. By the time, Barack Obama became President, there were eight hundred detainees at Gitmo; only three had been convicted and at least one other had been so badly tortured, that he never could have been brought to court. Examples from American history and artistic expression illustrate the folly of fighting a war on terror though indiscriminate torture and beatings to death. One of the most respected interrogators in World War II was a German, Hans Scharff, a member of the Luftwaffe (Air Force), who possessed language proficiency, relaxed casual conversation and empathy. It is ironical that after the war the American Air Force invited him to lecture on his experiences.[23] In *Taxi to the Dark Side* as the credits roll, the filmmaker's father, Frank, who was an interrogator of Japanese war prisoners in that war and never considered torture as an option, appears to rise from his deathbed and warn that the terrorists have already won if the Americans have reinvented themselves in their mirror image.

Torture Does not Work*

Several commentators deplored the "abuse" of prisoners but then qualified their judgment by noting that it was not as bad as what Saddam had done. Given the American government's high-mindedness for invading Iraq, this kind of rationalization can be dismissed as self-serving and sanctimonious.[24] Although the appalling mistreatment by American forces cannot be equated with the degree of barbarity that Cheka and Gestapo officials inflicted on their prisoners, recent revelations and the memoirs of those who suffered under those barbaric regimes do reveal disturbing parallels—as well as differences. The dehumanization of Iraqi detainees through forced nudity, hooding and the

---

* Porter Goss, CIA Director 2004-06

sadistic photographing of suspected "terrorists" does recall the erasure of personal identity of the "subhuman" racial enemies and enemies of the people. American, conservative columnist, Andrew Sullivan, detailed the nature of the torture that, among other barbaric treatments, included threats to family members, even children, that echoes the treatment of security forces in the Soviet Union and Nazi Germany. He also noted that the methods they employed were once considered war crimes by the U.S. when they were perpetrated by the Nazis.[25]

Even so, America was not a police state and there was a degree of accountability. Eleven soldiers from Abu Ghraib were tried under the Uniform Code of Military Justice and convicted for mistreatment of prisoners—the word torture was never used—and aggravated assault and battery; the ringleader, Sergeant Graner was given a dishonourable discharge and sentenced for physical and sexual abuse to prison for ten years. None of the detainees they assaulted or abused were even interrogated. In their account of the trial that in no way minimized the egregious treatment, a prosecutor and investigator argued that the accused should have been disciplined through administrative action rather than been held accountable to a criminal standard. They attributed the abuse to a lack of training and an absence of leadership. More controversially, they concluded that these soldiers acted on their own, that there were no direct orders from above, and that the Bush administration was not criminally culpable. This conclusion contradicted the reams of documentation, which were the memos from the CIA, the FBI and the Department of Defence, the Standard Operating Procedure manuals, and the later 2008 Armed Services Report authored by Senators Carl Levin and John McCain, that dismissed the few bad apples theory and rightly attributed the degrading treatment of detainees to senior officials in the military and the Bush administration whose abdication of responsibility was unconscionable. Rumsfeld, in particular, bore a heavy responsibility as he set the tone for the horrors that transpired at Abu Ghraib.[26]

In 2004 many Americans believed that the abuse of Iraqis was not all that serious—at least from the photographs that originally appeared—especially set against the gruesome attacks committed against Westerners. That attitude stems in part from the differences between a secular Western worldview and Islamic culture. The latter abhors sexual nudity and public sex. The sight of naked men and women being sexually humiliated by their male and female captors and forced to simulate anal sex or fellatio with other men was deeply shaming. (The public did not see photographs of Muslim men sodomized by soldiers.) In the Muslim mind, sexual transgressions were comparable to the torture and mutilation suffered by prisoners during Saddam's regime at the same prison. For many Muslims, the cruelty and degradation toward Iraqis at Abu Ghraib deepened their anti-Americanism and besmirched the high-sounding American moral ideals that retroactively justified the war.

The spread of those lurid pictures throughout the Arab world, along with images of American soldiers shooting unarmed Iraqis, was fuel for insurgency recruiters from Syria to Yemen as young radicalized men, many of whom had no previous military experience, found ways to cross the border into Iraq. The killers of the beheaded Nicholas Berg mirrored the American impulse for revenge when they reported that they were responding to the "satanic degradation" visited upon Iraqi prisoners.[27] Over the next couple of years, some Iraqis were outraged by the immense media coverage given to the plight of a Westerner kidnapped and murdered because it skewed the American public's understanding of the suffering of the Iraqi people as their country haemorrhaged from the bloodbath of sectarian killings and cleansing of neighbourhoods. The American public had difficulty in understanding that the horror inflicted on Westerners like Berg did not occur in a vacuum and that one outrage spawned another.

The American military also paid a steep price for the Abu Ghraib scandal. Other members of Graner's unit felt the scandal diminished their service in Iraq. As one of them later remarked, "Everybody needs his time over there to mean or count for something," not to be shamed or humiliated. If the government ordered the abuse, "then it means nothing. And now we live with ghosts and demons that will haunt us for the rest of our lives." On a more global level, American behaviour permitted the most repressive states to justify their brutal methods by citing America's example.[28] When Americans tortured and murdered thereby dishonouring the Geneva Conventions that prohibit cruel and inhuman treatment, they became like the enemy and, in John Quincy Adam's slightly edited words, "no longer the rulers of their spirit." Veterans from past wars warn, as did Senator John McCain, a

Vietnam veteran and former prisoner-of-war, that "The mistreatment of prisoners harms us more than our enemies" underscoring that America's international reputation could be torpedoed. Not only would American soldiers be in for a more difficult time, but also the use of torture endangered American lives by alienating potential allies since actionable intelligence relies on support from the local community.[29]

Torture also inflicted scars upon the individual perpetrators. Ordinary soldiers, who had been trained for a combat mission, found their circumstances changed shortly after the occupation began and, out of frustration and boredom, often succumbed to mistreating detainees. When often limited to patrolling neighbourhoods, they rounded up "suspects" and took them to makeshift prisons inside military bases where soldiers resorted to aggressive "monstering" techniques to scare them. Whether they slammed prisoners into walls, imposed stress positions, inflicted "compliance blows" or forced them to drink water "until [they] could not breathe," the purpose was to punish and inflict pain without causing lasting damage. Often this harsh treatment was not to secure actionable intelligence but as one soldier recalled later, "the only thing that really does excite you is when you get to...torture someone." And the reason: "We were doing things because we could." When Army reservist, Charles Graner, spoke to the media before his trial for offences committed at Abu Ghraib to announce "We're going to find out what kind of monster I am today," he likely had his tongue firmly planted in his cheek and played to the stereotypes of his audience. After soldiers returned home, some, however, began to reflect on what they had done. One remorseful soldier (who later committed suicide) acknowledged that it was reckless "to give that much power and responsibility to a bunch of guys who were full of hate and resentment."[30] As the psychologist, Dr. Philip Zimbardo, observed, when individuals are able to exercise arbitrary power "situational forces can work to transform even some of the best of us into Mr. Hyde monsters without the benefit of Dr. Jekyll's chemical elixir."[31]

In the corridors of power, torture in the short term served to reinforce the administration's case to invade Iraq. The Egyptians extracted information under torture from the chief of an al-Qaeda training camp who confessed that close ties existed between Iraq and al-Qaeda and that the former had trained the latter in bomb-making and poisoned gasses. The confession turned out to be a fabrication. This data was merely one thread of the gossamer-thin case that Bush's first Secretary of State, Colin Powell, presented before the U.N. to justify the invasion of Iraq. The 2009 release of four torture memos, one that focused on the treatment of Abu Zubaydah, also supported the contention that coercion was not only counterproductive to national security, but the application of torture was politically motivated. Believed to be one of the top men in al-Qaeda, Abu Zubaydah, captured in 2002, was dispatched to an overseas detention site in Thailand. The purpose was not, as later determined, to obtain information that would prevent future attacks but rather to coerce him into confessing to a link between al-Qaeda and Iraq that would serve the administration's agenda of, in Frank Rich's words, a "ticking timetable for selling the war in Iraq: it wanted to pressure Congress to pass a war resolution before the 2002 election." In short, torture was used to exploit public anger over September 11 and hoodwink the public into supporting a war that had nothing to do with those attacks.[32]

Politics aside, there is little evidence that what Bush designated as an "alternative set of procedures" to interrogate prisoners produced any actionable intelligence. Former FBI agent, Ali Soufan, a Lebanese-born former American officer in the FBI, publicly argued that the abuse of a terror suspect was counterproductive. Based on his career in counterterrorism, non-confrontational interview methods that incorporated "rapport building" and a knowledge of the language, culture, history of the region and al-Qaeda had been much more effective in identifying operatives, uncovering plots and saving lives. Offering tea and fruit took the suspect out his comfort zone because he expected to be subjected to harsh methods. In the spring of 2002 in a safe house, he and another FBI colleague interviewed the wounded Abu Zubaydah, nursed his wounds and gained his respect. The FBI agents obtained a treasure trove of information about specific individuals, notably the name of Khalid Sheikh Mohammed (KSM), who originally conceived the idea for the 9/11 strikes, and the identity of the so-called dirty bomber, Jose Padilla. They also acquired details about the strikes on New York and Washington that only confirmed information received but not acted upon by the CIA in the summer of 2001. Yet they were ordered aside by a CIA team and a contractor who stripped Zubaydah and subjected him to the abusive interrogation methods cited above; they produced no results except the refusal of Zubaydah to cooperate. When an enraged Soufan reported to his superiors that the "borderline torture" was ineffective, unreliable and a violation of the country's core values, he was ordered home. No longer an agent, he continued to write op-eds, provide congressional testimony and write a book to rebut the proponents of enhanced interrogation techniques (without naming Cheney) to prove that its more muscular methods not only failed to provide any valuable information on future attacks or the capture of senior al-Qaeda operatives but they also neutralized the work of skilled interrogators. The advocates of enhanced interrogation argued that its use on Khalid Sheikh Mohammed foiled an attack on the West Coast. But Soufan revealed that KSM's arrest occurred two months after the jihad plot had derailed and that his information was outdated. More importantly, he did not reveal information about a plot he would have known about, the bombing of the Marriot Hotel in Jakarta that did occur five months after he was arrested.[33]

Similarly, Matthew Alexander (a pseudonym), an Air Force major, sent with a team of interrogators to Iraq in 2006, has argued that harsh illegal methods have cost more American lives (soldiers) than were lost in the 9/11 attacks. Although his team was philosophically divided between employing the old "fear-and-control" methods that dehumanize the detainees, and the new approach that searches out the motives of the detainee combined with establishing a measure of respect for the individual, Alexander was convinced that the more robust interrogation techniques caused more harm than good. Becoming like the enemy in order to defeat him by displaying hatred and malice was incompatible with American principles and provided an incentive to join the insurgency. He interrogated over thirteen hundred foreign fighters and Sunni Iraqis who consistently told him that their motivation for wanting to kill Americans was the treatment of prisoners at Abu Ghraib and Guantánamo Bay. He found that by respecting the prisoners and their culture, including apologizing to them for mistakes that Americans had made earlier in the war, and by avoiding any form of humiliation or aggressive tactics, he could establish a rapport with them and slip into any role or "doppelganger" that would elicit crucial information. One of his most important intelligence breakthroughs enabled the military to identify the location and drop bombs on Abu Musab al Zarqawi's farmhouse, killing the thuggish religious fanatic, who was head of al-Qaeda in Iraq and responsible for the beheadings of Westerners. Yet the official story promoted during the Bush years, despite evidence to the contrary, was that aggressive tactics saved lives.[34] In reality, the administration did incalculable damage to its historical ideals and global reputation, as well as sanctioned sadism in the military culture and the intelligence community.

The Politics of Fear

For seven years, Bush, supported by Congress, trampled civil liberties and at times damaged the system of due process within America's own borders. Reflecting the public's willingness to trust the President after the trauma of September 11, Congress heeded Bush's request and quickly passed The Patriot Act in October 2001 with only a single dissenting Senate voice. Although the law usefully ensured that there would be better communication among the intelligence agencies and allowed the FBI to become an intelligence-gathering organization, it also featured draconian procedures. The law violated privacy rights by expanding the government's ability to wiretap, secretly read data of American organizations, and search individuals without showing probable cause or without oversight by independent judges.

The no-fly lists appeared to be a sensible mechanism for screening out suspected terrorists, but its application produced injustices, embarrassments and overlooked genuine terrorists. A plane carrying a British citizen, Yusuf Islam, formerly known in the musical world as Cat Stevens and respected for his humanitarian work, was rerouted. Islam was removed from the plane and interrogated for hours because his name appeared on a No Fly List, provoking criticism from the UK's then foreign minister, Jack Straw. Because the late Senator Edward Kennedy's name was close to an alias used by a suspected terrorist, he was on a no-fly list and was prevented from flying several times. The law also violated due process, without the opportunity for bail or access to an attorney, when it allowed for the detention of both citizens and non-citizens if they were suspected of being enemy combatants. As a result, almost three thousand people were rounded up, arbitrarily detained incommunicado, subjected to physical and verbal abuse, and harsh interrogation simply because they were Muslim or Arab, then quietly released or deported days or months later; only a few were charged with offences, unrelated to terrorism.[35] Since sections of the law contained sunset clauses, meaning that they would expire in four years, proponents of the law sought to make them permanent. Strong political support, particularly in the House of Representatives, ensured the passage of a second Patriot Act that Bush signed into law in March 2006. The entire Muslim population became much more carefully monitored and suspicion of foreigners remained high. In this climate of fear, police and prosecutors with media fanfare regularly announced the arrest of suspects for plotting major terrorist acts. These criminal investigations were often politicized by the Bush executive only to have the cases collapse because of the lack of evidence.

The Bush administration also retaliated against critics of its policies. Officials in the vice-president's office launched a smear campaign against retired American ambassador, Joseph Wilson, after he wrote an op-ed piece in the *New York Times* that challenged a statement made by Bush in a State of the Union address. Administration officials, Karl Rove and Richard Armitage, did more damage to national security as it endangered lives and overseas operations when they outed Wilson's wife, Valerie Plame, a covert CIA operative effectively ending her career. Rove publicly admitted that she was "fair game," even though one of her jobs was to stop Iran from acquiring nuclear weapons. The administration also threatened to prosecute the *New York Times* when the newspaper disclosed the administration's secret surveillance programme that many of its own lawyers thought was illegal. By overplaying the fear of terrorism, and combating terrorism with means often ethically and legally dubious, as well as yielding few pragmatic successes, the administration Gothicized the threat while their actions did little to protect national security.

By contrast, European countries investigated suspected terrorists without overheated political rhetoric.[36] In Spain and Britain, without colour-coded alerts, effective intelligence and police work prevented terrorist attacks, notably the alleged operation to detonate liquid-fuel bombs on transatlantic aircraft in the summer of 2006. A combination of British intelligence, Pakistani intelligence and Scotland Yard thwarted the Heathrow plot. No Western country is more threatened by a terrorist attack than the UK. A 2009 intelligence report indicated that two thousand citizens or residents posed a "serious threat to security."[37] Yet Britain dropped the label "war on terror" three years before President Obama did and was able to secure the release or transfer of nine British subjects from Guantanamo.

Motivated to improve the optics of his administration by appearing with Senator John McCain who had lobbied for a ban on torture, Bush signed into law a tepid anti-torture bill on December 30, 2005. But hours later, Bush directed the Executive Branch to disregard it even though the law stripped the federal courts of jurisdiction to consider petitions of habeas corpus filed by detainees at Guantánamo that would allow them to mount a court challenge of the state to provide reasons for their detention. The Supreme Court responded in 2004 and 2006 by rendering decisions which declared that enemy combatants were entitled to due process. The President could not unilaterally flout the rule of law by ignoring international law, specifically the Geneva Conventions that bar cruel treatment, degradation and torture, unless authorized by Congress. Regrettably, Congress capitulated to Bush's demands by passing the retrograde Military Commissions Act of 2006 that enabled authorities to detain and imprison individuals indefinitely (including legal residents of the United States) without ever charging them with a crime or providing them with an opportunity to prove their innocence. The law also provided retroactive immunity to officials who order or carry out torture. The absence of due process prompted one Canadian expert on terror to compare this law to Stalinist show trials, since the objective of the trials was not to determine guilt or innocence but to provide retributive justice.[38]

Nonetheless, despite his administration's belligerent rhetoric, trials of suspected terrorists did occur in federal civilian courts and there was a ninety percent conviction rate of the three hundred cases since 9/11. After being given their constitutional rights, providing valuable intelligence about training sites and a willingness to testify in other trials, the accused were convicted and received lengthy sentences. Among them, Zacarias Moussaoui, who pleaded guilty to conspiracy to attack the United States and Richard Reid, the shoe bomber who was apprehended when a flight attendant noticed a man trying to set fire to his shoes, were incarcerated for life. The American-born, John Walker Lindh, who was tried through the prism of fear after 9/11, arguably, however, received a prejudicial trial and an unjust sentence of twenty years.[39]

If the federal courts worked reasonably well, the same cannot be said for the military courts. Even though in trying suspected terrorists some would argue they possess advantages over civilian trials—hearsay evidence and testimony based on a coercive interrogation can be admitted—there were only three military trials and they were a fiasco. One of the accused received a life sentence but only served six months plus the time that he had already served, the second was sentenced to six months in addition to the time served and the third was given nine months following a plea bargain.*

"Their pain is not our pain"**

The ability of the state to short-circuit due process and condone, if not approve, the harsh treatment of detainees can only be understood in the context of the inability of a significant segment of the American population to understand or empathize with Islamic sensibilities. Even before the attacks on New York, Washington and rural Pennsylvania, Muslims were assailed, particularly during the First Gulf War, which prompted President

---

* In the first three years of the Obama administration, there were convictions for terrorist acts in both civilian and military courts. According to Jane Mayer writing in *The New Yorker*, the same prominent Republicans who applauded the due process of the civilian trials during the Bush era now exploited the miasma of fear and hysteria of critics. They objected to trying in a New York federal court the notorious Khalid Sheikh Mohammed, leaving the misleading impression that the accused would only receive justice in a military court. In response to political and public pressure, the Attorney General, Eric Holder capitulated. Jane Mayer, "The Trial," *The New Yorker*, February 15 and 22, 2010. For a different perspective, Shawcross, *Justice and the Enemy*, 119-123 notes that Obama might have prejudiced a civilian trial by stating that he was confident that KSM would be found guilty and face the death penalty.

** [Torture] presupposes, it requires, it craves the abrogation of our capacity to imagine others' suffering, dehumanizing them so much that their pain is not our pain. It demands this of the torturer...but also demands of everyone else the same distancing, the same numbness, on the part of those who know and close their eyes, those who do not want to know and close their eyes." Ariel Dorfman

George H. W. Bush to insist that "death threats, physical attacks, vandalism, religious violence and discrimination against Arab Americans must end." His use of the bully pulpit had the positive effect of reducing these assaults. But shortly after 9/11, Muslims again were the target of harassment, hateful and suspicious stares, physical assaults, and discrimination in the workplace and educational institutions. American Muslims and one Sikh (mistaken for a Muslim or an Arab) were murdered, the perpetrators boasting about the need for revenge. Like his father, George W. Bush condemned these attacks. Although he was sharply criticised by evangelical Christians, he stood with Muslim leaders, and in a highly publicized speech at an Islamic Centre proclaimed that "Islam is peace."[40] Yet efforts to challenge stereotypes about Muslims did not deter popular culture from reinforcing them. Indeed, the November 2001 meeting between Karl Rove and Hollywood executives was an effort by the White House to encourage the film industry to promote patriotism and the Bush message.

Films have long conditioned Americans to stereotype Arabs as prurient despots, venal oil sheiks and gun-wielding terrorists. The scholar, Jack Shaheen, who spent decades analyzing over one thousand films, concluded that prior to September 11, the vast majority portraying Arabs demonize them. Consider the 1976 Academy award-winning *Network*: a newsman rants that Arabs are "medieval fanatics [who are] simply buying us" and there is "not a single law in the books to stop them," even though in reality the 1980 Commerce Department figures indicated that OPEC investment in the U.S. accounted for less than one percent of foreign investment. In the 1998 *The Siege*, Arabs and Muslims are depicted as fifth columnists who, despite deceptive appearances, are "sleepers" preparing for the day when they unleash a tsunami of violence against Americans, a trope that continued in popular culture after 9/11. The 2000, *Rules of Engagement*, reveals the consequence of the public's penchant for stereotyping Arabs as terrorists: when American Marines shoot almost one hundred Arab men, women and children, audiences respond with applause and cheers.[41] Shaheen examined about one hundred post-September 11 films and, although a surprising one-third reveal complexity and avoid racist stereotypes, he concluded that the majority reflected the negative attitudes that Americans harboured toward Arabs, Muslims and Sikhs contributing to more hate crimes being directed against them. The ease and speed with which Americans were prepared for war in March, 2003, prompted the *Los Angeles Times*' film critic to wonder whether films that are "hardwired into our psyches" reinforce the xenophobia and the war fever.[42] His musing is speculative but the fact remains that a large segment of the public craved revenge for the loss of three thousand innocent lives on that terrible day in September. Since "Arabs" had been responsible for those deaths, many Americans were predisposed to welcome an attack "to desecrate the skyline of a representative Arab city and dole out misery to generic Arabs."[43] Under these circumstances, it was easy to blur the image of bin Laden with the "madman," Saddam Hussein.

Perhaps even more than film, television has shaped popular perceptions about terrorism and the use of torture. Consider the phenomenal success of the hyper-patriotic counter-terror drama, *24*, which reached a much wider audience and transcended its primetime status to become a cultural touchstone for the moral, legal and utilitarian ramifications of the forcible interrogation techniques of terrorist suspects during the Bush era. To a large extent, the appeal of the television series rested on the classic thriller trope: the ticking time-bomb plot, and an aggressive interrogation that must be applied to avert a disaster and save hundreds, perhaps thousands of lives, even though experienced FBI interrogators and defence lawyers for Guantánamo Bay detainees have argued this scenario is a fantasy and never occurs in real life.[44] Written by a Hollywood conservative who had no experience in intelligence matters or interrogation, the super heroic Jack Bauer, a former Special Forces soldier experienced in under-the-radar operations, commits illegal acts, including murder and torture. While committing spectacular derring-do operations in defence of his country and President, in the tradition of Dirty Harry, Bauer extracts through torture, vital information from his victims "for the greater good," while weak-kneed liberals flail around helplessly prattling on about the need for due process. When the villains apply torture, they are, however, motivated by sadism and vengeance. The series was most successful in reinforcing and exploiting the public's fear following reports about terrorist cells and suicide bombings. For three years, government officials spewed out uncontested anti-Arab and anti-Muslim slurs that in effect justified Bauer's use of violence against these "fanatics." One measurement of *24*'s influence was that in 2007, sixty-eight percent of Americans told Pew Research pollsters that torture was an acceptable option. A February, 2011, CNN poll found that fifty percent of respondents supported "harsh interrogation procedures," including water-boarding. The Fox programme that featured *24* was seriously discussed at a brainstorming session by interrogators at Guantánamo

Courtesy of Photofest

The Fox network's seven-year television series, 24, vividly captured and reinforced the belief that enhanced interrogation of suspected terrorists produces positive results despite evidence to the contrary in the real world. In 24, which operates on the dubious premise of the ticking-bomb scenario, Special Agent, Jack Bauer always extracts the information he is seeking after he assaults or tortures someone.

Bay as different techniques were bandied about. The extent of its popularity among the military prompted the dean of the Military Academy at West Point to meet with the producers of the show to request that changes be made because it was encouraging misperceptions among the soldiers who wonder "if torture is wrong, what about *24?*"[45]

This perception that torture is acceptable was not limited to soldiers or military cadets. Even a Supreme Court Judge, Antonin

Scalia, approved of the rough justice handed out by Bauer. In a panel discussion held in Canada, Scalia expressed skepticism about judicial oversight of overaggressive intelligence agents when they believe the threat of a terrorist attack exists. Referring to a specific episode in which Bauer tortures a suspect who subsequently provides valuable information: "Jack Bauer saved Los Angeles....He saved hundreds of thousands of lives. Are you going to convict Jack Bauer? I don't think so....So the question is... whether we believe in these absolutes, and ought we [to] believe in these absolutes." Scalia's belief that a television series reflected reality was shared by Michael Chertoff, a former judge and at that time Secretary of Homeland Security, even though he did not explicitly endorse torture.[*]

Their hard-line views were diametrically different from those of Margaret Stock, a professor of national security at West Point, who at one time worked in counterterrorism. She contended that the programme was a fantasy in that the audience knows that everything Bauer plans will be realized when, in reality, these operations are "messier" given that initial perceptions can be erroneous "because you are getting bad translations that don't make any sense." She recommended that Hollywood focus less on harsh interrogation techniques and more on dramatizing the importance of foreign languages to further effective intelligence work. The Canadian jurist, Justice Dennis O'Connor, who spent two years investigating the Syrian detention of Canadian citizen Maher Arar, went even further in his repudiation of abusive interrogation. In his exoneration of Arar, O'Connor was unequivocal that "torture can never be an instrument to fight terror, for torture is an instrument of terror."[46]

Hard-right polemicists in the media disdained these liberal

---

[*]   A powerful antidote to the melodrama of *24* is Showtime's television series *Homeland*. Its theme—countering jihadist terrorism—is similar, but the treatment is vastly more complex and nuanced. In this updated version of the Manchurian Candidate trope, the central characters are both sympathetic and flawed. Both the CIA operative and the veteran whom she regards as a mole, a soldier imprisoned for eight years, have been traumatized by their experiences in Iraq. As the series evolves, they increasingly mirror one another's psychological state. *Homeland* also seems to endorse the beliefs of Ali Soufan and others who contend that the best way to obtain information from suspected terrorists is to establish a human connection.

views and justified enhanced interrogation treatments against detainees at Abu Ghraib. Shock jocks like Rush Limbaugh reviled the detainees as "sick," perverted" and "less than human." Not surprisingly, he regarded waterboarding as a "no brainer" since it could save lives—the frequently cited mantra to justify its use despite the lack of evidence that it did have that effect. Michael Savage, another popular radio host, derided the detainees as "sub-human" and "vermin" and suggested that forcible conversion to Christianity is "probably the only thing that can turn them into human beings." As part of the pit-bull cultural war permeating America, the polemical Anne Coulter, among others, blamed the shenanigans on "girly boys" and feminism.[47] Philosopher Susan Neiman suggested that the photo antics of Lynndie London at Abu Ghraib would set the nascent women's movement in Arab countries back decades since they confirmed men's worst nightmare of what female power could do. Both of these views are skewed as they do not take into account the expert testimony presented at London's court martial, which indicated that far from being a feminist, she possessed a "compliant personality" who would do anything to please Graner, her lover at the time. One expert testified that she was more like a battered wife or an abused child, testimony that gave credence to the view that London was not an abuser of detainees but that Graner was abusing her.[48] None of this evidence became part of the national conversation.

In the toxic atmosphere of 2004, any critic of the treatment of detainees or even the strategic conduct of war was excoriated for undermining the American military. The tabloid pundit, Bill O'Reilly, on Fox News, who had already compared the Quran to *Mein Kampf*, called liberals and protestors traitors who should be incarcerated. When a liberal Democrat, Senator Dick Durban, appalled by an FBI report on the treatment of suspected terrorists at Guantánamo, compared it to that meted out by repressive totalitarian regimes, he was anathematized on talk radio as "a piece of excrement...that needs to be scraped off the sidewalk and eliminated."[49] The hysterical outbursts by supporters of harsh interrogation techniques reveal their incapacity to reflect upon the damage that American actions have inflicted not only on the Iraqi people but how they are a betrayal of America's own ideals and mirror the actions of their enemies. And these methods did not produce—notwithstanding the fantasies dramatized in *24*—valuable, actionable intelligence.

If the conservative media assailed critics who compared the treatment of detainees to that conducted by the agents of earlier totalitarian regimes, distinguished academics also defended the right to "lite torture" and "torture warrants." Michael Ignatieff, former Director of the Harvard University Carr Centre for Human Rights and former leader of the Liberal Party of Canada argued that coercion and the violation of rights for terror suspects may be necessary and that sleep deprivation was an acceptable technique. Alan Dershowitz, a Harvard law professor, contended that judges should issue torture warrants licensing authorities to torture "cunning beasts of prey." More controversially, two Australian academics, argued that it was not only pragmatically desirable but morally defensible, indicating that "punishing the innocent and torturing the culpable is, in fact, no worse than other activities we condone."[50] This line of reasoning comes dangerously close to those arguments advanced by apologists for the brutal treatment of "enemies" in the Soviet Union and Nazi Germany who were discussed in earlier chapters.

If academics were lowering the legal bar for terrorist suspects, evangelical Christians assailed Muslims per se and equated Islam with totalitarian regimes. By demonizing them as less than human, the "sand-nigger" *other*, they projected their fears and hatred onto Muslims much as the Nazis and the Soviets had toward their enemies. A leading evangelical admitted in 2003 that "Muslims have become the modern-day equivalent of the Evil Empire." Franklin Graham delivered the invocation and sermon at George W. Bush's 2001 inauguration and reappeared at White House functions. He characterized Christianity and Islam as "eternal enemies" that are locked in a "classic struggle that will end with the second coming of Christ." Pat Robertson, the Christian broadcaster who used the *700 Club* as his personal platform, indicted Islam for "seeking world domination" and the Prophet Mohammed as "a wild-eyed fanatic...a killer" and said that Muslims were "worse than Nazis." Then he irresponsibly contended that there was little that distinguished radical Islamism from moderate Islam even referring to bin Laden as one of the "true disciples of the teachings of the Quran." Equally damaging statements were made by a senior American officer, Lieutenant General William Boykin, in charge of the hunt for bin Laden, who told an Oregon, Florida congregation, that *jihadists* "will only be defeated if we come to them in the name

461

of Jesus." None of these gentlemen was willing to acknowledge the chilling passages in the Bible or the Torah that called for the death of infidels and the slaughter of others who were not among those chosen by God. For those American officials trying to win the hearts and minds of Muslims in the Middle East, the general's provocative remarks were deeply troubling because they "confirmed [the Muslim] conspiracy theory that the war on terrorism really is a war on Islam."[51]

If public opinion did not share General Boykin's sentiments, it was not exorcised about them either. American outrage at the images of Abu Ghraib was more an exception to the general indifference or short-lived hostility to alleged acts of American misconduct in Iraq. After the Haditha massacre of civilians was reported, which the military initially attempted to blame on insurgents, public outrage waned after a military investigation absolved the eight Marines from any wrong doing. According to a *Washington Post* report, civilian losses were "the cost of doing business, and the Marines needed to get 'the job done' no matter what it takes." Bloggers, as well, rallied around them, indicating that they were following the rules of engagement and referred to the incident as the Haditha "hoax."[52]

The public indifference to what happened at Haditha was a snapshot of a lack of empathy toward Iraqi suffering. Little attention was given to the estimated one hundred thousand Iraqi civilians who lost their lives, not unlike the lack of concern for Iraqi pain during the imposition of sanctions in the 1990s. The American media rarely reported or commented on the death of Iraqi civilians. Most journalists were embedded and produced coverage largely sympathetic to the military. On the rare occasion that Iraqi civilian losses were mentioned, the American media attributed them to other Iraqis because of "ancient hatreds" and ignored or downplayed the victims of collateral damage inflicted by their soldiers in firefights or at checkpoints. Occasionally, an exception occurred when an incident went viral such as the Apache helicopter that killed twelve individuals, including two Reuters' employees, and wounded two children.[53] The most common public response displayed a callous insensitivity: the Iraqis were "ingrates" for not appreciating American sacrifices in liberating them from a tyrant. The lack of media imagery documenting Iraqi pain; the inability of combatants and the media to distinguish between insurgents and civilians; the dehumanization of the Iraqi people, especially given that they were Arab and (primarily) Muslim; and ethnocentrism, the inability to identify with people unlike themselves, all contributed to that indifference.

Restraining the Darker Impulses

The late historian, Tony Judt, reminded us that if we compare the memoirs of those who survived imprisonment and torture in the Soviet Union, with those who suffered degrading treatment authorized by Bush and the Congress, we may well ask, is there any real difference?[54] The administration apologists who defended its actions by raising the distinction between the rule of law and "exceptional circumstances," thereby condoning, if not encouraging, the hyper-aggressive behaviour, would have vehemently rejected the implications of Judt's rhetorical question. In one sense they were right; there is a difference. Not everyone at Abu Ghraib acted in an unprofessional and undisciplined manner; master-at-arms, William J. Kimbro, who led three U.S. Navy dog teams, exercised integrity by refusing to participate in this excrescence, despite considerable pressure to conform.[55] And in a 2008 controversial and close decision, the Supreme Court delivered a stinging rebuke to the Bush administration by declaring a key part of the Military Commissions Act to be unconstitutional because it denied detainees a fundamental procedural right of habeas corpus to petition the courts to challenge their designation as enemy combatants. In the words of conservative Justice, Anthony Kennedy: the "laws and the Constitution...survive, and remain in force, in extraordinary times."

When checks and balances are placed on the state's capacity to abuse other human beings even purported enemies, some Americans place hope in the power of institutions and the sentiments of powerful officials to restrain man's darker impulses. When Alberto Moro, the former General Counsel to the Navy, testified before the Senate Armed Services Committee in June, 2008, he argued that there was little to distinguish between "cruelty and torture, for cruelty can be as effective as torture in savaging human flesh and spirit and in violating human dignity. Our efforts should be focused not merely on banning torture, but on banning cruelty."[56] The Gothic images captured on film in Abu Ghraib, those of cruelty and sadism that shook Americans out of their smug complacency that their presence in Iraq was fundamentally a force for good, haunted American political discourse and the testimony of many participants in these wars. Moro's argument was by no means the end of the debate as Bush supporters during the Obama era seized upon news developments to claim that the Bush programmes were justified to protect national security.

A plea for America to adhere to international humanitarian law and its own constitution does not foreclose the possibility that some of the detainees were genuine security risks. The release of a large trove of 2010 confidential documents by WikiLeaks revealed that the vast majority of detainees were either innocent or Taliban foot soldiers who were caught up in the fog of war. But a small percentage of those assessed between 2002 and 2008 were deemed high security risks and some were mistakenly released and resumed terrorist activity, including some who became candidates for the Saudi Arabian rehabilitation programme. These disclosures, however, strengthen rather than weaken the argument that humane treatment and a more stringent due process be followed in the assessment of these inmates.

The death of bin Laden, and early press reports that some valuable information was achieved to identify the nickname of his courier through enhanced interrogation techniques, revived the debate over the value of torture. Apologists for the Bush administration like John Woo argued that they have been vindicated—that harsh methods led directly to bin Laden's compound. The critics say that there is no way to prove this assertion. Enhanced interrogation was a stain on America and a violation of its laws and the Constitution. Based on his conversation with CIA Director, Leon Panetta, John McCain revealed in a *Washington Post* op-ed piece that the first piece of evidence as to the description of the courier came from a detainee held in another country, who, it is believed was not tortured. McCain also reiterated that those who were waterboarded or harshly interrogated provided false and misleading information.* (He does not mention that such information was used by the Bush administration to justify the Iraqi war). Most

---

* Peter Bergen in *Manhunt* is adamant that the CIA under Obama relied less on detainee information and more on the interception of cell phone conversations, spies on the ground and satellite pictures to track the whereabouts of bin Laden.

importantly, he stated that this debate should not be framed in utilitarian terms but as a fundamental moral question about what defines America. If those who fight this war sacrifice their best selves, what distinguishes Americans from their current and former enemies?[57]

20

Epilogue

The Gothic Mode in World War II

If I had not seen it I could hardly believe that you could find souls so monstrous that they would commit murder for
the sheer fun it....For there you have the
farthest point that cruelty can reach.

—*"On Cruelty"*
Montaigne,

Hitler and Stalin were brooding Gothic men of violence who presided over terrorist regimes. Yet despite their vast ideological differences, they retained a mutual re-gard for each other. During his war of extermination against Judeo–Bolshevism, Hitler could barely disguise his admiration for the "exceptional" leader. Although he loathed "Jewish Bolsheviks" and dismissed Russians as "Redskins," he privately expressed his "unconditional respect" for Stalin: Jews were notable victims of his show trials. Hitler also admired Stalin for eliminating the Russian bourgeoisie, who were "worthless for mankind." Using Gothic lan-guage, he characterized Stalin as "half beast, half giant." Stalin's in-difference to his people—"they can rot for all he cares"—mirrored his own feelings about the German people. Hitler, who placed stock on phrenology, conceded after watching newsreels of Stalin that his Soviet counterpart "has a good face" and that he believed he could negotiate with his "kindred soul."[1] Stalin for his part had praised Hitler for purging the SA, which served as a model for his elimination of rivals within the Party. Moreover, his trust in Hitler was so great in 1941 that he discounted Soviet and British intelligence that indicated that German troops had invaded the Soviet Union, a miscalculation that could have destroyed Soviet power.

Courtesy of Photofes

The 1990 film Europa Europa, *based on the real life travails of the Jewish Solomon Perel, who managed to survive the war by spending time in both a Soviet orphanage and the Hitler Youth movement. After witnessing one of his Soviet fellow students being shot by German soldiers, he dreams of Hitler and Stalin dancing together. In one sense, the dream reveals the teenager's confusion about his personal identity; on another level, it underscores the director, Agnieszka Holland's view that one tyrant was the double for the other.*

As the doppelganger for each other, Stalin and Hitler shared a similar abiding contempt for liberalism, since even apparent difference was tantamount to treason. Both adopted Lenin's aphorism, "whoever is not for us is against us"[2] and the same drive to eliminate worldviews that valued the individual and human empathy. They would rid the world of what each decided was filth and corrupt, convinced that they were ordained as the agent to decide who lived and who died. In their joint invasion of Poland in

September 1939, both also revealed an uncanny ability to tap into the base instincts of others.

The Cauldron of Hatred in Poland

Hitler and his fellow gangsters utilized the conditions of war to exercise their contempt and hatred for those they deemed genetically and racially inferior. Taking full advantage of the opportunistic and cynical Nazi–Soviet Pact signed between Germany and the Soviet Union, the Wehrmacht seized Poland's western and central areas within a month. By September 17, 1939, in accordance with the agreement, the Soviets seized without resistance its eastern part. Caught in the eye of the hurricane between the German and Soviet invasions, Poles suffered the theft of their possessions, the burning of their homes, and the requisition of forced labour and mass killings. Whether under Nazi or Soviet control, Poles were whipsawed by these brutal regimes that imposed the death penalty for the most minor infringement and followed a similar pattern of arbitrary arrest and execution or deportation of Polish intellectuals who might lead a future nationalistic renewal. Throughout the "bloodlands" among the ethnic mix in Poland, the Ukraine and Belarus, both predatory powers dragooned young men to serve their masters in the local police. The alternatives were starvation, deportation or forced labour.[3] At the same time, both powers possessed an unerring capacity to exploit ethnic, class and cultural cleavages by coercing locals to collaborate in killing Jews or acting as spies. Soviets exploited class tensions between Polish landlords and Ukrainian peasants. Both at the time and later, the Poles denied their collaboration, preferring to see themselves primarily as victims.

Although the Nazis and the Soviets mirrored each other in the brutality they inflicted on indigenous peoples, ideology dictated certain differences. The Germans ruthlessly enforced their racial laws, particularly on the nearly two million Poles, mostly forced labourers, who were resettled and housed in primitive camps in Germany. Racially undesirable male Slavic Poles were publicly hanged if denounced for a sexual liaison or even an inappropriate fraternization. Non-Aryan women were further vilified. Despite evidence of harassment, sexual slavery and the rape of Slavic women, Nazi sources maligned them as predators, as potential

destroyers of the race, who used their sexual wiles to lure unsuspecting German men to their ruin.[4] Any suggestion of sexual
impropriety by a Polish woman frequently led to her deportation
to a concentration camp. The Soviets, however, motivated more
by class warfare, secularized churches and synagogues and confiscated private property which devastated farms.

Under Soviet rule, Jews were stripped of their property and
thousands were deported to the interior in greater proportion than
any other ethnic group. There they experienced a death rate of
twenty-five to thirty percent. Nonetheless, because the state was
now the sole employer (until the German armies overran it in June
1941), it allowed a small Jewish minority to become militiamen,
teachers and foremen—positions that would not have been possible under Polish rule. Poles mistakenly inferred that Jews were
collaborators and Bolsheviks and therefore enemies of Poland, un-
warranted assumptions that existed throughout and after the war.
Reality was much more differentiated because as the Soviets entered Poland, the Ukrainian and Byelorussian minorities and the
Poles initially perceived the Soviets as liberators.[5] Those who welcomed them were soon disabused of Soviet benign intentions as
they deported or killed the Polish military, political and social
elites. After escaping from the German occupied west, Jews, some
of whom possessed first hand knowledge of Nazi atrocities, recognized that the Soviets were the lesser evil. Poles found it expedient to stigmatize Jews rather than to recognize their own naïveté.
Subsequently, when the German–Soviet war commenced in June
1941, non-Jewish Poles experienced the German army as "liberators." Although contemptuous of Slavic peoples, Germans knew
how to exploit local tensions and feral instincts.

The endemic anti-Semitism in prewar Poland and the Germans'
ability to channel that hostility enabled them to find Poles willing to murder Jews during the early phase of the Shoah. They exploited Polish anger further by forcing Jews to hang Poles as a
deterrent to joining the resistance. One of the most barbarous epi-
sodes occurred on June 10, 1941 in the town of Jedwabne, formerly
held by the Soviets under the 1939 pact but now occupied by the
Germans. Having received tacit approval from their new masters,
motivated by greed and their hatred for the "killers of Christ," half
of the Christian adult male population, with their wives and children's encouragement, participated in the murder and mutilation

of 1600 Jews of their town. In the carnival of death that followed, men, women and children were hacked to death with knives, nail-studded clubs and axes: the rest were rounded up, humiliated, beaten and locked into a barn that was then torched.

It was commonly believed that the massacre was the work of the German Gestapo until the 2000 Polish language publication of *Neighbors: The Destruction of the Jewish Community in Jedwabne, Poland* by the historian Jan T. Gross. By drawing upon primarily Polish Gentile sources, Gross has convincingly refuted this mis-perception. While a few Germans stood by taking pictures, Poles were the sole perpetrators of this atrocity. The book unleashed a firestorm of heated debate in Poland where it was first pub-lished, and an angry exchange in literary journals in America and Britain. Although educated Poles have largely accepted his con-clusions, including the then President, Aleksander Kwasniewski, the book's revelations unleashed primitive responses. As if to jus-tify the murders, some apologists asserted that all the Jews killed were Communists or believed to be Communists. Based on the testimony in post-war Stalinist courts of survivors and peasants in nearby villages, Gross, however, demolishes the widely held assumption that Jews were Stalinist collaborators. With four bio-graphical profiles, Gross elucidates how those who were accused of murdering Jews worked for the Stalinists for twenty months be-fore serving the Germans. They thought it expedient to realign their worldview to make the transition to working with the Soviet apparatchiks after the war seamless. He also posits that these in-dividuals were most likely to become allies of the Party and work for the Soviets later as part of the police or security apparatus. He concludes that "*anti-Semites rather than Jews were instrumen-tal in establishing the Communist regime after the war*" and that they were the "indigenous lumpenproletariat...who served the so-cial backbone of Stalinism in Poland." Yet right-wing xenophobic Polish spokesmen, including the authors of *One Hundred Lies of [Jan] Gross*, believed that the Polish-born Gross, who immigrat-ed to America 1968, had besmirched the honour of the country. Similarly, the former President, Lech Walesa reviled Gross as "a mediocre writer...a Jew who tries to make money." In Jedwabne today, there are two monuments that commemorate the war. One refers to the sixteen hundred Jews killed by Nazis but even more revealing, the other, erected in post-1989 Poland, pays tribute to one hundred and eighty people who were murdered between 1939 and 1956 by the security police of the Nazis and the Communists. No effort has been made to claim responsibility for what took place in July 1941. Despite the willingness of the intelligentsia to recognize that Jewish history should be incorporated into the Polish narrative, the ghost of anti-Semitism that was endemic in pre-war Poland, partly encouraged and sanctioned by the Catholic Church, appears to still hover over the country.*

Poles prided themselves on their refusal to collaborate with Germans. They recall that five thousand of their numbers were honoured as Righteous Gentiles and that pogroms happened elsewhere, in Russia and the Baltic Republics, but not in Poland. Those who acknowledged that pogroms did occur argue that they were the work of a small minority. Yet these comforting perceptions do not always square with the evidence. Relatively few Poles (or Ukrainians) came to the assistance of fleeing Jews when the SS was persecuting them. Either they were frightened bystanders or active collaborators. True, the price for assisting a Jew, particularly in Poland, was steep: the protector risked death for not only himself, but also his family. Still, thousands of Poles risked and incurred death by joining an underground resistance group. Those Poles, who were later praised as Righteous Gentiles because they offered assistance to desperate Jews during the war, became themselves victims of disgraceful treatment meted out by other Poles. For years these courageous men and women feared being exposed to their countrymen as "Jew lovers"; some had to flee their homeland while others who remained became potential targets for robbery, given the widespread belief that Jews had wealth and thus their protectors had acquired some of it. Individuals who protected Jews were held in contempt and socially ostracized by the vast majority of Gentile Poles. A family that sheltered seven Jews in Jedwabne feared their neighbours more than the Germans. They were hounded after the war—the wife, severely beaten—forcing them to move from place to place before emigrating to America.

---

* One encouraging sign, however, is that the 2009 publication of the powerful drama, *Our Class*, by Tadeusz Slbodzianek, based on what occurred at Jedwabne, a play that has been staged in Poland, Israel, Ireland, England and Toronto, received in 2010 the NIKE Literary Award, one of the most prestigious Polish literary awards, as the best book of the year.

Gross insightfully suggests that this hatred stemmed from guilt. Helpful Poles were "embarrassing witnesses to crimes that had been committed against Jews. They could point to the illicit material benefits that many continued to enjoy as a result of these crimes."[6]

Although anti-Semitism trafficked through Polish society, the situation on the ground was often more complicated than what is recounted. There were anti-Semites who deplored the Nazis' barbarous treatment of the Jews, of whom ninety percent were murdered during the war. Anti-Semites joined underground organizations for the express purpose of assisting Jews. By 1942 the Zegota organization was providing Jews with false documents and financially supporting a few thousand families in hiding. Some Jews were hidden inside homes or, if they could pass as Aryan, were schooled in their new identity as Roman Catholics. An estimated forty thousand Jews were assisted in this way. Some religious orders took in children and the priests and nuns paid the highest price if they were caught. The Home Army executed Poles who informed on or blackmailed Jews. The vast majority of these Polish Gentiles who rescued an estimated 160,000 to 240,000 Jews were anti-Semites.[7] Despite their theological hostility toward the "Christ-killers," and that Jews spoke Yiddish, which was reminiscent of the Nazis' language, these Polish Catholics at least retained their humanity.

These Poles did not represent the majority. A vivid eyewitness account from a respected local physician related how Polish crowds impassively watched as Jews were rounded up and shot. Worse, peasants joined in on the "Jew-hunts" because

> a psychosis took hold of them and they emulate the Germans in that they don't see a human being in Jews, only some pernicious animal, that has to be destroyed by all means, like dogs sick with rabies, or rats.[8]

On a larger scale, the Poles offered nothing to help the Warsaw ghetto uprising in the spring of 1943. Worse was the fate of those few who managed to escape through the sewers of Warsaw to join the Polish underground Home Army: almost without exception they were killed by Poles. When the Jews were not recognized as human beings, the plainsong of horror and depravity became permissible. At the same time, the courage of those who attempted to rescue Jews in a country that experienced the most brutal treatment in Nazi-occupied Europe should be recognized.

In the immediate post-war era, the two hundred thousand Polish Jews (three and one half million perished), who survived the Shoah, faced malicious anti-Semitism when the Communist Party extended its power over Poland. Besides confronting hostility in the workplace and when they sought to reclaim plundered property, they endured the resurgence of pogroms, the worst being in the city of Kielce where the blood libel charge surfaced once more. An eleven-year-old Christian boy disappeared from his home, Unbeknownst to his parents, he had gone to relatives in a nearby village for a few days. Upon his return, he informed his family that he had been kidnapped by Jews and held in a cellar where there were fifteen murdered children. As the news of this canard spread, a large mob proceeded to murder Jews, some of them survivors of the Nazi death camps. When the carnage ended, over forty were dead and more than eighty injured. With the exception of one prominent bishop, who was rebuked by his colleagues, the Catholic Church refused to condemn anti-Semitism and the blood libel. At the parish priest level, some asserted that Jews deserved divine punishment for their role in the crucifixion of Christ. Church leaders believed that the Jews were the authors of their own misfortune as they held powerful positions, particularly in the Security Police, in the abhorred Communist government. They were unwilling to condemn the murder of fifteen hundred Polish Jews or inform the population that the blood libel was a fabrication. Indeed, seven hundred years after Pope Innocent IV had declared that accusations of ritual murder against Jews were fraudulent, Stefan Wyszynski, a future bishop of Lublin asserted that the "matter of blood was not settled."[9]

Most sectors of the population believed that the Jews were vampires or Communists and responsible for Polish subjugation. The implication was that they deserved their fate. Yet visceral, post-war anti-Semitism predated any Communist attempts to take power in Poland. When communism was imposed from Moscow, there were Jews in the Polish administration, but their status was always precarious; indeed, it turned when Stalin launched his own anti-cosmopolitan campaign against Jews.[10] In a later monograph, Gross argues that traumatized survivors represented a shameful reproach to the many Poles who colluded with the Nazis through their betrayal and denunciation, their theft and extortion of Jewish property and in their murder of Jews. Poles feared Jews not because of what the latter had inflicted upon them, but vice versa. Their spectral-like appearance after the war startled their former neighbours: "'So'—followed by their first name...you are still alive?'" reminding them that Poles had been perpetrators and not the undisputed victims or resistance heroes they wanted to believe they were. The Jewish survivors aroused fear "that they might have to account for themselves," as perpetrators or bystanders who subsequently acquired Jewish property. They could have addressed that fear by mourning their Jewish neighbours' deaths. Their failure to undertake this form of redress meant that their shame would only be expiated if the Jews were "gotten rid of for good."[11] Another interpretation is that German behaviour during the Holocaust emboldened Poles to act on desires that they had previously held in check. Regardless, the silence in the post-war era around the Holocaust and ethnic cleansing (replicated less violently in 1957 and 1968 when the Jews, under the cover of anti-Zionism were driven out of Poland) is symptomatic of the difficulty that the over twenty thousand Jews and the Gentiles have encountered with regard to entering into a meaningful dialogue about reconciliation.

That said, Poles suffered a massive loss of life during the war. Dismembered by the Nazis and the Soviets, Poland saw the decapitation of its elites—the intelligentsia, clergy and military. In March 1940 Stalin ordered the murder of twenty-two thousand Polish citizens including over four thousand Polish officers shot in the head and buried in a mass grave in the Katyn forest. When the grave was discovered by Germans in 1943, the Soviets denied any involvement claiming that the executions were the work of the Germans. It was not until 1990 that President Mikhail Gorbachev acknowledged Soviet responsibility for this war crime. In 1992 Russian President Boris Yeltsin gave copies of the Politburo decision to Polish President, Lech Walesa. Both Churchill and Roosevelt had been complicit in this crime; when apprised of the killings at Katyn, they did everything possible to ensure that these mass murders were not made public lest it strain their alliance with Stalin. Although there has been some backsliding in Russian media by placing the blame on the Nazis, in April 2010, Prime Minister Putin and his counterpart Donald Tusk attended a memorial to honour the twenty-two thousand individuals who perished at Katyn.

Similarly, Hitler used the war as a pretext to exterminate civilian Poles and Jews. In 1939 he linked the fate of the Poles to the Jews: "the *volkisch* state must...take the decision either to seal off these racially alien elements in order not again to allow the blood of our people to be debased," or they must be transferred and make that land "available to our people's comrades." According to Goebbels, Hitler felt that the Poles were more "animal than human." In the fall of 1939, sixty-five thousand Poles and Jews were killed in Poland's German sector. For every German casualty at the hands of Poles, at least fifty Polish civilians were executed. In the fall of 1939, tens of thousands of educated Poles were killed. In the summer of 1940 on Hitler's orders, thirty-five hundred Polish intellectuals and three thousand professional criminals were shot in a forest outside Warsaw.[12] Large numbers of Poles not murdered were forcibly driven from their land. In order to make room for ethnic Germans, who were to be repatriated from Eastern Europe, Poles were either abducted for slave labour in the Reich or herded out of the newly incorporated territories into ghettoes in a fractured Poland called the General Government. In response, urged by Moscow Radio, the Polish Home Army staged a rebellion in August 1944 in Warsaw to coincide with the advancing Soviet troops. In the subsequent uprising over a quarter of a million Polish fighters and civilians were massacred, sent to concentration camps or to Germany as forced labourers, while the Soviet army that had steamrolled across Eastern Europe stopped at the eastern suburbs of Warsaw and did not intervene. As Stalin would only be satisfied with a puppet government, he allowed Hitler's forces to carry out the heinous deeds. By the end of the war, over two million ethnic Poles, along with 500,000 Ukrainians and Byelorussians living in Poland, were executed or perished in concentration or death camps.

"The Darkness Enveloped Us"*

U nder cover of war, Hitler seized his opportunity to exterminate the Jews. The Germans herded Jews from western Poland into ghettos where starvation, humiliation and the threat of death loomed as daily threats. Deportations to the new hermetically sealed reservation in the Lublin region in eastern Poland were so stringent that the Jews were not allowed to take with them food, extra underwear or even coats; often the frostbitten toes and fingers of survivors had to be amputated. Surrounded by barbed wire and Nazi guards, home became "a vast concentration camp, with congestion, stench, poverty, disease, and chaos unparalleled on earth."[13] The drive to populate the ghettos halted briefly as Nazi paladins considered sending all European Jews to a tropical island off the coast of Africa after the defeat of France, but the plan collapsed when Britain remained undefeated. Transport by trainloads resumed and thousands were sent to the ghettoes—euphemistically termed "Jewish residential districts" by the Germans—in Lodz and Warsaw, the two largest among the four hundred created in German-occupied Europe. The purpose was to deliver as many of the "rabble" to their death or, as explicitly acknowledged by Himmler, to conditions where "the plague will creep in and they'll croak."[14] In addition to random killings, their debilitation, through starvation and infestation by lice that rendered them susceptible to typhus, decimated the Jews. Amid this devastation, one problem for the Nazis and public health physicians was how to limit the disease to the ghetto. Physicians revealed the extent to which the medieval stereotype of the Jew persisted: because he disregarded cleanliness, the Jew was a plague carrier. Their fear of it spreading led to the decision to seal the Warsaw ghetto and sever its inhabitants contact with the outside world. As Jews were deprived of any economic opportunity to earn a living, and with the influx of new refugees, conditions worsened and the fears of the physicians became a self-serving prophesy as a massive outbreak of disease occurred. Even the occasional doctor, who did not share Nazi ideology, supported the execution of individuals caught outside the wall for fear of the Jew as a disease carrier. Quarantine surfaced as the best guarantee of preventing the spread of disease, at least with increased food, soap and coal

---

* Eli Wiesel

for the ghetto. The overwhelming majority rejected this proposition believing that Germans could only be protected from the Jewish virus if Jews were eliminated. Although physicians were not directly responsible for the decision to ratchet up the suppression, they contributed to that decision. Their views were not essentially different from those of Hitler who had long argued that Jews were vermin.[15] Minimal rations killed many while Hitler's decision in June 1941 to invade the Soviet Union sealed the fate for Jews, gradually allowing for their removal to vans with gas facilities, or death camps and the eventual liquidation of the ghettos. The mass expulsions, death by hunger and disease, and random killings would yield their systematic extermination.

Himmler and Heydrich assembled the Einsatzgruppen, the mobile killing squads that consisted primarily of fanatical members of the security services and the SS. In order to prepare his men for their "moral duty," Himmler relied on the standard SS indoctrination which denied the victims any shred of humanity. Jews were but "a mere approximation to humanity, with humanoid facial features—yet mentally and spiritually of a lower order than any animal" subhuman because they possessed "the nameless urge to destroy." The Einsatzgruppen filled trenches, ravines and pits in Russia, the Ukraine, Byelorussia and the Baltic states, with the naked bodies of more than 1.3 million Jews, many of them elderly men and women and children. The most notorious crime of these murderous squads was the June 1941 massacre of over thirty-three thousand Jews in two days in a ravine at Babi Yar, outside Kiev, in part inspired by the decision of the NKVD to blow-up their own headquarters in Kiev after the Germans occupied the city.* Before they were pitilessly annihilated, the victims were robbed, often tortured and women in particular, subjected to the humiliation of parading naked before their executioners and raped despite all the propaganda about the dangers of miscegenation. When they were not shooting Jews at close range, they executed thousands of alleged partisans, gypsies and Polish intellectuals.

---

*   A few weeks later, the NKVD repeated this act in Odessa, killing almost ninety Romanian military and civilian personnel. The Romanians, the only non-German country to occupy a Soviet city and the region around it, took revenge on the Jews by murdering 220,000 Jews en route to ghettos or concentration camps overseen by the Romanian state. Charles King, *Odessa: Genius and Death in a City of Dreams* (New York: W.W. Norton & Company, 2011), 202–203.

Byelorussia cleansed the entire intelligentsia class, many of whom were Jews, from its population.

Older members of the lower middle class supplemented the killing squads, the so-called German "police battalions." With little ideological predisposition, they participated in the shootings of at least thirty-eight thousand Jews and in ghetto clearing operations that deported some forty-five thousand more to the death camps at Treblinka. Motivated by a plethora of reasons—peer pressure, the brutalization of war, the impulse to revenge German war causalities, deference to authority and anti-Semitism—most participated in the killings even when they were given the option to be excused from these duties. Fear that their careers as police officers would be jeopardized, that their colleagues would stigmatize them as cowardly, and that their actions were sanctioned by the authorities were powerful incentives for them to perform their distasteful jobs. But no individual was sanctioned for not participating in what was a voluntary activity. After some initial hesitation, the routine killing of defenceless Jews brutalized the killers. No one gave the order to hurl a child against a wall; sadists did it because they enjoyed doing it.[16] Since Germany was at war, they could delude themselves that Germany was a beleaguered country surrounded by a sea of enemies backed by international Jewry.

One particularly insidious feature about the Nazi genocidal machine was how it successfully co-opted thousands of Slavic people, whom they actually despised, to expedite their crimes. Support for the Germans from local contingents, particularly Lithuanians and Ukrainians, motivated by a hatred of Bolshevism and by the Judeophobic belief that Jews were the "shedders of blood of Christian children," melded the ingredients for systematic mass murder. In Lithuania alone, between one-half and two-thirds of its Jews, about 140,000, were murdered by indigenous Lithuanian forces.[17] Even for those who indifferently stood by, there is little evidence that their passivity bred internal conflict. Their collusion abetted the unremitting remorselessness with which the Nazi genocide was directed against the Jews. From 1941 the Shoah, in the words of one historian, "proceded year after year, village by village, town after town, seeking and destroying like some hideous science-fiction monster."[18]

This monster was able to wreak its savagery because Hitler had melded Jews with the Soviet enemy who were "bestial" and "the scourge of mankind." Jews were responsible for turning Russia into "a plague centre," and therefore both must be excised from Europe.[19] The ideology of blood purity dictated that the war on the Eastern Front would be one of annihilation: "We will recuperate the good blood, which we can make use of, and incorporate it among us, [but with Jewish and Slavic blood], gentlemen—you may call this cruel, but nature is cruel—we will destroy this blood."[20] Shortly before his death, Hitler maintained that the extermination of the Jewish "poisoners" should take priority over all else.

Frontline soldiers were lashed by severe wartime conditions that ranged from extreme weather to unremitting political indoctrination and a system of harsh discipline that resulted in over thirteen thousand executions. As a result, they fully absorbed the Nazi hatred toward the "subhuman' enemy."[21] Based on a representative sample, their letters reveal the extent to which Hitler's apocalyptic either-or diatribes against a titanic foe in *Mein Kampf* and later public speeches were internalized. One soldier described the struggle with the Soviet Union as the "greatest battle of the spirit ever experienced by humanity...waged for the existence or downfall of Western man and the highest values which a people consciously carry on its shield." Some soldiers' perceptions of this enemy resembled the caricatured version of the Jews paraded in Streicher's scurrilous *Der Stürmer.* Indeed, copies of the tabloid appeared on the front to the delight of some of the soldiers. According to a *New York Times* report as early as 1936, Streicher urged Germans to "go to the bloody path" and exterminate the Jews.[22] Reading its pages in the light of their experiences only reinforced their determination, in the words of another soldier, to "liberate the world from this plague...and not return until we have uprooted all evil and destroyed the centre of the Jewish–Bolshevik 'world of do-gooders.'" [23]

For most of their lives, these young men had been marinated in the vile propaganda churned out by Hitler, Streicher and Goebbels. As soldiers they waged war with unprecedented ferocity on the Eastern Front, believing that gratuitous torture, mutilation and genocide were justifiable. Their demonization of the enemy is also evidence of their distorted perception of reality and the extent to which they reshaped themselves to accommodate their Führer's maniacal hatred. The fanaticism they exhibited in their letters and actions—among other crimes they participated in the murder of over three million Soviet POWs in open pens by starvation, exposure or disease—are grim reminders of the large shadow that Hitler's racist dementia cast in the war of "annihilation."

Under that spectre of evil resided the industrialized mass killing. Rudolf Höss, the psychopathic commandant of Auschwitz, boasted at his post-war trial that his bailiwick was "the greatest institution for human annihilation." His bravado exemplified the extremity of what Hannah Arendt labelled radical evil. She understood that what distinguished the violence of a totalitarian state was not just the number of people killed but the motivation and methods of the perpetrators. Their goal was to destroy the humanity of and any residue of free will in the prisoners—to make human beings truly superfluous—before annihilating them. As Auschwitz survivor, Primo Levi, incisively stated, the German purpose was "to annihilate us first as men in order to kill us more slowly afterwards." Unlike the Gulag in which the Soviet apparatchiks made some effort to ensure that the zeks made an economic contribution to the war effort, the Nazis admitted their death camps served no utilitarian interest and, to their own peril, disregarded the expertise that the Jews could have provided them. Even in the vast majority of the camps that housed, at their peak, nearly eight million POWs and foreign labourers, many of them dragooned when their labour was deemed essential to the war effort; tens of thousands were driven to a slow death through maltreatment, starvation and disease. The Nazis could not bring themselves to preserve life by improving the deteriorating working and living conditions even at a time when the outcome of the war was still in doubt. They became fixated on changing human nature itself; the camps became laboratories using "scientific" standards to obliterate every trace of human dignity, even the recognition that fellow beings were human beings. In one sense, the administrators and guards were caught in the same net of "lunacy and unreality" as those they exterminated. In another sense, the Nazi effort to erase the humanity of its inmates failed. In his survey of the literature of camp survivors in both the Nazi and Soviet camps, Tzvetan Todorov documents that quiet acts of compassion and mutual assistance made it possible for individuals to survive.[24]

The extermination camp emerged because gas chambers eliminated the need to watch men, women and children die. The perpetrators were not even required to dispose of the bodies.

That awful task was left to a group of Jews who were given a temporary reprieve to sort out the bodies, strip them of gold fillings and cut the women's hair prior to incinerating them. Unlike the camps in Germany and Austria, as dreadful as they were, the infamous death camps in the east primarily served to facilitate the Final Solution through immediate liquidation of entire, mainly Jewish families. Belsen, Sobibor and Treblinka were exclusively death camps where one million five hundred thousand Jews died but the most infamous, Auschwitz–Birkenau operated both as extermination centre and a slave labour camp. Although significant sites of extermination, the number of victims in these killing machines was fewer than those who died elsewhere. Over one-half of the victims who perished, both Jews and non-Jews, were shot in the east—Poland, the Baltic Republics and the Soviet Union, especially in the Ukraine and Byelorussia—or died from maltreatment in prison camps.[25]

The German-born political philosopher, Eric Voegelin, who had diagnosed the Nazis in the 1930s as having a satanic force with a fanatical ideology escaped from Austria four months after the *Anschluss*. In his post-war analysis of National Socialism, Voegelin recognized that the regime, its leader, a "grotesque marginal figure," was impervious to reason and surrounded by non-entities. It therefore depended on the "evil rabble" to maintain it in power. Infected with a "spiritual sickness," that rabble primarily consisted of the morally defective elites in the churches, civil service and in the universities who became principal players and beneficiaries of this criminal regime. But the "evil rabble" also applied to "the simple man," who had lost his decency, "when disorder arises somewhere and the society is no longer holding together."[26]

Since the line between the elites and the less sophisticated frequently blurred, Voegelin's insights are applicable to the perpetrators of mass killing. Some members of the Einsatzgruppen dealt with their guilt by indulging in binge drinking, sex in brothels and—with impunity—in illicit sex with racial aliens while others became disgruntled. Paul Blodel, who presided over the notorious massacres at Babi Yar, did not possess the ideological certainty to sustain him but instead showed signs of inner turmoil. A man of weak nature, he compensated for his lack of conviction by indulging in an orgy of killing in order to gain acceptance, and by coping with his guilt with excessive alcohol. When he later came to trial in

1951, he deployed the lamest of defences—his job had been mentally taxing, the numbers he was accused of killing were too high, he had been too ill in hospital to have carried out these offences—that could not save him from being executed.[27] The vast majority remained fanatical true believers, convinced of the righteousness of their deeds—a legitimate act of German self-defence against the scourge of Bolshevism—or attempted to project culpability onto the Poles. Not a single SS officer arrested after the war demonstrated any remorse. Nor did those who evaded arrest; for reasons of self-protection, some publicly denounced the Nazi regime but they never wavered in their inner convictions.[28] If one of them had undergone a post-war emotional collapse, it would have been more related to an unsettling trauma, one that is vividly captured in a *Twilight Zone* episode, "Death's-Head Revisited." A swaggering defiantly unrepentant SS captain returns years later to Dachau to reminisce about how he tortured and killed prisoners. There he is confronted by the ghost of one of those he killed, is tried by other ghosts, and for his crimes experiences emotionally the pain he inflicted upon them. Driven insane, the authorities are mystified by the cause. Perhaps only in drama can such a collision occur between a psychopath and his victims.[*]

Given their mutual admiration, it should not be a surprise that Stalin imbibed the spirit of his doppelganger during the early days of the Cold War. He seemed determined to expedite, in his own way, the programme that Hitler had not fully accomplished. Rather than repeating the Nazi form of a biological racism to eliminate a people with "poisoned" blood, Stalin took a different approach to address the alleged disloyalty of "rootless cosmopolitans." He reached back into the Russian past to revive and fan the atavistic fear of Jews sucking the blood out of Gentiles. In 1953 he encouraged in Georgia a re-enactment of a ritual that he had heard about as a child. The secret police permitted a woman to run through

---

[*]   Kurt Gerstein might be considered an exception. As an expert on prussic acid, he visited Belzec and witnessed the gassing of prisoners, and was horrified. On the train back to Berlin, he met a Swiss diplomat and provided him with full details of the operation. But Gerstein was not a typical SS officer given that he had joined the elite group to uncover its dark secrets after he discovered that a family member had become a victim of the euthanasia programme. After the war, the French moved him to a Paris prison as a suspected war criminal where in a distraught state, he hanged himself.

the streets of Tbilisi screaming that Jews had been caught murdering Christian children so that their blood could be drained and used for making matzo.[29] By this time, several Jews had already been arrested, tortured and executed; fifteen of the most prominent were subjected to a show trial in the so-called Doctors' Plot in the summer of 1952.* What might have been the most tragic case of ethnic cleansing and the murder of Soviet Jews on a colossal scale was only aborted by the death of Stalin in March 1953.

In the 2000 film *Shadow of a Vampire*, E. Elias Merhige re-imagines the creation of F. W. Murnau's *Nosferatu*. But his fictional Murnau (John Malkovich) is willing to enter into a Faustian bargain with a vampire (Willem Dafoe) to play the actor Max Schreck with the proviso that the undead creature be able to feast on the self-sacrificing Greta (Catherine McCormack). When the rat-faced vampire exceeds the arrangement, Murnau continues to film in the pursuit of his artistic vision oblivious to the carnage around him. When he says "if it's not in the frame, it doesn't exist," Murnau is emblematic of Hitler, Lenin and Stalin. Each regarded people as putty to be moulded into the society he envisioned and would sacrifice anyone from that frame who threatened his political vision. It is no coincidence that Lenin considered film the ultimate art form with which to mobilize the masses, Stalin vetted every film, and Hitler saw himself as an artist in which his canvas was the German people. If the artist-as-director that mirrored the vampire in *Shadow of a Vampire* lives on in celluloid, the dictators in real life—to continue with the vampire metaphor—were ultimately staked in the heart. In their different ways, the Soviet and the Nazi regimes collapsed. Germany decided that a moral reckoning was needed if it was to be integrated into the international community.

In contrast to post-communist Russia, beginning in the late 1960s German Chancellor Konrad Adenauer insisted that a prerequisite for a healthy German democracy depended upon Nazism being remembered rather than forgotten. German states subsequently

---

* A fictional rendering of this wave of terror set in Leningrad in 1952 and how it affected a hospital paediatrician and his family—the intangible apprehension they experienced before the dreaded late-night knock on the door, his conveyor belt interrogation and his arduous journey to the Gulag—is powerfully portrayed in Helen Dunmore's 2010 *The Betrayal* (Penguin Books).

mandated the teaching of the history of the Third Reich, including the extermination of the Jews, be a requirement for all students. More important in erasing the collective amnesia of the 1950s was the 1979 German screening of an American television mini-series *Holocaust* that was watched by an estimated twenty million viewers—over half the adult population. At Bayreuth, Wieland Wagner in the 1950s, and until his death in 1966, made every effort to strip away the iconography that had been associated with the Third Reich by presenting leaner productions. After the creation of the Federal Republic of Germany in 1990, Germany accelerated the process to face the evil of its past. Germans established memorials, among them former concentration camps to commemorate the victims, staged exhibitions and plays, and made films* with the intention of integrating the horrors of the past into the collective everyday present. Despite its prohibition in the constitution, the courts built up a body of law that justified the retroactive punishment for offences committed in the Nazi era and during the GDR (East Germany) provided it was done through regular courts and respected the rule of law. To ignore these heinous transgressions would be, in the words of the novelist and law professor, Bernhard Schlink, to "violate the commonly held conviction of all people concerning the worth and dignity of human beings."[30] Despite its different attitude toward retroactive justice, Americans generally shared these assumptions. After 9/11, however, ideology trumped evidence and due process was marginalized. Whether a fundamental shift has occurred since 2008 continues to be part of the ongoing discourse, but a few tentative reflections can be ventured.

---

* In 1946 Germans began exploring its country's guilt for Nazi war crimes with *The Murderers Are Among Us*. In this tradition, the 1990 *Nasty Girl* is a standout. Based on the life of Anja Rosmus who eventually decamped to America, the film charts her trajectory from school girl to adulthood. She becomes obsessed with finding out the truth about what occurred in her hometown during the Nazi era, only to incur the hostility of her older neighbours.

The Gothic Impulse
During the Obama Era

I like temperate and moderate natures
—"Of Moderation"
Montaigne

The consequences of National Socialism and Stalinism during World War II posed an existential threat to liberal democracies. The long-term effects of the age of terrorism and misguided wars reveal more hopeful signs—a fading of the Gothic impulse on security issues following the 2008 presidential election of Barack Obama. This did not signify that the world was a less dangerous place or that Obama shied away from ordering aggressive actions against American enemies. His "no drama" demeanour, however, displayed greater subtlety and deliberation in weighing the options and was less prone to demonization and adventurism.[*]

---

[*] In his eloquent Nobel Peace acceptance speech in December 2009, Obama offered insights into his nuanced political philosophy, among them a defence of the just war that includes both national self-defence and humanitarian assistance to others, ideas that subsequently guided his actions. Although he paid respect to the power of non-violence—"there's nothing weak—nothing passive—nothing naive—in the creed and lives of Gandhi and King," he also recognized that "evil does exist in the world. A non-violent movement could not have halted Hitler's armies. Negotiations cannot convince al Qaeda's leaders to lay down their arms." As a result, "force may be sometimes necessary...[given] the imperfections of man and the limits of reason." And although

Obama demonstrated a greater respect for Muslims in the wider world. In his Cairo speech, he used Arab phrases and quotations from the Quran in providing a counter-narrative to the familiar refrain that the West was waging a relentless war on Islam. While encouraging the forces of liberation during the 2011 Arab Spring, he abandoned the swagger of the previous administration by not threatening an Iraq-style intervention in Libya. His cautious back-seat approach of limiting U.S. involvement in the NATO air raids contributed to the demise of the megalomaniac Muammar Gaddafi while earning praise from the Libyans. He implemented a bilateral agreement signed in 2008 by his predecessor by withdrawing troops from Iraq, a decision that respected Iraqi sovereignty even though the grim sectarian hatred continued.

In this spirit of pragmatism, Obama adopted a more nuanced strategic refocus in South Asia. The results, however, have been mixed in delivering peace and security to the region. Abandoning the rhetoric of waging a war on terror and the vehemence of the moral posturing, Obama focused instead on eliminating al-Qaeda and its allies. After identifying the Afghan–Pakistan frontier area as the epicentre of the most serious terrorist threats to the international community and in an effort to keep "boots off the ground," Obama adopted a lethal counterterrorism strategy for dismantling this organization. It relied on high-tech intelligence gathering followed by commando raids and the dramatic increase in the number of pitiless drone missile strikes into the tribal areas of Pakistan (as well as deploying them against al-Qaeda affiliates in Yemen and Somalia). As a result, nearly two thousand militants were killed and, according to a cache of documents found in bin Laden's compound, the strategy seemed to be achieving its goal; the al-Qaeda leader acknowledged that the drone was "the only weapon that [was] hurting us." But despite their precision and the reduction of collateral damage, these strikes also killed civilians, and an estimated one thousand since 2004, and did not prevent further suicide attacks or deter jihadist recruitment.[31] Yet, despite the twenty

---

acknowledging that as head of state he "reserves the right to act unilaterally if necessary to defend [his] nation," he is also convinced that adhering to "international standards, strengthens those who do, and isolates and weakens those who don't." The full text can be found at http://www.nobelprize.org/nobel_prizes/peace/laureates/2009/obama-lecture_en.html

billion dollars in aid that America provided for Pakistan in the last decade, and Obama's greater diplomatic pressure and deployment of civilian mentoring, a hapless civilian government was no match for the Pakistani army. The military and intelligence elites, and an increasingly angry public, contended that America's drone attacks, and the killing of bin Laden, violated Pakistan's sovereignty. As a result of the "trust deficit," they regarded the U.S. as a greater threat to the state than their ancient enemy India, sometimes forgetting that the country had more to fear from a jihadist insurgency within.

In Afghanistan, Obama deployed thirty thousand more troops to degrade the Taliban and set a deadline for withdrawal. He rightly recognized that a clear victory was not possible. President Karzai is locked into an increasingly acrimonious relationship with the American government at the highest diplomatic levels. His re-election was pockmarked with massive fraud and he showed no evidence of reining in the culture of corruption—Transparently International consistently rated Afghanistan as one of the most egregiously corrupt countries in the world. One effect of pumping money into the country has been that only a small percentage of international funds earmarked for agricultural projects to replace the eradicated poppy fields reach their intended destination.[32] Considered the chief perpetrator of civilian casualties and noted for its capacity for intimidation and striking terror, the Taliban alienated the Afghan population; their support for the organization remains at seven percent. Yet a BBC/ABC poll at the end of 2010 showed an increase in Afghan support for attacks on foreign troops and there is more support for a negotiated settlement, and who can blame them. Afghans are aware that eventually the Americans will leave and its government—it is most unlikely that Karzai will exert control over the whole country—cannot provide the necessary security to prevent suicide bombings, high profile attacks and assassinations of local and high-level officials. The insurgents' message—you cannot trust this government to protect you—is effective. But who will an alternative government include—the warlords and the narco-Mafias, the supporters of the former Amir, Mullah Omar? In view of the seemingly intractable difficulties—the historical weight of tribalism, theocracy and kleptocracy—the coalition goal of nation building has been abandoned. After a Sisyphean decade, the most that Obama can achieve with his commitment to maintain troops until 2014 is to prevent the re-establishment of terrorist sanctuaries

Long before Obama ordered a special operation team to assassinate him, Osama bin Laden had lost much of his sheen as a pious and romantic warrior in the developing world apart from Pakistan's tribal areas. It bears repeating that transnational jihadism represented a fringe element within jihadism because its ideology and tactics not only could never persuade the larger Muslim community; indeed its actions alienated them. Along with the different Taliban factions, whose interests at the time of writing may or may not be regional, they had killed thousands of Muslims in suicide attacks, roadside bombs and executions. Spokesmen who initially had supported al-Qaeda shifted and declared that its bombings in Muslim nations were illegitimate—between 2004 and 2009 eighty-five percent of its victims were Muslims—and that terrorism directed against civilians in the West was wrong. The closure of Abu Ghraib in 2006, an emblem of American contempt for Arabs and a recruiting poster for insurgency, and its reopening in 2009 under Iraqi control also contributed to the diminished appeal of al-Qaeda. Increasingly, Arabs recognized that it did not offer a positive vision of the future.

Osama bin Laden's death was announced May 1, 2011, sixty-six years to the day of Hitler's. Although security experts believed al-Qaeda no longer represented an indomitable global threat, bin Laden's demise did not mean the al-Qaeda franchises in sub-Sahara Africa would be incapable of wreaking havoc. Radicalized by American actions in the Middle East and South Asia, the low-tech amateurs and freelancers ferreted out soft targets. As the *9/11 Commission Report* correctly warned, not even the death of al-Qaeda leaders would end the menace of terrorism. The ideology does indeed retain a currency among a small minority in the Muslim world who remain committed to attacking American officials in the Middle East. Bin Laden's charisma and financial means, however, would no longer draw new recruits, nor would the tattered organization be able to conceal the fractious internal conflicts between, for example, Egyptian and the Arabian Peninsula terrorists. The defiance and opposition that bin Laden personified took a battering blow with his death. Terrorists did not die for the divisive Ayman al-Zawahiri (the current head) but for the autocratic bin Laden, to whom they swore absolute loyalty. He inspired

489

them by forsaking a life of easy comfort to fight the Soviet Union in Afghanistan and then took on America (until he retreated in the last years of his life to a comfortable safe house in a garrison town near the capital of Pakistan). Moreover, the Arab Spring captured the global imagination and shattered the founding rationale of al-Qaeda: that change could only come through violence.[33]

After September 11, the West hoped that Arab–Muslim countries would engage in an open dialogue about alternatives to Islamist radicalism. Instead, ossified dictatorships found it useful to keep alive the fears of extremism as a foil; they allowed it to persist and refused to countenance free elections and the separation of powers. Their reasoning was "better us than the devil of fanaticism." Yet these corrupt states with their crony capitalism fuelled extremism within a stagnant order and vicious suffocation of independent centralist parties. In the seismic-looking events of the Arab Spring, citizens took to the streets to topple autocrats throughout the region and wash clean its despotism. With dictators increasingly being toppled, there is potential for a civil society to grow that could midwife a democracy and the rule of law provided the security forces are defanged and diversity is permitted. A year later, a counter-revolutionary phase of entrenched forces eclipsed the initial bliss-to-be-alive euphoria. The mafia-like Assad family in Syria was willing to kill as many civilians as necessary and invoke a regional conflagration if they could cling to power. Throughout the region, the population's quest for dignity and economic growth has been stalled by tensions between secularists and Islamists. Given the particularities of each country and the complexities of the Islamist landscape, there was no assurance that the aspirations of those who risked (and lost) their lives would not be dashed by old religious, sectarian or clan conflicts. In Egypt with the military determined to maintain power, an Islamist was elected President; the illiberal Muslim Brotherhood won one-half of the seats in Parliament, and the ultra-conservative fundamentalist Salafist Party carried twenty-five percent. The latter, that rejects twenty-first century modernity, posed a threat to secular liberals (many of whom were the Facebook idealists who initiated the demonstrations against Mubarak) and to the Christian Coptic minority. By early 2012 over 100,000 Copts had left the country following the overthrow of Mubarak. Perhaps the greatest threat the Salafists presented was to the more pragmatic governing Muslim

Brotherhood by inciting, along with other fringe groups, violent anti-American demonstrations in an effort to destabilize post-Mubarak Egypt. They did not want the Brotherhood—who needed American money—to succeed. The fundamental conflict over how to define political Islam (that was replicated with variations in the other states that experienced the Arab Spring) was, however, obscured and misinterpreted by segments of the American media and prominent politicians who regarded the riots as expressions of Muslim intolerance and anti-Americanism, and evidence that Obama's rapprochement with the Islamic world had failed. This distortion mirrored the perception of Muslims who believed that a crudely amateurish, online anti-Islam trailer was sanctioned by the American government and evidence of its ongoing war with Islam.* A more thoughtful interpretation—that a profound philosophical conflict existed between the values of the Muslim community and American free speech absolutism—was rarely discussed in the American media. Yet the upside to this historical transformation was that issues like the humiliating treatment of women and the vile anti-Semitism in the Arab world, which had percolated underground in the *ancien régimes*, were openly being debated and challenged. Turkey, an economic powerhouse in the region, the most liberal and Westernized Islamic state—despite jailing dissident journalists—by encaging the military and being more receptive to pluralism, demonstrated that Islam and modernity could coexist. Turkey and not clerical Iran** could serve as a model for the region. How the West responded to the changing dynamics—refraining from equating Islamists with terrorists—would go a long way in determining the nature of Western–Middle Eastern relationships.

Ironically, bin Laden was killed not long after a million people flooded into Tahrir Square in Cairo. Men and women, religious and secular were prepared to die, not for a caliphate but for justice and dignity, a repudiation of his nihilist credo. If bin Ladenism did not

---

* The film only went viral after an Egyptian T.V. host with Salafist sympathies uploaded it from the Web and showed clips on his show realizing its inflammatory effects.

** This is not to suggest that Iran will not attempt to court Egypt and forge a new relationship given that Ali Khamenei, the current Supreme Leader in Iran, translated the works of Sayyid Qutb into Farsi.

constitute the existential threat of Nazism and the Soviet Union during the Cold War, it did share some of their more unsavoury features: anti-Semitism, illiberalism, the cult-like embrace of charismatic leaders and the insidious use of modern propaganda methods. Just as the West celebrated the collapse of Nazism and the Soviet Union, it can derive some comfort from the widely accepted belief that bin Laden's death has substantially weakened transnational jihadism. It is fitting that bin Laden's final resting place is in the Arabian Sea given that President Bush shortly after 9/11 predicted that bin Laden and al-Qaeda would be assigned to "history's unmarked grave of discarded lies."[34]

Unlike the Bush team which merely dismissed American and international law, Obama's administration attempted to balance the rule of law and due process with national security. The results have largely disappointed his base who believed that he has repudiated much of what he campaigned for in the 2008 election. To his credit, he prohibited torture, closed the so-called black sites, ended rendition as a means of outsourcing torture, released the formerly secret torture memos, and has made changes to the Freedom of Information Act that would allow the victims' experience to be publically recognized. Above all, he has refrained from using the politics of fear. Yet he reneged on his promise to close Guantánamo, even though it was the Senate that played the "fear card" by overwhelmingly voting to keep the prison open indefinitely and to block the transfer of its prisoners to American soil. He signed into law a security measure that would allow the military to detain indefinitely without trial terrorist suspects arrested on American soil. Most controversially, he approved the dramatic escalation of drone attacks provoking criticism that he was more interested in killing his enemies than capturing them. According to a *New York Times* report in late May 2012, Obama unilaterally ordered the targets for lethal force in drone attacks in Yemen, Somalia and Pakistan assisted only by aides and a group of security experts. He even authorized the killing of two American citizens in Yemen through a missile strike. They were both incendiary internet demagogues, and there is some evidence that Anwar al-Awlaki was involved in inciting would-be murderers in Britain and the U.S. While the president must defend American security—and sometimes that involves killing the enemy—by conducting a take-no-prisoner policy he risks losing the good will of the international community and besmirching a bedrock of the country's judicial system—that of due process. By failing to embrace transparency and accountability over the use of drones, he threatens to undermine America's democratic legitimacy.[35]

I f American realpolitik trumped the Gothic impulse in global security issues, the cacophony and hyper-partisanship in American domestic politics heightened its feverish temperature. A narrow, monolithic view of Islam festered in America that was in part inspired by the belief of certain hard-right commentators that Muslim hordes had weakened Europe to the threat that Nazis had posed to Europe in the 1940s. Popular among conservative pundits was a book by the Egyptian-born writer, Bat Ye'or, entitled *Eurabia: The Euro-Arabian Axis*, which outlined a conspiracy theory that a secret organization has "engineered Europe's irreversible transformation through hidden channels" into "a fundamentally anti-Christian, anti-Western and anti-Semitic...cultural appendage of the Arab Muslim world."[36] That such a hysterical reaction, which bears a striking resemblance to the *Protocols* could be taken seriously by Mark Steyn, (*America Alone: The End of the World as We Know It*) and by online authors—Pamela Geller of "Atlas Shrugs" and Robert Spencer of "Jihad Watch"—was testimony to the alarmist sentiments in America. With their nativist rhetoric,* these authors promoted the demographic error and fuelled fears that Muslims are endowed with a fertility gene which will allow them to "takeover" in the West. More disturbingly, they propagated the canard that all Muslims were ideological Islamists. *Globe and Mail* columnist, Doug Saunders wrote a powerful rebuttal to the popular delusions disseminated by the Muslim-bashing

---

* Although these alarmist conservatives were not responsible for the mass murder of primarily young people, among them Muslims, by the Norwegian, Anders Breivik, a "Christian" mirror to bin Laden, who believed that he was acting on behalf of Christian–Jewish Europe, he named them as well as Fox News, the *Wall Street Journal* and *Maclean's* magazine in his lengthy cut-and-paste manifesto as inspiration for his "war against the Islamisation of Europe." Anti-Muslim activists raised over seventeen million dollars from neo-conservative foundations to send DVD copies of *Obsession: Radical Islam's War* to twenty-eight million voters in swing states. The film content is an exact replication of Breivik's manifesto. His contribution was to append a violent conclusion.

crowd. His carefully presented, well-documented arguments, supported by both scholarly and intelligence sources, were in sharp contrast to, for instance, Mark Steyn's "sarcastically-driven political commentary" and incendiary rhetoric categorizing Islam as a "bloodthirsty faith." Saunders persuasively contended that devout Muslims, who immigrated to the West, did not become terrorists. These nihilists were "religious novices" who had joined peer groups for personal reasons. Indeed, Muslims were as patriotic as non-Muslims, shared universal values and defined themselves more by their national identity than by their religion.[37]

Fear of and hostility toward Muslims accelerated after Obama's 2008 presidential election. During his presidency, a substantial number of Americans denied his Presidential legitimacy—he was not born in America, he was a Muslim or that he was too sympathetic to Muslims—all expressions of sublimated racism. When these rumours were combined with a lack of awareness about Muslims, paranoia and demagoguery lurched toward the precincts of power. The Republican, Peter King, presided over a congressional hearing into the "home-grown radicalization" of American Muslims. His committee raised the spectre of a McCarthyite witch hunt against American Muslims by tarring an entire community—"an enemy living amongst us"—with guilt by association. .Republican presidential wannabe, Michelle Bachman, even alleged that the Muslim Brotherhood had infiltrated the Obama administration. The unspoken assumption that American Muslims were waging jihad by stealth clashed with the reality that Muslims provided the largest number of tips to the FBI tracking terror suspects. Although Muslims constituted less than one percent of the population and were more integrated into American society than in European countries, they were the victims of fourteen percent of religious discrimination cases involving employment and educational opportunities. Combining suspicion and histrionics, Americans increasingly rejected the building of new mosques despite the burning of them. A frenzied furor raged over the construction of a proposed Muslim community centre close to the site of the 9/11 attacks. No wonder that polls indicated that one third of Americans believed that all Muslims should carry identity cards. Public officials pandered to these fears when Republicans supported the ban on the building of mosques. The hostility that conservative activists directed toward Muslims was also extended to

Obama. According to one poll taken in August 2011, thirty-one percent of Americans and fifty-three percent of Republicans believed that Obama "sympathized with the goals of Islamic fundamentalists who want to impose Islamic law around the world."[38]

Following the election of Obama, the political culture became more bitterly polarized by rancid scorched-earth assaults. A large swathe of the take-no-prisoners style of talk radio and Fox News launched a jihad against liberals, Democrats and the centrist President Obama who was increasingly regarded as the anti-Christ.* They resorted to hyperbole and outrageous untruths, a phenomenon that might be labelled tabloid Gothic, which has resulted in the deterioration of political discourse. This stridency saturated the health care debate. Popular spokespersons for the hard right such as Sarah Palin demonized President Obama and conjured up the hallucinogenic spectre of "death panels" that will determine whether elderly people live or die.[39] The absurdity of this canard could only work on a people who have been conditioned to believe that, except during the prosecution of a war, the expansion of the national government in the lives of people threatened individual rights, even as they benefited from government Social Security and Medicare programmes. Or on a people who have surrendered to binary thinking—us and them, good and bad, black and white, civilization and barbarism. If Palin's outburst was born out of ignorance, the bombast practised by Newt Gingrich, a Republican Presidential candidate, was much more insidious because as a former history professor, he was not oblivious to the power of demagoguery. When he demonized Democrats as "secular socialists who represent a threat just as dangerous as Nazi Germany or the Soviet Union," he knew that his hyperventilation was inflating opponents into ideological enemies and singing the hymnal of the Tea Party constituency that has lobotomized American politics by insisting on constitutional and

---

* Vigorous partisanship has a long pedigree in American politics but the digital age, including the Internet, has enabled the media to saturate everyday life in ways previously inconceivable. Fox News has its liberal opinion-based counterpart in MSNBC, but critics contended that the latter is not as ideologically driven and as prone to misinform viewers as the former and that MSNBC adheres more to professional standards. Paul Starr, "Governing in the Age of Fox News," *Atlantic Monthly*, January/February, 2010; Brian Stelter, "Study: Some News Viewers were Misinformed, *New York Times*, December 17, 2010.

political purity, and by regarding any form of compromise as treason. Another candidate, Rick Santorum, turned a policy difference about religion and contraceptives into Armageddon by suggesting that the "crushing" of faith was comparable to the horrors of the guillotines during the French Revolution. When he analogized the 2012 presidential election with that of 1933, he was implying that the re-election of Obama would be cataclysmic, comparable to the Nazi takeover of Germany.

A more perceptive reminder of the power of history can be found in Stephen King's absorbing 2011 novel *11/22/63*. A high school teacher is given the opportunity to time travel back to the late 1950s and alter history. He starts with altering the private life of a particular family and ends in an effort to change the public life of America by preventing the Kennedy assassination. The protagonist discovers that history is inimical to change; those who try pay a high price, and if successful, the outcome may not be for the better. The novel's premise is based on the conceit that human effort to effect historical change will encounter tenacious resistance. The utopian experiments in the Soviet Union and Nazi Germany to change human nature failed miserably, in part because they repeated the worst features of their respective histories. More importantly, their creeds required their citizens to look past the humanity of the designated outcasts, who were regarded as impediments to the regimes' drive toward the purified paradise. After their unconditional defeat in April 1945, the Germans recognized that if a historical pattern was to be fundamentally altered, they had to repudiate every vestige of National Socialism. For the most part they have succeeded—a few neo-Nazis still perpetrate violent crimes—but fascism in diluted forms remains a viable political option in some European countries. In the Czech Republic, Slovakia and Hungary, right-wing political parties and journalists, who serve as "active promoters and practitioners," promulgate hatred and exclusion against the Roma. Consider as well the continuities from Tsarist Russia, the Soviet era to Putin, and from the early Cold War and the post 9/11 era; and contemporaneously—Obama's America, the Middle East and South Asia. One reason for continuing these autocratic or destructive historical threads rather than cutting or redirecting them may be that the monsters and the ghosts that King suggests "are real and within us, and sometimes they win." That is why the Gothic remains relevant. The uncanny may seem more pertinent to fiction, but King's insight transcends the imaginary world. The monsters from the Russian past lurked in the shadows during the Soviet experiment and contributed, along with an untenable "scientific" ideology, to its destruction. Blood as a prerequisite for citizenship in Germany has receded, but the ghost of racism hovers over Europe—at least thirty political parties are calling for a "pure European identity—and racism remains a volatile issue in America. Blood purity and the fear of miscegenation may have lost its potency, and a U.S. Senator's malicious allusion in the 1890s to a black male as "a fiend, a wild beast, seeking whom he may devour" would never be repeated publicly, but the perception of young black males as a menace to society—given their high incarceration rate—still percolates in the white collective psyche. Television and the blogosphere attest to the culture's demonization of the *other* and to psychic vampirism. When his adversaries turn Obama into "an alien, a Manchurian Candidate with a diabolical hidden agenda," the dark double is alive and palpable. The online image of Obama perched in the pantheon of evil, alongside Hitler and Stalin, is a powerful reminder of how historical ghosts and the dark spirit of the Gothic stalk current politics—and American life.[40]

Notes

Further Reading

Index

Endnotes

Preface

1   Lynne Viola, *The Unknown Gulag: The Lost Worlds of Stalin's Special Settlements* (Oxford: Oxford University Press, 2007), 1.

2   A fuller explanation of psychic vampirism is provided in *That Line of Darkness*, Vol. I, *The Shadow of Dracula and the Great War* (Kingston: Encompass Editions, 2011), 91.

3   J. Arch Getty, "Stalin as Prime Minister: power and the Politburo," in *Stalin: A New History*, ed. Sarah Davies and James Harris (Cambridge: Cambridge University Press, 2005), 105–06. Getty's title conveys the flavour of his argument that despite differences with Western governments, Stalin, in his consultation with senior officials, acted in a manner similar to a British Prime Minister (Margaret Thatcher) conferring with her ministers. Ian Kershaw, *Hitler 1889-1936: Hubris* (London: Penguin Books, 1998), 519.

4   Viola, *The Unknown Gulag*, 184–188; Richard Overy, *The Dictators: Hitler's Germany and Stalin's Russia* (London: Allen Lane/ Penguin Books, 2004), 173; Alex Danchev, *On Art And War And Terror* (Edinburgh: Edinburgh University Press, 2009), 4.

Introduction

1   Lynne Viola, *The Unknown Gulag: The Lost Worlds of Stalin's Special Settlements* (Oxford: Oxford University Press, 2007), 1.

2   A fuller explanation of psychic vampirism is provided in *That Line of Darkness*, Vol. I, *The Shadow of Dracula and the Great War* (Kingston: Encompass Editions, 2011), 91.

3   J. Arch Getty, "Stalin as Prime Minister: power and the Politburo," in *Stalin: A New History*, ed. Sarah Davies and James Harris (Cambridge: Cambridge University Press, 2005), 105–06. Getty's title conveys the flavour of his argument that despite differences with Western governments, Stalin, in his consultation with senior officials, acted in a manner similar to a British Prime Minister (Margaret Thatcher) conferring with her ministers. Ian Kershaw, *Hitler 1889-1936: Hubris* (London: Penguin Books, 1998), 519.

4   Viola, *The Unknown Gulag*, 184–188; Richard Overy, *The Dictators: Hitler's Germany and Stalin's Russia* (London: Allen Lane/ Penguin Books, 2004), 173; Alex Danchev, *On Art And War And Terror* (Edinburgh: Edinburgh University Press, 2009), 4.

5   David Livingstone Smith, *Less than Human: Why We Demean, Enslave, and Exterminate Others* (New York: St Martins Press, 2011), especially Chapters One and Four.

6   David Punter, *The Literature of Terror* Second Edition Vol. II (London: Longman, 1996), 197.

7   Punter, *The Literature of Terror*, 183–184; Livingstone Smith, *Less than Human*, 129–131; Overy, *The Dictators*, 265–348.

8   One exception is Alan Bullock, a biographer of Hitler who in an interview commented: "if *he* isn't evil, who is?" Ron Rosenbaum, *Explaining Hitler: The Search for the Origins of his Evil* (New York: Random House, 1998), 86. Michael Burleigh comes close when he refers to the "blackness of their souls" in describing Nazi mass murderers. Michael Burleigh, *Moral Combat: A History of World War II* (London: HarperPress, 2010), 410.

9   Susan Neiman, *Moral Clarity: A Guide for Grown-Up Idealists* (Orlando: Harcourt, Inc, 2008), 336–337.

10   Neiman, *Moral Clarity*, 341, 344, 368–370.

11   Elizabeth Young-Bruehl, *Hannah Arendt: For Love of the World* (New Haven: Yale University Press, 1982), 221, 205; see also Richard J. Bernstein, "Are Arendt's Reflections on Evil Still Relevant?" in *Politics in Dark Times: Encounters with Hannah Arendt*, ed. Seyla Benhabib (Cambridge: Cambridge University Press, 2010), 296, 298 and Samantha Power, "The Lesson of Hannah Arendt," *New York Review of Books*, April 29, 2004.

12   Jeffrey Jerome Cohen, "Monster Culture (Seven Theses)," in *Monster Theory: Reading Culture*, ed. Jeffrey Jerome Cohen (Minneapolis: University of Minnesota Press, 1996), 7. Gothic specialist, Carol Senf in *Bram Stoker* (Cardiff: University of Wales Press, 2010), 85 asserts that despite the efforts to eliminate it, evil prevails and often results from the compulsion to destroy what is different.

13   Zygmunt Bauman, *Modernity and the Holocaust* (Ithaca New York: Cornell University Press, 1989), 91–92; Amir Weiner, "Nature, Nurture and Memory in a Socialist Utopia: Delineating the Soviet Socio-Ethnic Body in the Age of Socialism," *The American Historical Review* Vol. 104, (October 1999): 1114–1155.

14   Punter, *The Literature of Terror* Vol. I (London: Longman, 1996), 1.

15   Alexander N. Yakovlev, *A Century of Violence in Soviet Russia*, trans. Anthony Austin (New Haven: Yale University Press, 2002), 3.

16   David Punter, *The Literature of Terror: The Gothic Tradition Second Edition*, Vol. I (London: Longman, 1996), 5.

17   Timothy Snyder, *Bloodlands: Europe between Hitler and Stalin* (New York: Basic Books, 2010).

18   Richard Lourie, *The Autobiography of Joseph Stalin* (Washington DC: Counterpoint, 1999); Vadim Z. Rogovin, *Stalin's Terror 1937–1938:*

Political Genocide in the USSR, trans. Frederick S. Choate (Oak Park, MI: Mehring Books, 2009) presents a compelling case that Stalin feared Trotsky. The latter's writings and the considerable support he attracted not only internationally but within the Soviet Union was, according to Rogovin, the basis of that fear.

19   Bruno Bettelheim, *The Informed Heart* (*New York: Avon Books*, [1960] 1971), 151. Bettelheim, who spent time in both Dachau and Buchenwald concentration camps, specifically applied this term to prisoners who were convinced that they had no hope of ever leaving except as a corpse. Bernstein, "Are Arendt's Reflections on Evil Still Relevant?" 297.

20   Joachim C. Fest, *The Face of the Third Reich* trans. Michael Bullock (Middlesex: Penguin Books 1985), 119.

21   Orlando Figes, *The Whisperers: Private Life in Stalin's Russia* (New York: Henry Holt and Company/Metropolitan Books, 2007), xxxii.

22   Lev Kopelev, *Ease My Sorrows: A Memoir* trans. Antonina W. Bouis (New York: Random House, 1983), 48. Kopelev relays a conversation with a fellow prisoner who had survived the ordeal of working in the Kolyma gold mines. If zeks (inmates) were not being shot there or gone mad, most lost their brains and souls and had nothing left except the "bread share, lunch, stove, sleep [and] bread again."

23   Robert Jay Lifton, *Thought Reform and the Psychology of Totalism: A Study of "Brainwashing" in China* (New York: W. W. Norton & Company, 1961), 429.

24   Avishai Margalit, *On Compromise and Rotten Compromises* (Princeton: Princeton University Press, 2010), 189, 185–186.

25   Dave Grossman, *On Killing: The Psychological Cost of Learning to Kill in War and Society* (Boston: Little, Brown and Company, 1995), 251–52.

Chapter 1

1   Norman Cohn, *Warrant for Genocide: The Myth of the Jewish World-Conspiracy and the Protocols of the Elders of Zion* (Ann Arbor, Michigan: Scholars Press, 1981), 34–35; on page 83 Cohn offers evidence that Rachkovksy, a master forger, was the brainchild behind the Protocols.

2   Selections from the Protocols are cited in Cohn, *Genocide,* 62–64 and Marks, *How Russia Shaped the Modern World: From Art to Anti-Semitism, Ballet to Bolshevism* (Princeton: Princeton University Press, 2003), 150–51.

3   Catherine Merridale, *Night of Stone: Death and Memory in Russia* (London: Granta Books, 2000), 80.

4   Shlomo Lambroza, "The pogroms of 1903–1906," in Pogroms: Anti-Jewish Violence in Modern Russian History, ed. John D. Klier and Shlomo Lambroza (Cambridge: Cambridge University Press, 1992), 214.

5   Robert Service, *Russia: A History of Twentieth-Century Russia* (Cambridge: Harvard University Press, 1997), 15.

6   Merridale, *Night of Stone,* 81–2; Orlando Figes, *A People's Tragedy: A History of the Russian Revolution* (New York: Viking Penguin, 1997), 186.

7   Marks, *How Russia Shaped the Modern World,* 148.

8   Lambroza, "The pogroms of 1903–1906," 225.

9   Lambroza, "The pogroms of 1903–1906," 226.

10   Marks, *How Russia Shaped the Modern World,* 145; Figes, *A People's Tragedy,* 197.

11   Figes, *A People's Tragedy,* 197.

12   Cohn, *Genocide,* 115; Eric Stephen Bronner, *A Rumour about the Jews: Reflections on anti-Semitism and the Protocols of the learned elders of Zion* (New York: St Martin's Press, 2000), 92–93; Marks, *How Russia Shaped the World,* 144.

13   Figes, *A People's Tragedy,* 208; Joan Neuberger, *Hooliganism: Crime, Culture, and Power in St Petersburg,* 1900–1914 (xBerkley: University of California Press, 1993), 231.

14   Laura Engelstein, *The Keys to Happiness: Sex and the Search for Modernity in* Fin-de-Siècle *Russia* (Ithaca: Cornell University Press, 1992), 300. The ritual targeting of Jews is acknowledged in *Dark Star,* Alan Furst's 1991 espionage novel, in which the chief character, a Polish–Jewish survivor of the pogroms, comments that the only benefit that the Tsar provided for the Russian peasantry was to allow them to beat up Jews.

15   Albert S. Lindemann, *The Jew Accused: Three Anti-Semitic Affairs Dreyfus, Beilus, Frank,* 1894–1915 (Cambridge: Cambridge University Press, 1995), 187–88.

16   David I. Kertzer, *The Popes against the Jews: The Vatican's Role in the Rise of Modern Anti-Semitism* (New York: Alfred A. Knopf, 2001), 236.

17   Lindemann, *The Jew Accused,* 191.

18   David Fromkin, *Europe's Last Summer: Who Started the Great War in 1914?* (New York: Alfred A. Knopf, 2004), 6.

19   Wendy Slater, *The Many Deaths of Tsar Nicholas II: Relics, re-mains and the Romanovs* (London: Routledge, 2007).

20   James Hughes, *Stalinism in a Russian Province: A Study of Collectivization and Dekulakization in Siberia* (London: Macmillan Press, 1996), 5.

21   Stephen P. Frank, "Confronting the Domestic Other: Rural Popular Culture and Its Enemies in Fin-De-Siècle Russia," in *Cultures in Flux: Lower Class Values, Practices, and Resistance in Late Imperial Russia,* ed. Stephen P. Frank and Mark D. Steinberg (Princeton: Princeton University Press, 1994), 74–107.

22   Overy, *The Dictators,* 123.

23   Steven A. Barnes, *Death and Redemption: The Gulag and the Shaping of Soviet Society* (Princeton: Princeton University Press, 2011), 14–16.

Chapter 2

1   Figes, *A People's Tragedy,* 268.

2   Robert D. Warth, *Nicholas II: The Life and Reign of Russia's Last Monarch* (Westport Conn.: Praeger 1997), 150.

3   Figes, *A People's Tragedy,* 33.

4   Boris Kolonitskii, "The Desacralization of the Monarchy Rumours and 'Political Pornography' during World War I," trans. Nathaniel Knight in *Language and Revolution: Making Modern Political Identities,* ed. Igal Halfin, (London: Frank Cass, 2002), 58, 64.

5   Figes, *A People's Tragedy,* 284.

6   Edward Radzinsky, *The Rasputin File,* trans. Judson Rosengrant (New York: Doubleday, 2000), 262, 407.

7   Richard Pipes, *The Russian Revolution* (New York: Vintage Books, 1990), 259.

8   Richard Cullen, *Rasputin: The role of Britain's Secret Service in his torture and murder* (London: Dialogue, 2010), 183, 204.

9   Figes, *A People's Tragedy,* 20.

10   Christopher Read argues that the vast majority of workers condemned these actions because they perceived them to be a threat to the revolution. Orlando Figes argues that the street violence was a more generalized phenomenon. C. Read, *From Tsar to Soviets: The Russian People and their Revolution, 1917–21* (London: University College, 1996), 86–88, Figes, *People's Tragedy,* 316–23.

11   Figes, *A People's Tragedy,* 321.

12   Orlando Figes and Boris Kolonitskii, *Interpreting the Russian Revolution: the Language and Symbols of 1917* (New Haven: Yale University Press, 1999), 169.

13   Figes, *Interpreting the Russian Revolution,* 154.

14   Figes, *A People's Tragedy,* 349

15   Figes, *A People's Tragedy,* 350.

16   The Mensheviks were orthodox Marxists who believed that a bourgeois revolution was a necessary precondition to a socialist one that would ultimately occur once the contradictions of capitalism became clear to the proletarian working class. They most resembled the socialist parties throughout Europe. The Socialist Revolutionaries were a peasant party that largely subscribed to the same tenets. Both believed that support for the Provisional Government was necessary in order to avert a civil war. The Bolsheviks especially after Lenin arrived in Petrograd in April from Switzerland maintained that the dictatorship of the proletariat should prepare to assume power almost immediately. He unequivocally contended that the Bolsheviks should not support the Provisional Government. Although initially he had little support, Lenin was assisted by the prolongation of the war and demoralized soldiers and poorer workers who were really responding to the Bolshevik slogan for Peace, Land and Bread rather than Lenin per se. For the vast majority of people trying to survive, these sophisticated distinctions meant little. .

17   Figes, *Interpreting the Russian Revolution*, 169–70.

18   Engelstein, *Keys to Happiness*, 322.

19   Victoria E. Bonnell, *Iconography of Power: Soviet Political Posters under Lenin and Stalin* (Berkeley: University of California Press, 1997) 202, and Figure 5.5; Stephen White, *The Bolshevik Poster* (New Haven: Yale University Press, 1988), 57, Plate 1.14.

20   Figes, *A People's Tragedy*, 50, 161, 117.

21   Figes, *A People's Tragedy*, 161.

22   Ronald Grigor Suny, *The Soviet Experiment: Russia, the USSR, and the Successor States* (Oxford: Oxford University Press, Second Edition, 2011), 83–84; Figes, A *People's Tragedy,* 564.

23   Nicolas Werth, "A State against Its People: Violence, Repression, and Terror in the Soviet Union," in *The Black Book of Communism: Crimes, Terror, Repression,* ed. Stéphane Courtois et al., trans. Jonathan Murphy and Mark Kramer (Cambridge: Harvard University Press, 1999), 570.

24   Radzinsky, *The Rasputin File*, 278

25   Peter Kenez, "Pogroms and White ideology in the Russian Civil War," in *Pogroms: Anti-Jewish Violence*, 304–05.

26   Robert Service, *Lenin: A Biography* (London: Macmillan, 2000), 394; Figes, *People's Tragedy*, 677

27   Hiroaki Kuromiya, *Freedom and Terror in the Donbas: A Ukrainian-Russian Borderland, 1870-1990s* (Cambridge: Cambridge University Press, 1998), 111.

28   Figes, A *People's Tragedy*, 678–79.

29   Figes, *A People's Tragedy*, 83, 87.

30   Richard Pipes, ed., *The Unknown Lenin: From the Secret Archive* (New Haven: Yale University Press, 1996), 19, 86.

31   Bernice Glatzer Rosenthal, *The Occult in Russian and Soviet Culture,* ed. Bernice Glatzer Rosenthal, (Ithaca: Cornell University Press, 1997), 399

32   Pipes, *The Unknown Lenin*, 50; Lenin's more measured comment is cited in Lars T. Lih, *Lenin* (London: Reaktion Books, 2011), 175. In a review of *The Unknown Lenin*, Lih is highly critical of Pipes' misuse and selectivity of released Lenin documents. Having worked through 400-odd documents himself, Lih contends that Pipes' book is "chock full of errors" and "is too often unreliable and should be avoided." *Canadian American Slavic Studies*, Summer Fall, 2001, 301–306.

33   Maxim Gorky, *Untimely Thoughts: Essays on Revolution, Culture, and the Bolsheviks 1917–1918*, trans. intro. Herman Ermolaev (New York: PS Eriksson, 1968), 85, 146, 122.

34   Francois Furet, *The Passing of an Illusion: The Idea of Communism in the Twentieth Century*, trans. Deborah Furet (Chicago: The University of Chicago Press, 1999), 96–97.

35   Pipes, *The Russian Revolution*, 802

36   Thomas, *Solzhenitsyn,* 24

37   Donald Rayfield, *Stalin and His Hangman: An Authoritative Portrait of a Tyrant and Those Who Served Him* (London: Viking Books, 2004), 55.

38   Christopher Read, *From Tsar to Soviets: The Russian People and their Revolution* (London: UCL Press, 1996), 202; I. N. Steinberg, *In the Workshop of the Revolution* (New York: Rinehart & Company, Inc., 1953, 223.

39   Werth, "State against Its People," *Black Book of Communism*, 57.

40   Steinberg, *In the Workshop of the Revolution,* 224.

41   Werth, "State against Its People," *Black Book of Communism*, 69, 79

42   Solomon Volkov, *Saint Petersburg* (New York: Simon & Schuster, 1995), 210; Dmitri Volkogonov, *Lenin: Life and Legacy*, trans. Harold Shukman (London: HarperCollins, 1994), 238.

43   Bertram D. Wolfe, *The Bridge and the Abyss: The Troubled Friendship of Maxim Gorky and V.I. Lenin* (New York: Frederick Praeger, 1967), 68.

44   Figes, *A People's Tragedy,* 525.

45   Pipes, *The Russian Revolution,* 800.

46   Robert Gellately, *Lenin, Stalin and Hitler: The Age of Social Catastrophe* (New York: Alfred A. Knopf, 2007), 137.

47   Figes, *A People's Tragedy*, 524.

48   Steinberg, *In the Workshop of the Revolution,* 145–46; Figes, *A People's Tragedy*, 536.

49   Pipes, *The Russian Revolution*, 794–95, 820.

50   Applebaum, *Gulag*, xvi, xxxiv; Gorky, *Untimely Thoughts*, 142.

51   Service, *Stalin*, 169–70; Gellately, *Lenin, Stalin and Hitler*.70; D. M. Thomas, *Alexander Solzhenitsyn: A Century in His Life* (New York: St. Martin's Press, 1998), 33.

52   Figes, *A People's Tragedy*, 646

53   Pitirim A. Sorokin *Leaves of a Russian Diary—and Thirty Years Later* (Boston: The Beacon Press, 1950), 233,193

54   Pipes, *The Russian Revolution*, 836.

Chapter 3

1   Service, *Lenin: A Biography,* 454.

2   Robert Service, *Stalin: A Biography* (Cambridge Mass.: Belknap Press/ Harvard University Press, 2005), 208–09, 214.

3   Lynne Viola, *Peasant Rebels under Stalin: Collectivization and the Culture of Peasant Resistance* (New York: Oxford University Press, 1996), 16.

4   Volkogonov, *Lenin*, 342.

5   Marks, *How Russia Changed the World,* 281; Snyder, *Bloodlands*, 25.

6   Service, *Stalin,* 257–58; Figes, *The Whisperers*, 82.

7   Jonathan Glover, *Humanity: A Moral History of the Twentieth Century* (London: Jonathan Cape, 1999), 261; Conquest, *The Great Terror,* 22; Conquest, *Harvest of Sorrow,* 113; Glover, *Humanity*, 261–62; J Arch Getty and Oleg V. Naumov, trans. Benjamin Sher, *The Road to Terror: Stalin and the Self-destruction of the Bolsheviks, 1932-1939* (New Haven, Yale University Press, 1999), 45–50.

8   Piers Brendon, *The Dark Valley: A Panorama of the 1930s* (New York: Alfred A. Knopf, 2000), 230.

9   Geoffrey Hosking, *Russia and the Russians: A History* (Cambridge: Harvard University Press, 2001), 462.

10   Solzhenitsyn, *The Gulag Archipelago* vols. 1–2, 56; Brendon, *The Dark Valley*, 238; Figes, *The Whisperers*, 85; Robert C. Tucker *Stalin in Power: The Revolution From Above, 1928-41* (New York: Norton, 1990), 178; Viola, *Peasant Rebels*, 36–37.

11   Brendon, *The Dark Valley*, 235.

12   Sheila Fitzpatrick and Yuri Slezkine, ed., trans. Yuri Slezkine, *In the Shadow of Revolution: Life Stories of Russian Women from 1917 to the Second World War* (Princeton: Princeton University Press, 2000), 241.

13   Robert Chandler, *Everything Flows,* Vasily Grossman (New York: New York Review of Books, 2009), 213, n. 58.

14   Grossman, *Everything Flows*, trans. Robert Chandler, 118–120.

15   Lynne Viola, *The Best Sons of the Fatherland: Workers in the Vanguard of Soviet Collectivization* (New York: Oxford University Press, 1987, 139,118; Merle Fainsod, *Smolensk under Soviet Rule* (Cambridge: Harvard University Press, 1958), 248; Fitzpatrick, *In the Shadow of Revolution*, 273.

16   Lewis Siegelbaum and Andrei Sokolov, *Stalinism as a Way of Life: A Narrative in Documents* (New Haven: Yale University Press, 2000), 50; Figes, *The Whisperers*, 103–110.

17   Barnes, *Death and Redemption,* 96–97.

18   Viola, *Peasant Rebels*, 35, 39–42.

19   Viola, *Peasant Rebels*, 88, 145.

20   Snyder, *Bloodlands*, 29; Viola, *Peasant Rebels*, 69.

21   Tucker, *Stalin*, 185.

22   Viola, *Best Sons*, 128–29.

23   Hosking, *Russia*, 452.

24   Viola, *Peasant Rebels*, 171.

25   Ilya Ehrenburg, *The Second Day,* trans. Liv Tudge (Moscow: Raduga Publishers, 1984), 286.

26   Figes, *People's Tragedy*, 641; cited in Jochen Hellbeck, "Writing, Struggling, Becoming: Stalin-Era Autobiographical Texts," *The Russian Review* 60 no. 3 (2001): 351; Glover, *Humanity*, 256.

27   Nadezhda Mandelstam, *Hope Against Hope*, trans. Max Hayward (London: Penguin Books, 1973), 159.

28   Lev Kopelev, *To be Preserved Forever*, trans. and ed. Anthony Austin (Philadelphia: J.B. Lippincott and Company, 1977), 13.

29   Kopelev, *The Education of a True Believer*, trans. Gary Kern (New York: Harper & Row, 1980), 235.

30   Fitzpatrick, *Stalin's Peasants*, 129.

31   Applebaum, *Gulag*, 47.

32   Gellately, *Lenin, Stalin and Hitler*, 229; Conquest, *Harvest of Sorrow*, 226; Conquest, *The Great Terror*, 311, 339.

33   Mark Mazower, *Dark Continent: Europe's Twentieth Century* (London: Allen Lane, 1998), 50.

34   Ben Kiernan, *Blood and Soil: A World History of Genocide and Extermination from Sparta to Darfur* (New Haven: Yale University Press, 2007), 507; Conquest, Harvest of Sorrow, 218–19.

35   Conquest, *Harvest of Sorrow*, 196; Snyder, *Borderlands*, 42–46.

36   Kenneth Sherman, "Varlam Shalamov: Poet of the Frozen Inferno," *Queen's Quarterly* 111/4 (Winter 2004) 559; Conquest, *Harvest of Sorrow*, 231.

37   Merridale, *Night of Stone*, 218.

38   Miron Dolot, *Execution by Hunger: The Hidden Holocaust* (New York: W.W. Norton & Company, 1985), 204, 198.

39   Grossman, *Everything Flows*, 136.

40   Tucker, *Stalin in Power*, 192.

41   Grossman, *Everything Flows,* 133; Donald Rayfield, *Stalin and His Hangman: An Authoritative Portrait of a Tyrant and Those Who Served Him* (London: Viking Books, 2004), 184.

42   Victor Kravchenko, *I Chose Freedom: The Personal and Political Life of a Soviet Official* (New York: Charles Scribner's Sons, 1946), 130. Tucker, *Stalin in Power*, 195.

43   Boris Pasternak, *Doctor Zhivago.* Translated from the Russian by Richard Pevear and Larissa Volokhonsky (New York: Pantheon Books, 2010), 451.

44   Roy Medvedev, *Let History Judge: The Origins and Consequences of Stalinism*, revised and expanded Edition, ed. and trans. George Shriver (New York: Columbia University Press, 1989), 243–244.

45   Tucker, *Stalin in Power*, 193–94.

46   Conquest, *Harvest of Sorrow*, 259.

47   Jeffrey Brooks, *"Thank You, Comrade Stalin!" Soviet Public Culture from Revolution to Cold War* (Princeton: Princeton University Press, 2000), 58.

48   Merridale, *Night of Stone*, 200.

49   Snyder, Bloodlands, 54; Arthur Koestler, *The Yogi and the Commissar: Essays on the Modern Dilemma with a New Preface by the Author* (New York: Macmillan, 1965), 128–29; Arthur Koestler, *The Invisible Writing: An Autobiography* (Boston: The Beacon Press, 1954), 151–52.

50   Michael Scammell, Koestler*: A Literary and Political Odyssey of a Twentieth-Century Skeptic* (New York: Random House, 2009), 93.

51   Koestler, *The Invisible Writing*, 52–53, 154. George Orwell also recognized the power of this lie in Spain. He was probably saved from a NKVD firing squad or a show trial had he not been in hospital with a bullet wound in the neck. Based on his observations of Soviet cynicism

and the murder of those whom it could not control and the difficulties he incurred when he attempted to set the record straight in *Homage to Catalonia*, Orwell was inspired to write his dystopian novel *Nineteen Eighty-Four*. It was based upon the premise that historical truth could rarely be salvaged from the layers of mendacity and ordure heaped over it.

52   Snyder, *Bloodlands*, 51; Tim Snyder, "Holocaust: The Ignored Reality," *The New York Review of Books*, July 16, 2009. Eric D. Weitz, *A Century of Genocide: Utopias of Race and Nation* (Princeton: Princeton University Press, 2003), 71; Tucker, *Stalin in Power*, 195; Applebaum, *Gulag*, xix; Donald Rayfield, "The Ukrainian Famine of 1933: Manmade Catastrophe, Mass Murder, or Genocide," in *Holodomor: Reflections on the Great Famine of 1932-1933 in Soviet Ukraine* ed. Lubomyr Y. Luciuk (Kingston, Ontario: The Kashtan Press, 2008), 89; Robert Conquest, *The Great Terror: A Reassessment* (New York: Oxford University Press, 1990), 20.

53   David Satter, *It was a Long Time Ago, and it Never Happened: Russia and the Communist Past* (New Haven: Yale University Press, 2012), 224, 226.

54   Rayfield, "The Ukrainian Famine," 87–105 and Hiroaki Kuromiya, "The Great Famine: The Issue of Intentionality," 115–128, both in *Holodomor*.

56   Tucker, *Stalin*, 535.

Chapter 4

1   Modris Eksteins, *Rites of Spring: The Great War and the Birth of the Modern Age* (Toronto: Lester & Orpen Dennys, 1989), 304.

2   Vitaly Shentalinsky, *The KGB's Literary Archive*, trans. John Crowfoot (New York: Martin Kessler Books, 1996), 252–53.

3   David-Fox, *Showcasing the Great Experiment*, 142–144; Shentalinsky, *Archive*, 246, 261; Tovah Yedlin, *Maxim Gorky: A Political Biography* (Westport, Connecticut: Praeger, 1999), 190.

4   Applebaum, *Gulag*, 55.

5   Elizabeth Astrid Papazian, *Manufacturing Truth: The Documentary Moment in Early Soviet Culture* DeKalb: Northern Illinois University Press, 2009), 140–146; Yedlin, *Gorky*, 188, 191; David Remnick, "Seasons in Hell," *The New Yorker*, April 14, 2003; David-Fox, *Showcasing the Great Experiment*, 152, 155–156.

6   Solzhenitsyn, *The Gulag Archipelago*, vol. 2, 62–63; David-Fox, *Showcasing the Great Experiment*, 155.

7   Yedlin, *Gorky*, 190.

8   Cynthia A. Ruder, *Making History for Stalin: The Story of the Belomor Canal* (Gainesville: University Press of Florida, 1998), 44.

9   Orlando Figes, *Natasha's Dance: A Cultural History of Russia* (Toronto: Penguin Books, 2002), 476.

10   Merridale, *Night of Stone*, 125; Aileen Kelly, "In the Promised Land," *New York Review of Books*, November 29, 2001; Papazian, *Manufacturing Truth*, 126; David-Fox, *Showcasing the Great Experiment*, 148.

11   Greg Carleton, "Genre in Socialist Realism," *Slavic Review* 53 no. 4 (Winter 1994): 994–995; Barnes, *Death and Redemption*, 14.

12   Figes, *The Whisperers*, 197, 193.

13   Applebaum, *Gulag*, 65.

14   Solzhenitsyn, *The Gulag Archipelago, 1918–1956*, vols. 3, 4, trans. Thomas P. Whitney (New York: Harper & Row, 1975), Vol. 2, 82, 85; Amir, "Nature, Nurture and Memory in a Socialist Utopia," *American Historical Review:* 1131; Barnes, *Death and Redemption*, 77, 72, 91, 11–12. Gennady Andreev-Khomiakov, who was released two years short of his ten year sentence in the notorious SLON wrote in his memoir:

> Life in the camps convinced me that the renowned 'reforging through work and education' could only serve to corrupt people. Hungry, often driven by the survival instinct, shifting and dodging, we learned to hate work and the knout instead of to love them. We learned how to deceive the knout, [a whip used for flogging] feigning resignation to it, even praising it; but still we could not come to love them. You cannot command love.

Bitter Waters: Life and Work in Stalin's Russia, trans. and introduction by Ann E. Healy (Boulder: Westview Press, 1997), 138.

15   Carleton, "Socialist Realism," 998–99.

16   Yedlin, Gorky; Arkady Vaksberg, *The Murder of Maxim Gorky: A Secret Execution*, trans. Todd Bludeau (New York: Enigma Books, 2007).

17   Tucker, *Stalin*, 536.

18   Kravchenko, *Freedom*, 304.

19   Janusz Bardach and Kathleen Gleeson, *Surviving Freedom after the Gulag* (Berkeley: University of California Press, 2003), 101–02.

20   Shentalinsky, *Literary Archive*, 1

21   S. J. Taylor, *Stalin's Apologist* (New York: Oxford University Press, 1990), 185.

22   Taylor, *Stalin's Apologist*, 298, 207, 219.

23   Malcolm Muggeridge, *Chronicles of Wasted Time* (London: Collins, 1972), 255–56; Muggeridge is also cited in Snyder, *Bloodlands*, 56.

24   Taylor, *Stalin's Apologist*, 240. Other American journalists lost their illusions. William Henry Chamberlin, who once had regarded the Soviet Union as a beacon of hope "left convinced that the absolutist Soviet state...is a power of darkness and evil with few parallels in history." Tim Tzouliadis, *The Forsaken: An American Tragedy in Stalin's Russia* (New York: Penguin Press, 2008), 74.

25   David-Fox, *Showcasing the Great Experiment,* 110–111.

26   David-Fox, *Showcasing the Great Experiment,* 116.

27   Furet, *The Passing of an Illusion,* 147.

28   Conquest, *Harvest of Sorrow,* 314–15.

29   David-Fox, *Showcasing the Great Experiment*, 211, 279, Michael Holroyd, *Bernard Shaw* Vol. 3 *1918–50: The Lure of Fantasy* (London: Chatto & Windus), 224, and Caute, *Fellow-Travellers*, 120.

30   David-Fox, *Showcasing the Great Experiment*, 216–217, 219; David Caute, *The Fellow-Travellers: Intellectual Friends of Communism* (New Haven: Yale University Press, 1988), 108, 117–118; Andreev-Khomiakov, *Bitter Waters*, 2, 133.

31   Barnes, *Death and Redemption,* 86; Andreev-Khomiakov, *Bitter Waters*, 42. In 1920, Bertrand Russell was not fooled by the illusion that democratically elected soviets ruled in the name of the workers. He recognized that behind this façade was the dictatorship of the Party that was detested as a tyrannical government at home, but how it had already become a symbol of liberation abroad. Furet, *Passing of an Illusion*, 91–92. Unlike so many from the political left, Russell was too much a gadfly to subscribe to utopian socialism but remained a staunch critic of the Soviet Union.

By 1928, Serge's critical faculties earned him expulsion from the Party whereby he retreated into fictional writing and research into the early days of the Revolution. In 1933, he was arrested and he and his family were sent to the remote village of Orenberg, an early outpost of the Gulag network. With intellectuals and trade unionists taking up his cause in France, Stalin was sufficiently embarrassed to allow Serge to emigrate. Among his many writings remains a classic account of a show trial, *The Case of Comrade Tulayev.*

32   Tucker, *Stalin,* 361; David–Fox, *Showcasing the Great Experiment,* 218.

33   Tzouliadis, *The Forsaken.*

34   Muggeridge, *Chronicles,* 244.

35   David-Fox, *Embracing the Great Experiment,* 282–284; Paul Robeson Jr., *The Undiscovered Paul Robeson: Quest for Freedom, 1939–1976* (Hoboken, New Jersey: John Wiley & Sons, Inc, 2010), 152–155.

36   Furet, *Passing of an Illusion,* 148.

37   Cesarani, *Arthur Koestler*, 105.

38   Tucker, *Stalin*, 353–354.

39   Snyder, *Bloodlands*, x–xi. In the first six and one half years after the Nazis came to power they killed about ten thousand people while the Stalinist regime starved millions and shot about a million.

40   George Orwell, *As I Please, 1943–45: The Collected Essays Journalism and Letters of George Orwell* Vol. 3, ed. Sonia Orwell and Ian Angus (London: Secker & Warburg, 1968), 240 (italics in original).

41   André Gide, *Return to the U.S.S.R.*, trans. Dorothy Bussy (New York: Alfred A. Knopf, 1937), 45–46.

42   Michael David-Fox, "The Fellow-Travelers Revisited: 'The Cultured West' through Soviet Eyes," *The Journal of Modern History* 75 (June 2003). Solzhenitsyn relates the story that at end of a Party district conference, a tribute to Stalin was required. The ovation went on for over ten minutes no delegate daring to stop even if exhausted because NKVD men were looking to see who would stop first. Then after eleven minutes, the director of a paper factory aware of the falsity stopped and sat down. Instantly everyone stopped. That night he was visited by the NKVD and on the pretext of another charge received ten years in the camps. *The Gulag*, vol. 1, 69–70.

43   Andreev-Khomiakov, *Bitter Waters*, 133.

44   Gide, *U.S.S.R.*, 42.

45   Figes, *Natasha's Dance*, 460.

46   Denise J. Youngblood, *Movies for the Masses: Popular Cinema and Soviet Society in the 1920* (Cambridge University Press, 1992), 174.

47   Bonnell, *Iconography of Power*, 118–119, Plate 4.

48   David King, *The Commissar Vanishes: The Falsification of Photographs and Art in Stalin's Russia* (New York: Henry Holt, Metropolitan Books, 1997), 31, 28–29.

49   King, *Commissar Vanishes*, 28–29, 87, 98, 94.

50   King, *Commissar Vanishes*, 94, 66–69.

51   David-Fox, *Showcasing the Soviet Experiment*, 141; Fitzpatrick, *Stalin's Peasants*, 262.

52   Fitzpatrick, *Everyday Stalinism*, 66.

53   Martin Malia, *Russia under Western Eyes: From the Bronze Horsemen to the Lenin Mausoleum* (Cambridge: Harvard University Press, 1999), 307.

54   Furet, *Passing of an Illusion*, 290. Gide's comment appears in a slightly altered version in *The God that Failed*, ed. Richard Crossman (New York: Harper and Row, 1965), 168.

Chapter 5

1   Lih, *Lenin,* 176–177. The figure of eight thousand is cited in Pipes, *The Unknown Lenin* 153 and Figes, *A People's Tragedy,* 748–49. Lih in his review of Pipes' book draws upon Jonathan W. Daly, "'Storming the Last Citadel': The Bolshevik Assault on the Church 1922," in *The Bolsheviks in Russian Society,* ed. Vladimir N. Brovkin (New Haven, CT: Yale University Press, 1997), 235–68 that substantially reduces that number, Lih, *Canadian–American Slavic Studies,* Summer Fall 2001, 301–06.

2   Figes, *The Whisperers,* 33.

3   Tucker, *Stalin in Power,* 78.

4   Brooks, *Comrade Stalin,* 136.

5   Oleg V. Khlevniuk, *Master of the House: Stalin and his Inner Circle,* trans., Nora Seligman Favorov (Stanford: Stanford University, 2009), 8–9, 16–17.

6   Tatyana Tolstaya, "In Cannibalistic Times," *New York Review of Books,* April 11, 1991.

7   Tucker, *Stalin in Power,* 309.

8   Roman Brackman, *The Secret File of Joseph Stalin: A Hidden File* (London: Frank Cass, 2001), 198, 8.

9   Service, *Stalin,* 230. For his analysis of the "beaten" speech see 272–73.

10   Tucker, *Stalin in Power,* 166.

11   J. Arch Getty and Oleg V. Naumov, *Stalin and the Self-Destruction of the Bolsheviks, 1932–1939,* trans., Benjamin Sher (New Haven: Yale University Press, 1999), 56–58.

12   Khlevniuk, *Master of the House,* 125, 110.

13   Volkov, *Saint Petersburg,* 415.

14   Khlevniuk, *Master of the House,* 171–72

15   William Taubman, *Khrushchev: The Man and his Era* (New York: W.W. Norton & Company, 2003), 98.

16   Brendon, *Dark Valley,* 472.

17   Service, *Stalin,* 285; Rogovin, *Stalin's Terror,* 73–82, 46.

18   Simon Sebag Montefiore, *Stalin: Court of the Red Tsar* (London: Weidenfeld & Nicolson, 2003), 168–176.

19   Conquest, *The Great Terror,* 122.

20   Service, *Russia,* 231.

21   Montefiore, *Stalin,* 214.

22   Amir Weiner, "Nature, Nurture, and Memory in a Socialist Utopia," 1121.

23   Vadim Volkov, "The Concept of Kul'turnost' Notes on the Stalinist civilizing process," in *Stalinism New Directions*, ed. Sheila Fitzpatrick (London: Routledge, 2000), 226.

24   Fitzroy Maclean, *Eastern Approaches* (London: Jonathan Cape, 1966), 119-20, 84; cited in Lars T. Lih, "Melodrama and the Myth of the Soviet Man," in *Imitations of Life: Two Centuries of Melodrama in Russia*, ed. Louise McReynolds and Joan Neuberger (Durham: Duke University Press, 2002), 201-02, Trotsky's article in Rogovin, *Stalin's Terror*, 50-51.

25   Koestler, *The Invisible Writing*, 395.

26   Stephen F. Cohen, "The Afterlife of Nikolai Bukharin" introduction to *This I Cannot Forget: Memoirs of Nikolai Bukharin's Widow* by Anna Larina (New York: W.W. Norton & Company, 1993), 18-19.

27   Brooks, *Comrade Stalin*, 140.

28   Ibid, 140.

29   Ibid, 134.

30   Montefiore, *Stalin*, 206.

31   Service, *Stalin*, 281; Montefiore, *Stalin*, 207.

32   Taubman, *Khrushchev*, 104; Montefiore, *Stalin*, 222, 240.

33   Taubman, *Khrushchev*, 99.

34   Taubman, *Khrushchev*, 124; Figes, *The Whisperers*, 239.

35   Brackman, *Secret File of Stalin*, 328.

36   Edward Crankshaw, intro and commentary, trans. ed. Strobe Talbott, *Khrushchev Remembers* (Boston: Bantam Books, 1971), 117. He attempted to rewrite history by destroying incriminating documents. According to testimony given in 1988, 261 pages of his papers were burned in July 1954.

37   Brendon, *Dark Valley*, 475.

38   Brent, *Stalin's Last Crime*, 174.

39   Montefiore, *Stalin*, 242.

40   Kravchenko, *Freedom*, 291.

41   Alex de Jonge, *Stalin and the Shaping of the Soviet Union* (New York: Morrow, 1986), 367.

42   Figes, *The Whisperers*, 279.

43   Janusz Bardach and Kathleen Gleeson, *Man is Wolf to Man: Surviving the Gulag* (Berkeley: University of California Press, 1998), 137; Grossman, *Everything Flows*, 89; Montefiore, Stalin, 323.

44   Rogovin, *Stalin's Terror*, 136.

45   Elliott Mossman, ed., *The Correspondence of Boris Pasternak and Olga Freidenberg 1910-54* (New York: Harcourt Brace Jovanovich, 1982), 163.

46 Merridale, *Night of Stone,* 252.

47 Kravchenko, *Freedom,* 206, 235.

48 Sarah Davies, *Popular Opinion in Stalin's Russia: Terror, Propaganda, and Dissent 1934-41* (Cambridge: Cambridge University Press), 86.

49 Mandelstam, *Hope against Hope,* 410–11.

50 Davies, *Popular Opinion,* 87.

51 Ibid, 125.

52 Elena Bonner, *Mothers and Daughters,* trans. Antonina W. Bouis (New York: Random House, 1992).

53 Brooks, *Comrade Stalin,* 141.

54 Siegelbaum, *Stalinism,* 321.

55 Sheila Fitzpatrick, "Signals from Below: Soviet Letters of Denunciation in the 1930s,"in *Accusatory Practices: Denunciation in Modern European History 1789-1989,* ed Sheila Fitzpatrick and Robert Gellately (Chicago: University of Chicago Press, 1997), 102.

56 Tolstaya, "In Cannibalistic Times," *New York Review of Books,* 6.

57 J. Arch Getty, "Afraid of Their Shadows: The Bolshevik Recourse to Terror, 1932–38," in *Stalinism before the Second World War: New Avenues of Research,* ed. Manfred Hildermeier (Munich: R Oldenbourg Verlag, 1998), 176–178; Siegelbaum, *Stalinism, 33; Ernst Fischer, An Opposing Man,* trans. Peter and Betty Ross (London: Allen Lane, 1974), 300.

58 Montefiore, *Stalin,* 206.

59 Figes, *The Whisperers,* 279.

60 Richard Taylor and William Powell, ed., "Stalin, Molotov and Zhdanov on Ivan the Terrible, Part Two," in *The Eisenstein Reader,* trans. Richard Taylor (London: BFI, 1998), 160, 162.

61 Kaufmann, *Khrushchev,* 214.

62 Brent, *Stalin's Last Crime,* 173 (my emphasis); Service, *Stalin,* 341.

63 Adam Hochschild, *The Unquiet Ghost: Russians Remember Stalin* (New York: Viking, 1994), 82–88.

64 Siegelbaum, *Stalinism,* 235.

65 Bonner, *Mothers and Daughters,* 324, 317.

66 Figes, *The Whisperers,* 262.

67 Montefiore, *Stalin,* 281.

68 Montefiore, *Stalin,* 283..

69 Albert Reiss ed. *Molotov Remembers: Inside Kremlin Politics* (Chicago: Ivan R. Dee, 1993), 160.

Chapter 6

1   Siegelbaum, *Stalinism*, 223.

2   Brendon, *Dark Valley,* 477; Hiroaki Kuromiya, *Stalin* (London: Pearson/Longman, 2005), 125.

3   Snyder, *Bloodlands*, 81–83; Gorky cited in Amir, "Nature, Nurture and Memory in a Socialist Utopia," 1145.

4   Snyder, *Bloodlands*, 95–96, 102; Nicolas Werth, "The Mechanism of a Mass Crime: The Great Terror in the Soviet Union, 1937–38," in *The Specter of Genocide: Mass Murder in Historical Perspective*, ed. Robert Gellately and Ben Kiernan (Cambridge UK: Cambridge University Press, 2003), 237. Barry McLoughlin, "Mass Operations of the NKVD, 1937–8: A Survey," in *Stalin's Terror: High Politics and Mass Repression in the Soviet Union*, ed. Barry McLoughlin and Kevin McDermott (New York: Palgrave Macmillan, 2003), 118–152. Rayfield, *Stalin*, 302. Figes, *The Whisperers*, 240–41, Eric D. Weitz, A *Century of Genocide: Utopias of Race and Nation* (Princeton: Princeton University Press, 2003), 66.

5   Tzouliadis, *The Forsaken*, 8, 134–35, 107.

6   Brent, *Inside the Stalin Archives*, 195. For an excellent overview of the different types of camps that evolved from the 1920s to the war years, see Barnes, *Death and Redemption*.

7   Mikhail Bulgakov, *The Master & Margarita*, trans. Diana Burgin & Katherine Tiernan O'Connor (El Camino Capistrano: Ardis, 1995), 192.

8   Tzouliadis, *The Forsaken*, 267, 262, 363.

9   Eugenia Ginzburg, *Journey into the Whirlwind*, trans. Paul Stevenson and Max Hayward (New York: Harcourt Brace Jovanovich, 1967).

10   Suzanne Rosenberg, *Soviet Odyssey* (Toronto: Oxford University Press, 1988), 131.

11   Figes, *The Whisperers*, 242.

12   Kravchenko, *Freedom*, 214.

13   Figes, *The Whisperers,* 255.

14   Bardach, *Man is Wolf to Man,* 30.

15   Mandelstam, *Hope Against Hope*, 385; Conquest, *The Great Terror*, 256.

16   Rosenberg, *Soviet Odyssey,* 52–53, 130, 198–99.

17   Shentalinsky, *Literary Archive*, 25, 53; Merridale, *Night of Stone*, 260–61.

18   Mandelstam, *Hope against Hope,* 101.

19   Arthur Koestler, *Darkness at Noon,* trans. Daphne Hardy (Middlesex, England: Penguin Books, [1940] 1985), 41.

20 Koestler, *Darkness at Noon,* 128, 130.

21 Ginzburg, *Into the Whirlwind*, 45,177.

22 Ginzburg, *Into the Whirlwind*, 66.

23 Solzhenitsyn, *Gulag*, Vols. III–IV, 93.

24 Applebaum, *Gulag*, 282–83.

25 Bardach, *Man is Wolf to Man,* 183.

26 Brendon, *Dark Valley*, 485.

27 Ginzburg, *Into the Whirlwind*, 353–354.

28 Applebaum, *Gulag*, 172.

29 Lev Razgon, *True Stories*, trans. John Crowfoot (Dan Point, California: Ardis Publishers, 1997), 210–211.

30 Razgon, *True Stories*, 213–214.

31 Colin Thubron, *In Siberia* (New York: HarperCollins, 2000), 40.

32 Bardach, *Man is Wolf to Man,* 223.

33 Werth, "State Against its People," in *The Black Book of Communism*, 226.

34 Conquest, *The Great Terror*, 328–329.

35 Tzouliadis, *The Forsaken*, 208.

36 Hochschild, *Unquiet Ghost,* 272–73.

37 Eugenia Ginzburg, *Within the Whirlwind*, trans. Ian Boland (New York: Harcourt Brace Jovanovich, 1981), 71–72; Merridale, *Night of Stone*, 237.

38 Barnes, *Death and Redemption*, 10, 75–76.

39 Razgon, *True Stories,* 162; Applebaum, *Gulag*, 332.

40 Miriam Dobson, *Khrushchev's Cold Winter: Gulag Returnees, Crime, and the Fate of Reform after Stalin* (Ithaca: Cornell University Press, 2009), 6.

41 Dobson, *Khrushchev's Cold Summer*, 95, 150, 158; Stephen F. Cohen, *Soviet Fates and Lost Alternatives: From Stalinism to the New Cold War* (New York: Columbia University Press, 2009), 42.

42 Nanci Adler, *The Gulag Survivor: Beyond the Soviet System* (New Brunswick, U.S.A.: Transactions, 2002), 112–114.

43 Figes, *The Whisperers*, 600–01, Adler, *Gulag Survivor*, 223, 220–221.

44 Merridale, *Night of Stone*, 243–44.

45 Figes, *The Whisperers*, 578.

46 Kuromiya, *Stalin*, 207.

47 Hochschild, *The Unquiet Ghost*, 34.

48 Figes, *The Whisperers*, 266–67.

49 Ginzburg, *Within the Whirlwind,* 266.

50   Bardach, *Man is Wolf to Man*, 207.

51   Ginzburg, *Journey to the Whirlwind*, 75.

52   Ginzburg, *Within the Whirlwind*, 153.

53   Applebaum, *Gulag*, 518. Pechuro is also interviewed by the producers of the 1995 CNN series, *The Cold War*.

54   Bardach, *Surviving Freedom*, 13, 26.

55   David Remnick, *Lenin's Tomb: The Last Days of the Soviet Empire* (New York: Vintage Books, 1994), 42–46; Leon Aron, "The 'Mystery' of the Soviet Collapse," *Journal of Democracy* V17: 2. (April 2006), 29.

56   Orlando Figes, "Vlad the Great," *The New Statesman*, November 27, 2007; Nanci Adler, "The Future of the Soviet Past Remains Unpredictable: The Resurrection of Stalinist Symbols Amidst the Exhumation of Mass Graves," *Europe-Asia Studies* v.57 No. 8 (Dec. 2005): 1100; Satter, *It was a Long Time Ago*, 227–228, 216.

57   As a prominent beneficiary of this trove of documents, Figes extensively drew upon them for his magisterial *The Whisperers* and he was understandably angry about the theft of the archives. See Orlando Figes, "Putin vs. the Truth," *New York Review of Books*, April 30, 2009. It should not surprise anyone that *The Whisperers* has not been published in Russia although that may have more to do with self censorship rather than state censorship.

58   Catherine Merridale, "Amnesia Nation," *Index on Censorship* 34:2 (2005): 82; Alexei Levinson, "The Great Terror's Long Shadow," *Open Democracy*, June 13, 2011.

59   Barnes, *Death and Redemption*, 265–266 n. 28, Solzhenitsyn, *Gulag*, 1:176–177; Cohen, *Soviet Fates*, 59.

60   Merridale, *Night of Stone*, 417–18. See also two perceptive reviews, Anne Applebaum, "After the Gulag," *The New York Review of Books*, Vol. 49, No. 16, October 24, 2002, and Lewis Siegelbaum, "Witness Protection," *London Review of Books*, April 12, 2008. In his review of *The Whisperers*, Siegelbaum compares the Figes commentary of one of the oral witnesses with the interview itself that is on his colleague's website and makes the perceptive point that Figes and his interviewers were not neutral interlocutors: they were trying to extract material that revealed their anger against Stalin and even resorted to badgering the witnesses when they did not receive the information they wanted. It does not seem to occur to any of these scholars that the witness might have at one time held conflicting attitudes toward Stalin but given the passage of years and the improvement of his life and that of his family, it was psychologically preferable to dispense with his anger toward Stalin.

Chapter 7

1   Robert Cecil, The *Myth of the Master Race: Alfred Rosenberg and Nazi Ideology* (London: B.T. Batsford Ltd, 1972), 17–18, 72–73.

2   Konrad Heiden, *Deührer: Hitler's Rise to Power,* trans. Ralph Manheim (Boston: Houghton Mifflin Company, 1944), 100, 10. Heiden on page 133 provides specific examples of the similarities in ideas and language of the Protocols with Hitler's own speeches.

3   Roger Griffin, *A Fascist Century: Essays by Roger Griffin,* ed. Matthew Feldman (Houndmills, Basingstroke, Hampshire: Palgrave Macmillan), 2008, 81.

4   Griffin, *Modernism and Fascism,* 320.

5   Joachim C. Fest, *Hitler,* trans. Richard and Clara Winston (New York: Random House, 1975), 9.

6   Alison Owings, *Frauen: German Women Recall the Third Reich* (New Brunswick, N. J.: Rutgers University Press), 1994, 9; Robert Gellately, *Backing Hitler: Consent and Coercion in Nazi Germany* (Oxford University Press, 2001), 3.

7   Melita Maschmann, *Account Rendered: A Dossier on my Former Self* (London: Abelard–Schuman, 1964), 197.

8   Koonz, *The Nazi Conscience,* 10.

9   One historian who would take exception to this statement is Daniel Jonah Goldhagen, *Hitler' Willing Executioners: Ordinary Germans and the Holocaust* (New York: Alfred A. Knopf, 1996). He contends that all Germans were racist "eliminationist" anti-Semites.

10   Martin Davidson, *The Perfect Nazi: Uncovering My SS Grandfather's Secret Past and How Hitler Seduced a Generation* (London: Viking, 2010), 148.

11   Griffin, *Fascist Century,* 101.

12   Peter Fritzsche, *Life and Death in the Third Reich* (Cambridge/ Mass.: Belknap Press, 2008), 64, 75.

Chapter 8

1   Thomas S. Grey, "The Jewish question," in *The Cambridge Companion to Wagner* (Cambridge: Cambridge University Press, 2008) 216–218; Hans R. Vaget, "Wagner, Anti-Semitism and Mr. Rose: Merkwürd Ger-Fall!" *The German Quarterly* 66 (2 1993).

2   Leon Botstein, "German Jews and Wagner," in *Richard Wagner and his World* ed. Thomas S. Grey (Princeton: Princeton University Press, 2009), 153; Pamela M. Potter, "Wagner and the Third Reich: myths and realities," in *The Cambridge Companion to Wagner* (Cambridge: Cambridge University Press, 2008), 244.

3   Stuart Spencer and Barry Millington, trans., ed. *Selected Letters of Richard Wagner* (London: J.M. Dent & Sons Ltd, 1987), 221–222. Wagner's animosity toward the French stemmed in part from his belief that Jewish capitalists had exploited the Revolutions of 1848 for their own materialistic purposes. During the Franco–Prussian war in 1870, in a fit of chauvinistic frenzy, Wagner hoped that Bismarck would not be deterred from razing Paris and commented that "the burning of Paris would be a symbol of the world's liberation at last from the pressures of all that is base." His hatred of Roman Catholicism was in keeping with Chancellor Bismarck's strategy during the 1870s to unite the country by persecuting the enemy within by banishing priests and nuns from the country, closing their schools and expropriating their property. Wagner expressed his illiberalism by opining that freedom of the press should be denied the Jesuits: "they should utterly be wiped out, the schools made free, all the people stirred up by the priests should be shut down." *Cosima Wagner's Diaries:* Vol. 1 (London: Collins, 1978), 258, 214.

4   Jacob Katz, *The Darker Side of Genius: Richard Wagner's Anti-Semitism* (Hanover: University Press of New England, 1986), 36.

5   Alex Ross, *New Yorker*, "The Unforgiven," August 10, 1998, 68.

6   Bryan Magee, *Wagner and Philosophy* (London: Allen Lane, 2000), 350.

7   Katz, *Darker Side of Genius*, 69 and in Jonathan Carr, *The Wagner Clan* (London: Faber and Faber Ltd., 2007), 72, 75.

8   Jürgen Kühnel, "The Prose Writings," in *Wagner Handbook* ed. Ulrich Muller and Peter Wapnewski, trans. John Deathridge (Cambridge: Harvard University Press, 1992), 613, 597.

9   Derek Watson, *Richard Wagner: A Biography* (New York: Schirmer Books, 1979), 119, 304.

10   Marc A. Weiner, *Richard Wagner and the Anti-Semitic Imagination* (Lincoln: University of Nebraska, 1995), 181.

11   Watson, *Wagner*, 304.

12   Goldhagen, *Hitler's Willing Executioners*, 68–69.

13   George Mosse, *Toward the Final Solution: A History of European Racism* (New York: H. Fertig, 1985), 102–03; Jay Y. Gonen, *The Roots of Nazi Psychology: Hitler's Utopian Barbarism* (Lexington: The University Press of Kentucky, 2000), 64.

14   Magee, *Wagner and Philosophy*, 375.

15   Michael Tanner, *Wagner* (London: HarperCollins, 1996), 93; Thomas S. Grey, "The Jewish Question," in *The Cambridge Companion to Wagner*, ed. Thomas S. Grey (Cambridge: Cambridge University Press, 2008), 212–13.

16   Kim Cherin, "Is Wagner Good for the Jews," *Tikkun*, January, February, 2002.

17   *Cosima Wagner's Diaries:* Vol. II (London: Collins, 1980), 622, 771.

18   Dieter Borchmeyer, "Critique as passion and polemic: Nietzsche and Wagner," in *Cambridge Companion to Wagner*, 192, 202, Magee, *Wagner and Philosophy*, 334.

19   Magee, *Wagner and Philosophy,* 59–60.

20   Magee, *Wagner and Philosophy,* 179.

21   Hannu Salmi, *Imagined Germany: Richard Wagner's National Utopia* (New York: Peter Lang, 1999), 50–53.

22   Jonathan Carr, *The Wagner Clan* (London: Faber and Faber Ltd., 2007), 87.

23   Frederic Spotts, *Bayreuth: A History of the Wagner Festival* (New Haven: Yale University Press, 1994), 84.

24   Arthur Herman, *The Idea of Decline in Western History* (New York: The Free Press, 1997), 72.

25   Paul Lawrence Rose, *Wagner: Race and Revolution* (Yale University Press, 1992), 191.

26   Hans R. Vaget, "Wagner, Anti-Semitism and Mr. Rose: Merkwürd Ger-Fall!" *The German Quarterly* 66 (2 1993) and Edward Said, *London Review of Books*, February 11, 1993; Joachim Kohler, *Wagner's Hitler: The Prophet and his Disciple*, trans. Ronald Taylor (Cambridge: Polity Press); Weiner, *Wagner*, 90, 140.

27   Grey, "The Jewish Question," 213.

28   Tanner, *Wagner*, 28.

29   Rose, *Wagner*, 69.

30   Philip Kitcher and Richard Schacht, *Finding an Ending: Reflections on Wagner's Ring* (Oxford: Oxford University Press, 2004), 64–71.

31   Joseph Horowitz, "Nothing approaching caricature," *Times Literary Supplement*, August 21, 1998, 7.

32   Joachim Köhler, *Wagner's Hitler: The Prophet and his Disciple*, trans. intro. Ronald Taylor (Cambridge: Polity Press, 2000), 203.

33   M. Owen Lee, *Wagner's Ring: Turning the Sky Around* (New York: Limelight Editions, 1994), 78.

34   Magee, *Wagner and Philosophy*, 179, 85; Joseph Horowitz, "The Specter of Hitler in the Music of Wagner," *The New York Times*, November 8, 1998, 38.

35   Horowitz, "Nothing approaching caricature," 17.

36   Magee, *Wagner and Philosophy,* 183–84.

37   Horowitz, "Nothing," 17; Grey, "The Jewish Question," 214.

38 Kitcher, *Finding an Ending*, 168.

39 Kitcher, *Finding an Ending*, 180–181.

40 Ross, "The Ring and the Rings," *The New Yorker*, December 15, 2003.

41 Ross, "The Unforgiven," *The New Yorker*.

42 Carr, *Wagner Clan*, 187–88; Potter, "Wagner and the Third Reich," 237.

43 Ben Macintyre, *Forgotten Fatherland: The Search for Elisabeth Nietzsche* (London: Macmillan, 1992), 109.

44 Spotts, *Bayreuth*, 166.

45 Potter, "Wagner and the Third Reich," in *Cambridge Companion to Wagner*, 241; Stephen McClatchie, "Performing Germany in Wagner's *Die Meistersinger von Nürnberg*," in *Cambridge Companion to Wagner*, 147.

46 Frederic Spotts, *Hitler and the Power of Aesthetics* (London: Hutchinson, 2002), 113; Nike Wagner, *The Wagners: The Dramas of a Musical Dynasty*, trans. Ewald Osers and Michael Downes (London: Weidenfeld & Nicholson, 2000), 157; Brendon, *Dark Valley*, 107.

47 Albert Speer, *Inside the Third Reich* (New York: Avon Books, 1971), 598; David Denby, *The New Yorker* February 7, 2005.

48 Roy Pateman, *Chaos and Dancing Star: Wagner's Politics, Wagner's Legacy* (Boston: University Press of America, 2002), 260.

49 Joachim Kohler, *Richard Wagner: The Last of the Titans*, trans. Stewart Spencer (New Haven: Yale University Press, 2004), xiii, 327.

50 Wagner, *The Wagners*, 206; Brigitte Hamann, *Winifred Wagner: At the Heart of Hitler's Bayreuth*, trans. Alan Bance (London: Granta Books, 2005), 61.

51 Hamann, *Winifred Wagner*, 101; Carr, *The Wagner Clan*, 149.

52 Nike Wagner, *The Wagners*, 204.

53 Nike Wagner, *The Wagners*, 206–07.

54 Köhler, *Wagner's Hitler*, 29.

55 Guido Knopp, *Hitler's Women*, trans. Angus McGeoch (New York: Routledge, 2003), 180.

56 Nike Wagner, *The Wagners*, 206–07.

57 Spotts, *Bayreuth*, 141–42; Nike Wagner; *The Wagners*, 160–161.

58 Joachim Fest, *Speer: The Final Verdict*, trans. Ewald Osers and Alexandra Dring (London: Weidenfeld & Nicolson, 2001), 47, 360.

59 Wagner, *The Wagners*, 164.

60 Carr, *The Wagner Clan*, 285; Nike Wagner, *The Wagners*, 166.

Chapter 9

1   Geoffrey G. Field, Evangelist *of Race: The Germanic Vision of Houston Stewart Chamberlain* (New York: Columbia University Press, 1981), 403–04 and Niall Ferguson, *War of the World: Twentieth Century Conflict and the Descent of the West* (New York: Penguin Press, 2006), 254.

2   Niall Ferguson, *The War of the World*, 255.

3   Phillipe Burrin, "Nazi AntiSemitism: Animalization and Demonization," in *Demonizing the Other: Antisemitism, Racism, and Xenophobia*, ed. Robert S. Wistrich (Amsterdam: Harwood Academic, 1999), 226.

4   Klaus Theweleit, *Male Fantasies, Vol. 2: Male Bodies: Psychoanalyzing the White Terror*, trans. Stephen Conway, Erica Carter and Chris Turner (Minneapolis: University of Minnesota Press, 1989) 13.

5   Gunter Hartung, "Artur Dinter: A Successful Fascist Author in Pre-Fascist Germany" in *The Attractions of Fascism: Social Psychology and the Aesthetics of the 'Triumph of the Right*, ed. John Milful (New York: Berg, 1990), 109.

6   Victor Klemperer, *I Shall Bear Witness: The Diaries of Victor Klemperer 1933–1941*, Abridged and trans. Martin Chalmers (London: Phoenix Paperback, 1998), 307.

7   Dennis E. Showalter, *Little Man, What Now?* (Hamden Connecticut: Archon Books, 1982), 196; Klaus Theweleit, *Male Fantasies, Vol. 2: Male Bodies: Psychoanalyzing the White Terror*, trans. Stephen Conway, Erica Carter and Chris Turner (Minneapolis: University of Minnesota Press, 1989), 12; Randall L. Bytwerk, *Julius Streicher* (New York: Stein and Day, 1983), 145–46.

8   Linda Williams, "When the Woman Looks," in *Re-vision: Essays in Feminist Film Criticism*, ed. Mary Ann Doane et al (Los Angeles: American Film Institute, 1984), 89.

9   Heiden, *Der Führer*, 583–84.

10   Bytwerk, *Streicher*, 48.

11   Benno Müller-Hill, *Murderous Science: Elimination by scientific selection of Jews, Gypsies, and others, Germany 1933–45*, trans. George R. Fraser (Oxford: Oxford University Press, 1988), 90.

12   Adolf Hitler, *Mein Kampf* trans. Ralph Manheim (Boston: Houghton Mifflin Company, 1971), 239, 400, 30, italics in the original; Klaus P. Fischer, *The History of an Obsession: German Judeophobia and the Holocaust* (New York: Continuum, 1998), 137.

13   Hitler, *Mein Kampf*, 562, 325, 412, 316.

14   Robert Wistrich, *Hitler's Apocalypse: Jews and the Nazi Legacy* (London: Weidenfeld & Nicolson, 1985), 17, Heiden; *Der Führer*, 259; Richard J. Evans, *Rituals of Retribution: Capital Punishment in Germany 1600-1987* (Oxford University Press, 1996), 626.

15   Carl Zuckmayer, *A Part of Myself,* trans, Richard and Clara Winston (New York: Harcourt, Brace Jovanovich, 1970), 271–72.

16   Fest, *The Face of the Third Reich*, 399.

17   Hitler, *Mein Kampf*, 251; George L Mosse, *Nazi Culture: Intellectual, Cultural and Social Life in the Third Reich* (New York: Grosset & Dunlap, 1968), 39; H. G. Baynes, *Germany Possessed* (London: Jonathan Cape, 1941), 298.

18   Hitler, *Mein Kampf*, 305, 326. In the first citation, he adds that the Jew was a "sponger who like a noxious bacillus keeps spreading as soon as a favourable medium invites him." In the second, he adds "where he killed or starved about thirty million people with positively fanatical savagery, in part amid inhuman tortures in order to give a gang of Jewish journalists and stock exchange bandits domination over a great people."

19   Hitler, *Mein Kampf,* 252; Rosenbaum, *Explaining Hitler*, 189.

20   Klemperer, *I Will Bear Witness*, October 5, 1935, 134–35; Koonz, *Nazi Conscience*, 178.

21   Douglas Starr, *Blood: An Epic History of Medicine and Commerce* (New York: Alfred A. Knopf, 1998), 72.

22   Marion A. Kaplan, *Between Dignity and Despair: Jewish Life in Nazi Germany* (New York: Oxford University Press, 1998), 80–81.

23   *Friedlander, Nazi Germany and the Jews*, 122.

24   One of his Himmler's District leaders was overheard to say, "If I looked like Himmler, I would not talk about race." Peter Padfield, *Himmler Reichführer SS* (New York: Henry Holt, 1990), 80.

25   Tom Segev, *Soldiers of Evil: The Commandants of the Nazi Concentration Camps*, trans. Haim Waitzman (New York: McGraw-Hill Book Company, 1987), 80.

26   Burleigh, *The Third Reich*, 192–96.

27   Segev, *Soldiers of Evil*, 89–90.

28   Guido Knopp, *Hitler's Henchmen*, trans. Angus McGeoch (Sutton Publishing, 2000), 143; Segev, *Soldiers of Evil*, 74.

29   Michael Burleigh, *The Third Reich: A New History* (New York: Hill and Wang, 2000), 234; Lisa Pine, *Nazi Family Policy, 1933-45* (New York: Berg, 1997), 44–45; Ute Frevert, *Women in German History: From Bourgeois Emancipation to Sexual Liberation* trans. Stuart Mckinnon-Evans (Oxford: Berg, 1989), 237; Burleigh, *Racial State,* 252; Evans, *The Third Reich in Power*, 520.

Chapter 10

1   This is the thesis, one that is totally compatible with mine, presented by Sheila Faith Weiss in *The Nazi Symbiosis: Human Genetics and Politics in the Third Reich* (Chicago: University of Chicago Press, 2010).

2   Evans, *Rituals of Retribution,* 434–437.

3   Weiss, *The Nazi Symbiosis,* 84.

4   Michael Burleigh, *Death and Deliverance: 'Euthanasia' in Germany 1900–45* (Cambridge University Press, 1994), 17, 19.

5   Burleigh, *Death and Deliverance,* 21–3.

6   Alfred Kelly, *The Descent of Darwinism*: *Popularization of Darwinism in Germany 1860–1914* (Chapel Hill: University of North Carolina Press, 1981), 118.

7   Hitler, *Mein Kampf,* 404.

8   Michael Burleigh and Wolfgang Wippermann, *The Racial State: Germany 1933–45* (Cambridge: Cambridge University Press, 1992), 141–42.

9   Evans, *Rituals of Retribution,* 441–442.

10   Clarence Lusane, *Hitler's Black Victims: The Historical Experiences of Afro-Germans, European Blacks, Africans and African Americans in the Nazi Era* (New York: Routledge, 2002), 51.

11   Proctor, *Nazi War on Cancer,* 58; Kater, *Doctors under Hitler,* 237.

12   Robert Jay Lifton, *The Nazi Doctors: Medical Killing and the Psychology of Genocide* (New York: Basic Books, 1986), 31.

13   Overy, *The Dictators,* 246; Gellately, *Backing Hitler,* 93; Burleigh, *Racial State,* 138.

14   Weiss, *Nazi Symbiosis,* 101; Lusane, *Hitler's Black Victims,* 138–141.

15   Robert Proctor, *Racial Hygiene: Medicine under the Nazis* (Cambridge, Harvard University Press, 1988), 133; Overy, *The Dictators,* 251.

16   Müller-Hill *Murderous Science,* 23.

17   Starr, *Blood,* 75–76.

18   Proctor, *Racial Hygiene,* 124–25.

19   Speer, *Inside the Third Reich,* 92.

20   Hitler, *Mein Kampf,* 414–415, 430.

21   Paul Weindling, *Health, Race and German Politics between National Unification and Nazism 1870–1945* (Cambridge: Cambridge University Press, 1989), 491–92.

22   Robert Proctor, *Nazi War on Cancer* (Princeton N.J.: Princeton University Press, 1999), 120.

23   Proctor, *Nazi War on Cancer*, 209, 241.

24   Lionel B. Steiman, *Paths to Genocide: Antisemitism in Western History* (London: Macmillan Press, 1998), 142.

25   Geoffrey Cocks, *Psychotherapy in the Third Reich: The Göring Institute* (New Brunswick: [U.S.A.] Transaction Publishers, 1997), 104, 238–239. James E, Goggin and Eileen Brockman Goggin, *Death of a "Jewish Science:" Psychoanalysis in the Third Reich* (West Lafayette, Indiana: Purdue University Press), 2001, 94–96.

26   Weindling, *Health, race and German politics*, 500; Lisa Pine, *Nazi Family Policy, 1933–45* (New York: Berg, 1997), 42–43.

27   John Weiss, *Ideology of Death: Why the Holocaust Happened* (Chicago: J.R. Dee, 1996), 317.

28   Paul Weindling, "Understanding Nazi Racism: Precursors and Perpetrators," in *Confronting the Nazi Past: New Debates on Modern German History*, ed. Michael Burleigh (London: Collins & Brown, 1996), 75.

29   Max Weinreich, *Hitler's Professors: The Part of Scholarship in Germany's Crimes against the Jewish people* (New York: Yiddish Scientific Institute, 1946), 6.

30   Edwin Black, *IBM and the Holocaust: The Strategic Alliance between Nazi Germany and America's most Powerful Corporation* (New York: Crown Publishers, 2001), 8, 154.

31   Jonathan Peter Spiro, *Defending the Master Race: Conservation, Eugenics and the Legacy of Madison Grant* (Burlington V: University of Vermont Press, 2009), 149–153, 157; cited in Kühl, *Nazi Connection,* 85; cited in Black, *War Against the Weak,* 90, 251–252.

32   Claudia Koonz, "Eugenics, Gender, and Ethics in Nazi Germany: The Debate about Involuntary Sterilization 1933–1936," in *Revaluating the Third Reich*, ed. Thomas Childers and Jane Caplan (New York: Holmes & Meier, 1993), 68.

33   Stefan Kühl, *The Nazi Connection: Eugenics, American Racism, and German National Socialism* (New York: Oxford University Press, 1994), 39.

34   Kühl, *The Nazi Connection,* 46; Wendy Kline, *Building a Better Race: Gender, Sexuality, and Eugenics from the Turn of the Century to the Baby Boom* (Berkeley: University of California Press, 2001), 106.

35   Kühl, *Nazi Connection,* 48–50, 62.

36   Kline, *Building a Better Race,* 59; David Neiwert, *The Eliminationists: How Hate Talk Radicalized the American Right* (PoliPointPress, 2009), 204–208; *Patrick Buchanan, State of Emergency:*

The Third World Invasion and Conquest of America (New York: Thomas Dunne Books/St Martin's Press, 2006).

37   Weiss, *The Nazi Symbiosis*, 244, 309, 120.

38   Weindling, *Health, race and German politics*, 310; Michael H. Kater, *Doctors under Hitler* (Chapel Hill: The University of North Carolina Press, 1989), 233, 236.

39   Kühl, *The Nazi Connection*, 103.

40   It should be noted that there were exceptions. A French doctor with strong religious connections refused to join in medical work because such activities were "contrary to [her] conception as a doctor." When asked whether if she could not see the difference with "these people" she responded by stating "that there were several other people different from [her] starting with him." She did not expect to survive Auschwitz but in her remaining time, she was determined to remain a human being. She was not, however, punished or killed by Mengele or the other doctors and survived her ordeal. Lifton, *Nazi Doctors*, 297–98

Chapter 11

1   Michael Stürmer, *The German Century* (London: Weidenfeld & Nicholson, 1999), 153.

2   Snyder, *Bloodlands*, 61.

3   Koonz, *Nazi Conscience*, 33; Ian Kershaw, *The 'Hitler Myth': Image and Reality in the Third Reich* (Oxford: Oxford University Press, 1989), 36, 108.

4   Fest, *Speer,* 40.

5   Heiden, *Der Fuhrer*, 106.

6   Brandon Taylor, "Post-Modernism in the Third Reich," in *The Nazification of Art: Art, Design, Music, Architecture and Film in the Third Reich*, ed. Brandon Taylor and Wilfred van der Will (Winchester, Hampshire: Winchester Press), 1990, 129.

7   Hitler, *Mein Kampf*, 475.

8   Fritz Stern, *Dreams and Delusions: Drama of German History* (New York: Alfred A Knopf, 1987), 134.

9   William L. Shirer, *Berlin Diary: The Journal of a Foreign Correspondent* (New York: Alfred A. Knopf, 1943), 15, 17, 25; Kershaw, *Hitler*, 133.

10   Stephen H. Roberts, *The House that Hitler Built* (London: Methuen, 1939), 139.

11   Griffin, *Modernism and Fascism*, 277.

12   Overy, *The Dictators*, 129.

13   Sebastian Haffner, *The Ailing Empire: Germany from Bismarck to Hitler,* trans. Jean Steinburg (New York: Fromm International, 1989), 185–86.

14   George Orwell, *The Collected Essays: Journalism and Letters of George Orwell, Volume II; My Country Right or Left, 1940–43,* ed. Sonia Orwell and Ian Angus (London; Sacker & Warburg, 1968), 13–14.

15   Alex de Jonge, *Weimar Chronicle: Prelude to Hitler* (New York: New American Library, 1978), 216.

16   Klaus Petersen, "The Harmful Publications (Young Persons) Act of 1926: Literary Censorship and the Politics of Morality in the Weimar Republic," *German Studies Review* 15 no. 3 (October 1992): 507–08, 518.

17   Uli Linke, *Blood and Nation: The European Aesthetics of Race* (Philadelphia: University of Pennsylvania Press, 1999), 208.

18   Klaus P. Fischer, *Nazi Germany: A New History* (New York: Continuum, 1996), 366

19   Katerina Clark and Karl Schlögel, "Mutual Perceptions: Stalin's Russia in Nazi Germany—Nazi Germany in the Soviet Union," in *Beyond Totalitarianism: Stalinism and Nazi Germany Compared,* ed. Michael Geyer and Sheila Fitzpatrick (Cambridge: Cambridge University Press, 2009), 427.

20   Petersen, "Harmful Publications,"520.

21   Taylor, *Film Propaganda,* 144; Stern, *Dreams and Delusions,* 160.

22   Koonz, *Nazi Conscience,* 59.

23   Rüdiger Safranski, *Martin Heidegger: Between Good and Evil,* trans. Ewald Osers (Cambridge: Harvard University Press, 1998), 203.

24   Gellately and Nathan Stoltzfus, "Social Outsiders and the Construction of the Community of the People" in *Social Outsiders in Nazi Germany,* 3.

25   Roger Griffin, "Party Time: The Temporal Revolution of the Third Reich," *History Today* 4/16 (1999): 48.

26   Dieter Thomä "The Difficulty of Democracy: Rethinking the Political in the Philosophy of the Thirties (Genlen, Schmitt, Heidegger)," in *Nazi Germany and the Humanities,* ed. Wolfgang Bialas and Anson Rabinbach (Oxford: One World Publications, 2007), 92.

27   Bambach, *Heidegger's Roots,* 36.

28   Herman Philipse, *Heidegger's Philosophy of Being: A Critical Interpretation* (Princeton: Princeton University Press, 1998), 253.

29   Safranski, *Heidegger,* 232, 228, 227.

30   The most provocative critique of Heidegger, suggesting he be excluded from the ranks of a philosopher because his political project was to use philosophy to legitimatize Nazism, is Emmanuel Faye,

Heidegger: The Introduction of Nazism into Philosophy in light of the Unfinished Seminars of 1933-1935 (New Haven: Yale University Press, 2009). Critical but less accusatory include Charles Bambach, *Heidegger's Roots: Nietzsche, National Socialism and the Greeks* (Ithaca: Cornell University Press,) 2003, Richard Wolin, *The Politics of Being: The Political Thought of Martin Heidegger* (New York: Columbia University Press, 1990), Iain Thomson, "'Heidegger and National Socialism," *A Companion to Heidegger*, ed. Hubert L. Dreyfus and Mark A. Wrathall (Oxford: Blackwell Publishing), 2005. Herman Philipse, *Heidegger's Philosophy of Being*. Yet his biographer, Rüdiger Safranski, continues to maintain the distinction between a deeply-flawed human being and respect for his ideas and enormous influence.

31 Karl Löwith, *My life in Germany before and after 1933: A Report*, trans. Elizabeth King (London: The Athlone Press, 1994), 60.

32 Philipse, *Heidegger's Philosophy of Being*, 265–66.

33 Faye, *Heidegger*, 15–17. Faye quotes from Nazi philosophers writing in the 1920s that influenced Heidegger. John Gray, an astute modern philosopher, suggests that Heidegger's yearning to belong best explains his involvement with the Nazis. *Straw Dogs: Thoughts on Humans and Other Animals* (London: Granta Books, 2002), 50.

34 Faye, *Heidegger*, 97–98, 68–69, 138–39.

35 Gray, *Straw Dogs*, 255; Thomas Sheehan, "Heidegger and the Nazis," *New York Review of Books*, June 16, 1988.

36 Bambach, *Heidegger's Roots*, 53.

37 Peter Gay, *Weimar Culture: The Outsider as Insider* (New York: Harper & Row, 1968), 82–83.

38 Safranski, *Martin Heidegger*, 227; Philipse, *Heidegger's Philosophy of Being*, 496 n. 171; Faye, *Heidegger*, 30.

39 Safranski, *Heidegger*, 226–27; Safranski, *Martin Heidegger*, 231.

40 Koonz, *Nazi Conscience*, 46; Philipse, *Heidegger's Philosophy of Being*, 248.

41 Richard Wolin, *Heidegger's Children: Hannah Arendt, Karl Löwith, Hans Jonas and Herbert Marcuse* (Princeton University Press, 2001), 8.

42 Wolin, *The Politics of Being*, 89, 91; Stern, *Hitler*, 95, Safranski, *Heidegger*, 250.

43 Faye, *Heidegger*, 71.

44 Safranski, *Heidegger*, 231.

45 Bambach, Heidegger's Roots, 70

46 Iain Thomson, "Heidegger and National Socialism," *A Companion to Heidegger*, ed. Hubert L. Dreyfus and Mark A. Wrathall (Oxford: Blackwell Publishing), 2005, 44; Wolin, *Politics of Being*, 4.

47   Bambach, Heidegger's Roots, 129; Koonz, Nazi Conscience, 49.

48   Thomas Sheehan, "Heidegger and the Nazis," *New York Review of Books*, June 16, 1988, 44.

49   Safranski, *Heidegger*, 253–54.

50   Thomas Sheehan, "A Normal Nazi," *New York Review of Books*, January 14, 1993, 34.

51   Wolin, *Politics of Being*, 92.

52   Faye, *Heidegger*, 53.

53   Victor Farias, *Heidegger and Nazism* (Philadelphia, Temple University Press, 1989), 130; Faye, *Heidegger*, 66.

54   Faye, *Heidegger*, 203–04.

55   Bambach, *Heidegger's Roots*, 153.

56   Löwith, *My life in Germany before and after 1933,* 60–61.

57   John D. Caputo, "Heidegger's Revolution: An Introduction to an Introduction to Metaphysics," in *Heidegger toward the Turn: Essays on the Work of the 1930s*, ed. James Risser (Albany: State University of New York: 1999), 57.

58   Faye, *Heidegger*, 53.

59   Farias, *Heidegger*, 217

60   Safranski, *Heidegger*, 289; Caputo, "Heidegger's Revolution," 60.

61   Wolin, *Politics of Being*, 104–105.

62   Wolin, *Politics of Being*, 125–26; Caputo, "Heidegger's Revolution," 65.

63   Philipse, *Heidegger's Philosophy of Being,* 273–74; Safranski, *Martin Heidegger,* 327.

64   Adam LeBor, *Surviving Hitler: Choices Corruption and Compromise in the Third Reich* (London: Simon & Schuster, 2000), 119.

65   Wolin, *The Politics of Being,* 129.

66   Ott, *Martin Heidegger,* 32.

67   Thomä, "The Difficulty of Democracy," 92. Heidegger's comment about democracy was omitted from the 1961 edition and has only become available posthumously.

68   Faye, *Heidegger*, 168, 140, 143–44, 295.

69   Heidegger, *Being and Time;* Stern, *Hitler*, 96.

70   Faye, *Heidegger*, 117.

71   Safranski, *Heidegger*, 290.

72   Faye, *Heidegger*, 305.

73   Gordon A. Craig, *The Germans* (New York: Meridian, 1991), 145.

74   Martin Heidegger, "Creative Landscape: Why Do We Stay in the Provinces?" *Weimar Republic Sourcebook*, ed. Anton Kaes, Martin Jay

and Edward Dimenberg (Berkeley: University of California Press, 1994), 427.

75   Stapel, "The Intellectual and His People," *Weimar Republic Sourcebook*, 423–24.

76   Ott, *Martin Heidegger*, 167.

77   Hill, "Un-German Literature," 32–33.

78   Detlev J.K. Peukert, *Inside Nazi Germany: Conformity, Opposition and Racism in Everyday Life*, trans. Richard Deveson (London: Penguin Books, 1989), 24.

79   Daniel Guérin, *The Brown Plague: Travels in Late Weimar and early Nazi Germany*, trans. and intro by Robert Scgwartzwald (Durham: Duke University Press, 1994), 105.

80   Koonz, *The Nazi Conscience*, 46; Adam Kirsch, "The Jewish Question: Martin Heidegger," *New York Times*, April 29, 2010.

Chapter 12

1   Götz Ally, *Hitler's Beneficiaries: Plunder, Racial War, and the Nazi Welfare State* trans. Jefferson Chase (New York: Henry Holt and Company, 2006).

2   Richard J. Evans, *The Third Reich in Power 1933–1939* (New York: Penguin Press, 2005), 468–473.

3   Overy, *Dictators*, 209.

4   Peter Fritzsche and Jochen Hellbeck, "The New Man in Stalinist Russia and Nazi Germany" in *Beyond Totalitarianism*, 327–335. Before Sebastian Haffner (his real name was Raimund Pretzel) could graduate from law school in 1933, he was required to attend boot camp at which he not only sang Nazi songs, heard talks and received a taste of military training, but he also was exposed to a sinister comradeship. It became the "means for the most terrible dehumanization [because it]...admitted no thoughts, just mass feelings of the most primitive sort...and decomposed all the elements of individuality and civilization." If anyone challenged the crudity or the lack of individuality of comradeship, he was subjected to brutal corporal punishment by the group. Sebastian Haffner, *Defying Hitler: A Memoir*, trans. Oliver Pretzel (London: Weidenfeld & Nicolson, 2002, 285–91.

5   Jürgen Trimborn, trans. Edna McCown, *Leni Riefenstahl: A Life* (New York, Faber and Faber, 2007), 35.

6   Steven Bach, *Leni: The Life and Work of Lenin Riefenstahl* (New York: Alfred A. Knopf, 2007), 77; Trimborn, *Leni Riefenstahl*, 47; Eric Rentschler, *The Ministry of Illusion: Nazi Cinema and its Aftermath* (Cambridge: Harvard University Press, 1996), 45.

7   Bach, *Leni*, 80–81.

8   *Leni Riefenstahl: A Memoir*, (New York: St. Martin's Press, [1987], 1992 English translation), 101–02.

9   Bach, *Leni*, 191.

10   Ruth Starkman, "Mother of all Spectacles," *Film Quarterly* Vol.51 No.2 (Winter 1997–98): 21.

11   Bach, *Leni: Leni*, 91; *Memoir*, 107.

12   Bach, *Leni*, 123.

13   Bach, *Leni*, 140.

14   Ralf Georg Reuth, *Goebbels*, trans. Krishna Winston (New York: Harcourt Brace & Company, 1993), 232.

15   Fest, *Hitler*, 513.

16   David Clay Large, *Nazi Games: The Olympics of 1936* (New York: W.W. Norton, 2007), 308.

17   Large, *Nazi Games*, 309.

18   Deborah E. Lipstadt, *Beyond Belief: The American Press and the Coming of the Holocaust* (New York: The Free Press, 1986), 80, 84–85.

19   Griffin, "Party Time," 48.

20   Bach, *Leni*, 198.

21   Knopp, *Henchmen*, 28–29.

22   Eksteins, *Rites of Spring*, 304.

23   Rentschler, *Ministry of Illusion*, 152.

24   Alexandra Richie, *Faust's Metropolis: A History of Berlin* (London: Carroll & Graf Publishers, 1998), 455.

25   Rentschler, *Ministry of Illusion*, 122; William Moritz "Film Censorship during the Nazi Era," in *'Degenerate Art': The Fate of the Avant-Garde in Nazi Germany*, ed. Stephanie Barron (Los Angeles County Museum of Art: Abrams, 1994), 188.

26   Richard Taylor, *Film Propaganda: Soviet Russia and Nazi Germany* (London: I.B. Tauris, 1998), 152.

27   Richard J. Evans, *The Third Reich at War 1939–1945* (London: Penguin, 2008), 9, 14–15.

28   Uli Linke, *Blood and Nation: The European Aesthetics of Race* (Philadelphia: University of Pennsylvania Press, 1999), 199.

29   Peter Adam, *Art of the Third Reich* (New York: Harry N. Abrams, Inc., 1992), 148.

30   David Welch, *Propaganda and the German Cinema 1933–45* (Oxford: Clarendon Press, 1983), 103–04.

31   Erich Michaud, *The Cult of Art in Nazi Germany* trans. Janet Lloyd (Stanford: Stanford University Press, 2004), 152.

32   Erik Larson, *In the Garden of Beasts: Love, Terror, and an American Family in Hitler's Berlin* (New York: Crown, 2011), 359.

33   Reuth, *Goebbels*, 53.

34   Omer Bartov, *The 'Jew' in Cinema: From the Golem to Don't Touch My Holocaust* (Bloomington: Indiana University Press, 2005), 13.

35   Larson, *Garden of the Beasts*, 258.

36   Michele C. Cone, "Vampires, Viruses, and Lucien Rebatet: Anti-Semitic Art Critics during Vichy," in *The Jew in the Text: Modernity and the Construction of Identity*," ed. Linda Nochlin & Tamar Garb, (London: Thames and Hudson, 1991), 180.

37   Klemperer, *Witness*, 442; Nicholas Reeves, *The Power of Film Propaganda: Myth or Reality* (London: Cassell, 1999), 117.

38   Linda Schulte-Sasse, *Entertaining the Third Reich: Illusions of Wholeness in Nazi Cinema* (Durham: Duke University Press, 1996), 79.

39   Rentschler, *Ministry of Illusion*, 156; Schulte-Sasse, *Entertaining the Third Reich*, 62–63.

40   Rentschler, *Ministry of Illusion*, 163.

41   Wistrich, *Hitler's Apocalypse*, 36.

42   Reeves, *The Power of Film Propaganda*, 114.

43   David Culbert, "The Impact of Anti-Semitic Film Propaganda on German Audiences: *Jew Suss* and *The Wandering Jew* (1940)," in *Art Culture, and Media Under the Third Reich*, ed. Richard A. Etlin (Chicago: University of Chicago Press, 2002), 147, 154.

44   Ian Kershaw, "How effective was Nazi Propaganda?" in *Nazi Propaganda: The Power and the Limitations*, ed. David Welsh (London: Croom Helm, 1983), 371; Reeves, *Film Propaganda*, 118.

45   Fritzsche, Life and Death in Third Reich, 286.

46   Bartov, *The 'Jew' in Cinema*, 138–141.

47   Griffin, *Modernism and Fascism*, 308.

Chapter 13

1   Haffner, *Defying Hitler*, 144.

2   Evans, *Rituals of Retribution*, 605.

3   Overy, *The Dictators*, 204; Evans, *Rituals of Retribution*, 625–27, 630.

4   Rosenbaum, *Explaining Hitler*, 40, 43.

5   Eve Rosenhaft, *Beating the Fascists? The German Communists and Political Violence 1929–1933* (Cambridge: Cambridge University Press, 1983), 214.

6   Kershaw, *Hitler 1889–1936*, 501.

7   Kershaw, *Hitler, 460,* Gellately, *Backing Hitler,* 54.

8   Gellately, *Backing Hitler,* 41, 50.

9   Klemperer, *I Shall Bear Witness,* 51.

10   Larson, *Garden of Beasts* on page 3–4 offers a grisly example of an American physician, Joseph Schachno, who was beaten with a whip until the skin was flayed from his body because of anonymous denunciation that he might be a potential enemy of the state. Larson also provides several examples of Americans assaulted on the streets by storm troopers who refused to offer the Hitler salute or turned their back on SA parades.

11   Tucker, *Stalin in Power,* 275.

12   Amir Weiner, *Making Sense of War: The Second World War and the Fate of the Bolshevik Revolution* (Princeton: Princeton University Press, 2001), 235.

13   Overy, *Dictators,* 294–95.

14   Kershaw, *The 'Hitler Myth',* 92–93; Klemperer, *Witness,* 91.

15   Evans, *The Third Reich in Power,* 80.

16   Burleigh, *The Third Reich,* 184; Robert Gellately, *The Gestapo and German Society: Enforcing Racial Policy 1933–1945* (Oxford: Clarendon Press, 1990), 131, 42.

17   Evans, *Rituals of Retribution,* 679–81; Burleigh, *Third Reich,* 171.

18   Eric Johnson, *Nazi Terror: The Gestapo, the Jews and Ordinary Germans* (London: John Murray, 1999), 172–73.

19   Overy, *Dictators,* 600.

20   Fritzsche, *Life and Death in the Third Reich,* 42; Hannah Arendt, *Totalitarianism: Part Three of the Origins of Totalitarianism* (San Diego: A Harvest Book: [1966] 1976), 143, 147–148.

21   Burleigh, *Third Reich,* 204; Arendt, *Totalitarianism,* 145, 149, 151–53; Bettelheim, *The Informed Heart,* 128.

22   Klemperer, *I Shall Bear Witness,* 10.

23   Kaplan, *Between Dignity and Despair,* 18–20; Evans, *Third Reich in Power,* 95; Arendt, Totalitarianism, 145.

24   Geoffrey J. Giles, "The Institutionalization of Homosexual Panic in the Third Reich," in *Social Outsiders,* 250; Burleigh, *Racial State,* 196–197; Gellately, *Backing Hitler,* 115; Modris Eksteins, *Solar Dance: Genius, Forgery, and the Crisis of Truth in the Modern Age* (Toronto: Knopf Canada, 2012), 228.

25   Gellately, *Backing Hitler,* 92.

26   Nikolaus Wachsmann, "From Indefinite Confinement to Extermination: 'Habitual Criminals' in the Third Reich," in *Social Outsiders in Nazi Germany,* ed. Gellately, 165–191.

27 Elizabeth Heineman, *What Difference does a Husband Make in Nazi and Postwar Germany?* (Berkeley: University of California Press, 1999), 28.

28 Annette F. Timm, "The Ambivalent Outsider: Prostitution, Promiscuity, and VD Control Nazi Berlin," in *Social Outsiders in Nazi Germany*, 205-06.

29 Burleigh, *Third Reich*, 372; Sybil H. Milton, "Gypsies' as Social Outsiders in Nazi Germany," in *Social Outsiders*, 217.

30 Gellately, *Backing Hitler*, 99.

31 Segev, *Soldiers of Evil*, 192.

32 Gellately, *Backing Hitler*, 52-56.

33 Gellately, *Backing Hitler*, 65.

34 Gellately, *Backing Hitler*, 259.

35 Evans, *Rituals of Retribution*, 665-66.

36 Stürmer, *The German Century*, 159-60.

37 Gellately, *Gestapo and German Society*, 181-84; Overy, *Dictators*, 213.

38 Gellately, *Backing Hitler*, 137-140; Gellately, *Gestapo and German Society*, 149; Vandana Joshi, *Gender and Power in the Third Reich: Female Denouncers and the Gestapo [1933-45]* (Houndmills: Palgrave Macmillan, 2003), 55-56, 81.

39 Fritzsche and Hellbeck, "The New Man in Stalinist Russia and Nazi Germany," in *Beyond Totalitarianism*, 328; Fritz Stern, *Five Germanys I have Known* (New York: Farrar, Straus and Giroux, 2006), 107.

40 Gellately, *Backing Hitler*, 135.

41 Gellately, *Gestapo and German Society*, 204.

42 Johnson, *Nazi Terror*, 93.

43 Evan Burr, Bukey, *Hitler's Austria: Popular Sentiment in the Nazi Era 1938-45* (Chapel Hill: University of North Carolina Press, 2000), 134.

44 Zuckmayer, *A Part of Myself*, 50-51.

45 George Clare, *Last Waltz in Vienna: The Destruction of a Family 1842-1942* (London: Macmillan, 1981), 191.

46 Kaplan, *Between Dignity and Despair*, 120.

47 Friedländer, *Nazi Germany*, 272.

48 Michael Blumenthal, *The Invisible Wall: Germans and Jews: a personal exploration* (Washington D.C.: Counterpoint, 1998), 366-374 especially 374.

49 Friedländer, *Nazi Germany*, 132.

50   David Bankier, *The Germans and the Final Solution: Public Opinion under Nazis* (Oxford: Blackwell, 1996), 86.

51   Theodore S. Hamerow, *On the Road to the Wolf's Lair: German Resistance to Hitler* (Cambridge: Harvard University Press, 1997), 226–27.

52   Wibke Bruhns, *My Father's Country: The Story of a German Family*, trans. Shaun Whiteside (London: William Heinemann, 2008), 241–42.

53   Peter Gay, *My German Question: Growing up in Nazi Berlin* (New Haven: Yale University Press, 1998), 128, 134.

54   Maschmann, *Account Rendered*, 56, 40.

55   Black, *IBM*, 144.

56   Klemperer, *Witness*, 394; Haffner, *Defying Hitler*, 116.

57   Maschmann, *Account Rendered*, 221.

58   Bruhns, *My Father's Country*, 220.

Chapter 14

1   Originally jihad meant both a spiritual internal struggle against one's ego and military action for either defensive purposes or to spread the faith. Violent Islamists have abandoned the word's original intent and have recently used it to justify war against the infidel until he accepts Islam or prepares to pay a tribute.

2   David Punter and Glennis Byron, *The Gothic* (Malden, MA: Blackwell, 2004), 263–264.

3   Richard Devetak, "The Gothic scene of international relations: ghosts, monsters, terror and the sublime after September 11," *Review of International Studies* 31 (2005): 637. The epithets that Bush used to describe Hussein and bin Laden are taken from this essay. Devetak astutely compares the speeches of Bush to the horrified responses of Edmund Burke to the French Revolution and to the language used by Gothic writer Edgar Allan Poe in *The Fall of the House of Usher*.

4   John Quincy Adams, July 4, 1821, a speech he delivered to the House of Representatives. Devetak, "The Gothic scene of international relations," 640.

5   Jane Mayer, *The Dark Side: The Inside Story of How the War on Terror Turned into a War on American Ideals* (New York: Doubleday, 2008), 174.

Chapter 15

1   David J. Skal, *The Monster Show: A Cultural History of Horror* (New York: W.W. Norton & Company, 1993), 216.

2   For example, Kathleen Taylor, *Brainwashing: The Science of Thought Control* (Oxford: Oxford University Press, 2004).

3   Lawrence Wright, *The Looming Tower: Al-Qaeda and the Road to 9/11* (New York: Alfred A. Knopf, 2006), 14.

4   Bruce Cumings, *The Korean War: A History* (New York: Modern Library, 2010), 137–39.

5   Cumings *The Korean War*, 166–167; John Tirman, *The Deaths of Others: The Fate of Civilians in America's Wars* (Oxford: Oxford University Press, 2011), 288–294, 122.

6   John Lewis Gaddis, *The Cold War: A New History* (New York: Penguin Press, 2005), 45. Gaddis presents a chilling counter-factual scenario in which Soviet bombers attack South Korean cities; MacArthur orders American pilots to drop atomic bombs on Vladivostok and Chinese cities. European countries formally withdraw from NATO as mushroom clouds are reported over West German cities. 49.

7   Matthew M. Aid, *The Secret Sentry: The Untold History of the National Security Agency* (New York: Bloomsbury Press, 2009), 36.

8   Kevin Baker, "Stabbed in the back! The past and future of a right-wing myth," http://www.harpers.org/archives/2006/06/0081080.

9   Beverly Merrill Kelley, *Reelpolitik II: Political Ideologies in '50s and '60s Film* (Lanham, MD: Rowman & Littlefield, 2004), 185.

10   *New York Times*, April 21, 1950, cited in Cumings, *Korean War*, 254.

11   Michael J. Hogan, *A Cross of Iron: Harry S. Truman and the Origins of the National Security State,* 1945–1954 (Cambridge: Cambridge University Press, 1998), 254–255; Ellen Schrecker, *Many Are the Crimes: McCarthyism in America* (Boston: Little, Brown and Company, 1998), 210–211.

12   Stephen J. Whitfield, *The Culture of the Cold War* (Baltimore: Johns Hopkins University Press, 1991), 36; Larry Ceplair, *Anti-Communism in Twentieth-Century America: A Critical History* (Santa Barbara, California: Praeger. 2011), 16.

13   Raymond B. Lech, *Broken Soldiers* (Urbana: University of Illinois Press, 2000), 70, 124.

14   Susan L. Carruthers, *Cold War Captives: Imprisonment, Escape and Brainwashing* (Berkeley: University of California Press, 2009, 212–213; Eugene Kinkead, *In Every War but One* (Westport Conn.: Greenwood Press, 1959), 1,148, 17.

15   David Seed, *Brainwashing The Fictions of Mind Control: A Study of Novels and Films since World War II* (Kent; Kent University Press, 2004), 29, 31.

16   Adam J. Zweiback, "The 21 'Turncoat GIs': Nonrepatriations and the political culture of the Korean War," *The Historian* Vol. 60 (1998): 357–58; Carruthers, *Cold War Captives*, 175, 195.

17   Zweiback, "Turncoat GIs:" 358.

18   Kelley, *Reelpolitik II*, 214.

19   Tim Weiner, *Legacy of Ashes: The History of the CIA* (New York: Doubleday, 2007), 65, 555. H.P. Albarelli Jr., *A Terrible Mistake: The Murder of Frank Olson and the CIA's Secret Cold War Experiments* (Chicago: Trine Day LLC, 2009), 686–687, 350–358, 693.

20   Abbot Gleason, *Totalitarianism: The Inner History of the Cold War* (New York: Oxford University Press, 1995), 97.

21   Bruce I. Kaufman, *The Korean War* (Westport, CT: Greenwood Press, 1999), 29; Lech, *Broken Soldiers*, 150.

22   Kelley, *Reelpolitik II*, 186.

23   A major exception is *The United States and Biological Warfare: Secrets from the Early Cold War* (Bloomington: Indiana University, 1999) by Canadian historians Stephen Endicott and Edward Hagerman. They present with circumstantial evidence the case that an American covert operation did drop infected insects, spiders and feathers in northeast China that did cause a plague and cholera in February and March 1953. The 2002 German documentary *Codename Artichoke* also strongly suggests that there was some truth in the original confessions of those who claimed that the U.S. resorted to biochemical warfare.

24   Albert D. Biderman, *March to Calumny: The Story of American POWs in the Korean War* (New York: Macmillan, 1963), 136; Biderman, "Efforts of Communist Indoctrination Attempts: Some Comments Based on Air Force Prisoner-of-War Study," *Social Problems* Vol. 6, No. 4 (Spring 1959) 304–313; Robert J. Lifton, "Home by Ship: Reaction Pattern of American Prisoners of War Repatriated," *American Journal of Psychiatry* 110 (April, 1954): 732–39.

25   Susan Sontag, *Against Interpretation and Other Essays* (New York: Farrar, Straus & Giroux, [1961] 1966), 221

26   Carruthers, *Cold War Captives*, 206; Louis Menard, "Brainwashed," *The New Yorker*, September 15, 2003; Kelley, *Reelpolitik II*, 212; Cumings, *Korean War*, 85.

27   Momism in Wylie's polemic, *Generation of Vipers*, is referenced in Carruthers, *Cold War Captives*, 208–209.

That the Manchurian candidate syndrome retained its power is evident from an anecdote about Senator John McCain during the 2000 American election primaries. When asked by reporters why he had changed his mind and decided to run against George W. Bush in the Republican primaries, McCain, who had spent six years in a POW camp in North Vietnam, replied, "I was sitting in a room and Angela Lansbury turned over a queen of diamonds." His droll response delighted the press, but did not help him in the primaries. Indeed, because of McCain's reconciliation with Vietnam protestors and his dismissal of the notion of POW's still alive in Vietnam, many on the political right labelled *him* as a Manchurian Candidate. Jonathan Alter, *Newsweek*, February 21, 2000, 30.

28   Carruthers, *Cold War Captives*, 234.

29   Anne Collins, *In the Sleep Room: The Story of the CIA Brainwashing in Canada* (Toronto: Key Porter Books, 1988), 109.

30   Allen M. Hornblum, *Acres of Skin: Human Experiments at Holmesburg Prison* (New York: Routledge, 1998), xi–xii, xvi, 242; James H. Jones, *Bad Blood: The Tuskegee Syphilis Experiment* (Toronto: Maxwell MacMillan, 1993), 12, 27 Collins, *In the Sleep Room*, 113; Harvey M. Weinstein, *Psychiatry and the CIA: Victims of Mind Control* (Washington, DC: American Psychiatric Press, 1990), 94–96.

31   Naomi Klein, *The Shock Doctrine: The Rise of Disaster Capitalism* (Toronto: Random House, 2007), 40–41.

32   Klein, *The Shock Doctrine*, 42.

33   Weinstein, *Psychiatry and the CIA*, 222–23.

34   Weinstein, *Psychiatry and the CIA*, 36.

35   John Marks, *The Search for the "Manchurian Candidate": The CIA and Mind Control* (New York: Times Books, 1979), 133–37. The plight of Linda Macdonald is profiled in "A tragic failure of will" by Allan Fotheringham, *Maclean's*, March 18, 1991, 68.

36   Klein, *The Shock Doctrine*, 29, 53.

37   Klein, *The Shock Doctrine*, 44.

38   Raymond B. Lech, *Tortured into Fake Confession: The Dishonouring of Korean War Prisoner Col. Frank H. Schwable, USMC* (Jefferson: McFarland & Company, 2011), 80.

39   Mayer, *The Dark Side*, 158, 161.

40   Mayer, *The Dark Side*, 161.

41   Thomas B. Byers, "Kissing Becky: Masculine Fears and Misogynist Moments in Science Fictions Films," *Arizona Quarterly* Vol. 45, No. 3 (Autumn 1987): 83.

42   Carruthers, *Cold War Captives*, 15.

Chapter 16

1   Wright, *Looming Tower*, 12.

2   Jeffrey Herf, *Nazi Propaganda and the Arab World* (New Haven: Yale University Press, 2009), 255–259.

3   Juan Cole, *Engaging the Muslim World* (Houndmills, Basingstroke Hampshire: Palgrave Macmillan, 2009), 58–59 and John W. Dower, *Cultures of War: Pearl Harbor/ Hiroshima/ 9-11/Iraq* (New York: W.W. Norton), 2010, 304.

4   John Calvert, *Sayyid Qutb and the Origins of Radical Islamism* (London: Hurst and Company. 2010), 224, 241–243.

5   Fawaz A. Gerges, *The Rise and Fall of Al-Qaeda* (New York: Oxford University Press, 2011), 30–31, 43; Calvert, *Qutb*, 15, 291–292.

6   The *9/11Report* makes the most explicit connection between Qutb and bin Laden: "Bin Laden also heavily relies heavily on the Egyptian writer Sayyid Qutb....Bin Laden shares Qutb's stark view, permitting him and his followers to rationalize even unprovoked mass murder as righteous defence of an embattled faith." Thomas H. Kean and Lee H. Hamilton, *9/11Report: The National Commission on Terrorist Attacks Upon the United States* (New York: St. Martin's Press, 2004), 51 Calvert, *Qutb*, 295.

7   Jessica Stern, *Terror in the Name of God: Why Religious Militants Kill* (New York: Ecco, 2003), 264.

8   Gerges, *Al-Qaeda,* 55–58.

9   Peter L Bergen, *The Longest War: The Enduring Conflict between America and Al-Qaeda* (New York: Free Press, 2011), 27; Peter L .Bergen, *Holy War, Inc.: Inside the Secret World of Osama Bin Laden* (New York: Free Press, 2001), 78, 99.

10   Wright *Looming Tower*, 305–06; Gilles Kepel, *The War for Muslim Minds: Islam and the West*, trans., Pascale Ghazaleh (Cambridge, Mass.: Harvard University Press, 2004), 105–06.

11   Gerges, *Al Qaeda,* 90–101, 60–61; Fawaz A. Gerges, *Journey of the Jihadist: Inside Muslim Militancy* (Orlando: Harcourt, Inc., 2006), 203–04, 214–220.

12   John F. Burns, "A Reporter's Quest for Osama bin Laden, the Unholy Grail," *New York Times*, May 8, 2011.

13   Ahmed Rashid, *Descent into Chaos: The United States and the Failure of Nation Building in Pakistan, Afghanistan, and Central Asia* (New York: Viking, 2008), 235, 227.

14   Jason Burke, *9/11Wars* (London: Allen Lane, 2011), 347–349, 309.

15   Lifton, *Thought Reform,* 429.

16   Stern, *Terror in the Name of God,* 261–262.

17   Tarek Fatah, *Chasing the Mirage: The Tragic Illusion of an Islamic State* (Mississauga, ON: John Wiley and Sons), 2008, 254–257.

18   Seth G. Jones, *In the Graveyards of Empires: America's War in Afghanistan* (New York: W. W. Norton & Company, 2009), 284.

19   Jytte Klausen, *The Cartoons that Shook the World* (New Haven: Yale University Press, 2009), 22, 91, 101; Burke, *9/11 Wars* 232; Irshad Manji, *Allah, Liberty & Love* (Toronto: Random House Canada, 2011), 160–169.

20   Ian Buruma, *Murder in Amsterdam: The Death of Theo van Gogh and the Limits of Tolerance* (London: Penguin Books), 2006, 139–40.

21   Tarek Fatah, *The Jew is not my Enemy: Unveiling the Myths that Fuel Anti-Semitism* (Toronto: McClelland and Stewart), 2010, 20–21, 109, 26.

22   Will Eisner, *The Plot: The Secret History of the Protocols of Zion* (New York: W. W. Norton & Company, 2005), 3.

23   Youssef H. Abour-Enein, *Militant Islamist Ideology: Understanding the Global Threat* (Annapolis, Maryland: Naval Institute Press, 2110), 81; Lisa Miller, *Heaven: Our Enduring Fascination with the Afterlife* (New York: HarperCollins, 2010), 82–83.

24   Jason Burke, "The Making of a Suicide Bomber," *Sunday Observer*, January 20, 2008; Kepel, *The War for Muslim Minds*, 8

25   Simon Baron-Cohen, *The Science of Evil: On Empathy and the Origins of Cruelty* (New York: Basic Books, 2011), 153.

Chapter 17

1   Joseph J. Ellis, "Finding a Place for 9/11 in American History," *New York Times,* January 28, 2006; Ferguson, *Colossus,* 27. Ferguson writes: "Malignant though it is Islamic fundamentalist terrorism remains a far less potent threat to the United States than the Soviet Union once was." For an excellent, trenchant article that ridicules the comparison of the terrorist threat with that confronted by the West during the 1939–45 war is by Tony Judt, "What We Have learned, If Anything?" *New York Review of Books,* May 1, 2008. Peter L. Bergen quotes with disapproval the hyperbolic comment made by the prominent neoconservative, Richard Perle, that the "West faced victory or holocaust" *Manhunt: The Ten-Year Search for Bin Laden from 9/11 to Abbottabad* (New York: Crown Publishers, 2012), 254. Benjamin R. Barber, "Hannah Arendt between Europe and America: Optimism in Dark Times," in *Politics in Dark Times,* 259–276. Barber is particularly scathing of *Terror and Liberalism* by Paul Berman who, according to Barber, misguidedly uses the totalitarian label to describe Saddam Hussein's regime and radical Islamists. Barber concedes that radical Islam does practice terrorism but the criteria of political scientists, especially Arendt, to designate a totalitarian state does not apply to the authoritarian regimes of the Middle East and to decentralized, antistatist and marginalized terrorists who resist even the concept of government and politics. 272–76.

2   Dower, *Cultures of War*, 437.

3   Robert Draper, "And He Shall Be Judged," Gentleman's Quarterly, http://men.style.com/gq/features/top

Another chilling example is from Ephesians 6:13: "Therefore put on the full armour of God so that when the day of evil comes, you may be able to stand your ground and, after you have done everything, to stand." Dower, Cultures of War, 86. .

4   Gray, *Black Mass,* 115.

5   Reinhold Niebuhr, *The Irony of American History* with a new introduction by Andrew J. Bacevich (Chicago: University of Chicago Press, [1952] 2008), 133, 173, 3, 16.

6   Dower, *Cultures of War,* 293, 307, 83.

7   Dower, *Cultures of War,* 293, 59–60, 83; Bergen, *The Longest War,* 58.

8   Richard A. Clarke, *Against All Enemies: Inside America's War on Terror* (New York: Free Press, 2004), 30, 232.

9   Stephen Holmes, *The Matador's Cape: America's Reckless Response to Terror* (Cambridge: Cambridge University Press, 2007), 2.

10   Peter N. Stearns, *American Fear: The Causes and Consequences of High Anxiety* (New York: Routledge, 2006), 59.

11   John Mueller, "Simplicity and Spook: Terrorism and the Dynamics of Threat Exaggeration," *International Studies Perspective* 6 (2005), 224.

12   Caroline Joan [Kay] Picart and Cecil Greek, "Profiling the Terrorist as a Mass Murderer," in *Monsters in and Among Us: Towards A Gothic Criminology,* ed. Joan [Kay] Picart and Cecil Greek (Madison: Dickinson University Press 2007), 266–268.

13   These places are specifically mentioned by bin Laden in an essay he wrote on the cusp of the Iraq war. Steve Coll, *The Bin Ladens: An Arabian Family in the American Century* (New York: The Penguin Press, 2008), 570.

14   Dinesh D'Souza, *The Enemy at Home: The Cultural Left and its Responsibility for 9/11* (New York: Broadway Books, originally published by Double Day, 2007, 2008), 279.

15   Michael Otterman and Richard Hil, *Erasing Iraq: The Human Costs of Carnage* (London: Pluto Press, 2010), 33. Bergen, *Holy War,* 222–23. Chalmers Johnson, *Nemesis: The Last Days of the American Republic* (New York: Henry Holt and Company, 2006), 26–29.

16   Dower, *Cultures of War,* 70.

17   Susan Sontag, "First Impressions," *New Yorker,* September 24, 2001, 32.

18   Craig Seligman, Sontag & Kael (New York: Counterpoint, 2004), 97–98.; Koch cited Susan Faludi, *The Terror Dream: Fear and Fantasy in Post 9/11 America* (New York: Metropolitan Books/Henry Holt and Company, 2007), 29. *The New Republic* ran an article that began, "What do Osama bin Laden, Saddam Hussein and Susan Sontag have in common?" In a subsequent interview, Sontag made it clear that she did not subscribe to the view that America "had it coming." The vitriol that Sontag experienced is similar to that endured by Jeremiah Wright, the one-time pastor of Barack Obama, during the 2008 presidential primary. Obama's opponents culled twenty seconds out of context from two sermons delivered after September 11 2001 and in March 2003 that implied that he hated America. Yet his message was that aggressive foreign policies can have dangerous consequences for America.

19   Neiman, *Moral Clarity,* 370.

20   Faludi, *The Terror Dream,* 25, 9, 47.

21   Tirman, *The Deaths of Others,* 217.

22   Scott Lucas, *The Betrayal of Dissent: Beyond Orwell, Hitchens and the New American Century* (London: Pluto Press, 2004), 125.

23   Anonymous, *Imperial Hubris: Why the West is Losing the War on Terror* (Washington D. C.: Brassey's Inc., 2004), 165; Clarke, *Against All Enemies,* 244–45.

24   Dower, *Cultures of War,* 74.

25   Burke, *9/11 Wars,* 504. Burke puts the number of civilian deaths until mid-May 2011 between 14,000 and 17,000 and at least three or four times that number wounded or permanently disabled. That number includes the deaths inflicted by insurgents. The political scientist, John Tirman estimates 9,000 Afghan deaths can be directly attributed to the American military. Tirman, *Deaths of Others,* 279.

26   For a full account of this raid see Dominic Streatfeild, *A History of the World Since 9/11* (London: Atlantic Books, 2011), 83–111.

27   Steve Coll, *Ghost Wars: The Secret History of the CIA Afghanistan and bin Laden from the Soviet Invasion to September 10, 2001* (New York: Penguin Press, 2004), 17.

28   For an excellent profile of three of the new breed of Islamist's ideologues see Lawrence Wright, "The Master Plan," *New Yorker,* September 4, 2006; Bergen, *Manhunt,* 138, 143.

29   Bergen, *The Longest War,* 317.

30   The youngest member of the Afghan National Assembly, Malalai Joya, told Canadian professor Michael Byers in September 2006 that the election was a "sham" and lamented "the corruption that was siphoning off billions of dollars of much-needed foreign aid." She also said that "liberation should be achieved in a country by the people themselves."

Michael Byers, *Intent for a Nation: A relentlessly optimistic manifesto for Canada's role in the world* (Vancouver: Douglas & McIntyre, 2007), 46.

31   Rashid, *Descent into Chaos,* 329–330.

32   Cole, *Engaging the Muslim World,* 190. Cole reports that one in seven Pashtun farmers in Helmand who saw their poppy fields eradicated had to sell one of their children, usually a girl. Burke, *9/11 Wars,* 317. Rory Stewart, who knows the country well, has noted that when the Taliban were left alone they alienated the local population by "living parasitically, lecturing puritanically and failing to deliver." Rory Stewart, "When Less is Best," New York Times, March 20, 2007, Op-Ed.

33   Ahmed Rashid, "Pakistan on the Brink," June 11, 2009, "The Afghanistan Impasse," October 8, 2009, *New York Review of Books*; *Bergen, The Longest War,* 256, 331.

34   Sarah Chayes, *The Punishment of Virtue: Inside Afghanistan After the Taliban* (New York: Penguin Press, 2006).

Chapter 18

1   Pepe Escobar, "Mistah McChrystal—he dead," *Asia Times Online,* June 25, 2010; Joseph Conrad, *Heart of Darkness and the Secret Sharer* (Toronto: Bantam Books, [1902] 1981), 123.

2   Conrad, *Heart of Darkness,* 101,123.

3   Wright, *The Looming* Tower, 337–338. Al-Qaeda considered Massoud such a threat that Zawahiri arranged for his assassination that occurred on September 9, 2001.

In an interview aired on CBS *60 Minutes* on April 29, 2007, the former CIA chief, George Tenet, reported that he received intelligence on July 10, 2001 of a significant terrorist attack in the coming weeks or months. He met with Condoleezza Rice, then national security advisor, and after the briefing felt that he had finally gotten the full attention of the administration. Whether Rice passed on the urgency of Tenet's warnings is unknown.

4   Aid, *The Secret Sentry,* 214, 219. See also interview of Richard Clarke by Lesley Stahl, *60 Minutes,* CBS, March 21, 2004.

5   Examples of this jingoistic frenzy abound. The *New York Times* columnist, Thomas Friedman, demanded that the French be voted "Off the Island" (out of the Security Council) for daring to be so presumptuous as to oppose America's drive for war. Among the more outrageous efforts at dehumanization was a doctored front-page photo in a New York tabloid that replaced the heads of the French and German UN representatives with weasel faces and the irascible journalist, Christopher Hitchens who described then French President, Jacques Chirac, as a "positive monster of conceit" and a "rat that tried to roar." Wilfried

Mausbach, "Forlorn Superpower: European Reactions to the American Wars in Vietnam and Iraq," in *Iraq and the Lessons of Vietnam Or, How Not to Learn from the Past* ed. Lloyd C. Gardner and Marilyn B. Young (New York: The New Press, 2007), 79.

6   *Aid, Secret Sentry*, 245; Ron Suskind, *The One Percent Doctrine: Deep inside America's Pursuit of its Enemies since 9/11* (New York: Simon and Schuster, 2006), 62; Morris Berman, *Dark Ages: The Final Phase of Empire* (New York: W.W. Norton & Company, 2006), 211.

7   Ron Suskind, *The Way of the World: A Story of Truth and Hope in an Age of Extremism* (Toronto: Double Day Canada, 2008), 180–82, 364–367.

8   Suskind, *Way of the World*, 374–80.

9   Danner, *The Secret Way to War*, 8.

10   *The 9/11 Commission Report: Final Report on the National Commission on Terrorist Attacks Upon the United States* (New York: W.W. Norton, 2004), 61.

11   James Bamford, *A Pretext for War: 9/11, Iraq, and the abuse of America's Intelligence Agencies* (New York: Doubleday, 2004), 368–71.

12   Kanan Makiya, *The Republic of Fear: The Politics of Modern Iraq* (Berkeley: University of California Press, 1998), ix–xxxiii, 47. In contrast to the original 1989 publication written under the pseudonym, Samir al-Khalil, in this paperback edition, he has used his own name. He adds a powerful new introduction that reveals how Iraq, after the 1991 Gulf War, was dismantled by UN sanctions, turning the country from a totalitarian state into a criminal one. As indicators of Hussein's diminished power to inculcate fear, he cites the large number of rank-and-file soldiers who deserted and the defections of high ranking officials. But the "tin-pot" dictator tried to compensate by adding draconian punishments such as branding for desertion and cultivating sectarian differences. Kanan Makiya, *The Republic of Fear: The Politics of Modern Iraq* (Berkeley: University of California Press, 1998), ix–xxxiii.

13   Kanan Makiya, *Cruelty and Silence: War, Tyranny, Uprising and the Arab World* (New York: W.W. Norton and Company, 1993), 18.

14   Tirman, *The Deaths of Others*, 200.

15   Russ Hoyle, *Going to War: How Misinformation, Disinformation, and Arrogance Led America into* Iraq (New York: St. Martin's Press, 2008), 232; Glenn Greenwald, *A Tragic Legacy* (New York: Crown Publishers, 2007), 105–106.

16   Jeffrey Record, "The Use and Abuse of History: Munich, Vietnam and Iraq," *Survival* 49: 1, Spring 2007, 149.

17   Hoyle, *Going to War,* 234; Susan A. Brewer, *Why America Fights: Patriotism and War Propaganda from the Philippines to Iraq* (Oxford: Oxford University Press, 2009), 244; Greenwald, *A Tragic Legacy,* 110.

18   Bamford, *A Pretext for War*, 377; Benjamin & Simon, *Next Attack*, 171; Mark Danner, "How Bush Really Won," *New York Review of Books,* January 13, 2005, 51; Stearns *American Fear*, 214.

19   Ron Suskind, "Without a Doubt," *New York Times Magazine,* October 17, 2004; Mark Danner, *The Secret Way to War: The Downing Street Memo and the Iraq's War Buried History* (New York: The New York Review of Books, 2006), 25.

20   Frank Rich, *The Greatest Story Ever Sold: The Decline and Fall of Truth From 9/11 to Katrina* (New York: Penguin Press, 2006), 166–174; Brewer Why America Fights, 264, 8.

21   Stearns, *American Fear*, 212. Two reporters from the Knight-Ridder newspapers under the Washington bureau editor, John Walcott, were asking probing questions of their sources within the intelligence community regarding the credibility of the 'revelations' about the Iraqi defectors that should have been done by the New York and Washington based print and television outlets. Unfortunately, some of their newspapers failed to print their stories preferring to run material from the *New York Times*. The Knight-Ridder reports are documented in Rich, *The Greatest Story Ever Sold*, 192–93 and *Bill Moyer's Journal: Buying the War*, PBS, April 25, 2007.

The liberal *New Republic* and the neoconservative *Weekly Standard* adopted the same position: that the president would be guilty of surrender in the war on international terrorism if he did not make a concerted effort to topple Hussein. Rich, *The Greatest Story Ever Sold*, 28. Eric Beehlert argues in *Lapdogs: How the Press Rolled Over for Bush* that Bush had an easy time with the press and television networks. Prior to September 11, they consistently ignored his failings while ramping up criticism of Democrats from Clinton to Kerry during the 2004 Presidential election in part because reporters have been intimidated for years from a "deep-pocketed Republican media noise machine" that has sought to destroy an independent free press and because a reporter's career could be red-lined if he appeared too far-left or critical of Republicans. Instead of being a neutral watchdog to assure accountability from those wielding power, journalists served more as courtesans (New York: Free Press, 2006,) 3.

22   Rich, *The Greatest Story Ever Sold*, 79. The late historian, Tony Judt, argued that liberals, acting more like a sieve rather than a filter, became Bush's "useful idiots" because they provided the "ethical fig-leaf for the "brutish polices" of the neo-conservatives. "The Strange

Death of Liberal America," *London Review of Books*, September, 20, 2006.

23   Gareth Porter, "Manufacturing the Threat to Justify Aggressive War in Vietnam and Iraq," in *Iraq and the Lessons of War from Vietnam*, 101; Frank Rich, "Return to the Scene of the Crime," *New York Times*, August 27, 2006, Week in Review.

24   Brewer, *Why America Fights*, 244. One of the major architects of the war, Paul Wolfowitz, did believe that the overthrow of Saddam Hussein would have a domino effect of ending tyranny and ushering democracy into the Middle East while liberals like Michael Ignatieff cautiously supported a military operation on humanitarian grounds. But support for democracy or human rights arguments were not tendered by administration officials to prepare the public for an invasion of Iraq because they reasoned, probably correctly, that Americans would *only* support a war if they were terrified into believing that the Iraq dictator was a real threat to their national security. Indeed as a vigorous exponent of the invasion, Wolfowitz mainly hyped bogus intelligence and a non-existent September 11-Saddam connection.

During the 1980–88 Iran-Iraq war in which American official policy was one of neutrality, Hussein was the recipient of American intelligence in the Gulf, and military and financial largess because the administration was alarmed about the Islamic regime in Iran. President Reagan sent Donald Rumsfeld twice as a special envoy in December 1983 and in March 1984 to Iraq, the first time to provide psychological support and establish the framework for later American military aid that included the U.S. providing directly or indirectly cluster bombs, anthrax and other biological weapons material. The visit led to a meeting with the Iraqi dictator, one in which the Rumsfeld later said that he "cautioned" Saddam about using "poison gas," but there is no mention of this in the minutes of his meetings. When American intelligence confirmed that Hussein had deployed poison gas against Iran and Kurdish insurgents, Rumsfeld undeterred negotiated in his second meeting the building of an oil pipeline, and in the interest of realpolitik, avoided raising the issue of how American aid was being used. In an attempt to malign the patriotism of his critics accusing them of appeasing dictators, he might have looked at himself in the mirror and recall how he cozied up to the "butcher" of Iraq.

25   Paul Craig Roberts, "A Threat Greater than Terrorism," www. counterpunch.org roberts03212005.html.

26   Margaret MacMillan, *The Uses and Abuses of History* (Toronto: Viking Canada, 2008), 160–161.

27   Daniel Benjamin and Steven Simon, *The Next Attack: The Failure of the War on Terror and a Strategy for Getting it Right* (New York: Owl

Book/Henry Holt and Company, 2006) persuasively develop this argument in chapter seven.

28 Coll, *The Bin Ladens*, 568.

29 Kathryn S. Olmstead, *Real Enemies: Conspiracy Theories and the American Democracy, World War I to 9/11* (Oxford: Oxford University Press, 2009), 213.

30 Suskind, *The One Percent Doctrine*, 27. Mahmood believed that nuclear weapons should spread to other Islamic countries and trigger an end-of-days scenario and the "beatific triumph of Islam." Among the critics who vehemently argue that the war against Iraq diluted the war on terror are Clarke, *Against all Enemies,* Scheuer, *Hubris* and Benjamin & Simon, *The Next Attack*. Perhaps the most devastating critique of Bush's war in Iraq fuelling terrorism came with the release in the fall of 2006 of the CIA's own report on global terrorism.

31 David Cole, "Are We Safer?" *The New York Review of Books*, Vol. 53, Number 4, March 9, 2006. Experts on terrorism provided compelling empirical evidence that terrorist attacks around the world by jihadists groups rose by 607 percent in the average yearly rate since the invasion of Iraq. They also asserted that the capture and killing of two-thirds of the Al-Qaeda leadership in late 2001 in Afghanistan, not the war in Iraq, prevented further attacks on America. Peter Bergen and Paul Cruickshank, "The Iraq Effect: War Has Increased Terrorism Sevenfold Worldwide," *Mother Jones,* March, 2007.

32 Benjamin & Simon, *Next Attack*, 42; Seth G. Jones, *In the Graveyard of Empires: America's War in Afghanistan* (New York: WW Norton, 2009), 282. The Taliban first deployed suicide bombings after they became a component of the insurgency in Iraq. In Afghanistan the recruits to carry out these missions are often the disabled, the most vulnerable and marginalized sectors of the population, in which few services are available to rehabilitate them after three decades of war. That Al-Qaeda paid several thousand dollars to the families of suicide bombers might explain why it was so easy to find recruits.

33 The National Museum, where fifteen-thousand objects were looted in 2003, reopened in February 2009 even though only a quarter of what had been pilfered had been retrieved by the opening.

34 Otterman, *Erasing Iraq*, 5.

35 Rajiv Chandrasekaran, *Imperial Life in the Emerald City: Inside Iraq's Green Zone* (New York: Alfred A. Knopf, 2006), 153.

36 Michael Schwartz, *War Without End: The Iraq War in Context* (Chicago: Haymarket Books, 2008), 39–40.

37 Dower, *Cultures of War*, 445, 414.

38 Klein, *The Shock Doctrine*, 420–430.

39   Conrad, *Heart of Darkness,* 104–105.

40   Devetak, "The Gothic scene of international relations," 635–37.Thomas E. Ricks, *Fiasco: The American Military Adventure in Iraq* (New York: The Penguin Press, 2006), 431. His point is reinforced by the "Harpers Index" that as of March 2006, the percentage of soldiers who state that the war was retaliation for Saddam's role in the 9/11 attacks was eighty-five percent. *Harpers,* May 2006; Brewer, *Why America Fights,* 265–66; Joshua E. S. Philips, *None of Us Were Like This Before: American Soldiers and Torture* (London: Verso, 2010), 38.

41   Conrad, *Heart of Darkness,* 123.

42   Gray, *Black Mass,* 28.

43   Danchev, *On Art And War And Power,* 220.

44   Jeremy Scahill, *Blackwater: The Rise of the World's Most Powerful Mercenary Army* (New York: Nation Books, 2007), 107–08.

45   Dahr Jamail, *Beyond the Green Zone: Dispatches from an Unembedded Journalist in Occupied Iraq* (Chicago: Haymarket Books, 2007), 73–83, 130–141. Scahill, *Black Water,* 133–144. Cockburn is quoted by Scahill on page 143. Schwartz, *War Without End,* 86–87 on collective punishment apart from Fallujah and 92–119 on Fallujah. "Patrick Cockburn, "Toxic Legacy of U.S. assault on Falluja 'worse' than Hiroshima," *The Independent,* July 24, 2010.

46   During summer of 2006, death squads were responsible for more killings—often preceded by grisly torture—than the foreign and Sunni insurgents, America's ostensible enemies. These squads, which operated under the auspices of the Interior Ministry, had been established by a corrupt and thuggish Bayan Jabr who became Finance Minister. When he was originally appointed Minister for Housing and Reconstruction after the fall of Saddam, two Americans working with him were appalled by his methods and requested that Bremer fire him, but instead they were dismissed. Ken Silverstein, "The Minister of Civil War: Bayan Jabr, Paul Bremer and the rise of the Iraqi death squads," *Harpers,* August, 2006. For the violence in May 2007 see Thomas E. Ricks, *The Gamble: General David Patraeus and the American Military Adventure in Iraq, 2006–2008* (New York: Penguin Press, 2009), 179.

47   Klein, *The Shock Doctrine,* 451.

48   Christian Caryl, "What about the Iraqis?" *The New York Review of Books,* Vol. 54, Number 1, January 11, 2007; Tirman, *Deaths of Others,* 242.

49   Burke, *9/11 Wars,* 271–279.

50   Andrew Bacevich, "Obama Wants Us To Forget the Lesson of Iraq," *New Republic,* August 31, 2010.

51   Cole, *Engaging the Muslim World*, 124; Otterman, *Erasing Iraq*, 169–70; Joseph Stiglitz and Linda Bilmes, *The Three Trillion Dollar War: The True Cost of the Iraq Conflict* (New York: W.W. Norton and Co., 2008), 133, 136.

52   Schwartz, *War Without End*, 269.

53   Ricks, *The Gamble*, 296, 324.

54   Cole, *Engaging the Muslim World,* 118–119.

55   Kanan Makiya, "How Did I Get Iraq Wrong," *Slate*, http//www.slate.com/id/2186763/

56   According to Pentagon statistics as reported by the Associated Press, as of the first six months of 2012, one suicide has occurred daily.

57   Diana Priest, "Soldier Suicides at Record Level," *Washington Post*, January 31, 2008; Justine Sharrock, *Tortured: When Good Soldiers Do Bad Things* (Hoboken, N.J.: John Wiley & Sons, Inc., 2110), 128, 204; Philips, *None of Us*, 186–188, 195.

This focus on damaged soldiers does not take into account the number of combatants who appeared to flourish in Iraq. In his memoir, David Bellavia recounts how he willingly descended into the "darkest parts of the human soul," "surrender[ed] to the insanity around [him]" and rode "its wave wherever it" took him, even to "madness." He excelled in kinetic face-to-face combat in Falluja. When he returned, he experienced no nightmares or regrets except for the loss of comrades. David Bellavia and John R. Bruning, *House to House: An Epic Memory of War* (New York: Free Press, 2007), 113.

Chapter 19

1   Clarke, *Against All Enemies,* 24; McCoy, *A Question of Torture,* 113.

2   William Shawcross, *Justice and the Enemy: Nuremberg, 9/11, and the trial of Khalid Sheikh Mohammed* (New York: Public Affairs, 2011), 61. Shawcross vigorously and sometimes shamelessly defends the Bush administration's security policies, including the right to torture. He does not differentiate between the hardened al-Qaeda, the conscripted foot soldiers in Afghanistan or those who were kidnapped and sold to the Americans. Not only does he even hint that the vast majority were innocent, he compares them to Nazi and Communist mass murders. Lawyers who represent them, he vilifies as engaging in "lawfare" against the American government. He praises Obama when he maintained his predecessor's policies and criticizes him when he did not. Agamben is cited in Joanna Bourke, *What It Means to Be Human: Reflections from 1791 to the Present* (London: Virago Press, 2011), 157.

3   For an excellent discussion of how Franz Kafka's novel *The Trial* and his short story, "In the Penal Colony" applies to the detainees at Abu Ghraib and Guantanamo see Danchev *On Art And War And Terror*, 172–196.

4   Dilawar's life and death are extensively profiled in Philips, *None of Us*, 22–32, 41, 47.

5   David Cole and Jules Lobell, *Less Safe, Less Free: Why America is Losing the War on Terror* (New York: The Free Press, 2007), 103–104. Even during the Vietnam War when the Viet Cong defied conventional rules of war by torturing prisoners, including John McCain, and often fighting without uniforms, the United States developed a process of status hearings to separate real civilians from prisoners of war. A similar process was used in the first Gulf War. Mayer, *Dark Side*, 121.

6   Klein, *The Shock Doctrine*, 366–67; Bourke, *What It Means to Be Human*, 157.

7   Moazzam Begg, *Enemy Combatant: My Imprisonment at Guantanamo, Bagram and Kandahar* (New York: The New Press, 2006).

8   Murat Kurnaz, *Five Years of My Life: An Innocent Man in Guantanamo* with Helmut Kuhn, trans. Jefferson Chase. (New York: Palgrave Macmillan, 2008); Kurnaz is also featured in the 2011 German/ Swiss/ Canadian documentary, *The Guantanamo Trap*.

9   Dower, *Cultures of War*, 81.

10   Shawcross, *Justice and the Enemy* on page 204 states that only twenty-eight al Qaeda suspects were subjected to enhanced interrogation techniques.

11   Philip Zimbardo, *The Lucifer Effect: Understanding How Good People Turn Bad* (New York: Random House, 2007), 410–411.

12   Alfred W. McCoy, *A Question of Torture: CIA Interrogation, from the Cold War to the War on Terror* (New York: Henry Holt and Company, 2006), 109; Mayer *Dark Side*, 165–66. In Vietnam, as part of the infamous Phoenix Programme under the auspices of the CIA up to 20,000 Viet Cong suspects were assassinated or summarily executed after being tortured with methods such as extreme sensory deprivation, electric shock treatments and waterboarding. Later administrators and operatives admitted that half of those killed "were not even Party members and they never captured a "high-ranking Viet Cong agent." McCoy also asserts that the CIA revived three components of the old Phoenix Programme through the creation of the Scorpions for counterinsurgency: torture, assassination and the recruitment of native mercenaries. McCoy, "Torture in the Crucible of Counterinsurgency," in *Iraq and the Lessons of Vietnam*, 241, 262.

13 Louis Begley, *Why the Dreyfus Affair Matters* (New Haven: Yale University Press, 2009), 42; Hynes, *The Soldiers Tale*, 252; Bergen, *The Longest War*, 108.

14 Zimbardo, *The Lucifer Effect*, 336–337, 414, 412; Kurnaz, *Five Years*, 176–178.

15 Philips interviewed the man who may or may not be the photographed hooded man that claims he was given electroshocks. He was difficult to verify because this technique leaves few marks on the epidermis and damage under the skin disappears in a matter of weeks. *None of Us*, 143–44.

16 Mark Danner, "Torture and Truth," *The New York Review of Books,* June, 10, 2004; Mayer, *Dark Side*, 169; Tirman, *Deaths of Others*, 230.

17 Seymour Hersh, "The Gray Zone," *The New Yorker*, May 24, 2004.

18 Lila Rajiva, *The Language of Empire: Abu Ghraib and the American Media* (New York: Monthly Review Press, 2005), 135; Ian Buruma, "Ghosts," *New York Review of Books*, Vol. LV, Number 11, June 26, 2008; Danchev, *On Art And War and Terror*, 188.

19 Sharrock, *Tortured*, 110–118.

20 Danchev, *On Art And War And Terror,* 176.

21 Mayer, *Dark Side*, 148, 168; Klein, *The Shock Doctrine*, 444–45; Danner, "US Torture;" Burke, *9/11 Wars*, 93.

22 Bergen, *Longest War*, 100.

23 Philips, *None of Us*, 165–166.

24 Some columnists were outraged. Thomas Friedman of the *New York Times*, who had been earlier seduced into supporting the war by the administration's argument about the existence of Saddam Hussein's cache of WMD's and its threat to America, became almost apoplectic by the torture revelations emerging from Guantánamo Bay: "Just shut it down and then plow it under. It has become worse than an embarrassment. I am convinced that more Americans are dying and will die if we keep the Gitmo prison open than if we shut it down." McCoy, *Question of Torture*, 180.

25 *The Sunday Times*, October 7 and December 23, 2007.

One example of a memoir that reveals how the degrading abuses meted out by Stalinists in Czechoslovakia are shockingly similar those approved by the Bush administration is by Artur London, *The Confession*, trans. Alastair Hamilton (New York: Morrow, 1970).

26 Christopher Graveline and Michael Clemens, *The Secrets of Abu Ghraib Revealed: American Soldiers on Trial* (Washington, D.C.: Potomac Books, Inc., 2010), 300–301; Sharrock, *Tortured*, 241; Danchev, *On Art And War And Terror*, 186; Caldwell, *Fallgirls*, 165–166.

27   Burke, *9/11 Wars*, 168–174, 136.

28   Sharrock, *Tortured,* 101; Jane Mayer, "The Battle for a Country's Soul," *New York Review of Books*, August 14, 2008. Mayer's essay convincingly argues that the Bush administration's coercive tactics have not worked, that they have damaged the rule of law and American interests abroad, and that some of the most penetrating critics were conservative Republican lawyers who once worked within the administration.

29   Neiman, *Moral Clarity*, 366; Philips, *None of Us*, 155.

30   Graveline, *The Secrets of Abu Ghraib Revealed,* 213; Philips, *None of Us*, 37, 39, 64–66.

31   Zimbardo, "Revisiting the Stanford Prison Experiment: A Lesson in the Power of Situation," *Chronicle of Higher Education*, March 30 2007.

32   Initially Ibn al-Shaykh al-Libi's interrogation by the FBI employing non-invasive methods yielded valuable information but when the CIA took over and outsourced him for torture in Egypt, he finally gave his assailants what they wanted to hear. One year later al-Libi recanted his confession: "They were killing me. I had to tell them something." For an analysis of the treatment of "high value detainees" see Mark Danner, "US Torture: Voices from the Black Sites," *New York Review of Books*, April 9, 2009. Frank Rich, "The Banality of Bush White House Evil," *New York Times*, Op-Ed, April 25, 2009.

33   Mayer. *Dark Side*, 134–138, 155; Ali Soufan, "My Tortured Decision," *New York Times*, Op-ed, April 22, 2009; Soufan, "What Torture Never Was," *New York Times*, September 6, 2009; Bergen, *The Longest War*, 110; Ali Soufan, *The Black Banners: The Inside Story of 9/11 and the War Against al Qaeda* (New York: W.W. Norton, 2011), 368–69.

34   Matthew Alexander with John R. Bruning, *How to Break a Terrorist: The U.S. Interrogators Who Used Brain, Not Brutality to Take Down the Deadliest Man in Iraq* (New York: Free Press, 2008); Scott Horton, "'The American Public has a Right to Know That They Do Not Have to Choose Between Torture and Terror': Six questions for Matthew Alexander, author of *How to Break a Terrorist*," http://harpers.org/archive/2008/12hbc

Musab al-Zarqawi was the Jordanian-born criminal turned terrorist who rose to worldwide prominence when he was mistakenly named by Colin Powell at the UN in February 2003 as the link between Saddam Hussein's regime and al-Qaeda. His role as a master strategist for al-Qaeda was bogus given that he headed his own rival organization. His connections were with Iran who was using him to achieve hegemony over Iraq. He was distrusted by Osama bin Laden, a response that deepened when al-Zarqawi's visceral hatred toward Shiites eventuated in his organizing suicide truck bombings on Shiite shrines and mosques and fomenting sectarian conflict. An excellent article on al-Zarqawi is "The Short, Violent Life of Abu Musab Al-Zarqawi" by Mary Anne Weaver, *Atlantic Online* July-August, 2006; Bergen, *Longest War*, 160–164.

Even during the latter years of the second Bush administration, there were insiders including Bush's Secretary of State, Condoleezza Rice, working to rein in the excesses of Cheney, Rumsfeld and their coterie by fighting legal judgements that allowed enhanced interrogation techniques and trying to close Guantánamo. When Cheney lambasted Obama, he was really attacking the lawyers within his former administration whose work had made it possible for Obama to build upon and package his own plan to the country. David Brooks, "Cheney lost to Bush," *New York Times*, May 22, 2009.

One fully operational and potentially disastrous post-September 11 plan that involved a hydrogen cyanide attack on the New York subways was aborted not because detainees were tortured but because a mole within al-Qaeda informed the CIA that Zawahiri called the plan off because it could not top the shock effect of the earlier attacks. Suskind, *One Percent Solution*, 217–220.

35   Michael Welch, *Scapegoats of September 11th: Hate Crimes & State Crimes in the War on Terror* (New Brunswick, New Jersey: Rutgers University Press, 2006), 159–161, 87–95.

36   A good example of restrained language occurred in the summer of 2007 after the botched bombings in London and Glasgow. Avoiding framing the issue as a clash of civilizations or a war on terror, then Prime Minister, Gordon Brown, referred to the attackers as a "few extremists" whose "terrorist cause...is unacceptable to mainstream people in every faith in every part of the world." Generally, the public responses to these attacks have been much more measured than in the States.

37   Bergen, *The Longest War*, 244.

38   Tom Quiggin, "The Show trials will go on," *Ottawa Citizen*, March 1, 2008.

39   A comprehensive examination of the Lindh case that outlines how media reports distorted his case and how the evidence was so flimsy that the prosecutors dropped the terrorist-related charges can be found in Tom Junod, "Innocent," *Esquire*, February 15, 2010 http://www.esquire.com/features/ESQ0706JLINDH_106.

40   Ariel Dorfman, "Forward: The Tyranny of Terror: Is Torture Inevitable in Our Century and Beyond?" in *Torture: A Collection,* ed. Sanford Levinson (New York: Oxford University Press, 2004), 8–9; Lori

Peek, *Behind the Backlash: Muslim Americans after 9/11* (Philadelphia: Temple University Press, 2011), 23–27, Chapter Four, 60–102.

41   Jack G. Shaheen, *Reel Bad Arabs: How Hollywood Vilifies a People* (Northampton Mass.; Olive Branch Press, [2001] 2009), 374, 21. The trope of Arabs as fifth columnists was a central premise in Season Four (2004–2005) of *24*.

42   Jack G. Shaheen, *Guilty: Hollywood's Verdict on Arabs after 9/11* (Northampton Mass.; Olive Branch Press, 2008), xix.

43   Holmes, *The Matador's Cape*, 327.

44   That the ticking-bomb scenario is a fantasy with respect to terrorist attacks is unequivocally stated in *Taxi to the Dark Side*. There were, however, a couple of criminal cases in Germany where this drama played itself out, both involving the kidnapping of a young child. In the first case in 1988, after the kidnapper received the ransom and then was arrested, he refused to reveal, until the police beat him, the whereabouts of the boy, and they subsequently found the boy alive in a wooden box. In 2002, the Frankfurt Deputy Police Chief threatened to torture the accused if he did not reveal the location of the child. The accused then admitted that the child was dead. The officer was charged with coercion, a misdemeanour. In the more classic terrorist scenario, in which supposedly torture foiled an attempt to blow up eleven trans-Pacific aircraft in 1995, the case is shrouded in controversy because the facts of the case are in dispute. In 1995, after the Manila police resorted to physical and psychological torture, a suspect confessed to this plot. Commentators from across the American political terrain, including law professor, Alan M. Dershowitz, who had written a book arguing the case for "torture warrants," cited this case as an example of the necessity of occasionally applying torture to an accused. But according to the historian, Alfred McCoy, the Manila police quickly found the important information on the accused's laptop, and that later accounts of his sixty-seven days of torture were police fabrications. Claudia Card, *Confronting Evils: Terrorism, Torture and Genocide* (Cambridge: Cambridge University Press, 2010), 191. McCoy, *A Question of Torture*, 110–112.

45   Jane Mayer, "Whatever it takes: the politics of the man behind '24,'" *The New Yorker*, February, 19, 2007; Shaheen, *Guilty*, 49; Sharrock, *Torture*, 2.

46   Scalia and Stock are cited in Philips, *None of Us*, 102–104. I have slightly altered Philip's phrasing and punctuation of the Scalia quotation; Colin Freeze, *Globe and Mail*, June 30, 2007. If any country has experienced a large dose of terrorist attacks surely that dubious honour must go to Israel. Yet in a remarkable 1999 case, *The Public Committee Against Torture v. The State of Israel*, the Israeli Supreme Court argued that the rule of law and civil liberties were vital to a democratic nation's

security concerns if that meant that "at times democracy fights with one hand tied behind her back." This is not a lesson that former Vice-President Dick Cheney and his associates absorbed.

47 Livingstone Smith, *Less than Human*, 22–23. Rajiva, *Language of Empire*, 25. The stridently evangelical and populist character of the cultural wars is similar to the tensions that currently bedevil the Arab and Muslim worlds between fundamentalists and secularists. In America, it has become a take-no-prisoners vendetta waged by the political and religious Right who have vowed to "take back" and restore an older purer American society. It has sunk its fangs into the penetrable hides of the secular forces of modernity, epitomized by what they view as liberal East Coast godless and intellectual elites.

48 Neiman, *Moral Clarity*, 367; Caldwell, *Fallgirls*, 156–157.

49 Baker, "Stabbed in the back,"

50 Bourke, *What It Means to Be Human,* 152–156.

51 Ronald Wright, *What is America: A History of the New World Order* (London: Alfred A. Knopf, 2008), 198; Lee Marsden, *For God's Sake: The Christian Right and US Foreign Policy* (London: Zed Books, 2008), 62, 233–34; Benjamin and Simon, *The Next Attack*, 272–75.

52 Tirman, *Deaths of Others*, 304–306.

53 Tirman, *Deaths of Others*, 262–63. After a careful analysis of the different groups who did body counts of Iraqi civilians, Tirman concludes that the epidemiological study undertaken by a physician, who was a former military officer, and his team of statisticians, which puts the losses closer to over 655,000, is the most reliable. He adds the caveat that only when the war is fully over will there be anything like an accurate count. 325–336.

Erasing Iraq, 104–107. One embedded reporter who did communicate how the war impacted the Iraqi people was Evan Wright from *Rolling Stone* who later said that most Americans' view of war "is too sanitized." Had American audiences been more familiar with the Apache helicopter video, later titled "Collateral Murder" by Julian Assange of the muckraking WikiLeaks, of the strafing of individuals, a van and buildings in a Baghdad street, they might have had a greater appreciation of the reality of urban warfare in Iraq. One of the most chilling aspects of this July, 2007 twenty-four-minute video, rarely seen on American television but received over nine million hits on YouTube, is the callous attitude of the pilots who comment on what they see on the ground as though they were playing a video game. Nonetheless, it is hard to distinguish between combatants and civilians, and the long-lensed camera could be perceived as a weapon. Moreover, the video offers no context. There is no mention that the members of the battalion on the ground in the previous month experienced over one hundred and fifty attacks and roadside bombs, and that four of their company had been killed and nineteen wounded. Despite these flaws, the military behaved badly. Before the video went viral, the military lied about what happened and later exonerated the soldiers by stating that they had followed the rules of engagement. Yet two of the soldiers involved in the incident on the ground apologized to the Iraqi people for their role in the occupation. Tirman, *Deaths of Others*, 343; Raffi Khatchadourian, "No Secrets," *The New Yorker*, June 7, 2010.

54   Mayer. *Dark Side*, 134–138; Ali Soufan, "My Tortured Decision," *New York Times*, Op-ed, April 22, 2009; Mayer, *Dark Side*, 155; Stephen Grey, "America's Gulag," *The New Statesman*, May 17, 2004. Sharrock, *Tortured*, 183; Tony Judt, "What have We Learned, If Anything," *New York Review of Books*, May 8, 2008.

55   Danchev, *On Art And War And Terror*, 212–213.

56   Philips, *None of Us*, 155.

57   John McCain, "Bin Laden's death and the debate over torture," *The Washington Post*, May 11, 2011

Chapter 20

1   Brackman, *Secret File of Stalin*, 340; Overy, *Dictators*, 230; Claudia Schmolders, *Hitler's Face: The Biography of an Image*, trans. Adrian Dalib (Philadelphia: University of Pennsylvania Press, 2006), 126; Adolf Hitler, *Hitler's Table Talk, 1941–44: His Private Conversations*, trans. ed. Norman Cameron and R.H. Stevens, intro. H.R. Trevor-Roper (New York: Enigma Books, 2000), 624.

2   Suny, *The Soviet Experiment,* 141.

3   Snyder, *Bloodlands*, 398.

4   Doris L. Bergen, "Sex, Blood, and Vulnerability, Women Outsiders in German Occupied Europe," in *Social Outsiders*, 276.

5   Jan T. Gross, "A Tangled Web: Confronting Stereotypes Concerning Relations between Poles, Germans, Jews and Communists," in *The Politics of Retribution in Europe: World War 11 and its Aftermath*, ed. István Deák, Jan T. Gross, and Tony Judt (Princeton: Princeton University Press, 2000), 92–100.

6   Jan T. Gross, *Fear: Anti-Semitism in Poland after Auschwitz, An Essay in Historical Interpretation* (New York: Random House, 2006), 45; Gross, *Neighbors*, 84–86, 100–01.

7   Burleigh, *Moral Combat*, 468–470.

8   Gross, "A Tangled Web," 91.

9   Gross, *Fear*, 135, 149.

10 "Their ethnic background was a colossal liability and an impediment to their careers, from every point of view." Gross, *Fear*, 222.

11 Gross, *Neighbors*, 100; Gross, *Fear*, 245, 36, 248, 258.

12 Ian Kershaw, *Hitler 1936–1945: Nemesis* (London: Allen Lane, 2000), 237, 245; see also Evans, *The Third Reich at War*, 15, 44; Burleigh, *Third Reich*, 442.

13 Richard Breitman, *The Architect of Genocide: Himmler and the Final Solution* (Hanover NH: University Press of New England, 1992), 81.

14 Burleigh, *The Third Reich*, 587.

15 Christopher Browning, *The Path to Genocide: Essays on Launching the Final Solution* (Cambridge: University of Cambridge, 1992), 148–161.

16 Christopher R. Browning, *Ordinary Men: Reserve Police Battalion 101 and the Final Solution in Poland* (New York: HarperPerennial, 1992), 142. Browning drew upon the same archival material but arrives at fundamentally different conclusions than Daniel Jonah Goldhagen in *Hitler's Willing Executioners*. Goldhagen argues that the police battalions were representative of "eliminationist" anti-Semitic German society even before Hitler came to power. These ex-police officers not only enjoyed the killings but also tortured their victims before killing them. From the evidence that both scholars present, this judgment of the battalions is accurate, but to argue that they are representative of all the killers is questionable. What is more untenable is that they represented all of society, a judgment hard to prove. Equally problematic is Goldhagen's insistence that anti-Semitism alone rather than a cluster of factors, that Browning discusses, can explain these barbarous actions. These battalions had no difficulty in killing Christian Poles. Perhaps most contentious is his argument that only Germans were imbued with a blind hatred of Jews. Although he briefly acknowledged the participation of locals in the killing squads, he does not take into account the brutal cruelty of the Croatian fascists, the Ustasha movement, behaviour that shocked even the Germans or the ruthlessness of the Romanian Iron Guard. There is nothing about the behaviour of the French, who exceeded SS quotas in deporting foreign Jews to their certain death. In a later 1998 edition, Browning writes an Afterword that offers a convincing rebuttal to Goldhagen's monocausal analysis and offers a more nuanced perspective stating at one point that because "these policemen were 'willing executioners' does not mean that they 'wanted to be genocidal executioners.'" *Ordinary Men*, 216. For the voluntary nature of killings by these former policemen and SS officers, see Burleigh, *Moral Combat*, 401.

17 Burleigh, *Third Reich*, 606.

18   Richard Overy, "Girl in a hayloft," *TLS*, November 8, 2002, 9.

19   Kershaw, *Hitler 1936–45*, 470.

20   Fest, *Hitler*, 685.

21   American surveys of POWs revealed that more than two-thirds of the soldiers expressed belief in the Führer in August and late November 1944, and that "blind faith" in him was the single most important element in the state of mind of soldiers. This mentality enabled them to shift "responsibility for their own crimes to their victims." Omer Bartov, *Hitler's Army: Soldiers, Nazi, and War in the Third Reich* (New York: Oxford University Press, 1992), 145, 147.

22   Black, *IBM*, 125.

23   Bartov, *Hitler's Army*, 96, 83, 161, 163.

24   Hynes, *Soldiers Tale*, 263; Gellately, *Backing Hitler*, 207. Fest, *Hitler*, 682; Arendt *Totalitarianism*, 156; Tzvetan Todorov, *Facing the Extreme: Moral Life in the Concentration Camps* (New York: Henry Holt and Company: 1996).

25   Timothy Snyder, "Holocaust: Ignored Reality," *New York Review of Books*, July 16, 2009; Snyder, *Bloodlands*, 382.

26   Eric Voegelin, *Hitler and the Germans* (Columbia: University of Missouri Press, 1999), 105; cited in Gross in *Neighbors*, 105.

27   Hilary Earl, *The Nuremberg SS-Einsatzgruppen Trial, 1945–1958: Atrocity, Law, and History* (Cambridge: Cambridge University Press, 2009), 163–167.

28   Hans Safrian, *Eichmann's Men*, trans. Ute Stargardt (Cambridge: Cambridge University Press, 2010), 219; One powerful example is Davidson's grandfather in *The Perfect Nazi*, xviii. Psychiatric causalities were not limited to members of the Einzatzgruppe. Despite propaganda efforts by psychiatrists to ensure that the Wehrmacht was untainted by war neurosis, there is plenty of evidence that ordinary soldiers experienced it particularly on the Eastern Front. When the Red Army launched a six-day artillery barrage, the doctors reported "a complete state of exhaustion...among all men of the battalion...as a result of a far too great mental and nervous strain....The men are completely indifferent and apathetic, partly suffering from fits of crying, and are not to be cheered up by this or that phrase. Food is being eaten only in disproportionately small quantities." Bartov, *Hitler's Army*, 21.

29   Brackman, *Secret File of Stalin*, 386.

30   Bernard Schlink, *Guilt about the Past* (Toronto: Anansi Press, 2010), 60.

31   Bergen, *The Longest War*, 332–333; Gerges, *Al-Qaeda*, 25.

32   Robert Draper, "Opium Wars," *National Geographic*, February, 2011.

33   Fareed Zakaria, "When Terror Loses its Grip," *Time*, May 20, 2011.

34   Bergen, *Manhunt*, 261.

35   Jo Becker and Scott Shane, "Secret 'Kill List' Proves a Test of Obama's Principles and Will," *New York Times*, May 29, 2012; Shawcross, *Justice and the Enemy*, 210–211; David Cole, "Obama and Terror: The Hovering Questions," *New York Review of Books*, July 12, 2002; Larry Siems, *The Torture Report: What the Documents say about America's Post 9/11 Torture Program* (*OR Books, 2012.*)

36   Burke, *The 9/11 Wars*, 217.

37   Doug Saunders, *Myths of the Muslim Tide: Do Immigrants Threaten the West?* (New York: Alfred A. Knopf Canada, 2012), 22, 100–102. The footnote reference to the inflammatory DVD is on page 31. See also Saunders "The 'Eurabia' myths deserve a debunking" and "Exposing Dangerous Fictions," *The Globe and Mail*, September 20, 2008 and July 30, 2011.

38   Saunders, *Myths of the Muslim Tide*, 33.

39   The origin of this distortion in what became the Patient Protection and Affordable Care Act was a provision, sponsored by a Democrat and Republican, that Medicare would cover a voluntary or optional conversation that could occur every five years between a patient and a doctor about living wills, power of attorney and end-of-life treatment preferences. It did not take long before this proposal was twisted beyond recognition. Not only was the conversation now mandatory but, in a perverse echo from Nazi eugenics, seniors were being put in a position of being put to death by their government. The most egregious misrepresentation occurred when Sarah Palin used the term "death panels" on her Facebook page where she stated that "bureaucrats can decide, based on their 'level of productivity in society,' whether they are worthy of health care. Such a system is downright evil." Earl Blumenauer, "My Near Death Panel Experience," *New York Times*, November 15, 2009.

40   Porter, *The Ghosts of Europe*, 256; George M. Frederickson, *The Black Image in the White* Mind: *The Debate on Afro-American Character and Destiny, 1877–1914* (Middleton, Conn: Wesleyan University Press, 1971), 276; E. J. Dionne Jr., "President Obama as an alien," *Washington Post*, February 23, 2012.

Further Reading

You're talking as though I was crossing a moral line from
which there's no turning back. You must remember this is
routine for me. I've arrested many innocent men and women.
I hunted people down for the State, good people, knocking
on doors without knowing anything about the suspect except
their name was on a list.

—Agent Six
Tom Rob Smith

A complete bibliography is available on my website http://www.
thatlineofdarkness.com and on the Encompass Editions site at
http://www.encompasseditions.com

In the first volume I cited selected novels and monographs that
I found particularly valuable. For the second volume, I offer reflections on mysteries and thrillers set in the historical eras discussed
in the book. These novels are grounded in vivid atmospherics and
period detail, and are populated by interesting, often conflicted,
characters who must navigate the treacherous political terrain in
which they live. They are also great reads.

Morley Torgov's *The Mastersinger From Minsk* (Toronto:
Dundurn, 2012) is set in Munich 1868 where the composer Richard
Wagner is preparing for the opening of his comic opera, *Die
Meistersinger*. A poison-pen letter to Wagner and a series of murders, including those of cast members, engage the sleuthing skills
of Inspector Hermann Preliss. An absorbing read that captures the
monumental egotism and rank anti-Semitism of Wagner and, yet
because of Preliss' operatic interests, the novel conveys the maj-
esty and beauty of the opera. The real mystery is the intentions of
the unknown tenor with the golden voice who wins the role of the
young knight.

Philip Kerr's expertly researched Berlin noir series feature the
Nazi-hating, wise-cracking, Bernie Gunther, a world-weary former
criminal investigator, whose idiosyncratic moral code—he has no
qualms about killing in cold blood a killer that he feels will not receive justice in the courts—has enabled him to survive the Third
Reich. His travails include overcoming the obstacles of Nazi officials after he foils a conspiracy of renegade SS officers who commit

a series of blood-ritual killings of Aryan teenage girls in an effort to incite a pogrom against Berlin's Jews, a stint himself in the SS in the killing fields of the Eastern Front, and internment in a Soviet POW camp. In his eighth novel, *Prague Fatale* (New York: G. P. Putnam's Sons, 2012), he spends a weekend at the behest of the newly-appointed, *Reichsprotektor* of Bohemia and Moravia, Reinhard Heydrich, investigating a murder in his villa outside Prague. What Gunther does not initially realize is that Heydrich is using him to ferret out a spy within the German ranks. Previous novels explore the fascist mentality of the different security services which operated in the early Cold War in South America, Cuba and on both sides of the Iron Curtain in Europe.

David Downing's train station series from *Zoo Station* (New York: Soho Press, 2007) to his fifth *Lehrter Station* (New York: Soho Crimes, 2012) features John Russell, an Anglo-American freelance journalist and former communist with divided loyalties—an anti-Nazi German lover and a German son—who is willing to work for the Soviet, American and British security services. In this amoral netherworld, he must deceive, lie and even kill and yet he retains his decency. Downing manages to convey in *Zoo Station* the personal relationships against the backdrop of 1939 Berlin before the outbreak of war—his lover is an actress who works in state-sanctioned plays and films and his son is a member of the Hitler Youth movement—where he is confronted with an American colleague's suspicious death from "suicide" after uncovering a story about the euthanizing of disabled children. In the chaos of post-war Berlin in *Lehrter*, Russell has to navigate through the treacherous terrain of the American and Soviet security services where his life is endangered by both: he threatens to expose how the former work with reinvented SS officers in order to smuggle out certain Germans from the Soviet Zone and the latter Stalinists are looking to eliminate anyone who is not a true believer. From its powerful evocation of Nazi Germany to its aftermath, the five books are presented in chronological order and therefore should be read as one long novel: in the riveting fifth instalment, Downing pulls together the threads from the previous novels.

William Ryan's investigator is Captain Alexei Korlev, a conscientious police officer who tries to pursue justice and avoid the pitfalls of Stalinist politics. A secret Believer who also places his faith in a better future life in the Soviet Union, he is also a pragmatist concerned about self-preservation. In *The Holy Thief* (New York: Minotaur Books, 2010) set in 1936 Moscow on the cusp of the Great Terror, the investigation becomes complicated when it leads to suspects within the NKVD. In *The Darkening Field*, (New York: Minotaur Books, 2012) primarily set in 1937 Odessa, a dead woman is a lover of the Commissar of Internal Security, the feared Nikolai Yezhov. Korlev enters a moral quagmire when he uncovers what may be a genuine counter-revolutionary plot. A trademark of both books is that what begins as a mystery—in the first a grisly murder, the second a mysterious suicide—inevitably becomes intermeshed with the treacherous Stalinist terrain.

Tom Rob Smith's trilogy, beginning with the edgy thriller of 1950s Stalinism, *Child 44* (New York: Grand Central Pub., 2008) that features as its protagonist, Leo Demidov, a loyal security officer of the MGB (the successor of the NKVD) whose motto—cruelty is a virtue—rationalizes the heinous acts inflicted on "ideological enemies" to protect the security of the state and for the greater good of its citizens. In a country where the only real crime is espionage, the official message is that under socialism the state has provided a crime-free utopia. There emerges a child serial killer that challenges the perception that such a crime could only occur in the decadent West: the perpetrator is deemed "clearly sick" and the mentally ill are ideologically suitable targets for torture, while the "normal" killer is able to continue with his mayhem. When Demidov watches the torture of an innocent veterinarian and hears of his later execution, his faith is shaken, and further undermined when the MGB accuses his wife of being an enemy of the state with which he refuses to support. Forced into internal exile, Demidov goes on the lam to hunt his quarry. In doing so, he unravels the fabric of his own past. The second, *The Secret Speech* (New York: Grand Central Pub., 2009), set in 1956 when de-Stalinization turns Demidov into a state criminal pursued by former Gulag inmates, explores a topsy-turvy state of affairs that requires Demidov to live with his guilt and atone for his past collusion with evil. Finally, *Agent Six* (New York: Grand Central Pub., 2012) examines the toxicity of the Cold War played out in 1950 Moscow, New York City during the early 1960s—one of the characters is obviously based on Paul Robeson, Afghanistan before and after the Soviet invasion and again in New York when the thriller turns into a mystery. If commitment to an ideology causes one to shred his humanity—on both sides of the ideological divide—the reverse proves to be true when individuals put people before the greater cause.

Robert Littell's *The Stalin Epigram* (New York: Simon & Schuster, 2009) is not a thriller in a conventional sense, but his novel vividly captures the atmosphere of fear and paranoia of the 1930s, and the sadism and terror of the Lubyanka. The central character is the bohemian, idealistic and naive poet, Osip Mandelstam, who made the mistake of writing a sarcastic poem about Stalin which the security police acquire. He is arrested and in a dreamlike sequence Mandelstam imagines having a conversation with Stalin who is grotesque—physically repulsive, crude, indifferent to human life and thuggish—yet fiendishly savvy. The novel might inspire some readers to search out Nadezhda Mandelstam's *Hope Against Hope: A Memoir*, the classic account of her husband.

Joseph Kanon, who may be best known for his *The Good German*, released *Istanbul Passage* (New York: Atria Books, 2012) in which the city is awash in espionage and the site of Jewish rescue operations during the war—so tragic that it sends one of the characters into a catatonic state where she remains, perhaps permanently. As the novel opens, the war is over but the intrigue continues as the geo-political dividing lines shift. The protagonist, Leon Bauer, an expatriate American businessman who has done undercover work is assigned to turn over to the Americans a Soviet defector. The man in question is a Romanian who committed atrocious war crimes and the mission entrusted to Bauer is far more dangerous than he anticipated. His determination to protect the Romanian and not judge him both frustrates and earns the respect of the reader. What is fascinating about the novel is its insight into neutral Istanbul during and after the war and the role of the different intelligence communities to protect and advance their national interests.

Julia Spencer-Fleming's *One Last Soldier* (New York: Minotaur Books, 2011) investigates the psychological damage done to soldiers who served time in Iraq. Her major character is a rector who has returned to her parish in the Adirondacks after her tour of duty. Although on the surface she is coping better than others who are part of a support group to which she belongs, she finds that her combat flashbacks, and dependence on drugs and alcohol, threaten to imperil her judgment and her personal relationship with the town's police chief. A mystery forms the background for this engrossing read about the psychological struggles that ex-veterans face as they attempt to reintegrate into their community.

Index

photo by Keith Penner

Robert Douglas, born in London, Ontario, has a BA and MA from the University of Toronto. He taught history and social sciences for the Durham and Peel Boards of Education, and at Branksome Hall, a Toronto independent girl's school. It was his love of teaching a Western Civilization programme, combined with a passion for international travel, wide reading and conversation, which inspired the two volumes of *That Line of Darkness*: *The Shadow of Dracula and the Great War* and *The Gothic from Lenin to bin Laden*. Writing became a complement to teaching for the purpose of reaching a larger audience.

In addition to professional responsibilities, he enjoys swimming, cycling and walking, particularly the cities of New York, and London, and on the Continent. He always ferrets out interesting second-hand bookstores, stimulating theatre and art galleries that become the subject of wonderful conversation over good food and wine. For twenty-five years, he and his wife, Gayle, have hosted monthly dinner soirees that explore a diverse range of political–social and artistic topics.

ENCOMPASS EDITIONS, founded in 2009 and
based in Kingston, Ontario, Canada, is dedicat-
ed to providing access to traditional publishing to a wider spectrum of writers than is often
the case—writers in the United States, Canada,
the United Kingdom and the European Union.
Although Encompass does not accept unsolicit-
ed manuscripts, the company relies upon several agents who work closely with writers of
every level of experience. This policy permits
Encompass to focus on what it does best: publish
books good to read. You can visit the Encompass
website at www.EncompassEditions.com
or contact editor Robert Buckland at
words@encompasseditions.com

CPSIA information can be obtained at www.ICGtesting.com
Printed in the USA
LVOW060125220113

316612LV00003B/17/P

9 781927 664001